Not For Tourists™ Guide to **BOSTON**

P9-ARX-060

2007

Not For Tourists Inc

Published and designed by:
Not For Tourists, Inc.
NFT.—Not For Tourists. Guide to BOSTON 2006
www.notfortourists.com

Publisher
Jane Pirone

Information Design
Jane Pirone
Rob Tallia
Scot Covey
Ben Bray

Managing Editor
Rob Tallia

Database Manager
Ben Bray

City Editor
Harry Kelly

Writing and Editing
Andrea Calabratta
Knox Gardner
Ann Jackman
Harry Kelly

Joy Mazzola
Sarah Shemkus
Jason Warner

Research
Michael Dale
Manny Rodriguez
Sho Spaeth

Graphic Design/Production
Jeanette Rodriguez
Chesley Andrews
Scot Covey
Jonathan Levy
Nick Trotter
Lisette de Orbegoso

Research Intern
Lily Chu

Graphic Design Intern
Aaron Schielke

Proofing
Dorothy Ball
Jennifer Keeney Sendrow

Sales & Marketing
Alli Hirschman
Erin Hodson
Annie Holt
Nate Walker

NFT would like to thank
Diana Pizzari for her hard
work and dedication over the
past five years—best of luck!

Printed in China
ISBN#0-9778031-2-0 $14.95
Copyright © 2006 by Not For Tourists, Inc.

Every effort has been made to ensure that the information in this book is as up-to-date as possible at press time. However, many details are liable to change—as we have learned. The publishers cannot accept responsibility for any consequences arising from the use of this book.

Not For Tourists does not solicit individuals, organizations, or businesses for listings inclusion in our guides, nor do we accept payment for inclusion into the editorial portion of our book; the advertising sections, however, are exempt from this policy. We always welcome communications from anyone regarding ANYTHING having to do with our books; please visit us on our website at www.notfortourists.com for appropriate contact information.

Dear NFT User,

Welcome to the 2007 edition of NFT Boston. This book, already the ultimate user's manual to Boston, has somehow just become **even more ultimate**. Using a combination of hard work, good people and common sense, we've added all sorts of cool new content to NFT Boston, including …

- new maps for **Dorchester**, **Mattapan**, **Hyde Park**, **West Roxbury** and **Roslindale**.

- **scales** on all maps, **cross-streets** for all listings, and "**open 24-hours**" icons for the night owls.

- even **kitchen closing times**, pages on **Berklee** College of Music and continuing education programs, where to find **WiFi**, **Internet connections** and **self storage**, and where to **rent a van or truck**.

Whoa!

We're helped by the generous contributors called out on the facing page, who sent in their suggestions and corrections to make this book even better. All of this means that NFT Boston helps you navigate just about anything. We love it – and if you're reading a display copy of this book right now, you really should buy it.

If there is anything that **you** would like to see in the next edition of NFT Boston, please visit our website at **www.notfortourists.com** and let us know. Your feedback is important to us, and contributes mightily to the integrity of this book.

Here's hoping you find what you need,

Jane, Rob, & Harry

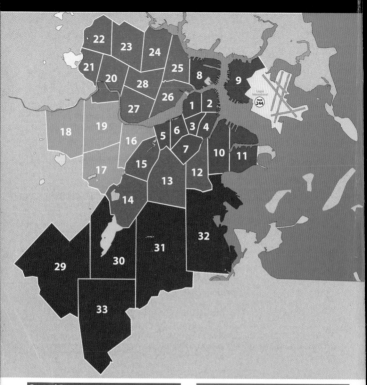

Boston Area Driving Map
and **Downtown Boston Map**
foldout, last page

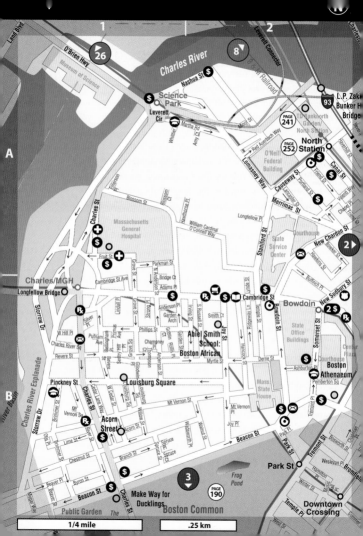

Once home to elite Boston Brahmins, Beacon Hill still has some of the most expensive real estate in America. Charming brick row houses reflect a long and storied history; where the State House stands, John Hancock once grazed cows. The star of the Charles River skyline is the Leonard P. Zakim Bunker Hill Bridge, the world's widest cable-stayed bridge. The West End, once a bustling working-class neighborhood, is now a charmless tract of high-rise buildings.

$ Banks

- **Bank of America** • 104 Canal St [Valenti]
- **Bank of America** • 161 Cambridge St [Joy St]
- **Bank of America** • 3 Center Plz [Cambridge St]
- **Bank of America (ATM)** • 125 Nashua St [Storrow]
- **Bank of America (ATM)** • 200 Portland St [Valenti]
- **Bank of America (ATM)** • 243 Charles St [Fruit]
- **Bank of America (ATM)** • 45 Charles St [Chestnut St]
- **Cambridge Trust** • 65 Beacon St [Charles St]
- **Citizens Bank** • 1 Center Plz [Cambridge St]
- **Citizens Bank (ATM)** • 122 Cambridge St [Temple St]
- **Citizens Bank (ATM)** • 250 Cambridge St [Garden St]
- **Citizens Bank (ATM)** • 55 Fruit St [N Grove]
- **Citizens Bank (ATM)** • Boston Museum of Science • Science Park [Monsignor O' Brien Hwy]
- **Sovereign Bank** • 1 Beacon St [Tremont St]
- **Sovereign Bank** • 125 Causeway St [Canal St]
- **Sovereign Bank** • 67 Beacon St [Charles St]
- **Sovereign Bank (ATM)** • 1 Ashburton Pl [Somerset St]
- **Sovereign Bank (ATM)** • 27 Beacon St [Park St]

Donuts

- **Dunkin' Donuts** • 106 Cambridge St [Bowdoin]
- **Dunkin' Donuts** • 111 Causeway St [Friend]
- **Dunkin' Donuts** • 125 Nashua St [Storrow]
- **Dunkin' Donuts** • 22 Beacon St [Bowdoin]

✚ Emergency Rooms

- **Massachusetts Eye and Ear Infirmary** • 243 Charles St [Fruit]
- **Massachusetts General** • 55 Fruit St [N Grove]

O Landmarks

- **Abiel Smith School** • 46 Joy St [Smith Ct]
- **Acorn Street** • b/w West Cedar St & Willow St, running parallel to Chestnut St
- **Boston Athenaeum** • 10 1/2 Beacon St [Somerset St]

- **Leonard P Zakim Bunker Hill Bridge** • I-93 & Charles River
- **Longfellow Bridge** • Cambridge St & Charles St
- **Louisburg Square** • b/w Mt Vernon St & Pinckney St
- **Make Way for Ducklings** • Charles St & Beacon St
- **Massachusetts General Hospital** • 55 Fruit St [N Grove]
- **TD Banknorth Garden** • 150 Causeway St [Beverly]

Libraries

- **West End** • 151 Cambridge St [Lynde]

Ⓡ Pharmacies

- **CVS** • 155 Charles St [Silver Pl]
- **CVS** • 191 Cambridge St [S Russell]
- **CVS** • 2 Center Plz [Cambridge St] ⌚
- **Gary Drug** • 59 Charles St [Mount Vernon St]

⬡ Police

- **District A-1** • 40 New Sudbury St [Bulfinch]

✉ Post Offices

- **Charles Street Station** • 136 Charles St [Revere St]
- **John F Kennedy Station** • 25 New Chardon St [Bulfinch]
- **State House Station** • 24 Beacon St [Park St]

⬢ Schools

- **Advent School** • 15 Brimmer St [Pinckney]
- **Boston Children's School** • 8 Whittier Pl [Martha]
- **Suffolk University** • 8 Ashburton Pl [Somerset St]

Supermarkets

- **Whole Foods Market** • 181 Cambridge St [Joy St]

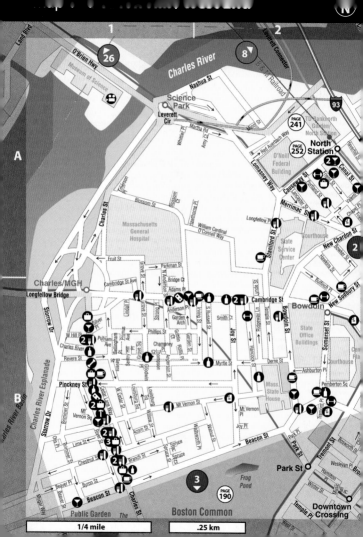

Sundries / Entertainment

Locals praise the community feel of the square mile that constitutes Beacon Hill. While the West End caters mostly to work-a-day suits, a diverse array of restaurants and shops line Charles and Cambridge Streets on Beacon Hill. Pubs like Seven's and The Four's cater to sports fans, but Cheers mainly draws tourists. The Public Garden and Boston Common function as this neighborhood's backyard.

Coffee

- **Bagels Etc •** 70 Staniford St [Longfellow Pl]
- **Capital Coffee House •** 122 Bowdoin St [Ashburton]
- **Starbucks •** 1 Charles St [Beacon St]
- **Starbucks •** 222 Cambridge St [Irving St]
- **Starbucks •** 97 Charles St [Pinckney]
- **Tammy's Place •** 25 New Sudbury St [Bulfinch]

Copy Shops

- **Copy Clone •** 31 Mt Vernon St [Hancock St]
- **FedEx Kinko's •** 2 Center Plz [Cambridge St] ♿
- **Jaguar Graphics & Print •** 129 Portland St [Valenti]
- **Johnson's Printing •** 15 Tremont Pl [Beacon St]

Gyms

- **Beacon Hill Athletic Club •** 261 Friend St [Causeway]
- **Beacon Hill Athletic Club •** 3 Hancock St [Cambridge St]
- **Boston Sports Club •** 1 Bulfinch Pl [Bowdoin]
- **Fitcorp •** 1 Beacon St [Tremont St]

Hardware Stores

- **Charles Street Supply •** 54 Charles St [Mount Vernon St]

Liquor Stores

- **Beacon Capitol Market •** 32 Myrtle St [Joy St]
- **Beacon Hill Wine & Spirits •** 63 Charles St [Mount Vernon St]
- **Charles Street Liquors •** 143 Charles St [Silver Pl]
- **DeLuca's Market & Wine Shop •** 11 Charles St [Branch]
- **Demetri Brothers Liquor & Gifts •** 53 Revere St [Grove St]
- **Jobi's Liquors •** 170 Cambridge St [Joy St]
- **Mccormack's Liquors •** 82 Hancock St [Mount Vernon St]
- **Simmons Liquor Store •** 210 Cambridge St [S Russell]
- **Swetts Liquors •** 3 Somerset St [Beacon St]

Movie Theaters

- **Mugar Omni Theatre •** Science Park [Monsignor O'Brien Hwy]

Nightlife

- **21st Amendment •** 150 Bowdoin St [Mount Vernon St]
- **6B •** 6 Beacon St #B [Tremont Pl]
- **Beacon Hill Pub •** 149 Charles St [Silver Pl]
- **Boston Beer Works •** 112 Canal St [Valenti]
- **Cheers •** 84 Beacon St [Brimmer]
- **The Four's •** 166 Canal St [Causeway]

- **Greatest Bar •** 262 Friend St [Causeway]
- **The Harp •** 85 Causeway St [Portland]
- **Hill Tavern •** 228 Cambridge St [Irving St]
- **Seven's •** 77 Charles St [Mount Vernon St]
- **Sullivan's Tap •** 168 Canal St [Causeway]

Pet Shops

- **Fi-Dough •** 103 Charles St [Pinckney]

Restaurants

- **75 Chestnut •** 75 Chestnut St [River St]
- **Angus Beef Steakhouse •** 107 Merrimac St [Lancaster St]
- **Anthem •** 138 Portland St [Valenti]
- **Artu •** 89 Charles St [Pinckney]
- **Beacon Hill Bistro •** 25 Charles St [Chestnut St]
- **Café Podima •** 156 Cambridge St [Hancock St]
- **The Federalist •** XV Beacon Hotel • 15 Beacon St [Somerset St]
- **Figs •** 42 Charles St [Chestnut St]
- **Grotto •** 37 Bowdoin St [Cambridge St]
- **Harvard Gardens •** 316 Cambridge St [Grove St]
- **Hungry I •** 71 1/2 Charles St [Mount Vernon St]
- **King & I •** 145 Charles St [Silver Pl]
- **Lala Rokh •** 97 Mt Vernon St [W Cedar]
- **Ma Soba •** 156 Cambridge St [Hancock St]
- **Panificio •** 144 Charles St [Silver Pl]
- **The Paramount •** 44 Charles St [Chestnut St]
- **Phoenicia •** 240 Cambridge St [Garden St]
- **Pierrot •** 272 Cambridge St [Anderson St]
- **Ristorante Toscano •** 41 Charles St [Chestnut St]
- **Torch •** 26 Charles St [Branch]
- **Upper Crust •** 20 Charles St [Branch]
- **Viva Burrito •** 66 Staniford St [Longfellow Pl]

Shopping

- **Black Ink •** 101 Charles St [Pinckney]
- **DeLuca's Market •** 11 Charles St [Branch]
- **Eugene Galleries •** 76 Charles St [Mount Vernon St]
- **The Flat of the Hill •** 60 Charles St [Mount Vernon St]
- **Hilton's Tent City •** 272 Friend St [Causeway]
- **Moxie •** 51 Charles St [Mount Vernon St]
- **The Red Wagon •** 69 Charles St [Mount Vernon St]
- **Savenor's Market •** 160 Charles St [Cambridge St]
- **Wish •** 49 Charles St [Mount Vernon St]

Video Rental

- **Fred's Video Beacon Hill •** 63A Charles St [Mount Vernon St]
- **Mike's Movies •** 250 Cambridge St [Garden St]

Map 1 • **Beacon Hill / West End**

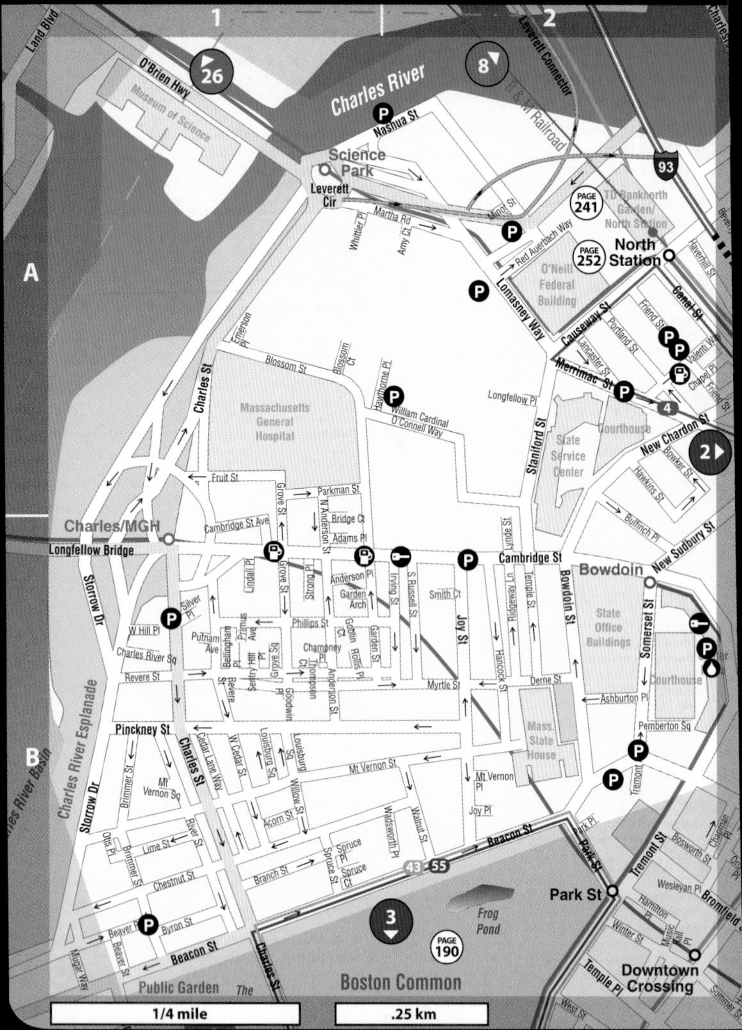

Ⓝ

1 **2**

Land Blvd

O'Brien Hwy

26

Museum of Science

Charles River

Nashua St

8▼

Leverett Connector

MBTA Railroad

93

Science Park

Leverett Cir

Martha Rd

Amy Ct

West St

PAGE 241 TD Banknorth Garden/ North Station

PAGE 252 **North Station**

Whittier St

Blossom St

Fruit St

Blossom Ct

O'Neill Federal Building

Causeway St

Merrimac St

Lancaster St

Portland St

Friend St

Nashua St

Valenti Way

Chardon St

4

Longfellow Pl

Lomasney Way

Staniford St

Longfellow Pl

Courthouse

State Service Center

New Chardon St

2▶

Bowker St

Hawkins St

Bulfinch Pl

New Sudbury St

A

Massachusetts General Hospital

William Cardinal O'Connell Way

Emerson Pl

Grove St

Parkman St

N Anderson St

Bridge Ct

Adams Pl

Cambridge St Ave

Charles/MGH

Longfellow Bridge

Storrow Dr

Charles St

Lindall Pl

Grove St

Irving St

Anderson Pl

Garden Arch

S Russell St

Phillips St

Goffe St

Garden St

Smith Ct

Cambridge St

Temple St

Hancock St

Bowdoin

Somerset St

State Office Buildings

Courthouse

B

Charles River Esplanade

Storrow Dr

Charles River Basin

W Hill Pl

Silver Pl

W Cedar St

Revere St

Primus Ave

Putnam Ave

Charles River Sq

Brimmer St

Pinckney St

Mt Vernon Pl

Cedar Lane Way

W Cedar St

Charles St

Lime St

River St

Byron St

Beaver St

Beaver Pl

Chestnut St

Beacon St

Public Garden

The

Phillips St

Grove St

Bowdoin St

Beverly

Garden Ct

Anderson St

Goodwin Pl

Champney Pl

Chambers St

Thompson

Lindall Ct

Louisburg Sq

Willow St

Acorn St

Mt Vernon St

Walnut St

Branch St

Spruce Pl

Spruce St

Spruce Ct

Myrtle St

Joy St

Derne St

Mass. State House

Mt Vernon St

Joy Pl

Ridgeway Ln

Hancock St

Temple St

Bowdoin St

Ashburton Pl

Derne St

Pemberton Sq

Tremont St

Courthouse

43 55

3▼

PAGE 190

Boston Common

Beacon St

Park St

Frog Pond

Park St

Winter St

Temple Pl

Bosworth St

Province St

Wesleyan Pl **Bromfield**

Hamilton Pl

Downtown Crossing

West St

Tremont St

1/4 mile **.25 km**

Public transit (or your own two feet) remains the best way to travel in this high-traffic, parking-scarce neighborhood. If you simply must drive, be prepared for the havoc wreaked by never-ending construction, particularly at the intersection where Cambridge and Charles Streets converge at the exit from Storrow Drive. Route 93 takes you to points north and south, while Storrow runs east and west. Cross the Longfellow Bridge to get to Cambridge.

Subway

- **Bowdoin**
- **Charles/MGH**
- **Downtown Crossing**
- **North Station**
- **Park Street**
- **Science Park**

Bus Lines

- **4** • North Station—World Trade Center via Federal Courthouse
- **43** • Ruggles Station—Park & Tremont Streets
- **55** • Jersey & Queensberry Streets—Copley Square or Park & Tremont Streets

Car Rental

- **Avis** • 3 Center Plz [Cambridge St] • 617-534-1400
- **Dollar** • Government Ctr • 209 Cambridge St [S Russell] • 617-723-8312

Car Washes

- **Professional Auto Detailers** • 1 Center Plz [Cambridge St]

Gas Stations

- **Exxon** • 239 Cambridge St [Blossom St] ⏰
- **Gulf** • 296 Cambridge St [Strong]
- **Mobil** • 150 Friend St [Valenti]

Parking

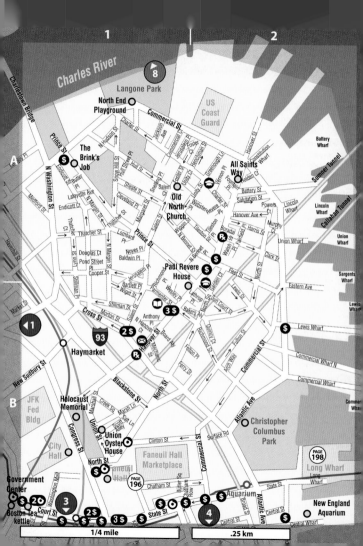

Charles River

1

2

Charlestown Bridge

8

Langone Park

North End Playground

Commercial St

US Coast Guard

Battery Wharf

A

Prince St

N Washington St

$ The Brink's Job

N Hudson St

Charter St

Commercial St

Snow Hill St

Hull St

Salem St

Old North Church

All Saints Way

Hanover St

Sumner Tunnel

Lincoln Wharf

Lincoln Tunnel
Callahan Tunnel

Union Wharf

Sargents Wharf

Lewis Wharf

Medford St

Endicott St

Lafayette Ave

N Margin St

Cleveland Pl

Prince St

Hanover Ave

R

Thatcher St

Margin St

Cooper St

Noyes Pl
Baldwin Pl

Paul Revere House $

Fleet St

North St

Eastern Ave

Douglas Ct
Pond Street

Jerusalem Pl

Bartlett Pl
Wiget St

Stillman St

Cross St

Morton St

Anthony

2 $

Haymarket

93

Blackstone St

North St

R

Commercial St

Commercial Wharf N

Commercial Wharf

1

Market St

Stillman St

New Sudbury St

JFK
Fed
Bldg

B

Holocaust
Memorial

Congress St

City
Hall

Union St

Union
Oyster
House

North St

$

Clinton St

Surface Rd

Faneuil Hall
Marketplace

PAGE
196

Atlantic Ave

Christopher
Columbus
Park

Commer
Wha

Long Wharf

PAGE
198

Long
Wharf

Government
Center

$ 2

Boston Tea
kettle

3

Court St

2 $

3 $

State St

4

Aquarium

Atlantic Ave

State
Wharf

Central St

$

New England
Aquarium

Central Wharf

1/4 mile

.25 km

Despite its yuppification, the North End is still code for best manicotti you'll ever know and octogenarians playing chess on the narrow sidewalks. The Big Dig's finishing touch, the Rose Kennedy Greenway, should be completed by about 2009, rejoining the North End with Faneuil Hall and its hordes of tourists and office workers. Quincy Market's food court is a must-try for lunch on the go-go-go.

$ Banks

- **Bank of America** • 260 Hanover St [Parmenter]
- **Bank of America** • 60 State St [Kilby St]
- **Bank of America (ATM)** • 2 Atlantic Ave [High St]
- **Bank of America (ATM)** • 283 Causeway St [Endicott St]
- **Bank of America (ATM)** • 4 Commercial St [State]
- **Bank of America (ATM)** • 48-50 Salem St [Morton St]
- **Bank of America (ATM)** • 64-66 Cross St [Salem St]
- **Century Bank** • 136 State St [India St]
- **Century Bank** • 275 Hanover St [Richmond St]
- **Citizens Bank** • 28 State St [Congress]
- **Citizens Bank** • 315 Hanover St [Prince]
- **Citizens Bank** • 53 State St [Congress]
- **Citizens Bank (ATM)** • 1 Boston Pl [Court]
- **Citizens Bank (ATM)** • 1 Cambridge St [Sudbury]
- **Citizens Bank (ATM)** • 1 State St [Washington St]
- **Citizens Bank (ATM)** • 100 City Hall Plz [Cambridge St]
- **Citizens Bank (ATM)** • 177 State St [McKinley]
- **Citizens Bank (ATM)** • 342 Hanover St [N Bennet St]
- **Citizens Bank (ATM)** • 92 State St [Broad]
- **First National Bank of Ipswich** • 33 State St [Congress]
- **Sovereign Bank** • 287 Hanover St [Richmond St]
- **Sovereign Bank** • 75 State St [Kilby St]
- **Sovereign Bank** • Central Wharf [Central St]
- **Sovereign Bank (ATM)** • 1 Union St [North St]

Donuts

- **Dunkin' Donuts** • 1 Congress St [North St]
- **Dunkin' Donuts** • 1 Fleet Ctr [Hanover St]
- **Dunkin' Donuts** • 100 City Hall Plz [Cambridge St]
- **Dunkin' Donuts** • 111 State St [Broad]
- **Dunkin' Donuts** • 2 City Hall Sq [Cambridge St]
- **Dunkin' Donuts** • 20 North St [Scott Aly]

Landmarks

- **All Saints Way** • Battery St & Hanover St
- **Boston Tea Kettle** • 63 Court St [Cambridge St]
- **The Brink's Job** • 165 Prince St [Causeway]
- **Christopher Columbus Park** • Atlantic Ave
- **City Hall** • 1 City Hall Plz [Cambridge St]
- **Faneuil Hall** • Congress St at North St
- **Holocaust Memorial** • Congress St at Union St [Congress]
- **New England Aquarium** • Central Wharf [Central St]
- **North End Playground** • Commercial St & Foster St
- **Old North Church** • 193 Salem St [Hull St]
- **Paul Revere House** • 19 North Sq [Garden Ct St]
- **Union Oyster House** • 41 Union St [Marshall St]

Libraries

- **North End** • 25 Parmenter St [Hanover St]

Pharmacies

- **CVS** • 218 Hanover St [Cross St]
- **Green Cross Pharmacy** • 393 Hanover St [Clark St]

Post Offices

- **Hanover Street Station** • 217 Hanover St [Cross St]

Schools

- **Eliot Elementary** • 16 Charter St [Unity St]
- **St John** • 9 Moon St [Lewis St]

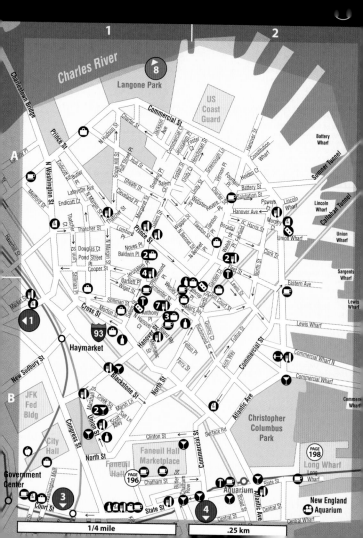

Though you can't walk into a bad meal in the North End, several high-priced establishments serving fashionably small portions have followed the yupsters in. To keep it real, try L'Osteria. Stay for dessert: Mike's is world-famous for a reason; Modern Pastry fills its cannoli in front of you; hit Caffe Vittoria for atmosphere. By night, young professionals reemerge at Faneuil Hall and hit the dance floors—hard.

Coffee

- **Anne-Marie's Place •** 251 Causeway St [Medford St]
- **Boston Bean Stock Coffee •** 97 Salem St [Wiget]
- **Caffe Paradiso •** 255 Hanover St [Richmond St]
- **Caffe Victoria •** 296 Hanover St [Prince]
- **Contrata's •** 396 Hanover St [Salutation]
- **Red Barn Coffee Roasters •** 1 Faneuil Hall Sq [S Market]
- **Seattle's Best Coffee •** 200 State St [Atlantic Ave]
- **Starbucks •** 2 Atlantic Ave [High St]
- **Starbucks •** 2-4 Faneuil Hall Marketplace [Commercial St]
- **Starbucks •** Boston Long Wharf Marriott • 296 State St [Atlantic Ave]
- **Starbucks •** 63 Court St [Cambridge St]
- **Starbucks •** 84 State St [Kilby St]

Copy Shops

- **AlphaGraphics •** 74 Canal St [Valenti]
- **Fedex Kinkos •** 60 State St [Kilby St]
- **Harborside Copy •** 338 Commercial St [Murphy]
- **Sir Speedy Printing Center •** 77 N Washington St [Thacher St]
- **Staples •** 25 Court St [Tremont St]
- **The UPS Store •** 71 Commercial St [Cross St]

Farmer's Markets

- **City Hall Plaza (May-Nov, Mon 11-6, Wed 11-6) •** City Hall Plz at Cambridge St [Cambridge St]

Gyms

- **Beacon Hill Athletic Club •** 85 Atlantic Ave [High St]

Hardware Stores

- **Boston Hardware •** 16 Fleet St [Garden Ct St]
- **Brookstone •** 200 State St [Atlantic Ave]
- **Salem Street True Value •** 89 Salem St [Wiget]

Liquor Stores

- **Cirace's Liquor •** 173 North St [Moon]
- **Federal Wine & Spirits •** 29 State St [Devonshire]
- **Martignetti Liquors •** 64 Cross St [Morton St]
- **Wine Bottega (wine only) •** 341 Hanover St [Prince]
- **Wine Cave •** 33 Union St [Marshall St]

Movie Theaters

- **Simons IMAX Theatre •** Central Wharf [Central St]

Nightlife

- **Bell in Hand Tavern •** 45 Union St [Marshall St]
- **Black Rhino •** 21 Broad St [Central St]
- **Black Rose •** 160 State St [Commercial St]
- **Boston Rocks •** 245 Quincy Market
- **Boston Sail Loft •** 80 Atlantic St [High St]
- **Club Q •** 25 Union St [North St]
- **Green Dragon Tavern •** 11 Marshall St [Hanover St]
- **McFadden's •** 148 State St [India St]
- **Ned Devine's •** Quincy Market [S Market]
- **Paddy O's •** 33 Union St [Marshall St]
- **Parris •** Quincy Market [S Market]
- **Pete's Pub •** 108 Blackstone St [Hanover St]
- **Purple Shamrock •** 1 Union St [North St]
- **The Rack •** 24 Clinton St [Blackstone]
- **Sanctuary •** 189 State St [McKinley]
- **Tia's on the Waterfront •** 200 Atlantic Ave [State]
- **Vertigo •** 126 State St [Broad]

Restaurants

- **Antico Forno •** 93 Salem St [Wiget]
- **Billy Tse •** 240 Commercial St [Atlantic Ave]
- **Bonne Chance •** 77 Canal St [Valenti]
- **Boston Sail Loft •** 80 Atlantic Ave [High St]
- **Bova's Bakery •** 134 Salem St [Prince] ⏰
- **Bricco •** 241 Hanover St [Cross St]
- **Caffe Paradiso •** 255 Hanover St [Richmond St]
- **The Daily Catch •** 323 Hanover St [Prince]
- **Galleria Umberto •** 289 Hanover St [Richmond St]
- **Green Dragon Tavern •** 11 Marshall St [Hanover St]
- **Haymarket Pizza •** 106 Blackstone St [Hanover St]
- **Houston's •** 60 State St [Kilby St]
- **L'Osteria •** 104 Salem St [Bartlett Pl]
- **La Famiglia Giorgio's •** 112 Salem St [Cooper]
- **La Summa •** 30 Fleet St [McClellan Hwy]
- **Lucca •** 226 Hanover St [Cross St]
- **Mamma Maria •** 3 North Sq [Garden Ct St]
- **McCormick & Schmick's •** Faneuil Hall Marketplace [S Market]
- **Pizzeria Regina •** 11 1/2 Thacher St [N Margin]
- **Prezza •** 24 Fleet St [Garden Ct St]
- **Ristorante Fiore •** 250 Hanover St [Parmenter]
- **Sage •** 69 Prince St [Salem St]
- **Sel de la Terre •** 255 State St [Atlantic Ave]
- **Taranta •** 210 Hanover St [Cross St]
- **Theo's Cozy Corner •** 162 Salem St [Tileston St]
- **Union Oyster House •** 41 Union St [Marshall St]
- **Via Valverde •** 233 Hanover St [Cross St]

Shopping

- **Bova's Bakery •** 134 Salem St [Prince] ⏰
- **Brooks Brothers •** 75 State St [Kilby St]
- **Dairy Fresh Candies •** 57 Salem St [Morton St]
- **Fresh Cheese •** 81 Endicott St [Stillman St]
- **Green Cross Pharmacy •** 393 Hanover St [Clark St]
- **Holbrows Flowers •** 100 City Hall Plz [Cambridge St]
- **Karma •** 26 Prince St [Hanover St]
- **Maria's Pastry Shop •** 46 Cross St [Morton St]
- **Mike's Pastry •** 300 Hanover St [Prince]
- **Modern Pastry •** 257 Hanover St [Richmond St]
- **Monica's Salumeria •** 130 Salem St [Prince]
- **Newbury Comics •** 1 Washington Mall [Court]
- **Roche-Bobois •** 585 Commercial St [Hull St]
- **Salumeria Italiana •** 151 Richmond St [North St]
- **Salumeria Toscana •** 272 Hanover St [Parmenter]
- **Stanza dei Sigari •** 292 Hanover St [Prince]

Video Rental

- **Beantown Video •** 372 Commercial St [Salutation]
- **North End Video •** 292 North St [Moon]
- **Video Cinema •** 62 Salem St [Stillman St]

(15)

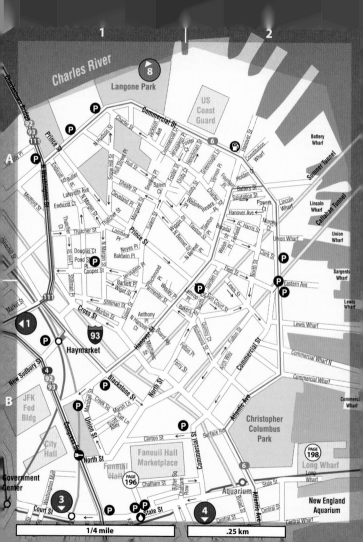

Map 2

Don't drive unless you want to spend 40 minutes looking for a parking spot at which you'll invariably be ticketed. Some garages and lots dot the area if you're willing to spend the dough. Best bet: take the Green Line to Haymarket or Government Center to get to the North End and Faneuil Hall, respectively.

Subway

- • Aquarium
- • Haymarket
- • State

Bus Lines

- **4** • North Station—World Trade Center via Federal Courthouse
- **6** • Boston Marine Industrial Park—South Station/ Haymarket Station
- **92** • Assembly Square Mall—Downtown via Sullivan Square Station, Main Street
- **93** • Sullivan Square Station—Downtown via Bunker Hill Street & Haymarket Station
- **111** • Woodlawn or Broadway & Park Ave— Haymarket Station via Mystic River/Tobin Bridge

Car Rental

• **Enterprise** • 1 Congress St [North St] • 617-723-8077

Car Washes

• **Bradford Auto Park & Wax** • 75 State St [Kilby St]

Gas Stations

• **Mobil** • 420 Commercial St [Holden Ct]

Parking

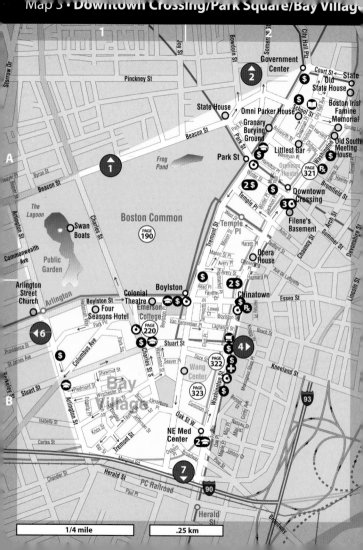

Map 3 • Downtown Crossing/Park Square/Bay Village

1

Government Center
2

Court St — State
Old State House
Boston Irish Famine Memorial
Old South Meeting House
PAGE 321
Downtown Crossing
Filene's Basement

State House
Omni Parker House
Granary Burying Ground
Littlest Bar
Orpheum Theatre

Park St
1

Frog Pond

Boston Common
PAGE 190

Swan Boats

The Lagoon

Public Garden

Temple Pl
Opera House

Boylston
2

Chinatown
Essex St

Arlington Street Church

Colonial Theatre
Boylston St
Emerson College
PAGE 220

4

PAGE 322

6

Four Seasons Hotel

Stuart St

Wang Center
PAGE 323

Bay Village

93

Kneeland St

90
7

NE Med Center
2

Herald St
PC Railroad
Broadway
Herald St

1/4 mile   .25 km

Map

19

Sadly, the City is determined to "develop" away what little remains of the old character of Washington Street between Downtown Crossing and New England Medical Center. The Opera House is an impressive symbol of a thriving Theater District, but high-end development here makes the Combat Zone even more of a distant memory. Bay Village, a tiny 19th-century enclave, has practically no commercial space, making it pleasantly serene after a snowstorm.

$ Banks

- **Bank of America** • 157 Stuart St [Warrenton St]
- **Bank of America** • 6 Tremont St [Court]
- **Bank of America** • 710 Washington St [Kneeland]
- **Bank of America (ATM)** • 11 Winter St [Winter Pl]
- **Bank of America (ATM)** • 175 Tremont St [Aveery St]
- **Bank of America (ATM)** • 58 Winter St [Tremont St]
- **Bank of America (ATM)** • 630 Washington St [Essex]
- **Bank of America (ATM)** • 80 Boylston St [Tremont St]
- **Cathay Bank** • 621 Washington St [Hayward Pl]
- **Citizens Bank** • 73 Tremont St [Beacon St]
- **Citizens Bank (ATM)** • 1 Milk St [Washington St]
- **Citizens Bank (ATM)** • 120 Tremont St [Hamilton Pl]
- **Citizens Bank (ATM)** • 750 Washington St [Kneeland]
- **Sovereign Bank** • 30 Winter St [Winter Pl]
- **Sovereign Bank** • 61 Arlington St [St James Ave]
- **Sovereign Bank (ATM)** • 600 Washington St [Hayward Pl]
- **Sovereign Bank (ATM)** • 769 Washington St [Kneeland]

◉ Donuts

- **Dunkin' Donuts** • 127 Tremont St [Park St]
- **Dunkin' Donuts** • 417 Washington St [Winter St]
- **Dunkin' Donuts** • 426 Washington St [Winter St]
- **Dunkin' Donuts** • 630 Washington St [Essex]
- **Dunkin' Donuts** • 750 Washington St [Kneeland]
- **Dunkin' Donuts** • 8 Park Plz [Boylston St]
- **Dunkin' Donuts** • 80 Boylston St [Tremont St]
- **Honey Dew Donuts** • 426 Washington St [Winter St]

✚ Emergency Rooms

- **Tufts-New England Medical Center** • 750 Washington St [Kneeland]

◉ Landmarks

- **Arlington Street Church** • 351 Boylston St [Arlington St]
- **Boston Irish Famine Memorial** • School St & Washington St
- **Colonial Theater** • 106 Boylston St [Tremont St]
- **Four Seasons Hotel** • 200 Boylston St [Charles St]
- **Granary Burying Ground** • Tremont St & Park St
- **Old South Meeting House** • 310 Washington St [Milk St]
- **Old State House** • 206 Washington St [Court]
- **Omni Parker House** • 60 School St [Chapman]
- **Opera House** • 539 Washington St [Ave de Lafayette]
- **State House** • Beacon St at Park St
- **Swan Boats** • Arlington St & Boylston St
- **Wang Center** • 270 Tremont St [Hollis St]

◧ Libraries

- **Kirstein Business** • 20 City Hall Ave [Pi]

℞ Pharmacies

- **CVS** • 631 Washington St [Essex]

◉ Schools

- **Boston Renaissance Charter** • 250 Stuart St [Church St]
- **Emerson College** • 120 Boylston St [Boylston Pl]
- **Josiah Quincy Elementary** • 885 Washington St [Oak St W]
- **Josiah Quincy Upper School** • 900 Washington St [Pine St]
- **New England School of Law** • 154 Stuart St [Warrenton St]
- **Suffolk University Law School** • 120 Tremont St [Hamilton Pl]

◉ Supermarkets

- **C-Mart** • 692 Washington St [Kneeland]

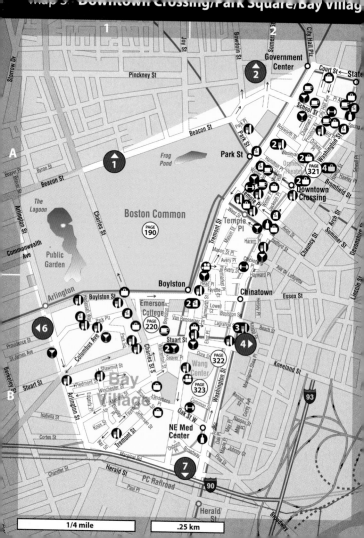

Starrow Dr

Pinckney St

Joy St

Bowdoin St

Somerset St

City Hall Plz

Court St → State

Government Center

2

School St

Beacon St

Park St

Park St

1

Wesleyan

2

Orpheum Theater

PAGE 321

4

Washington St

Bromfield St

Frog Pond

Downtown Crossing

2

Byron St

Beaver St

Temple Pl

Boston Common

PAGE 190

West St

Avon St

Summer St

Chauncy St

The Lagoon

Charles St

Tremont St

Mason St

Harem

Washington St

Bedford St

Commonwealth Ave

Public Garden

Boylston St

Mason St

Avery St

Chicken

Hayward Pl

Ave de Lafayette

Arlington St

Arlington

Boylston St

Boylston

Head St

Essex St

Lincoln St

Chinatown

Fayette

6

Boylston Way

Park Plz

Columbus Ave

Emerson College

PAGE 220

Van Rensselaer Pl

2

Lowell

Boylston St

Lagrange

Beach St

Providence St

St James Ave

Stuart St

Stuart St

2

Seaver St

Dore St

3

4

Kneeland St

Berkeley St

Piedmont St

Shawmut St

Winchester St

Wang Center

PAGE 322

Washington St

Marginal Rd SB

93

Bay Village

Melrose St

Jefferson St

Carleton

PAGE 323

Common St

Bennet St

Nassau St

Isabella St

Knox St

Oak St W

Pleasant St

Cortes St

Tremont St

Ogden Pl

NE Med Center

Broadway

Johnny Ct

Chandler St

Herald St

7

90

PC Railroad

Paul St

Herald St

Broadway

| 1/4 mile | .25 km |

Sundries / Entertainment

Map 3

Filene's may have been swallowed by the company that owns Macy's, but downstairs Filene's Basement (which hasn't been associated with Filene's for decades) still packs in shoppers trawling for bargains. The best way to finish a Downtown Crossing shopping excursion during the week is with a scrumptious Chilean sandwich from Chacarero (take-away only). If you'd rather sit down for a top-end meal, try Aujourd'hui, Excelsior or, across the Common, No. 9 Park.

Coffee

- **Bill's Coffee Shop** • 1 City Hall Ave
- **Rachel's Kitchen** • 12 Church St [Fayette St]
- **Starbucks** • 12 Winter St [Washington St]
- **Starbucks** • 143 Stuart St [Warrenton St]
- **Starbucks** • 240 Washington St [Water]
- **Starbucks** • 27 School St [Province St]
- **Starbucks** • 62 Boylston St [Tremont St]
- **Tremont Tea Room (tea only)** • 48 Winter St [Tremont St]

Copy Shops

- **ABC Printing** • 487 Washington St [Temple Pl]
- **BFS Business Printing** • 10 Park Plz [Providence]
- **Copy Cop** • 260 Washington St [Water]
- **Emerson College Print Copy Center** • 201 Tremont St [Boylston St]
- **FedEx Kinko's** • 125 Tremont St [Park St]
- **Mail Boxes Etc** • 276 Washington St [Spring Ln]
- **Sir Speedy Printing Center** • 20 Province St [Province St]
- **Staples** • 25 Winter St [Winter Pl]
- **The UPS Store** • 198 Tremont St [Boylston St]

Gyms

- **Bally Total Fitness** • 17 Winter St [Winter Pl]
- **Sports Club LA** • 4 Avery St
- **Wang YMCA of Chinatown** • 8 Oak St W [Tremont St]
- **Women's Fitness of Boston** • 27 School St [Province St]

Liquor Stores

- **Boston Liquor Depot** • 861 Washington St [Oak St W]
- **Merchants Wine & Spirits** • 6 Water St [Washington St]
- **Wine Cellar** • 497 Washington St [Temple Pl]

Movie Theaters

- **Loews Boston Common** • 175 Tremont St [Avery St]
- **Wang Center** • 270 Tremont St [Hollis St]

Nightlife

- **Aria** • 246 Tremont St [Stuart]
- **Big Easy** • 1 Boylston Pl [Boylston St]
- **Chaps** • 101 Warrenton St [Stuart]
- **Felt** • 533 Washington St [Ave de Lafayette]
- **Intermission Tavern** • 228 Tremont St [Stuart]
- **Jacque's** • 79 Broadway [Winchester St]
- **Matrix** • 275 Tremont St [Hollis St]
- **MJ O'Connor's** • 27 Columbus Ave [Park Sq]
- **Mojitos Lounge** • 48 Winter St [Tremont St]
- **Parker's Bar** • 60 School St [Chapman]
- **Roxy** • 279 Tremont St [Common]
- **Rumor** • 100 Warrenton St [Stuart]
- **Teatro** • 177 Tremont St [Head]
- **Venu** • 100 Warrenton St [Stuart]
- **West Street Grille** • 15 West St [Washington St]
- **Whiskey Park** • 64 Arlington St [Providence]

Restaurants

- **Aujourd'hui** • 200 Boylston St [Charles St]
- **Buddha's Delight** • 5 Beach St [Washington St]
- **Chacarero** • 426 Washington St [Winter St]
- **Dedo** • 69 Church St [Piedmont]
- **Emperor's Garden** • 690 Washington St [Lagrange]
- **Excelsior** • 272 Boylston St [Hadassah]
- **Herrera's Mexican Grille** • 11 Temple Pl [Tremont St]
- **Intermission Tavern** • 228 Tremont St [Stuart]
- **Jacob Wirth** • 31 Stuart St [Dartmouth St]
- **Know Fat** • 530 Washington St [Ave de Lafayette]
- **Legal Sea Foods** • 26 Park Plz [Hadassah]
- **Locke-Ober** • 3 Winter Pl [Winter St]
- **Mantra** • 52 Temple Pl [Tremont St]
- **McCormick & Schmick's** • 34 Columbus Ave [Park Sq]
- **New Saigon Sandwich** • 696 Washington St [Kneeland]
- **No 9 Park** • 9 Park St [Beacon St]
- **Penang** • 685 Washington St [Lagrange]
- **Pigalle** • 75 Charles St S [Stuart]
- **Rachel's Kitchen** • 12 Church St [Fayette St]
- **Rock Bottom Brewery** • 115 Stuart St [Tremont St]
- **Sam LaGrassa's** • 44 Province St [Bosworth]
- **Silvertone Bar & Grill** • 69 Bromfield St [Tremont St]
- **Smith & Wollensky** • 101 Arlington St [Stuart]
- **Teatro** • 177 Tremont St [Head]
- **Tequila Mexican Grill** • 55 Bromfield St [Tremont St]
- **Via Matta** • 79 Park Plz [Hadassah]

Shopping

- **Beacon Hill Skate Shop** • 135 Charles St S [Fayette St]
- **Borders** • 10 School St [Washington St]
- **Bromfield Camera & Video** • 10 Bromfield St [Washington St]
- **City Antiques** • 362 Tremont St [Jefferson St]
- **City Sports** • 11 Bromfield St [Washington St]
- **DSW** • 385 Washington St [Bromfield]
- **Eddie Bauer Outlet** • 500 Washington St [West St]
- **H&M** • 350 Washington St [Franklin St]
- **Jack's Joke Shop** • 226 Tremont St [Stuart]
- **LJ Peretti** • 2 1/2 Park Sq
- **Macy's** • 450 Washington St [Temple Pl]
- **Marshall's** • 350 Washington St [Franklin St]
- **Old Town Camera** • 226 Washington St [Court]
- **Staples** • 25 Court St [Tremont St]
- **Staples** • 25 Winter St [Winter Pl]
- **TJ Maxx** • 350 Washington St [Franklin St]
- **Windsor Buttons** • 35 Temple Pl [Tremont St]

Video Rental

- **Kung Fu Video** • 365 Washington St [Bromfield]

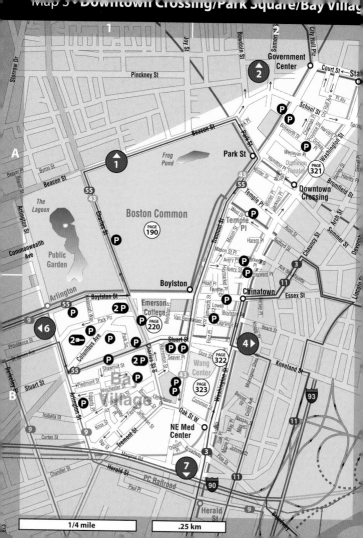

Map 5 • Downtown Crossing/Park Square/Bay Village

This area is well served by the T and buses, and now that the Silver Line is running, there's less reason than ever to drive around here. Note that Tremont Street runs in only one direction until it intersects with, uh, Tremont Street, and that Washington Street north of Temple Place in Downtown Crossing is a pedestrian mall closed to traffic.

Map 1

Subway

- **Arlington**
- **Boylston**
- **Chinatown**
- **Downtown Crossing**
- **Government Center**
- **NE Medical Center**
- **Park Street**

Bus Lines

- **3** · Boston Marine Industrial Park—South Station/ Haymarket Station
- **9** · City Point—Copley Square via Broadway Station
- **11** · City Point—Downtown, Bayview Route
- **43** · Ruggles Station—Park & Tremont Streets
- **55** · Jersey & Queensberry Streets—Copley Square or Park & Tremont Streets

Car Rental

- **Budget** · Motor Mart Garage · 24 Park Plz · 617-497-3669
- **Hertz** · 30 Park Plz · 617-338-1500

Parking

With the demolition of the Central Artery, work has started on the Rose Kennedy Greenway, a mixed-use green space that will pull together the heart of the Financial District and the buildings along the waterfront, much like a nice rug. Like all Chinatowns, Boston's Chinatown bustles. For an introduction, stroll and window-shop along Beach Street and its cross-streets.

Banks

- **Asian American Bank & Trust** • 68 Harrison Ave [Beach St]
- **Bank of America** • 100 Federal St [Franklin St]
- **Bank of America** • 125 High St [Pearl St]
- **Bank of America** • 175 Federal St [High St]
- **Bank of America** • 65 Franklin St [Arch St]
- **Bank of America (ATM)** • 0 Post Office Sq [Congress]
- **Bank of America (ATM)** • 1 Financial Ctr [Summer]
- **Bank of America (ATM)** • 1 Post Office Sq [Water]
- **Bank of America (ATM)** • 30 Rowes Wharf [High St]
- **Bank of America (ATM)** • 730 Atlantic Ave [Beach St]
- **Bank of America (ATM)** • 79 Summer St [Otis St]
- **Banknorth Massachusetts** • 15 Broad St [Doane]
- **Banknorth Massachusetts** • 75 Federal St [Franklin St]
- **Boston Private Bank & Trust** • 10 Post Office Sq [Water]
- **Century Bank** • 24 Federal St [Milk St]
- **Century Bank** • 280 Atlantic Ave [Central St]
- **Citizens Bank** • 1 Financial Ctr [Summer]
- **Citizens Bank** • 40 Summer St [Arch St]
- **Citizens Bank** • 6 Ave de Lafayette [Chauncy St]
- **Citizens Bank** • 77 Franklin St [Arch St]
- **Citizens Bank (ATM)** • 650 Atlantic Ave [Essex]
- **Citizens Bank (ATM)** • 700 Atlantic Ave [East St]
- **Eastern Bank** • 101 Federal St [Matthews]
- **Eastern Bank** • 265 Franklin St [Oliver]
- **One United Bank** • 133 Federal St [Milton Pl]
- **Sovereign Bank** • 1 Federal St [Milk St]
- **Sovereign Bank** • 100 Oliver St [High St]
- **Sovereign Bank** • 125 Summer St [Bedford]
- **Sovereign Bank** • 2 South Station Concourse [Essex]
- **Sovereign Bank** • 43 Kneeland St [Harrison Ave]
- **Sovereign Bank** • 61 Harrison Ave [Beach St]
- **Sovereign Bank (ATM)** • 160 Federal St [Milton Pl]
- **Sovereign Bank (ATM)** • 300 Congress St [Dot Ave]
- **Wainwright Bank & Trust** • 63 Franklin St [Arch St]

Donuts

- **Dunkin' Donuts** • 10 Winthrop Sq [Devonshire]
- **Dunkin' Donuts** • 101 Summer St [Lincoln St]
- **Dunkin' Donuts** • 16 Kneeland St [Shea]
- **Dunkin' Donuts** • 176 Federal St [High St]
- **Dunkin' Donuts** • 265 Franklin St [Oliver]
- **Dunkin' Donuts** • 70 E India Row [Atlantic Ave]
- **Honey Dew Donuts** • South Station • 700 Atlantic Ave [East St]

⭘ Landmarks

- **Boston Harbor Hotel** • 70 Rowes Wharf [High St]
- **Chinatown Gate** • Beach St & Hudson St
- **Custom House Tower** • 3 McKinley Sq [Central St]
- **Federal Reserve** • 600 Atlantic Ave [Summer]
- **South Station** • Atlantic Ave & Summer St

℞ Pharmacies

- **CVS** • 340 Washington St [Bromfield]
- **CVS** • 55 Summer St [Chauncy St]
- **PharmaCare Specialty Pharmacy** • 35 Kneeland St [Harrison Ave]
- **Tai Tung Pharmacy** • 256 Harrison Ave [Johnny]
- **Walgreens** • 70 Summer St [Otis St]

Post Offices

- **Fort Point Station** • 25 Dorchester Ave [Summer]
- **Lafayette Station** • 7 Ave de Lafayette [Chauncy St]
- **Milk Street** • 31 Milk St [Arch St]

Schools

- **Tufts University School of Medicine** • 136 Harrison Ave [Harvard St]

Supermarkets

- **C-Mart** • 109 Lincoln St [Tufts]
- **Super 88** • 73 Essex St [Oxford St]

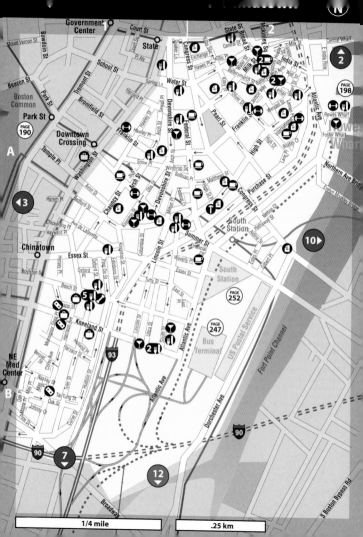

Sundries / Entertainment

Although there are plenty of worthwhile restaurants in Chinatown, you might consider Chau Chow City for dim sum, Taiwan Café for the real deal, Ocean Wealth for seafood, or Shabu-Zen for Japanese hot pot. For late-night bites, remember that neighbors News and South Street Diner serve well into the night. Some of Boston's top restaurants, including Radius, Julien, and Meritage, call the Financial District home.

Map 4

Coffee

- **Bean & Leaf Company** •
  20 Custom House St [India St]
- **Boston Coffee Exchange** •
  32 Summer St [Hawley St]
- **Jake's Beantown Café** •
  64 Broad St [Custom]
- **Peet's Coffee & Tea** • 176 Federal St
  [High St]
- **Starbucks** • 1 Federal St [Milk St]
- **Starbucks** • 1 Financial Ctr [Summer]
- **Starbucks** • 1 Federal Pl
  [High St]
- **Starbucks** • 101 Federal St [Matthews]
- **Starbucks** • 211 Congress St [High St]

Copy Shops

- **Air Graphics** • 89 Broad St [Franklin St]
- **BFS Business Printing** •
  282 Congress St [Dot Ave]
- **Copy Cop** • 1 International Pl
  [High St]
- **Copy Cop** • 101 Summer St
  [Lincoln St]
- **Copy Cop** • 13 Congress St [State]
- **Copy Cop** • 180 High St
  [Batterymarch St]
- **Copy Cop** • 85 Franklin St [Devonshire]
- **FedEx Kinko's** • 10 Post Office Sq
  [Water]
- **FedEx Kinko's** • 211 Congress St
  [High St]
- **Litigation Document Productions** •
  61 Batterymarch St, Fl 4 [Wendell St]
- **News Clips Etc Inc** • 42 Chauncy St
  [Bedford]

Gyms

- **Boston Sports Club** • 10 Franklin St
  [Washington St]
- **Fitcorp** • 100 Summer St [Bedford]
- **Fitcorp** • 125 Summer St [Bedford]
- **Fitness International** •
  1 International Pl [High St]
- **Langham Hotel Health Club** •
  250 Franklin [Oliver]
- **Rio Sports Club** • 52 Summer St
  [Arch St]
- **Rowes Wharf Health Club & Spa** •
  70 Rowes Wharf [High St]

Hardware Stores

- **Hardware Outlet** • 51 High St
  [Federal St]

Nightlife

- **An Tain** • 31 India St [Milk St]
- **Aqua** • 120 Water St [Kilby St]
- **Elephant & Castle** •
  161 Devonshire St [Milk St]
- **Good Life** • 28 Kingston St [Bedford]
- **JJ Foley's** • 21 Kingston St [Summer]
- **Jose McIntyre's** • 160 Milk St
  [India St]
- **Les Zygomates** • 129 South St [Tufts]
- **Mr Dooley's Boston Tavern** •
  77 Broad St [Custom]
- **News** • 150 Kneeland St [Utica St]
- **Rowes Wharf Bar** •
  Boston Harbor Hotel •
  70 Rowes Wharf [High St]
- **Times Restaurant and Bar** •
  112 Broad St [Wendell St]
- **Umbria** • 295 Franklin St
  [Batterymarch St]

Pet Shops

- **Aqua World (fish only)** • 20 Tyler St
  [Kneeland]

Restaurants

- **Andale** • 125 Summer St [Bedford]
- **Chau Chow City** • 83 Essex St [Ping]
- **J Pace & Son** • 1 Federal St [Milk St]
- **Julien** • Langham Hotel •
  250 Franklin [Oliver]
- **Les Zygomates** • 129 South St [Tufts]
- **Meritage** • 70 Rowes Wharf [High St]
- **Milk Street Café** • 50 Milk St
  [Devonshire]
- **New Shanghai** • 21 Hudson St
  [Kneeland]
- **News** • 150 Kneeland St [Utica St]
- **Noodle Alcove** • 10 Tyler St [Beach St]
- **Ocean Wealth** • 8 Tyler St [Beach St]
- **Osushi** • 101 Arch St [Snow Pl]
- **Peach Farm** • 4 Tyler St [Beach St]
- **Peking Tom's** • 25 Kingston St
  [Summer]
- **Pho Hoa** • 17 Beach St [Shea]
- **Pizza Oggi** • 131 Broad St [Wendell St]

- **Pressed Sandwiches** • 2 Oliver St
  [Milk St]
- **Radius** • 8 High St [Summer]
- **Sakurabana** • 57 Broad St [Broad]
- **Shabu-Zen** • 16 Tyler St [Beach St]
- **South Street Diner** • 178 Kneeland St
  [South St]
- **Sultan's Kitchen** • 116 State St [Broad]
- **Taiwan Café** • 34 Oxford St [Oxford Pl]
- **Umbria** • 295 Franklin St
  [Batterymarch St]

Shopping

- **Anna's Dessert House** •
  66 Harrison Ave [Beach St]
- **Boston Costume Company** •
  69 Kneeland St [Tyler St]
- **Silky Way Boston** • 38 Kneeland St
  [Harrison Ave]

Video Rental

- **Beijing Video (Chinese)** •
  30 Kneeland St, 4th Fl [Shea]
- **Top Ten Video Music (Chinese)** •
  219 Harrison Ave [Oak St]
- **Universe Video (Chinese)** •
  5 Knapp St [Shea]

27

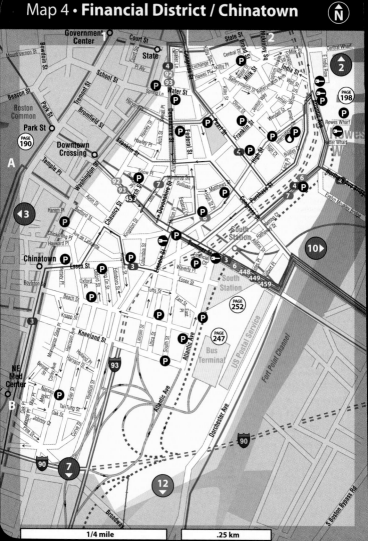

Map 2

The Dig may be over, and all of the lanes in O'Neill Tunnel may finally be open, but just the same there's still plenty of surface road construction in the Financial District to routinely snarl traffic. If you don't absolutely need to drive around here, don't, especially during rush hour.

Subway

- **Chinatown**
- **Downtown Crossing**
- **Park Street**
- **South Station**
- **State**

Bus Lines

- **3** • Boston Marine Industrial Park—South Station/ Haymarket Station
- **4** • North Station—World Trade Center via Federal Courthouse
- **6** • Boston Marine Industrial Park—South Station/ Haymarket Station
- **7** • City Point—Otis & Summer Streets via Northern Avenue & South Station
- **92** • Assembly Square Mall—Downtown via Sullivan Square Station, Main Street
- **93** • Sullivan Square Station—Downtown via Bunker Hill Street & Haymarket Station
- **448** • Marblehead—Haymarket, Downtown Crossing, or Wonderland
- **449** • Marblehead—Haymarket, Downtown Crossing, or Wonderland
- **459** • Marblehead—Haymarket, Downtown Crossing, or Wonderland

Car Rental

- **Alamo** • 270 Atlantic Ave [Central St] • 617-557-7179
- **Dollar** • Boston Harbor Hotel • 30 Rowes Wharf [High St] • 617-367-2654
- **Hertz** • South Station Amtrak • Summer St & Atlantic Ave • 617-338-1503
- **National** • 70 E India Row [Atlantic Ave] • 617-557-7179
- **Select Car Rentals** • 1 Lincoln St [Bedford] • 617-737-0371

Car Washes

- **Eddie's Professional Auto Detailers** • 1 International Pl [High St]

P Parking

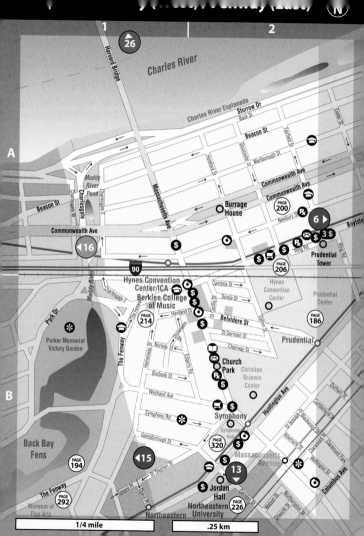

Map 5

Traffic on Mass Ave! MassPIRG on Newbury Street! Berklee students between classes! This area is fraught with minor perils, but that's because there's a lot going on. The striking group of buildings that comprises the Christian Science Center, together with the Pru and 111 Huntington (the "Daily Planet"), looks great at night. The long, Soviet-looking structure facing the Mother Church on Mass Ave is Church Park, a luxury apartment building.

$ Banks

- **Bank of America** • 133 Massachusetts Ave [Boylston St]
- **Bank of America** • 285 Huntington Ave [Gainsborough]
- **Bank of America** • 855 Boylston St [Gloucester]
- **Bank of America (ATM)** • 161 Massachusetts Ave [Belvidere St]
- **Bank of America (ATM)** • 221 Massachusetts Ave [Clearway]
- **Bank of America (ATM)** • 346 Huntington Ave [Opera]
- **Bank of America (ATM)** • 800 Boylston St [Fairfield St]
- **Bank of America (ATM)** • 90 Massachusetts Ave [Comm Ave]
- **Citizens Bank (ATM)** • 141 Massachusetts Ave [Boylston St]
- **Citizens Bank (ATM)** • 281 Huntington Ave [Gainsborough]
- **Citizens Bank (ATM)** • 800 Boylston St [Fairfield St]
- **Citizens Bank (ATM)** • 900 Boylston St [Gloucester]
- **Sovereign Bank** • 279 Massachusetts Ave [Westland]
- **Sovereign Bank** • 800 Boylston St [Fairfield St]
- **Sovereign Bank (ATM)** • 799 Boylston St [Fairfield St]

✹ Community Gardens

◉ Donuts

- **Dunkin' Donuts** • 1108 Boylston St [Hemenway St]
- **Dunkin' Donuts** • 153 Massachusetts Ave [Belvidere St]
- **Dunkin' Donuts** • 283 Huntington Ave [Gainsborough]
- **Dunkin' Donuts** • 333 Newbury St [Hereford]
- **Dunkin' Donuts** • 434 Massachusetts Ave [Columbus]

○ Landmarks

- **Burrage House** • 314 Commonwealth Ave [Hereford]
- **Christian Science Center** • 175 Huntington Ave [W Newton]
- **Church Park** • 221 Massachusetts Ave [Clearway]
- **Hynes Convention Center** • 900 Boylston St [Gloucester]
- **Jordan Hall** • 30 Gainsborough St [Huntington]
- **Prudential Tower** • 800 Boylston St [Fairfield St]
- **Symphony Hall** • 301 Massachusetts Ave [Huntington]

📖 Libraries

- **The Mary Baker Eddy Library** • 200 Massachusetts Ave [Clearway]

℞ Pharmacies

- **CVS** • 231 Massachusetts Ave [Clearway]
- **CVS** • 240 Newbury St [Fairfield St]
- **Walgreens** • 841 Boylston St [Fairfield St] ⌚

✉ Post Offices

- **Astor Station** • 207 Massachusetts Ave [Clearway]
- **Prudential Center Post Office** • 800 Boylston St [Fairfield St]

🏫 Schools

- **Berklee College of Music** • 1140 Boylston St [Hemenway St]
- **Boston Conservatory** • 8 The Fenway [Boylston St]
- **City on a Hill Charter** • 320 Huntington Ave [Opera]
- **Kingsley Montessori** • 30 Fairfield St [Comm Ave]
- **New England Conservatory** • 290 Huntington Ave [Gainsborough]
- **Newman Preparatory** • 245 Marlborough St [Exeter St]

🛒 Supermarkets

- **Trader Joe's** • 899 Boylston St [Gloucester]
- **Whole Foods Market** • 15 Westland Ave [Edgerly Rd]

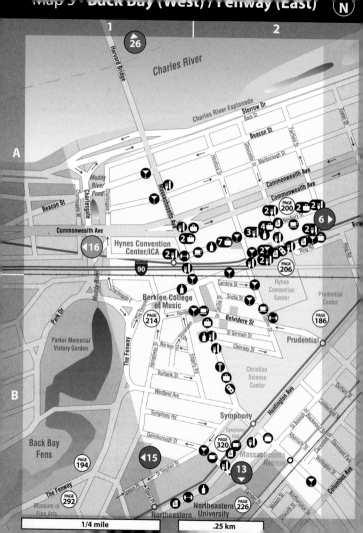

Map 3 · **Back Bay (West) / Fenway (East)** (N)

Charles River

Harard Bridge

(26)

Charles River Esplanade

Storrow Dr

Back St

Beacon St

1

Marlborough St

Commonwealth Ave

Commonwealth Ave

A

Muddy River Pond

Charlesgate

Beacon St

Charlesgate W

Massachusetts Ave

Newbury St

PAGE 200

(6)

Bow

Commonwealth Ave

(16)

Hynes Convention Center/ICA

Ring Rd

90

PAGE 206

Hynes Convention Center

Cambria St

Scotia St

Prudential Center

PAGE 186

Berklee College of Music

PAGE 214

Havila

Belvidere St

St Germain St

Prudential

2

Park Dr

Clearway St

Norway St

Burbank St

Christian Science Center

Huntington Ave

Durham St

B

Westland Ave

Symphony Rd

Symphony

Symphony Hall

Gainsborough St

PAGE 320

Massachusetts Avenue

(15)

St Stephen St

(13)

PAGE 226

Back Bay Fens

PAGE 194

The Fenway

PAGE 292

Museum of Fine Arts

Northeastern

Northeastern University

Columbus Ave

1/4 mile

.25 km

Map 5

Trident Booksellers and Café is a terrific spot for brunching and browsing. Get earthy (or just drink) at Other Side Cosmic Café. Beer drinkers who can handle Tunnel-level stereo volume and a touch of attitude should try Bukowski's. Also try Clio or Café Jaffa for dinner (depending on your budget for the evening). Berklee students often sit in at Wally's, joining more established musicians to play live jazz most nights of the week.

☕ Coffee

- **Espresso Royale** • 286 Newbury St [Gloucester]
- **Espresso Royale** • 44 Gainsborough St [Huntington]
- **Starbucks** • 151 Massachusetts Ave [Haviland St]
- **Starbucks** • 273 Huntington Ave [Gainsborough]
- **Starbucks** • 350 Newbury St [Mass Ave]
- **Starbucks** • Sheraton Hotel • 39 Dalton St [Scotia]

📋 Copy Shops

- **FedEx Kinko's** • 900 Boylston St [Gloucester]
- **Gnomon Copy** • 325 Huntington Ave [Opera]
- **Sir Speedy Printing Center** • 827 Boylston St [Fairfield St]
- **The UPS Store** • 263 Huntington Ave [Gainsborough]
- **The UPS Store** • 304 Newbury St [Hereford]

🏋 Gyms

- **Boston Fitness & Swim Club** • 39 Dalton St [Scotia]
- **Boston Sports Club** • 361 Newbury St [Mass Ave]
- **Central YMCA** • 316 Huntington Ave [Gainsborough]

🔧 Hardware Stores

- **Economy Hardware** • 219 Massachusetts Ave [Clearway]

🍸 Liquor Stores

- **Bauer Wine & Spirits** • 330 Newbury St [Hereford]
- **Choice Mart** • 181 Massachusetts Ave [St Germain]
- **Costello's** • 1084 Boylston St [Mass Ave]
- **DeLuca's Market** • 239 Newbury St [Fairfield St]
- **Huntington Wine & Spirits** • 301 Huntington Ave [Gainsborough]

🍷 Nightlife

- **Bukowski's** • 50 Dalton St [Scotia]
- **Crossroads** • 495 Beacon St [Mass Ave]
- **Dillon's** • 955 Boylston St [Hereford]
- **Kings** • 10 Scotia St [St Cecilia]
- **The Last Drop** • 421 Marlborough St [Mass Ave]
- **Lir** • 903 Boylston St [Gloucester]
- **Match** • 94 Massachusetts Ave [Newbury St]
- **Our House East** • 52 Gainsborough St [St Stephen]
- **Pour House** • 907 Boylston St [Gloucester]
- **Sonsie** • 327 Newbury St [Hereford]
- **TC's Lounge** • 1 Haviland St [Mass Ave]
- **Top of the Hub** • Prudential Center • 800 Boylston St [Fairfield St]
- **Wally's Café** • 427 Massachusetts Ave [Columbus]

🍴 Restaurants

- **Bangkok City** • 167 Massachusetts Ave [Belvidere St]
- **Bangkok Cuisine** • 177A Massachusetts Ave [St Germain]
- **Betty's Wok & Noodle Diner** • 250 Huntington Ave [Mass Ave]
- **Cactus Club** • 939 Boylston St [Hereford]
- **Café Jaffa** • 48 Gloucester St [Boylston St]
- **Capital Grille** • 359 Newbury St [Mass Ave]
- **Casa Romero** • 30 Gloucester St [Newbury St]
- **Clio** • 370A Commonwealth Ave [Mass Ave]
- **Croma** • 269 Newbury St [Gloucester]
- **Island Hopper** • 91 Massachusetts Ave [Newbury St]
- **L'Espalier** • 30 Gloucester St [Newbury St]
- **Lir** • 903 Boylston St [Gloucester]
- **Other Side Cosmic Café** • 407 Newbury St [Mass Ave]
- **Pour House** • 909 Boylston St [Gloucester]
- **Shanti: Taste of India** • 277B Huntington Ave [Gainsborough]
- **Sonsie** • 327 Newbury St [Hereford]
- **Spike's Junkyard Dogs** • 1076 Boylston St [Mass Ave]
- **Tapeo** • 266 Newbury St [Gloucester]
- **Top of the Hub** • 800 Boylston St [Fairfield St]
- **Trident Booksellers & Café** • 338 Newbury St [Hereford]
- **Vinny T's** • 867 Boylston St [Gloucester]
- **Wine Cellar** • 30 Massachusetts Ave [Marlborough]

🛍 Shopping

- **Army Barracks** • 328 Newbury St [Hereford]
- **Back Bay Bicycle** • 366 Commonwealth Ave [Mass Ave]
- **CD Spins** • 324 Newbury St [Hereford]
- **Daddy's Junky Music** • 159 Massachusetts Ave [Belvidere St]
- **DeLuca's Market** • 239 Newbury St [Fairfield St]
- **Economy Hardware** • 219 Massachusetts Ave [Clearway]
- **Emack & Bolio's** • 290 Newbury St [Gloucester]
- **John Fluevog** • 302 Newbury St [Hereford]
- **Johnson Artist Materials** • 355 Newbury St [Mass Ave]
- **JP Licks** • 352 Newbury St [Mass Ave]
- **Luna Boston** • 286 Newbury St [Gloucester]
- **Matsu** • 259 Newbury St [Fairfield St]
- **Newbury Comics** • 332 Newbury St [Hereford]
- **Orpheus** • 362 Commonwealth Ave [Mass Ave]
- **Sephora** • 800 Boylston St [Fairfield St]
- **Sweet-N-Nasty** • 90 Massachusetts Ave [Comm Ave]
- **Trident Booksellers & Café** • 338 Newbury St [Hereford]
- **Urban Outfitters** • 361 Newbury St [Mass Ave]
- **Utrecht Art Supply Center** • 333 Massachusetts Ave [St Botolph]
- **Virgin Megastore** • 360 Newbury St [Mass Ave]

📹 Video Rental

- **Blockbuster** • 235 Massachusetts Ave [Clearway]
- **Hollywood Video** • 899 Boylston St [Gloucester]

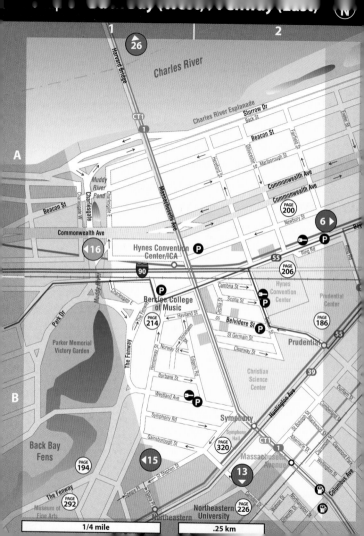

Map 5

Traffic is always nasty on Mass Ave during the week. On weekends Mass Ave becomes a parking lot, so avoid driving around here on Saturdays and Sundays if at all possible. And remember: there's no left turn from inbound Boylston Street onto Mass Ave. Few spots in Boston make it so easy for traffic cops to fill their quotas.

Subway

- **Massachusetts Avenue**
- **Hynes Convention Center (B,C,D)**
- **Prudential (E)**
- **Symphony (E)**

Bus Lines

- **CT1** · Central Square, Cambridge—BU Medical Center/BU Medical Campus
- **1** · Harvard/Holyoke Gate—Dudley Station via Massachusetts Avenue & BU Medical Center
- **9** · City Point—Copley Square via Broadway Station
- **39** · Forest Hills Station—Back Bay Station via Huntington Avenue
- **55** · Jersey & Queensberry Streets—Copley Square or Park & Tremont Streets

Car Rental

- **Avis** · 41 Westland Ave [Edgerly Rd] · 617-534-1400
- **Enterprise** · 800 Boylston St [Fairfield St] · 617-262-8222
- **Select Car Rental** · 39 Dalton St [Scotia] · 617-236-6088

Gas Stations

- **Shell** · 584 Columbus Ave [Mass Ave] ☺

Parking

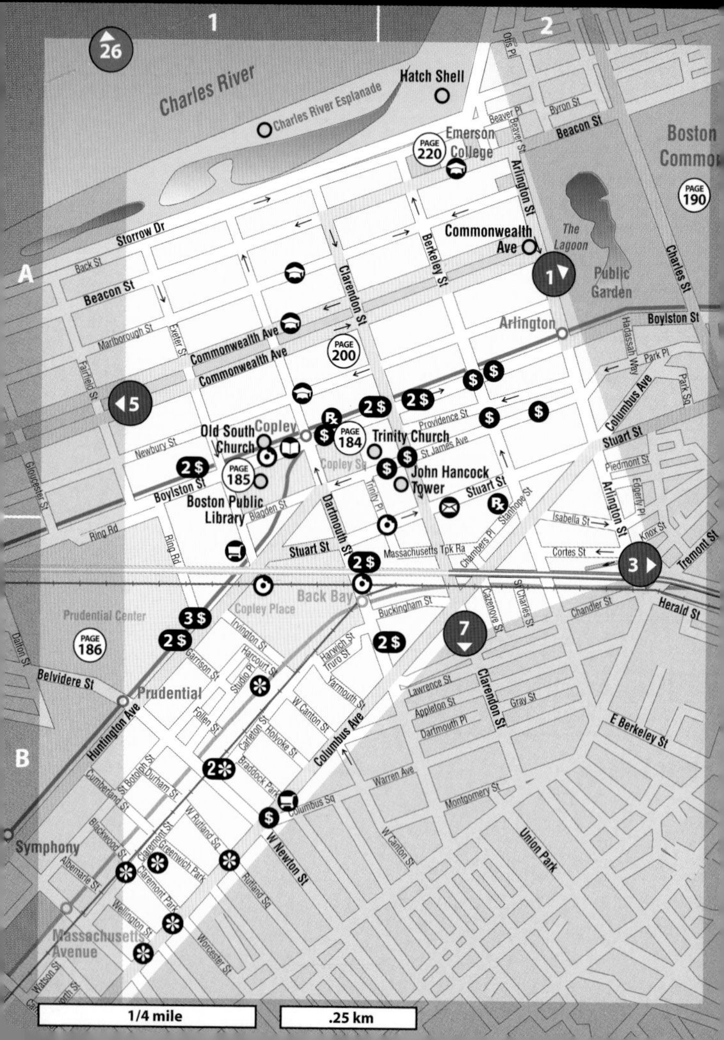

Map 6 • **Back Bay (East) / South End (Upper)**

1

2

26

Charles River

Hatch Shell

Charles River Esplanade

PAGE 220

Emerson College

Beaver Pl

Beacon St

Otis Pl

Byron St

Boston Common

PAGE 190

Storrow Dr

Commonwealth Ave

Arlington St

Berkeley St

Clarendon St

The Lagoon

Public Garden

1

A

Back St

Beacon St

Marlborough St

Commonwealth Ave

Commonwealth Ave

PAGE 200

Arlington

Boylston St

Hadassah Way

Park Pl

Park Sq

Columbus Ave

Exeter St

Fairfield St

Providence St

St. James Ave

2 $

2 $

$ $

$

Stuart St

Piedmont St

Arlington St

Columbus Ave

5

Newbury St

Old South Church

Copley

PAGE 184

Trinity Church

R

Eldredge Pl

Isabella St

Cortes St

3

Gloucester St

2 $

Boylston St

PAGE 185

Dartmouth St

Clarendon St

Copley St

$

John Hancock Tower

Trinity St

St. James Ave

Boston Public Library

Blagden St

Stuart St

R

Chambers Pl

Stanhope St

King St

Tremont St

Herald St

Ring Rd

Ring Rd

Stuart St

Massachusetts Tpk Rd

2 $

Back Bay

Copley Place

Buckingham St

St Charles St

Cazenove St

Chandler St

Prudential Center

PAGE 186

3 $

2 $

Irvington St

Harcourt St

Hannah St

Truro St

Yarmouth St

7

Lawrence St

Appleton St

Gray St

2 $

Clarendon St

E Berkeley St

Belvidere St

Prudential

Huntington Ave

Cumberland St

St Botolph St

Durham St

Carleton St

Holyoke St

Columbus Ave

W Canton St

Dartmouth Pl

Warren Ave

Montgomery St

Union Park

Symphony

2 ❋

$

W Newton St

W Rutland Sq

Braddock Park

Columbus Ave

W Concord St

W Center St

❋

Albemarle St

Westland Ave

Blackwood St

St Stephen St

Symphony Rd

Greenwich Park

Greenwich St

W Newton St

Massachusetts Avenue

❋

❋

❋

❋

❋

❋

Wadsworth St

Worcester St

E Berkeley St

1/4 mile

.25 km

This area features the "top" of Newbury Street, whose mix of locals, tourists, and international students and slackers keeps its merchants busy. Also here are boulevards inspired by 19th-century Paris, Trinity Church, the Hancock Tower, and some of Boston's best hotels. Diverse architecture in an attractive setting makes Copley Square a popular brown-bag lunch spot.

$ Banks

- **Bank of America** • 210 Berkeley St [St James Ave]
- **Bank of America** • 557 Boylston St [Clarendon St]
- **Bank of America** • 699 Boylston St [Exeter St]
- **Bank of America (ATM)** • 101 Huntington Ave [Garrison St]
- **Bank of America (ATM)** • 110 Huntington Ave [Harcourt]
- **Bank of America (ATM)** • 130 Dartmouth St [Columbus]
- **Bank of America (ATM)** • 145 Dartmouth St [Stuart]
- **Bank of America (ATM)** • 31 St James Ave [Arlington St]
- **Bank of America (ATM)** • 465 Columbus Ave [W Newton]
- **Bank of America (ATM)** • 745 Boylston St [Exeter St]
- **Boston Private Bank & Trust** • 500 Boylston St [Clarendon St]
- **Citizens Bank** • 426 Boylston St [Berkeley St]
- **Citizens Bank** • 535 Boylston St [Clarendon St]
- **Citizens Bank** • 607 Boylston St [Dartmouth St]
- **Citizens Bank (ATM)** • 101 Huntington Ave [Garrison St]
- **Citizens Bank (ATM)** • 111 Huntington Ave [Garrison St]
- **Citizens Bank (ATM)** • 145 Dartmouth St [Stuart]
- **Citizens Bank (ATM)** • 200 Clarendon St [St James Ave]
- **Citizens Bank (ATM)** • 717 Boylston St [Exeter St]
- **Sovereign Bank** • 575 Boylston St [Dartmouth St]
- **Sovereign Bank (ATM)** • 100 Huntington Ave [Harcourt]
- **Sovereign Bank (ATM)** • 200 Clarendon St [St James Ave]
- **Wainwright Bank & Trust** • 155 Dartmouth St [Stuart]

✴ Community Gardens

◉ Donuts

- **Dunkin' Donuts** • 145 Dartmouth St [Stuart]
- **Dunkin' Donuts** • 2 Copley Pl [Dartmouth St]
- **Dunkin' Donuts** • 430 Stuart St [Trinity]
- **Dunkin' Donuts** • 715 Boylston St [Exeter St]

○ Landmarks

- **Boston Public Library** • 700 Boylston St [Exeter St]
- **Charles River Esplanade**
- **Commonwealth Ave** • Arlington St to Mass Ave
- **Hatch Shell** • Esplanade [Congress]
- **John Hancock Tower** • 200 Clarendon St [St James Ave]
- **Old South Church** • 645 Boylston St [Dartmouth St]
- **Trinity Church** • 206 Clarendon St [St James Ave]

🕮 Libraries

- **Boston Public Library** • 700 Boylston St [Exeter St]

℞ Pharmacies

- **CVS** • 587 Boylston St [Dartmouth St] ♨
- **Statscript Pharmacy** • 21 Stanhope St [Berkeley St]

✉ Post Offices

- **Back Bay Annex Station** • 390 Stuart St [Clarendon St]

🏫 Schools

- **Commonwealth** • 151 Commonwealth Ave [Dartmouth St]
- **Fisher College** • 118 Beacon St [Berkeley St]
- **Learning Project Elementary** • 107 Marlborough St [Clarendon St]
- **Snowden International High** • 150 Newbury St [Dartmouth St]

🛒 Supermarkets

- **Shaw's** • 53 Huntington Ave [Exeter St]
- **South End Food Emporium** • 469 Columbus Ave [W Newton]

(37)

Map 6 • **Back Bay (East) / South End (Upper)**

Sundries / Entertainment

If you're hungry around here, you won't be starved for choices. Consider grabbing a great sandwich at Parish Café, a curry at House of Siam, or, if you're operating on an expense account, Grill 23. If you're just thirsty, grab a cocktail at Lush Lounge. Graphic design junkies should check out the incredible collection at the International Poster Gallery.

☕ Coffee

- **The Kiosque** • 600 Boylston St [Dartmouth St]
- **Marie's Place** • 390 Stuart St [Clarendon St]
- **Starbucks** • Westin Hotel • 10 Huntington Ave [Dartmouth St]
- **Starbucks** • Copley Place • 110 Huntington Ave [Harcourt]
- **Starbucks** • 165 Newbury St [Dartmouth St]
- **Starbucks** • 441 Stuart St [Trinity]
- **Starbucks** • 443 Boylston St [Berkeley St]
- **Starbucks** • 755 Boylston St [Fairfield St]
- **Tealuxe** • 108 Newbury St [Clarendon St]

📋 Copy Shops

- **BFS Printers** • 320 Stuart St [Columbus]
- **Copy Cop** • 601 Boylston St
- **FedEx Kinko's** • 187 Dartmouth St [St James Ave] ♿
- **Fedex Kinko's** • 575 Boylston St [Dartmouth St]
- **Pro Print** • 410 Boylston St [Berkeley St]
- **The UPS Store** • 110 Huntington Ave [Harcourt]
- **The UPS Store** • 398 Columbus Ave [W Canton]

🚜 Farmer's Markets

- **Copley Square (May-Nov; Tues 11 am-6 pm. Fri 11 am-6 pm)** • Copley Sq at St James Ave

🏋 Gyms

- **Body Evolver Health Fitness Center** • 364 Boylston St [Arlington St]
- **Boston Sports Club** • 501 Boylston St [Clarendon St]
- **Columbus Athletic Club** • 209 Columbus Ave [Berkeley St]
- **Fitcorp** • 800 Boylston St [Fairfield St]
- **Fitness Together** • 36 Newbury St [Berkeley St]
- **HealthWorks Fitness Center** • 441 Stuart St [Trinity]

🔧 Hardware Stores

- **Brookstone** • 100 Huntington Ave [Harcourt]
- **Park True Value Hardware** • 233 Newbury St [Fairfield St]

🍷 Liquor Stores

- **Best Cellars** • 745 Boylston St [Exeter St]
- **Clarendon Wine** • 563 Boylston St [Clarendon St]
- **The Wine Emporium** • 474 Columbus Ave [W Newton]

🍸 Nightlife

- **Anchovies** • 433 Columbus Ave [Braddock]
- **Champions** • Marriott • 110 Huntington Ave [Harcourt]
- **City Bar** • Lenox Hotel • 61 Exeter St [Boylston St]
- **Clery's** • 113 Dartmouth St [Columbus]
- **Club Café** • 209 Columbus Ave [Berkeley St]
- **Rattlesnake** • 384 Boylston St [Berkeley St]
- **Rise** • 306 Stuart St [Columbus]
- **Saint** • 90 Exeter St [Blagden]
- **Vox Populi** • 755 Boylston St [Fairfield St]

🍴 Restaurants

- **33** • 33 Stanhope St [Clarendon St]
- **Abe & Louie's** • 793 Boylston St
- **b.good** • 131 Dartmouth St [Columbus]
- **Bangkok Blue** • 651 Boylston St [Dartmouth St]
- **Blackfin Chophouse & Raw Bar** • 116 Huntington Ave [Garrison St]
- **Bomboa** • 35 Stanhope St [Cahners]
- **Brasserie Jo** • 120 Huntington Ave [W Newton]
- **Charlie's Sandwich Shoppe** • 429 Columbus Ave [Holyoke St]
- **Claremont Café** • 535 Columbus Ave [Claremont Pk]
- **Davio's** • 75 Arlington St [Stuart]
- **Domani** • 51 Huntington Ave [Exeter St]
- **Grill 23 & Bar** • 161 Berkeley St [Stuart]
- **House of Siam** • 542 Columbus Ave [Worcester St]
- **Jae's** • 520 Columbus Ave [Concord Sq]
- **Jae's** • 711 Boylston St [Exeter St]
- **L** • 234 Berkeley St [Newbury St]
- **Laurel** • 142 Berkeley St [Columbus]
- **Legal Sea Foods** • 800 Boylston St [Fairfield St]
- **Mistral** • 223 Columbus Ave [Cahners]
- **Montien** • 63 Stuart St [Huntington]
- **Osushi** • 10 Huntington Ave [Dartmouth St]
- **Parish Café** • 361 Boylston St [Arlington St]
- **Rouge** • 480 Columbus Ave [W Newton]

🛍 Shopping

- **All Things Chocolate** • 31 St James St [Arlington St]
- **Amazing Express** • 57 Stuart St [Huntington]
- **Anthropologie** • 799 Boylston St [Fairfield St]
- **Brooks Brothers** • 46 Newbury St [Berkeley St]
- **City Sports** • 480 Boylston St [Clarendon St]
- **Crate & Barrel** • 777 Boylston St [Fairfield St]
- **First Act Guitar Studio** • 745 Boylston St [Exeter St]
- **Hempest** • 207 Newbury St [Exeter St]
- **International Poster Gallery** • 205 Newbury St [Exeter St]
- **Kitchen Arts** • 161 Newbury St [Dartmouth St]
- **Lindt Master Chocolatier** • 704 Boylston St [Exeter St]
- **Lord & Taylor** • 760 Boylston St [Fairfield St]
- **Louis Boston** • 234 Berkeley St [Newbury St]
- **Lush** • 166 Newbury St [Dartmouth St]
- **Marc Jacobs** • 81 Newbury St [Clarendon St]
- **Marshall's** • 500 Boylston St [Clarendon St]
- **Neiman Marcus** • 5 Copley Pl [Dartmouth St]
- **Paper Source** • 338 Boylston St [Arlington St]
- **Saks Fifth Avenue** • 1 Ring Rd [Waltham]
- **Shreve, Crump & Low** • 440 Boylston St [Berkeley St]
- **Stil** • 170 Newbury St [Dartmouth St]
- **Tannery** • 400 Boylston St [Berkeley St]
- **Teuscher Chocolates of Switzerland** • 230 Newbury St [Fairfield St]
- **Tweeter Etc** • 350 Boylston St [Arlington St]
- **Winston Flowers** • 131 Newbury St [Dartmouth St]

Map 6

39

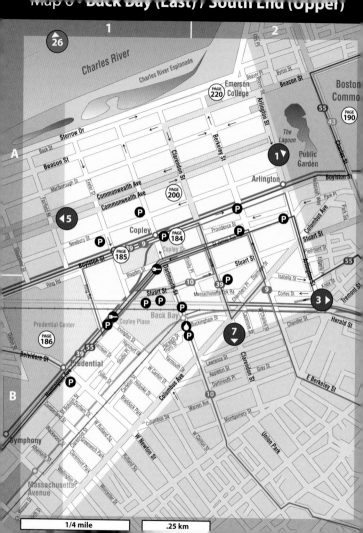

In Boston, jaywalking is a time-honored pastime, especially around the Pru and along Boylston and Newbury Streets. Back Bay is generally well-served by public transportation, even though (somewhat unusually) no buses actually run down Comm Ave. Street parking? Good luck.

Subsway

■ · **Arlington**
■ · **Copley**
■ · **Back Bay**

Bus Lines

9 · City Point—Copley Square via Broadway Station

10 · City Point—Copley Square via Andrew Station & BU Medical Area

39 · Forest Hills Station—Back Bay Station via Huntington Avenue

43 · Ruggles Station—Park & Tremont Streets

55 · Jersey & Queensberry Streets—Copley Square or Park & Tremont Streets

Car Rental

· **Dollar** · Mariott Copley Place ·
110 Huntington Ave [Harcourt] · 617-578-0025

· **Hertz** · 10 Huntington Ave [Dartmouth St] · 617-338-1506

· **Hertz** · Back Bay Station Amtrak ·
145 Dartmouth St [Stuart] · 617-338-1500

Car Washes

· **Magic Touch** · 131 Dartmouth St [Columbus]

Parking

The South End is America's largest Victorian neighborhood, has the city's largest gay population, and, after years of gentrification, is now actually a "destination" spot for visitors to Boston. All this hipness, of course, makes the South End more expensive than it was a decade ago, forcing some residents to move. Perhaps the development of BU Medical Center's "biosafety" research lab will keep housing prices in check.

$ Banks

- **Bank of America** • 557 Tremont St [Waltham]
- **Bank of America (ATM)** • 393 Massachusetts Ave [St Botolph]
- **Century Bank (ATM)** • BU Dental School • 100 E Newton St [Harrison Ave]
- **Century Bank (ATM)** • BU Parking Garage • 710 Albany St [E Concord]
- **Century Bank (ATM)** • BU Med School • 715 Albany St [E Concord]
- **Citizens Bank** • 1355 Washington St [Waltham]
- **Citizens Bank (ATM)** • 840 Harrison Ave [E Springfield]
- **Mercantile Bank** • 1320 Washington St [Rollins St]
- **Sovereign Bank** • 521 Tremont St [Dwight]
- **Sovereign Bank (ATM)** • 818 Harrison Ave [Worcester St]

Community Gardens

Donuts

- **Dunkin' Donuts** • 1138 Washington St [E Berkeley]
- **Dunkin' Donuts** • 616 Massachusetts Ave [Shawmut Ave]

Emergency Rooms

- **Boston Medical Center** • 1 Boston Medical Ctr Pl [Mass Ave]

Landmarks

- **Cathedral of the Holy Cross** • 1400 Washington St [Union Pk St]
- **SoWa Building** • 450 Harrison Ave [Thayer St]

Libraries

- **South End** • 685 Tremont St [W Newton]

Pharmacies

- **Boston Medical Outpatient Pharmacy** • 720 Harrison Ave [E Brookline]
- **CVS** • 400 Tremont St [Herald]
- **Tremont Drug** • 610 Tremont St [W Dedham]
- **Walgreens** • 1603 Washington St [Rutland]

Police

- **District D-4** • 650 Harrison Ave [E Dedham]

Post Offices

- **Cathedral Station** • 59 W Dedham St [Shawmut Ave]

Schools

- **Cathedral Grammar** • 595 Harrison Ave [Malden]
- **Cathedral High** • 74 Union Park St [Harrison Ave]
- **Joseph J Hurley Elementary** • 70 Worcester St [Tremont St]
- **William Blackstone Elementary** • 380 Shawmut Ave [W Dedham]
- **William McKinley** • 90 Warren Ave [Columbus]

Supermarkets

- **Foodie's Urban Market** • 1421 Washington St [Upton]
- **Ming's Supermarket** • 1102 Washington St [E Berkeley]
- **Super 88** • 50 Herald St [Washington St]

The South End is loaded with terrific bars and restaurants. Consider starting your night at Delux, a beloved neighborhood bar. Then take your friends to Joe V's for Italian, or perhaps Aquitaine if you're in the mood for French. After a few bottles of wine, roll over to Pho Republique to continue the fun. For the morning after, treat your stomach to breakfast at Mike's City Diner. If you're still alive after all that, call us.

Map
7

☕ Coffee

- **Francesca's** • 564 Tremont St [Union Pk St]
- **Haley House Bakery & Café** • 23 Dartmouth St [Montgomery St]
- **Starbucks** • 627 Tremont St [W Canton]

📄 Copy Shops

- **FedEx Kinko's** • 715 Albany St [E Concord]
- **Stratografix** • 1200 Washington St [Perry St]

🌸 Farmer's Markets

- **South End at the Open Market** (May 23-Oct; Sun 9 am-4 pm) • 540 Harrison Ave [Savoy St]

💪 Gyms

- **Boston Sports Club** • 560 Harrison Ave [Rollins St]

🔨 Hardware Stores

- **Warren Hardware** • 470 Tremont St [E Berkeley]

🍾 Liquor Stores

- **Brix Wine Shop** • 1284 Washington St [Savoy St]
- **Wine Emporium** • 607 Tremont St [Dartmouth St]

🍸 Nightlife

- **Delux Café** • 100 Chandler St [Clarendon St]
- **Eagle** • 520 Tremont St [Dwight]
- **Franklin Café** • 278 Shawmut Ave [Hanson]
- **Pho Republique** • 1415 Washington St [Union Pk St]

🐾 Pet Shops

- **The Pet Shop Girls** • 12 Union Park St [Shawmut Ave]
- **Polka Dog Bakery** • 256 Shawmut Ave [Milford]
- **s'Poochies Spa & Boutique** • 400 Tremont St [Herald]

🍴 Restaurants

- **Addis Red Sea** • 544 Tremont St [Waltham]
- **Aquitaine** • 569 Tremont St [Union Pk St]
- **B&G Oysters** • 550 Tremont St [Waltham]
- **Caffe Umbra** • 1395 Washington St [Union Pk St]
- **Delux Café** • 100 Chandler St [Clarendon St]
- **Dish** • 253 Shawmut Ave [Milford]
- **El Triunfo** • 147 E Berkeley St [Harrison Ave]
- **Emilio's** • 536 Tremont St [Hanson]
- **Equator** • 1721 Washington St [W Springfield]
- **flour bakery + café** • 1595 Washington St [Rutland]
- **Franklin Café** • 278 Shawmut Ave [Hanson]
- **Garden of Eden** • 571 Tremont St [Union Pk St]
- **Hamersley's Bistro** • 553 Tremont St [Waltham]
- **Joe V's** • 315 Shawmut Ave [Union Pk St]
- **The Little Window** • 42 Plympton St [Harrison Ave]
- **Masa** • 439 Tremont St [Appleton St]
- **Metropolis Café** • 584 Tremont St [Upton]
- **Mike's City Diner** • 1714 Washington St [W Springfield]
- **Morse Fish** • 1401 Washington St [Union Pk St]
- **Nicole's** • 639 Tremont St [W Canton]
- **Nightingale** • 578 Tremont St [Upton]
- **Pho Republique** • 1415 Washington St [Union Pk St]
- **Picco** • 513 Tremont St [E Berkeley]
- **Red Fez** • 1222 Washington St [Perry St]
- **Sibling Rivalry** • 523 Tremont St [Dwight]
- **Stella** • 1525 Washington St [E Brookline]
- **Thai Village** • 592 Tremont St [Upton]
- **Tremont 647** • 647 Tremont St [W Brookline]
- **Union Bar and Grille** • 1357 Washington St [Waltham]

🛍 Shopping

- **Aunt Sadie's** • 18 Union Park St [Shawmut Ave]
- **Bobby from Boston** • 19 Thayer St [Harrison Ave]
- **Brix Wine Shop** • 1284 Washington St [Savoy St]
- **The Butcher Shop** • 552 Tremont St [Waltham]
- **Community Bicycle Supply** • 496 Tremont St [E Berkeley]
- **Fresh Eggs** • 58 Clarendon St [Chandler St]
- **Ilex** • 73 Berkeley St [Chandler St]
- **Kosmos Market** • 683 Tremont St [W Newton]
- **Lekker** • 1317 Washington St [Rollins St]
- **Lionette's** • 577 Tremont St [Union Pk St]
- **Picco** • 513 Tremont St [E Berkeley]
- **Posh** • 557 Tremont St [Waltham]
- **South End Formaggio** • 268 Shawmut Ave [Milford]
- **Uniform** • 511 Tremont St [E Berkeley]

🎲 Video Rental

- **Mike's Movies** • 630 Tremont St [W Canton]

Street parking north of Washington Street is a disaster, a situation compounded by the paucity of parking lots and garages. Visitors should strongly consider using the Silver Line, particularly to go to any spot on or near Washington Street.

Subway

- NE Medical Center
- Herald St
- E Berkeley St
- Union Park St
- Newton St
- Worcester Sq
- Massachussetts Ave
- Lenox St
- Melnea Cass Blvd

Bus Lines

- **CT1** • Central Square, Cambridge—BU Medical Center/BU Medical Campus
- **CT3** • Beth Israel Deaconess Medical Center—Andrew Station via BU Medical Center
- **1** • Harvard/Holyoke Gate—Dudley Station via Mass Ave & BU Medical Center
- **8** • Harbor Point/UMass—Kenmore Station via South End Medical Area
- **9** • City Point—Copley Square via Broadway Station
- **10** • City Point—Copley Square via Andrew Station & BU Medical Area
- **43** • Ruggles Station—Park & Tremont Streets
- **47** • Central Square, Cambridge—Broadway Station via South End Medical Area

Gas Stations

- **Mobil** • 273 E Berkeley St [Albany St] ⊗
- **Stop N Gas** • 970 Washington St [Herald]
- **Sunoco** • 976 Washington St [Herald]

Parking

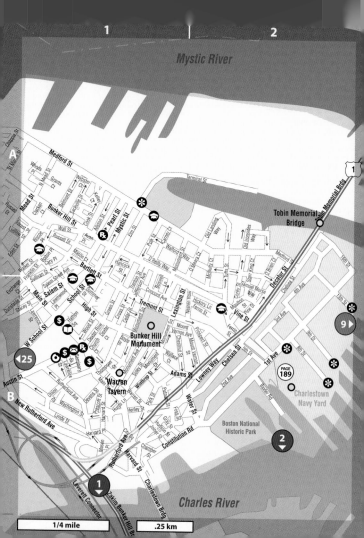

Mystic River

1

2

Medford St

Terminal St

Bunker Hill St

Pearl St

Mystic St

Tobin Memorial
Bridge

Mead St

Bartlett St

Salem St

School St

High St

Tremont St

Lexington St

Vine St

Decatur St

Bunker Hill
Monument

Main St

W. School St

25

Austin St

Warren
Tavern

Adams St

Lowney Way

Chelsea St

1st Ave

PAGE
189

9

Charlestown
Navy Yard

New Rutherford Ave

Rutherford Ave

Constitution Rd

Boston National
Historic Park

2

Harvard St

Water St

Leverett Connector

Zakim Bunker Hill Br

Charlestown Bdg

1

Charles River

1/4 mile

.25 km

Map 3

In most cities, Charlestown would be a gem of preservation (and gentrification). It has views, well-preserved colonial homes, Bunker Hill, and the *USS Constitution*. But it's tough to stand out in Boston and a bit tricky for anyone to get here. Separated from the rest of the city by highways, train yards, and water, Charlestown is a quiet neighborhood drifting toward hardscrabble on the edges.

Banks

- **Citizens Bank** • 5 Austin St [Warren St]
- **Citizens Bank (ATM)** • 140 Main St [Church Ct]
- **Co-Operative Bank** • 201 Main St [Hathon]

Community Gardens

Donuts

- **Dunkin' Donuts** • 11 Austin St [Warren St]

Landmarks

- **Bunker Hill Monument** • Monument Ave [High St]
- **Charlestown Navy Yard** • Constitution Rd & Warren St
- **Tobin Memorial Bridge** • US-1
- **Warren Tavern** • 2 Pleasant St [Main]

Libraries

- **Charlestown** • 179 Main St [Wood St]

Pharmacies

- **CVS** • Bunker Hill Mall • 5 Austin St [Warren St]
- **High Pharmacy** • 54 High St [Green St]

Post Offices

- **Charlestown** • 23 Austin St [Lawrence St]

Schools

- **Charlestown High** • 240 Medford St [Polk]
- **Clarence R Edwards Middle** • 28 Walker St [High St]
- **Harvard-Kent Elementary** • 50 Bunker Hill St [Moulton St]
- **The Holden School** • 8 Pearl St [Wesley St]
- **Warren Prescott Elementary** • 50 School St [Bartlett St]

Mystic River

1   2

A

Medford St
Woods
St
Grants
Ct
Mead St
Mead St
Webster St
Belmont
St
Russell St
Forrest St
Eden St
Bunker Hill St
Clinkston
St
Franklin St
Sackville St
Pearl St
Mystic St
Elm St
Terminal St
Old Landing Way
Medford St
Decatur St
Old Ironsides Way
16th St
13th St
12th St

Bartlett St
Mason Ct
Cary Pl
Salem St
Salem Street Ave
Hancock St
Avon
Wall Pl
Fox St
Walford Way
O'Reilly Way
Gardner Ct
Corey St
Medford Ct
Tufts St
Samuel Morse Way
Chelsea St
4th Ave
5th Ave

Main St
School St
High St
Lynmwood
Harbon
Wood Row
Concord St
Tremont St
Lexington St
Warren St Now
Vine St
Ferrin St
Cross St
3rd Ave
6th Ave
7th Ave

Sullivan St
Green St
Cedar St
Monument Ave
Mount Vernon Ave
Prospect St
Hickory Ln

W School St
Seminary
Lawrence St
Monument Sq
Winthrop St
Adams St
Lowney Way
Chelsea St
2nd Ave
Baxter Rd
8th Ave

◄25

Thompson
Soley St
Pleasant St
Mead St
Water St

Austin St
Rutherford Ave
Devens St
Washington St
Harvard St
Henley St
First Ave

B
New Rutherford Ave
Union St
Lynde St
Pratt St
Harvard Pl
Chambers St
Constitution Rd

Mason St
Harvard St

Leverett Connector
Zakim Bunker Hill Br
Charlestown Brdg

Charles River

Tobin Memorial Bridge
1

9 ►

PAGE
189

Charlestown
Navy Yard

Boston National
Historic Park

2
▼

1

1/4 mile   .25 km

Map 3

Two notable restaurants along Charlestown's City Square are Todd English's Olives and Meze Estiatorio. Views of the city can't be beat while eating oysters at the recently upscaled Tavern on the Water. For plotting revolution after visiting Bunker Hill, nothing's better than the Warren Tavern, one of the oldest bars in the country and watering hole of many of our favorite patriots.

Coffee

- **Coffee Shop** • 1 Thompson Square [Austin]
- **Sorelle** • 100 City Sq [Park St]

Farmer's Markets

- **Charlestown (July-Oct; Wed 2 pm-7 pm)** • Main St & Austin St

Gyms

- **Boston Young Men's Christian Union** • 48 Boyle St [Pleasant St]
- **Curves** • 5 Austin St [Warren St]

Liquor Stores

- **Bunker Hill Liquors** • 200 Bunker Hill St [Green St]
- **Charlestown Liquors** • 10 Thompson Sq [Austin]
- **McCarthy Brothers Liquors** • 9 Moulton St [Bunker Hill St]

Nightlife

- **Sullivan's Pub** • 85 Main St [Monument Ave]
- **Tavern on the Water** • 1 Pier 6 at E 8th St
- **Warren Tavern** • 2 Pleasant St [Main]

Restaurants

- **Figs** • 67 Main St [Monument Ave]
- **Ironside Grill** • 25 Park St [Warren St]
- **Jenny's Pizza** • 320 Medford St [Allston St]
- **Meze Estiatorio** • 100 City Sq [Park St]
- **Navy Yard Bistro & Wine Bar** • 1 1st Ave [3rd St]
- **Ninety Nine** • 29 Austin St [Lawrence St]
- **Olives** • 10 City Sq [Main]
- **Paolo's Trattoria** • 251 Main St [Lawnwood]
- **Sorelle** • 1 Monument Ave [Main]
- **Sorelle** • 100 City Sq [Park St]
- **Tangierino** • 83 Main St [Monument Ave]
- **Warren Tavern** • 2 Pleasant St [Main]

Shopping

- **A Wild Flower** • 73 Main St [Monument Ave]
- **Bunker Hill Florist** • 1 Thompson Sq [Austin]
- **Doherty's Flowers** • 223 Main St [School St]
- **The Joy of Old** • 85A Warren St [Pleasant St]

In the middle of winter, it's a long, bitter hike into Charlestown from the Orange Line stops at Community College or Sullivan Square. You might consider busses from Haymarket as a quicker alternative, with the 92 bus getting you up Main Street and the 93 bus to the Navy Yard. A great summer alternative is to mix it up with the tourists on the City Water Taxi from Long Wharf.

Bus Lines

92 • Assembly Square Mall—Downtown via
Sullivan Square Station, Main St

93 • Sullivan Square Station—Downtown via
Bunker Hill Street & Haymarket Station

111 • Woodlawn or Broadway & Park Ave—
Haymarket Station via Mystic River/Tobin Bridge

Gas Stations

• **Shell** • 1 Rutherford Ave [N Washington] ℗

P Parking

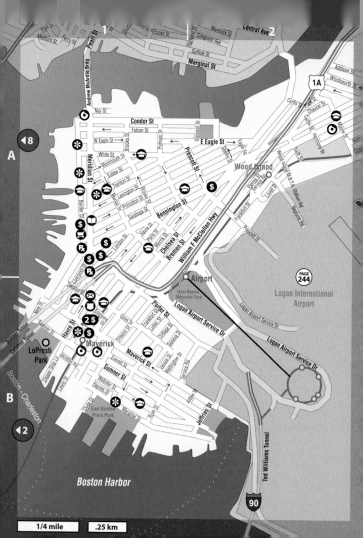

With more residents deciding to relocate to East Boston, attracted by cheaper housing costs and knock-out views of the skyline, hammers are louder in Eastie these days than the jets at Logan. Once predominantly an Italian-American enclave, Eastie is now home to a diverse and vibrant Latin American community. Maverick Square is busy, but you'll want to make the walk up to Day Square to get a better sense of the turf.

Banks

- **Bank of America (ATM)** • 3-11 Porter St [Central Sq]
- **Bank of America (ATM)** • 47 Maverick Sq [Sumner St]
- **Citizens Bank** • 26 Central Sq [Bennington]
- **East Boston Savings Bank** • 1 Bennington St [Porter St]
- **East Boston Savings Bank** • 10 Meridian St [Maverick St]
- **East Boston Savings Bank (ATM)** • 294 Bennington St [Chelsea St]
- **Eastern Bank (ATM)** • 246 Border St [Lexington St]
- **Sovereign Bank** • 2 Meridian St [Maverick St]

Community Gardens

Donuts

- **Betty Ann's** • 565 Bennington St. [Moore]
- **Dunkin' Donuts** • 13 Maverick Sq [Sumner St]
- **Honey Dew Donuts** • 12 Maverick Sq [Sumner St]
- **Honey Dew Donuts** • 470 Meridian St [Condor]

O Landmarks

- **LoPresti Park** • Sumner St

Libraries

- **East Boston** • 276 Meridian St [Princeton St]

Pharmacies

- **CVS** • 210 Border St [Saratoga St] ⊗
- **Walgreens** • 1 Central Sq [Meridian St] ⊗

Police

- **District A-7** • 69 Paris St [Emmons St]

Post Offices

- **East Boston Station** • 50 Meridian St [Paris St]

Schools

- **Dante Alighieri Elementary** • 37 Gove St [Paris St]
- **Donald McKay Elementary/Middle** • 122 Cottage St [Maverick St]
- **East Boston Central Catholic** • 69 London St [McClellan Hwy]
- **East Boston High** • 86 White St [Eutaw]
- **Hugh Roe O'Donnell Elementary** • 33 Trenton St [Marion St]
- **James Otis Elementary** • 218 Marion St [Morris]
- **Patrick J Kennedy Elementary** • 343 Saratoga St [Putnam St]
- **Samuel Adams Elementary** • 165 Webster St [Ruth]
- **St Mary Star of the Sea Elementary** • 58 Moore St [London St]
- **Umana/Barnes Middle** • 312 Border St [Eutaw]

Supermarkets

- **Shaw's** • 246 Border St [Lexington St]

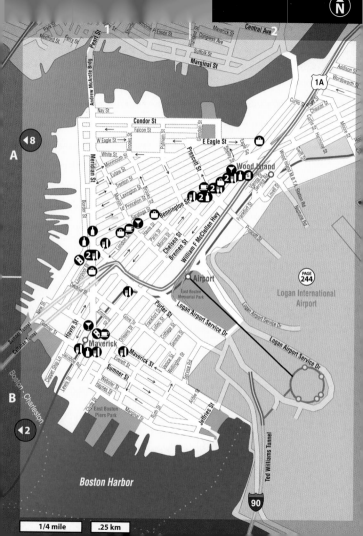

Sundries / Entertainment

Map 9

Pañerias, rotisseries, and taquerias outnumber the many fine Italian bakeries and cafés. The Peruvian spit chicken at the Ricon Limeno in Day Square is a best bet, while the Salvadoran El Buen Gusto offers a more refined dining experience close by. People from all over town drive to Santarpio's for pizza. Shopping has a distinct Latin American flavor, with small stores selling piñatas, saint votives, and soccer kits.

Coffee

- **La Sultana** • 40 Maverick Sq [Winthrop St]
- **Peaches & Cream** • 73 Bennington St [London St]
- **Spinelli's** • 282 Bennington St [Prescott St]

Copy Shops

- **The UPS Store** • 2 Neptune Rd [Bennington]

Liquor Stores

- **Castillo Liquors** • 228 Meridian St [Saratoga St]
- **Clipper Ship Wine & Spirits** • 17 Maverick Sq [Sumner St]
- **Day Square Liquor** • 288 Bennington St [Chelsea St]
- **Kappy's Liquors** • 216 Border St [Saratoga St]
- **Neptune Liquors** • 1 Neptune Rd [Bennington]

Nightlife

- **Kelly Square Pub** • 84 Bennington St [Marion St]
- **Pony Lounge** • 411 Chelsea St [Shelby]
- **Trainor's Café** • 127 Maverick St [Paris St]

Restaurants

- **Café Belo** • 254 Bennington St [Prescott St]
- **Café Italia** • 150 Meridian St [London St]
- **Café Meridian** • 271 Meridian St [Princeton St]
- **El Buen Gusto** • 295 Bennington St [Chelsea St]
- **Jeveli's** • 387 Chelsea St [Bennington]
- **La Frontera** • 290 Bennington St [Chelsea St]
- **La Terraza** • 19 Bennington St [Porter St]
- **Rincon Limeno** • 409 Chelsea St [Shelby]
- **Santarpio's Pizza** • 111 Cheslea St [Porter St]
- **TacoMex** • 65 Maverick Sq [Sumner St]
- **Taqueria Cancun** • 192 Sumner St [Maverick Sq]

Shopping

- **Brazilian Soccer House** • 110 Meridian St [London St]
- **Globos y Fiesta** • 52A Bennington St [London St]
- **Lilly's Flower Shop** • 512 Saratoga St [Chelsea St]
- **Liverty Stadium Bookstore** • 268 Bennington St [Prescott St]
- **Lolly's Bakery** • 158 Bennington St [Brooks]
- **Salvy the Florist** • 8 Chelsea St [Maverick St]

Video Rental

- **Blockbuster** • 184 Border St [Central Sq]
- **Maverick Audio & Video** • 25 Maverick Sq [Sumner St]

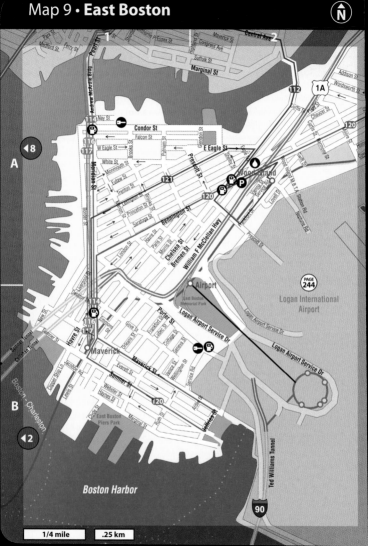

Map 9 • **East Boston**

N

Park St
Medford St
Ferry St
Pearl St
Shelby St
Thorne St
Essex St
Orleans St
Congress Ave
Maverick St
Central Ave
1

Suffolk St
Marginal St
Highland St

112
1A

Curtis St
Addison St
Wordsworth St

Chaucer St
Curtis St
Byron St
120

A
8

Nay St
Condor St
Falcon St
E Eagle St
W Eagle St
Brooks St
Putnam St
Lamson St
Prescott St
116
117

Meridian St
White St
Monmouth St
Eutaw St
Trenton St
121
120
Wood Island M.B.T.A. Station Rd
Bayswater Rd
P
Wood Island
Vienna St
London St

Border St
Lexington St
Princeton St
Saratoga St
Bennington St
Brooks St
Paris St
Marion St
Moore St
Havre St
Chelsea St
Bremen St
Prescott St
Neptune Rd
Walley St

William F McClellan Hwy

PAGE
244

Logan International
Airport

Sumner Tunnel
Callahan Tunnel
Boston – Charlestown

Decatur St
Havre St
Havre St
Emmons St
114
116
117
Maverick

Gove St
Porter St
Frankfort St
Lubec St
Cottage St
Everett St
Border St
London St
Paris St
Orleans St
Maverick St
Airport
East Boston
Memorial Park
Logan Airport Service Dr
Logan Airport Service Dr
Logan Airport Service Dr

Navy St
Sumner St
Clipper Ship Ln
Jeffries St
Lamson St
Lewis St
Webster St
Haynes St
Seaver St
Maverick St
Sumner St
Bremen St
Wordsworth St
Marginal St
Fifth St
Jeffries St
120

B
2

East Boston
Piers Park

Boston Harbor

Ted Williams Tunnel
I-90
90

| 1/4 mile | .25 km |

Blue train to Wonderland! You'll get off well before the beach at the busy Maverick stop or Wood Island, the closest stop to Day Square. Driving means the Callahan Tunnel. Be sure to stay in the right lane for the first exit out of the tunnel. Bang a right onto Chelsea Street to get to Maverick Square, or left to Day Square. Bicycle options include water taxis or the year-round MBTA ferries from Logan to Long Wharf.

Subway

- ███ • **Maverick**
- ███ • **Airport**
- ███ • **Wood Island**

Bus Lines

- **112** • Wellington Station—Wood Island Station via Central Ave, Mystic Mall & Admiral's Hill
- **116** • Wonderland Station—Maverick Station via Revere St
- **117** • Wonderland Station—Maverick Station via Revere St
- **120** • Orient Heights Station—Maverick Station via Bennington St
- **121** • Wood Island Station—Maverick Station via Lexington

🔑Car Rental

- **Affordable Auto Rental** • 84 Condor St [Brooks] • 617-561-7000

💧Car Washes

- **Squikee Clean** • 452 Bremen St [Bennington]

⛽Gas Stations

- **Citgo** • 110 Service Rd [Mass Tpke]
- **Getty** • 331 Bennington St [Bremen St]
- **Mobil** • 396 Chelsea St [Shelby]
- **Mobil** • 470 Meridian St [Condor] 🕐
- **Shell** • 52 Meridian St [Paris St] 🕐

🅿Parking

Map 10 South Boston (West) / TOWN.MAP

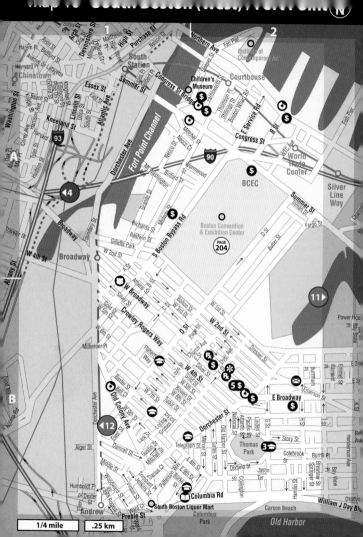

No matter what signs in this area say, please -- please -- do not call it "SoBo." This part of South Boston, which includes the Fort Point area, is home to artist communities, high-priced condos, the Boston Convention and Exhibition Center, and the first museum built in Boston in 100 years, the Institute for Contemporary Art. New hotels and other commercial spaces are slated to open over the next few years.

Map 1

Banks

- **Bank of America** • 460 W Broadway [Dorchester St]
- **Bank of America (ATM)** • 332 Congress St [Sleeper]
- **Boston Private Bank & Trust** • 157 Seaport Blvd [B]
- **Citizens Bank** • 441 W Broadway [F]
- **Citizens Bank (ATM)** • 405 W Broadway [F]
- **Citizens Bank (ATM)** • 415 Summer St [D]
- **Citizens Bank (ATM)** • 482 W Broadway [Dorchester St]
- **Citizens Bank (ATM)** • 555 E Broadway [H]
- **Eastern Bank** • 470 W Broadway [Dorchester St]
- **Mt Washington Bank** • 430 W Broadway [F]
- **Sovereign Bank** • 474 W Broadway [Dorchester St]
- **Sovereign Bank (ATM)** • 330 Congress St [Sleeper]

Community Gardens

Donuts

- **Dunkin' Donuts** • 268 Summer St [A St]
- **Dunkin' Donuts** • 330 Congress St [Sleeper]
- **Dunkin' Donuts** • 482 W Broadway [Dorchester St]
- **Dunkin' Donuts** • 75 Old Colony Ave [C]

Landmarks

- **Boston Convention & Exhibition Center** •
  415 Summer St [D]
- **Children's Museum** • 300 Congress St [Sleeper]
- **Institute of Contemporary Art** •
  100 Northern Ave [Fan Pier]
- **South Boston Liquor Mart** • 295 Old Colony Ave
  [Jenkins]

Libraries

- **Washington Village** • 1226 Columbia Rd [Mercer St]

Pharmacies

- **CVS** • 423 W Broadway [F]
- **Prescription Shoppe** • 378 W Broadway [E]

Police

- **District C-6** • 101 W Broadway [A St]

Post Offices

- **South Boston Station** • 444 E 3rd St [Emerson St]

Schools

- **Excel High** • 95 G St [E 6th]
- **James Condon Elementary** • 200 D St [W 5th]
- **Michael J Perkins Elementary** • 50 Burke St
  [Pilsudski]
- **Monument High** • 95 G St [E 6th]
- **Odyssey High** • 95 G St [E 6th]
- **Patrick F Gavin Middle** • 215 Dorchester St [W 5th]
- **St Augustine's** • 209 E St [Baxter]

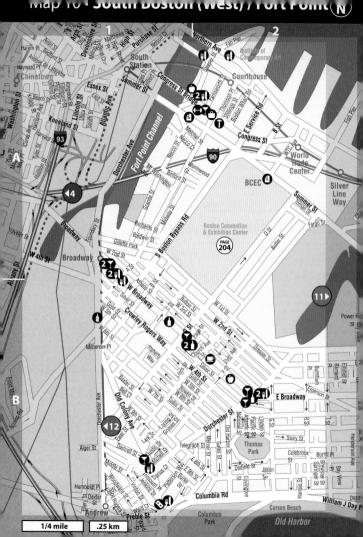

Map 10 · South Boston (West) / Fort Point N

1/4 mile   .25 km

New on the Dorchester Street scene is South, a welcome and reasonably priced upscale restaurant in the midst of Southie's excellent pub food offerings. Drinkin' establishments are great here—especially Lucky's and Shenanigans.

Coffee

- **Café Arpeggio** • 398 W Broadway [F]

Copy Shops

- **FedEx Kinko's** • 415 Summer St [D]
- **Sir Speedy Printing Centers** • 266 Summer St [A St]

Farmer's Markets

- **Children's Museum (July-Oct; Tues 4 pm-7 pm)** • 300 Congress St, in front of Children's Museum [Sleeper]
- **South Boston (July-Oct; Mon 12 pm-6 pm)** • 444 W Broadway [F]

Gyms

- **Focus Fitness** • 303 Congress St [Dot Ave]

Hardware Stores

- **Seaport Hardware** • 369 Congress St [Stillings]

Liquor Stores

- **Al's Liquors** • 226 W Broadway [C]
- **Leonid Wine Company** • 341 W Broadway [E]
- **New Bay View Liquors** • 108 Dorchester St [W 2nd]
- **O'Donoghue's Liquor Store** • 341 West Broadway [D]
- **Old Colony Wine** • 259 Dorchester Ave [W 5th]

Movie Theaters

- **Institute for Contemporary Art** • 100 Northern Ave [B]

Nightlife

- **Blackthorn Pub** • 471 W Broadway [Dorchester St]
- **The Cornerstone** • 16 W Broadway [Dot Ave]
- **The Junction** • 110 Dorchester St [W 2nd]
- **Lucky's** • 355 Congress St [A St]
- **The Quiet Man** • 11 W Broadway [Dot Ave]
- **Shenanigans** • 332 W Broadway [D]
- **Stadium** • 232 Old Colony Ave [Mitchell]

Restaurants

- **6 House** • 28 W Broadway [Dot Ave]
- **Amrheins** • 80 W Broadway [A St]
- **Barking Crab** • 88 Sleeper St [Northern Ave]
- **Blue Wave Bar & Grill** • 343 Congress St [Farnsworth]
- **The Daily Catch** • 2 Northern Ave [Sleeper]
- **Fresh Tortillas** • 475 W Broadway [Dorchester St]
- **Lucky's** • 355 Congress St [A St]
- **R&L Delicatessen** • 313 Old Colony Ave [Jenkins]
- **Salsa's Mexican Grill** • 118 Dorchester St [W B'way]
- **Stadium** • 232 Old Colony Ave [Mitchell]
- **Teriyaki House** • 32 W Broadway [Dot Ave]

Shopping

- **Machine Age** • 354 Congress St [A St]

Video Rental

- **Blockbuster** • 267 Old Colony Ave [Patterson]

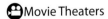

Parking here is hard to find and mostly residential. The Red Line and the Silver Line graze this area, and don't get you very close to Broadway, so to get to Broadway from Back Bay or the South End consider taking the 9 bus.

Subway

- **South Station**
- **Broadway**
- **Andrew**
- **Courthouse**
- **World Trade Center**
- **Silver Line Way**
- **BCEC**

Bus Lines

- **CT3** • Beth Israel Deaconess Medical Center—Andrew Station via BU Medical Center
- **3** • Boston Marine Industrial Park—South Station/Haymarket Station
- **4** • North Station—World Trade Center via Federal Courthouse
- **5** • City Point—McCormack Housing via Andrew Station
- **6** • Boston Marine Industrial Park—South Station/Haymarket Station
- **9** • City Point—Copley Square via Broadway Station
- **10** • City Point—Copley Square via Andrew Station & BU Medical Area
- **11** • City Point—Downtown, Bayview Route
- **47** • Central Square, Cambridge—Broadway Station via South End Medical Area

Car Washes

- **Super Shine Auto Wash** • 39 Old Colony Ave [C]

Gas Stations

- **Exxon** • 79 W Broadway [A St]
- **Hess** • 151 Old Colony Ave [D] ⏰
- **Shell** • 302 W Broadway [D]

Parking

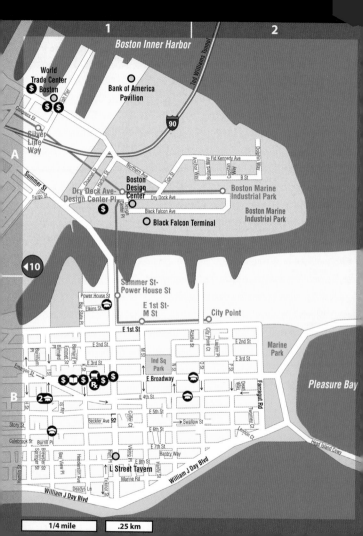

For that little bit of Irish you have, bring it here to Southie. Like many Boston neighborhoods, the ethnic makeup here is slowly changing, but this is still the proud home of the second-largest St. Patrick's Day celebration in the country. Populated with classic triple-deckers and surrounded by pleasant, scenic views of the beach, Southie has a unique charm.

$ Banks

- **Bank of America** • 636 E Broadway [Emerson St]
- **Citizens Bank (ATM)** • 713 E Broadway [K St]
- **First Trade Union Bank** • 10 Drydock Ave [Design Ctr Pl]
- **First Trade Union Bank** • 753 E Broadway [L]
- **Mt Washington Bank** • 708 E Broadway [K St]
- **Sovereign Bank (ATM)** • 1 Seaport Ln [Northern Ave]
- **Sovereign Bank (ATM)** • 2 Seaport Ln [Northern Ave]

Donuts

- **Dunkin' Donuts** • 200 Seaport Blvd [WTC]

Landmarks

- **Bank of America Pavilion** • 290 Northern Ave [Mass Tpke]
- **Black Falcon Terminal** • 1 Black Falcon Ave [Design]
- **Boston Design Center** • 1 Design Center Pl [Black]
- **L Street Tavern** • 658 E 8th St [L]
- **World Trade Center Boston** • 200 Seaport Blvd [WTC]

Libraries

- **South Boston** • 646 E Broadway [Emerson St]

Pharmacies

- **Brooks** • 710 E Broadway [K St]

Schools

- **Gate of Heaven** • 609 E 4th St [I St]
- **Joseph P Tynan Elementary** • 640 E 4th St [I St]
- **Oliver Hazard Perry Elementary** • 745 E 7th St [N]
- **St Brigid's** • 866 E Broadway [O St]
- **St Peter's** • 518 E 6th St [I St]
- **Uphams Corner Charter** • 7 Elkins St [Summer]

Supermarkets

- **Stop & Shop** • 713 E Broadway [K St]

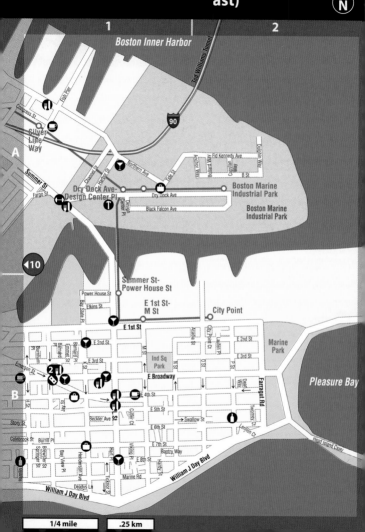

During the summer months, Bank of America Pavilion holds a great concert series. Just off the map to the east lies Fort Independence Park, a popular gathering spot in the summer and home to its eponymous Civil War-era fort (tours available). Good beer spots abound here, and you can count on No Name Restaurant for reliable seafood.

Coffee

- **Java House** • 566 E Broadway [H]
- **Sidewalk Café** • 764 E 4th St [M St]
- **Starbucks** • 601 Congress St [D]

Gyms

- **Boston Athletic Club** • 653 Summer St [W 1st]

Hardware Stores

- **Backstage True Value** • 21 Drydock Ave [Tide]

Liquor Stores

- **East Side Market** • 474 E 8th St [Winfield]
- **Jimmy's Korner** • 143 P St [E 6th]

Nightlife

- **Boston Beer Garden** • 734 E Broadway [L]
- **Corner Tavern** • 645 E 2nd St [K St]
- **Harpoon Brewery** • 306 Northern Ave [Harbor]
- **L Street Tavern** • 658 E 8th St [L]
- **Murphy's Law** • 837 Summer St [E 1st]
- **Playwright** • 658 E Broadway [K St]

Restaurants

- **Aura** • Seaport Hotel • 1 Seaport Ln [Northern Ave]
- **Boston Beer Garden** • 732 E Broadway [L]
- **Café Porto Bello** • 672 E Broadway [K St]
- **Kelly's Landing** • 81 L St [E 4th]
- **L Street Diner** • 108 L St [E 5th]
- **No Name Restaurant** • 15 Fish Pier Rd [Northern Ave]
- **Playwright** • 658 E Broadway [K St]
- **Summer Street Grille** • 653 Summer St [W 1st]

Shopping

- **EP Levine** • 23 Drydock Ave [Tide]
- **Miller's Market** • 336 K St [E 7th]
- **Stapleton Floral** • 635 E Broadway [Emerson St]

Video Rental

- **Hub Video** • 613 E Broadway [Emerson St]

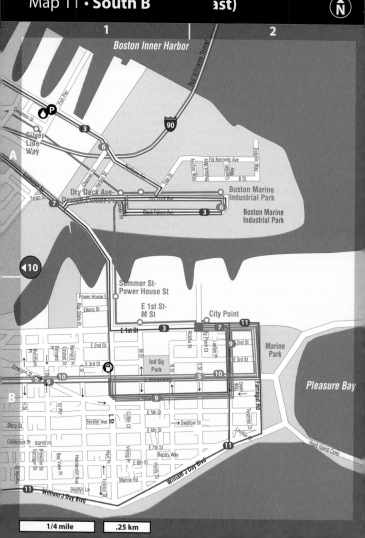

Map 11 · **South B** **(ast)**

N

Boston Inner Harbor

P

Congress St

Fish Pier

Silver
Line
Way

90

Fid Kennedy Ave

MW Bolling Way

Anchor Way

Bullard St

Capstan Way

B St

Dolphin Way

Fargo St

Dry Deck Ave-
Design Center Pl

Channel St

Harbor St

Fox St

Dry Dock Ave

Black Falcon Ave

Boston Marine
Industrial Park

Black Falcon Ave

Boston Marine
Industrial Park

10

Summer St-
Power House St

Power House St

Bay State Pl

Elkins St

E 1st St-
M St

E 1st St

City Point

Marine
Park

Pleasure Bay

Burnham Pl

Emerson St

E 2nd St

Barnard Pl

Emmet Pl

Barnard Pl

E 3rd St

M St

N St

O St

Ardsilla St

City Point Ct

Gavdin Pl

2nd St

E 3rd St

P

Ind Sq
Park

Carry Shores

Farragut Rd

Dean Way

Story St

H St

G St

F St

Beckler Ave

Collier Ct

E 5th St

Twomey Ct

Denton Pl

Head Island Cswy

Colebrook St

Burrill St

Bay View Pl

Brewster St

Springer St

Helden Pl

507 Ave

Hart Pl

Vinton St

E 6th St

E 7th St

Bantry Way

Swallow St

Story St

Hardy St

Marine Rd

E 8th St

William J Day Blvd

Deadys Ln

William J Day Blvd

1/4 mile

.25 km

This area, which used to be accessible to the car-deprived only by bus or a long hike from the Red Line is now much easier to get to with the addition of Silver Line stops. If you drive, do be careful where you park your car during snowy winter days. Spots aren't allowed to be saved, but tell that to the people who shoveled out a space…

Subway

- · **Silver Line Way**
- · **Northern Ave - Harbor St**
- · **Northern Ave - Tide St**
- · **Dry Dock Ave - Design Center Pl**
- · **Summer St - Power House St**
- · **E 1st St - M St**
- · **City Point**

Bus Lines

- **3** · Boston Marine Industrial Park—
  South Station/Haymarket Station
- **5** · City Point—McCormack Housing via
  Andrew Station
- **6** · Boston Marine Industrial Park—
  South Station/Haymarket Station
- **7** · City Point—Otis & Summer Streets via
  Northern Avenue & South Station
- **9** · City Point—Copley Square via
  Broadway Station
- **10** · City Point—Copley Square via
  Andrew Station & BU Medical Area
- **11** · City Point—Downtown, Bayview Route

⬤ Car Washes

· **Mr Perfection** · 1 Seaport Ln [Northern Ave]

🅿 Gas Stations

· **Exxon** · 57 L St [E 3rd]

🅿 Parking

Map 72 Newmarket, Massachusetts Ave

N

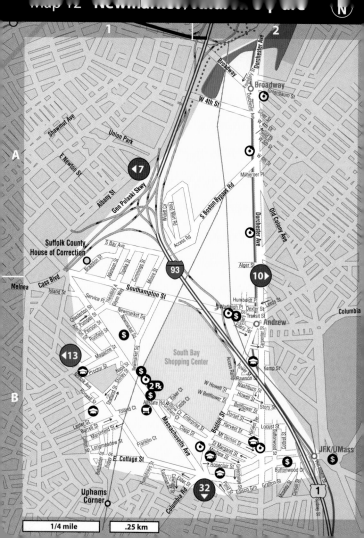

1/4 mile   .25 km

Every city has a bleak staging area and Newmarket is Boston's. Food distributors, u-store warehouses, and the big box chains at South Bay Shopping Center are the heart of this commercial and industrial area. Unless you've got a trip to Target or are visiting family at the Suffolk County House of Correction, you'll find only the fraying edges of Southie, Dorchester, and Roxbury worth a deeper look.

$ Banks

- **Bank of America** • 1104 Massachusetts Ave [Newmarket]
- **Bank of America (ATM)** • 150 Mount Vernon St
- **Bank of America (ATM)** • 8 Allstate Rd [Mass Ave]
- **Citizens Bank** • 60 Newmarket Sq [Mass Ave]
- **Citizens Bank (ATM)** • 863 Columbia Rd [Buttonwood]
- **Mt Washington Bank** • 501 Southampton St [Ellery St]

◉ Donuts

- **Doughboy Deli** • 220 Dorchester Ave [W 5th]
- **Dunkin' Donuts** • 1100 Massachusetts Ave [Newmarket]
- **Dunkin' Donuts** • 22 W Broadway [Dot Ave]
- **Dunkin' Donuts** • 256 Boston St [Roseclair]
- **Dunkin' Donuts** • 510 Southampton St [Ellery St]
- **Dunkin' Donuts** • 847 Dorchester Ave [Mount Vernon St]
- **Watermark Doughnut** • 370 Dorchester Ave [D]

◯ Landmarks

- **Suffolk County House of Correction** • 20 Bradston St [Southampton]

℞ Pharmacies

- **Stop & Shop** • 8B Allstate Rd [Mass Ave]
- **Target** • 7 Allstate Rd [Mass Ave]

◉ Schools

- **Boston Collegiate Charter** • 11 Mayhew St [Boston St]
- **Community Academy Middle** • 76 Shirley St [Roswell]
- **Roger Clap Elementary** • 35 Harvest St [Boston St]
- **Samuel W Mason Elementary** • 150 Norfolk Ave [Proctor]
- **St Mary's Elementary** • 52 Boston St [Father Songin]
- **William E Russell Elementary** • 750 Columbia Rd [Pond St]

◉ Supermarkets

- **Super 88** • 101 Allstate Rd [Mass Ave]

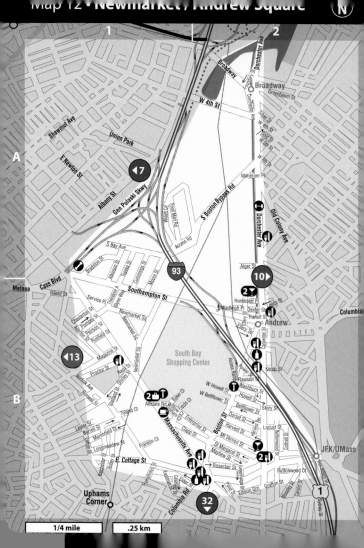

Nothing makes you appear sexier than taking a date to a hidden den of romance. 224 Boston Street wows with trendy South End vibe and reasonable prices. With its frightening high-crime exterior, the sophistication and live fado of Cape Verdean Restaurante Laura must be a bit like sneaking past St. Peter. And it would be a shame to overlook the tiny Café Polonia and its authentic Polish cuisine.

Coffee

- **Starbucks** • Target • 7 Allstate Rd [Mass Ave]
- **Sugar Bowl** • 837 Dorchester Ave [Mount Vernon St]

Gyms

- **Gold's Gym** • 323 Dorchester Ave [W 7th]

 Hardware Stores

- **Home Depot** • 5 Allstate Rd [Mass Ave]
- **PJ O'Donnell & Co** • 115 Boston St [Washburn St]

Liquor Stores

- **Andrew Square Liquors** • 605 Dorchester Ave [Boston St]
- **Cape Verdean Liquors** • 690 Columbia Rd [Elder]

Nightlife

- **Aces High** • 551 Dorchester Ave [Dexter St]
- **Dot Tavern** • 840 Dorchester Ave [Harvest St]
- **Sports Connection Bar** • 560 Dorchester Ave [Leeds]

Pet Shops

- **Skipton Kennel & Pet Center** • 70 Southampton St [Bradston]

Restaurants

- **224 Boston Street** • 224 Boston St [St Margaret]
- **Alex's Pizza** • 580 Dorchester Ave [Leeds]
- **Avenue Grille** • 856 Dorchester Ave [Mount Vernon St]
- **Baltic Deli & Café** • 632 Dorchester Ave [Father Songin]
- **Café Polonia** • 611 Dorchester Ave [Boston St]
- **Restaurante Laura** • 688 Columbia Rd [Elder]
- **Singh's Roti Shop** • 692 Columbia Rd [Elder]
- **Taqueria Casa Real** • 860A Dorchester Ave [Mount Vernon St]
- **Venetian Garden** • 1269 Massachusetts Ave [Columbia Rd]
- **Victoria** • 1024 Massachusetts Ave [Newmarket]
- **World Seafood Restaurant** • 400 Dorchester Ave [D]

Shopping

- **Home Depot** • 5 Allstate Rd [Mass Ave]
- **Little Tibet** • 1174 Massachusetts Ave [Willow Ct]
- **Marshall's** • 8D Allstate Rd [Mass Ave]

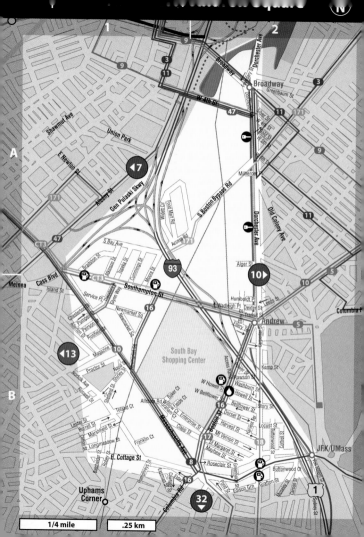

This largely commercial and industrial area isn't well served by public transportation. If you need to get to the South Bay Shopping Center without driving, take the 10 bus from Andrew Square or Copley. If you're out for a stroll, make sure to leave the JFK/UMass T stop to the north onto Columbia Road.

Subway

- **Broadway**
- **Andrew**
- **JFK/UMass**

Bus Lines

- **CT3** • Beth Israel Deaconess Medical Center—Andrew Station via BU Medical Center
- **3** • Boston Marine Industrial Park—South Station/Haymarket Station
- **5** • City Point—McCormack Housing via Andrew Station
- **8** • Harbor Point/UMass—Kenmore Station via South End Medical Area
- **9** • City Point—Copley Square via Broadway Station
- **10** • City Point—Copley Square via Andrew Station & BU Medical Area
- **11** • City Point—Downtown, Bayview Route
- **16** • Forest Hills Station—Andrew Station or UMass via Columbia Road
- **17** • Fields Corner Station—Andrew Station via Uphams Corner & Edward Everett Square
- **18** • Ashmont Station—Andrew Station via Fields Corner Station
- **47** • Central Square, Cambridge—Broadway Station via South End Medical Area
- **171** • Dudley Station—Logan Airport via Andrew Station

Car Rental

- **Enterprise** • 230 Dorchester Ave [W 5th] • 617-268-1411
- **Hertz Local Edition** • 371 Dorchester Ave [D] • 617-268-4660

Car Washes

- **Bubbles Car Wash** • 90 Southampton St [Mass Ave]
- **Scrubadub Auto Wash** • 25 W Howell St [Boston St]

Gas Stations

- **Gulf** • 888 Dorchester Ave [Columbia Rd] ☉
- **Independent** • 150 Southampton St [Topeka]
- **Mobil** • 85 Southampton St [Bradston] ☉
- **Shell** • 10 Howard Johnson Plz [Howard Ave]
- **Texaco** • 820 Columbia Rd [Dot Ave]

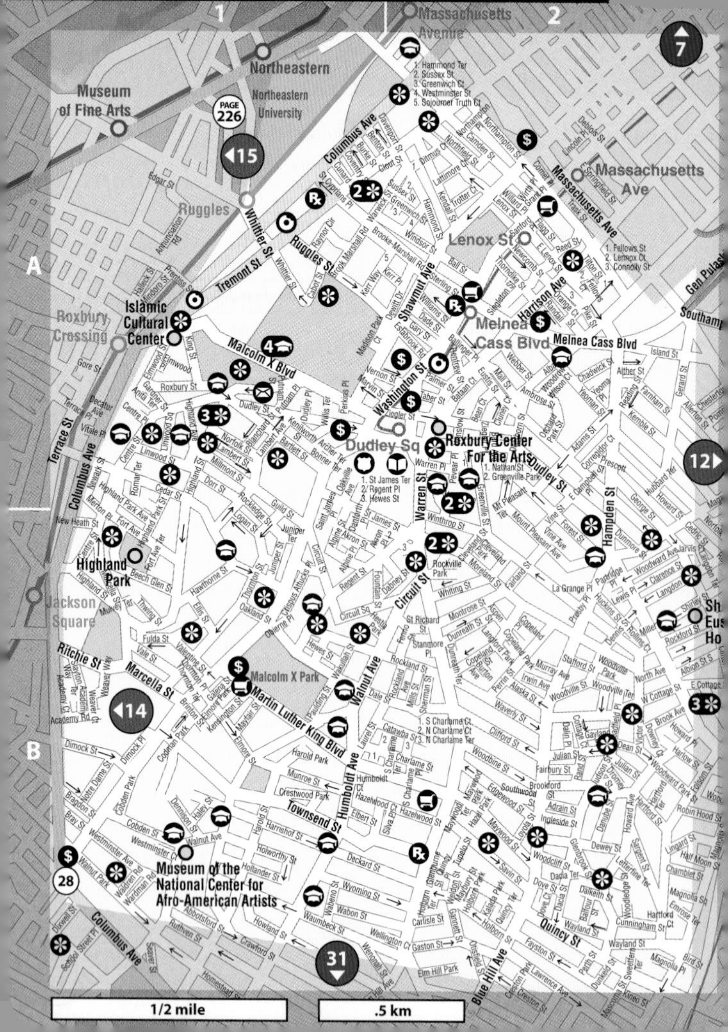

Map 13 · **Roxbury**

1

Massachusetts
Avenue

2

7

Northeastern

Museum
of Fine Arts

PAGE
226

15

Northeastern
University

Columbus Ave

1. Hammond Ter
2. Sussex St
3. Greenwich St
4. Westminster St
5. Sojourner Truth Ct

$

Massachusetts
Ave

Ruggles

Whittier St

Ruggles St

Tremont St

Lenox St

1. Fellows St
2. Lenox Ct
3. Connolly St

Roxbury
Crossing

Islamic
Cultural
Center

Malcolm X Blvd

4

Shawmut Ave

Washington St

Melnea
Cass Blvd

Melnea Cass Blvd

Gen Pulaski

Southam

Island St

Terrace St

Columbus Ave

Roxbury St

3

Dudley Sq

$

1. St James St
2. Regent Pl
3. Mewes St

Warren Pl

Roxbury Center
For the Arts

Dudley St

1. Nathan St
2. Greenville Park

2

12

Hampden St

A

Warren St

Circuit St

Rockville
Pl

2

La Grange Pl

Sh
Eus
Ho

Highland
Park

Jackson
Square

Ritchie St

Marcella St

14

Malcolm X Park

Martin Luther King Blvd

$

Walnut Ave

Humboldt Ave

1. S Charlame Ct
2. N Charlame Ct
3. N Charlame St

Townsend St

Harold Park

3

B

$

28

Museum of the
National Center for
Afro-American Artists

Columbus Ave

Quincy St

Blue Hill Ave

31

Elm Hill Park

1/2 mile

.5 km

There's a beauty to Roxbury under the grime of urban blight. Dudley Square is Roxbury's commercial center, but more businesses are finding opportunity closer to the busy Orange Line or along Blue Hill Avenue. The National Center of Afro-American Art, the largest mosque in New England, and the view from Fort Hill are among the many reasons not to overlook Roxbury.

 $ Banks

- **Bank of America** • 114 Dudley St [Washington St]
- **Bank of America (ATM)** • 1762 Washington St [Mass Ave]
- **Bank of America (ATM)** • 39 Warren St [Ziegler]
- **Citizens Bank** • 2343 Washington St [Marvin St]
- **Sovereign Bank** • 3060 Washington St [Walnut Pk]
- **Sovereign Bank** • 330 Martin Luther King Blvd [Washington St]
- **Sovereign Bank (ATM)** • 1010 Harrison Ave [Melnea]

Community Gardens

Donuts

- **Dunkin' Donuts** • 1131 Tremont St [Ruggles St]
- **Dunkin' Donuts** • 1350 Tremont St [Prentiss]
- **Dunkin' Donuts** • 2360 Washington St [Roxbury]

Landmarks

- **Highland Park** • Fort Ave & Beech Glen
- **Islamic Cultural Center** • 1 Malcolm X Blvd [Roxbury]
- **Museum of the National Center for Afro-American Artists** • 300 Walnut Ave [Cobden]
- **Roxbury Center for Arts** • 182 Dudley St [Harrison Ave]
- **Shirley-Eustis House** • 33 Shirley St [Clifton St]

Libraries

- **Dudley** • 65 Warren St [Dudley St]

Pharmacies

- **Kornfield Drug** • 2121 Washington St [Williams St]
- **Ruggles Square Pharmacy** • 1123 Tremont St [Ruggles St]
- **Walgreens** • 416 Warren St [Townsend]

Police

- **District B-2** • 135 Dudley St [Warren St]

Post Offices

- **Roxbury Station** • 55 Roxbury St [Shawmut Ave]

Schools

- **Boston Adult Academy** • 55 New Dudley St [King St]
- **Boston Day and Evening Academy** • 20 Kearsarge Ave [Warren St]
- **Boston Latin Academy** • 205 Townsend St [Humboldt Ave]
- **Carter Development Center** • 396 Northampton St [Columbus]
- **David A Ellis Elementary** • 302 Walnut Ave [Cobden]
- **Eliot Educational Center** • 56 Dale St [Walnut Ave]
- **George Lewis Middle** • 131 Walnut Ave [Dale]
- **Henry Dearborn Middle** • 35 Greenville St [Dudley St]
- **Henry L Higginson Elementary** • 160 Harrishof St [Haley]
- **James P Timilty Middle** • 205 Roxbury St [Centre St]
- **John Winthrop Elementary** • 35 Brookford St [Dromey]
- **Madison Park Technical Vocational High School** • 55 Malcom X Blvd [Roxbury]
- **Nathan Hale Elementary** • 51 Cedar St [Hawthorne St]
- **O'Bryant School of Math & Science** • 55 Malcom X Blvd [Roxbury]
- **Orchard Gardens K-8** • 906 Albany St [Webber]
- **Paige Academy** • 40 Highland Ave [Centre St]
- **Ralph Waldo Emerson Elementary** • 6 Shirley St [Dudley St]
- **Roland Hayes School of Music** • 55 Malcom X Blvd [Roxbury]
- **Roxbury Charter High** • 18 Hulbert St [Regent St]
- **Roxbury Community College** • 1234 Columbus Ave [Cedar St]
- **St Patrick Elementary** • 131 Mt Pleasant Ave [Blue Hill]
- **William Monroe Trotter Elementary** • 135 Humboldt Ave [Wyoming]

Supermarkets

- **People's Tropical Food** • 1830 Washington St [Lenox]
- **Tropical Foods** • 2101 Washington St [Williams St]

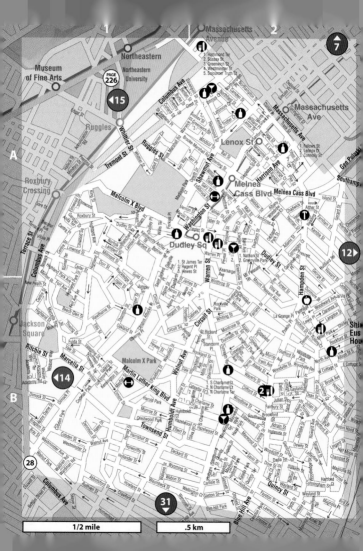

If you're hankering for Dominican food, it doesn't get better than the summertime flavors of Merengue. Flames has upscaled in its second location on Blue Hill Avenue. Butterfly Coffee is a great new addition for commuters at Roxbury Crossing and those of you brushing up on your Ethiopian. While lacking in restaurant density, many lunch counters serve soul food, jerk, and Hispanic delicacies, making good finds for the adventuring set.

Farmer's Markets

- **Dudley Town Common**
  (Jun-Oct; Tues & Thurs 4 pm-7 pm) •
  Dudley St & Blue Hill Ave

Gyms

- **Body by Brandy Fitness Center** •
  2181 Washington St [Ruggles St]
- **Roxbury Family YMCA** •
  285 Martin Luther King Blvd [Walnut Ave]

Hardware Stores

- **Hampden Supply Co** • 101 Hampden St [Adams St]

Liquor Stores

- **Brothers Liquors** • 616 Shawmut Ave [Lenox]
- **Caribbean Liquors** • 527 Dudley St [North Ave]
- **Folgers Liquors** • 2665 Washington St [Cedar St]
- **Garden Liquors** • 276 Warren St [Waverly St]
- **Giant** • 2371 Washington St [Roxbury]
- **Hollywood Liquors** • 950 Tremont St [Davenport]
- **Liquor Land** • 874 Harrison Ave [Northampton St]
- **Simon's Liquor** • 2169 Washington St [Ruggles St]
- **Warren Liquors** • 368 Warren St [Maywood St]

Nightlife

- **C&S Tavern** • 380 Warren St [Maywood St]
- **El Mondonguito** • 221 Dudley St [Greenville St]
- **Slade's** • 958 Tremont St [Davenport]

Restaurants

- **Bob the Chef's** • 604 Columbus Ave [Northampton St]
- **Breezeway Bar and Grill** • 153 Blue Hill Ave [Julian]
- **Merengue** • 156 Blue Hill Ave [Julian]
- **Pepper Pot** • 208 Dudley St [Winslow]
- **Roxbury Rotisserie** • 475 Dudley St [Shirley]
- **Stash's Grille** • 150 Dudley St [Warren St]

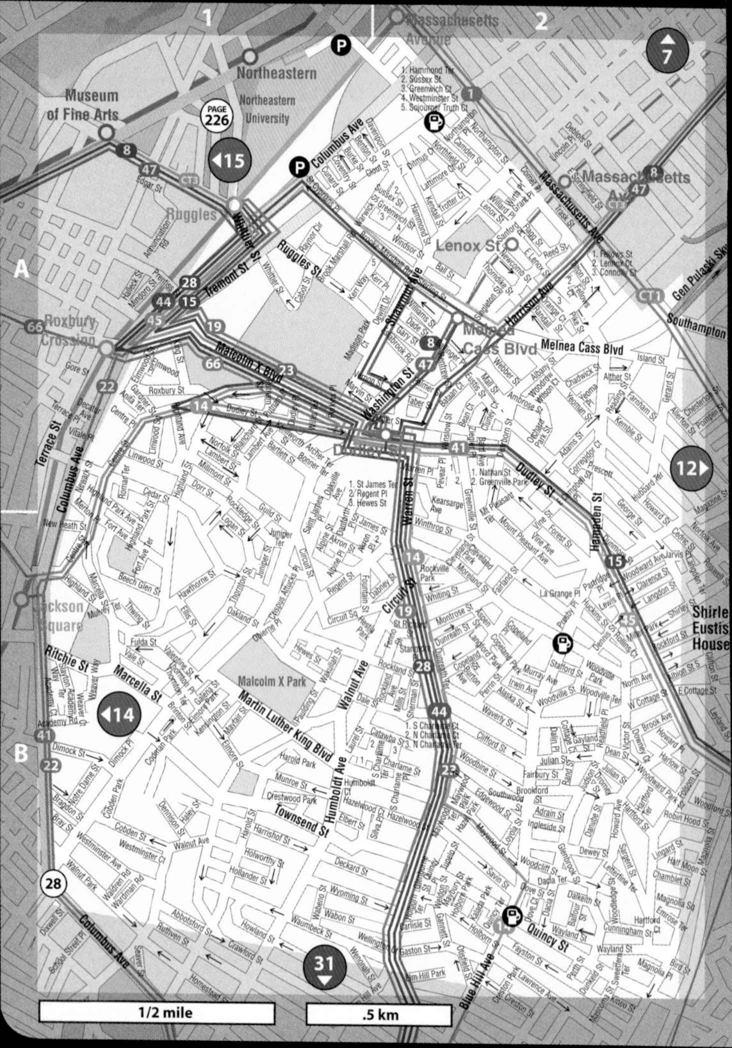

Map 13 · **Roxbury**

Map 13 · Roxbury

Museum of Fine Arts

Northeastern
Northeastern University

Massachusetts Avenue

1. Hammond Ter
2. Sussex St
3. Greenwich Ct
4. Westminster St
5. Sojourner Truth St

Columbus Ave

Ruggles

Massachusetts Ave

Lenox St

Ruggles St

1. Francis St
2. Lennox St
3. Connor St

Tremont St

Malcolm X Blvd

Melnea Cass Blvd
Melnea Cass Blvd

Gen Pulaski Sky
Southampton

Roxbury Crossing

Harrison Ave

Roxbury St

Martin Luther King Blvd

1. St James Ter
2. Regent Pl
3. Hewes St

Dudley St

1. Nathan St
2. Greenville Park

Washington St

Shirley
Eustis
House

Warren St

Circuit St

Rockville Park

La Grange St

Jackson Square

Ritchie St

Marcella St

Malcolm X Park

Martin Luther King Blvd

Walnut Ave

Humboldt Ave

1. S Charlotte St
2. N Charlotte St
3. N Charlotte St

Harold Park

Humboldt

Crestwood Park

Townsend St

Columbus Ave

Quincy St

1/2 mile   .5 km

Map 13

Potholed and neglected, Roxbury's thicket of streets makes for fiendishly difficult travel. Considering how many people call the neighborhood home, the public transportation is woefully inadequate. Unless you skirt the parameter on the Orange Line or the pleasant Southwest Corridor bike trail, you'll likely head through Dudley Station, the busy bus hub packed with loiterers.

Subway

- **Massachusetts Ave**
- **Ruggles**
- **Roxbury Crossing**
- **Jackson Square**
- **Northeastern (E)**
- **Museum (E)**
- **Ruggles (E)**
- **Mass Ave**
- **Lenox St**
- **Melnea Cass Blvd**
- **Dudley Square**

Bus Lines

- **CT1** • Central Square, Cambridge—BU Medical Center/BU Medical Campus
- **CT3** • Beth Israel Deaconess Medical Center—Andrew Station via BU Medical Center
- **1** • Harvard/Holyoke Gate—Dudley Station via Massachusetts Ave & BU Medical Center
- **8** • Harbor Point/UMass—Kenmore Station via South End Medical Area
- **14** • Roslindale Square—Heath Street via Dudley Station, Grove Hall & American Legion Hwy
- **15** • Kane Square or Fields Corner Station—Ruggles Station via Uphams Corner
- **19** • Fields Corner Station—Ruggles Station via Grove Hall & Dudley Streets
- **22** • Ashmont Station—Ruggles Station via Talbot Ave & Jackson Square
- **23** • Ashmont Station—Ruggles Station via Washington Street
- **28** • Mattapan Station—Ruggles Station via Dudley Station
- **41** • Centre & Eliot Streets—JFK/Umass Station via Dudley Station, Centre Street & Jackson Square Station
- **44** • Jackson Square Station—Ruggles Station via Seaver Street & Humboldt Avenue
- **45** • Franklin Park Zoo—Ruggles Station via Blue Hill Avenue
- **47** • Central Square, Cambridge—Broadway Station via South End Medical Area
- **66** • Harvard Square—Dudley Station via Allston & Brookline

℗ Gas Stations

- **Citgo** • 294 Blue Hill Ave [Quincy St]
- **Eagle Oil** • 67 Blue Hill Ave [Moreland]
- **Sunoco** • 785 Tremont St [Northampton St] ♿

℗ Parking

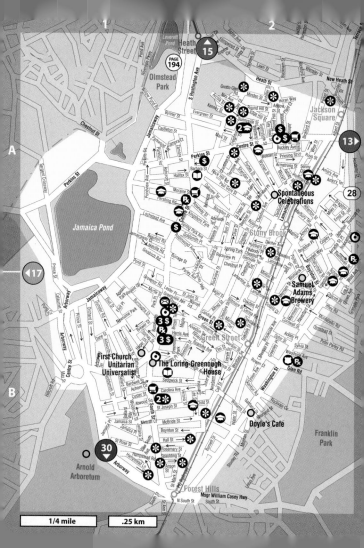

Despite the threat of gentrification, Jamaica Plain is still home to a diverse population of artists, students, lesbians, and immigrants. Upscale restaurants, locals' dives, and hipster lounges exist side by side on the same block. Stunning Jamaica Pond forms part of the city's Emerald Necklace, and the Arnold Arboretum and Franklin Park Zoo are great places to be outside. Colorful festivals are a highlight of the summer months.

Map 1

$ Banks

- **Bank of America** • 315 Centre St [Walden St]
- **Bank of America** • 677 Centre St [Seaverns]
- **Boston Private Bank & Trust (ATM)** • 403 Centre St [Barbara]
- **Citizens Bank** • 696 Centre St [Burroughs St]
- **Citizens Bank (ATM)** • 301 Centre St [Seaverns]
- **Citizens Bank (ATM)** • 684 Centre St [Seaverns]
- **Hyde Park Cooperative Bank** • 733 Centre St [Harris Ave]
- **People's Federal Savings Bank** • 725 Centre St [Harris Ave]
- **Roxbury Highland Bank** • 515 Centre St [Spring Pk Ave]
- **Wainwright Bank & Trust** • 687 Centre St [Seaverns]

Community Gardens

Donuts

- **Dunkin' Donuts** • 1926 Columbus Ave [Walnut Pk]
- **Dunkin' Donuts** • 315 Centre St [Walden St]
- **Dunkin' Donuts** • 684 Centre St [Seaverns]
- **Dunkin' Donuts** • 757 Centre St [Thomas St]

Landmarks

- **Arnold Arboretum** • 125 Arborway [Centre St]
- **Doyle's Café** • 3484 Washington St [Williams St]
- **First Church, Unitarian Universalist** • 6 Eliot St [Centre St]
- **The Loring-Greenough House** • 12 South St [Centre St]
- **Samuel Adams Brewery** • 30 Germania St [Brookside]
- **Spontaneous Celebrations** • 75 Danforth St [Boylston St]

Libraries

- **Connolly** • 433 Centre St [Paul Gore St]
- **Jamaica Plain** • 12 Sedgwick St [South St]

Pharmacies

- **CVS** • 467 Centre St [Boylston St]
- **CVS** • 704 Centre St [Burroughs St]
- **Egleston Square Pharmacy** • 3090 Washington St [Beethoven]
- **Samuels Pharmacy** • 46 Woodside Ave [Washington St]

Police

- **District E-13** • 3345 Washington St [Green St]

Post Offices

- **Jamaica Plain Station** • 655 Centre St [Myrtle St]

Schools

- **Blessed Sacrament Elementary** • 30 Sunnyside St [Westerly]
- **Compass** • 26 Sunnyside St [Westerly]
- **Egleston High** • 3134 Washington St [School St]
- **Ellis Mendell Elementary** • 164 School St [Copley]
- **English High** • 144 McBride St [Call]
- **Greater Egleston Community High** • 80 School St [Weld]
- **James Curley Elementary** • 40 Pershing Rd [Centre St]
- **John F Kennedy Elementary** • 7 Bolster St [Wyman St]
- **Louis Agassiz Elementary** • 20 Child St [South St]
- **Mary E Curley Middle** • 493 Centre St [Pershing]
- **Nativity Prep** • 39 Lamartine St [Roys]
- **Our Lady of Lourdes Elementary** • 54 Brookside Ave [Minton]

Supermarkets

- **Harvest Co-op Market** • 57 South St [Custer]
- **Hi-Lo** • 450 Centre St [Moraine]
- **Stop & Shop** • 301 Centre St [Walden St]

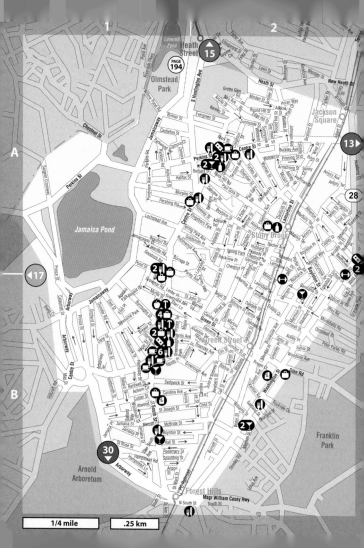

Centre Street functions as the main artery in JP, lined with restaurants and shops of all kinds. The Milky Way, the Brendan Behan Pub, and Zon's cluster at the Hyde Square end of Centre, while Doyle's, The Midway Café, and James' Gate are closer to Forest Hills T stop. The area around Jackson Square offers the flavors of its Puerto Rican, Dominican, and Cape Verdean communities, as does Washington Street.

☕ Coffee

- **Cha Fahn (tea only)** • 763 Centre St [Greenough Ave]
- **Emack & Bolio's** • 736 Centre St [Thomas St]
- **June Bug Café** • 403A Centre St [Barbara]
- **Sweet Finnish** • 761 Centre St [Eliot St]

🖨 Copy Shops

- **Fresh Copy** • 64 South St [Carolina Ave]
- **Schell Printing** • 3399 Washington St [Green St]

🍎 Farmer's Markets

- **Jamaica Plain (July-Oct; Tues 12 pm- 5 pm, Sat 12 pm- 3 pm)** • 677 Centre St [Seaverns]

🏋 Gyms

- **Mike's Fitness** • 284 Amory St [Porter St]
- **YMCA Egleston Square Youth Center** • 3134 Washington St [School St]

🔧 Hardware Stores

- **Hardware City** • 656 Centre St [Myrtle St]
- **Yumont True Value Hardware** • 702 Centre St [Burroughs St]

🍾 Liquor Stores

- **Blanchard Liquors** • 741 Centre St [Harris Ave]
- **Chauncy Liquor Mart** • 3100 Washington St [Beethoven]
- **Egleston Liquors** • 3086 Washington St [Beethoven]
- **Foerster's Market & Liquors** • 78 Boylston St [Danforth St]
- **Hyde Square Wine & Liquor** • 391 Centre St [Sheridan St]

🍸 Nightlife

- **Brendan Behan Pub** • 378 Centre St [Sheridan St]
- **Costello's Tavern** • 723 Centre St [Harris Ave]
- **Doyle's Café** • 3484 Washington St [Williams St]
- **Jeanie Johnston Pub** • 144 South St [Hall St]
- **Midway Café** • 3496 Washington St [Williams St]
- **Milky Way Lounge & Lanes** • 403 Centre St [Barbara]
- **Samuel Adams Brewery** • 30 Germania St [Brookside]

🍴 Restaurants

- **Ban Chiang House** • 707 Centre St [Burroughs St]
- **Bella Luna** • 405 Centre St [Barbara]
- **Bon Savor** • 605 Centre St [Pond St]
- **Bukhara** • 701 Centre St [Burroughs St]
- **Café D** • 711 Centre St [Burroughs St]
- **Centre Street Café** • 699 Centre St [Burroughs St]
- **Cha Fahn** • 763 Centre St [Greenough Ave]
- **Dogwood Café** • 3712 Washington St [Arborway]
- **Doyle's Café** • 3484 Washington St [Williams St]
- **Great Wall** • 779 Centre St [Eliot St]
- **James's Gate** • 5 McBride St [South St]
- **JP Seafood Café** • 730 Centre St [Harris Ave]
- **La Pupusa Guanaca** • 378 Centre St [Sheridan St]
- **Purple Cactus Burrito & Wrap** • 674 Centre St [Seaverns]
- **Sorella's** • 388 Centre St [Sheridan St]
- **Tacos El Charro** • 349 Centre St [Westerly]
- **Ten Tables** • 597 Centre St [Pond St]
- **Wonder Spice Café** • 697 Centre St [Burroughs St]
- **Zesto's** • 460 Centre St [Boylston St]
- **Zon's** • 2 Perkins St [Perkins Sq]

👜 Shopping

- **Boing! JP's Toy Shop** • 729 Centre St [Harris Ave]
- **Boomerangs** • 716 Centre St [Burroughs St]
- **Bread & Butter Baking Co.** • 3346 Washington St [Green St]
- **CD Spins** • 668 Centre St [Starr Ln]
- **City Feed and Supply** • 66 Boylston St [Chestnut Ave]
- **Eye Q Optical** • 7 Pond St [Centre St]
- **Fat Ram's Pumpkin Tattoo** • 380 Centre St [Sheridan St]
- **Ferris Wheels Bicycle Shop** • 66 South St [Carolina Ave]
- **Fire Opal** • 683 Centre St [Seaverns]
- **Gadgets** • 671 Centre St [Seaverns]
- **JP Licks** • 659 Centre St [Starr Ln]
- **Petal & Leaf** • 461 Centre St [Moraine]
- **Pluto** • 603 Centre St [Pond St]

📀 Video Rental

- **Columbus Video** • 1967 Columbus Ave [Washington St]
- **Video Underground** • 389 Centre St [Sheridan St]
- **Videosmith** • 672 Centre St [Seaverns]

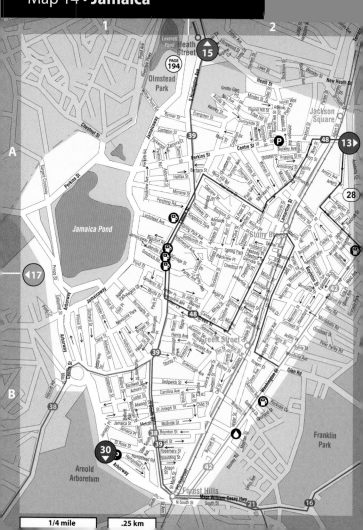

Driving is fairly convenient in JP, thanks to the quick flow of traffic on the Riverway and the abundance of free parking. Locals use the 39 bus, running down Centre Street as often as the Orange Line. But in this eco-conscious neighborhood, biking, skating, and walking are very popular (and PC) forms of transportation. Southwest Corridor Park has a bike trail that runs alongside the Orange Line all the way downtown.

Subway

- **Jackson Square**
- **Stony Brook**
- **Green St**
- **Forest Hills**
- **Heath St (E)**

Bus Lines

- **16** · Forest Hills Station—Andrew Station or UMass via Columbia Road
- **21** · Ashmont Station—Forest Hills Station via Morton Street
- **38** · Wren Street—Forest Hills Station via Centre & South Streets
- **39** · Forest Hills Station—Back Bay Station via Huntington Avenue
- **42** · Forest Hills Station—Ruggles Station via Washington Station & Dudley Square
- **48** · Jamaica Plain Loop Monument—Jackson Square Station via Green Street

Car Washes

- **Jamaica Plain Car Wash** · 3530 Washington St [Rossmore]

Gas Stations

- **Citgo** · 3055 Washington St [Walnut Pk]
- **Citgo** · 531 Centre St [Goldsmith Pl]
- **Citgo** · 561 Centre St [Lakeville]
- **Hatoff's** · 3440 Washington St [Union Ave]
- **Independent** · 525 Centre St [Goldsmith Pl]
- **Independent** · 581 Centre St [Goodrich]

Parking

Longwood is home to a number of nationally prominent medical institutions, including Dana-Farber and the Brigham. Rising above Tremont Street and Huntington Avenue, residential Mission Hill gives families, young professionals, and students attending Harvard Medical, Mass College of Art, and the other nearby schools some great views of the Mission Church Basilica and the rest of Boston.

$ Banks

- **Bank of America** • 1614 Tremont St [Wigglesworth]
- **Bank of America** • 333 Longwood Ave [Binney St]
- **Bank of America (ATM)** • 1643 Tremont St [Wigglesworth]
- **Bank of America (ATM)** • 300 The Fenway [Palace]
- **Bank of America (ATM)** • 360 Huntington Ave [Opera]
- **Bank of America (ATM)** • 550 Huntington Ave [Ruggles St]
- **Bank of America (ATM)** • 610 Huntington Ave [St Alphonsus]
- **Bank of America (ATM)** • 621 Huntington Ave [Tetlow]
- **Bank of America (ATM)** • MBTA Roxbury Crossing • Tremont St & Columbus Ave
- **Citizens Bank** • 1628 Tremont St [Wigglesworth]
- **Citizens Bank (ATM)** • 1620 Tremont St [Wigglesworth]
- **Citizens Bank (ATM)** • Boston Children's Hospital • 300 Longwood Ave [Blackfan]
- **Citizens Bank (ATM)** • 33 Kilmarnock St [Boylston St]
- **Citizens Bank (ATM)** • 75 Francis St [Vining]
- **Sovereign Bank** • 6 Francis St [Huntington]
- **Sovereign Bank (ATM)** • 350 Longwood Ave [Brookline Ave]
- **Sovereign Bank (ATM)** • 58 Forsyth St [Greenleaf]

✴ Community Gardens

◎ Donuts

- **Dunkin' Donuts** • 115 Forsyth St [Greenleaf]
- **Dunkin' Donuts** • 1420 Boylston St [Kilmarnock]
- **Dunkin' Donuts** • 1620 Tremont St [Wigglesworth]
- **Dunkin' Donuts** • 1631 Tremont St [Wigglesworth]
- **Dunkin' Donuts** • 350 Longwood Ave [Brookline Ave]
- **Dunkin' Donuts** • 360 Huntington Ave [Opera]
- **Mike's Donuts** • 1524 Tremont St [Carmel]

✚ Emergency Rooms

- **Brigham and Women's Hospital** • 75 Francis St [Vining]
- **Children's Hospital** • 300 Longwood Ave [Blackfan]

◐ Landmarks

- **Diablo Glass & Metal** • 123 Terrace St [Cedar St]
- **Isabella Stewart Gardner Museum** • 280 The Fenway [Palace]
- **Mission Church Basilica** • 1545 Tremont St [Pontiac]
- **Museum of Fine Arts** • 465 Huntington Ave [Museum Rd]
- **Warren Anatomical Museum** • 10 Shattuck St [Binney St]

📖 Libraries

- **Parker Hill** • 1497 Tremont St [Burney]

℞ Pharmacies

- **Brooks** • 1295 Boylston St [Yawkey]
- **CVS** • 300 Longwood Ave [Blackfan]
- **CVS** • 350 Longwood Ave [Brookline Ave]
- **Walgreens** • 1630 Tremont St [Wigglesworth]

✉ Post Offices

- **Mission Hill Station** • 1575 Tremont St [S Whitney]

🎓 Schools

- **Boston Latin School** • 78 Ave Louis Pasteur [Longwood]
- **David Farragut Elementary** • 10 Fenwood Rd [Huntington]
- **Emmanuel College** • 400 The Fenway [Ave Louis Pasteur]
- **Harvard Medical** • 25 Shattuck St [Binney St]
- **Harvard School of Dental Medicine** • 188 Longwood Ave [Palace]
- **Harvard School of Public Health** • 677 Huntington Ave [Washington St]
- **Health Careers Academy** • 360 Huntington Ave [Opera]
- **James Hennigan Elementary** • 200 Heath St [Schiller]
- **Manville** • 3 Blackfan Cir [Longwood]
- **Massachusetts College of Art** • 621 Huntington Ave [Tetlow]
- **Massachusetts College of Pharmacy and Health Sciences** • 179 Longwood Ave [Palace]
- **Mission Hill** • 67 Alleghany St [Parker St]
- **New Mission High School** • 67 Alleghany St [Parker St]
- **Northeastern University** • 360 Huntington Ave [Opera]
- **Roxbury Preparatory Charter** • 120 Fisher Ave [Hayden St]
- **School of the Museum of Fine Arts** • 230 The Fenway [Evans Rd]
- **Simmons College** • 300 The Fenway [Palace]
- **Wentworth Institute of Technology** • 550 Huntington Ave [Ruggles St]

🛒 Supermarkets

- **Star Market** • 33 Kilmarnock St [Boylston St]
- **Stop & Shop** • 1620 Tremont St [Wigglesworth]

91

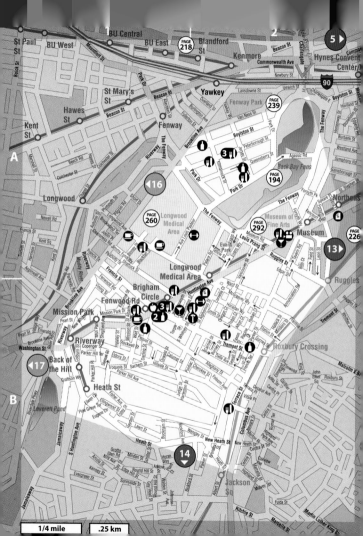

Tucked inside the Fenway are some good restaurants that reflect the low-key character of this neighborhood, such as tiny twosome El Pelon Taqueria and Rod Dee. Penguin Pizza makes delicious pies with creative combinations of toppings. Our favorite place for a pint around Mission Hill and Longwood is Flann O'Brien's.

Coffee

- **Brigham Circle Diner** • 737 Huntington Ave [Francis St]
- **Red Bean Coffee Roasters** • 350 Longwood Ave [Brookline Ave]
- **Starbucks** • Children's Hospital • 283 Longwood Ave [Blackfan]

Copy Shops

- **Mail Boxes Etc** • 360 Huntington Ave [Opera]
- **The Print House** • 660 Huntington Ave [Washington St]

Farmer's Markets

- **Mission Hill (11:30 am-6 pm)** • Huntington Ave & Tremont St

Gyms

- **Custom Fitness** • 75 St Alphonsus St [Smith St]
- **Fitcorp** • 77 Ave Louis Pasteur [Longwood]

Hardware Stores

- **AC Hardware** • 1562 Tremont St [St Alphonsus]

Liquor Stores

- **Bradley Liquors** • 1383 Boylston St [Kilmarnock]
- **Brigham Liquors** • 732 Huntington Ave [Calumet]
- **Dara's Wine & Spirits** • 750 Huntington Ave [Fenwood]
- **Fuentes Market and Liquor Store** • 680 Parker St [Gurney]
- **Jersey Street Liquors** • 48 Queensberry St [Jersey]
- **Mission Hill Liquors** • 1623 Tremont St [Wigglesworth]

Movie Theaters

- **Museum of Fine Arts** • 465 Huntington Ave [Museum Rd]

Nightlife

- **Curtin's Roadside Tavern** • 1592 Tremont St [Worthington St]
- **Flann O'Brien's** • 1619 Tremont St [Wigglesworth]
- **Linwood Grill & BBQ** • 69 Kilmarnock St [Queensberry]
- **Machine** • 1256 Boylston St [Yawkey]
- **Punter's Pub** • 450 Huntington Ave [Parker St]
- **Ramrod** • 1254 Boylston St [Yawkey]

Restaurants

- **Bravo** • 465 Huntington Ave [Museum Rd]
- **Brigham Circle Diner** • 737 Huntington Ave [Francis St]
- **Brown Sugar Café** • 129 Jersey St [Queensberry]
- **Chacho's** • 1502 Tremont St [Burney]
- **El Pelon Taqueria** • 92 Peterborough St [Kilmarnock]
- **Huntington Pizza & Café** • 764 Huntington Ave [Wait]
- **Il Mondo Pizza** • 682 Huntington Ave [Wigglesworth]
- **Linwood Grill & BBQ** • 81 Kilmarnock St [Queensberry]
- **Longwood Grille & Bar** • 342 Longwood Ave [Brookline Ave]
- **Mississippi's** • 103 Terrace St [Cedar St]
- **Penguin Pizza** • 735 Huntington Ave [Francis St]
- **Rod Dee II** • 94 Peterborough St [Kilmarnock]
- **Solstice Café** • 1625 Tremont St [Wigglesworth]
- **Sorento's** • 86 Peterborough St [Kilmarnock]
- **Squealing Pig** • 134 Smith St [Washington St]

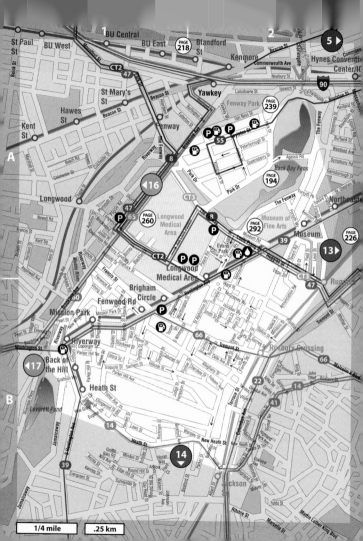

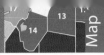

In an ideal world, a tram line would run down the middle of Boylston Street. This would ease the game-day crunch on the Green Line and provide better access to the Fens and the area around the intersection of Park Drive and Brookline Avenue. If you're going to see the Sox, don't count on street parking in the Fenway neighborhood itself.

Subway

- **Northeastern (E)**
- **Museum of Fine Arts (E)**
- **Longwood Medical Area (E)**
- **Brigham Circle (E)**
- **Fenwood Rd (E)**
- **Mission Park (E)**
- **Riverway (E)**
- **Back of the Hill (E)**
- **Heath (E)**
- **Roxbury Crossing**

Bus Lines

- **CT2** • Sullivan Station—Ruggles Station via Kendall/MIT
- **CT3** • Beth Israel Deaconess Medical Center—Andrew Station via BU Medical Center
- **8** • Harbor Point/UMass—Kenmore Station via South End Medical Area
- **8** • Roslindale Square—Heath Street via Dudley Station, Grove Hall & American Legion Hwy
- **22** • Ashmont Station—Ruggles Station via Talbot Avenue & Jackson Square
- **39** • Forest Hills Station—Back Bay Station via Huntington Avenue
- **41** • Centre & Eliot Streets—JFK/UMass Station via Dudley Station, Centre Street & Jackson Square Station
- **47** • Central Square, Cambridge—Broadway Station via South End Medical Area
- **60** • Chestnut Hill—Kenmore Station via Brookline Village & Cypress Street
- **65** • Brighton Center—Kenmore Station via Washington Street, Brookline Village
- **66** • Harvard Square—Dudley Station via Allston & Brookline

Car Washes

- **Athens Shell** • 525 Huntington Ave [Louis Prang St]

Gas Stations

- **Exxon** • 1420 Boylston St [Kilmarnock]
- **Getty** • 1600 Tremont St [Wigglesworth]
- **Independent** • 634 Huntington Ave [St Alphonsus]
- **Mobil** • 1301 Boylston St [Yawkey]
- **Shell** • 1241 Boylston St [Yawkey]
- **Shell** • 525 Huntington Ave [Louis Prang St]
- **Texaco** • 914 Huntington Ave [S Huntington]

Parking

Map 13 **Kenmore Square / Brookline (East)**

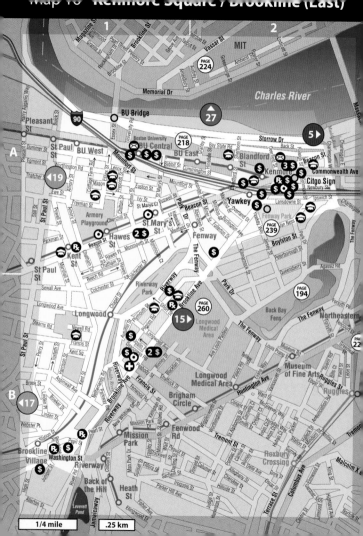

Under the watchful triangular eye of the revamped Citgo sign, the Kenmore Square area is notable for sprawling Boston University, the nightclub scene on Lansdowne Street, and, of course, Fenway Park. Beyond Fenway and the core of Kenmore Square, urban bustle gives way to the more serene residential neighborhoods of affluent Brookline.

$ Banks

- **Bank of America** • 410 Brookline Ave [Longwood]
- **Bank of America** • 540 Commonweath Ave [Kenmore]
- **Bank of America** • 771 Commonwealth Ave [Saint Mary's St]
- **Bank of America (ATM)** • 1024A Beacon St [Saint Mary's St]
- **Bank of America (ATM)** • 201 Brookline Ave [Park Dr]
- **Bank of America (ATM)** • 4 Brookline Pl [Brookline Ave]
- **Bank of America (ATM)** • 542 Commonwealth Ave [Brookline Ave]
- **Bank of America (ATM)** • 660 Beacon St [Comm Ave]
- **Brookline Savings Bank** • 1016 Beacon St [Saint Mary's St]
- **Brookline Savings Bank** • 160 Washington St [White Pl]
- **Century Bank** • 512 Commonwealth Ave [Kenmore]
- **Century Bank** • 771 Commonwealth Ave [Saint Mary's St]
- **Century Bank (ATM)** • Hotel Commonwealth • 500 Commonwealth Ave [Kenmore]
- **Century Bank (ATM)** • Barnes & Noble • 660 Beacon St [Comm Ave]
- **Century Bank (ATM)** • 770 Commonwealth Ave [Saint Mary's St]
- **Citizens Bank** • 435 Brookline Ave [Longwood]
- **Citizens Bank** • 560 Commonwealth Ave [Beacon St]
- **Citizens Bank (ATM)** • 1 Deaconess Rd [Pilgrim Rd]
- **Citizens Bank (ATM)** • 49 Lansdowne St [Ipswich St]
- **Citizens Bank (ATM)** • 542 Commonwealth Ave [Brookline Ave]
- **Mercantile Bank** • 61 Brookline Ave [Lansdowne]
- **Sovereign Bank** • 552 Commonwealth Ave [Brookline Ave]

Donuts

- **Dunkin' Donuts** • 1008 Beacon St [Saint Mary's St]
- **Dunkin' Donuts** • 1108 Beacon St [Hawes St]
- **Dunkin' Donuts** • 457 Brookline Ave [Longwood]
- **Dunkin' Donuts** • 530 Commonwealth Ave [Brookline Ave]

Emergency Rooms

- **Beth Israel Deaconess Medical Center** • 110 Francis St [Brookline Ave]

O Landmarks

- **BU Bridge** • Essex St & Mountfort St
- **Citgo Sign** • Commonwealth Ave & Beacon St
- **Fenway Park** • 4 Yawkey Wy [Brookline Ave]

Pharmacies

- **PharmaCare Specialty Pharmacy** • 330 Brookline Ave [Short St]
- **Pierce Apothecary** • 1180 Beacon St [Kent St]
- **Village Pharmacy** • 1 Brookline Pl [Brookline Ave]

Post Offices

- **Boston University** • 775 Commonwealth Ave [Mountfort]
- **Kenmore Station** • 11 Deerfield St [Comm Ave]

Schools

- **Amos A Lawrence** • 27 Francis St [St Albans]
- **Ansin Religious School of Ohabei Shalom** • 1187 Beacon St [Marshall St]
- **Boston Arts Academy** • 174 Ipswich St [Lansdowne]
- **Boston University** • 1 Sherborn St [Comm Ave]
- **Fenway High** • 174 Ipswich St [Lansdowne]
- **Ivy Street** • 200 Ivy St [Essex]
- **Kids Are People Elementary** • 656 Beacon St [Comm Ave]
- **Neha/Lubavitch School for Girls** • 9 Prescott St [Lenox]
- **New England Hebrew Academy** • 9 Prescott St [Lenox]
- **New England School of Photography** • 537 Commonwealth Ave [Brookline Ave]
- **Wheelock College** • 200 Riverway [Short St]
- **The Winsor School** • 103 Pilgrim Rd [Short St]

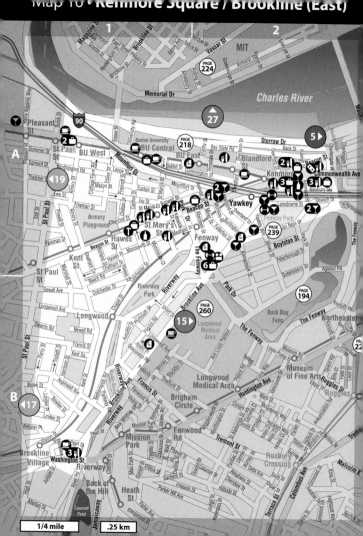

Map 10 • Kenmore Square / Brookline (East)

Lansdowne Street offers an ample selection of clubs and bars, including several 18-plus nights. For non-clubbers, Elephant Walk or Great Bay are elegant dining options. However, for those lucky enough to score tickets, the best entertainment in the area is still a game or concert at Fenway. For a secret stroll, go looking for sublime Beech Park, just over the border in Brookline.

☕ Coffee

- **Espresso Royale** • 736 Commonwealth Ave [Saint Mary's St]
- **Java Stop** • 4 Brookline Pl [Brookline Ave]
- **Starbucks** • Beth Israel Hospital • 364 Brookline Ave [Short St]
- **Starbucks** • 595 Commonwealth Ave [Sherborn St]
- **Starbucks** • 775 Commonwealth Ave [Mountfort]
- **Starbucks** • 874 Commonwealth Ave [Armory]

📋 Copy Shops

- **FedEx Kinko's** • 115 Cummington St [Babbitt]
- **Minuteman Press** • 132 Brookline Ave [Burlington]
- **Staples** • 401 Park Dr [Brookline Ave]
- **The UPS Store** • 423 Brookline Ave [Longwood]

🏋 Gyms

- **Boston Sports Club** • 201 Brookline Ave [Park Dr]
- **Curves (Women only)** • 2 Brookline Pl #201 [Brookline Ave]
- **Gold's Gym** • 71 Lansdowne St [Brookline Ave]

🔧 Hardware Stores

- **Economy Hardware** • 1012 Beacon St [Saint Mary's St]

🍾 Liquor Stores

- **Wine Gallery** • 516 Commonwealth Ave [Kenmore]
- **Wine Press** • 1024 Beacon St [Saint Mary's St]

🎬 Movie Theaters

- **AMC Theatres Fenway 13** • 201 Brookline Ave [Park Dr]

🍸 Nightlife

- **An Tua Nua** • 835 Beacon St [Munson]
- **Audubon Circle** • 838 Beacon St [Munson]
- **Avalon** • 15 Lansdowne St [Ipswich St]
- **Axis** • 13 Lansdowne St [Ipswich St]
- **Bill's Bar and Lounge** • 5 1/2 Lansdowne St [Ipswich St]
- **Boston Billiard Club** • 126 Brookline Ave [Burlington]
- **Cask 'n' Flagon** • 62 Brookline Ave [Lansdowne]
- **The Dugout** • 722 Commonwealth Ave [Saint Mary's St]
- **Embassy** • 36 Lansdowne St [Ipswich St]
- **Foundation Lounge** • 500 Commonwealth Ave [Kenmore]
- **Game On!** • 82 Lansdowne St [Brookline Ave]
- **Jillian's** • 145 Ipswich St [Lansdowne]

- **The Modern** • 36 Lansdowne St [Ipswich St]
- **PJ Kilroy's** • 822 Beacon St [Munson]
- **T's Pub** • 973 Commonwealth Ave [Crowninshield]
- **Tequila Rain** • 3 Lansdowne St [Ipswich St]
- **Tiki Room** • 1 Lansdowne St [Ipswich St]
- **Who's on First?** • 19 Yawkey Wy [Brookline Ave]

🍴 Restaurants

- **Ankara Café** • 472 Commonwealth Ave [Kenmore]
- **Audubon Circle** • 838 Beacon St [Munson]
- **Bertucci's** • 4 Brookline Pl [Brookline Ave]
- **Boston Beer Works** • 61 Brookline Ave [Lansdowne]
- **Café Belo** • 636 Beacon St [Raleigh]
- **Chef Chang's House** • 1004 Beacon St [Saint Mary's St]
- **Cornwall's** • 654 Beacon St [Comm Ave]
- **Eastern Standard** • 528 Commonwealth Ave [Kenmore]
- **Elephant Walk** • 900 Beacon St [Park Dr]
- **Ginza** • 1002 Beacon St [Saint Mary's St]
- **Great Bay** • 500 Commonwealth Ave [Kenmore]
- **India Quality** • 484 Commonwealth Ave [Kenmore]
- **New England Soup Factory** • 2 Brookline Pl [Brookline Ave]
- **Noodle Street** • 627 Commonwealth Ave [Sherborn St]
- **Petit Robert Bistro** • 468 Commonwealth Ave [Kenmore]
- **Sol Azteca** • 914A Beacon St [Park Dr]
- **Taberno de Haro** • 999 Beacon St [Saint Mary's St]

🛍 Shopping

- **Artemisia** • 506 Commonwealth Ave [Kenmore]
- **Bed Bath & Beyond** • 401 Park Dr [Brookline Ave]
- **Best Buy** • 401 Park Dr [Brookline Ave]
- **Blick Art Materials** • 401 Park Dr [Brookline Ave]
- **Boston Bicycle** • 842 Beacon St [Arundel]
- **Economy Hardware** • 1012 Beacon St [Saint Mary's St]
- **Guitar Center** • 750 Commonwealth Ave [Saint Mary's St]
- **Hunt's Photo and Video** • 520 Commonwealth Ave [Kenmore]
- **Nantucket Natural Oils** • 508 Commonwealth Ave [Kenmore]
- **Nuggets** • 486 Commonwealth Ave [Kenmore]
- **REI** • 401 Park Dr [Brookline Ave]
- **Ski Market** • 860 Commonwealth Ave [Armory]
- **Staples** • 401 Park Dr [Brookline Ave]
- **Tomb/5W!TS** • 186 Brookline Ave [Park Dr]
- **Tweeter Etc** • 880 Commonwealth Ave [Armory]
- **University Computers** • 533 Commonwealth Ave [Brookline Ave]

🎲 Video Rental

- **Blockbuster** • 532 Commonwealth Ave [Brookline Ave]

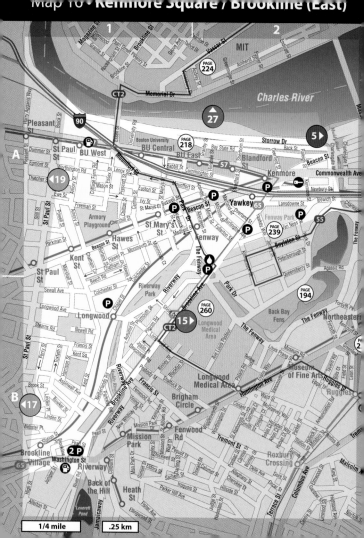

Map 10 • Kenmore Square / Brookline (East)

The Green Line T stops around Kenmore Square and BU are frequently overrun by students and baseball fans, so B train riders might prefer the 57 bus during peak school and game hours. For parking, trawl Bay State Road and Cummington Street or head further west on Comm Ave.

Subway

- ■ **Kenmore**
- ■ **Blandford St** (B)
- ■ **BU East** (B)
- ■ **BU Central** (B)
- ■ **BU West** (B)
- ■ **St Paul St** (B)
- ■ **St Mary's St** (C)
- ■ **Hawes St** (C)
- ■ **Kent St** (C)
- ■ **St Paul St** (C)
- ■ **Fenway** (D)
- ■ **Longwood** (D)
- ■ **Brookline Village** (D)

Bus Lines

- **CT2** • Sullivan Station—Ruggles Station via Kendall/MIT
- **55** • Jersey & Queensberry Streets—Copley Square or Park & Tremont Streets
- **57** • Watertown Yard—Kenmore Station via Newton Corner & Brighton Center
- **65** • Brighton Center—Kenmore Station via Washington Street, Brookline Village

Car Rental

- **Select Car Rental** • 500 Commonwealth Ave [Kenmore] • 617-532-5060

Car Washes

- **Advance Auto Detailing** • 401 Park Dr [Brookline Ave]

Gas Stations

- **Gulf** • 25 Washington St [Brooklin Pl] ♿
- **Mobil** • 850 Commonwealth Ave [Armory]

P Parking

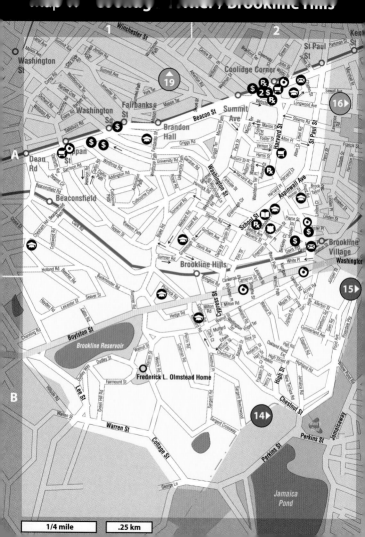

Map 6 Coolidge Corner, Brookline Hills

1/4 mile   .25 km

Map 17 15 14

With easy access to independent stores and neighborhood restaurants, as well as relaxed residential areas perfect for leisurely strolls, Coolidge Corner combines the best of city living with the benefits of suburban life. Brookline Hills is quiet and tree-lined, with plenty of large homes that date to the early 1900s.

$ Banks

- **Bank of America** • 1319 Beacon St [Harvard St]
- **Bank of America (ATM)** • 1624 Beacon St [Washington St]
- **Banknorth Massachusetts** • 1641 Beacon St [University Rd]
- **Brookline Cooperative Bank** • 264 Washington St [Davis Ave]
- **Brookline Savings Bank** • 1340 Beacon St [Harvard St]
- **Brookline Savings Bank** • 1661 Beacon St [Winthrop Rd]
- **Sovereign Bank** • 1 Harvard St [Kent St]
- **Sovereign Bank** • 1341 Beacon St [Harvard St]

Donuts

- **Dunkin' Donuts** • 1316 Beacon St [Harvard St]
- **Dunkin' Donuts** • 1671 Beacon St [Winthrop Rd]
- **Dunkin' Donuts** • 20 Boylston St [High St]
- **Dunkin' Donuts** • 265 Boylston St [Cameron St]
- **Dunkin' Donuts** • 8 Harvard St [Kent St]

O Landmarks

- **Frederick L Olmstead Home** • 99 Warren St [Welch]

Libraries

- **Brookline Main Library** • 361 Washington St [Goodwin Pl]

Rx Pharmacies

- **CVS** • 1322 Beacon St [Harvard St]
- **CVS** • 294 Harvard St [Green St]
- **CVS** • 400 Washington St [Cypress St]
- **Walgreens** • 1324 Beacon St [Harvard St]

Police

- **Brookline Police Department** • 350 Washington St [Thayer St]

Post Offices

- **Brookline Branch** • 1295 Beacon St [Pleasant St]
- **Brookline Village Branch** • 207 Washington St [Station]

Schools

- **Boston Graduate School of Psychoanalysis** • 1581 Beacon St [Washington St]
- **Brookline High** • 115 Greenough St [Davis Ave]
- **Israeli Complementary School** • 50 Sewall Ave [Charles St]
- **John D Runkle** • 50 Druce St [Buckminster]
- **Maimonides** • 34 Philbrick Rd [Boylston St]
- **Pierce** • 50 School St [Washington St]
- **St Mary of the Assumption** • 67 Harvard St [Kent St]
- **William H Lincoln** • 19 Kennard Rd [Boylston St]

Supermarkets

- **Star Market** • 1717 Beacon St [Tappan]
- **Stop & Shop** • 155 Harvard St [Harris St]
- **Trader Joe's** • 1317 Beacon St [Harvard St]

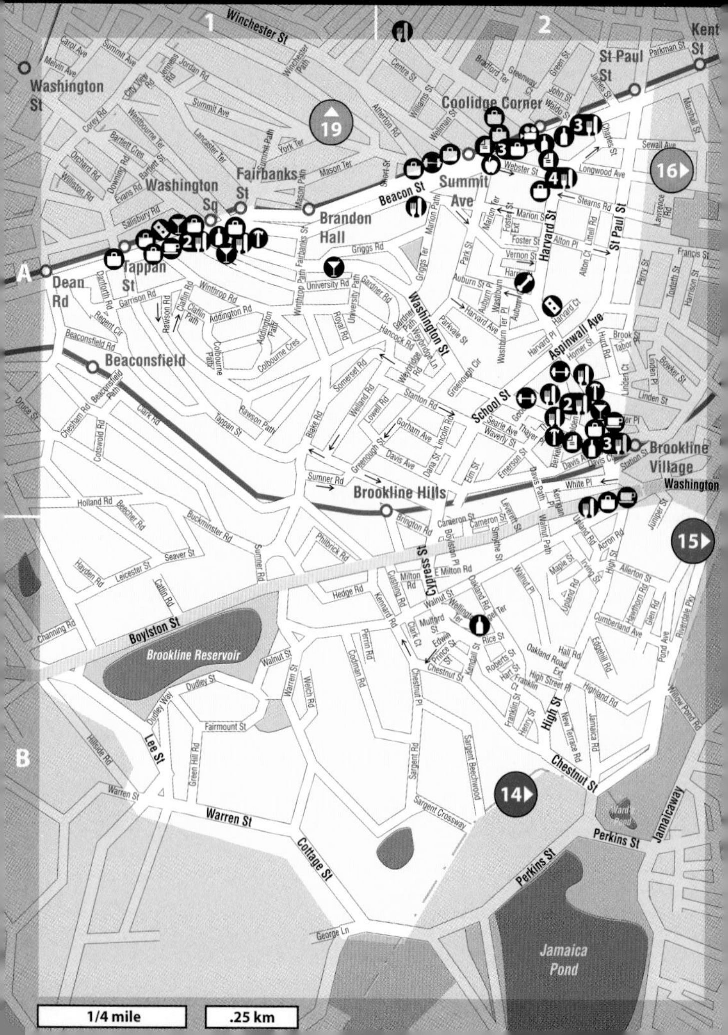

Map 19 • Coolidge Corner / Brookline Hills

1

2

Kent St

Winchester St

Centre St

St Paul St

Parkman St

Washington St

Coolidge Corner

19

Fairbanks St

Washington Sq

Summit Ave

16

Beacon St

Brandon Hall

Summit Ave

Longwood Ave

Webster St

Marion St

Stearns Rd

St Paul St

Francis St

Harvard St

Dean Rd

Tappan St

Foster St

Vernon St

Auburn St

Harvard Ave

Aspinwall Ave

Beaconsfield

Brook St

Tabor Pl

Linden St

Brookline Village

Washington

School St

Beacon St

Washington St

University Rd

Griggs Rd

Winthrop Rd

Colbourne Cres

Pleasant St

White Pl

Brookline Hills

Sumner Rd

Davis Ave

Gorham Ave

Cypress St

15

Holland Rd

Beebe Ct

Brookmister St

Seaver St

Philbrick Rd

Milton Rd

Milton Rd

Cameron St

Boylston St

Brookline Reservoir

Walnut St

Rice St

Chestnut St

High St

Lee St

Fairmount St

Warren St

14

Chestnut St

Perkins St

Jamaicaway

Cottage St

Warren St

George Ln

Jamaica Pond

B

A

1/4 mile   .25 km

This neighborhood features one of Greater Boston's most beloved movie houses, the Coolidge Corner Theater, where an eclectic slate of mostly independent films plays in meticulously restored art deco surroundings. For food at value prices, Rani Indian Bistro or local favorite Anna's Taqueria are good bets.

☕ Coffee

- **Athan's Bakery** • 1621 Beacon St [Washington St]
- **Nancy's Café & Bakery** • 220 Washington St [Davis Ct]
- **Starbucks** • 15 Harvard St [Webster Pl]
- **Starbucks** • 1655 Beacon St [Winthrop Rd]

🖨 Copy Shops

- **FedEx Kinko's** • 1370 Beacon St [Centre St]
- **Mail Boxes Etc** • 258 Harvard St [Beacon St]
- **The UPS Store** • 288 Washington St [Holden St]

🍎 Farmer's Markets

- **Brookline (June-Oct; Thurs 1:30 pm-dusk)** • Centre St at Beacon St [Beacon St]

🏋 Gyms

- **Beacon Hill Athletic Club** • 279 Washington St [Holden St]
- **Fitness Together** • 1404 Beacon St [Winchester St]
- **Fitness Unlimited** • 62 Harvard St [Kent St]

🔨 Hardware Stores

- **Atlas Paint & Supply** • 294 Washington St [Holden St]
- **Brookline Storefront** • 33 Harvard St [Pierce]
- **Connelly's Hardware** • 706 Washington St [Beacon St]

🍷 Liquor Stores

- **Best Cellars (Wine only)** • 1327 Beacon St [Harvard St]
- **Foley's Liquor Store** • 228 Cypress St [Rice St]
- **Food Center Liquors** • 10 Harvard Sq [Andem]
- **Gimbel's Liquors** • 1637 Beacon St [University Rd]
- **London Wine** • 1300 Beacon St [Pleasant St]
- **Wine Gallery** • 375 Boylston St [Brington]

🎬 Movie Theaters

- **Coolidge Corner Theatre** • 290 Harvard St [Green St]

🍸 Nightlife

- **The Last Drop** • 596 Washington St [Griggs Rd]
- **Matt Murphy's Pub** • 14 Harvard St [Webster Pl]
- **The Public House** • 1648 Beacon St [Washington St]
- **Washington Square Tavern** • 714 Washington St [Beacon St]

🐾 Pet Shops

- **Brookline Grooming & Pet Supplies** • 148 Harvard St [Harris St]

🍴 Restaurants

- **Baja Betty's Burritos** • 3 Harvard Sq [Andem]
- **Boca Grande** • 1294 Beacon St [Pleasant St]
- **Bottega Fiorentina** • 41 Harvard St [Andem]
- **Brookline Family Restaurant** • 305 Washington St [Holden St]
- **Café Mirror** • 362 Washington St [Goodwin Pl]
- **Café St Petersburg** • 236 Washington St [Davis Ct]
- **Chef Chow's House** • 230 Harvard St [Webster St]
- **Dok Bua** • 411 Harvard St [Fuller St]
- **Fireplace** • 1634 Beacon St [Washington St]
- **Fugakyu** • 1280 Beacon St [Pleasant St]
- **Golden Temple** • 1651 Beacon St [University Rd]
- **Khao Sarn** • 250 Harvard St [Longwood]
- **La Morra** • 48 Boylston St [High St]
- **Matt Murphy's Pub** • 14 Harvard St [Webster Pl]
- **Pho Lemongrass** • 239 Harvard St [Webster St]
- **Rani Indian Bistro** • 1353 Beacon St [Webster St]
- **Rod Dee** • 1430 Beacon St [Summit Ave]
- **Seoul Kitchen** • 349 Washington St [Thayer St]
- **Tsunami** • 10 Pleasant St [John St]
- **Village Fish** • 22 Harvard St [Webster Pl]
- **Village Smokehouse** • 1 Harvard St [Kent St]
- **Washington Square Tavern** • 714 Washington St [Beacon St]

🛍 Shopping

- **Athan's Bakery** • 1621 Beacon St [Washington St]
- **Beacon Kosher** • 1706 Beacon St [Williston]
- **Bowl & Board** • 1354 Beacon St [Webster St]
- **EC Florist & Gifts** • 224 Washington St [Davis Ct]
- **Emack & Bolio's** • 1663 Beacon St [Winthrop Rd]
- **Eureka Puzzles** • 1354 Beacon St
- **Marathon Sports** • 1638 Beacon St [University Rd]
- **Paper Source** • 1361 Beacon St [Webster St]
- **Party Favors** • 1356 Beacon St [Webster St]
- **Petropol** • 1428 Beacon St [Summit Ave]
- **Pier 1 Imports** • 1351 Beacon St [Webster St]
- **Russian Village** • 1659 Beacon St [Winthrop Rd]
- **Serenade Chocolates** • 5 Harvard St [Andem]
- **Ten Thousand Villages** • 226 Harvard St [Sewall Ave]
- **Wild Goose Chase** • 1431 Beacon St [Summit Ave]
- **Zathmary's** • 299 Harvard St [Green St]

📀 Video Rental

- **Hollywood Video** • 111 Harvard St [Harvard Ct]
- **Movieworks** • 1658 Beacon St [Winthrop Rd]

Brookline is eminently drivable, and parking in the Coolidge Corner area is usually easy to find and reasonably priced. There's one catch: overnight street parking is essentially forbidden. A better alternative may be the T: the Green Line's C and D trains offer access to most of the area.

Subway

- **Kent St (C)**
- **St Paul St (C)**
- **Coolidge Corner (C)**
- **Summit Ave (C)**
- **Brandon Hall (C)**
- **Fairbanks St (C)**
- **Washington Sq (C)**
- **Tappan St (C)**
- **Dean Rd (C)**
- **Brookline Village (D)**
- **Brookline Hills (D)**
- **Beaconsfield (D)**

Bus Lines

- **60** • Chestnut Hill—Kenmore Station via Brookline Village & Cypress Street
- **65** • Brighton Center—Kenmore Station via Washington Street, Brookline Village
- **66** • Harvard Square—Dudley Station via Allston & Brookline

Car Washes

- **Effective Car Detail** • 40 Aspinwall Ave [Harvard St]
- **Scrubadub Auto Wash** • 143 Harvard St [Harris St]

Gas Stations

- **Mobil** • 198 Harvard St [Marion St]
- **Mobil** • 345 Boylston St [Cypress St] ⚡

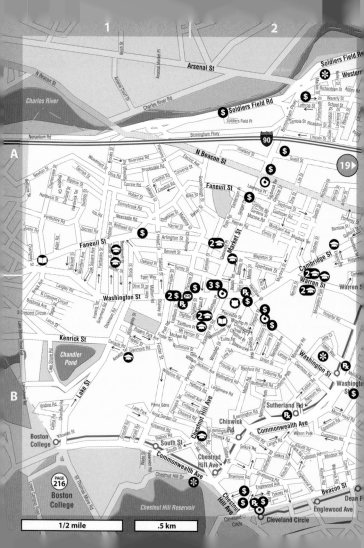

Brighton is the more sedate half of the Allston-Brighton duo but, like its rowdier neighbor, it attracts plenty of college students and young professionals. Narrow, tangled residential streets surround the cluster of shops and restaurants on Washington Street in Brighton Center.

Banks

- **Bank of America** • 315 Washington St [Waldo Ter]
- **Bank of America** • 350 Chestnut Hill Ave [Englewood]
- **Bank of America** • 5 Chestnut Hill Ave [Washington St]
- **Bank of America (ATM)** • 175 Market St [N Beacon]
- **Bank of America (ATM)** • 225 Washington St [Snow St]
- **Bank of America (ATM)** • 401 Washington St [Dighton]
- **Cambridge Trust (ATM)** • 2 Soldiers Field Rd [Soldiers Field Pl]
- **Citizens Bank** • 2000 Beacon St [Sutherland]
- **Citizens Bank** • 35 Washington St [Monastery]
- **Citizens Bank** • 414 Washington St [Parsons]
- **Citizens Bank (ATM)** • 1912 Beacon St [Ayr]
- **Citizens Bank (ATM)** • 241 Market St [Cypress Rd]
- **Mercantile Bank** • 423 Washington St [Parsons]
- **People's Federal Savings Bank** • 435 Market St [Surrey]
- **People's Federal Savings Bank (ATM)** • 20 Guest St [Market St]
- **People's Federal Savings Bank (ATM)** • 236 Faneuil St [Arlington St]
- **Sovereign Bank** • 30 Birmingham Pkwy [Waverly St]
- **Sovereign Bank** • 415 Market St [Henshaw]
- **Sovereign Bank (ATM)** • 250 Washington St [Shepard St]

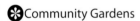 Community Gardens

Donuts

- **Dunkin' Donuts** • 1955 Beacon St [Ayr]
- **Dunkin' Donuts** • 214 N Beacon St [Market St]
- **Dunkin' Donuts** • 235 Washington St [Shannon]
- **Dunkin' Donuts** • 350 Washington St [Academy Hill]

Libraries

- **Brighton** • 40 Academy Hill Rd [Peaceable]
- **Faneuil** • 419 Faneuil St [Bigelow St]

Pharmacies

- **Brooks** • 399 Market St [Henshaw]
- **CVS** • 1927 Beacon St [Ayr]
- **CVS** • 427 Washington St [Eastburn St]
- **Melvin Pharmacy** • 1558 Commonwealth Ave [Melvin Ave]
- **Sutherland Pharmacy** • 1690 Commonwealth Ave [Wilson Pk]

Police

- **District D-14** • 301 Washington St [Wirt]

Post Offices

- **Brighton** • 424 Washington St [Parsons]

Schools

- **Alexander Hamilton Elementary** • 198 Strathmore Rd [Lothian]
- **Another Course to College** • 20 Warren St [Nevins]
- **Boston Community Leadership Academy** • 20 Warren St [Nevins]
- **Brighton High** • 25 Warren St [Monastery]
- **Conservatory Lab Charter** • 25 Arlington St [Leicester]
- **James Garfield Elementary** • 95 Beechcroft St [Hester]
- **Kennedy Day School Program** • 30 Warren St [Monastery]
- **Mary Lyon Elementary/Middle** • 50 Beechcroft St [Hester]
- **Mesivta High School of Greater** • 34 Sparhawk St [Bentley]
- **Mount St Joseph Academy** • 617 Cambridge St [Eleanor]
- **Shaloh House Hebrew Day** • 29 Chestnut Hill Ave [Dighton]
- **St. Columbkille Elementary** • 25 Arlington St [Leicester]
- **Thomas A Edison Junior High** • 60 Glenmont Rd [Willoughby St]
- **William H Taft Middle** • 20 Warren St [Nevins]
- **Winship Elementary** • 54 Dighton St [Chestnut Hill Ave]

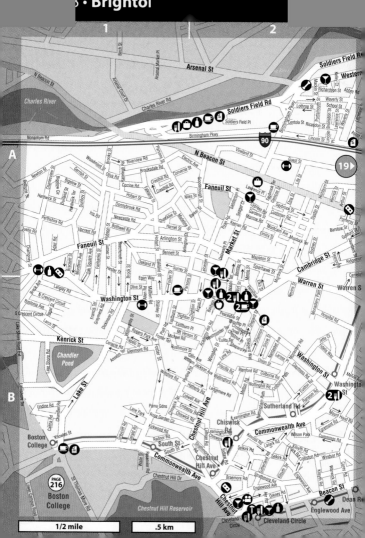

The Last Drop on Washington Street is the definition of a no-frills, neighborhood beer joint. If frills are more your style, try Soho, a modern, two-level club that tries to emulate Manhattan chic. Hungry? Grab some tapas and, of course, sangria at Tasca.

☕ Coffee
- **French Press Coffee** • 2201 Commonwealth Ave [Lake St]
- **Greenhouse Café** • 425 Washington St [Parsons]
- **Market Diner** • 34 Market St [Mass Tpke]
- **Starbucks** • 1660 Soldiers Field Rd [Soldiers Field Pl]

🖨 Copy Shops
- **Commonwealth Copy** • 132 Lincoln St [Antwerp]
- **FedEx Kinko's** • 252 Washington St [Shepard St]
- **Staples** • 1660 Soldiers Field Rd [Soldiers Field Pl]
- **The UPS Store** • 2193 Commonwealth Ave [Lake St]

🍎 Farmer's Markets
- **Brighton (July-Oct; Sat 12-4:30)** • 5 Chestnut Hill Ave [Washington St]

🏋 Gyms
- **Bally Total Fitness** • 25 Guest St [Life]
- **Beacon Hill Athletic Club** • 470 Washington St [Allen St]
- **Oak Square YMCA** • 615 Washington St [Breck]

🔧 Hardware Stores
- **Cleveland Circle Hardware** • 1920 Beacon St [Ayr]

🍾 Liquor Stores
- **Dorr's Liquor Mart** • 354 Washington St [Chestnut Hill Ave]
- **Martignetti Liquors** • 1650 Soldiers Field Rd [Soldiers Field Pl]
- **Oak Square Liquors** • 610 Washington St [Breck]
- **Reservoir Wines & Spirits** • 1922 Beacon St [Ayr]
- **Walsh Wine & Spirits** • 313 Washington St [Waldo Ter]

🎭 Movie Theaters
- **National Amusements Circle Cinemas** • 399 Chestnut Hill Ave [Beacon St]

🍸 Nightlife
- **CitySide** • 1960 Beacon St [Sutherland]
- **Green Briar** • 304 Washington St [Wirt]
- **Irish Village** • 224 Market St [Saybrook St]
- **Joey's** • 416 Market St [Henshaw]
- **Mary Ann's** • 1937 Beacon St [Ayr]
- **Roggie's** • 356 Chestnut Hill Ave [Englewood]
- **Soho** • 386 Market St [Henshaw]

🐾 Pet Shops
- **No Bones About It** • 1786 Beacon St [Warwick Rd]
- **Toureen Kennels & Grooming Salon** • 505 Western Ave [Mackin]

🍴 Restaurants
- **Bamboo** • 1616 Commonwealth Ave [Washington St]
- **Bangkok Bistro** • 1952 Beacon St [Sutherland]
- **Bluestone Bistro** • 1799 Commonwealth Ave [Chiswick Rd]
- **Cityside Bar & Grill** • 1960 Beacon St [Sutherland]
- **Devlin's** • 332 Washington St [Waldo Ter]
- **Green Briar** • 304 Washington St [Wirt]
- **IHOP** • 1850 Soldiers Field Rd [N Beacon] ⏰
- **Jasmine Bistro** • 412 Market St [Henshaw]
- **Soho** • 386 Market St [Henshaw]
- **Tasca** • 1612 Commonwealth Ave [Washington St]

🛍 Shopping
- **Amanda's Flowers** • 347 Washington St [Academy Hill]
- **Boomerangs** • 298 Washington St [Wirt]
- **CompUSA** • 205 Market St [Lawrence Pl]
- **Staples** • 1660 Soldiers Field Rd [Soldiers Field Pl]

📀 Video Rental
- **Blockbuster** • 358 Chestnut Hill Ave [Englewood]
- **Brighton Video** • 596 Washington St [Brackett]
- **Hollywood Video** • 103 N Beacon St [Arthur]

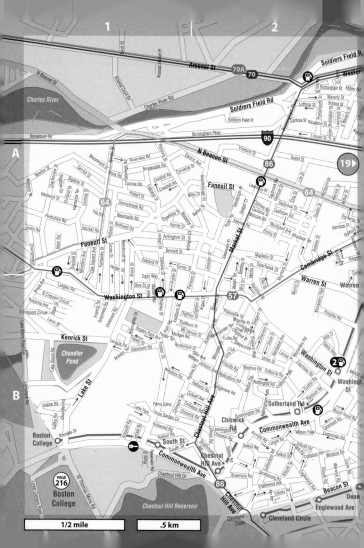

Map 1

The bus dominates public transportation in Brighton—the 57 bus brings riders into Kenmore Square, and the 64 bus and 86 bus lead into Cambridge and Somerville. The Green Line's C train creeps along the southern edge of Brighton to Cleveland Circle.

Subway

- **Warren St (B)**
- **Washington St (B)**
- **Sutherland Rd (B)**
- **Chiswick Rd (B)**
- **Chestnut Hill Ave (B)**
- **South St (B)**
- **Boston College (B)**
- **Englewood Ave (C)**
- **Cleveland Circle (C)**

Bus Lines

57 • Watertown Yard—Kenmore Station via Newton Corner & Brighton Center

64 • Oak Square—Central Square, Cambridge, or Kendall/MIT

70 • Cedarwood, N Waltham, or Watertown Square—University Park via Central Square

70A • Cedarwood, N Waltham, or Watertown Square—University Park via Central Square

86 • Sullivan Square Station—Cleveland Circle via Harvard/Johnson Gate

Car Rental

- **Rent A Wreck** • 2022 Commonwealth Ave [Gerald] • 617-254-9540

Gas Stations

- **Econogas** • 1550 Commonwealth Ave [Melvin Ave]
- **Exxon** • 433 Washington St [Eastburn St]
- **Gulf** • 1650 Commonwealth Ave [Mt Hood]
- **Gulf** • 195 Market St [N Beacon]
- **Gulf** • 455 Washington St [Malbert]
- **Mobil** • 500 Western Ave [Mackin]
- **Shell** • 332 Chestnut Hill Ave [Englewood]
- **Sunoco** • 602 Washington St [Breck]

Map 19 • Allston (South) / Brookline (North)

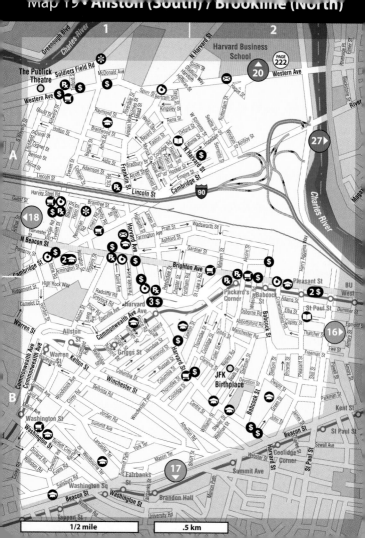

Crowded living and rowdy students define Allston for most. There's no place in the city where so many cheap eats, dive bars, and used goods are crammed into so few blocks. It's a dirty mashup and the city is better for it. It's also the primary home to newly-arrived Russian Jews, who add vitality to Brookline's Jewish culture and locus on Harvard Street.

$ Banks

- **Asian American Bank & Trust** • 230 Harvard Ave [Brainerd]
- **Bank of America** • 1237 Commonwealth Ave [Harvard Ave]
- **Bank of America (ATM)** • 1236A Commonwealth Ave [Harvard Ave]
- **Bank of America (ATM)** • 186 Brighton Ave [Quint]
- **Bank of America (ATM)** • 400 Western Ave [Litchfield St]
- **Bank of America (ATM)** • 881 Commonwealth Ave [Buick]
- **Bank of America (ATM)** • 957 Commonwealth Ave [Harry Agganis]
- **Century Bank** • 300 Western Ave [Everett St]
- **Century Bank (ATM)** • BU, Campus Convenience/ Sleeper Hall • 275 Babcock St [Gardner St]
- **Citizens Bank** • 315 Harvard St [Babcock]
- **Citizens Bank** • 429 Harvard St [Coolidge St]
- **Citizens Bank** • 60 Everett St [Harvester]
- **Citizens Bank (ATM)** • 1065 Commonwealth Ave [Alcorn]
- **Citizens Bank (ATM)** • 1219 Commonwealth Ave [Harvard Ave]
- **Citizens Bank (ATM)** • 157 Brighton Ave [Harvard Ave]
- **Citizens Bank (ATM)** • 289 Harvard St [Green St]
- **Citizens Bank (ATM)** • 370 Western Ave [Telford]
- **Citizens Bank (ATM)** • 509 Cambridge St [Barrows]
- **People's Federal Savings Bank** • 229 N Harvard St [Franklin St]
- **Sovereign Bank** • 487 Harvard St [Lawton]
- **Wainwright Bank & Trust** • 301 Harvard St [Babcock]

✳ Community Gardens

◉ Donuts

- **Dunkin' Donuts** • 1020 Commonwealth Ave [Babcock]
- **Dunkin' Donuts** • 179 Brighton Ave [Parkvale]
- **Dunkin' Donuts** • 209 N Harvard St [Western]
- **Dunkin' Donuts** • 210 Harvard Ave [Comm Ave]
- **Dunkin' Donuts** • 60 Everett St [Harvester]
- **Twin Do-Nuts** • 501 Cambridge St [Barrows]

○ Landmarks

- **John F Kennedy Birthplace** • 83 Beals St [Harvard St]
- **The Publick Theater** • 1400 Soldiers Field Rd [Western]

📖 Libraries

- **Coolidge Corner** • 31 Pleasant St [John St]
- **Honan-Allston** • 300 N Harvard St [Eatonia]

℞ Pharmacies

- **Brooks** • 181 Brighton Ave [Parkvale]
- **CVS** • 1266 Commonwealth Ave [Gorham St]
- **CVS** • 900 Commonwealth Ave [St Paul]
- **Osco** • 370 Western Ave [Telford]
- **Pelham Healthcare Services** • 280 Lincoln St [Eric]
- **Shaw's** • 1065 Commonwealth Ave [Alcorn]
- **Stop & Shop** • 60 Everett St [Harvester]

✉ Post Offices

- **Allston Station** • 47 Harvard Ave [Farrington]
- **Soldiers Field Station** • 117 Western Ave [Hague]

🎓 Schools

- **Bay Cove Academy** • 156 Lawton St [Abbottsford]
- **Beacon High** • 74 Green St [Dwight]
- **Congregation Kehillath Israel Religious School** • 384 Harvard St [Beals]
- **Edward Devotion** • 345 Harvard St [Shailer]
- **Harriet Baldwin Elementary** • 121 Corey Rd [Washington St]
- **Horace Mann School for the Deaf and Hard of Hearing** • 40 Armington St [Webley]
- **Jackson Mann Elementary** • 40 Armington St [Webley]
- **Lesley University** • 29 Everett St [Mass Ave]
- **Media and Technology Charter High** • 1001 Commonwealth Ave [Babcock]
- **Michael Driscoll** • 64 Westbourne Ter [Bartlett St]
- **St Herman of Alaska Christian** • 64 Harvard Ave [Farrington]
- **Thomas Gardner Elementary** • 30 Athol St [Brentwood]
- **Torah Academy** • 11 Williston Rd [Salisbury]

🛒 Supermarkets

- **Bazaar** • 424 Cambridge St [Rugg]
- **The Butcherie** • 428 Harvard St [Coolidge St]
- **Shaw's** • 1065 Commonwealth Ave [Alcorn]
- **Shaw's** • 370 Western Ave [Telford]
- **Stop & Shop** • 60 Everett St [Harvester]
- **Super 88** • 1 Brighton Ave [Malvern St]
- **Whole Foods Market** • 15 Washington St [Corey Rd]

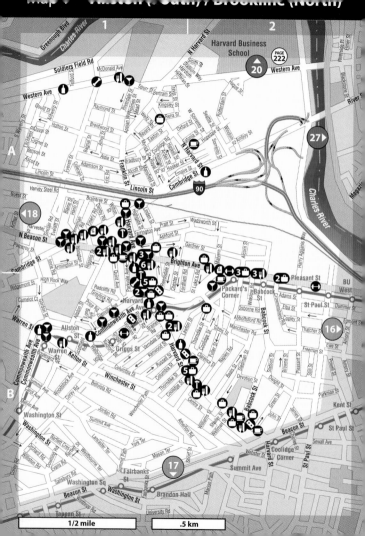

Map 7 — Allston (South), Brookline (North)

Allston Rock City! The rock clubs drive the crowd in Allston, with live music and DJs every night of the week. Check the Paradise, Harper's Ferry, Great Scott, and even the velvet rope at the Wonder Bar. Taps dominate the Sunset Grill and the Big Time. The restaurant gems of Allston are diamonds in the rough. Of the roughest, we can't get enough of the Pakistani tandoori at Madina Market's Kitchen.

☕ Coffee

- **Caffe LaScala** • 318 Harvard St [Babcock]
- **Infusions Tea Spa (tea only)** • 110 Brighton Ave [Linden St]
- **Peet's Coffee & Tea** • 285 Harvard St [Green St]
- **Starbucks** • Star Market • 1065 Commonwealth Ave [Alcorn]
- **Starbucks** • 277 Harvard St [Green St]
- **Starbucks** • 473 Harvard St [Lawton]

📋 Copy Shops

- **Signal Graphics** • 450 Cambridge St [Emery]
- **Staples** • 214 Harvard Ave [Comm Ave]
- **The UPS Store** • 1085 Commonwealth Ave [Malvern St]

🏋 Gyms

- **Boston Sports Club** • 15 Gorham St [Comm Ave]
- **HealthWorks Fitness Center** • 920 Commonwealth Ave [St Paul]
- **Wellbridge Health and Fitness Center** • 1079 Commonwealth Ave [Malvern St]

🔧 Hardware Stores

- **Aborn True Value** • 438 Harvard St [Coolidge St]
- **Economy Hardware** • 144 Harvard Ave [Glenville Ter]
- **Model Hardware** • 22 Harvard Ave [Cambridge St]

🍷 Liquor Stores

- **Allston Food and Spirits** • 223 Cambridge St [N Harvard]
- **Blanchard Liquors** • 103 Harvard Ave [Brighton Ave]
- **Brookline Liquor Mart** • 1354 Commonwealth Ave [Walbridge]
- **Hurley's** • 1441 Commonwealth Ave [Warren St]
- **Mall Discount Liquors & Wines** • 525 Harvard Ave [Verndale]
- **Marty's Liquors** • 193 Harvard Ave [Comm Ave]
- **Wine Shop** • 370 Western Ave [Telford]

🎤 Nightlife

- **Avenue Bar & Grille** • 1249 Commonwealth Ave [Royce Rd]
- **Big City** • 138 Brighton Ave [Harvard Ave]
- **Bus Stop Pub** • 252 Western Ave [N Harvard]
- **Common Ground** • 85 Harvard Ave [Gardner St]
- **Great Scott** • 1222 Commonwealth Ave [Harvard Ave]
- **Harper's Ferry** • 156 Harvard Ave [Harvard Ave]
- **Harry's Bar & Grill** • 1430 Commonwealth Ave [Kelton]
- **The Kells** • 161 Brighton Ave [Harvard Ave]
- **Kinvara Pub** • 34 Harvard Ave [Cambridge St]
- **Model Café** • 7 N Beacon St [Cambridge St]
- **O'Brien's** • 3 Harvard Ave [Cambridge St]
- **Our House** • 1277 Commonwealth Ave [Spofford]
- **Paradise Rock Club & Lounge** • 967 Commonwealth Ave [Harry Agganis]
- **Reel Bar** • 477 Cambridge St [Islington St]
- **Scullers Jazz Club** • Doubletree Hotel • 400 Soldiers Field Rd [Cambridge St]
- **Silhouette Lounge** • 200 Brighton Ave [Allston St]
- **Sports Depot** • 353 Cambridge St [Highgate]
- **Sunset Grill & Tap** • 130 Brighton Ave [Linden St]
- **Tonic** • 1316 Commonwealth Ave [Redford]
- **White Horse Tavern** • 116 Brighton Ave [Linden St]
- **Wonder Bar** • 186 Harvard Ave [Glenville Ter]

🐾 Pet Shops

- **The Pet Shop** • 165 Harvard Ave [Glenville Ave]
- **Petco** • 304 Western Ave [Everett St]

🍴 Restaurants

- **Anadolu Café** • 1022 Commonwealth Ave [Babcock]
- **Bagel Rising** • 1243 Commonwealth Ave [Harvard Ave]
- **Big City** • 138 Brighton Ave [Harvard Ave]
- **Bottega Fiorentina** • 313B Harvard St [Babcock]
- **Breakfast Club Diner** • 270 Western Ave [McDonald]
- **Brown Sugar Café** • 1033 Commonwealth Ave [Winslow Ave]
- **Buddha's Delight** • 404 Harvard St [Naples]
- **Buk Kyung II** • 151 Brighton Ave [Harvard Ave]
- **Café Brazil** • 421 Cambridge St [Denby]
- **Camino Real** • 48 Harvard Ave [Farrington]
- **Charlie's Pizza & Café** • 177 Allston St [Kelton]
- **El Cafetal** • 479 Cambridge St [Islington St]
- **Grasshopper** • 1 N Beacon St [Cambridge St]
- **Grecian Yearning** • 174 Harvard Ave [Glenville Ave]
- **Harry's Bar & Grill** • 1430 Commonwealth Ave [Kelton]
- **Indian Dhaba Roadside Diner** • 180 Brighton Ave [Parkvale]
- **La Mamma Pizza** • 190 Brighton Ave [Quint]
- **Madina Market's Kitchen** • 72 Brighton Ave [Chester St]
- **Paris Creperie** • 278 Harvard St [Green St]
- **Rangoli** • 129 Brighton Ave [Linden St]
- **Redneck's Roast Beef** • 140 Brighton Ave [Harvard Ave]
- **Reef Café** • 170 Brighton Ave [Parkvale]
- **Rubin's** • 500 Harvard St [Kenwood]
- **Saigon** • 431 Cambridge St [Denby]
- **Spike's Junkyard Dogs** • 108 Brighton Ave [Linden St]
- **Sunset Grill & Tap** • 130 Brighton Ave [Linden St]
- **Super 88 Food Court** • 1095 Commonwealth Ave [Malvern St]
- **Upper Crust** • 286 Harvard St [Green St]
- **V Majestic** • 164 Brighton Ave [Parkvale]
- **Zaftigs Delicatessen** • 335 Harvard St [Shailer]

🛍 Shopping

- **Berezka International Food Store** • 1215 Commonwealth Ave [Linden St]
- **Bicycle Bill's** • 253 N Harvard St [Easton]
- **Bob Smith's Wilderness House** • 1048 Commonwealth Ave [Winslow Rd]
- **Brookline News and Gift** • 313 Harvard St [Babcock]
- **Catering by Andrew** • 402 Harvard St [Naples]
- **City Housewares** • 434 Harvard St [Coolidge St]
- **City Sports** • 1035 Commonwealth Ave [Winslow Rd]
- **Clear Flour** • 178 Thorndike St [Lawton]
- **Coco Cosmetics** • 192 Harvard Ave [Glenville Ter]
- **Eastern Mountain Sports** • 1041 Commonwealth Ave [Winslow Rd]
- **Economy Hardware** • 144 Harvard Ave [Glenville Ter]
- **Herrell's Ice Cream** • 155 Brighton Ave [Harvard Ave]
- **In Your Ear** • 957 Commonwealth Ave [Harry Agganis]
- **International Bicycle Center** • 89 Brighton Ave [Reedsdale]
- **Israel Bookshop** • 410 Harvard St [Fuller St]
- **Jasmine Sola Warehouse Store** • 965 Commonwealth Ave [Harry Agganis]
- **JP Licks** • 311 Harvard St [Babcock]
- **Kolbo Fine Judaica** • 437 Harvard St [Coolidge St]
- **Kupel's Bake & Bagel** • 421 Harvard St [Fuller St]
- **New England Comics** • 131 Harvard St [Brighton Ave]
- **Pixi Accessories** • 175 Harvard Ave [Glenville Ave]
- **Re:Generation Records and Tattoo** • 155 Harvard Ave [Glenville Ave]
- **Richman's Zipper Hospital** • 318 Harvard St [Babcock]
- **Staples** • 214 Harvard Ave [Comm Ave]
- **Stingray Body Art** • 1 Harvard Ave [Cambridge St]
- **TJ Maxx** • 525 Harvard Ave [Verndale]
- **Urban Renewals** • 122 Brighton Ave [Linden St]
- **Vespa Boston** • 22 Brighton St [St Lukes]
- **Wulf's Fish Market** • 409 Harvard St [Fuller St]

📀 Video Rental

- **Blockbuster** • 473 Harvard St [Lawton]
- **Cinemasmith** • 279 Harvard St [Green St]
- **Korean Book & Video Renting Store (Korean & Japanese)** • 156 Harvard Ave [Glenville Ter]
- **Yes Brasil (Brazilian)** • 1287 Commonwealth Ave [Spofford]

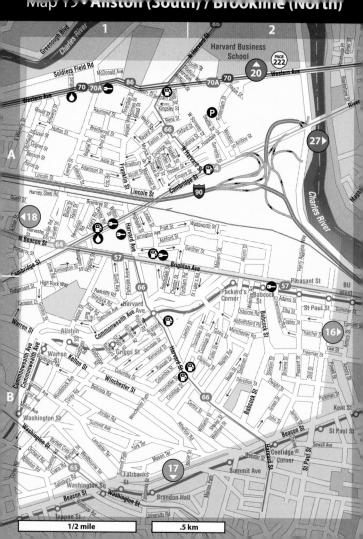

The Green Line doesn't get more crowded and unbearable than the B train to BC. Even being wedged in with the fresh face of affluence is little solace. Parking is notoriously difficult in Allston, so deal with the T or take a cab. Clubbing and busing go like this: 66 bus to Harvard, 64 bus to Central Square, and if you think it's faster than the T, 54 bus to Kenmore Square.

Subway

- ■ **St Paul St** (B)
- ■ **Pleasant St** (B)
- ■ **Babcock St** (B)
- ■ **Packard's Corner** (B)
- ■ **Harvard Ave** (B)
- ■ **Griggs St** (B)
- ■ **Allston St** (B)
- ■ **Warren St** (B)
- ■ **Washington St** (B)

Bus Lines

- **57** · Watertown Yard—Kenmore Station via Newton Corner & Brighton Center
- **64** · Oak Square—Central Square, Cambridge, or Kendall/MIT
- **65** · Brighton Center—Kenmore Station via Washington Street, Brookline Village
- **66** · Harvard Square—Dudley Station via Allston & Brookline
- **70** · Cedarwood, N Waltham, or Watertown Square—University Park via Central Square
- **70A** · Cedarwood, N Waltham, or Watertown Square—University Park via Central Square
- **86** · Sullivan Square Station—Cleveland Circle via Harvard/Johnson Gate

Car Rental

- **Budget** • 95 Brighton Ave [Linden St] • 617-497-3608
- **Enterprise** • 292 Western Ave [Everett St] • 617-783-2240
- **Enterprise** • 996 Commonwealth Ave [Babcock] • 617-738-6003
- **Hertz** • 414 Cambridge St [Denby] • 617-787-2894
- **Hertz Local Edition** • 226 Harvard Ave [Brainerd] • 617-566-9801
- **U-Save Auto & Truck Rental** • 25 Harvard Ave [Cambridge St] • 617-254-1000

Car Washes

- **Allston Car Wash** • 434 Cambridge St [Rugg]
- **Shield System Cloth Car Wash** • 365 Western Ave [Telford]

Gas Stations

- **Exxon** • 198 Western Ave [N Harvard]
- **Gulf** • 226 Harvard Ave [Brainerd]
- **Hess** • 100 Brighton Ave [Linden St]
- **Hess** • 219 Cambridge St [Higgins St]
- **Mobil** • 434 Cambridge St [Rugg]
- **Shell** • 445 Harvard St [Thorndike]
- **Sunoco** • 454 Harvard St [Thorndike]

Parking

Map 20 • Harvard Square / Allston (North)

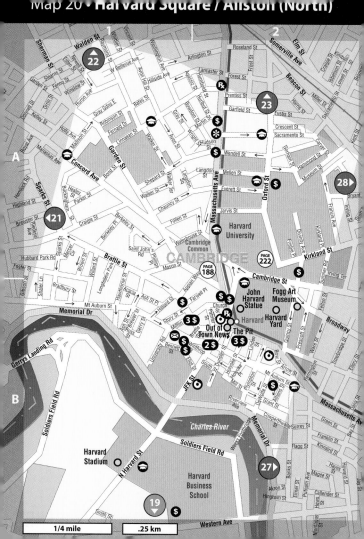

Map 2

Despite an onslaught of retail chain stores, Harvard Square still retains much of its eccentric charm, with speed chess players, quirky stores, and eclectic eateries. Stroll up Brattle Street to admire the magnificent houses, or step into Harvard Yard to escape into another world.

 Banks

- **Bank of America** • 1414 Massachusetts Ave [JFK]
- **Bank of America (ATM)** • 1 Mifflin Pl [Mt Auburn]
- **Bank of America (ATM)** • 1663 Massachusetts Ave [Hudson St]
- **Bank of America (ATM)** • 28 Eliot St [Winthrop St]
- **Bank of America (ATM)** • 45 Quincy St [Kirkland St]
- **Bank of America (ATM)** • 47 Oxford St [Everett St]
- **Bank of America (ATM)** • 67 Mt Auburn St [Linden St]
- **Bank of America (ATM)** • Spangler Ctr [Hague]
- **Cambridge Savings Bank** • 1374 Massachusetts Ave [Holyoke St]
- **Cambridge Savings Bank (ATM)** • 36 JFK St [Mt Auburn]
- **Cambridge Trust** • 1336 Massachusetts Ave [Holyoke St]
- **Cambridge Trust** • 1720 Massachusetts Ave [Garfield St]
- **Cambridge Trust (ATM)** • 124 Mt Auburn St [University Rd]
- **Citizens Bank** • 6 JFK St [Brattle Sq]
- **Citizens Bank (ATM)** • 1 Bennett St [Eliot St]
- **Citizens Bank (ATM)** • 1400 Massachusetts Ave [Dunster St]
- **Sovereign Bank** • 1420 Massachusetts Ave [Church St]
- **Sovereign Bank (ATM)** • 125 Mt Auburn St [University Rd]
- **Wainwright Bank & Trust** • 44 Brattle St [Story]

 Community Gardens

 Donuts

- **Dunkin' Donuts** • 1 Bow St [Mass Ave]
- **Dunkin' Donuts** • 65 JFK St [Eliot St]
- **Dunkin' Donuts** • Harvard MBTA • Massachusetts Ave & Brattle St

 Landmarks

- **Fogg Art Museum** • 32 Quincy St [B'way]
- **Harvard Stadium** • N Harvard St & Soldiers Field Rd
- **Harvard Yard** • b/w Broadway, Quincy St, Peabody St & Massachusetts Ave
- **John Harvard Statue** • Harvard Yard [Peabody St]
- **Out of Town News** • 0 Harvard Sq [JFK St]
- **The Pit** • 0 Harvard Sq [JFK St]

 Pharmacies

- **Brooks** • 1740 Massachusetts Ave [Prentiss]
- **CVS** • 1426 Massachusetts Ave [Church St]

 Post Offices

- **Harvard Square Station** • 125 Mt Auburn St [University Rd]

 Schools

- **Boston Archdiocesan Choir School** • 29 Mt Auburn St [Athens St]
- **Graham and Parks** • 44 Linnaean St [Aveon St]
- **Harvard Business** • Soldiers Field Rd [Soldiers Field Rd]
- **Harvard Law** • 1563 Massachusetts Ave [Waterhouse]
- **Harvard University** • 1350 Massachusetts Ave [Holyoke St]
- **Maria L Baldwin** • 28 Sacramento St [Sacramento Pl]
- **St Peter's** • 96 Concord Ave [Buckingham St]

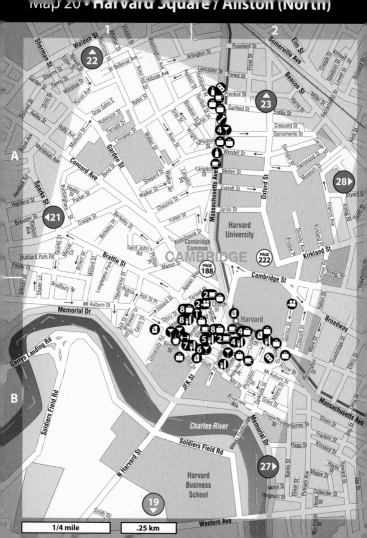

Map 20 • Harvard Square / Allston (North)

1/4 mile .25 km

If the superlative people-watching isn't enough, browse the bookshelves at the Coop, grab a beer at Grendel's, or indulge in L.A. Burdick's justly celebrated hot chocolate. For casual fare, nothing beats Mr. and Mrs. Bartley's Burger Cottage. If you want to dress up a little, try Harvest or Sandrine's.

Coffee

- **Algiers Coffee House** • 40 Brattle St [Story]
- **Au Bon Pain** • 1360 Massachusetts Ave [Holyoke St]
- **Dado Tea** (tea only) • 50 Church St [Palmer St]
- **Peet's Coffee & Tea** • 100 Mt Auburn St [JFK]
- **Simon's Coffee House** • 1736 Massachusetts Ave [Prentiss]
- **Starbucks** • 1662 Massachusetts Ave [Shepard St]
- **Starbucks** • 31 Church St [Palmer St]
- **Starbucks** • 36 JFK St [Mt Auburn]
- **Tealuxe** • 0 Brattle St [Hague]

Copy Shops

- **FedEx Kinko's** • 1 Mifflin Pl [Mt Auburn]
- **Gnomon Copy** • 1304 Massachusetts Ave [Linden St]
- **Gnomon Copy** • 99 Mt Auburn St [JFK]
- **Staples** • 57 John F Kennedy St [Winthrop St]

Farmer's Markets

- **Cambridge/Charles Square** (May-Nov; Fri 1 pm-6 pm, Sun 10 am-3 pm) • 1 Bennett St [Eliot St]

Gyms

- **Wellbridge Health and Fitness Center** • 5 Bennett St [Eliot St]

Hardware Stores

- **Dickinson Brothers True Value** • 26 Brattle St [Church St]

Liquor Stores

- **Harvard Wine** • 1664 Massachusetts Ave [Shepard St]
- **University Wine Shop** • 1739 Massachusetts Ave [Prentiss]

Movie Theaters

- **Brattle Theatre** • 40 Brattle St [Story]
- **Harvard Film Archive** • 24 Quincy St [B'way]
- **Loews Cineplex Harvard Square** • 10 Church St [Mass Ave]

Nightlife

- **Cambridge Common** • 1667 Massachusetts Ave [Hudson St]
- **Charlie's Kitchen** • 11 Eliot St [Mt Auburn]
- **Club Passim** • 47 Palmer St [Church St]
- **Grendel's Den** • 89 Winthrop St [JFK]
- **Hoffa's Swiss Alps** • 114 Mt Auburn St [Mifflin]
- **John Harvard's Brew House** • 33 Dunster St [Mt Auburn]
- **Lizard Lounge** • 1667 Massachusetts Ave [Hudson St]
- **Noir** • Charles Hotel • 1 Bennett St [Eliot St]
- **Redline** • 59 JFK St [Winthrop St]
- **Regattabar** • Charles Hotel • 1 Bennett St [Eliot St]
- **Shay's Lounge** • 58 JFK St [South St]
- **Temple Bar** • 1688 Massachusetts Ave [Sacramento St]
- **West Side Lounge** • 1680 Massachusetts Ave [Sacramento St]

Pet Shops

- **Cambridge Pet Care Center** • 1724 Massachusetts Ave [Garfield St]

Restaurants

- **9 Tastes** • 50 JFK St [Winthrop St]
- **Algiers** • 40 Brattle St [Story]
- **b. good** • 24 Dunster St [Mass Ave]
- **Border Café** • 32 Church St [Palmer St]
- **Caffe Paradiso** • 1 Eliot Sq [Mt Auburn]
- **Cambridge, 1** • 27 Church St [Palmer St]
- **Casablanca** • 40 Brattle St [Story]
- **Charlie's Kitchen** • 10 Eliot St [Winthrop St]
- **Chez Henri** • 1 Shepard St [Mass Ave]
- **Crazy Doughs** • 35 Dunster St [Mt Auburn]
- **Greenhouse Coffee Shop** • 3 Brattle St [Brattle Sq]
- **Grendel's Den** • 89 Winthrop St [JFK]
- **Harvest** • 44 Brattle St [Story]
- **Hi-Rise Bread Company** • 56 Brattle St [Hilliard St]
- **Hoffa's Swiss Alps** • 114 Mt Auburn St [Mifflin]
- **Iruña** • 56 JFK St [Winthrop St]
- **John Harvard's Brew House** • 33 Dunster St [Mt Auburn]
- **Mr & Mrs Bartley's Burger Cottage** • 1246 Massachusetts Ave [Plympton]
- **Pho Pasteur** • 35 Dunster St [Mt Auburn]
- **The Red House** • 98 Winthrop St [JFK]
- **Rialto** • 1 Bennett St [Eliot St]
- **Sabra Grill** • 20 Eliot Sq [JFK]
- **Sandrine's** • 8 Holyoke St [Mass Ave]
- **Shilla** • 57 JFK St [Winthrop St]
- **Tamarind Bay** • 75 Winthrop St [Dunster St]
- **UpStairs on the Square** • 91 Winthrop St [JFK]
- **Veggie Planet** • 47 Palmer St [Church St]

Shopping

- **Abodeon** • 1731 Massachusetts Ave [Prentiss]
- **Alpha Omega** • 1380 Massachusetts Ave [Holyoke St]
- **Berk's Shoes** • 50 JFK St [Winthrop St]
- **Black Ink** • 5 Brattle St [Brattle Sq]
- **Bob Slate** • 1288 Massachusetts Ave [Linden St]
- **Cambridge Naturals** • 1670 Massachusetts Ave [Hudson St]
- **Cardullo's Gourmet Shoppe** • 6 Brattle St [Brattle Sq]
- **City Sports** • 44 Brattle St [Story]
- **Crate & Barrel** • 48 Brattle St [Story]
- **Harvard Book Store** • 1256 Massachusetts Ave [Plympton]
- **Harvard Coop** • 1400 Massachusetts Ave [Dunster St]
- **Herrell's Ice Cream** • 15 Dunster St [Mass Ave]
- **Hidden Sweets** • 25 Brattle St [Church St]
- **LA Burdick Homemade Chocolates** • 52D Brattle St [Story]
- **Leavitt & Pierce** • 1316 Massachusetts Ave [Holyoke St]
- **Little Tibet** • 1174 Massachussets Ave [DeWolfe]
- **Museum of Useful Things** • 49 Brattle St [Farwell]
- **Newbury Comics** • 36 JFK St [Mt Auburn]
- **Nini's Corner** • 1394 Massachusetts Ave [Holyoke St]
- **Nomad** • 1741 Massachusetts Ave [Prentiss]
- **On Church Street** • 54 Church St [Palmer St]
- **Oona's** • 1210 Massachusetts Ave [Bow St]
- **Out of Town News** • 0 Harvard Sq [Church St]
- **Planet Records** • 54B JFK St [Winthrop St]
- **Proletariat** • 36 JFK St [Mt Auburn]
- **Staples** • 57 JFK St [Winthrop St]
- **Stereo Jack's** • 1686 Massachusetts Ave [Sacramento St]
- **Tannery** • 11A Brattle St [Brattle Sq]
- **Tealuxe** • 0 Brattle St [Hague]
- **Tess and Carlos** • 20 Brattle St [Church St]
- **Twisted Village** • 12B Eliot St [Winthrop St]
- **Urban Outfitters** • 11 JFK St [Brattle Sq]

Video Rental

- **Hollywood Express** • 1740 Massachusetts Ave [Prentiss]
- **Quick Flix** • 8 Bow St [Mass Ave]

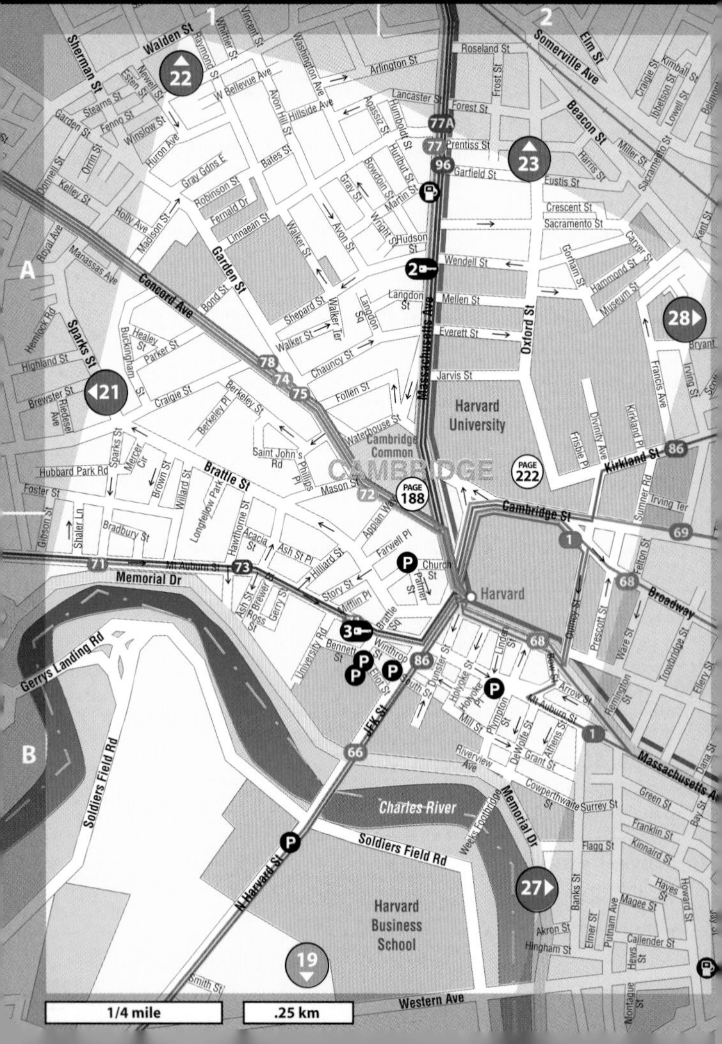

Map 20 • **Harvard Square / Allston (North)**

1

2

Sherman St

Walden St

22

Sorrel St

Newell St

Fenno St

Winslow St

Huron Ave

W Bellevue Ave

Avon St

Washington Ave

Arlington St

Roseland St

Somerville Ave

Elm St

Beacon St

Craigie St

Kimball St

Mellen St

Dickson St

Lowell St

Garden St

Stearns St

Gray Gdns E

Robinson St

Fernald Dr

Linnaean St

Bates St

Bond St

Lancaster St

Forest St

Prentiss St

Frost St

Miller St

Sacramento St

Eustis St

Crescent St

Sacramento St

77A

77

96

Garfield St

23

Hammond St

Hilliard Hillside Ave

Concord Ave

Garden St

Shepard St

Walker St

Chauncy St

Follen St

O Hudson St

Langdon St

Wendell St

Mellen St

Everett St

Jarvis St

Oxford St

Conant St

Museum St

28

Bryant St

Francis Ave

Irving St

A

Sparks St

Highland St

Brewster St

Foskett St

21

Healey St

Buckingham St

Parker St

Craigie St

78

74

75

Berkeley St

Berkeley Pl

Saint John's Rd

Waterhouse St

Cambridge Common

Harvard University

PAGE 222

Kirkland Rd

Irving Ter

Kirkland St

86

Hubbard Park Rd

Brown St

Willard St

Brattle St

Longfellow Park

Hawthorne St

Acacia St

Ash St Pl

Mason St

Appian Pl

CAMBRIDGE

72

PAGE 188

Cambridge St

1

69

Foster St

Mercer Cir

Sparks Pl

Bradbury St

71

Memorial Dr

73

Ash St

Willard St

Hilliard St

Story St

Griffin Pl

Farwell Pl

Church St

Palmer St

Harvard

68

Prescott St

Ware St

Broadway

B

Gerrys Landing Rd

Soldiers Field Rd

N Harvard St

3

Bennett St

University Rd

Winthrop St

86

Mt Auburn St

JFK St

Eliot St

S Flagg St

Mill St

Plympton St

Dunster St

Holyoke St

Linden St

68

Bow St

Arrow St

Auburn St

DeWolfe St

1

Massachusetts Ave

66

Charles River

Riverview Ave

Grant St

Memorial Dr

Cowperthwaite St

Surrey St

Banks St

Green St

Franklin St

Kinnaird St

27

Soldiers Field Rd

Flagg St

Hayes St

Magee St

Elmer St

Putnam Ave

St Paul St

Callender St

Hews St

Harvard Business School

19

Smith St

Western Ave

Akron St

Hingham St

Pleasant St

Montague St

1/4 mile

.25 km

All roads, or at least many bus routes and the Red Line, lead to Harvard Square. Throngs of pedestrians are sure to slow down those brave enough to drive, and parking is hard to find, though diligent circling—and a little bit of luck—usually yields results.

Subway

 · Harvard

Bus Lines

1 · Harvard/Holyoke Gate—Dudley Station via Massachusetts Avenue & BU Medical Center

66 · Harvard Square—Dudley Station via Allston & Brookline

68 · Harvard/Holyoke Gate—Kendall/MIT via Broadway

69 · Harvard/Holyoke Gate—Lechmere Station via Cambridge Street

71 · Watertown Square—Harvard Station via Mt Auburn Street

72 · Huron Avenue—Harvard Station via Concord Avenue

73 · Waverley Square—Harvard Station via Trapelo Road

74 · Belmont Center—Harvard Station via Concord Avenue

75 · Belmont Center—Harvard Station via Concord Avenue

77 · Arlington Heights—Harvard Station via Massachusetts Ave

77A · North Cambridge—Harvard Station, Local

78 · Arlmont Village—Harvard Station via Park Circle

86 · Sullivan Square Station—Cleveland Circle via Harvard/Johnston Gate

96 · Medford Square—Harvard Station via George Street & Davis Square

Car Rental

- **Alamo** · 1663 Massachusetts Ave [Hudson St] · 617-661-8747
- **Avis** · 1 Bennett St [Eliot St] · 617-534-1400
- **Hertz** · 24 Eliot St [Winthrop St] · 617-338-1520
- **National** · 1663 Massachusetts Ave [Hudson St] · 617-661-8747
- **Thrifty** · Harvard Square Hotel · 110 Mt Auburn St [Eliot St] · 617-876-2758

Gas Stations

- **Citgo** · 180 Western Ave [Travis]
- **Gulf** · 1725 Massachusetts Ave [Garfield St]

Parking

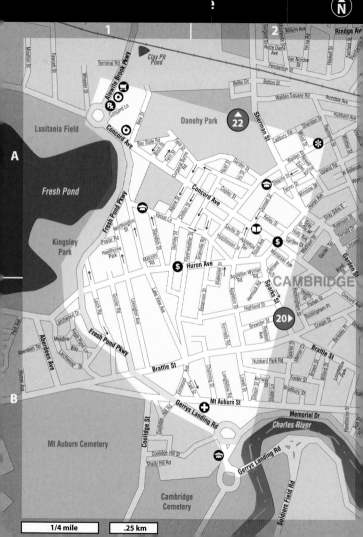

Tucked behind bustling Harvard Square, this hushed suburban community is nice for a pleasant house-viewing stroll, but little else. Still, the greenspace along Fresh Pond Parkway is a good place for a picnic, walk, or careful bike ride. Beautifully maintained Mt. Auburn Cemetery, a historic landmark, is celebrating its 175th anniversary with special events.

$ Banks

• **Cambridge Savings Bank (ATM)** • 168 Huron Ave
  [Manassas]
• **Cambridge Trust** • 353 Huron Ave [Chilton]

✳ Community Gardens

◉ Donuts

• **Dunkin' Donuts** • 201 Alewife Brook Pkwy [Terminal]
• **Dunkin' Donuts** • 517 Concord Ave [Concord Ln]

➕ Emergency Rooms

• **Mount Auburn** • 330 Mt Auburn St [Longfellow Rd]

📖 Libraries

• **Boudreau** • 245 Concord Ave [Donnell]

℞ Pharmacies

• **CVS** • 211 Alewife Brook Pkwy [Concord Ave] ♿

🎓 Schools

• **Buckingham Browne & Nichols** •
  80 Gerrys Landing Rd [Greenough Blvd]
• **Cambridge Montessori** • 161 Garden St [Walden St]
• **John M Tobin** • 197 Vassal Ln [Standish]

🛒 Supermarkets

• **Whole Foods Market** • 200 Alewife Brook Pkwy
  [Concord Ave]

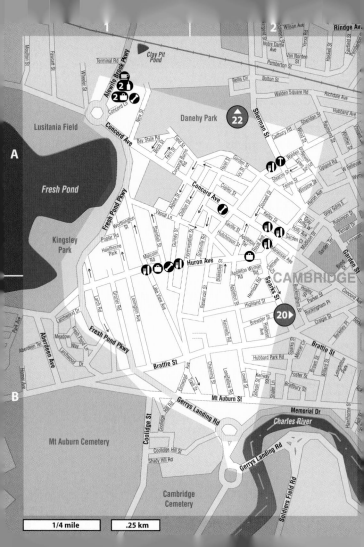

If you're a gourmand, and particularly if you're a cheese enthusiast, make the trip to Formaggio Kitchen. Don't forget to ask for free samples. For a quick bite along Huron Avenue, grab a slice at Armando's.

Coffee

- **Starbucks** • 220 Alewife Brook Pkwy [Concord Ave]

Hardware Stores

- **Masse's True Value Hardware** • 249 Walden St
  [Sherman St]

Liquor Stores

- **Kappy's Liquors** • 215 Alewife Brook Pkwy
  [Concord Ave]
- **Mall Discount Liquors & Wines** •
  202 Alewife Brook Pkwy [Concord Ave]

Pet Shops

- **Jeana's Dirty Dog Salon** • 298 Concord Ave
  [Walden St]
- **Pet Supply Outlet Store** • 211 Alewife Brook Pkwy
  [Concord Ave]
- **Raining Cats and Dogs** • 368 Huron Ave [Standish]

Restaurants

- **Armando's** • 163 Huron Ave [Concord Ave]
- **Aspasia** • 377 Walden St [Concord Ave]
- **Full Moon** • 344 Huron Ave [Chilton]
- **Hi-Rise Bread Company** • 208 Concord Ave [Huron]
- **Il Buongustaio** • 369 Huron Ave [Standish]
- **Trattoria Pulcinella** • 147 Huron Ave [Concord Ave]

Shopping

- **Formaggio Kitchen** • 244 Huron Ave [Appleton St]
- **Henry Bear's Park** • 361 Huron Ave [Standish]
- **Newbury Comics** • 211 Alewife Brook Pkwy
  [Concord Ave]
- **Staples** • 186 Alewife Brook Pkwy [Terminal]

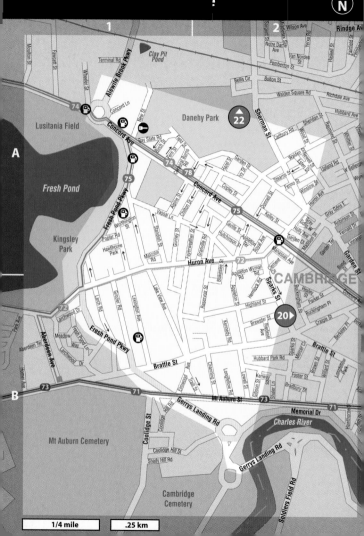

Unless you live here, you're not going to have an easy time parking.
You might snag a space on Huron Avenue, but that's about it. Red
Line stops are also far away, so to get here by public transportation
take one of the buses that originate at Harvard Square.

Bus Lines

- **71** • Watertown Square—Harvard Station via
  Mt Auburn Street
- **72** • Huron Avenue—Harvard Station via Concord
  Avenue
- **73** • Waverley Square—Harvard Station via
  Trapelo Road
- **74** • Belmont Center—Harvard Station via
  Concord Avenue
- **75** • Belmont Center—Harvard Station via
  Concord Avenue
- **78** • Arlmont Village—Harvard Station via
  Park Circle

Car Rental

- **Enterprise Rent A Car** • 48 New St [Concord Ave] •
  617-354-2302

Gas Stations

- **Citgo** • 199 Concord Ave [Huron]
- **Gulf** • 260 Lexington Ave [Worthington St]
- **Gulf** • 60 Lexington Ave [Brattle St]
- **Mobil** • 343 Fresh Pond Pkwy [Lake View Ave] ☺
- **Shell** • 603 Concord Ave [Wheeler]
- **Sunoco** • 515 Concord Ave [Concord Ln] ☺

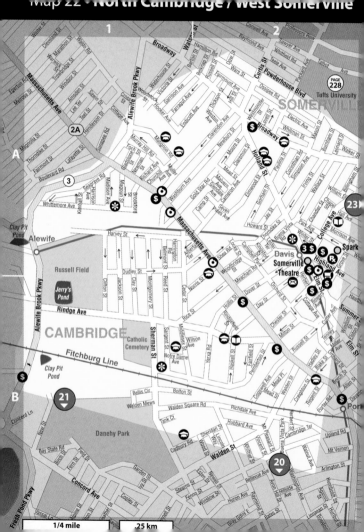

Map 2

Over the years, working-class Slummerville transformed into oh-so-hip Somerville, with Davis Square as its center. Blending urban culture with a small-town neighborhood feel, eclectic restaurants sit alongside old family businesses, a movie theater, diner, and ice cream shop. On warm nights, Davis fills with a mix of long-time residents, Tufts students, and young professionals. North Cambridge's great shops and restaurants are undeservedly overlooked because of their distance from the T.

$ Banks

- **Bank of America** • 406 Highland Ave [Grove St]
- **Bank of America (ATM)** • 1116 Broadway [Holland St]
- **Bank of America (ATM)** • 2168 Massachusetts Ave [Rindge Ave]
- **Bank of America (ATM)** • 2502 Massachusetts Ave [Cottage Pk]
- **Bank of America (ATM)** • 253 Elm St [Chester St]
- **Century Bank** • 2309 Massachusetts Ave [Meacham Rd]
- **Citizens Bank** • 212 Elm St [Bowers]
- **Citizens Bank (ATM)** • 1 Holland St [College]
- **Citizens Bank (ATM)** • 4 College Ave [Winter St]
- **First National Bank of Ipswich** • 2067 Massachusetts Ave [Walden St]
- **Middlesex Federal Savings** • 1 College Ave [Highland Ave]
- **Wainwright Bank & Trust** • 176 Alewife Brook Pkwy [Terminal]
- **Wainwright Bank & Trust** • 250 Elm St [Chester St]

❋ Community Gardens

◉ Donuts

- **Dunkin' Donuts** • 244 Elm St [Chester St]
- **Dunkin' Donuts** • 2480 Massachusetts Ave [Edmunds]
- **Dunkin' Donuts** • 2480 Massachusetts Ave [Washburn Ave]
- **Verna's Donut Shop** • 2344 Massachusetts Ave [Norris]

○ Landmarks

- **Somerville Theater** • 55 Davis Sq [Highland Ave]
- **Spark** • 50 Grove St [Winslow Ave]

📖 Libraries

- **O'Neill** • 70 Rindge Ave [Ringdefield]
- **Somerville West** • 40 College Ave [Morrison Ave]

℞ Pharmacies

- **Brooks** • 393 Highland Ave [Grove St]

✉ Post Offices

- **West Somerville** • 58 Day St [Herbert]

🏛 Schools

- **Benjamin Banneker Charter** • 21 Notre Dame Ave [Middlesex St]
- **Cambridge Friends** • 5 Cadbury Rd [Wood St]
- **American International School** • 45 Matignon Rd [Murray Hill Rd]
- **Matignon High** • 1 Matignon Rd [Churchill Ave]
- **North Cambridge Catholic High** • 40 Norris St [Cedar St]
- **Peabody** • 70 Rindge Ave [Ringdefield]
- **Powder House Community** • 1060 Broadway [Packard]
- **SCALE** • 167 Holland St [Cameron Ave]
- **Tufts University** • 169 Holland St [Cameron Ave]

🛒 Supermarkets

- **Sessa's Cold Cuts & Italian Specialties** • 414 Highland Ave [Grove St]

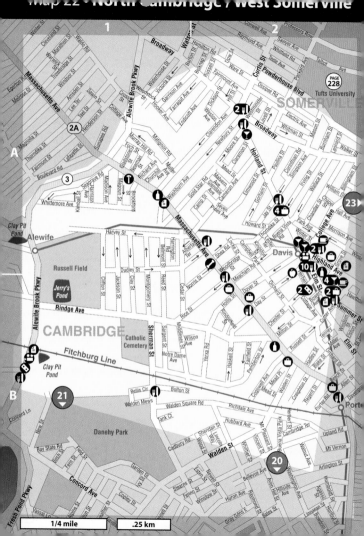

Whatever your taste in food and entertainment, you'll satisfy it here. Try the stylish French-Cambodian dishes at Elephant Walk, Out of the Blue's delicious inexpensive seafood, Redbones barbecue, or belly-warming momo from House of Tibet. Then catch national and local bands at Somerville Theater or Johnny D's, drink with local color at Sligo, or sip a Guinness to the strains of an Irish *sessúin* at the Burren. For comedy, don't miss Jimmy Tingle's Off-Broadway Theater.

Map 22

☕ Coffee

- **Au Petit Pain** • 11 College Ave [Winter St]
- **Starbucks** • 260 Elm St [Chester St]

🖨 Copy Shops

- **Budget Copy** • 2449 Massachusetts Ave [Gold Star Rd]
- **Sir Speedy Printing Center** • 260 Elm St [Chester St]
- **Staples** • 186 Alewife Brook Pkwy [Terminal]
- **The UPS Store** • 411 Highland Ave [Grove St]

🍎 Farmer's Markets

- **Somerville (May-Nov; Wed 12 pm-6 pm)** • Day St & Herbert St

🔧 Hardware Stores

- **City Paint & Supply** • 2564 Massachusetts Ave [Newman St]

🍾 Liquor Stores

- **Downtown Wine & Spirits** • 225 Elm St [Grove St]
- **Norton Beverage** • 2451 Massachusetts Ave [Gold Star Rd]
- **Pemberton Fruit Market** • 2172 Massachusetts Ave [Rindge Ave]

🎬 Movie Theaters

- **Loews Cineplex Fresh Pond** • 168 Alewife Brook Pkwy [Terminal]
- **Somerville Theatre** • 55 Davis Sq [Highland Ave]

🍸 Nightlife

- **The Burren** • 247 Elm St [Chester St]
- **Jimmy Tingle's Off-Broadway Theater** • 255 Elm St [Chester St]
- **Johnny D's Uptown** • 17 Holland St [Winter St]
- **PJ Ryan's** • 239 Holland St [B'way]
- **Redbones** • 55 Chester St [Herbert]
- **Sligo Pub** • 237A Elm St [Grove St]
- **Somerville Theatre** • 55 Davis Sq [Highland Ave]

🐾 Pet Shops

- **Animal Spirit** • 2348 Massachusetts Ave [Norris]

🍴 Restaurants

- **Amelia's Kitchen** • 1137 Broadway [Westminster St]
- **Anna's Taqueria** • 236 Elm St [Chester St]
- **Antonia's Italian Bistro** • 37 Davis Sq [Highland Ave]
- **Bhoja** • 235 Elm St [Grove St]
- **Café Barada** • 2269 Massachusetts Ave [Dover]
- **Dave's Fresh Pasta** • 81 Holland St [Irving St]
- **Diesel Café** • 257 Elm St [Chester St]
- **Diva Indian Bistro** • 246 Elm St [Chester St]
- **Elephant Walk** • 2067 Massachusetts Ave [Walden St]
- **Frank's Steak House** • 2310 Massachusetts Ave [Rice St]
- **Gargoyles on the Square** • 219 Elm St [Grove St]
- **House of Tibet** • 235 Holland St [B'way]
- **Jasper White's Summer Shack** • 149 Alewife Brook Pkwy [Rindge Ave]
- **Jose's** • 131 Sherman St [Bellis]
- **Joshua Tree** • 256 Elm St [Chester St]
- **Martsa on Elm** • 233A Elm St [Grove St]
- **Namaskar** • 236 Elm St [Chester St]
- **Nick's Roast Beef** • 20 College Ave [Winter St]
- **Out of the Blue** • 215 Elm St [Grove St]
- **Qingdao Garden** • 2382 Massachusetts Ave [Alberta]
- **Redbones** • 55 Chester St [Herbert]
- **Rosebud Diner** • 381 Summer St [Cutler Ave]
- **Sauce** • 400 Highland Ave [Grove St]
- **Soleil Café** • 1153 Broadway [Curtis]

🛍 Shopping

- **Asierica** • 2259 Massachusetts Ave [Dover]
- **Bicycle Exchange** • 2067 Massachusetts Ave [Walden St]
- **Black & Blues** • 89 Holland St [Simpson Ave]
- **CD Spins** • 235 Elm St [Grove St]
- **China Fair** • 2100 Massachusetts Ave [Walden St]
- **Chinook Outdoor Adventure** • 93 Holland St [Simpson Ave]
- **Cibeline** • 85 Holland St [Irving St]
- **McKinnon's Choice Meat Market** • 239A Elm St [Grove St]
- **Modern Brewer** • 2304 Massachusetts Ave [Rice St]
- **Nellie's Wildflowers** • 72 Holland St [Buena Vista Rd]
- **Poor Little Rich Girl** • 416 Highland Ave [Grove St]

📀 Video Rental

- **Blockbuster** • 180 Alewife Brook Pkwy [Terminal]
- **Hollywood Express** • 238 Elm St [Chester St]
- **West Coast Video** • 255 Elm St [Chester St]

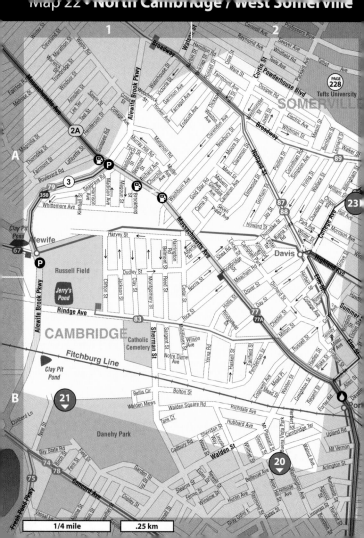

Map 22 • North Cambridge / West Somerville

1

2

Professors Row

Conwell Ave

Sawyer Ave

Raymond Ave

Whitfield Rd

Teele Ave

Talbot Ave

PAGE
228

Tufts University

SOMERVILLE

Winter St

Cleveland St

Walker Rd

Marathon St

Warwick St

Trowbridge St

Windsor Rd

Amsden St

Melrose St

Magnolia St

Thorndike St

Fairmont St

Boulevard Rd

Broadway

Walker St

Hamilton Rd

Watsonhouse Rd

Victoria St

Garrison Ave

Woodstock St

Moore Ave

Fairmount Ave

Ware St

Curtis St

Powderhouse Blvd

Ossipee Rd

Electric Ave

Whitman St

Mason St

Jackson St

Burnham St

Massachusetts Ave

2A

Lafayette Rd

Henderson St

Sartwell Ave

Cottage Ave

Clarendon Ave

Newbury St

Lindstrom Ave

Clyde St

Dickerson St

Moore St

Mead St

Elmwood St

Broadway

Paulina St

Irving St

Corinthian Rd

Simpson Ave

Wallace St

William St

89

3

Kimball St

Seagrave Rd

Harrison Ave

Madison Ave

Magoun St

Brookford St

Richard Ave

Churchill Ave

Gold Star Rd

Malvern Ave

Elm St

Cameron Ave

Gorham St

Chandler St

Orchard St

87
88

350

Whittemore Ave

Washburn Ave

Carol Ave

Seven Pines Ave

Howard St

Thorndike St

Kingston St

Banks St

Bigelow St

Winter St

Park Ave

23

Clay Pit
Pond

67

Alewife

Harvey St

Harrington Rd

Belmont St

Aberdeen Ter

Shea Rd

Locke St

Woodbridge St

Campbell Pk

Cutter Ave

Liberty Ave

Morrison Ave

Davis

Highland Ave

Russell Field

Dudley St

Jackson St

Clifton St

Clay St

Montgomery St

Reed St

Cedar St

Hollis St

Meacham Rd

Dover St

Day St

Chester St

Herbert St

Cottage Ave

Banks St

Summer

Jerry's
Pond

Rindge Ave

83

Sherman St

Catholic
Cemetery

Middlesex St

Pond St

Pemberton St

Wilson Ave

Verna St

Russell St

Milton St

Fitchburg Line

Notre Dame
Ave

Sargent St

Fairfield St

Haskell St

Creighton St

Porter Rd

CAMBRIDGE

Clay Pit
Pond

21

Bellis Cir

Walden Mews

Bolton St

Walden Square Rd

Tank Ct

Richdale Ave

Hubbard Ave

Mt Pleasant St

Cogswell Ave

Mead Pl

Lincoln Ave

Buena Vista Park

Cambridge Ter

Upland Rd

Concord Ln

Nye St

Cadbury Rd

Sheridan St

Lexington
Way

Whittier St

Vincent St

Mt Vernon

Danehy Park

Bay State Rd

Birch St

Ford St

Garden St

Stearns St

Walden St

Newell St

Huron Ave

Bellevue Ave

Avon Hillside Ave

Arlington St

20

75

74
78

Copley St

Concord Ave

Winslow St

Huron Ave

Bates St

B

A

B

1/4 mile   .25 km

Map 22

Forget driving or parking in Davis Square on weekends and during rush hour, when it gridlocks. Ditto for the area around Alewife. The Red Line serves both areas, and for the more athletically inclined, the Minuteman bike trail starts in Davis and passes through North Cambridge and Alewife on its way to Belmont. For North Cambridge haunts along Mass Ave and its side streets, get to know the 77 bus.

Subway

- ■ **Davis**
- ■ **Alewife**

Bus Lines

- 74 • Belmont Center—Harvard Station via Concord Avenue
- 75 • Belmont Center—Harvard Station via Concord Avenue
- 77 • Arlington Heights—Harvard Station via Massachusetts Avenue
- 77A • North Cambridge—Harvard Station Local
- 78 • Arlmont Village—Harvard Station via Park Circle
- 79 • Arlington Heights—Alewife Station via Massachusetts Avenue
- 83 • Rindge Ave—Central Square, Cambridge via Porter Square Station
- 87 • Arlington Center or Clarendon Hill—Lechmere Station
- 88 • Clarendon Hill—Lechmere Station via Highland Avenue
- 89 • Clarendon Hill—Sullivan Square Station via Broadway
- 90 • Davis Square—Wellington Station via Sullivan Square Station
- 96 • Medford Square—Harvard Station via George Street & Davis Square
- 350 • North Burlington—Alewife Station via Burlington

Car Washes

- **Cambridge Car Wash** • 2013 Massachusetts Ave [Regent St]

Gas Stations

- **Independent** • 2535 Massachusetts Ave [Rindge Ave]
- **Massachusetts Avenue Firestone** • 2480 Massachusetts Ave [Edmunds]
- **Mobil** • 2615 Massachusetts Ave [Alewife Brook]

Parking

Map 23 • **Central Somerville / Porter Square**

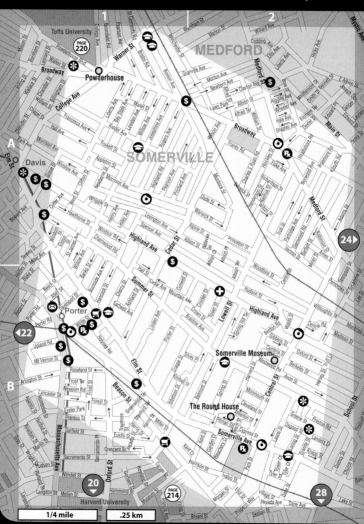

1/4 mile   .25 km

Porter Square may feel less polished than its brethren Harvard and Davis, but living space here and in neighboring Somerville is slightly more affordable. Shops and restaurants are concentrated on Mass Ave, and a diverse mix of young people, families, and townies populates the residential neighborhoods of Somerville.

$ Banks

- **Bank of America** • 1847 Massachusetts Ave [Upland]
- **Bank of America (ATM)** • 1815 Massachusetts Ave [Roseland]
- **Cambridge Savings Bank** • 53 White St [Elm St]
- **Cambridge Savings Bank (ATM)** • 36 White St [White St Pl]
- **Cambridge Savings Bank (ATM)** • 711 Somerville Ave [Elm St]
- **Central Bank** • 399 Highland Ave [Grove St]
- **Century Bank (ATM)** • 110 Medford St [Dexter St]
- **Citizens Bank (ATM)** • Somerville Ave & Massachusetts Ave
- **East Cambridge Savings Bank** • 285 Highland Ave [Cedar St]
- **Sovereign Bank** • 403 Highland Ave [Grove St]
- **Winter Hill Bank** • 5 Cutter Ave [Elm St]
- **Winter Hill Bank** • 691 Broadway [Boston Ave]

✳ Community Gardens

◉ Donuts

- **Dunkin' Donuts** • 1 White St [Somerville Ave]
- **Dunkin' Donuts** • 154 Highland Ave [Central St]
- **Dunkin' Donuts** • 504 Broadway [Hinckley]
- **Dunkin' Donuts** • 519 Somerville Ave [Park St]
- **Russ' Donuts** • 2 Highland Rd [Morrison Ave]

✚ Emergency Rooms

- **Somerville** • 230 Highland Ave [Tower St]

◯ Landmarks

- **Powderhouse** • College Ave & Broadway
- **The Round House** • 36 Atherton St [Beech St]
- **Somerville Museum** • 1 Westwood Rd [Central St]

℞ Pharmacies

- **Brooks** • 530 Somerville Ave [Park St]
- **CVS** • 36 White St [White St Pl] ♿
- **CVS** • 532 Medford St [Lowell St]

✉ Post Offices

- **Porter Square** • 1953 Massachusetts Ave [Allen St]

🚌 Schools

- **Benjamin G Brown** • 201 Willow Ave [Kidder]
- **John F Kennedy** • 5 Cherry St [Elm St]
- **St Anthony Elementary** • 480 Somerville Ave [Loring]
- **St Catherine's of Genoa** • 192 Summer St [Belmont St]
- **St Clement's Elementary** • 589 Boston Ave [Warner]
- **St Clement's High** • 579 Boston Ave [Warner]

🛒 Supermarkets

- **Star Market** • 275 Beacon St [Sacramento St]
- **Star Market** • 49 White St [White St Pl]

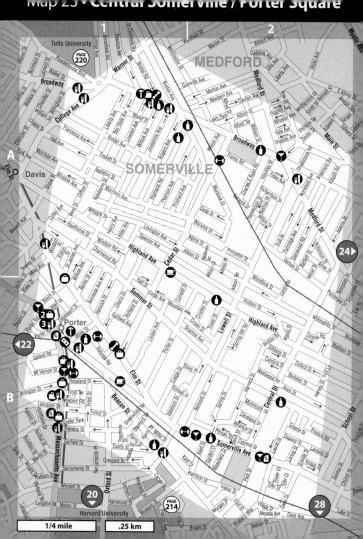

Map 23 • **Central Somerville / Porter Square**

The best bet for nearby entertainment is to hop on the Red Line and head one stop in either direction (toward Davis or Harvard). If you do stay local, sample hand-crafted pasta at the Cambridge outpost of Italian mini-chain Rustic Kitchen or hit Sky Bar, where there's live music almost every night.

Map 2

Coffee

- **Café Rossini** • 278 Highland Ave [Eastman]
- **Carberry's Bakery & Coffee House** • 187 Elm St [Windom]
- **Starbucks** • 711 Somerville Ave [Elm St]

Copy Shops

- **Gnomon Copy** • 1923 Massachusetts Ave [Davenport]
- **The UPS Store** • 1770 Massachusetts Ave [Lancaster St]
- **The UPS Store** • 519 Somerville Ave [Park St]

Gyms

- **Bally Total Fitness** • 1815 Massachusetts Ave [Roseland]
- **Curves** • 270 Cedar St [Murdock St]
- **Curves For Women** • 622 Somerville Ave [Kent St]
- **HealthWorks Fitness Center** • 35 White St [White St Pl]

Hardware Stores

- **City Paint & Supply** • 729 Broadway [Bristol Rd]
- **Tags Hardware** • 29 White St [White St Pl]

Liquor Stores

- **Ball Square Fine Wines & Liquors** • 716 Broadway [Willow Ave]
- **Blue Label Liquors** • 2 Carter St [Roland]
- **Crowley's Liquors** • 152 Boston Ave [Highland Rd]
- **Liquor World** • 13 White St [Somerville Ave]
- **O'Brian's Liquors** • 158 Highland Ave [Central St]
- **Seven Hills Wine & Spirits** • 288 Beacon St [Sacramento St]
- **Somerville Wine & Spirits** • 235 Highland Ave [Crocker]
- **Woody's Liquor** • 594 Somerville Ave [Garden Ct]
- **Woody's Liquors** • 523 Broadway [William St]

Nightlife

- **Christopher's** • 1920 Massachusetts Ave [Porter Rd]
- **On the Hill Tavern** • 499 Broadway [Medford St]
- **Samba Bar & Grill** • 608 Somerville Ave [Kent St]
- **Sky Bar** • 518 Somerville Ave [Park St]
- **Toad** • 1912 Massachusetts Ave [Porter Rd]

Pet Shops

- **Big Fish, Little Fish** • 55 Elm St [Cedar St]
- **Stinky's Kittens & Doggies Too** • 110 Bristol Rd [B'way]

Restaurants

- **Anna's Taqueria** • 822 Somerville Ave [Acadia Pk]
- **Blue Fin** • 1815 Massachusetts Ave [Roseland]
- **Broken Yolk** • 136 College Ave [B'way]
- **Christopher's** • 1920 Massachusetts Ave [Porter Rd]
- **Kaya** • 1924 Massachusetts Ave [Porter Rd]
- **Lil Vinny's** • 525 Medford St [Lowell St]
- **Lyndell's Bakery** • 720 Broadway [Willow Ave]
- **Naturals Café** • 187 Elm St [Windom]
- **Passage to India** • 1900 Massachusetts Ave [Porter Rd]
- **RF O'Sullivan's** • 282 Beacon St [Sacramento St]
- **Rustic Kitchen** • 1815 Massachusetts Ave [Roseland]
- **Sound Bites** • 708 Broadway [Willow Ave]
- **Sugar & Spice** • 1933 Massachusetts Ave [Davenport]
- **Tu y Yo** • 858 Broadway [Walker St]

Shopping

- **Ace Wheelworks** • 145 Elm St [Willow Ave]
- **Big Fish, Little Fish** • 55 Elm St [Cedar St]
- **Bob Slate** • 1975 Massachusetts Ave [Beech St]
- **Cambridge Music Center** • 1906 Massachusetts Ave [Porter Rd]
- **City Sports** • 1815 Massachusetts Ave [Roseland]
- **Joie de Vivre** • 1792 Massachusetts Ave [Arlington St]
- **Lyndell's Bakery** • 720 Broadway [Willow Ave]
- **Paper Source** • 1810 Massachusetts Ave [Arlington St]
- **Roach's Sporting Goods** • 1957 Massachusetts Ave [Allen St]

Video Rental

- **Blockbuster** • 1 Porter Sq [White St]

Map 23 • **Central Somerville / Porter Square**

Tufts University

PAGE 220

Broadway

MEDFORD

College Ave

Davis

A

Porter

B

77
77A

96

SOMERVILLE

80

2

24

88 90

22

87

85

83

20

PAGE 214

Harvard University

28

1/4 mile   .25 km

Guarded by a 46-foot steel kinetic sculpture (painted red to match the subway line), centrally located Porter Square T stop makes it easy to get from Porter to other corners of Cambridge or all the way into Boston. Street parking is generally plentiful.

Subway

■ **Porter**

Bus Lines

- **77** • Arlington Heights—Harvard Station via Massachusetts Avenue
- **77A** • North Cambridge—Harvard Station Local
- **80** • Arlington Center—Lechmere Station via Medford Hills
- **83** • Rindge Avenue—Central Square, Cambridge via Porter Square Station
- **85** • Spring Hill—Kendall/MIT Station via Summer Street & Union Square
- **86** • Sullivan Square Station—Cleveland Circle via Harvard/Johnson Gate
- **88** • Clarendon Hill—Lechmere Station via Highland Avenue
- **90** • Davis Square—Wellington Station via Sullivan Square Station
- **94** • Medford Square—Davis Square Station via W Medford & Medford Streets
- **96** • Medford Square—Harvard Station via George St & Davis Square
- **101** • Malden Center Station— Sullivan Square Station

Car Rental

- **Enterprise** • 377 Summer St [Cutter Ave] • 617-628-2266
- **Hertz** • 646 Somerville Ave [Lowell St] • 617-625-7958

Car Washes

- **Somerville Car Wash** • 680 Somerville Ave [Craigie St]
- **Titan Gas & Car Wash** • 590 Boston Ave [Harvard St]

Gas Stations

- **Gulf** • 367 Highland Ave [West St]
- **Gulf** • 583 Broadway [Alfred St]
- **Gulf** • 701 Somerville Ave [Elm St]
- **Sunoco** • 541 Broadway [William St]

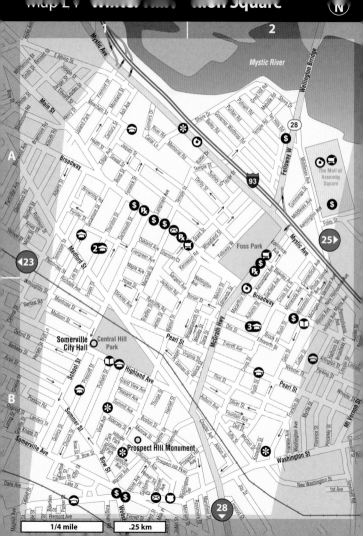

Comprising at least three of the seven hills of Somerville, this former grazing land now houses City Hall, the 93-year-old library, and the remnants of Somerville's working-class neighborhoods. There's little reason to visit Winter Hill unless you live there, but Union Square has thriving restaurants and nightlife. Don't miss the view of Boston from atop Prospect Hill, where America's first flag was raised in 1776. It's a great spot to catch the July 4th fireworks.

$ Banks

- **Bank of America (ATM)** • 5 Middlesex Ave [Main]
- **Bank of America (ATM)** • 68 Union Sq [Stone Ave]
- **Century Bank** • 102 Fellsway W [Shore]
- **Citizens Bank** • 338 Broadway [School St]
- **Citizens Bank** • 40 Union Sq [Warren Ave]
- **Citizens Bank** • 779 McGrath Hwy [Mystic Ave]
- **Citizens Bank (ATM)** • 321 Broadway [Temple St]
- **Sovereign Bank** • 125 Broadway [Wisconsin]
- **Sovereign Bank (ATM)** • 77 Middlesex Ave [Kensington Ave]
- **Winter Hill Bank** • 342 Broadway [School St]

Community Gardens

Donuts

- **Dunkin' Donuts** • 220 Broadway [McGrath Hwy]
- **Dunkin' Donuts** • 498 Mystic Ave [Butler Dr]
- **Dunkin' Donuts** • 76 Middlesex Ave [Kensington Ave]

Landmarks

- **Prospect Hill Monument** • Munroe St b/w Prospect Hill Ave & Walnut St
- **Somerville City Hall** • 93 Highland Ave [School St]

Libraries

- **Somerville East** • 115 Broadway [Michigan]
- **Somerville Main Library** • 79 Highland Ave [Prescott St]

Pharmacies

- **Brooks** • 299 Broadway [Marshall St]
- **Stop & Shop** • 779 McGrath Hwy [Mystic Ave]
- **Walgreens** • 343 Broadway [Dartmouth St]

Police

- **Somerville Police Department** • 220 Washington St [Merriam St]

Post Offices

- **Somerville Branch** • 237 Washington St [Bonner Ave]
- **Winter Hill Branch** • 320 Broadway [Marshall St]

Schools

- **Arthur D Healey** • 5 Meacham St [Ash Ave]
- **Cummings** • 42 Prescott St [Summer]
- **East Somerville Community** • 115 Pearl St [Rush]
- **Full Circle High** • 8 Bonair St [Royce Pl]
- **Lincoln Park Community** • 290 Washington St [Parker St]
- **Lincoln Park Community** • 50 Thurston St [Evergreen Ave]
- **Lincoln Park Community** • 8 Bonair St [Royce Pl]
- **Little Flower Elementary** • 17 Franklin St [Arlington St]
- **Next Wave Middle** • 8 Bonair St [Royce Pl]
- **Somerville High** • 81 Highland Ave [School St]
- **St Ann's** • 50 Thurston St [Evergreen Ave]
- **Winter Hill Community** • 115 Sycamore St [Evergreen Ave]

Supermarkets

- **Star Market** • 299 Broadway [Marshall St]
- **Stop & Shop** • 779 McGrath Hwy [Mystic Ave]

Map 14 • Winter Hill / Union Square

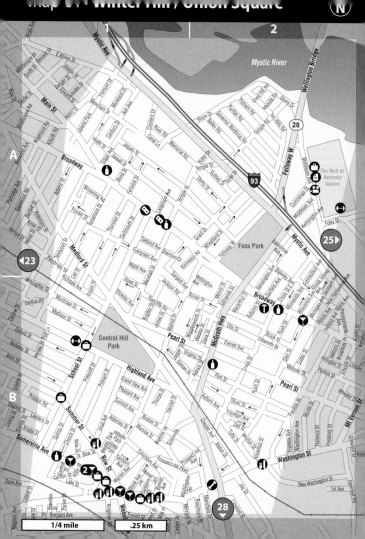

Map 24

Once upon a time, one of the few places to hear free live music was the Tir na Nog. It's still the best spot for music and a pint, but today you can also catch bands at P.A.'s Lounge and Sally O'Brien's across the street. Further down the road, Toast hosts DJs most nights. And depending on your mood, the Independent offers upscale dining on one side and a rowdy pub on the other.

Copy Shops

- **Staples** • 165 Middlesex Ave [Cummings St]

Farmer's Markets

- **Union Square** • Washington St & Somerville Ave

Gyms

- **World Gym** • 16 Sturtevant St [Assembly Sq Dr]
- **YMCA** • 101 Highland Ave [School St]

Hardware Stores

- **Robi Tool Sales** • 168 Broadway [Cross St]

Liquor Stores

- **Jerry's Liquor** • 329 Somerville Ave [Hawkins]
- **Joe's Liquors** • 156 Broadway [Rush]
- **Paul Revere Beverage** • 10 Main St [Edgar Ave]
- **Trans Liquor Mart** • 545 McGrath Hwy [Pearl St]
- **Winter Hill Liquor Mart** • 313 Broadway [Temple St]

Movie Theaters

- **Loews Cineplex Assembly Square** •
  35 Middlesex Ave [Foley]

Nightlife

- **The Independent** • 75 Union Sq [Stone Ave]
- **Khoury's State Spa** • 118 Broadway [Glen St]
- **PA's Lounge** • 345 Somerville Ave [Hawkins]
- **Sally O'Brien's** • 335 Somerville Ave [Hawkins]
- **Tir Na Nog** • 366A Somerville Ave [Kilby St]
- **Toast** • 70 Union Sq [Stone Ave]

Restaurants

- **Café Belo** • 120 Washington St [New Washington]
- **Great Thai Chef** • 255 Washington St [Bonner Ave]
- **Machu Picchu** • 25 Union Sq [Webster Ave]
- **Neighborhood Restaurant & Bakery** • 25 Bow St [Walnut St]
- **Sherman** • 257 Washington St [Webster Ave]
- **Taqueria la Mexicana** • 247 Washington St [Bonner Ave]

Shopping

- **Bombay Market** • 359 Somerville Ave [Kilby St]
- **Bostonian Florist** • 92 Highland Ave [School St]
- **Christmas Tree Shops** • 177 Middlesex Ave [Cummings St]
- **Mudflat Studio** • 149 Broadway [Minnesota]
- **Reliable Market** • 45 Union Sq [Warren Ave]
- **Ricky's Flower Market** • 9 Union Sq [Stone Ave]
- **Saini Sweet Shop** • 65 Summer St [School St]

Video Rental

- **BR Music & Video** • 323 Broadway [Langmaid]
- **Palmer Video** • 345 Broadway [Dartmouth St]

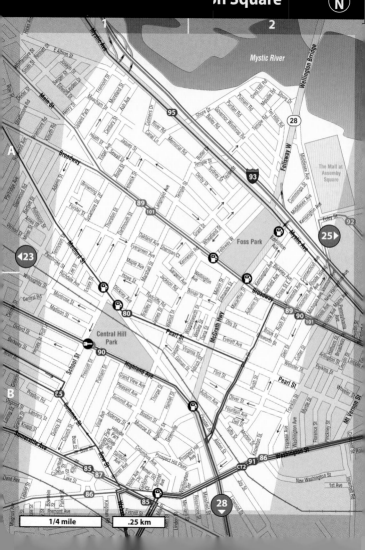

No matter what road you're on in Somerville, you'll always mysteriously end up in Union Square. A pinwheel of converging roads, including the city's oldest, Washington Street, it has always been more a way to get somewhere else than a destination. We hope a long-proposed T extension never sees the light of day, though this area's lack of accessibility has helped preserve its ethnic diversity.

Bus Lines

- **CT2** • Sullivan Station—Ruggles Station via Kendall/MIT
- **85** • Spring Hill—Kendall/MIT Station via Summer Street & Union Square
- **86** • Sullivan Sq Station—Cleveland Circle via Harvard/Johnson Gate
- **87** • Arlington Center or Clarendon Hill—Lechmere Station
- **89** • Clarendon Hill—Sullivan Square Station via Broadway
- **90** • Davis Square—Wellington Station via Sullivan Square Station
- **91** • Sullivan Square Station—Central Square, Cambridge via Washington
- **92** • Assembly Square Mall—Downtown via Sullivan Square Station, Main Street
- **95** • West Medford—Sullivan Square Station via Mystic Avenue
- **101** • Malden Center Station—Sullivan Square Station

Car Rental

- **Americar Auto Rental** • 90 Highland Ave [School St] • 617-776-4640

Gas Stations

- **Global Gas** • 345 Medford St [Pearl St]
- **Gulf** • 212 Broadway [McGrath Hwy]
- **Gulf** • 231 Washington St [Columbus]
- **Hess** • 709 McGrath Hwy [Blakeley] ⏰
- **Sunoco** • 258 Broadway [Walnut St]
- **Sunoco** • 434 McGrath Hwy [Greenville St]
- **Xtra Gas** • 360 Medford St [School St]

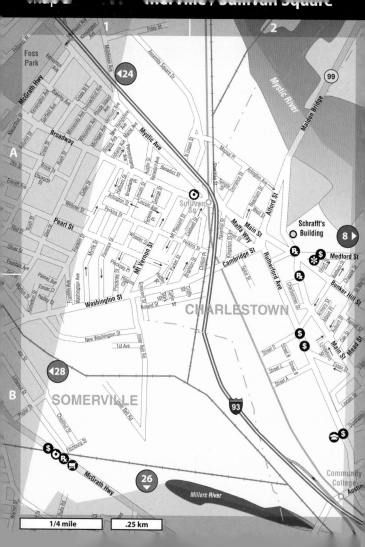

Map 3 ... nerville / Sullivan Square

Foss Park
McGrath Hwy
MacArthur
McGrath Ave
Kensington Ave
Cross St.
Garfield Ave
Walnut St

Assembly Square Dr

124

Foley St

2

Mystic River

Malden Bridge

99

Broadway
Minnesota Ave
Wisconsin Ave
Michigan Ave
Mississippi Ave
Rhode Island Ave
Connecticut Ave

Mystic Ave

New Hampshire Ave
Pennsylvania Ave
Maine Ave
Austin St
N Union St

Mossat Pl

Arlington Ave

A
Cross St
Brook St
Bush St

Center St

Hathorn St
Broadway
Pearson Ave
Benedict St
Lincoln Ave
Parsons George St

Linden Pl

Sherman St

Temple St
Devereaux St
West St
Beacham St

Allord St

Everett Ave
Ellsworth Ave

Webster St
Perkins St

Arlington St

⊙
Sullivan Sq

Haverhill St
Kingston St

Main St

Mafra Way

Schrafft's
Building ○

8 ▶

Pearl St
Glen St

Flint St

Oliver St

Franklin St
Merritt St
Blakes St

Wheeler St

Mt Vernon St
Perkins St
Cahuly St
Mt Pleasant St
Brighton St

Clifton Pl

Cambridge St

℞
℞

✳ Medford St
Short St
Bunker Hill St

Fountain Ave

Pinckney St
Higgins St

Parker St

Spice St

Linwood St

Chappie St

Palmer Ave
Turner Ct
Hadley Pl

Crescent St

Carter St
Clark St
Stark St

Rutherford Ave

Chelsea St

Polk St
Elm St

Bunker Hill St

Washington St

Roland St

CHARLESTOWN

Albion St
Cook St

Rusell St

Main St
Mead St

New Washington St

1st Ave

$
$

Street D
Street C
Street B

Lincoln St

28

Inner Belt Rd

Street B
Street A

93

Dunstable

B

SOMERVILLE

Chestnut St
Fitchburg St

McGrath Hwy

Inner Belt Rd

$
$℞⊙

26
▼

Millers River

🍴$

Community
College ○
Austin

| 1/4 mile | .25 km |

The historic Schrafft's Building, formerly the country's largest candy factory and a current landmark of local traffic reports, is not enough a reason to visit this neighborhood - a throughway, really, from Cambridge/Somerville to Charlestown. The character of this area is typified by Sullivan Square, which has been a busy transport hub for over 100 years.

Banks

- **Bank of America (ATM)** • 22 McGrath Hwy
  [Fitchburg]
- **Citizens Bank (ATM)** • 250 New Rutherford Ave
  [W School St]
- **East Cambridge Savings Bank (ATM)** •
  534 Medford St [Short St]
- **Sovereign Bank** • 437 Rutherford Ave [Essex]
- **St Jean's Credit Union** • 500 Rutherford Ave [St D]

✴ Community Gardens

◎ Donuts

- **Dunkin' Donuts** • Sullivan Sq Station •
  1 Broadway [Mystic Ave]
- **Dunkin' Donuts** • 14 McGrath Hwy [Fitchburg]

○ Landmarks

- **Schrafft's Building** • 529 Main St [Mishawum]

℞ Pharmacies

- **Brooks** • 14 McGrath Hwy [Fitchburg] ♻
- **Melrose Drug Center** • 462 Main St [Charbonnier]
- **Teamsters Care Pharmacy** • 552 Main St [Mishawum]

🏫 Schools

- **Bunker Hill Community College** •
  250 New Rutherford Ave [W School St]

🏪 Supermarkets

- **Shaw Market** • 14 McGrath Hwy [Fitchburg]

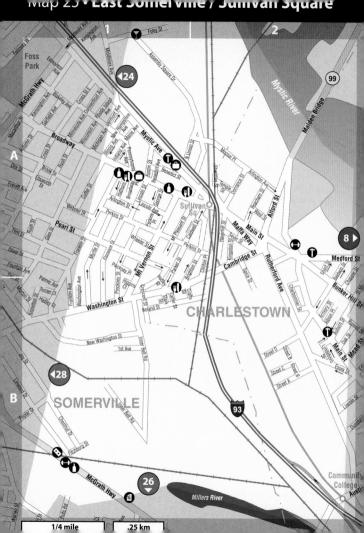

Map 23 • East Somerville / Sullivan Square

1

2

Foley St

Fellsway W

Kensington Ave

Edmunds Ave

Assembly Square Dr

Mystic River

Malden Bridge

99

Foss Park

McGrath Hwy

Washington Ave

Blakeley Ave

Garfield Ave

Cross St

Connecticut Ave

Rhode Island Ave

◀24

Minnesota Ave

Wisconsin Ave

Michigan Ave

Broadway

Mt Vernon Ave

Illinois Ave

New Hampshire Ave

Marne Ave

Mystic Ave

A

Otis St

Brook St

Road St

Everett Ave

Ellsworth St

Cutter Ave

Clifford St

Pennsylvania Ave

Austin St

Benedict Ave

Benedict St

N Union St

Mosel Pl

Arlington Ave

Dorrance St

Temple St

Arlington St

Broadway

Lincoln Ave

Sewall St

West St

Alford St

Webster St

Perkins St

Sullivan Sq

Main St

8 ▶

Pearl St

Florence St

Myrtle St

Franklin St

Wheeler St

Perkins St

Perkins Pl

Mt Pleasant St

Caldwell St

Haverhill St

Kingston St

Maffa Way

Medford St

Flint St

Glen St

Short St

Bunker Hill St

Oliver St

Pinckney Pl

Pinckney St

Mt Vernon St

Hadley

Brighton St

Clifton Pl

Cambridge St

Rutherford Ave

Charlestown St

Soxa St

Tufts St

Elm St

Almon St

Allston St

Elm St

Clay St

Fountain Ave

Palmer Ave

Turner Ct

Higgins

Pearl St

Crescent St

Crafts

Street

Roland St

CHARLESTOWN

Lincoln St

Essex St

Mead St

Main St

Hadley Cy

Washington St

New Washington St

1st Ave

Street D

Street C

Street B

Street A

Lincoln St

Joy St

Linwood St

28◀

Poplar St

B

SOMERVILLE

Chestnut St

Portland Belt Rd

93

Fitchburg St

McGrath Hwy

26 ▼

Millers River

Community College

Marten St

Foundry Rd

Marten Rd

1/4 mile   .25 km

Vinny's at Night might actually be the reason, if any exist, to visit this part of town. Don't be fooled by the convenience store frontage: in back lies a treasure trove of unreal Sicilian food. The Good Time Emporium is the ideal place for a good batting-cage heart-to-heart a la *Good Will Hunting* and other retro amusements.

Copy Shops

- **Go Ape** • 21 McGrath Hwy [Rufo]

Gyms

- **Fitcorp** • 529 Main St [Mishawum]
- **Gold's Gym** • 14 McGrath Hwy [Fitchburg]

Hardware Stores

- **Cunningham** • 545 Medford St [Short St]
- **Everett Supply & True Value Hardware** • 403 Main St [Auburn St]
- **Home Depot** • 75 Mystic Ave [N Union]

Liquor Stores

- **Bairos Liquors** • 78 Broadway [Hathorn]
- **Middlesex Beverages** • 30 Broadway [Mount Vernon St]
- **Sav-Mor Discount Liquors** • 15 McGrath Hwy [Rufo]

Nightlife

- **Good Time Emporium** • 30 Assembly Square Dr [Foley]

Restaurants

- **Beijing Taste** • 99A Cambridge St [Brighton St]
- **Mount Vernon** • 14 Broadway [Mt Pleasant St]
- **Vinny's at Night** • 76 Broadway [Hathorn]

Shopping

- **Home Depot** • 75 Mystic Ave [N Union]
- **Vinny's Superette** • 76 Broadway [Hathorn]

Video Rental

- **Hollywood Express** • 14 McGrath Hwy [Fitchburg]

Map 29 East Somerville, Sullivan Square

Foss Park

Mystic River

Malden Bridge

McGrath Hwy

Broadway

Sullivan Sq

Main St

Medford St

Bunker Hill St

CHARLESTOWN

Washington St

Rutherford Ave

SOMERVILLE

Main St

Mystic Ave

Mt Vernon St

Pearl St

New Washington St

1st Ave

Inner Belt Rd

McGrath Hy

Millers River

Community College Austin

1/4 mile   .25 km

Transportation

Sullivan Square Station is a major stop on the T's Orange Line and several bus routes. If driving, beware of the other drivers (true in all of Boston but must be highlighted here), confusing signage (ditto), multiple rotaries (ditto), and annoying traffic (you guessed it).

Subway

- **Community College**
- **Sullivan Sq**

Bus Lines

- **CT2** · Sullivan Station—Ruggles Station via Kendall/MIT
- **80** · Arlington Center—Lechmere Station via Medford Hills
- **86** · Sullivan Square Station—Cleveland Circle via Harvard/Johnson Gate
- **87** · Arlington Center or Clarendon Hill—Lechmere Station
- **88** · Clarendon Hill—Lechmere Station via Highland Avenue
- **89** · Clarendon Hill—Sullivan Square Station via Broadway
- **90** · Davis Square—Wellington Station via Sullivan Square Station
- **91** · Sullivan Square Station—Central Square, Cambridge via Washington Street
- **92** · Assembly Square Mall—Downtown via Sullivan Square Station, Main Street
- **93** · Sullivan Square Station—Downtown via Bunker Hill Street & Haymarket Station
- **95** · West Medford—Sullivan Square Station via Mystic Avenue
- **101** · Malden Center Station—Sullivan Square Station
- **104** · Malden Center Station—Sullivan Square Station
- **105** · Malden Center Station—Sullivan Square Station
- **109** · Linden Square—Sullivan Square Station via Glendale Square

Car Rental

- **Enterprise** · 37 Mystic Ave [N Union] · 617-625-1766

Gas Stations

- **Hess** · 123 Cambridge St [Parker St] ✪
- **Independent** · 339 Main St [Eden]
- **Mobil** · 386 Main St [Lyndeboro St]

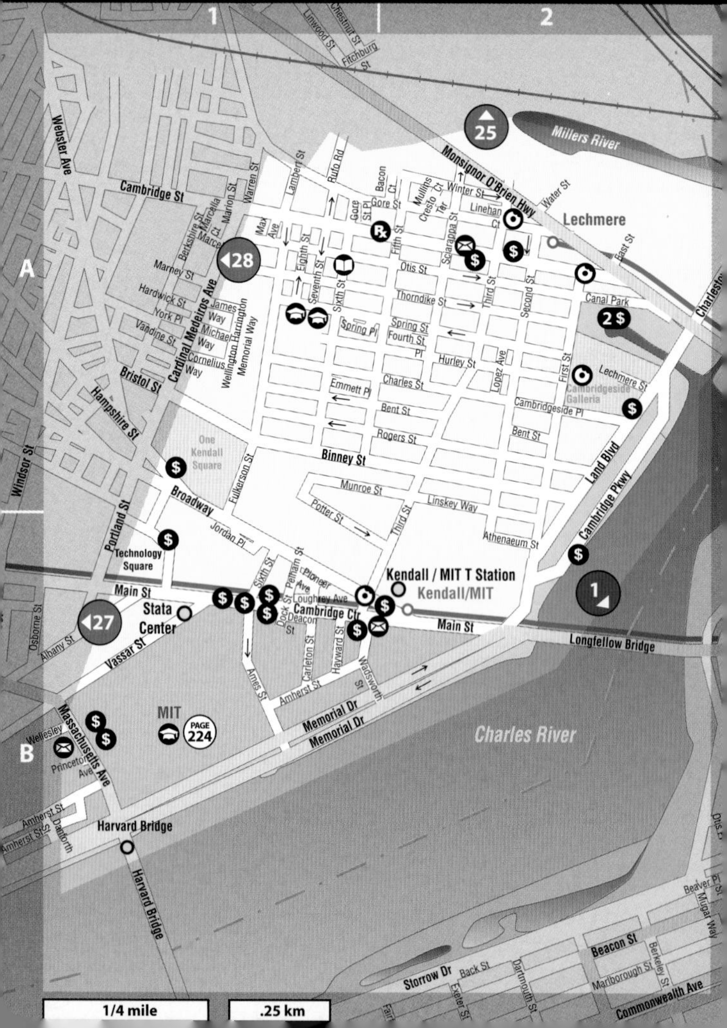

Map 26 · **East Cambridge/Kendall Square/MIT**

1
2

Webster Ave

Cambridge St

Millers River

Monsignor O'Brien Hwy

25

Lechmere

Limerick St
Fitchburg St
Chestnut St

Winter St
Water St

Beacon St
Gore St
Gore St

Berkshire St
Berkshire St
Marion St
Warren St
Lambert St
Auto Rd
Otis St
Ct
Mullin
Linehan

East St
Charlestown

Cambridge St

Marney Av
Max Ave
Marcella
Eighth St
Fifth St
Seventh St
Spring St
Sixth St

A

Hardwick St
James Way
Michael Way
Wellington
Memorial Way
Huntington
Cornelius

York St
Vardine St
Way

28

Thorndike St
Spring St
Fourth St
Pl

Third St
Sciarappa St

Scio
Second St
First St

Canal Park

2

Lechmere
St

Hampshire St

Bristol St

Emmett Pl

Charles St

Hurley St
Loper Ave

Cambridgeside
Galleria

Cambridgeside Pl

One
Kendall
Square

Bent St

Bent St

Rogers St

Land Blvd

Windsor St

Fulkerson St

Binney St

Munroe St

Linskey Way

Broadway

Portland St

Third St

Potter St

Jordan Pl

Athenaeum St

Cambridge Pkwy

Technology
Square

Main St

27

Stata
Center

Vassar St

Sixth St
Galileo
Ames St
Fifth St
Dock St
Pl
Wadsworth St
Carleton St

Pilgrim
Ave
Dock St

Kendall / MIT T Station
Kendall/MIT

Cambridge Ctr

Harvard St

Main St

1

Longfellow Bridge

Albany St

Osborne St

MIT

PAGE
224

Amherst St

Amherst Alley

Memorial Dr

Memorial Dr

Charles River

Massachusetts Ave

Wellesley

Princeton St

B

Amherst St
Dedham St
Amherst St

Harvard Bridge

Harvard Bridge

Storrow Dr

Back St

Beaver St

Mugar Way

Otis St

Fee St

Beacon St

Berkeley St

Marlborough St

Dartmouth St

Exeter St

Fairfield St

Commonwealth Ave

1/4 mile
.25 km

Once dominated by countless factories producing candy and candles, East Cambridge is now dominated by MIT and countless labs and tech companies. These eager beavers have a sweet tooth for sleek architecture, the most striking example being the Stata Center. The strip of green along Cambridge Parkway, not far from the Galleria and the Green Line, is a nice place to kill time by watching sailboats on the Charles on a sunny day.

Banks

- **Bank of America** • 100 Cambridgeside Pl [Land]
- **Bank of America** • 84 Massachusetts Ave [Vassar]
- **Bank of America (ATM)** • 150 Cambridge Park [Land]
- **Bank of America (ATM)** • 2 Canal Park [Land]
- **Bank of America (ATM)** • 4 Cambridge Ctr [Dock]
- **Bank of America (ATM)** • 600 Technology Sq [B'way]
- **Bank of America (ATM)** • 77 Massachusetts Ave [Amherst]
- **Boston Private Bank & Trust** • 1 Cambridge Ctr [Hayward St]
- **Cambridge Trust** • 326 Main St [Dock]
- **Century Bank (ATM)** • One Kendall Sq [Hampshire St]
- **Citizens Bank** • 225 Cambridge St [Third St]
- **East Cambridge Savings Bank** • 1 Canal Park [Land]
- **East Cambridge Savings Bank** • 292 Cambridge St [Sciarappa]
- **Sovereign Bank (ATM)** • 3 Cambridge Ctr [Dock]
- **Wainwright Bank & Trust** • 1 Broadway [Main]

Donuts

- **Dunkin' Donuts** • Sullivan Sq Station • 1 Broadway [Main]
- **Dunkin' Donuts** • 100 Cambridgeside Pl [Land]
- **Dunkin' Donuts** • 5 Third St [Monsignor O'Brien Hwy]
- **Dunkin' Donuts** • 99 Cambridge St [Carter St]

Landmarks

- **Harvard Bridge** • Massachusetts Ave [Memorial Dr]
- **Kendall / MIT T Station** • [Main]
- **Stata Center** • 32 Vassar St [Main]

Libraries

- **O'Connell** • 48 Sixth St [Thorndike]

Pharmacies

- **Ciampa Apothecary** • 425 Cambridge St [Fifth St]

Post Offices

- **East Cambridge Station** • 303 Cambridge St [Sciarappa]
- **Kendall Square Station** • 250 Main St [Hayward St]
- **MIT** • 84 Massachusetts Ave [Vassar]

Schools

- **Kennedy-Longfellow** • 158 Spring St [Seventh]
- **Massachusetts Institute of Technology** • 77 Massachusetts Ave [Amherst]

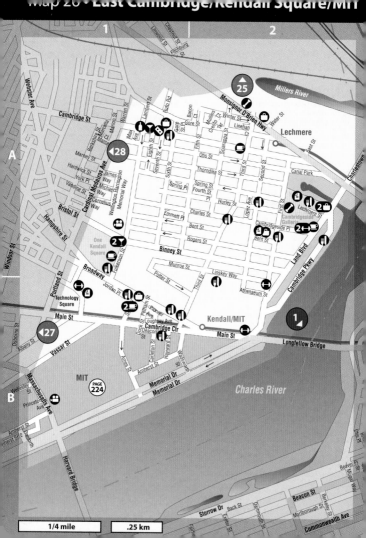

Map 26 • East Cambridge/Kendall Square/MIT

East Cambridge is home to Helmand, one of our favorite restaurants in all of Boston, and also our favorite movie complex, Kendall Square Cinema. Grab a beer at Cambridge Brewing Company after a film (or before, if called for). Cambridge Galleria is a suburban-style shopping palace—its Apple Store almost excuses the presence of yet another location of the preposterous Cheesecake Factory.

Coffee

- **Beantowne Coffee House** • One Kendall Sq [Hampshire St]
- **Starbucks** • 100 Cambridgeside Pl [Land]
- **Starbucks** • Marriott Hotel • 2 Cambridge Ctr [Hayward St]
- **Starbucks** • 6 Cambridge Ctr [Dock]
- **Sweet Touch** • 241 Cambridge St [Third St]

Copy Shops

- **FedEx Kinko's** • 600 Technology Sq [B'way]
- **Kendall Press** • 36 Charles St [Second St]
- **Minuteman Press** • 5 Cambridge Ctr [Dock]
- **The UPS Store** • One Kendall Sq [Hampshire St]

Gyms

- **Cambridge Racquet & Fitness Club** • 215 First St [Linskey]
- **Fitcorp** • 600 Technology Sq [B'way]
- **Fitness Works At Work** • 1 Main St [First St]

Hardware Stores

- **Brookstone** • 100 Cambridgeside Pl [Land]
- **Sears** • 100 Cambridgeside Pl [Land]

Liquor Stores

- **660 Liquors** • 660 Cambridge St [Max]

Movie Theaters

- **Landmark Kendall Square Cinema** • One Kendall Sq [Hampshire St]
- **MIT Film Series** • 77 Massachusetts Ave [Amherst]

Nightlife

- **Cambridge Brewing Company** • One Kendall Sq, Bldg 100 [Hampshire St]
- **Flattop Johnny's** • One Kendall Sq, Bldg 200 [Hampshire St]
- **Pugliese's** • 635 Cambridge St [Lambert St]

Pet Shops

- **Boston Tropical (fish and reptiles only)** • 243 Monsignor O'Brien Hwy [Sciarappa]
- **Petco** • 119 First St [Charles St]

Restaurants

- **Aceituna** • 605 W Kendall St [Athenaeum]
- **Bambara** • 25 Land Blvd [Cambridgeside]
- **Black Sheep Café** • 350 Main St [Dock]
- **The Blue Room** • One Kendall Sq [Hampshire St]
- **The Cheesecake Factory** • 100 Cambridgeside Pl [Land]
- **Court House Seafood** • 498 Cambridge St [Sixth]
- **Desfina** • 202 Third St [Charles St]
- **Helmand** • 143 First St [Bent St]
- **Legal Sea Foods** • 5 Cambridge Ctr [Dock]
- **Second Street Café** • 89 Second St [Spring]

Shopping

- **Apple Store** • 100 Cambridgeside Pl [Land]
- **Best Buy** • 100 Cambridgeside Pl [Land]
- **Calumet Photographic** • 65 Bent St [Second St]
- **Cambridge Antique Market** • 201 Monsignor O'Brien Hwy [Water]
- **Mayflower Poultry** • 621 Cambridge St [Eigth]

Video Rental

- **Video Oasis** • 625 Cambridge St [Eigth]

Parking at the Galleria is reasonably priced and handy if street parking is difficult to locate. Perennially confusing is the One Kendall Square complex not being located at Kendall Square—it's actually a few blocks up Broadway toward Cardinal Medeiros Avenue.

Subway

- **Lechmere**
- **Kendall/MIT**

Bus Lines

- **CT2** • Sullivan Square Station—Ruggles Station via Kendall/MIT
- **68** • Harvard/Holyoke Gate—Kendall/MIT via Broadway
- **69** • Harvard/Holyoke Gate—Lechmere Station via Cambridge Street
- **80** • Arlington Center—Lechmere Station via Medford Hills
- **85** • Spring Hill—Kendall/MIT Station via Summer Street & Union Square
- **87** • Arlington Center or Clarendon Hill—Lechmere Station
- **88** • Clarendon Hill—Lechmere Station via Highland Avenue

Car Rental

- **Enterprise** • 1 Broadway [Main] • 617-577-0404

Gas Stations

- **Shell** • 239 Monsignor O'Brien Hwy [Sciarappa]

Parking

Map 29 • Central Square / Cambridgeport Ⓝ

Harvard
University
PAGE
222

Cambridge St

Webster Ave

Hampshire St

Massachusetts Ave

Broadway

Prospect St

Cambridge
City Hall

Central

University Park

Necco
Building/
Novartis

Edgerton
& Strobe

Simmons
Hall

MIT
PAGE
224

Memorial Dr

Charles River

St Paul St

BU Bridge

Essex St

90

BU West

Storrow Dr

BU Central   Boston University

Commonwealth Ave

PAGE
218

BU East

Blandford
Street

Beacon St

1/4 mile   .25 km

Map 2

Love it or hate it, Central Square is the genuine center of Cambridge. This area's showcase development is University Park, a 27-acre mixed-use "campus" of residences and biotech companies. Sadly, the old Necco candy factory is now a Novartis research facility. If you're driving through this area, swing by eye-popping Simmons Hall. Cambridgeport looks more like old-school New England, but is in fact a very diverse part of already diverse Cambridge.

Banks

- **Bank of America** • 226 Main St [Wadsworth St]
- **Bank of America** • 727 Massachusetts Ave [Pleasant St]
- **Bank of America (ATM)** • 1000 Massachusetts Ave [Ellery St]
- **Bank of America (ATM)** • 139 Massachusetts Ave [Vassar]
- **Bank of America (ATM)** • 235 Main St [Hayward St]
- **Bank of America (ATM)** • 622 Massachusetts Ave [Essex]
- **Bank of America (ATM)** • 820 Memorial Dr [River St]
- **Cambridge Savings Bank** • 630 Massachusetts Ave [Essex]
- **Cambridge Trust** • 350 Massachusetts Ave [Blanche]
- **Citizens Bank** • 689 Massachusetts Ave [Temple St]
- **Citizens Bank (ATM)** • 20 Sidney St [Green St]
- **Sovereign Bank** • 515 Massachusetts Ave [Norfolk St]
- **Wainwright Bank & Trust** • 647 Massachusetts Ave [Prospect St]

✹ Community Gardens

⃝ Landmarks

- **Cambridge City Hall** • 795 Massachusetts Ave [Bigelow St]
- **Edgerton Center & Strobe Alley** • 77 Massachussetts Ave, MIT [Vassar]
- **Necco Building/Novartis** • 250 Massachusetts Ave [Landsdowne]
- **Simmons Hall** • 229 Vassar St [Concord Ave]
- **University Park** • Massachusetts Ave & Sidney St

📖 Libraries

- **Central Square** • 45 Pearl St [Franklin St]

℞ Pharmacies

- **Brooks** • 330 River St [Blackstone]
- **CVS** • 624 Massachusetts Ave [Essex]
- **Walgreens** • 625 Massachusetts Ave [Essex]

⃝ Police

- **Cambridge Police Department** • 5 Western Ave [Magazine St]

✉ Post Offices

- **Cambridge** • 770 Massachusetts Ave [Inman St]

🎓 Schools

- **Amigos Elementary** • 100 Putnam Ave [Magee]
- **Fletcher/Manyard Academy** • 225 Windsor St [B'way]
- **Henry Buckner** • 85 Bishop Richard Allen Dr [Norfolk St]
- **James F Farr Academy** • 71 Pearl St [Auburn St]
- **Martin Luther King Jr** • 100 Putnam Ave [Magee]
- **Morse School** • 40 Granite St [Pearl St]

🛒 Supermarkets

- **Harvest Co-op Market** • 581 Massachusetts Ave [Essex]
- **Star Market** • 20 Sidney St [Green St]
- **Trader Joe's** • 748 Memorial Dr [Pleasant St]
- **Whole Foods Market** • 340 River St [Blackstone]

Map 1 · Central Square / Cambridgeport

Sundries / Entertainment

Map 27

Not the obvious place to frolic the day away, Central's full of funk-venture by night. Seeing a rock show at the Middle East will earn you instant cool points. The Field pours a perfect pint of Boddingtons. River Gods is a sacrilegiously charming place to chill. Stop by Eastern Trading Company to check out their magical rotating racks of great vintage duds.

Coffee

- **1369 Coffee House** •
  757 Massachusetts Ave [Inman St]
- **Carberry's Bakery & Coffee House** •
  74 Prospect St [St Paul]
- **Dado Tea (tea only)** •
  955 Massachusetts Ave [Bay St]
- **Joe's Coffee Shop** •
  770 Massachusetts Ave [Inman St]
- **Mariposa Bakery** •
  424 Massachusetts Ave [Main]
- **Starbucks** • 655 Massachusetts Ave
  [Prospect St]

Copy Shops

- **Classic Copy & Printing** •
  678 Massachusetts Ave [Western]
- **Reproman Reprographics** •
  675 Massachusetts Ave [Temple St]
- **Sir Speedy Printing Center** •
  1001 Massachusetts Ave [Ellery St]
- **The UPS Store** •
  955 Massachusetts Ave [Bay St]

Farmer's Markets

- **Cambridgeport**
  (June-Oct; Sat 10:30-3:30) •
  Magazine St & Memorial Dr
- **Central Square**
  (May-Nov; Mon 12 pm-6 pm) •
  Bishop Richard Allen Dr at Norfolk St

Gyms

- **Boston Sports Club** •
  625 Massachusetts Ave [Essex]
- **Cambridge Family YMCA** •
  820 Massachusetts Ave [Bigelow St]
- **Cambridge Sports Club** •
  350 Massachusetts Ave [Blanche]
- **Curves** • 614 Massachusetts Ave [Essex]

Hardware Stores

- **Economy Hardware** •
  438 Massachusetts Ave [Main]
- **Pill Hardware** •
  743 Massachusetts Ave [Pleasant St]

Liquor Stores

- **Dana Hill Liquors** •
  910 Massachusetts Ave [Lee]
- **Libby's Liquors** •
  575 Massachusetts Ave [Essex]
- **Whole Foods Market** • 340 River St
  [Blackstone]

Nightlife

- **All Asia** • 334 Massachusetts Ave
  [Blanche]
- **Asgard** • 350 Massachusetts Ave
  [Blanche]
- **Cantab Lounge** •
  738 Massachusetts Ave [Pleasant St]
- **The Cellar** • 991 Massachusetts Ave
  [Dana St]
- **Enormous Room** •
  567 Massachusetts Ave [Pearl St]
- **The Field** • 20 Prospect Ave [Mass Ave]
- **The Middle East** •
  472 Massachusetts Ave [Douglas St]
- **Middlesex** • 315 Massachusetts Ave
  [State]
- **Miracle of Science** •
  321 Massachusetts Ave [State]
- **People's Republik** •
  880 Massachusetts Ave [Lee]
- **Phoenix Landing** •
  512 Massachusetts Ave [Brookline St]
- **Plough & Stars** •
  912 Massachusetts Ave [Hancock St]
- **River Gods** • 125 River St [Kinnaird]
- **TT the Bear's Place** • 10 Brookline St
  [Green St]
- **Western Front** • 343 Western Ave
  [Putnam Ave]

Restaurants

- **Asgard** • 350 Massachusetts Ave
  [Blanche]
- **Asmara** • 739 Massachusetts Ave
  [Pleasant St]
- **Atasca** • 50 Hampshire St [Webster Ave]
- **Brookline Lunch** • 9 Brookline St
  [Mass Ave]
- **Café Baraka** • 80 1/2 Pearl St
  [William St]
- **Carberry's** • 74 Prospect St [St Paul]
- **Cuchi Cuchi** • 795 Main St [Cherry St]
- **Dolphin Seafood** •
  1105 Massachusetts Ave [Remington]
- **Green Street Grill** • 280 Green St
  [Magazine St]
- **Hi-Fi Pizza & Subs** •
  496 Massachusetts Ave [Brookline St]
- **India Pavilion** • 17 Central Sq
  [Pleasant St]
- **La Groceria** • 853 Main St
  [Bishop Richard Allen Dr]
- **Mary Chung** •
  464 Massachusetts Ave [Douglas St]
- **Middle East** •
  472 Massachusetts Ave [Douglas St]
- **Miracle of Science** •
  321 Massachusetts Ave [State]
- **Moody's Falafel Palace** •
  25 Central Sq [Pleasant St]
- **Picante Mexican Grill** •
  735 Massachusetts Ave [Pleasant St]
- **Pu Pu Hot Pot** • 907 Main St [Columbia St]
- **Rendezvous** • 502 Massachusetts Ave
  [Brookline St]
- **Salts** • 798 Main St [Windsor St]
- **Sonora Mexican Grill** •
  319 Western Ave [Hews]
- **Tavern in the Square** •
  720 Massachusetts Ave [Temple St]
- **ZuZu!** • 474 Massachusetts Ave
  [Douglas St]

Shopping

- **Buckaroo's Mercantile** •
  5 Brookline St [Mass Ave]
- **Cambridge Bicycle** •
  259 Massachusetts Ave [Front]
- **Cheapo Records** •
  645 Massachusetts Ave [Prospect St]
- **Cremaldi's** • 31 Putnam Ave [Green St]
- **Economy Hardware** •
  438 Massachusetts Ave [Main]
- **Hubba Hubba** •
  534 Massachusetts Ave [Norfolk St]
- **Looney Tunes** •
  1001 Massachusetts Ave [Ellery St]
- **Massive Records** •
  1105 Massachusetts Ave [Remington]
- **Micro Center** • 730 Memorial Dr
  [Riverside Rd]
- **Pearl Art & Craft Supplies** •
  579 Massachusetts Ave [Essex]
- **Sadye & Company** •
  182 Massachusetts Ave [Albany St]
- **Shalimar** • 571 Massachusetts Ave
  [Pearl St]
- **Skippy White's** •
  538 Massachusetts Ave [Norfolk St]
- **Ten Thousand Villages** •
  694 Massachusetts Ave [Western]
- **Toscanini's** • 899 Main St [Columbia St]
- **University Stationery** •
  311 Massachusetts Ave [State]

Video Rental

- **Blockbuster** •
  541 Massachusetts Ave [Norfolk St]
- **Hollywood Express** •
  765 Massachusetts Ave [Inman St]

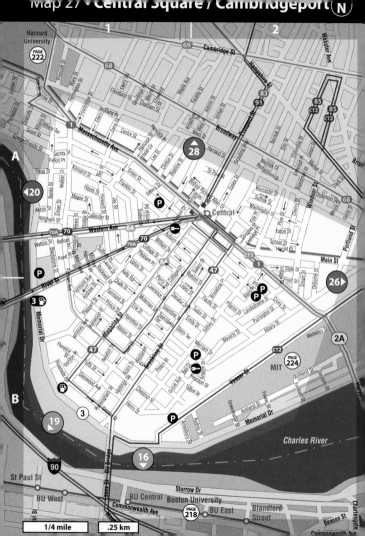

Map 27 • Central Square / Cambridgeport (N)

Harvard
University

PAGE
222

Cambridge St

Webster Ave

69

68

Hampshire St

83
91

85
CT2

85
CT2

Massachusetts Ave

Broadway

Bristo

28

Norfolk Ct
Richardson St

68

Windsor St

20

Western Ave

Central

64

70

70A

70

64

CT1

Main St

47

1

26

70A

70

River St

3

Memorial Dr

47

LandsDowne St

CT2

2A

PAGE
224

MIT

3

Memorial Dr

19

Charles River

3

16

90

St Paul St

BU West

Storrow Dr

BU Central Boston University

Commonwealth Ave

PAGE
218

BU East

Blandford
Street

Beacon St

Charlesgate

1/4 mile   .25 km

Without a Cambridge city sticker, parking around Central Square is not easy. If you don't mind dropping a couple of bucks, the parking garages in University Park will get you pretty close. The Cambridge Department of Public Works has a phone number you can call to "report a street or sidewalk" defect, tempting us to call them once a day to report "all of Mass Ave."

Subway

■ · **Central**

Bus Lines

- **CT1** · Central Square, Cambridge—BU Medical Center/BU Medical Campus
- **CT2** · Sullivan Station—Ruggles Station via Kendall/MIT
- **1** · Harvard/Holyoke Gate—Dudley Station via Massachusetts Avenue & BU Medical Center
- **47** · Central Square, Cambridge—Broadway Station via South End Medical Area
- **64** · Oak Square—Central Square, Cambridge, or Kendall/MIT
- **68** · Harvard/Holyoke Gate—Kendall/MIT via Broadway
- **69** · Harvard/Holyoke—Lechmere Station via Cambridge Street
- **70** · Cedarwood, N Waltham, or Watertown Square—University Park via Central Square
- **70A** · Cedarwood, N Waltham, or Watertown Square—University Park via Central Square
- **83** · Rindge Avenue—Central Square, Cambridge via Porter Square Station
- **85** · Spring Hill—Kendall/MIT Station via Summer Street & Union Square
- **91** · Sullivan Square Station—Central Square, Cambridge via Washington

Car Rental

- **Budget** · 66 Anglim St [Waverly St] · 617-497-3614
- **Enterprise** · 25 River St [Franklin St] · 617-547-7400

Gas Stations

- **Mobil** · 816 Memorial Dr [River St] ♻
- **Shell** · 207 Magazine St [Riverside Rd] ♻
- **Shell** · 820 Memorial Dr [River St] ♻
- **Sunoco** · 808 Memorial Dr [River St]

Parking

Straddling Cambridge and Somerville, Inman Square is an almost-hidden treasure at the center of the Cambridge/Somerville vortex. Colorful in every sense, and featuring a cross-cultural array of restaurants and bars, people from the rest of Boston are increasingly finding their way to Inman, particularly when they're hungry.

$ Banks

- **Bank of America (ATM)** • 120 Beacon St [Washington St]
- **Bank of America (ATM)** • 1400 Cambridge St [Antrim]
- **Cambridge Savings Bank** • 1378 Cambridge St [Hampshire St]
- **Cambridge Trust (ATM)** • 468 Broadway [Ware]
- **Citizens Bank** • 141 Portland St [B'way]
- **East Cambridge Savings Bank** • 1310 Cambridge St [Oak St]

Community Gardens

Donuts

- **Cambridge Coffee Shop** • 847 Cambridge St [Harding St]
- **Dunkin' Donuts** • Shell • 1001 Cambridge St [Windsor St]
- **Dunkin' Donuts** • 222 Broadway [Moore]
- **Dunkin' Donuts** • 282 Somerville Ave [Prospect St]

Emergency Rooms

- **Cambridge** • 1493 Cambridge St [Highland Ave]

O Landmarks

- **Julia Child's Home** • 103 Irving St [Bryant]

Libraries

- **Cambridge Main Library** • 359 Broadway [B'way Ter]
- **Valente** • 826 Cambridge St [Harding St]

Rx Pharmacies

- **Inman Pharmacy** • 1414 Cambridge St [Antrim]
- **Skenderian Apothecary** • 1613 Cambridge St [Roberts Rd]
- **Target** • 180 Somerville Ave [Mansfield]
- **Walgreens** • 16 Beacon St [Concord Ave]

Post Offices

- **Inman Square Station** • 1311 Cambridge St [Oak St]

Schools

- **Cambridge Rindge & Latin High** • 459 Broadway [Ware]
- **Cambridgeport** • 89 Elm St [Market St]
- **Castle** • 298 Harvard St [Lee]
- **King Open School** • 850 Cambridge St [Harding St]
- **Prospect Hill Academy Charter** • 15 Webster Ave [Everett St]
- **Rindge School of Technical Arts** • 459 Broadway [Ware]

Supermarkets

- **Farmer's Bounty** • 234 Elm St [Chester St]
- **Whole Foods Market** • 115 Prospect St [Harvard St]

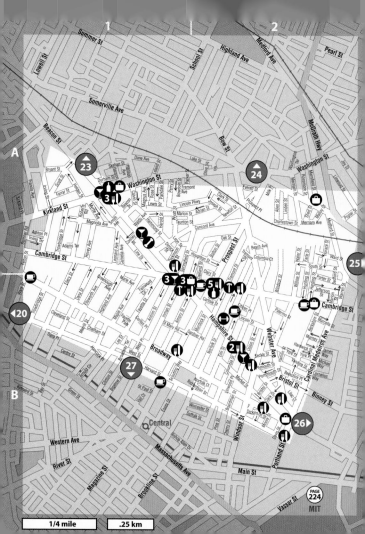

Sundries / Entertainment

Map 28

Eats and treats. Stop for a burger and your choice of 100+ beers at Bukowski's. Sample Dali's to-die-for tapas or East Coast Grill & Raw Bar's marvels from the sea. Curious shoppers will not regret spending time in Absolutely Fabulous or The Garment District, a fabulous thrift megastore whose basement sells clothes at $1 per pound.

Coffee

- **1369 Coffee House** • 1369 Cambridge St [Springfield]
- **Cambridge Coffee Shop** • 847 Cambridge St [Harding St]
- **Diesel Café** • 257 Elm St [Chester St]
- **Peet's Coffee & Tea** • Whole Foods • 115 Prospect St [Harvard St]
- **Starbucks** • 468 Broadway [Ware]

Gyms

- **Fitness Together** • 143 Hampshire St [Norfolk St]

Hardware Stores

- **City Paint & Supply** • 1149 Cambridge St [Norfolk St]
- **Inman Square Ace Hardware** • 1337 Cambridge St [Springfield]

Liquor Stores

- **Prospect Liquor** • 1226 Cambridge St [Prospect St]
- **Wine Cask** • 407 Washington St [Beacon St]

Nightlife

- **Abbey Lounge** • 3 Beacon St [Dickinson St]
- **B-Side Lounge** • 92 Hampshire St [Windsor St]
- **Bukowski's** • 1281 Cambridge St [Oakland St]
- **The Druid** • 1357 Cambridge St [Springfield]
- **Kirkland Café** • 425 Washington St [Beacon St]
- **Ryles Jazz Club** • 212 Hampshire St [Inman St]
- **Thirsty Scholar Pub** • 70 Beacon St [Cooney]

Pet Shops

- **Fi-Dough** • 70 Beacon St [Cooney]

 Restaurants

- **Amelia's Trattoria** • 111 Harvard St [Davis St]
- **Argana** • 1287 Cambridge St [Oakland St]
- **B-Side Lounge** • 92 Hampshire St [Windsor St]
- **Café Kiraz** • 119 Hampshire St [Columbia St]
- **City Girl Café** • 204 Hampshire St [Inman St]
- **Dali** • 415 Washington St [Beacon St]
- **East Coast Grill & Raw Bar** • 1271 Cambridge St [Oakland St]
- **Emma's Pizzeria** • 40 Hampshire St [Webster Ave]
- **EVOO** • 118 Beacon St [Washington St]
- **Koreana** • 154 Prospect St [B'way]
- **Magnolia's** • 1193 Cambridge St [Tremont St]
- **Midwest Grill** • 1124 Cambridge St [Norfolk St]
- **Ole Mexican Grill** • 11 Springfield St [Cambridge St]
- **Oleana** • 134 Hampshire St [Elm St]
- **Pho Lemon** • 228 Broadway [Clark St]
- **S&S Restaurant** • 1334 Cambridge St [Oak St]
- **Sweet Chili** • 1172 Cambridge St [Tremont St]
- **Toscanini and Sons** • 406 Washington St [Beacon St]

Shopping

- **Absolutely Fabulous** • 1309 Cambridge St [Oak St]
- **Christina's Homemade Ice Cream** • 1255 Cambridge St [Prospect St]
- **The Garment District** • 200 Broadway [Davis St]
- **Inman Square Market** • 1343 Cambridge St [Springfield]
- **Royal Pastry** • 738 Cambridge St [Marion St]
- **Target** • 180 Somerville Ave [Mansfield]
- **Wine Cask** • 407 Washington St [Beacon St]

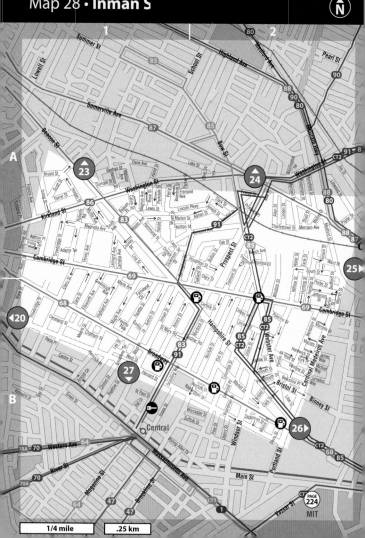

Can't get there by T, but it's easy enough to hop a bus or take a short walk from the Central or Kendall Square T stops. Parking is for the adventurous, though there are a couple of public lots. The neighborhood is a cyclists' mecca—drivers, take heed.

Bus Lines

- **CT1** • Central Square, Cambridge—BU Medical Center/BU Medical Campus
- **CT2** • Sullivan Station—Ruggles Station via Kendall/MIT
- **1** • Harvard/Holyoke Gate—Dudley Station via Massachusetts Avenue & BU Medical Center
- **47** • Central Square, Cambridge—Broadway Station via South End Medical Area
- **64** • Oak Square—Central Square, Cambridge, or Kendall/MIT
- **68** • Harvard/Holyoke Gate—Kendall/MIT via Broadway
- **69** • Harvard/Holyoke Gate—Lechmere Station via Cambridge Street
- **70** • Cedarwood, N Waltham, or Watertown Square—University Park via Central Square
- **70A** • Cedarwood, N Waltham, or Watertown Square—University Park via Central Square
- **80** • Arlington Center—Lechmere Station via Medford Hills
- **83** • Rindge Avenue—Central Square, Cambridge via Porter Square Station
- **85** • Spring Hill—Kendall/MIT Station via Summer Street & Union Square
- **86** • Sullivan Square Station—Cleveland Circle via Harvard/Johnson Gate
- **87** • Arlington Center or Clarendon Hill—Lechmere Station
- **88** • Clarendon Hill—Lechmere Station via Highland Avenue
- **90** • Davis Square—Wellington Station via Sullivan Square Station
- **91** • Sullivan Square Station—Central Square, Cambridge via Washington

Car Rental

- **U-Save Auto & Truck Rental** • 70 Prospect St
  [Webster Ave] • 781-321-3300

Gas Stations

- **Citgo** • 277 Broadway [Elm St]
- **Exxon** • 209 Broadway [Moore]
- **Hess** • 287 Prospect St [Hampshire St] ♿
- **Mobil** • 320 Broadway [Prospect St]
- **Shell** • 1001 Cambridge St [Windsor St]

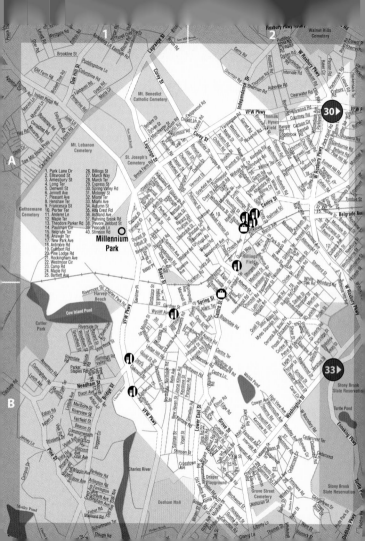

1

2

Roxbury Pkwy Roxbury   Walnut Hills
Cemetery

W Roxbury Pkwy

VFW Pkwy

30 ►   VFW P

Centre St

Belgrade Ave

33

Stony Brook
State Reservation

Mt. Lebanon
Cemetery

St. Joseph's
Cemetery

Corey St

Gethsemane
Cemetery

A

1. Park Lane Dr
2. Ellswood St
3. Amesbury St
4. Long Ter
5. Denwell St
6. Jennett Ave
7. Pleasant Ave
8. Henshaw Ter
9. Francesca St
10. Porter Ter
11. Anderer Ln
12. Maple Ter
13. Theodore Parker Rd
14. Paulman Cir
15. Belgrade Ter
16. Anawan Ter
17. New Park Ave
18. Ardmore Rd
19. Cuthbert Rd
20. Pine Lodge Rd
21. Rockingham Ave
22. Westmoor Cir
23. Camp Rd
24. Maple Rd
25. Bartlett Ave

26. Billings St
27. March Way
28. March Ter
29. Cypress St
30. Sprinvel Valley Rd
31. Moloney St
32. Miami Ter
33. Miami Ave
34. Autumn St
35. Alta Crest Rd
36. Ashland Ave
37. Running Brook Rd
38. Trevore Deddord St
39. Peacock Ln
40. Stimson Rd

Millennium
Park

Spring St

Needham St

Bridge St

VFW Pkwy

B

Cutler
Park

Cow Island Pond

Grove St

Washington St

Stony Brook
State Reservation

Charles River

Dedham Mall

Draper
Playground

Grove Street
Cemetery

Essentials

Over the past several years, a handful of community renovation projects have helped gussy up West Roxbury, a relatively quiet suburb-within-the-city. Among these projects is Millennium Park, which was developed on the site of the former Gardner Street Landfill. The park has several baseball fields, soccer fields, bike paths, walkways, and playgrounds. Its upper fields provide wonderful views, and each year the park's favorable winds attract the Boston Area Sport Kite Championships.

⊙ Landmarks
• **Millennium Park** • VFW Pkwy & Gardner St

Sundries / Entertainment

Commercial activity in West Roxbury is centered along Centre Street between Baker Street and West Roxbury Parkway. For a tasty lunch, try a sandwich from Real Deal or Spring Street Café.

🍴 Restaurants
• **Corrib Pub** • 2030 Centre St [Lagrange St]
• **Real Deal** • 1882 Centre St [Hastings St]
• **Samia Bakery** • 1894 Centre St [Hastings St]
• **Spring Street Café** • 320 Spring St [Billings St]
• **Tony's Place** • 188 Baker St [Wycliff Ave]
• **Vintage** • 1430 VFW Pkwy [Caledonian Ave]
• **West on Centre** • 1732 Centre St [Manthorne Rd]
• **West Roxbury Pub & Restaurant** • 1885 Centre St [Hastings St]

🛍 Shopping
• **Irish Cottage** • 1898 Centre St [Park St]
• **Jack Davis Florist** • 2097 Centre St [Temple St]

Transportation

The subway doesn't extend into West Roxbury, but to get there you can use the MBTA's Needham commuter rail line. Pick up the Needham line at the Forest Hills stop (on the T's Orange Line) and get off at either the Highland stop or the West Roxbury stop.

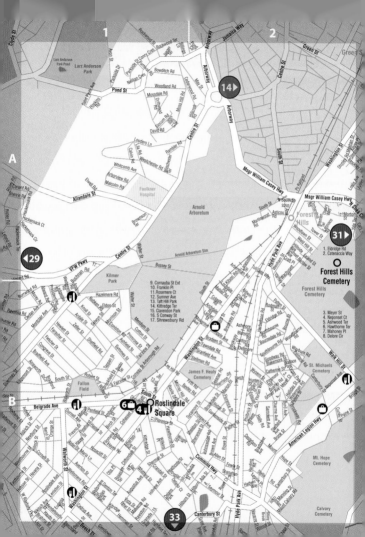

Essentials

By the mid-1980s Roslindale Square (also known as Roslindale Village) had largely fallen into disrepair, but thanks to a concerted effort by the city government and local businesses, together with strategic advice provided by the National Trust for Historical Preservation, Roslindale was given a new lease on life. Things turned out well enough for the NTHP to bestow its "Main Street" award on Roslindale Square, commending it for historic and aesthetic preservation during its economic revitalization.

⦿ Landmarks

- **Forest Hills Cemetery** • 95 Forest Hills Ave
- **Roslindale Square** • Washington St &
  Belgrade Ave

Sundries / Entertainment

The action here (such as it is) is centered around Roslindale Square, which, unbeknown to many Bostonians, has two terrific restaurants: Birch Street Bistro and Delfino.

🍴 Restaurants

- **Birch Street Bistro** • 14 Birch St [Corinth St]
- **Café Apollonia** • 146 Belgrade Ave [Metcalf St]
- **Delfino** • 754 South St [Taft Ct]
- **Diane's Bakery** • 9 Poplar St [South St]
- **Pleasant Café** • 4515 Washington St [Cedrus Ave]
- **Primavera** • 289 Walk Hill St [Canterbury St]
- **Village Sushi & Grill** • 14 Corinth St [Birch St]
- **Yucatan Tacos** • 1417 Centre St [Knoll St]

🛍 Shopping

- **18 Birch Street** • 18 Birch St [Corinth St]
- **Blooms & Greens** • 4014 Washington St [Lesher St]
- **Emack & Bolio's** • 2 Belgrade Ave [Birch St]
- **Exotic Flowers** • 609 American Legion Hwy [Canterbury St]
- **Formax Bread Baking Company** • 27 Corinth St [Cohasset St]
- **Solera** • 10 Corinth St [Birch St]
- **Village Books** • 751 South St [Taft Ct]
- **Zia** • 22 Birch St [Corinth St]

Transportation

To get to Roslindale without driving, you can either take the T's Orange Line to the Forest Hills stop and from there take an MBTA bus, or you can ride the commuter rail. The Needham commuter rail line stops in Roslindale at Roslindale Village and Bellevue.

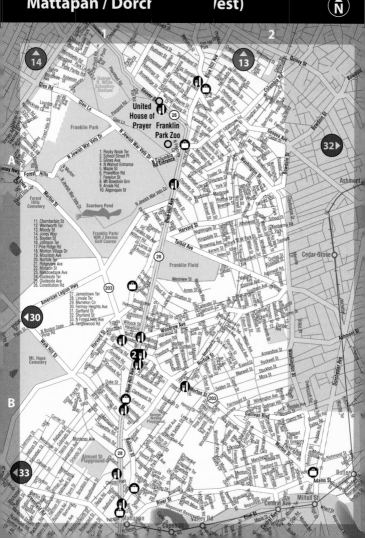

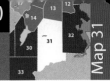
Essentials

Mattapan is mostly residential, a mix of single-family homes, triple-deckers, and city housing that's home to about 40,000 people. In particular, Mattapan is home to a growing Haitian-American community (the largest in Massachusetts), and has smaller communities whose roots are in many of the other nations of the Caribbean. It's not fancy, but hey – Boston City TV (aka The Menino Channel) comes here too.

⊙Landmarks

- **Franklin Park Zoo [Bear Cages]** •
  1 Franklin Park Rd
- **United House of Prayer** • 206 Seaver St

Sundries / Entertainment

Commercial activity in Mattapan clusters around Mattapan Square, which lies at the intersection of Blue Hill Avenue, River Street, and Cummins Highway. For patties and other West Indian treats, one of the many spots along Blue Hill Avenue will rock dem taste buds. Pit Stop Bar-B-Q, with its great ribs, represents for Morton Street.

🍴Restaurants

- **Ali's Roti** • 1188 Blue Hill Ave [Morton St]
- **Brothers** • 1638 Blue Hill Ave [River St]
- **Bon Appetit** • 1138 Blue Hill Ave [Livingstone St]
- **Flames** • 461 Blue Hill Ave [Georgia St]
- **Flames** • 663 Morton St [Rhoades St]
- **Hummingbird Grill** • 736 Blue Hill Ave [Esmond St]
- **Jamaica Jerk & Grill** • 1210A Blue Hill Ave [Landor Rd]
- **Lenny's Tropical Bakery** • 1195 Blue Hill Ave
  [Deering Rd]
- **Picasso Creole Cuisine** • 1296 Blue Hill Ave
  [Fessenden St]
- **Pit Stop Bar-B-Q** • 888A Morton St [Evans St]
- **Simco's on the Bridge** • 1509 Blue Hill Ave [Regis St]
- **United House of Prayer Kitchen** • 206 Seaver St
  [Elm Hill Ave]

🛍Shopping

- **Brigham's Ice Cream** • 1621 Blue Hill Ave [Fairway St]
- **Dark Horse** • 2297 Dorchester Ave [Adams St]
- **Hip Zepi USA** • 612 Blue Hill Ave [Columbia Rd]
- **Le Foyers Bakery** • 132 Babson St [Fremont St]
- **Rainbow Apparel** • 474 Blue Hill Ave [Geneva Ave]
- **Taurus Records** • 1282 Blue Hill Ave [Evelyn St]

Transportation

The T's Red Line passes through the JFK/UMass station before splitting into two branches. To get to the Mattapan T stop, choose an Ashmont-bound train. At the Ashmont station, the "it's not retro, it's old" Mattapan trolley will take you as far as Mattapan Square. The MBTA commuter rail's Fairmount line makes a stop at Morton Street.

Map 32 • **Dorchester (East)**

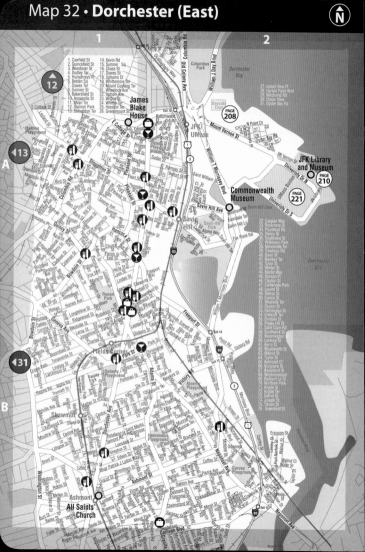

1. Cawfield St
2. Quincefield St
3. Wendover St
4. Dudley Ter
5. Humphreys St
6. Belden St
7. Dawes Ter
8. Sumner St
9. Bakersfield St
10. Annapolis St
11. Mvan Ter
12. Sumner Park
13. Sexton Ter

14. Kevin Rd
15. Sumner Sq
16. Chase St
17. Dawes St
18. Uphams Ct
19. Whittemore Ter
20. Mount Cushing Ter
21. Wheelock Ave
22. Upham Ave
23. Wilder St
24. Whitney St
25. Hession Ter
26. Greenmount St

12
113
431

James Blake House

E Cottage St

JFK / UMass

PAGE 208

Mount Vernon St

N Point Dr

Oyster Bay Rd

JFK Library and Museum

University Dr N

PAGE 210

PAGE 221

Commonwealth Museum

University Dr S

Savin Hill Cove

Savin Hill

Savin Hill Park

Dorchester Bay

32. Caspian Way
33. Rockmere St
34. Pearlstad Rd
35. Ormsy St
36. Southview St
37. Wilkinson Park
38. Melvinside Ter
39. Treadway Rd
40. Dunn St
41. Navaho Ter
42. Taylor St
43. Winter St
44. Martin Way
45. Duncan Pl
46. Clayton St
47. Centervale Park
48. Levant St
49. Jewen St
50. Eunice St
51. Westville
52. Dayton St
53. Remington St
54. Endicott Ter
55. Enndale St
56. Popes Hill St
57. Saint Clare Rd
58. Scottkeck St
59. Bloomington
60. Breeze St
61. Jervey St
62. Woodworth St
63. Walnut St
64. Taylor St
65. Ashmont Ct
66. Borgane St
67. Beaumont St
68. Westmoreland
69. Radford Ln St
70. Northam Park
71. Argyle St
72. Defnot St
73. Joseph St
74. Tilman St
75. Greenfield St

Freeport St

Fields Corner

Doherty Playground

Adams St

Alsen Playground

Shawmut

Dorchester Ave

Ronalsand St

Saint Marks

Hemenway Playground

Garvey Playground

Ashmont

All Saints Church

Gallivan Blvd

Neponset Ave

Map 32 • **Dorchester (East)**

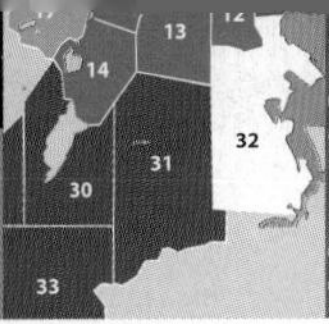

Map 32

Essentials

(In)famous for protecting turf, Dorchester is more a collection of distinct neighborhoods and ethnicities than a neighborhood itself. Uphams Corner, Savin Hill, Fields Corner, Ashmont, Codman Square, and Grove Hall are but a few of the areas that comprise Boston's largest district. Sure, it has a high crime rate and a lousy rep, but let's hope that the gentrification creeping down Dot Ave doesn't entirely rob Dorchester of its cred.

⊙ Landmarks

- **All Saints' Church** • 209 Ashmount St
- **Commonwealth Museum** • 220 Morissey Blvd
- **The James Blake House** • 735 Columbia Rd
- **John F Kennedy Library and Museum** • Morissey Blvd & Columbia Point

Sundries / Entertainment

Irish bars line Dot Ave; they lack tourists and charge three bucks for Guinness. Less Irish, but gayer, dBar is a great addition to the street. Mixed between them are the city's best pho houses. You'll find excellent Caribbean cuisine along Blue Hill Avenue and reggae dances at the Caribbean Cultural Center. Grove Hall and Uphams Corner are the areas to go for soul food.

Nightlife

- **Banshee** • 934 Dorchester Ave [Edison Grn]
- **dBar** • 1236 Dorchester Ave [Hoyt St]
- **Harp & Bard** • 1099 Dorchester Ave [Savin Hill Ave]
- **Lucky Strike Lanes** • 289 Adams St [Park St]

- **Moonlight Terrace** • 756 Dudley St [Belden St]
- **Phillips Old Colony House** • 780 Morrissey Blvd [Freeport St]
- **Sunrise** • 1157 Dorchester Ave [Dunn St]
- **Pho 2000** • 198 Adams St [Arcadia St]
- **Pho Hoa** • 1356 Dorchester Ave [Kimball St]
- **Resaurante Cesaria** • 266 Bowdoin St [Draper St]
- **Shanti: Taste of India** • 1111 Dorchester Ave [Savin Hill Ave]

🍴 Restaurants

- **Ashmont Grill** • 555 Talbot Ave [Ashmont St]
- **Ba-Le Restaurant** • 1052 Dorchester Ave [William St]
- **Blarney Stone** • 1505 Dorchester Ave [Park St]
- **CF Donovan's** • 112 Savin Hill Ave [Sydney St]
- **Charlie's Place** • 1740 Dorchester Ave [Semont Rd]
- **Chef Lee's II** • 554 Columbia Rd [Arion St]
- **Chris's Texas BBQ** • 1370 Dorchester Ave [Orchardfield St]
- **dbar** • 1236 Dorchester Ave [Hoyt St]

🛍 Shopping

- **Asian Bookstore** • 1392 Dorchester Ave [Greenwich St]
- **Colleen's Flowershop** • 912 Dorchester Ave [Grafton St]
- **Greenhill's Irish Bakery** • 780 Adams St [Henderson Rd]
- **P.J. Bait Shop** • 1397 Dorchester Ave [Greenwich St]

Transportation

In a word: Underserved! The Red Line tracks along the eastern side of Dorchester, roughly parallel to Dot Ave. From Ashmont, a trolley line wraps around to Mattapan Square. Buses run along Blue Hill Avenue; unfortunately, none of these buses directly connects Dorchester to Central Boston. The MBTA commuter rail's Fairmount line makes a stop at Uphams Corner and at Morton Street.

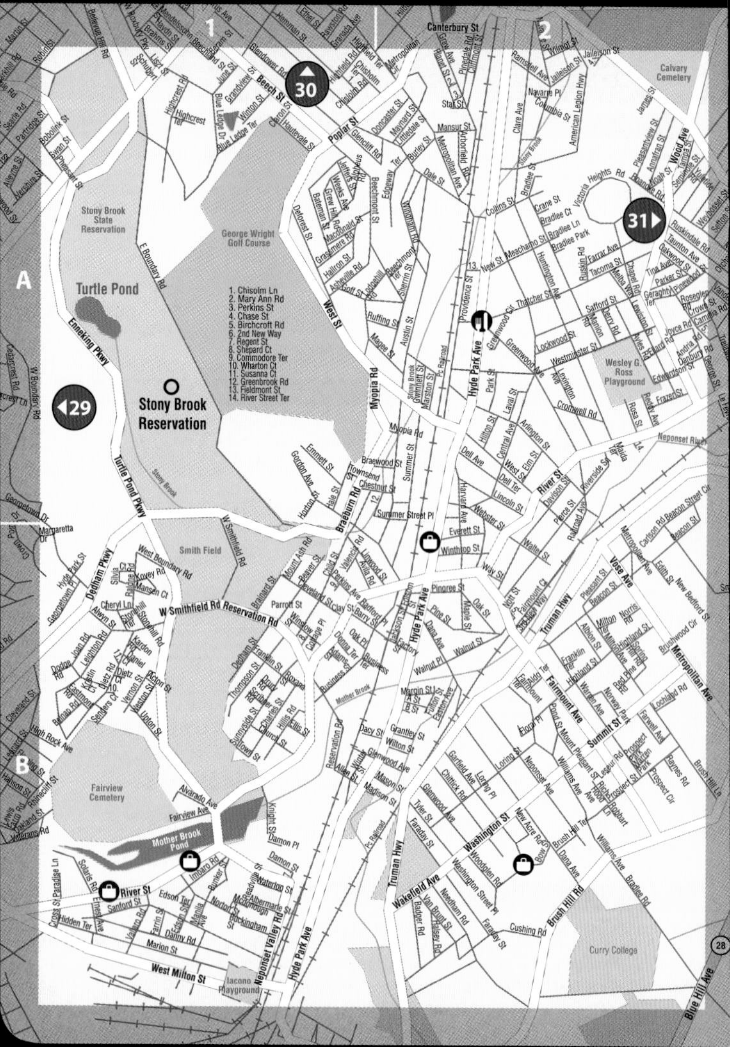

Map 33 • **Hyde Park**

1

Canterbury St

2

30

George Wright
Golf Course

Stony Brook
State
Reservation

Turtle Pond

A

Stony Brook
Reservation

1. Chisolm Ln
2. Mary Ann Rd
3. Perkins St
4. Chase St
5. Birchcroft Rd
6. 2nd New Way
7. Regent St
8. Shepard Ct
9. Commodore Ter
10. Wharton Ct
11. Susanna Ct
12. Greenbrook Rd
13. Fieldmont St
14. River Street Ter

29

31

Wesley G.
Ross
Playground

Calvary
Cemetery

Neponset Rd

Smith Field

Summer Street Pl

B

Fairview
Cemetery

Mother Brook
Pond

River St

West Milton St

Iacono
Playground

Curry College

28

Essentials

Almost as large as Franklin Park , Stony Brook Reservation covers 475 acres and includes low hills, dense woods, rock outcroppings, and marshland. The park's largest feature is Turtle Pond, where you can fish for perch and sunfish. There are also several miles of bicycle paths and the most extensive hiking opportunities within the city limits. Among the park's many recreational facilities is the John F. Thompson Center, New England's first recreational facility designed specifically to accommodate handicapped visitors.

O Landmarks

• **Stony Brook Reservation** • Washington St & Turtle Pond Pkwy

Sundries / Entertainment

If you're hungry, check out the Caribbean dishes at Angie's. If you're looking for entertainment, enjoy some bowling at Ron's. If you're not into bowling but you have pimped your ride, then you're at least able to cruise Hyde Park Avenue for hotties and doughnuts.

Restaurants

• **Angie's** • 984 Hyde Park Ave [Thatcher St]

Shopping

• **Capone Foods** • 14 Bow St [Garfield Ave]
• **Marascio's Market** • 1758 River St [Neponset Valley Pkwy]
• **Ron's Gourmet Ice Cream** • 1231 Hyde Park Ave [Everett St]
• **Tutto Italiano** • 1889 River St [Solaris Rd]

Transportation

To get to Hyde Park, take the MBTA commuter rail's Franklin line or Providence line. The Franklin line makes two stops in Hyde Park, at Fairmount and Readville. You can get on the Franklin line at South Station, which is served by the T's Red Line. Use the Providence line to reach the Hyde Park stop or the Readville stop. The Providence line stops at Forest Hills, where you can transfer from the T's Orange Line.

Overview

Copley Square is named after Boston-born portrait painter John Singleton Copley (1738-1815), America's first great artist. His portraits of America's founding fathers are on display at the Massachusetts Historical Society, across the street from the square, and at the Museum of Fine Arts. The Boston Marathon, held annually on Patriots Day (the third Monday in April), ends on Boylston Street. A BosTix outlet, the place to score discounted theater tickets, stands at the corner of Boylston Street and Dartmouth Street. The farmers' market fills the square Tuesdays and Fridays from 11 am to 6 pm, June through October. The Friends of Copley Square sponsors its annual Holiday Tree Lighting on the first Thursday after Thanksgiving. Summer months bring folk dancing performances to the square on Tuesday evenings.

Architecture & Sculpture

The Boston Public Library is America's oldest public library. The Renaissance-revival style structure holds within it over seven million books, as well as busts of famous writers and prominent Bostonians. Big bonus: it offers wireless Internet access. Across the square you'll find the neo-Romanesque Trinity Church, designed by notable architect H.H. Richardson. The stained glass windows alone are worth a trip inside.

John Hancock Tower

The John Hancock Mutual Life Insurance Company, which already inhabited buildings on Clarendon Street and Berkeley Street, needed more space to house its employees, so it opted to build a 60-story black glass tower. What better place to put it than next to the Public Library and an old church? Designed by architect I. M. Pei, and completed in 1976, the John Hancock Tower became famous for being the tallest building in New England, and simultaneously infamous for falling apart.

Locals were upset when a foundation collapse in the early stages of construction nearly sucked Trinity Church into the ground. They became outraged when, in January 1973, one of the building's 10,000-plus glass windows "popped off" and shattered on the ground below, followed by dozens more 500-pound window panes. All told, 65 panes fell onto the roped-off area below the building before workers changed the solder used to mount the windows. In the meantime, locals had dubbed the Hancock "The Plywood Palace," in reference to the black plywood sheets put in place to substitute for the fallen panes. Not long after, engineers discovered the building was in danger of being sheared in half by the wind, resulting in another expensive fix. Today, the Hancock Tower stands sturdy, tall, and proud, and locals have even grown to love it.

The observation deck on the 60th floor, originally opened to the public in response to community feedback, was permanently closed for security reasons after the events of September 11, 2001.

How to Get There—Driving

From the south, take I-93 N to Exit 18 (Massachusetts Avenue/Roxbury). Follow signs to Massachusetts Avenue and turn right. Turn right on Huntington Avenue, then left onto Dartmouth Street. From the north, take I-93 S to Exit 26 (Storrow Drive). Follow Storrow Drive west to the Copley Square exit. Turn right onto Beacon Street and, after two blocks, turn left onto Clarendon Street. After five blocks, turn right onto St. James Avenue.

This is one of two examples in the city (the other being the Pru) where the "look up, locate the giant building, and drive towards it" method of navigation works well.

How to Get There—Mass Transit

Take the Green Line to the Copley stop. Alternatively, take the Orange Line to the Back Bay stop, exit, and head to your right along Dartmouth Street. Again, if you're not sure which way to go, look for the giant glass building.

General Information

NFT Map: 6
Address: 700 Boylston St,
Boston, MA 02116
Phone: 617-536-5400
Website: www.bpl.org
Hours: Mon-Thurs: 9 am–9 pm, Fri-Sat:
9 am–5 pm, Sun: 1 pm–5 pm
(Oct-May)

Overview

The Boston Public Library, founded in 1848, was the country's first publicly-supported municipal library. The BPL was also the first public library to lend a book and the first to institute a children's room.

The BPL's main branch is the Central Library, composed of two august buildings adjacent to Copley Square that hold a lot more than just books. Facing Dartmouth Street, the McKim Building (the "old wing") was designed by noted 19th-century architect Charles Follen McKim and opened in 1895. The old wing, which houses the Research Library, is built around a delightful Italianate courtyard that offers readers a most un-library-like place to relax with a book. A set of murals painted by John Singer Sargent hangs inside. Sargent, better known for his portraits than for large installations, intended for these mammoth murals to be his masterpiece. There's also a set of allegorical murals by Pierre Puvis de Chavannes and the architecturally significant Bates Hall.

Opened to the public in 1972, the Johnson Building was designed by legendary architect Philip Johnson. The building, which houses the General Library, faces Boylston Street and is still referred to as the "new wing." The Johnson Building has less knock-out art than the McKim Building, but it does have the tiled architectural frieze *The Goose Girl*, which is worth seeking out if you're wandering through the building. The BPL offers guided tours of both the old and new wings.

Internet

If you're ever stuck without Internet access, head over to the Central Library. Both the old and new wings have PCs available for use by the general public. (All computers have Internet connections and Microsoft Office software.) The first floor of the new wing also has "express" PCs that limit use to 15 minutes—handy for a quick e-mail hit. Both buildings are also equipped with WiFi access.

For the Kids

The Central Library has an outstanding collection of materials for even the youngest readers. Most of these materials can be found in the Margret and H.A. Rey Children's Room, named for the creators of the beloved inquisitive simian, Curious George. The Children's Room also offers access to computers with Internet filtering software, which is helpful for protecting fragile little minds. For more information, check the website or call 617-859-2270.

Restaurants

The Central Library now has two restaurants to sate you during long hours of research. Novel, the fancier of the two restaurants, is set in a spacious room overlooking the courtyard in the center of the McKim Building. Next door to Novel, Sebastian's Map Room Café serves breakfast, lunch, and snacks. For reservations at Novel, or for additional information, call 617-385-5660. Note that food and drink are generally prohibited from the public areas of the Central Library, so chug your coffee before entering.

How to Get There—Driving

From the north or the south, take I-93 to Exit 26 (Storrow Drive). From Storrow Drive, take the Copley Square exit. The exit dead-ends at Beacon Street. Turn right on Beacon Street, drive four blocks to Exeter Street, and make a left. Drive along Exeter Street until you reach Boylston Street. The Central Library is on the corner of Boylston Street and Exeter Street.

From the west, take the Mass Pike (I-90 E) to Exit 22 (Prudential Center/Copley Square). Move to the right lane and follow the road in the tunnel toward Copley Square. The tunnel exits onto Stuart Street. Quickly move to the far left lane of Stuart Street and make a left at the next light onto Dartmouth Street. Drive through the next set of lights. The Central Library will be on the left.

Parking

The Central Library's location near Copley Square doesn't offer much in the way of street parking. If you're feeling unlucky, try the parking garage on Stuart Street between Dartmouth Street and Exeter Street.

How to Get There—Mass Transit

Take the T's Green Line to the Copley stop or the Orange Line to the Back Bay stop.

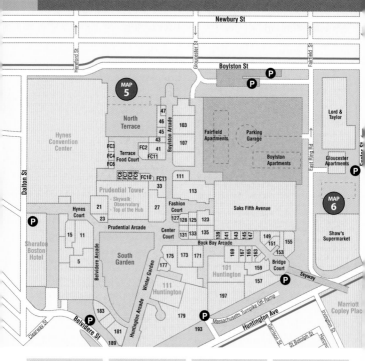

Stores

5 US Post Office
11 Ann Taylor Loft
15 Au Bon Pain
21 St Francis Chapel
23 Dunkin' Donuts
27 Ann Taylor
43 GameStop
45 Florsheim Shoes
46 Travel 2000
47 Truffles Fine Confections
103 Legal Sea Foods
107 Sephora
111 F Carriere
113 Talbots Collection

123 Olympia Sports
126 The Walking Company
127 The Body Shop
133 Johnston & Murphy
135 Aldo
139 Sunglass Hut
141 Teavana
143 Papyrus
145 Landau Collections
147 Optica
149 Barami
151 Kuhlman
153 L'Occitane
155 California Pizza Kitchen
157 Express Men

159 Crane & Co.
163 Lacoste
165 Yankee Candle
167 Swarovski
171 Levenger
175 Chico's Club Monaco
177 Franklin Covey
179 Barnes & Noble
181 The Sharper Image
183 Sovereign Bank
189 The Cheesecake Factory
193 Applebee's
197 FitCorp

Food Court

FC1 Pizzeria Regina
FC2 Panda Express
FC3 Paradise Bakery
FC4 Poulet Rotisserie Chicken
FC5 Boston Chowda
FC6 Flamers
FC7 Gourmet India
FC8 Sakkio Japan
FC9 Ben & Jerry's
FC10 Qdoba Mexican Grill
FC11 Louis Barry Florist

General Information

NFT Maps: 5 & 6
Address: 800 Boylston St, Boston, MA 02199
Phone: 1-800-SHOP-PRU or 617-236-3100
Website: www.prudentialcenter.com

Overview

The Prudential Center opened in 1965 and, at 52 stories, reigned as the city's tallest building until the 60-story John Hancock Tower was completed eleven years later. With the exception of the top two floors, which house an observation deck and a restaurant, the Prudential Tower is used mainly as office space. A street-level mall was opened in the 1990s and houses almost 50 shops including Saks Fifth Avenue and numerous restaurants and services. The "Pru" is also home to several apartment buildings and is connected to the Hynes Convention Center and the Sheraton Boston Hotel.

Skywalk and Top of the Hub

Other than shopping, the Prudential Center's main attractions are its Skywalk Observatory and Top of the Hub restaurant (both located in the Prudential Tower). The Skywalk is open daily from 10 am until 9:30 pm (8 pm in the winter). It offers spectacular views of Boston and its suburbs, as well as the harbor, Blue Hill, and—way off in the distance—Cape Cod. The Skywalk costs $10.50 adults, $8.50 seniors, and $7 children under 12. As you walk around the Skywalk, focus on the huge windows, which are marked to help you locate some of the more well-known features of the Boston skyline.

For a less informative, slightly more expensive, but extremely relaxing city view, walk two floors up from the Skywalk to the Top of the Hub restaurant and cocktail lounge. Entrees are pricey, but juice and cocktails from the bar are fairly priced and served with a spectacular view. For about $5 apiece—cheaper than the Skywalk—you can peer down at the city or across at the top of the John Hancock Tower with beverage in hand. The restaurant and lounge get busy at night, especially when the jazz band is playing. A casual but "anti-slob" dress code is in effect.

How to Get There—Driving

From the north, take I-93 S to Exit 26 (Storrow Drive) and follow it to the Copley Square exit on the left. Take a right onto Beacon Street and follow it to Exeter Street. Make a left onto Exeter Street and the Prudential Center Garage will be four blocks down on the right.

From the west, follow the Mass Pike (I-90 E) into Boston. Get off at Exit 22 (Copley Square/Prudential Center) and follow the signs for Prudential Center. This will take you directly to the Prudential Center Garage entrance on your right.

From the south, take I-93 N to Exit 26 (Storrow Drive) and follow to the Copley Square exit on the left. Take a right onto Beacon Street and follow it to Exeter Street. Take a left onto Exeter Street. The Prudential Center Garage will be four blocks down on the right.

If you get lost, try this: Look up. Find the giant building that says "Prudential" on top. Drive towards it.

How to Get There—Mass Transit

The Green Line will take you to the Prudential T stop on Huntington Avenue (E train only), the Copley stop on Boylston Street at Dartmouth Street, and the Hynes/ICA stop on Newbury Street at Mass Ave. The Orange Line and the MBTA Commuter Rail both stop at Back Bay Station, just across the street from Copley Place and a short walk away.

Overview

Cambridge Common was the center of rebel activity in the early years of the Revolution and has been a hub of political and social activity ever since. George Washington rallied the 16,000-man Continental Army under an elm tree on the green on July 3, 1775, and the area became the primary training ground for the troops.

William Dawes, along with Paul Revere and Dr. Samuel Prescott, rode his horse across the Common on his way to warn those in Lexington and Concord that "the regulars are coming" (not that "the British are coming"). While Revere inspired a famous poem and became the namesake of many American cities, Dawes was commemorated with some lousy bronze hoof prints in the pavement of the Common.

Three cannons that the colonists seized from the Lobsterbacks still sit by the flagpole. There's also a memorial to victims of the Irish Potato Famine.

Even with the addition of a playground and a softball field, this historical urban oasis remains an important place to voice ideas and protests. Just steps away from Harvard University, the Common's corner on Massachusetts Avenue has been used by activists protesting everything from the occupation of Iraq to Israelis in Palestine to the existence of SUVs.

Attractions

Relaxing and people-watching are, by far, the two best activities to undertake on the Common. With its prime location next to Harvard Square, you can feel like a Harvard student, without the excessive course fees and mandatory high IQ, though tree-shaded benches are available for reading if you want to play the part.

The park has a fenced-in playground located on the corner of Garden and Waterhouse Streets, where kids can frolic safely. The playground was last renovated in 1990 (including the addition of a wooden climbing structure, swings, bridges, slides, and benches/picnic tables) and is recommended for parents with children aged one to ten.

Sports

There's a softball field, soccer fields, and designated areas for other light recreation along with bike paths for cyclists, skaters, joggers, and walkers. Despite the close link between afternoon softball games and booze, the rules forbid alcoholic beverages on the ball field.

Parks & Places · **Charlestown Navy Yard**

General Information

NFT Map: 8
Address: 1st Ave, Charlestown, MA 02129
Phone: 617-242-5601 (Visitor Center);
617-242-5670 (USS Constitution)
Websites: www.nps.gov/bost/Visiting_Navy_Yard.htm
www.cityofboston.gov/freedomtrail/
ussconstitution.asp
www.charlestownonline.net/navyyard.htm
Hours: 10 am until 4 pm daily; free admission

Practicalities

The Charlestown Navy Yard is a must-see for anyone
who likes big ships or US naval history. The two main
attractions are the *USS Cassin Young* and "Old Ironsides"
herself, the *USS Constitution*. The yard was established in
1800 as one of the first naval shipyards in the country, and
the *Constitution* is almost as old as the country itself. When
the Navy retired the yard in 1974, the yard became part of
the Boston National Historic Park.

Attractions

Typical Fourth of July celebrations in Boston range from
backyard barbecues to beach sunbathing, but the Navy Yard
has its own unique tradition. Independence Day is celebrated
with the customary turning of the *Constitution*—an annual
practice in which the great vessel is tugged out of the dock
and rotated to ensure uniform weathering. The *Cassin Young*
has battle scars from its service in both World War II and the
Korean War. The nearby Commandant's House, the oldest
building in the Navy Yard, is no longer a private home, but
an elegant museum, which is open to the public.

How to Get There—Driving

From the north, take I-93 S to Exit 28 (Sullivan Square/
Charlestown), go under I-93, and follow signs to Sullivan
Square. Bear left at the first traffic light and drive into the
Sullivan Square rotary; take the second right onto Bunker
Hill Street, turn right onto Chelsea Street, and make an
immediate left onto Fifth Street. Drive one block (Fifth
Street dead-ends) and turn left onto First Avenue.

From the south, take I-93 N to Exit 26 (Storrow Drive) and
aim for the "North Station, USS Constitution" signs. Turn
left onto Martha Road (which becomes Lomasney Way),
left on Causeway Street, then left at N Washington Street,
and get into the right lane as quickly as possible. At the
end of the bridge, turn right onto Chelsea Street.

From the west, take the Mass Pike (I-90 E) to I-93 N, and
follow the directions above.

Parking

Though public transportation is strongly recommended
for this area, discounted parking with Boston National
Historical Park validation is available from the Nautica
Parking Garage across from the park's Visitor Center on
Constitution Road.

How to Get There—Mass Transit

Visitors can take a water shuttle to the Navy Yard from Long
Wharf for $1.50. For more information, see page [254].

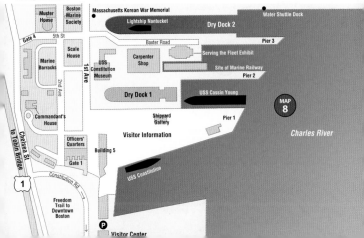

General Information

NFT Map:	3
Address:	147 Tremont Pl (between Temple Pl & West St)
Phone:	617-426-3115
Websites:	www.bostonusa.com
	www.cityofboston.gov/freedomtrail/
	bostoncommon.asp
	www.cityofboston.gov/parks/streettrees/
	inventories.asp

Overview

The nation's oldest public park, Boston Common was purchased by the Commonwealth of Massachusetts in 1634 to serve as livestock grazing ground. The city charged each household six shillings to pay for "the Commonage." (It was Tax-achusetts even back then!) People also used the Common—to watch others being hanged at the gallows (like them curse'ed Quakers), for public meetings, and for military drills. The gallows were removed in 1817 and cow grazing was officially banned in 1830, around the time that urban cow ownership began falling out of fashion. In 1910, the Olmsted brothers oversaw a massive landscape renovation, designating Boston Common as the anchor of the "Emerald Necklace," a system of connected parks that winds through many of Boston's neighborhoods. Boston Common is the beginning of the Freedom Trail and the Black Heritage Trail.

Boston Common embodies the spirit of the city around it. Tourists, students, lunching suits, homeless Bostonians, and strolling older folks all share the park. On the lawn, squirrels and pigeons fight the latest chapter in their centuries-old gang war, while ducks enjoy free bread from park-goers.

Adjacent to the park is the Public Garden, former swampland that was filled in 1837. The nation's first botanical garden, the

Public Garden's French style of ornamental beds and paths stand in sharp contrast to the Common's informal, pastoral English layout.

Activities

The Freedom Trail is a 2.5-mile path through central Boston that passes by 16 of the city's historic landmarks. You'll find detailed route maps and information at the Visitor Center on Boston Common. Many of the sites along the red-painted line offer free admission, others "recommend" a donation, and some actually charge.

Frog Pond serves as a part-time ice-skating rink in winter and a splashing pool for children in summer. The smooth paved paths that traverse the Common make it ideal for cyclists, rollerbladers, scooters, joggers, and walkers. Throughout the year, the park hosts concerts, plays, political rallies, and other formal and informal gatherings.

How to Get There

Tremont, Beacon, Charles, Park, and Boylston Streets bound Boston Common. Parking is available, believe it or not, under the Common on Charles Street. By car, take the Mass Pike (I-90) to the Copley Square exit. Go straight at the off ramp onto Stuart Street. Take a left onto Charles Street by the Radisson Hotel.

By mass transit, take the Green Line or the Silver Line bus to the Boylston T stop at the corner of Boylston Street and Tremont Street. This stop is heavily used by tourists and locals, so expect crowds. Another equally bustling option is to take the Red Line or Green Line to the Park Street T stop at the northeastern edge of the Common.

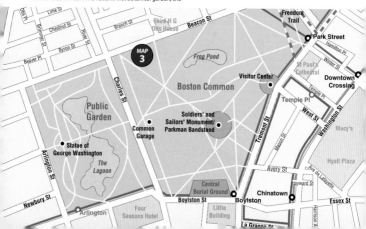

Freedom Trail & Black Heritage Trail

General Information

NFT Maps: 1, 2, 3, 4, 8
Address: Visitor Center, 147 Tremont Street, Boston, MA 02111
Freedom Trail: www.thefreedomtrail.org
Black Heritage Trail: www.afroammuseum.org/trail.htm
Walking Tours: Available daily during spring/summer/fall, 11 am, 12 pm, and 1 pm ($12 adults, $6 children, cash only)
Audio Tours: Available at the Visitor Center. $15 rental; 617-357-8300

Freedom Trail Overview

The Freedom Trail conveniently links several important colonial and post-colonial historical sites. Marked by a thick red path on the sidewalks, either painted or made of inlaid brick, the trail leads sightseers from the Visitor Center on Boston Common to the Charlestown Navy Yard on the opposite side of the Charles River. The 2.5-mile trek passes by 16 different sites, including the location of the Boston Massacre, Paul Revere's house, a couple of old cemeteries, and Bunker Hill. Walking tours leave the Visitor Center every 30 minutes and a complete trail walk usually lasts about 90 minutes. Audio tours are also available.

Trail Head: The Boston Common—America's oldest public park, 44-acre Boston Common is home to well-fed squirrels, pigeons, walkers, joggers, bikers, fat squirrels, dogs, ducks, and pigeons. See page 190.

1. **The State House**—The Massachusetts state government sits here in this gold-domed building on Beacon Hill—the oldest building in the city, in fact. Tour Hours: Mon–Fri 10 am–3:30 pm; 617-727-3676.

2. **Park Street Church**—The Evangelical Church was constructed in 1809 and has since stood as a testament to Bostonian faith. Lucky passersby may even be treated to a tirade being given from the outdoor pulpit. 617-523-3383. Traditional worship: 8:30 am and 11 am. Contemporary worship: 4 pm and 6 pm.

3. **Granary Burying Ground**—An epitaph here reads "Revere's Tomb" near the resting places of both John Hancock and Samuel Adams, along with a giant monolith paying tribute to the family of Boston-born Ben Franklin. This is the city's third-oldest burial ground. Open daily 9 am–5 pm.

4. **King's Chapel**—The chapel was built with the objective that it "would be the equal of any in England." Summer hours: Sun 2 pm–4 pm, Mon 9:30-4 pm, Tues-Wed 10 am–11:30 am and 1:30 pm– 4 pm, Thurs-Sat 10 am-4 pm; winter hours: Sat 10 am–4 pm. Entry is free but there's a $2 "suggested" donation. Services are held Wednesdays 12:15 pm and Sundays 9:45 am and 11 am; 617-227-2155.

King's Chapel Burying Ground—Older than the Granary and the final resting place of some of Boston's first settlers. Open daily, 9 am–5 pm.

5. **Benjamin Franklin's Statue/Site of the First Public School**—Boston Latin School, founded in 1635, is still open (but it's since moved to the Fenway). The old high school is considered the top public school in Boston. Sidewalks here are always packed with people going about their downtown routines, a reminder that Boston's past and present occupy the same small space.

6. **Old Corner Bookstore Building**—Built in 1712, this is one of Boston's oldest surviving structures. During the 19th century, the building housed the publisher of classic New England titles *Walden* and *The Scarlet Letter*.

7. **Old South Meeting House**—"Voices of Protest," a permanent exhibit in the house, speaks of generations who made history under one roof. Nov–Mar, 10 am–4 pm. Apr–Oct, 9:30 am–5 pm. Adults $5, students and seniors $4, children (6-18) $1, children under six free; 617-482-6439.

8. **Old State House**—The building's lush exterior will draw you inside, where the Bostonian Society houses a library along with its museum of Boston's past.
Library: Tues 11 am-4:30 pm, Wed and Thurs 10 am–4:30 pm, closed weekends and holidays. Daily use fee: non-members $10, college students $5.
Museum: 9 am–5 pm, extended hours in summer, closed New Year's Day, Thanksgiving, and Christmas Day. Adults $5, older adults (62+) $4, students (over 18) $4, children (6-18) $1; 617-720-1713.

9. **Site of the Boston Massacre**—Cobblestones now mark this historic site.

10. **Faneuil Hall**—Shopping mixed with history, with some eateries to boot. If you like touristy knick-knacks, this is the place to shop. Open daily 10 am–9 pm. Historical talks every thirty minutes, 9:30 am–4:30 pm. See page 196.

11. **Paul Revere House**—See how Boston's favorite patriot once lived. Keep in mind that when he lived there, the area wasn't filled with Italian restaurants. Apr 15–Oct 31, 9:30 am–5:15 pm. Nov 1–Apr 14, 9:30 am–4:15 pm. Closed Mondays in Jan–Mar and on Thanksgiving, Christmas Day, and New Year's Day. Adults $3, seniors and college students $2.50, children (5-17) $1; 617-523-2338.

12. **Old North Church**—It was on the Old North Church, the oldest church building in Boston, that two lanterns were placed the night before the battles at Lexington and Concord. As you may recall, it was "one if by land, two if by sea." The British took boats across the Charles to make their way towards the now-famous western villages, so two lanterns were hung. Winter hours: 9 am–5 pm daily. Summer hours: 9 am–6 pm daily; 617-523-6676.

13. **Copp's Hill Burying Ground**—The site began as a cemetery in the 1660s and was later used for public hangings (until the death penalty was outlawed in Massachusetts in 1984—or possibly even sooner than that). Open daily 9 am–5 pm.

14. **Bunker Hill Monument**—A 221-foot granite obelisk commemorates the Battle of Bunker Hill—the first major battle of the American Revolution. The monument sits atop Breed's Hill, where the misnamed battle actually took place. Exhibitions at the visitor's center explain how the battle came to be and how it was won. Hours: 9:30 am–4:30 pm daily; 617-242-5641.

15. **USS Constitution**—aka "Old Ironsides," America's oldest commissioned warship. Winter hours: Thurs–Sun, 10 am–3:50 pm. Summer hours: Tues-Sun: 10 am–3:50 pm. Tours depart every half hour; 617-242-5670. See Charlestown Navy Yard page 189.

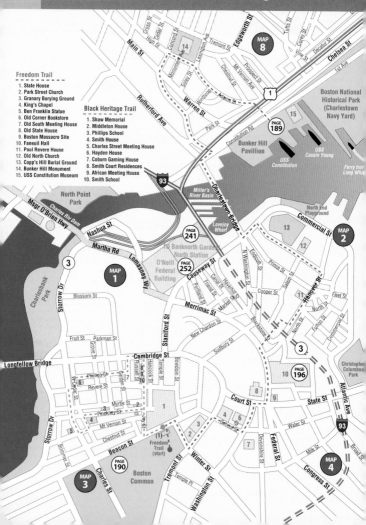

Freedom Trail & Black Heritage Trail

Freedom Trail

1. State House
2. Park Street Church
3. Granary Burying Ground
4. King's Chapel
5. Ben Franklin Statue
6. Old Corner Bookstore
7. Old South Meeting House
8. Old State House
9. Boston Massacre Site
10. Faneuil Hall
11. Paul Revere House
12. Old North Church
13. Copp's Hill Burial Ground
14. Bunker Hill Monument
15. USS Constitution Museum

Black Heritage Trail

1. Shaw Memorial
2. Middleton House
3. Phillips School
4. Smith House
5. Charles Street Meeting House
6. Hayden House
7. Coburn Gaming House
8. Smith Court Residences
9. African Meeting House
10. Smith School

Black Heritage Trail Overview

Running north from the State House, this trail recognizes the historical significance of Boston's African-American community. After the American Revolution, free blacks congregated in the area now known as the North Slope of Beacon Hill. In 1790, when the first federal census was taken, Massachusetts was the only state in the country to record no slaves. The historic homes on the Black Heritage Trail are private residences and are closed to the public, but the African Meeting House and the Abiel Smith School are open to visitors.

1. **Robert Gould Shaw and the 54th Regiment Memorial**—Located on Boston Common, this monument was built in 1897 in honor of the first all-black regiment that fought for the Union Army during the Civil War.

2. **George Middleton House**—(5-7 Pinckney St) George Middleton was the commander of an all-black military company during the Revolutionary War called the Bucks of America. His house, erected in 1797, is the oldest standing wooden structure on Beacon Hill.

3. **The Phillips School**—(Anderson & Pinckney Sts) One of the first Boston public schools to be integrated (in 1855) as a result of the historic court case *Roberts v. Massachusetts*, which opposed the racial segregation of the city's schools.

4. **John J. Smith House**—(86 Pinckney St) John J. Smith was born free in Virginia in 1820 and eventually moved to Boston where he opened a successful barbershop that catered to many wealthy white customers from all over the city. His shop served as a haven for anti-slavery debates and fugitive slaves.

5. **Charles Street Meeting House**—(Mt Vernon & Charles Sts) Built in 1807, the Charles Street Meeting House was originally the site of the segregated Third Baptist Church. After a failed attempt to desegregate the church, Timothy Gilbert and several other abolitionist sympathizers left to form the Free Baptist Church, the first integrated church in America.

6. **Lewis and Harriet Hayden House**—(66 Phillips St) Lewis and Harriet Hayden ran a boarding house out of their home, which was also a stop on the Underground Railroad. Lewis Hayden was an ardent African-American abolitionist and community leader who served as a delegate to the Republican Convention, fought for women's rights, and helped found the Museum of Fine Arts.

7. **John Coburn Gaming House**—(2 Phillips St) The site of one of the most lucrative Black-owned businesses in the city, the gaming house was built in 1843 and catered to Boston's white elite. John Coburn used the profits from the successful business to finance several abolitionist groups in the community, including the Massasoit Guards. Founded as an all-black military company to support the state's troops in case of war, the Guards also patrolled Beacon Hill to protect African-Americans from slave catchers.

8. **Smith Court Residences**—(3, 5, 7, 7A, & 10 Smith Ct) Five remaining wooden houses located on Beacon Hill's north slope were all purchased by middle-class African-Americans from white landowners.

9. **The African Meeting House**—(8 Smith Ct) Founded as a response to racial discrimination in Boston's religious communities, the African Meeting House remains the oldest standing Black church building in the country. The structure was built using labor and donations from the African-American community. It was used for religious services, as a safe haven for political discussion, and as a makeshift school for black children until the Abiel Smith School came into existence.

10. **Abiel Smith School**—(46 Joy St) Built in 1834 as the first schoolhouse in America to educate black school children, the Abiel Smith School was under-funded, overcrowded, and under-staffed. Substandant conditions led to *Roberts v. Massachusetts* and the desegregation of schools in 1855. Winter hours: 10 am–4 pm, Mon–Sat. Summer hours: 10 am–4 pm daily. Closed Thanksgiving, Christmas, and New Year's Day. Admission is free.

MAP 16

90

St Mary's St

Hawes St

Harvard St

St Paul St

Kent St

Beacon St

Fenway

Back Bay Fens

Prudential

Coolidge Corner

Riverway Park

Boylston St

Symphony

Summit Ave

Longwood

Riverway

Brookline Ave

Louis Pasteur St

Park Dr

Agassiz Rd

Fenway

Northeastern

Massachusetts Ave

Brandon Hill

BROOKLINE

Massachusetts Ave

Washington St

Aspinwall Ave

MAP 15

Museum

Huntington Ave

Longwood Med Area

Ruggles St

Ruggles

MAP 17

Brookline Village

Greenport

Brigham Cir

Brookline Hills

Fenwood Rd

Tremont St

Roxbury Crossing

Boylston St

Riverway

Malcolm X Blvd

Cypress St

Back of the Hill

Warren St

Olmsted Park

Willow Pond

Heath St

Heath St

Jackson Square

Ward's Pond

Centre St

Townsend St

Francis Parkman Dr

Jamaicaway

Huntington Ave

Perkins St

Columbus Ave

Quincy St

Jamaica Park

Jamaica Pond

Stony Brook

MAP 14

BOSTON

Centre St

Green St

Washington St

Pond St

Green Street

George R White Schoolboy Stadium

Walnut Ave

Pierpont Rd

Seaver St

• Main Gate

Franklin Park

Jewish War Veterans Dr

Glen Rd

Franklin Park Zoo

Columbia Rd

Arborway

Forest Hills

Centre St

Circuit Dr

Forest Hills St

William J Devine Golf Course

Dairy Rd

Arnold Arboretum

South St

Morton St

Scarboro Pond

Blue Hill Ave

MAP 31

Kilmer Park

Walter St

Bussey St

American Legion Hwy

Talbot Ave

MAP 30

Washington St

Hyde Park Ave

Forest Hills Cemetery

Walk Hill St

Franklin Field

General Information

NFT Maps: 14, 15, 16, 17, 30 & 31
Address: Two Brookline Pl, Brookline, MA 02445
Phone: 617-232-5374
Websites: www.emeraldnecklace.org
              www.cityofboston.gov/parks/necklace.asp

Overview

Known primarily for his work designing New York's Central Park, celebrated landscape architect Frederick Law Olmsted also created a beautiful string of Boston parks when he moved to Brookline in 1883. Olmsted's Necklace was designed as an uninterrupted five-mile walkway from Back Bay to Franklin Park, where Bostonians could stroll barefoot and without worry. The Necklace has been broken up over the years, both by the construction of the Casey Overpass near Franklin Park and by the conversion of the Riverway, Jamaicaway, and Arborway from pleasant carriage paths to major roads carrying highway-amounts of traffic. The city and conservation groups are putting together a "master plan" for the severed sections of the Necklace and together are trying to balance path restoration with traffic concerns. With the future construction of the Rose Kennedy Greenway where the Central Artery once stood, the idea is to link all of Boston's parks into an actual necklace.

Franklin Park

Spanning 500 acres, Franklin Park is the Necklace's largest park and was originally designed as a country retreat in the vein of Central Park in New York. Named after Benjamin Franklin, the park encompasses the Zoo (617-541-LION), one of the first public golf courses in the country (617-265-4084), 100 acres of woodland, and the seven-acre Scarboro Pond. The Franklin Park Zoo (not part of Olmsted's original plan), which opened in 1911, is home to the "Butterfly Landing," a butterfly enclosure open seasonally from June through September. The zoo made headlines in 2003, when adolescent gorilla "Little Joe" escaped from his enclosure—twice. The first time, he stayed on site. The second time, he ended up at a bus stop in Roxbury. Zoo entry: adults $9.50, children 5.50, seniors $8, half price the first Sat of each month; winter hours (Oct 1–Mar 31), 10 am–4 pm; summer hours, 10 am–5 pm weekdays, and 6 pm weekends and holidays; www.zoonewengland.com.

Arnold Arboretum

The oldest arboretum in the country, Arnold Arboretum is named after its financier, whaling tycoon and horticulturalist James Arnold. Visitors come primarily to stroll amongst the exotic greenery, which includes bonsai and lilac trees. Because Arnold left most of his estate to Harvard and the school uses the arboretum as a nature museum, it seems only fair for the city to allow the grand university to rent the land for just a dollar a year. Open every day until dusk, the visitor center is open 9 am–4 pm weekdays, 10 am–2 pm weekends (Nov-Feb); 9 am–4pm weekdays, 10 am–4 pm Sat, 12 pm–4 pm Sun, and closed holidays. Entry is free!

Jamaica Park

Wealthy Bostonites of yesteryear built their summer homes in this spot, called "the jewel in the Emerald Necklace" because of the 60-acre sparkling Jamaica Pond. The largest and purest body of water in Boston, the glacier-formed pond is fed by natural springs and is 90 feet deep in some places. The pond is so clean that it serves as a back-up city reservoir. What looks like a haunted house is actually Pinebank, the only building within the Emerald Necklace that pre-dates the park's creation. It sits in a state of disrepair and neglect, despite Boston Parks Department plans to protect the Victorian Gothic site from further deterioration. Joggers and dog-walkers share the 1.5 mile paved trail around the pond. Fishing is one of the most popular activities, and every year the City of Boston stocks the pond with trout, salmon, and indigenous pickerel, bass, hornpout, and perch. The boathouse rents canoes, sailboats, and rowboats, and, in winter, has a fireplace going. Around Halloween, the community organization Spontaneous Celebrations sponsors a lantern walk around the pond.

Olmsted Park

A joint project between the City of Boston and the Town of Brookline to link the two cities together, Olmsted Park showcases the landscape architect's unique design philosophy with a series of ponds and wooded paths that open onto expansive views that help you understand why Olmsted is the Boston Brahmin equivalent of a rock star. (The city boasts at least one Olmsted impersonator.) A great feature of the park is the human-made Muddy River, currently the site of a major dredging project. Leverett, Willow, and Ward's Ponds are more secluded and less crowded than nearby Jamaica Pond. A new bike/pedestrian path system on the Brookline side from Jamaica Pond to Boylston Street (Route 9) was recently completed.

Riverway Park

Hidden below the busy street level is the narrowest park in the system and also the only one that is completely human-made. Riverway lies in the valley of the Muddy River (the boundary between Boston and Brookline) and features several small islands, wooded paths, and pretty footbridges. Its steep tree-lined banks protect visitors from the city bustle above. Footbridges connect the Boston and Brookline sides, but these are poorly lit at night.

Back Bay Fens

Olmsted's first phase of the Necklace in 1878, the Back Bay Fens was a sewage-infested saltwater marsh on the verge of extinction when he stepped in, transforming the swampy area into a meandering brackish creek. The creation of the Charles River Dam in 1910 turned the Fens into a freshwater marsh. Today, the Fens has quite a few notable attractions, including recreation facilities, the Kelleher Rose Garden, War Memorials, and the Victory Garden. The Victory Garden was created in 1941, in an effort to grow extra food for troops, and is currently tended to by local green thumbs who shell out $20 per year to maintain personal plots. A former parking lot, the western end of the Fens was recently converted into green space. But it's a notorious local fact that more than mere gardening takes place on the grounds—think George Michael.

General Information

NFT Map: 2
Phone: 617-523-1300
Websites: www.faneuilhallmarketplace.com
    www.faneuilhall.com
    www.cityofboston.gov/freedomtrail/
    faneuilhall.asp
    www.nps.gov/bost/Faneuil_Hall.htm

Faneuil Hall

Faneuil Hall was built as a food and produce market/meeting hall by Boston's wealthiest merchant, Peter Faneuil, in 1742. It's a historically poignant section of commercial property: at this location, Samuel Adams rallied for independence (prior to his interest in brewing beer), the doctrine of "no taxation without representation" was established, and George Washington and company celebrated our country's freedom. In later years it was the site of abolitionist rallies. It's still both a commercial spot and a meeting place used by campaigning politicians, with shops in the basement and the first floor, the Great Hall on the second, and a museum on the third.

Since its inception, the Faneuil Hall Marketplace has been a major shopping arena, and it's now stocked with 100 stores and pushcarts and 17 sit-down restaurants as well as a gastronomic orgy of a food hall. The marketplace alone attracts more than 12 million visitors a year and hosts numerous events and shows. Local talent includes jugglers, mimes (yes, those, too), magicians, bands, and the occasional strolling Ben Franklin. If you're looking to be entertained while you shop, Faneuil Hall is your place.

Four buildings make up the marketplace: Faneuil Hall, Quincy Market, North Market, and South Market. Touristy and crowded at times, it's still one of the best and most visually pleasing places to buy souvenirs, shop in a mall-like environment, and try any number of local dishes. Standard mall stores occupy most of North and South Market, while local vendors and souvenir slingers can be found in the Hall or at pushcarts in Quincy Market. The Hall and all pushcarts are open Monday through Saturday from 10 am to 9 pm, and from noon to 6 pm on Sundays. Shopping hours in the other marketplaces vary by vendor. The Hall and all shops are closed on Christmas.

Quincy Market

Located directly behind Faneuil Hall, Quincy Market is where you go to chow down. The food court runs the length of the building and far exceeds a typical food court in both variety and quality of offerings. Whatever you crave, it's hard to go away disappointed. It is usually crowded at lunch, especially during the field trip and leaf-peeping seasons, so avoid peak hours if you're in a rush. Various sit-down bars and restaurants and pushcarts encircle the food court around the perimeter. The North Market and South Market, which stand on either side

of Quincy Market, have other places to sit for a meal, including the still-there Durgin Park.

Like many places in Boston, Quincy Market is built on landfill in what used to be Boston Harbor. Unlike other sections, when you're in Quincy Market, you're standing on bones. The butchers who used to occupy the wharves behind Faneuil Hall would let their unusable animal parts pile up, creating a sanitation nightmare. Then someone had the bright idea of throwing the bones in the water, which eventually helped fill the wharf area and allowed for the construction of Quincy Market.

Museum

Ancient and Honorable Artillery Company Museum; 617-227-1638; www.ahacsite.org

Located on Faneuil Hall's third floor, the museum and library showcase the history of the Ancient and Honorable Artillery Company. The oldest military organization in the US (and third-oldest in the world), this august body was established as the Military Company of Boston in 1637 and still holds military drills and participates in various ceremonial events. The museum proudly displays the company's artifacts. It is a unique collection that is well worth a visit for military and history buffs. The museum is open Monday–Friday; 9 am-3:30 pm.

How to Get There—Driving

From the south, take I-93 N to Exit 23 ("Government Center"). Upon exiting, follow the signs to the Aquarium. At Surface Road, turn left. Faneuil Hall will be on the right-hand side.

From the west, take the Mass Pike (I-90) to Exit 24B (I-93 N). From I-93, take Exit 23 ("Government Center") and follow the directions above.

From the north, take I-93 S to Exit 24A toward Government Center. Stay to the right, and follow the signs for Faneuil Hall. Immediately off the exit, turn right. Faneuil Hall will be directly in front of you.

Parking

There are over 10,000 parking spaces within a two-mile radius of Faneuil Hall. The 75 State Street garage near the intersection of State Street and Broad Street offers a $2 discount on weekdays with store validation, and $10 parking after 5 pm daily and on selected holidays with store validation.

How to Get There—Mass Transit

To get to Faneuil Hall Marketplace, take the T's Green Line to Government Center or Haymarket, the Blue Line to State or Aquarium, or the Orange Line to State or Haymarket.

Shopping

A Hat for Every Head (pushcart)
Ann Taylor
Bill Rodgers Running Center
Boston Logos (pushcart)
Boxers To Go (pushcart)
Celtic Weavers
Coach
Cuoio
Custom Caps
Fantasy Island
Harvest Fare (pushcart)
Head Games (pushcart)
La Cloche (pushcart)
Life is a Highway (pushcart)
Merry Trading Company (pushcart)
Nightshirts To Go (pushcart)
Nine West
Ocean Man (pushcart)
Orient Express (pushcart)
Orvis
Sacs (pushcart)
Sea Boston USA (pushcart)
Sock It To Me
Ulyssion Imports
Urban Outfitters
Victoria's Secret

Goods & Gifts

African Collections (pushcart)
ALFA Designs
Arman Time Company (pushcart)
Art for 'Em (pushcart)
Artists See Boston (pushcart)
Batik Adventure
Best of Boston
Boston Campus Gear
Boston Pewter Company
The Boston Sun Spot
Bostonian Society Museum Shop
Build-A-Bear Workshop
Camera Center
Cheers Gift Shop
The Christmas Dove
Conversations
Crabtree & Evelyn
Crate & Barrel
Destination Boston
Discovery Channel Store
Every Bead of My Heart (pushcart)
Exotic Flowers
Funusual
Gateway News
Geoclassics
Godiva Chocolatier
Happy Hangups
Henri's Glassworks
Illusions
Local Charm
Magnetic Chef (pushcart)

The Monkey Bar (pushcart)
Museum of Fine Arts Store
Musically Yours (pushcart)
Narnia
Origins
Scottie Connection
Sluggers Upper Deck Kiosk
(pushcart)
Stuck on Stickpins (pushcart)
Sunglass Hut & Watch Station
Swatch
Teeny Billboards (pushcart)
Touch of Irish (pushcart)
Wit Crafts (pushcart)
Yankee Candle Company

Food

A La Carte
Al Mercantino
Ames Plow Tavern
Aris Barbeque
Bangkok Express
Bistany International
Bombay Club
Boston & Maine Fish Co
Boston Chipyard
Boston Chowda
Boston Pretzel
Boston Rocks
Brown Derby Deli
Carol Ann's Bake Shop
Cheers Café
Columbo Frozen Yogurt Shoppe
Dick's Last Resort
Durgin Park Restaurant
El Paso Enchilada
Fisherman's Net
Jen Lai Rice & Noodle Company
Joey's Gelateria
Kilvert & Forbes
Kingfish Hall
La Pastaria
McCormick & Schmick's
Megumi
The Dog House
North End Bakery
Philadelphia Steak & Hoagie
Piccolo Panini
Pizzeria Regina
Plaza III, the Kansas City Steak House
The Prime Shoppe
Salty Dog Seafood Grill & Bar
Slugger's Dugout
Starbucks
Steve's Greek Cuisine
Steve's Ice Cream & Fudge
Ueno Sushi
Walrus and the Carpenter
West End Strollers
Zuma's Tex Mex Café

Bars & Entertainment

Cheers
Comedy Connection
Ned Devine's Irish Pub
Parris
Sam's Café
The Monkey Bar

Services

BosTix Ticket Booth
Faneuil Hall Marketplace
Information
City View Trolley Tours

Nearby Bars

The Atrium Lounge
Bell in Hand Tavern
Black Rose
Dockside Restaurant & Bar
Hennessey's
McFadden's
Kitty O'Shea's
The Rack
The Place
Purple Shamrock
Sissy K's
Union Oyster House
Vertigo

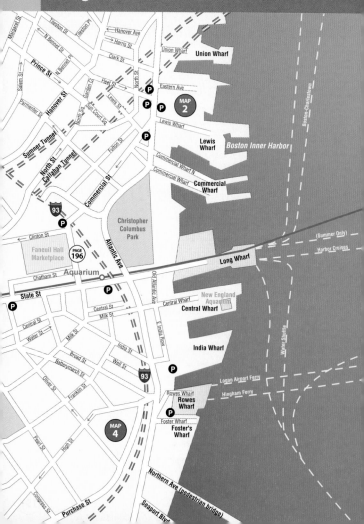

Overview

Originally named Boston Pier, Long Wharf juts into Boston Harbor at the bottom of State Street, while Rowes Wharf is farther south, near Broad Street. In the 1700s, Long Wharf extended more than one-third of a mile into Boston Harbor, but the dumping of urban landfill has resulted in a significant portion of the pier being surrounded by land rather than water. Purportedly the oldest continually operating wharf in the US, Long Wharf is the site of the Chart House, the oldest existing pre-Revolutionary War warehouse in Boston.

Attractions

During the warmer months, stop by the Landing Bar on Long Wharf for a drink in the sunshine. It's the perfect place to hang out and catch a Red Sox game on television after work or when you're waiting to board a ferry.

The New England Aquarium is located at nearby Central Wharf and operates an IMAX Theatre next door. The Aquarium allows scientists and researchers to study marine and aquatic habitats and to educate visitors about conservation issues. One of the most exciting events to participate in is a "release party," when an animal is returned to its natural habitat. Hours: 9 am–5 pm weekdays (6 pm summer), 9 am–6 pm weekends (7 pm summer). Closed Thanksgiving and Christmas Day. Adults $17.95, children (3-11) $9.95. www.neaq.org; 617-973-5200.

There are several whale-watching excursions that leave from the wharves. Whale-watching season starts in April and ends in the fall.

- Voyager III • Central Wharf • 617-973- 5206
- Boston Harbor Cruises • 63 Long Wharf • 617-227-4321
- Massachusetts Bay Lines Whale Watch • 60 Rowes Wharf • 617-542-8000

Long Wharf is also where you catch the Harbor Express boat to the Boston Harbor Islands. There are 34 islands in all, six of which are staffed and serviced by a free boat shuttle from the headquarters on Georges Island. These islands are still underutilized by locals and unfrequented by tourists. They vary in size, but most offer trails, old forts, diverse flora and fauna, camping (on Peddocks, Grape, Lovells, and Bumpkin), and great views of Boston and the harbor. Spectacle Island's past as a former quarantine island, glue factory, and garbage dump has been covered over with rubble from the Big Dig and transformed into an eco-friendly recreation spot. It is set to open in 2006. Of course, it was set to open in 2005, as well. The islands open seasonally, so check the website, www.bostonislands.com, or call 617-223-8666.

If you're prone to seasickness, or if watching whales isn't your bag, the newly-renovated Christopher Columbus Park is a short walk from Long Wharf. The playground for the little ones is top-notch, and its famous rose garden is dedicated to Rose Fitzgerald Kennedy. It's also a good viewing spot for the fireworks on First Night. Next door is Tia's, a popular after-work meat market bar in the summer.

Architecture

Rowes Wharf features a commanding arch that looks out onto Boston Harbor. The Wharf is a mixed-use complex that has won numerous design awards, including the Urban Land Institute's "Award for Excellence." The complex is shared by the Boston Harbor Hotel, 100 luxury condominiums, and offices. There is a little-known observation area on the ninth floor named the Forester Rotunda, offering views of both the city and harbor. Though not advertised, you can go through the hotel to gain access. In the summertime, a floating dock hosts outdoor concerts and movies under the stars.

Ferries

Both Long Wharf and Rowes Wharf serve as ferry terminals for the MBTA. F1 transports people to and from Rowes Wharf and Hingham Shipyard. F2 and F2H stop at Long Wharf, Logan Airport, and the Fore River Shipyard in Quincy. F2H also has limited service to Pemberton Point in Hull. F4, which travels to the Charlestown Navy Yard, also uses the Long Wharf terminus. The Harbor Express to Georges Island also leaves from Long Wharf. For more information on ferries, see page 254. For schedules and maps, go to www.mbta.com/traveling_t/schedules_boats.asp, or call 617-222-5000.

How to Get There—Driving

To Long Wharf from the north, take I-93 S, and get off at Exit 24A (Government Center/Aquarium). Follow signs to the Aquarium. From the south, take Exit 23 (Government Center) and follow signs to the Aquarium.

To Rowes Wharf from the north, take I-93 S and get off at Exit 23 (aim for South Station). Turn left onto Congress Street and immediately left onto Atlantic Avenue. The wharf is on the right, two blocks past the intersection of Congress Street and Atlantic Avenue.

From the south, take I-93 N to Exit 20, and follow signs to South Station. Once you drop onto Atlantic Avenue, proceed through the Congress Street intersection and drive two blocks. The wharf will be on your right.

Parking

There is very limited street parking in the area, so if you want to forego driving around to find a free spot, you should try one of the many parking garages that are all within walking distance of the various wharves. Parking fees can cost $25 or more, depending on how long you stay, though there are usually discounted rates on weekends and after 5 pm on weekdays. If you're willing to shell out the cash, here are a few nearby garages:

- The Rowes Wharf building features an underground discounted parking garage with an entrance on Atlantic Avenue.
- Harbor Garage at the Aquarium, 70 East India Row; 617-367-3847
- 75 State Street Garage, 75 State St (entrance on Broad St); 617-742-7275
- Dock Square Garage, 200 State St; 617-367-4373
- Laz Parking, 290 Commercial St; 617-367-6412
- Fetz Parking, 269 Commercial St; 617-367-1681
- 2 Atlantic Avenue Garage, 2 Atlantic Ave; 617-854-3365
- Standard Parking, 28 Atlantic Ave; 617-227-3713

How to Get There—Mass Transit

To Long Wharf, take the T's Blue Line to the Aquarium stop. To Rowes Wharf, take either the Blue Line to Aquarium or the Red Line to South Station.

Overview

Originally one of the least fashionable streets of Back Bay, Newbury Street has undergone quite a transformation, morphing into Boston's most popular shopping area and a good place to hang out and strut your stuff.

A beautiful stretch of real estate featuring late 19th- and early 20th-century architecture, Newbury Street runs eight blocks from the Public Garden west to Massachusetts Avenue. The cross streets run alphabetically from east to west, starting with Arlington, then Berkeley, Clarendon, etc. Stores pack the buildings along Newbury, which were originally designed for residential use, making for a lot of oddly shaped, quirky boutiques. Featuring shops for all ages and tax brackets, from the upper-class Armani to the youthful Urban Outfitters, there are countless ways to spend money here.

In the summertime, the cafés spill out onto the sidewalk, providing a nice environment for those who want to sit and relax, and increased difficulty for those who want to walk at regular speeds. For people-watching, Newbury Street is the best spot in Boston. A veritable human car crash, you get to see the "hippest" elements of every age group, from 80-year-olds to eight-year-olds, interacting and fighting for space on the same small sidewalk.

For an updated list of shops, see www.newbury-st.com. For a great take on the social aspects (such as they are) of Newbury Street, check out Macy Raymond's essay at www.notfortourists.com/boston.aspx.

History

The whole of Back Bay was swampland until about 1870, when workers completed a massive filling project. As a result, Back Bay is the only neighborhood in Boston to benefit from a modern concept called "urban planning." Streets actually cross each other at 90-degree angles, and at no point is there a traffic circle or an eight-way intersection. Unfortunately, fluctuations in the water table are rotting the wooden planks on which most of the area's structures sit. The result: Back Bay is sinking. It seems that Back Bay residents have more to worry about than the Hynes being converted into a casino.

The architecture on Newbury Street is fairly uniform, since most of the development occurred during the same half-century. Emmanuel Church, designed by Alexander Estey in 1862, was the first building completed on Newbury Street. The Church of the Covenant, built in 1865, houses some spectacular stained glass windows. Its Emmaus Window shines even in the dimmest of lights.

How to Get There—Driving

Newbury Street is easy to get to. From I-93 take Exit 26 to Storrow Drive. Take the exit for Arlington Street, and proceed up Arlington until you hit Newbury Street (right turn only, one-way). Newbury Street lies between Boylston Street and Commonwealth Avenue, so if you get twisted around use these larger streets as landmarks.

How to Get There—Mass Transit

From the T's Green Line you can get off at the Arlington stop, the Copley stop, or the Hynes/ICA stop. Note that the Green Line's E train breaks off the main track at Copley, so use the B, C, or D train to get to Hynes/ICA.

All addresses are on Newbury Street

Clothing

9 Months · 286 · maternity wear
A Pea in the Pod · 10 · maternity wear
Agnes b · 172 · French clothing for men and women
Akris Boutique · 16 · shoe store
Alan Bilzerian · 34 · designer clothes
Alan Rouleau Couture · 73 · custom tailoring
Aldo · 180 · shoes and leather goods
Allen Edmonds · 36 · shoes and cedar products
American Apparel · 138 · men's and women's clothing
American Eagle Outfitters · 201 · youth clothes
Ana Hernandez Bridal · 165 · bridal boutique
Ann Taylor · 18 · women's clothes
Aria Bridesmaids · 39 · wedding clothing
Army Barracks · 328 · military duds
Banana Republic · 28 · men's and women's clothing
Barbour by Peter Elliot · 134 · men's and women's clothing
BCBG Max Azaria · 71 · women's designer clothing
Bella Bridesmaid · 163 · wedding clothing
Benetton · 140 · men's and women's clothing
Best of Scotland · 115 · sweaters at mill prices
Betsey Johnson · 201 · designer clothes
Betsy Jenney of Boston · 114 · women's unusual designer clothes
Boutique Giorgio Armani · 22 · clothes

Boutique Longchamp · 139A · French handbags
Brooks Brothers · 46 · classy clothing for men and women
Burberry Limited · 2 · clothes for men and women
Calypso · 114 · women's clothing
Camper Shoes · 139 · shoes
Chanel · 5 · clothing and accessories
Chico's · 12 · women's clothing
Clifford Michael Design · 73 · women's clothing, wedding clothing
Cole Haan · 109 · men's and women's clothing
Cuoio · 115 · European shoes for women
Designer Shoes · 125 · designer shoes
Diesel · 339 · clothing
DKNY · 37 · clothing
Dress · 339 · women's clothing
Easter Wings · 244 · women's clothing
Ecco Newbury Street · 216 · shoes
Emporio Armani · 210-214 · men's and women's clothing
Ermenegildo Zegna · 39 · clothes
Fiandaca · 73 · couture clothing
Flair Bridesmaid Boutique · 129 · wedding clothing
Footstock · 133 · shoes
French Connection · 206 · men's and women's clothing
Gap · 201 · clothing
GapKids · 201 · children's clothing
Giani Versace Boutique · 12 · women's clothing, accessories and shoes
Gi Pore · 176 · women's clothing
Guess? · 80 · clothing
Hempest · 207 · hemp clothing
I Boutique · 251 · men's and women's clothing
In the Pink · 133 · women's clothing

Intermix · 186 · women's clothing
Jasmine Sola Shoes · 329 · shoes
Jessica McClintock · 201 · women's cocktail attire
John Fluevog Shoes · 302 · shoes
Joseph Ribkoff · 224 · women's clothing
Karmaloop Boston · 160 · men's and women's clothing
Kate Spade Shoes · 117 · shoes, purses, etc.
Kenneth Cole Productions · 128 · shoes
L'Elite · 276 · bridal boutique
La Boutique Reine · 134 · bridal boutique
Lester Harry's · 115 · bedding, children's and infant's clothing
Lingerie Studio · 264 · lingerie
LF Stores · 353 · women's clothing
Lucky Brand · 229 · denim
Luna Boston · 286 · accessories and handbags
Marc Jacobs · 81 · fashion
Matsu · 259 · handbags
Max Mara · 69 · women's clothing
Mudo · 205 · clothing
Nanette Lepore · 119 · women's clothing
Niketown · 200 · everything Nike
Oilily · 31 · Dutch clothing for women and children
Oilily Women's · 32 · women's clothes
Patagonia · 346 · clothing for the great outdoors
Petit Bateau · 171 · women's clothing
Queen Bee · 85 · women's clothing
Ralph Lauren · 95 · clothing
Relic · 116 · men's and women's clothing
Renaissance Room · women's clothing

All addresses are on Newbury Street

Clothing–*continued*

Riccardi Boutique • 116 • clothing
Rockport • 83 • shoes
Rugby Ralph Lauren • 342 • men's and women's clothing
Sean Store • 154 • men's clothing
Second Time Around Collections • 176 & 252 • new and consignment clothes
Serenella • 134 • European women's clothes
Sigrid Olsen • 141B • women's clothing
Stel's • 334 • men's and women's clothing, accessories and jewelry
Steve Madden • 324A • shoes and handbags
Stil • 170 • women's clothing
Sumner Chas • 16 • women's clothing
Thom Brown of Boston • 337 • shoes
Toppers • 230 • hats
Urban Outfitters • 361 • clothing
Vera Wang • 253 • wedding clothing
Whim Boutique • 253 • men's and women's clothing
Zrinka • 164 • women's clothing

Restaurants

29 Newbury • 29 • new American food
Ben & Jerry's • 174 • ice cream
The Capital Grille • 359 • steak house
Charley's Eating & Drinking Saloon • 284 • American food
Ciao Bella • 240 • Italian food
Daisy Buchanan's • 240 • bar
Dunkin' Donuts • 335 • donuts
Emack & Bolio's Ice Cream • 290 • ice cream
Emporio Armani Café • 214 • Italian cuisine
Espresso Royale Café • 286 • coffee house
The Jewel of Newbury • 254 • Italian food
JP Licks Ice Cream • 352 • local ice cream shop
Kashmir • 279 • Indian food
L'Aroma Café • 85 • coffee shop
Luigi and Roscoe's • American food
Newbury Pizza & Subs • 225 • pizza & subs
Piattini Wine Café • 226 • Italian food
Shino Express Sushi • 144 • Japanese food
Sonsie • 327 • international cuisine
Starbucks • 350 • coffee shop
Stephanie's on Newbury • 190 • American food
Steve's • 316 • Greek-American food
Tapeo • 268 • Spanish food
Tealuxe • 108 • tea bar
Thai Basil • 132 • Thai food

Wisteria House • 264 • Chinese-American cuisine
The Wrap • 247 • wraps and smoothies

Services

30 Newbury Spa • 30 • skin care, hair removal, hair salon
350 Newbury Tan • 350 • tanning
Acru Salon • 167 • beauty salon
Alexander's Salon • 163 • beauty salon
Annie Bulman Salon • 207 • hair salon
Anthony Pino Salon • 299 • hair salon
Avanti Salon • 11 • hair and skin care
Back Bay Framery and Photo • 303 • framing and photo finishing
Back Bay Hair Designs • 291 • hair salon
Bang & Olufsen • 30 • home audio/video systems
Beaucage Salon • 71 • salon for men and women
Beauty Rules • 274 • hair salon
BeBe Nail and Skin Salon • 154 • skin care, nail care
Bella Sante • 39 • day spa
BLU Salon on Newbury • 118 • hair salon
Boston Professional Teeth Whitening Spa • 75 • teeth whitening
Cellular One • 222 • mobile phone communications
Cherry Market • 349 • grocer
Christopher J Hawes Color Design Group • 36 • hair colorists
Cititan Baron's of Boston • 316 • tanning
Condom World • 332 • sexual novelties
Daryl Christopher Limited • 37 • beauty salon
Dekwa Elements of Hair • 132 • feng shui-inspired hair salon
DeLuca's Market • 239 • grocery store
Deuxieme Salon • 235 • hair salon
Diego • 143 • hair and nail services
Eclipse Salon Gallery • 164 • beauty salon
Elizabeth Grady Skin Care Salon • 11 • skin care
Enzo & Company • 135 • hair salon, skin care, nail care
Erez Levanon Salon • 69 • hair salon, nail care
Everbare Laser Hair Removal • 10 • laser hair removal
Fenway Sportszone • 306 • sports memorabilia
For Eyes Optical Co. • 222A • eyeglass store
G Spa Inc. • 35 • day spa, hair salon
Giuliano, The Spa for Beauty & Wellness • 338 • spa
Gorgeous Nails on Newbury • 245 • nail care
HairColorXperts • 297 • hair salon
Highlights Hair Salon • 286 • hair salon

Hollywood Nail and Skin Salon • 253 • day spa, skin care, nail care, hair removal
Hot Gossip • 207 • salon
I Soci Salon • 8 • beauty salon
James Joseph Salon • 168 & 30 • salon
James Patrick Salon • 121 • salon
Jean-Pierre Salon • 116 • salon
Jennifer's Nail & Skin Care • 224 • nail care, hair removal
Jerel Roberts Salon • 138 • hair coloring and styling
John Lewis • 97 • gold and silver craftsmen
Johnson Paint Company • 355 • art supplies
Jordan the Tailor • 271 • tailor
Kang's Corner Newbury Street • 314 • smoke shop, etc
Kosmetika European Skin Care • 77 • skin care
L'Atelier Salon • 174 • salon
La Tete Coiffure • 221 • salon
Laser Skin Center Medical Spa • 119 • skin care, hair removal
Laura's Nails & Spa • 215 • day spa, skin care, nail care, hair removal
Lauren's Nails and Skin Salon • 164 • nails and skin salon
Les Amis • 91 • salon
Mario Russo Salon at 9 Newbury • 45 • salon
Mechanique • 115 • salon
Mia's Nail Salon • 168 • manicures
Michaud Cosmetics • 69 • eyebrow shaping and cosmetics
Newbury Electrology • 271 • permanent hair removal
Newbury Natural Nails • 247 • nail salon
Newbury Tailoring Company • 129 • tailoring and alterations
Newbury Street Cingular Customer Center • 222 • mobile phone communications
Nora's Convenience Store • 303 • convenience store
The North Face • 326 • outdoor apparel and gear
Oasis Hair Salon • 9 • salon and spa
Peter & Yerem Hair • 205 • salon
Pierre Deux • 111 • French interior design
Pour Moi Skin & Body Salon • 105 • day spa
Rachel's Makeup & Eyebrow Studio • 176 • make-up, hair removal
Richard-Joseph Hair • 164 • salon
Roger E Lussier • 168 • framing
Safar Coiffures • 235 • salon
The Salon at 10 Newbury • 10 • salon
Salon 350 • 350 • hair salon
Salon Acote • 132 • men's and women's hairstyling
Salon Luiz • 115 • salon

Salon Marc Harris · 30 · hair salon
Salon Monet · 176 · hair salon
Salon Nordic Skin Care · 221 · skin care
Salon Persona · 301 · salon
Salon Pini · 231 · salon
Salon Red & Spa · 144A · hair salon, skin care, nail care
Salon Trio · 115 · nail care, hair removal
Secret Garden · 338 · florist
See · 125 · eyeglass store
Sleek Medspa · 228 · skin care, hair removal
Sprint-PCS Wireless · 330 · mobile phone communications
Starr Hair Studio · 114 · salon
Stephan Coiffeur · 305 · salon
Studio Tan · 350 · tanning
T-Mobile · 118 · mobile phone communications
Tanorama · 226 · tanning
Thy Nails & Skin Care Salon · 173 · nail care, hair removal
Town's Nails · 236 · nail care
UMI · 75 · salon
Vidal Sassoon · 14 · salon
Violet Skin Boutique · 257 · day spa, skin care, nail care
Wellesley Optical · 216 · eyeglass store
Winston Flowers · 131 · florist

Gifts & Miscellaneous

1154 Lill Studio · 220 · handbags
A Touch of France Gallery · 173 · art gallery
Acme Fine Art · 38 · bought and sold modern American art
Agatha Paris · 127 · jewelry
Alfred J. Walker Fine Art · 162 · art gallery
Alpha Gallery Inc. · 38 · art gallery
Appleton's · 134 · over 150 artists showcased
Arden Gallery · 129 · art gallery
Atelier Janiye · 165 · jewelry
Axelle Fine Arts · 91 · art gallery
Back Bay Estate Jewelers · 129 · antique jewelry
Back Bay Oriental Rugs · 154 · rugs
Barbara Krakow Gallery · 10 · art gallery
Bauer Wines Spirits · 330 · liquor store
Beadworks · 167 · make your own jewelry
Bellezza Home and Garden · 129 · Italian ceramics
Beth Urdang Gallery · 14 · art gallery
Bliss · 121 · home furnishings, cooking and dining
Boston Beat Records · 279 · record store
Brodney Antiques & Jewelry · 145 · antiques and jewelry
Buddenbrooks Fine & Rare Books · 31 · bookstore

Caravan International · 219 · gift shop
Cartier · 40 · jewelry
Chase Gallery · 129 · art gallery
Childs Gallery · 169 · art gallery
Comenos Fine Arts · 9 · art gallery
Commonwealth Fine Art · 236 · art gallery
CoSo Gallery's Gallery · 158 · art gallery
Diptyque · 123 · French perfumery
Domain Home Fashions · 7 · furniture
dona flor · 246 · home ceramics
Dorfman Jewelers · 24 · jewelry
DTR Modern Galleries · 167 · art gallery
Dyansen Gallery · 132 · art gallery
Erwin Pearl · 4 · jewelry
European Watch Co. · 232 · watch repair and shop
Felicia's Cosmetics · 314 · cosmetics
Firefly Jewelry and Gifts · 270 · jewelry and gift shop
Firestone and Parson · 8 · antique jewelry
Fresh · 121 · bath products
Galerie d'Orsay · 33 · art gallery
Gallery NAGA · 67 · art gallery
Guido Frame Studio · 118 · ready-to-frame prints
The Guild of Boston Artists · 162 · art gallery
Hope · 302 · unique gift shop
Howard Yezerski Gallery · 14 · art gallery
International Poster Gallery · 205 · poster art gallery
International Rugs · 171 · home furnishings
Jaboola · 291 · jewelry
Judi Rotenberg Gallery · 130 · art gallery
Judy Ann Goldman Fine Art · 14 · art gallery
Karyatis Greek Antiquity · 172 · jewelry
Kidder Smith Gallery · 131 · art gallery
Kiehl's · 112 · beauty products
Kinkade at Camelot · 221 · art gallery
Kitchen Arts · 161 · kitchen tools
Kitty World · 279 · Hello Kitty heaven
Knit and Needlepoint · 11 · crafts and sewing supplies
L'Attitude Gallery Sculpture Garden · 218 · art gallery
Lanoue Fine Art · 160 · art gallery
Lavender Home & Table · 173 · home and garden, bedding, antiques
Lush Cosmetics · 166 · beauty products
Madura Company · 144 · home furnishings, bedding
Marquit Andrea Fine Arts · 38 · art gallery
Mayan Weavers · 268 · Native American crafts
Mercury Gallery · 8 · art gallery
Miller Block Gallery · 14 · art gallery

Newbury Comics · 332 · music and video store
Newbury Fine Arts Gallery · 29 · art gallery
Newbury Yarns · 164 · crafts and sewing supplies
Nielsen Gallery · 179 · art gallery
O & Company · 161 · olive oil store
O'Brien Stephen B · 268 · art gallery
Pageo · 33 · Jewelry
Pepper Gallery · 38 · art gallery
Poggenpohl Boston Showroom · 135 · designer kitchens
Pottery Barn · 122 · home décor
Pratesi Linens · 110 · bed and bath linens
Prem-La · 211 · home and garden
Pucker Gallery · 171 · art gallery
Q Optical · 287 · glasses and sunglasses
Remedix · 299 · beauty products
Richardson-Clarke Gallery · 38 · art gallery
Robert Klein Gallery · 38 · art gallery
Robert Marc Newbury Street · 35 · glasses and sunglasses
Royka's Fine Arts Antiques Gallery · 213 · antiques
SAC Gallery · 175 · art gallery
Sajonian Sarkis · 273 · jewelry
Selletto · 244 · garden-inspired home décor
Shambala Tibet · 270 · Tibetan artifacts
Shu Uemura · 130 · beauty products
Simon Pearce Glass · 115 · glassware
Small Pleasures · 142 · jewelry
So Good Jewelry · 349 · jewelry
Solstice · 168 · glasses and sunglasses
St. George Gallery · 245 · art gallery
Sugar Heaven · 218 · candy
Sunglass Hut International · 182 · sunglasses store
Teuscher Chocolates of Switzerland · 230 · chocolates
Time & Time Again · 273 · watch store
Timeless Teas · 85 · tea
Trident Booksellers and Café · 338 · bookstore and café
Victoria Munroe Fine Art · 179 · art gallery
Virgin Megastore · 360 · music and video store
VOSE Galleries of Boston Inc. · 238 · art gallery
Watch Boston · 217 · jewelry
Waterworks · 103 · bathroom accessories
Wavetime Watch · 273 · watch store
Zoe · 279 · home décor

Parking Garages

Danker Donohue Garage · 341
Fitz Inn Auto Parks · 149

Boston Convention & Exhibition Center

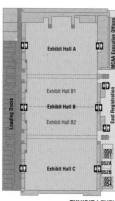

EXHIBIT LEVEL

Exhibit Hall A

Exhibit Hall B1

Exhibit Hall B

Exhibit Hall B2

Exhibit Hall C

MCAA Executive Offices

East Registration

Loading Docks

050
051
052A
052B
053
054

MAP 10

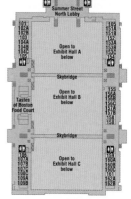

MEETING LEVEL 1

Entrance Plaza

Summer Street
North Lobby

Open to
Exhibit Hall A
below

Skybridge

Tastes
of Boston
Food Court

Open to
Exhibit Hall B
below

Skybridge

Open to
Exhibit Hall C
below

101
102A
102B
103
104A
104B
104C
105

106
107A
107B
107C
108
109A
109B

105
151A
151B
152
153A
153B
153C
154

155
156A
156B
156C
157A
157B
158
159

159
160A
160B
160C
161
162A
162B

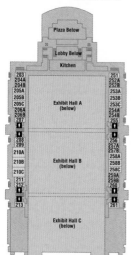

MEETING LEVEL 2

Plaza Below

Lobby Below

Kitchen

Exhibit Hall A
(below)

Exhibit Hall B
(below)

Exhibit Hall C
(below)

203
204A
204B
205A
205B
205C
206A
206B
207

208
209
210A

210B

210C

211
212
213

251
252A
252B
253A
253B
253C
254A
254B
255

256
257A
257B
258A
258B
258C
259A
259B
260
261

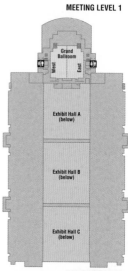

BALLROOM LEVEL

Grand
Ballroom

West   East

Exhibit Hall A
(below)

Exhibit Hall B
(below)

Exhibit Hall C
(below)

General Information

NFT Map: 10
Address: 415 Summer St,
Boston, MA 02210
Phone: 617-954-2000
Fax: 617-954-2299
Websites: www.mccahome.com
www.advantageboston.com

Overview

It took longer than expected to complete (what doesn't in this town?) and was plagued by cost overruns and contractor squabbling, but the Boston Convention & Exhibition Center finally opened in June 2004. In our humble opinion, it was worth the wait. Designed by noted architect Rafael Viñoly, the BCEC, which stands near Fort Point Channel on Summer Street (about a half-mile from South Station), is a stunning addition to the South Boston waterfront landscape.

Put simply, the BCEC is gargantuan. With 516,000 square feet of contiguous exhibition space, 160,000 square feet of flexible meeting space, more than 80 meeting rooms, and a 40,000 square-foot grand ballroom, the building covers an overall area of 1.7 million square feet. The BCEC now holds the coveted title of New England's Largest Man-Made Space and is big enough to hold 16 football fields.

The new complex is the centerpiece of the city's initiative to attract more convention business to Boston. As the old real estate mantra goes, it's all about "location, location, location," and a prime selling point for the BCEC is its proximity to both South Station and Logan Airport. Only two miles from Logan, the BCEC is closer to its city airport than the convention center of any other American city.

Services

The BCEC is used for large-scale conferences, meetings, and exhibitions. To schedule an event and be assigned a personal coordinator, contact the sales department on 617-954-2411 or sales@advantageboston.com.

Catering services at the BCEC are provided by Aramark. If you are planning a catered event, contact Aramark on 617-954-2482.

How to Get There—Driving

The BCEC is easy to reach from the Mass Pike (I-90). From the Pike, take Exit 25 (South Boston). Turn right onto Congress Street, then right onto D Street, then the second right onto Summer Street. The BCEC will be immediately on the left. It's hard to miss.

From the south, take I-93 N, get off at Exit 20, follow the signs to I-90 E and Exit 25. Follow the directions above.

From the north, take I-93 S, get off at Exit 23 (Purchase Street/South Station), proceed straight onto Purchase Street at the end of the exit ramp, and take a left onto Summer Street at South Station. Drive about a mile down the road to D Street and make a right.

Parking

If you must drive, you'll probably be dropping your car in a garage or fenced parking lot. The establishments listed below are the closest to the BCEC.

EDIC Garage • 10 Drydock Ave, 617-722-4300
Fitz-Inn Auto Parks • 10 Necco St, 617-426-1556
Fitz-Inn Auto Parks • 30-60 Necco St, 617-426-1556
Fitz-Inn Auto Parks • 17-31 Farnsworth St, 617-737-8161
Stanhope Garage • 338 Congress St, 617-338-5657
Stanhope Garage • 381 Congress St, 617-426-5326
Sunpark • 28 Northern Ave, 617-737-0910
Transpark • 390 Congress St, 617-737-3363
Transpark • 25 Northern Ave, 617-451-7732

How to Get There—Mass Transit

The Silver Line stops at the BCEC (alight at the World Trade Center stop, escalate to the top entrance, and traverse the bridge). To connect to the Silver Line from points other than Logan Airport, take the T's Red Line to South Station. The BCEC is only a few hundred yards away from South Station, so if you want to stretch your legs take a stroll across Fort Point Channel instead of transferring to the Silver Line.

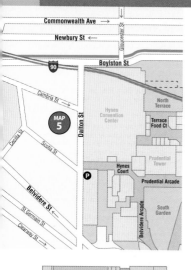

PLAZA LEVEL

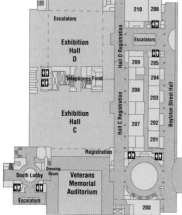

SECOND LEVEL

THIRD LEVEL

General Information

NFT Map:	5
Address:	900 Boylston St, Boston, MA 02115
Phone:	617-954-2000
Websites:	www.mccahome.com
	www.advantageboston.com

Overview

The John B. Hynes Veterans Memorial Convention Center is a relatively small center, with just 193,000 square feet of exhibit space, a 25,000-square-foot ballroom, and 37 meeting rooms. The Hynes is conveniently located in Back Bay with many hotels, historical sites, and tourist attractions within close proximity. Only a short walk from the Green Line's Hynes Convention Center/ICA stop, it is easily accessible by public transportation.

Once the big name in town for would-be conventioneers, the Hynes Convention Center now plays second fiddle to the Boston Convention and Exhibition Center (see page [204]). Because the Hynes adjoins the Prudential complex and sits in the midst of a few thousand hotel rooms, it continues to attract convention business, focusing on mid-size meetings and letting the biggest fish (like the International Boston Seafood Show) swim to the Southie Starship. A state commission was convened in 2004 to determine whether the Hynes should continue to operate as a convention center, be converted into retail, sold to the highest bidder, etc., but as of press time, no decisions have been made.

Services

The Hynes is used for conferences, meetings, exhibitions, and most other events where groups of people gather. To schedule an event and be assigned a personal coordinator, contact the sales department by phone on 617-954-2411, or by email at sales@massconvention.com.

Catering services at the Hynes are provided by Aramark. If you are considering planning a catered event, contact Aramark on 617-954-2330.

How to Get There—Driving

The Hynes is only four miles from Logan Airport. Two major roadways, I-93 and the Mass Pike (I-90), will deliver you close to the venue. From I-93, take Exit 26 (Storrow Drive). Follow Storrow Drive for about two miles to the Fenway/Kenmore exit and head towards Fenway. Continue to the first set of lights and merge left onto Boylston Street.

From the Mass Pike, take Exit 22 (Prudential/Copley Place), stay left as you exit, and turn onto Huntington Avenue. At the next set of lights (Belvidere Street), take a right, follow the curve, and bear right onto Dalton Street. At the lights, turn right onto Boylston Street.

The main entrance to the Hynes is at 900 Boylston Street and is easily accessible to taxis and buses via an access lane, which is set apart from Boylston Street.

Parking

There are numerous parking garages within a three-block walk of the Hynes, totaling more than 4,500 spaces. There is metered parking available around the Hynes and adjacent streets, but these spots are hard to come by.

- **Prudential Center Parking Garage**,
  800 Boylston St, up to three hours for $8, 3-4 hours for $15, and 4-5 hours for $18. Parking for up to 10 hours costs $29, and the daily maximum is $38. 617-236-3060.
- **Copley Place Parking Garage**,
  100 Huntington Ave (corner of Huntington Ave & Dartmouth St), $6 per hour, $28 for 3-10 hours, but only $7 for three hours with validation. 617-369-5025.
- **Boston Marriott Hotel Copley Place**,
  100 Huntington Ave, valet parking only, $39 per day. 617-236-5800.
- **Westin Copley Place Parking Garage**,
  10 Huntington Ave, $15 for 1 hour, $23 for 2-3 hours, and $28 for 3-8 hours. 617-262-9600.
- **Colonnade Hotel Parking Garage**,
  120 Huntington Ave, $8 per hour, $19 for 3–12 hours. $32 for overnight parking. 617-424-7000.
- **Back Bay Hilton Hotel Parking Garage**,
  40 Dalton St, $10 for 1 hour, $20 for 2-3 hours, $22 for 3–12 hours. $30 for overnight parking. 617-236-1100.

How to Get There—Mass Transit

The subway stops just two blocks away from the Hynes. Take the Green Line (B, C, or D train) to the Hynes Convention Center/ICA stop. Once you get off the subway, exit at any entrance and follow signs to the Hynes.

General Information

NFT Map: 32
Address: 200 Mt Vernon St, Columbia Point
             Boston, MA 02125
Phone: 617-474-6000 (Bayside Expo)
             617-474-6544 (Executive Conference Center)
Website: www.baysideexpo.com

Overview

Located three miles from downtown Boston, the Expo Center was once "New England's largest conference center and hotel complex," but has now ceded that crown to the much larger Boston Convention and Exhibition Center in Southie. Built on the site of a bankrupt mall and ringed by parking lots, the stark white, square Expo Center didn't win any design awards, but the building is functional, allowing visitors to focus on the boat, auto, RV, trade, or flower show that attracted them there in the first place.

The center's single-level exhibit space includes 18 meeting rooms, a full-service restaurant, lounge, cafeteria, and concessions. While they are convenient, on-site vendors' price-to-quality ratios are not the best. A small cup of coffee costs more than $2—and that's for the standard stuff, not a chic, unpronounceable foreign blend. An alternative would be to tailgate in the Expo Center's immense parking lot, but that will cost you, too ($12, to be precise), making the T the best choice for thrifty show-goers.

Adjacent to the exhibit space, the Executive Conference Center has everything an executive could wish for (well, almost everything), such as T-1 Internet access, wireless LAN, and wireless phone and video conferencing.

On nice days, be sure to take a drive around the back to the center's "bayside," where there are pleasant views of grassy Old Harbor, South Boston, and planes landing at Logan Airport.

The Doubletree Hotel (240 Mt Vernon St; 617-822-3600) markets itself to business travelers and vacationing tourists alike. This 197-room hotel's loftier rooms offer both city and ocean views. In addition to standard hotel amenities such as a fitness room, lounge, and a tour/recreation desk, the Doubletree Club offers free chocolate chip cookies at check-in.

How to Get There—Driving

From the south, take I-93 N to Exit 14. Stay in the right lane and follow Morrissey Boulevard. At the third set of lights, take a right onto Mt. Vernon Street. Follow the signs and take the third left into the Bayside Expo main entrance.

From the north and west, take the Mass Pike (I-90) E to I-93 S. Get off I-93 at Exit 15 (Columbia Road). Stay in the left lane and take a left off the ramp. Go three-quarters of the way around the rotary and bear right onto Day Boulevard. Proceed past the Massachusetts State Police barracks and take the first right into the Bayside Expo north entrance.

Parking

Don't be fooled into off-site parking by the shifty folks at the Sovereign Bank parking lot across the street from the Expo Center. If you do, you'll have to lug your stuff across the street, only to walk by dozens of available spaces in the Expo Center lot. Make sure you follow the signs for on-site parking at Bayside Expo Center. Parking costs $12 on show days.

How to Get There—Mass Transit

Take the Red Line T or MBTA Commuter Rail to the JFK/UMass station. The Expo Center is directly across the street. The red "Beantown Trolley" runs from the T stop to the front entrance of the Expo Center, a distance of about a half-mile.

Bayside Expo & Conference Center

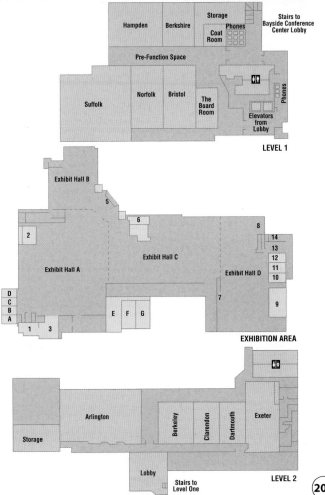

LEVEL 1

Hampden | Berkshire | Storage | Phones
Coat Room

Stairs to Bayside Conference Center Lobby

Pre-Function Space

Suffolk | Norfolk | Bristol | The Board Room

Phones

Elevators from Lobby

EXHIBITION AREA

Exhibit Hall B

5

6

2

8

14
13
12
11
10

Exhibit Hall A

Exhibit Hall C

Exhibit Hall D

9

D
C
B
A

7

1 3

E F G

LEVEL 2

Arlington

Berkeley | Clarendon | Dartmouth

Exeter

Storage

Lobby

Stairs to Level One

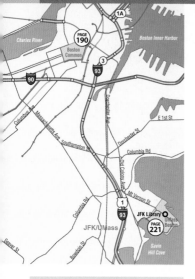

The library, which overlooks Boston Harbor from windswept Columbia Point, was designed by architect I.M. Pei (who also designed the Christian Science Center next to the Pru). The centerpiece of the complex is a nine-story concrete tower fronted by a glass-enclosed pavilion. The adjacent Stephen E. Smith Center, used for educational programs and conferences, opened in 1991. Outside on the lawn sits *Victura*, JFK's 26-foot sloop.

What's Inside

The JFK Library holds 8.4 million pages of presidential papers, 180,000 still photographs, six million feet of film and videotape, and 15,000 catalogued museum objects. The library also houses the world's most comprehensive collection of the papers and mementos of Ernest Hemingway but they are available to professional researchers only. If you are a scholar who seeks access to Papa's papers, check the library's website to review the restrictive rules.

The library's Centennial Room displays rotating exhibits showcasing the Kennedy White House's embrace of cultural values and the arts. Visitors can watch a 17-minute film about the Kennedy administration before entering the main exhibit space. On weekends, the 2 pm showing of the introductory film is replaced by a 30-minute film about JFK's brother/attorney general, Robert F. Kennedy. Visitors can also watch a 20-minute film about the Cuban Missile Crisis.

A museum café serves light meals and snacks from 9 am to 5 pm, and the gift shop is open during visiting hours.

How to Get There—Driving

The JFK Library is off Morrissey Boulevard next to the UMass Boston campus. From the north or the south, take I-93 to Exit 14 (Morrissey Boulevard) and follow the signs. From the west, take the Mass Pike (I-90) east to the intersection with I-93. Take the exit toward I-93 S, get off I-93 at Exit 14, and follow the signs. The library provides free on-site parking.

How to Get There–Mass Transit

Take the T's Red Line to the JFK/UMass stop. A free shuttle bus runs between the T stop and the library. Shuttle buses run every 20 minutes between 8 am and 5 pm.

General Information

Address: Columbia Point
              Boston, MA 02125
Phone: 617-514-1600
Website: www.jfklibrary.org
Hours: 9 am-5 pm daily except Thanksgiving,
              Christmas, and New Year's Day
Admission: Adults $10, seniors and students
              $8, children $7, free for children 12 and
              under

Overview

The John F. Kennedy Library and Museum, dedicated to our 35th president on October 20, 1979, houses 21 permanent exhibits examining the life and work of JFK, his administration, his family, and his legacy. The library is one of eleven presidential libraries administered by the National Archives and Records Administration, a federal government agency. The library draws approximately 200,000 visitors each year.

General Information

Mass Audubon:
781-259-9500; www.massaudubon.org
Wellfleet Bay Wildlife Sanctuary:
508-349-2615; www.wellfleetbay.org
Cape Cod National Seashore Salt Pond Visitor Center:
508-349-3785; www.nps.gov/caco

Overview

There are few places in the world where you can describe where you live by pointing to a part of your anatomy. Jutting out from the mainland like a flexing arm, Cape Cod is home to 15 towns, with a permanent population of roughly 220,000 that swells to over 550,000 in the summer months. The Cape's entrance is approximately 50 miles southeast of Boston, making the sandy beaches and picturesque shoreline a favorite summer getaway for Bostonians.

Grey days on the Cape can be almost as enjoyable as those of the sunny variety, with the mist, fog, and calm seas conjuring images of sailors and fishermen past. On some summer days, bright blue skies give way to smogsets over distant Boston that are so pretty you'll wish everyone in the city drove an Escalade.

The Cape is not entirely serene—summer travelers from the mainland can expect lengthy traffic delays just past Plymouth, where the overburdened Bourne and Sagamore bridges offer passage over the Cape Cod Canal. In an effort to relieve congestion and reduce bridge backup times, the Sagamore rotary is being replaced with a direct connection from Route 3 South onto the Sagamore Bridge. It might be more streamlined, but it ain't going to reduce the amount of cars heading to the Cape on Saturday mornings. Construction is scheduled to be complete by early 2007. Sixty-five miles east at the Cape's end sits bustling and bawdy Provincetown, home to the largest, loudest, and proudest gay community on the East Coast. If Cape Cod isn't your bag, ferries can transport you south of the Cape to olde-timey Nantucket Island or old-moneyed Martha's Vineyard.

The Towns

The Cape, about 70 miles in length, is often divided into three regions: Flexing your arm, the bicep is the Upper Cape, the area just above the elbow is the Mid Cape, and the forearm out to the fingertips is the Outer Cape. To confuse you in proper Bostonian fashion, the Outer Cape is sometimes called the Lower Cape even though it sits north of the Upper Cape. For convenience, we'll tack "the Islands" on to this list, making this section "the Cape and the Islands," just like the TV weather people refer to it.

The Upper Cape—Includes the Falmouth, Mashpee, Sandwich, and Bourne areas. Close to the historical settlement of Plymouth, and about 55 miles from downtown Boston, lie the Bourne and Sagamore bridges, which carry traffic over the Cape Cod Canal and onto the Cape. Here lies the beginning of the cranberry bog and seasonal tourist life. For the best views and smoothest journey, avoid the highways and take surface routes such as 28A that take you close to the water. If you're a

film buff, you might consider a visit to Woods Hole, where part of the movie *Jaws* was filmed.

The Mid Cape—Includes Dennis, Yarmouth, and Barnstable and its seven villages: Hyannis, Osterville, Centerville, Cotuit, West Barnstable, Barnstable Village, and Marstons Mills. Almost 70% of the Cape's permanent population resides in the Hyannis area, so the downtown remains busy throughout the year. Hyannis is home to the JFK Museum and the Ocean Street Docks, with ferries and tour boats leaving regularly in the summer for the islands of Nantucket and Martha's Vineyard. Much of the Mid Cape now lacks rustic charm, opting instead to reek of parking lot and chain store. Take the Old King's Highway (Route 6A) if you want to stay in the Cape mood.

The Outer Cape—Home of the peaceful Cape Cod National Seashore, Nickerson State Park, and the quiet towns of Brewster, Orleans, Eastham, Wellfleet, Chatham, Harwich, and Truro, it's difficult to imagine the spectacle sitting at the tip of the Outer Cape: Provincetown. At land's end sits one of the most "out" towns, where gay couples are as plentiful as seagulls, and you'll never be sure whether that person strutting down the street is Cher or some dude dressed as Cher—but it's probably the latter. After a day in the sun, cruise into P-town for a night of revelry. Gay or straight, the town knows how to party. For full effect, visit during Carnival in August. More information is available at www. provincetown.com.

The Islands—Martha's Vineyard and Nantucket each possess a distinct feel. Nantucket, only three by nine miles, is a quaint New England destination where tourists roam the cobble-stoned streets year-round. In addition to shops and galleries, the downtown is home to the Nantucket Whaling Museum. The natural beauty of Nantucket is stunning. Martha's Vineyard is well known for great beaches, ocean vistas, and the seaside villages of Oak Bluffs, Chilmark, Edgartown, and Tisbury. It's even better known for its well-heeled rich folk and the Kennedy Compound.

Want to start an instant argument on the Cape and Islands? Bring up the Cape Wind Project. Energy developers want to put over 100 windmills, each taller than the Statue of Liberty, in the shallow waters between the Cape, the Vineyard, and Nantucket. The windmills could generate enough electricity for the majority of the Cape and the Islands under normal conditions. The idea sounds like a winner, but wealthy landowners with waterfront property don't want their view ruined, so the fight goes on.

Lighthouses

Varying in shape, size, and functionality, lighthouses are a significant Cape Cod attraction. If you have time to visit a lighthouse or two, we recommend the Nobska Point Lighthouse at Woods Hole, an oft-photographed white tower at the southwestern tip of Cape Cod, the Cape Cod (Highland) Lighthouse in North Truro, or the Chatham Lighthouse on the southeastern corner of the Cape.

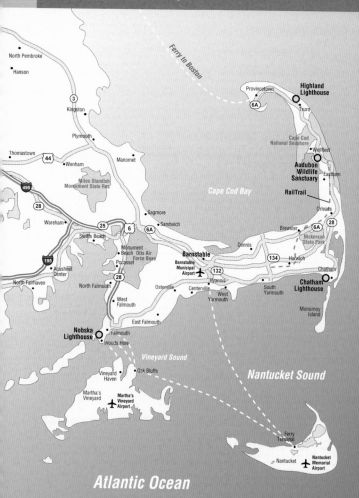

The Outdoors

After waiting all that time in traffic to get out to the Cape, you'll be eager to get outside and enjoy it. If the water calls, you can splash about at one of the Cape's many bay or ocean beaches, take a boat out to sea, dive or snorkel in the bay, canoe or kayak, parasail, or enjoy one of the whale- or seal-watching excursions offered.

Flora and fauna enthusiasts come here to explore the lush plant and animal life at the Cape's many sanctuaries. The Audubon Society's Wellfleet Bay Wildlife Sanctuary is the only sanctuary with a visitors center. It boasts 1,000 acres of woodlands, wetlands, and grasslands that attract an exciting variety of wildlife, including songbirds and shorebirds. Five miles of scenic trails wind through the various habitats, while the Nature Center includes "green" elements such as solar heating and composting toilets. Inside the nature center, you'll find two 700-gallon aquariums that feature the underwater worlds of the salt marsh and tidal flats. Other sanctuaries on the Cape include Long Pasture near Barnstable, Skunknett River near Osterville, Sampson's Island (accessible only by private boat from local marinas and town landings), and Ashumet Holly near Falmouth. The Cape Cod National Seashore Salt Pond visitor center in Eastham offers guided tours and nature walks through the salt marshes.

Monomoy Island, established in 1944 as a National Wildlife Refuge, is a barrier island that sits ten miles south of Chatham. It is prime habitat for migratory birds and a seal population that has grown in recent years. It is not uncommon to sit on Nauset beach to the north and see seals swimming regularly along the shoreline, which wasn't the case ten years ago. Monomoy has hiking trails and birdwatching opportunities as well as commercial boat tours for seal-watching. Check out www.fws.gov/northeast/monomoy/.

Sports

Cape Cod is an ideal location for sport fishing. Charters and tours are available and, for those looking to have a little fun on the water, ships such as the *Yankee* offer party cruises, perfect for those who hate lugging around a heavy cooler. Be warned: Drinking and water sports are not always the best combo.

Landlubbers should know that golf is popular here. There are a dozen or so courses on the Cape, varying in price, size, and level of difficulty. One universal trait: They're all busy all the time in the summer. Biking is another favorite pastime in the area, with free trails including the epic 26-mile RailTrail at Cape Cod National Park. The trail runs along the bed of a defunct railroad (hence the name) from Dennis (get on at Route 134 just south of Exit 9 from Route 6) to the South Wellfleet General Store.

Diehard baseball fans shouldn't miss the 103-year-old Cape Cod League, where top college athletes are recruited to play in the summer, many of whom go on to the majors. Thurman Munson, Nomar Garciaparra, Barry Zito, and other stars once played for one of the league's ten teams. Attending one of their early evening games is what summer is all about. Bring your beach chair, grab a hot dog, and watch the little kids scramble for foul balls.

Ferries

If the idea of crawling along in weekend or holiday traffic doesn't appeal to you, there's another option for getting across to the Cape. A number of ferry companies provide services between Boston and Cape Cod, from point to point on the Cape, and between the Islands.

Bay State Cruises Fast Ferry •
617-748-1428 • www.boston-ptown.com
Bay State offers two different services to Provincetown from the World Trade Center pier. Daily service in the summer (May 19–Oct 2) is provided by the Provincetown III, with boats leaving Boston three times per day—8 am, 1 pm, and 5:30 pm—and returning at 11:30 am, 4 pm, and 9 pm. The journey costs only 1.5 hours and costs $43 one-way and $68 round-trip (and an extra $5 each way if you're taking your bike with you). If you're on a budget, you might opt for the Provincetown II (service runs June through September)—a 3-hour boat that leaves at 9:30 am Saturday and Sunday, (June 24–Sept 3) and costs a mere $18 one-way, $29 round-trip. The boat leaves P-town at 3:30 pm.

Boston Harbor Cruises Provincetown Fast Ferry •
617-227-4321 • www.bostonharborcruises.com
The oldest ferry company in Boston offers a luxury high-speed catamaran ferry cruise with concierge service from Long Wharf in Boston to MacMillan Wharf in Provincetown. Travel time is 90 minutes and the fare costs $45 one-way, $70 return. Ferry times vary depending on the day of the week and the season, but in peak times, the ferries leave at 9 am, 2 pm, and 6:30 pm from Thursday to Sunday (returning from P-town at 11 am, 4 pm, and 8:30 pm). On most other days between May 25 and October 1, ferries leave at 9 am and either 2 pm or 4 pm. Check the website for schedules.

Hy-Line Cruises •
800-492-8082 • www.hy-linecruises.com
Hy-Line provides ferry service between Hyannis, Nantucket, and Martha's Vineyard. The high-speed *Grey Lady* catamaran zips between Hyannis and Nantucket year-round. Ferries leave Hyannis for Nantucket daily at 6:10 am, 9 am, 1:30 pm, and 6:10 pm. Tickets cost $16.50 one-way, $33 round-trip, $5 each way for bikes. Ferries for Martha's Vineyard leave at 9:15 am. Tickets cost $16.50 one-way and $33 round-trip.

Island Queen Ferry •
508-548-4800 • www.islandqueen.com
The 600-passenger ferry *Island Queen* travels between Falmouth Harbor (Falmouth Heights Road) and Martha's Vineyard from May to mid-October. The journey takes about 35 minutes and costs $12 return ($6 for bikes). The boat sails daily approximately once every hour and a half in the summer months between 9 am and 6 pm.

Steamship Authority •
508-693-9130 • http://steamshipauthority.com
Steamship provides year-round service between Martha's Vineyard and Woods Hole, Nantucket, and Hyannis, and between Martha's Vineyard and New Bedford. Tickets cost $6.50 one-way for adults, $3.50 one-way for children 5-12, $3 one-way for bikes, and between $35 and $50 one-way per vehicle (depending on size). Check the website for schedule information.

Berklee College of Music

1. 130 Massachusetts Avenue
2. Berklee Performance Center
3. 150 Massachusetts Avenue
4. 155 Massachusetts Avenue
5. 171 Massachusetts Avenue
6. The Berklee Bookstore
7. 20 Belvidere Street
8. 9 Belvidere Street
9. 1140 Boylston Street
10. 22 The Fenway
11. 98 Hemingway Street
12. Boston Architectural Center
13. 931 Boylston Street
14. 264-270 Commonwealth Avenue

Berklee College of Music

General Information

NFT Map: 5
Address: 1140 Boylston St, Boston, MA 02215
Phone: 617-266-1400
Website: www.berklee.edu

Overview

Berklee is the largest independent music college in the world and calls itself the "premier institution for the study of contemporary music." Founded in 1945 by pianist and MIT-trained engineer Lawrence Berk, the school became accredited in 1973. Berklee offers four-year degrees as well as diploma programs that allow students to forego the liberal arts and focus exclusively on music. Facilities include more than 250 private practice rooms. In addition to performance, students study Music Business/Management, Music Education, and Music Therapy. During the summer, the school offers specialized programs including Berklee in Los Angeles.

The college enrolls close to 4,000 students, with the highest percentage (about 26%) of international students of any college in the United States. The student body is a funky, diverse lot, with many musicians from Japan, Korea, Germany, Switzerland, and Brazil. They tend to congregate on Mass Ave, particularly by the Virgin Megastore at the corner of Newbury Street. Tracy Bonham, Melissa Etheridge, Patty Larkin, Branford Marsalis, and Bruce Hornsby are among Berklee's notable alumni. At the 2006 Grammy Awards, seven Berklee alums took home golden gramophones.

Tuition

In the 2005-2006 academic year, tuition fees amounted to $21,790 and housing was an additional $11,690 per year. However, costs vary between degree and diploma programs, and additional fees may apply. Berklee awards $10.5 million in scholarships each year.

Sports

There are no college-level athletics at Berklee, but student clubs do offer soccer, basketball, softball, and yoga, among others. Nearby fitness facilities, including the YMCA, the Tennis and Racquet Club, and Boston Kung-Fu Tai-Chi Institute offer discounted rates for students. Much more popular than sports are the 350-plus student music ensembles in an impressive range of styles.

Culture on Campus

Housed in the historic Fenway Theater, the 1,200-seat Berklee Performance Center (BPC) stands as one of the finest concert halls on the East Coast. Located at 136 Massachusetts Avenue near the intersection with Boylston Street, the BPC offers numerous performances by major concert promoters as well as faculty and student concerts throughout the year. To attend a performance, check out the Event Calendar at www.berkleebpc.com or call the box office at 617-747-2261.

Departments

Admissions..617-747-2047
Financial Aid................617-747-2274 or 800-538-3844
Registrar..617-747-2240
Housing..617-747-2292
Alumni Relations..............................617-747-2236
Berklee Performance Center 617-747-2474
Library...617-747-2258

Colleges & Universities · **Boston College**

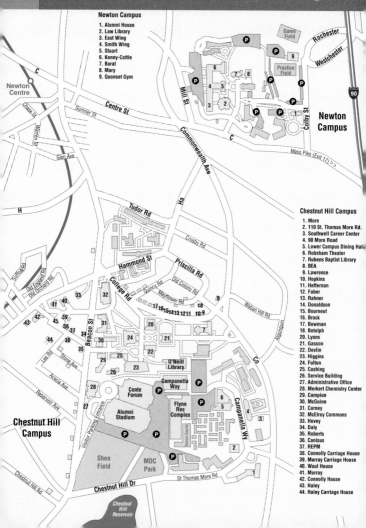

Newton Campus

1. Alumni House
2. Law Library
3. East Wing
4. Smith Wing
5. Stuart
6. Kenny-Cottle
7. Barat
8. Mary
9. Quonset Gym

Newton Campus

Chestnut Hill Campus

Chestnut Hill Campus

1. More
2. 110 St. Thomas More Rd.
3. Southwell Career Center
4. 90 More Road
5. Lower Campus Dining Hall
6. Robsham Theater
7. Rubens Baptist Library
8. BEA
9. Lawrence
10. Hopkins
11. Heffernan
12. Faber
13. Rahner
14. Donaldson
15. Bourneuf
16. Brock
17. Bowman
18. Botolph
19. Lyons
20. Gasson
21. Devlin
22. Higgins
23. Fulton
24. Cushing
25. Service Building
26. Administrative Office
27. Merkert Chemistry Center
28. Campion
29. McGuinn
30. Carney
31. Carney
32. McElroy Commons
33. Hovey
34. Daly
35. Roberts
36. Canisius
37. REPM
38. Connolly Carriage House
39. Murray Carriage House
40. Waul House
41. Murray
42. Connolly House
43. Haley
44. Haley Carriage House

General Information

Main Campus:	140 Commonwealth Ave, Chestnut Hill, MA 02467
Newton Campus:	885 Centre St, Newton Campus, MA 02459
Phone:	617-552-8000
Website:	www.bc.edu

Overview

It all began one day in Paris in 1534, when a group of students at the University of Paris got together and decided to combine their devotion to God with their commitment to bettering society. They called themselves the Society of Jesus, or the Jesuits. A few centuries later, in 1863, three Jesuits opened a college in the South End and cleverly named it Boston College. The college began with just 22 students, but even then the Jesuit profs envisioned a grander institution that would integrate intellectual development with religious and ethical growth.

Over the past century-and-a-half, the school has drifted a bit, both geographically and ethically. Once located in Boston proper, the school now sits six miles to the west, sprawling over 116 acres in Chestnut Hill and another 40 in Newton. And while the college is still officially Jesuit through and through, today's BC students aren't known for being particularly pious or devout.

BC's 9,000 undergraduates and 4,700 graduate students have a bit of a bad reputation among locals and students at other area colleges—the stereotype pegs all BC guys as binge-drinking jock wannabees sporting backwards baseball caps, more likely to be looking for a fight than searching for knowledge. It is widely rumored that the girls' appetite for Abercrombie & Fitch is matched only by their thirst for peach schnapps. Overlooked by naysayers is BC's excellent academic reputation. Its 11 colleges, schools, and institutes offer degree programs in more than fifty fields of study, and *U.S. News & World Report* rated BC the 37th best college in the country. In 2003, two BC students were selected as Rhodes Scholars and a school-record of 14 Fulbright Grants were awarded to graduating seniors.

Tuition

In the 2005-2006 academic year, undergraduate tuition amounted to $30,950 with room and board an additional $10,000 or so. Add on books, lab fees, and personal expenses. Graduate student tuition, fees, and expenses vary by college. However, approximately 65% of students receive financial aid.

Sports

Boston College has been hailed by *U.S. News & World Report* as having one of the top 20 overall college sports programs. Supporting 34 varsity and 34 club and intramural sports, the college boasts a diverse and strong athletic department. The varsity teams all compete at the NCAA Division I level. In 2004, the football team won the Continental Tire Bowl, making it BC's fourth consecutive bowl win. The biggest game every year is against Notre Dame. The men's hockey team has been perennially successful, winning the national championship in 2001 and losing in the semifinals of the Frozen Four in 2004.

Culture on Campus

The Robsham Theater Arts Center is Boston College's creative center. Built in 1981, the theater seats 591 people. The building also includes a black box theater that seats 150-200 people. The three main departments housed in the facility are the Department of Theater Arts, the Robsham Dance and Theater Company, and the Boston Liturgical Dance Ensemble. The university presents four faculty-directed and two student-directed productions each year, and 20 musical and dance groups perform throughout the year.

Another source of culture at Boston College is the McMullen Museum of Art. Located on the first floor of Devlin Hall, the museum is housed in one of the many Neo-Gothic buildings on the main campus. Aside from its notable permanent collection, the museum has frequent exhibitions of international and scholarly importance from all periods and cultures. The museum is free and open to the public. Hours: Mon–Fri 11 am–4 pm and Sat–Sun 12 pm–5 pm.

Departments

Undergraduate Admissions	617-552-3100
A&S Graduate Admissions	617-552-3265
Carroll Graduate School of Management	617-552-3920
Connell School of Nursing	617-552-4928
Law School Admissions	617-552-4350
Lynch School of Education	617-552-4214
Graduate School of Social Work	617-552-4024
Student Services	617-552-3300
	800-294-0294
Athletic Departments and Tickets	617-552-GoBC
O'Neill Library	617-552-4470

Colleges & Universities · **Boston University**

General Information

NFT Map: 16
Address: One Sherborn St, Boston, MA 02215
Phone: 617-353-2000
Website: www.bu.edu

Overview

If you really want to go to school *in* Boston, BU is the school for you. Consisting of a strip of buildings along Commonwealth Avenue, BU's campus doesn't win any points for style, beauty, or landscape architecture (since that would require having a clearly defined landscape). Aside from several thousand red banners on the lampposts that say "Boston University," and a larger than usual concentration of jaywalking young folk along Comm Ave, there's little indication that you've even entered BU's domain.

The fourth-largest private university in the country, the school's "campus" is the learning center for all students and the residence of many of its 29,000 undergraduates and grad students. The upshot of the ill-defined BU campus is that its students are truly living in the city. BU students make the best of the little green space they have. "The Beach," a strip of greenery on the inbound side of Storrow Drive (which runs along the Charles), is a springtime hot-spot for socializing and sunbathing.

When the university was founded in 1839, it was intended to be theological school for ministers of the Methodist Episcopal Church. As the years went by, the university expanded its curriculum in order to accommodate the needs and interests of its growing student population. Today, there are 17 schools and colleges and 60 different degree programs. Boston University students represent all 50 states, as well as 143 countries. BU also holds the distinction of having the most property owned by a non-government institution in the City of Boston.

Longtime president and infamous curmudgeon John Silber stepped down in 1996 after more than thirty years of leading the school to wherever he pleased. His replacement, former NASA chief Daniel Goldin, was called off the job even before he began his first day due to conflicting ideas about how the university should be run. Goldin said he took the job on the condition that Silber would not occupy a seat on the board of trustees. The Executive Committee balked at this stipulation and, after a little mud was slung, Goldin's termination was signed, thereby embarrassing the university in national headlines. Following the reign of an interim president since the resignation of Jon Westling in 2002, BU's tenth and current president, Robert A. Brown, was inaugurated to the post in April 2006.

Tuition

Undergraduate tuition costs run at about $29,988 per year with room and board an additional $9,680. Add on books, lab fees, and personal expenses. Graduate student tuition, fees, and expenses vary by college.

Sports

Notwithstanding the termination of the university's football program in 1997, the Terriers have quite an impressive athletics department. With 23 NCAA Division I varsity sports, Boston University provides a rich environment for sports lovers. The department prides itself on its equal emphasis on women's and men's varsity sports. The men's varsity ice hockey team is, by far, the most popular sports team at BU, with the most enthusiastic community support. There is fierce competition every year for the Beanpot—the "New England Invitational" tournament. In the past 53 years, BU has won the Beanpot 26 times, with Boston College being their biggest rival for the title. The university's hockey and basketball teams play in the Agganis Arena, a spiffy new facility that also hosts other sporting and entertainment events.

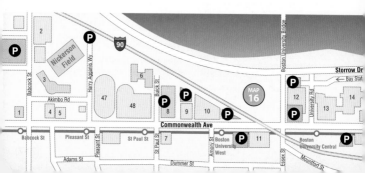

Culture on Campus

The first university to have a music program, BU remains committed to the arts. The Boston University Art Gallery is located at 855 Commonwealth Avenue. Although the gallery has no permanent collection, the architecture of the building is like an exhibit unto itself. Alluding to both the Classical and the Medieval, the columns that adorn the façade are a rare beauty and have attracted many people on that basis alone. You would never guess that the building is actually a converted Buick dealership. If this piques your interest, you'll be happy to learn that the gallery is open and free to the public, but only during the academic school year: Tues–Fri 10 am–5 pm and Sat–Sun 1 pm–5 pm.

Departments

Undergraduate Admissions	617-353-2300
Graduate Admissions	617-353-2696
Graduate School of Management	617-353-2670
School of Medicine	617-638-4630
School of Law	617-353-3100
School of Education	617-353-4237
School of Public Health	617-353-4640
School of Social Work	617-353-3765
Athletic Department and Ticket Office	617-353-GoBU
Mugar Memorial Library	617-353-3704

Building Legend

1. 1019 Commonwealth Ave (major residence)
2. Case Athletic Center
3. West Campus (major residence)
4. Office of Housing
5. Media Group
6. 10 Buick St (major residence)
7. Center for English Language and Orientation Programs
8. Comptroller; Financial Assistance; Registrar; Student Health Services
9. College of General Studies
10. College of Fine Arts; University Art Gallery
11. School of Hospitality Administration; Metropolitan College Academic departments and other programs
12. Boston University Academy
13. George Sherman Union; Dean of Students
14. Mugar Memorial Library; University Information Center
15. School of Law
16. Metropolitan College; Summer Term
17. School of Theology; University Professors Program
18. Marsh Chapel
19. Photonics Center
20. College of Arts and Sciences
21. School of Social Work
22. Graduate School of Arts and Sciences
23. The Tsai Performance Art Center
24. The Castle
25. Warren Towers (major residence)
26. Office of Information Technology
27. College of Engineering
28. Sargent College of Health and Rehabilitation Sciences
29. College of Communication
30. School of Education
31. Morse Auditorium
32. Biological and Physics Research Buildings
33. The Towers (major residence)
34. Chancellor's Office; President's Office; Provost's Office; Development and Alumni Relations
35. School of Management
36. 575 Commonwealth Ave (major residence)
37. Metcalf Science Center
38. Admissions Reception Center
39. Kenmore Classroom Building
40. Shelton Hall (major residence)
41. International Students and Scholars Office; Martin Luther King, Jr Center
42. University Computers
43. Barnes & Noble at BU
44. Hotel Commonwealth
45. Miles Standish Hall (major residence)
46. Danielsen Hall (major residence) (off map)
47. Agganis Arena
48. Fitness and Recreation Center

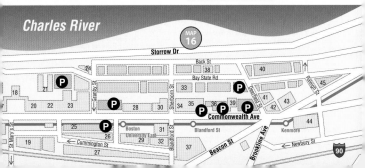

1. Ansin Building
2. Cutler Majestic Theatre
3. Little Building
4. Walker Building
5. Tufte Performance and Production Center
6. Student Campus Center
7. Student Residence
8. Student Union
9. Student Residence
10. Student Residence
11. Piano Row Residence

General Information

NFT Maps: 3 & 6
Address: 120 Boylston St, Boston, MA 02116
Phone: 617-824-8500
Website: www.emerson.edu

Overview

Emerson College is the country's only comprehensive college or university dedicated solely to communication and the arts in a liberal arts context. In close proximity to Boston's Theater District, Emerson is near all of the city's major media interests. Founded as a small oratory school in 1880, Emerson has expanded its curriculum over the years to include other forms of communication. Today Emerson specializes in communication, marketing, communication sciences and disorders, journalism, the performing arts, the visual and media arts, and writing literature and publishing. Emerson also operates semester-study programs in Los Angeles and the Netherlands.

The college enrolls about 3,000 full-time undergraduates and 1,000 graduate students, many of whom can be found sporting funky haircuts and smoking outside Emerson buildings between classes. Students take pride in their award-winning radio station, WERS (88.9 FM). Most alumni go on to pursue careers in the communications and entertainment fields. Notable alumni include talk show host Jay Leno, actor Denis Leary, and entrepreneur and make-up artist Bobbi Brown.

Tuition

In the 2005-2006 academic year, undergraduate tuition fees were $24,064. Room and board costs about $10,000. Add on books, service fees, activity fees, and personal expenses. Graduate student tuition, fees, and expenses vary by the number of credits taken.

Sports

Although Emerson does have an athletic department, it has never been one of the school's top priorities. Since most of the students attending Emerson College are interested primarily in the fields of communications and performing arts, sports are considered nothing more than a lighthearted diversion. Still, Emerson College sponsors 13 men's and women's varsity teams that compete in the NCAA's Division III.

Culture on Campus

Because Emerson considers itself an arts school, it takes great pride in its theater. The aptly named Majestic Theatre was built in 1903 as an opera house. In 2001, the college closed the theater temporarily for renovation and reopened its doors in 2003. Today, the historic venue seats 1,200 people and has become an integral part of the campus. Not only does it provide a venue for all types of productions by Emerson students, it serves the greater New England community. It hosts more operas than any other theater in New England and is the top stop for most touring dance companies. To visit the theater or check out a performance, go to the theater box office located at 219 Tremont Street in Boston or call 617-824-8000.

Departments

Undergraduate Admissions Office	617-824-8600
Graduate Admissions Office	617-824-8610
Majestic Theatre	617-824-8000 or 800-233-3123
Athletics Department	617-824-8690
Fitness Center	617-824-8692
Library	617-824-8668

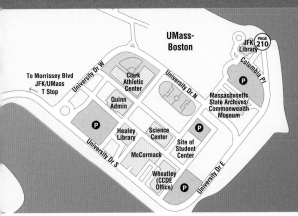

General Information

Address: 100 Morrissey Blvd, Boston, MA 02125
Phone: 617-287-5000
Website: www.umb.edu

Overview

The University of Massachusetts Boston is one of five UMass campuses. The campus opened in 1982 when UMass acquired Boston State College. The campus has been described as a sensibly priced, high-quality college that provides excellent academic programs to people from all walks of life. UMass Boston aims "to bring technical, intellectual, and human resources to the community."

The school's most famous alum is Boston Mayor Thomas M. Menino. Not exactly renowned for his oratory skills, he is nevertheless a well respected champion of the low-income neighborhoods. Menino graduated from UMass Boston at the age of 45 in 1988 with a degree in community planning. UMass Boston's campus, which has been described as a "concrete jungle," is only three miles from downtown Boston and is easy to reach by public transportation. (Take the Red Line to JFK/UMass Station.)

Tuition

Recent controversial tuition hikes have put undergraduate tuition costs at about $20,720 per year for out-of-towners and $9,666 for in-state residents. Graduate tuition costs run at about $20,732 per year for out-of-towners and $10,580 for in-state residents.

Sports

The University of Massachusetts Boston offers 14 varsity sports, including basketball, soccer, lacrosse, and ice hockey. All teams compete in the NCAA's Division III. The Beacon Fitness Center is open to all students and staff free of charge. The UMass teams are called the Beacons, carry the slogan "Follow the Light," and have been named All-Americans 93 times in seven sports. UMass Boston provides a community service program which offers, for free or at very low cost, the use of all athletic facilities and coaches to the general public.

Culture on Campus

The current Performing Arts Department is actually a conglomerate of three previously separate theater arts, music, and dance departments. Music courses provide grounding in music theory, history, and performance. Private music lessons are also available for one credit. The college Jazz Band, Chamber Orchestra, and Chamber Singers all give public performances at the end of each semester.

Departments

Undergraduate Admissions 617-287-6100
Graduate Admissions 617-287-6400
Graduate College of Education 617-287-7600
College of Nursing & Health Sciences ... 617-287-7500
Performing Arts Department 617-287-5640
Athletic Department 617-287-7801
Healey Library 617-287-5923
Honors Program 617-287-5520
Jazz Band 617-287-6990

1. Quad Athletic Facility
2. Hilles Library
3. Harkness Commons/Child
4. Pound Hall/Administration
5. Maxwell-Dworkin/Pierce
6. Areeda/Langdell Hall/Library
7. Pierce
8. Austin
9. Jefferson Lab
10. Music Building
11. Science Center/Cabot Science Library
12. Hoffman Lab/Mallinckrodt Lab/
    Naito/Gibbs/Converse/Conant Lab
13. 38 Oxford/42 Oxford
14. Biological Labs
15. Fairchild Biochemistry Lab
16. Memorial Hall Sanders Theatre
17. Graduate School of Design/Gund Hall
18. Fogg Art Museum/Busch-Reisinger Museum
19. Carpenter Center
20. Barker Center
21. Loeb Library
22. Lamont Library
23. Widener Library
24. Adams House/Westmorely
25. American Repertory Theatre/
    Loeb Drama Center
26. Brattle Theatre
27. Taubman
28. One Eliot/Littauer/Belfer
29. Malkin Athletic Center
30. Amelia Tataronis Rieman
    Center for the Performing Arts

31. Beren Tennis Center
32. Dillon Field House
33. Briggs Cage
34. Blodgett Pool
35. Bright Hockey Center
36. Murr Center
37. Gordon Indoor Track
    & Tennis Facility
38. Cotting
39. Morgan Hall
40. Baker Library
41. Aldrich
42. Dean's House
43. Shad Hall
44. Chapel
45. Rock Center
46. Cumnock
47. Spangler Center
48. Burden
49. Baker Hall
50. McCollum
51. McArthur
52. Kresge

PAGE 188

MAP 20

General Information

NFT Map: 20
Address: University Hall, Cambridge, MA 02138
Phone: 617-495-1000
Website: www.harvard.edu

Overview

You've probably heard quite a bit about Harvard. Chances are, you associate it with academic excellence, cutting-edge research, red brick, and students with at least two roman numerals after their names.

That stereotype hits the nail at least partly on the head. Founded in 1636, Harvard remains the richest and most revered university in the country (and perhaps even the world). True to myth, its pool of 19,000+ undergrads and grad students include children of royalty, famous actors, heirs, heiresses, and an assortment of other fortunate sons and daughters. But the truth is that these folks are more the exception than the rule. Harvard's deep pockets have allowed it to offer generous scholarships and increase the cultural and financial diversity of its student population. The same loot helps them net world-class professors in each of its 11 schools and colleges.

With the goal of properly housing and educating "the best of the best" in all fields from arts and humanities to business and technology, Harvard is hungry for more than just talented minds. The university continues to gobble up land in Cambridge and across the river in Allston, disgruntling some locals.

Perhaps Harvard needs more space for its livestock. A phrase coined to mock the local accent states that you cannot "pahk the cah in Havahd Yahd," since automobile traffic is prohibited there. However, an old contract clause allows each full professor to pasture one cow in the Yard. Assistant faculty members are allowed a sheep. Luckily for Harvard, no professor in recent memory has taken advantage of this opportunity.

Tuition

For the 2005-2006 academic year, undergraduate tuition, room, board, and college fees amount to $41,675. Graduate school tuition varies depending on the program.

Sports

Athletics at Harvard began around 1780, when a small group of students began challenging each other to wrestling matches, thereby starting an early version of *Fight Club*. Since then, the spirit of athletic competition has remained integral to the Harvard experience. Harvard introduced its crew team in 1844, and won its first championship just two years later. Since then, the men's heavyweight and lightweight crew teams have won 11 championships between them and the women's lightweight crew team has won five championships.

Years ago, Harvard was a football powerhouse, always ranked among the top ten in the nation. Harvard still consistently tops the Ivy League, and games against the likes of Yale continue to fill century-old Harvard Stadium on fall afternoons. The men's tennis team has also been a source of pride in the athletic department, consistently producing top-class players, many of whom have gone on to play professionally. In the fall of 2004, the team captured their second consecutive Eastern College Athletic Conference title.

Not all jocks are dumb: Since 1920, Harvard athletes have netted 44 Rhodes Scholarships.

Not all nerds suck at sports: More than 100 Harvard athletes have participated in the Olympics.

Culture on Campus

Harvard boasts four art museums, each showcasing art from different parts of the world. The university also runs an extensive music and theater program. Music department performances are held in the prestigious Sanders Theater, renowned for its acoustics and design. Aside from hosting most of the orchestral and choral performances by Harvard groups, Sanders Theatre is also a popular venue for professional groups such as the Boston Philharmonic, the Boston Chamber Music Society, and the Boston Baroque.

Harvard's various dance troupes perform at the Amelia Tataronis Rieman Center for the Performing Arts.

The country's only not-for-profit theater company housing a resident acting company and an international training conservatory, the American Repertory Theater (A.R.T.) operates out of the Harvard University campus.

A building shaped suspiciously like "Linguo, the Grammar Robot" of *Simpsons* fame houses the offices of the Harvard Lampoon on Mt. Auburn Street. Graduates of this famed humor publication have gone on to work for *Saturday Night Live*, *The Simpsons*, and *Late Night with Conan O'Brien*. (O'Brien himself is a Harvard alum.)

Departments

Undergraduate Admissions	617-495-1551
Graduate School of Arts and Sciences	617-495-1814
Graduate School of Education	617-495-3414
Kennedy School of Government	617-495-1100
Harvard Law School	617-495-3100
Harvard Medical School	617-432-1000
Harvard Business School	617-495-6000
Athletics Department Ticket Office	877-GO-HARVARD or 617-495-2211
Sanders Theatre	617-496-2222

Colleges & Universities · **MIT**

General Information

NFT Maps: 26 & 27
Address: 77 Massachusetts Ave, Cambridge, MA 02139
Phone: 617-253-1000
Website: www.mit.edu

Overview

Just down the Chuck River from Harvard, MIT is one of the top tech schools in the world. The school's 1,000 faculty and 10,000 slide-rule-bearing graduate and undergraduate students inhabit a 153-acre "factory of learning" that features both neoclassical domes and some of the most aggressively modernist buildings in Boston (including the Stata Center, designed by world-renowned architect Frank Gehry).

MIT profs are infamous for assigning massive amounts of work, but some students can't seem to get enough of engineering, spending their downtime planning and executing "hacks," tech-

nically elaborate pranks. A frequent target of hackers is MIT's Great Dome. In 1994, a replica of an MIT police cruiser appeared atop the dome. In 1996, it was adorned with a gigantic beanie cap complete with a fully functioning propeller. Just before the release of Star Wars Episode One: The Phantom Menace, students decorated the dome to look like the robot R2-D2. Harvard is another frequent target of hackers. During a 1990 Harvard-Yale football game, players and spectators alike were surprised when an 8.5' x 3.5' rocket-propelled banner with the letters MIT sprang up from under the end zone as Yale lined up to kick a field goal.

Tuition

In the 2004-05 academic year, undergraduate tuition fees cost $32,300. Room and board totaled $9,500.

Sports

Whoever said science nerds can't play sports was totally right. Nevertheless, they keep trying, posting moderate success in both Division II and III. Believe it or not, MIT actually boasts the largest num-

1. Pierce Laboratory
2. Fluid Dynamics Laboratory/ Dept of Mathmatics
3. Maclaurin Buildings
4. Maclaurin Buildings
5. Pratt School
6. Eastman Laboratories
6B. Solvent Storage
7. Rogers Building
7A. Rotch Library Extension
8. 21 Ames Street
9. Center for Advanced Educational Services
10. Maclaurin Building/Alumni Center
11. Homberg Building
12. 60 Vassar Street
12A. Waste Chemical Storage
13. Bush Building
14. Hayden Memorial Library
16. Dorrance Building
17. Wright Brothers Wind Tunnel
18. Dreyfus Building
24. Advanced Nuclear Systems/ Center for Experimental Study Group Dept of Nuclear Engineering
26. Compton Laboratories
31. Sloan Laboratories
32. Stata Center
33. Guggenheim Laboratory
34. EG & G Education Center
35. Sloan Laboratory
36. Fairchild Building

37. McNair Building
38. Fairchild Building
39. Brown Building
41. Lean Aerospace Initiative
42. Power Plant
43. Power Plant Annex
44. Cyclotron
46. Brain and Cognitive Sciences
48. Parsons Laboratory
50. Walker Memorial
51. Wood Sailing Pavilion
54. Green Building
56. Whitaker Building
57. MIT Alumni Pool
62. Alumni Houses: Munroe Hayden Wood
64. Alumni Houses: Walcott Bemis Goodale

66. Landau Building
68. Koch Biology Building
E1. Gray House
E2. Senior House
E15. Wiesner Building
E17. Mudd Building
E18. Ford Building
E19. Ford Building
E25. Whitaker College
E28. Publications and References
E32. 28 Carleton Street
E33. Rinaldi Tile
E34. Earth Resources Library

E38. Suffolk Building
E39. MIT Press
E40. Muckley Building
E42. Hayward St. Garage
E48. Office of the Treasurer
E51. Tang Center
E52. Sloan Building
E53. Hermann Building
E55. Eastgate

West Campus

MAP 27

Briggs Field

ber of NCAA-sponsored programs in the nation, and the coaches and students have received numerous awards for sports excellence. The heavyweight crew squads and the men's cross-country and track teams have garnered accolades for the university.

Culture on Campus

In a time when art and technology are often indistinguishable, it's not hard to believe that MIT has a happening arts program, too. We highly recommend a visit to the MIT Museum. Holographic images, scientific photographs, and mechanical sculptures with names like "Untitled Fragile Machine" show just how beautiful math-type stuff can be.

The Weisner Building (designed by I.M. Pei and housing the Media Laboratory) opened in 1985 and was used, for much of its first decade, to explore digital video and multimedia. The Media Lab allows for interdisciplinary research, and the developing focus of study is on how electronic information affects our daily lives—how we use it to think, express, and communicate ideas. Many of the Media Lab's research projects are made possible through corporate sponsorship, and the lab fosters a positive relationship between academia and industry.

According to the MIT website, the Media Lab "houses a gigabit fiber-optic plant that connects a heterogeneous network of computers, ranging from fine-grained, embedded processors to supercomputers." Unfortunately, in its role as an academic research laboratory, the Media Lab is not able to accommodate visits from the general public.

Departments

Undergraduate Admissions	617-253-4791
Graduate Admissions	617-253-2917
School of Humanities, Arts, and Social Sciences	617-253-3450
School of Engineering	617-253-3291
School of Science	617-253-8900
Sloan School of Management	617-253-2659
Office of the Arts	617-253-4003
Athletic Department	617-253-4498

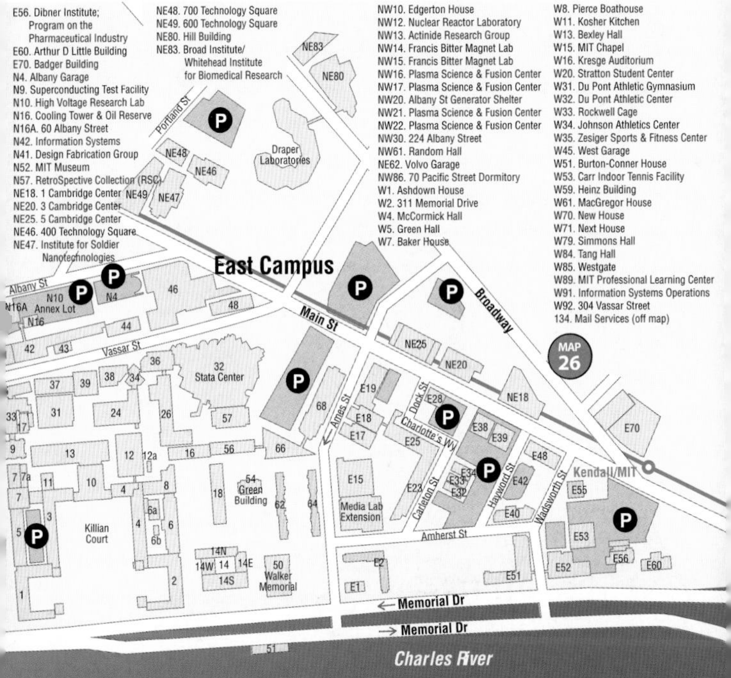
E56. Dibner Institute; Program on the Pharmaceutical Industry
E60. Arthur D Little Building
E70. Badger Building
N4. Albany Garage
N9. Superconducting Test Facility
N10. High Voltage Research Lab
N16. Cooling Tower & Oil Reserve
N16A. 60 Albany Street
N42. Information Systems
N41. Design Fabrication Group
N52. MIT Museum
N57. RetroSpective Collection (RSC)
NE18. 1 Cambridge Center
NE20. 3 Cambridge Center
NE25. 5 Cambridge Center
NE46. 400 Technology Square
NE47. Institute for Soldier Nanotechnologies
NE48. 700 Technology Square
NE49. 600 Technology Square
NE80. Hill Building
NE83. Broad Institute/ Whitehead Institute for Biomedical Research
NW10. Edgerton House
NW12. Nuclear Reactor Laboratory
NW13. Actinide Research Group
NW14. Francis Bitter Magnet Lab
NW15. Francis Bitter Magnet Lab
NW16. Plasma Science & Fusion Center
NW17. Plasma Science & Fusion Center
NW20. Albany St Generator Shelter
NW21. Plasma Science & Fusion Center
NW22. Plasma Science & Fusion Center
NW30. 224 Albany Street
NW61. Random Hall
NE62. Volvo Garage
NW86. 70 Pacific Street Dormitory
W1. Ashdown House
W2. 311 Memorial Drive
W4. McCormick Hall
W5. Green Hall
W7. Baker House
W8. Pierce Boathouse
W11. Kosher Kitchen
W13. Bexley Hall
W15. MIT Chapel
W16. Kresge Auditorium
W20. Stratton Student Center
W31. Du Pont Athletic Gymnasium
W32. Du Pont Athletic Center
W33. Rockwell Cage
W34. Johnson Athletics Center
W35. Zesiger Sports & Fitness Center
W45. West Garage
W51. Burton-Conner House
W53. Carr Indoor Tennis Facility
W59. Heinz Building
W61. MacGregor House
W70. New House
W71. Next House
W79. Simmons Hall
W84. Tang Hall
W85. Westgate
W89. MIT Professional Learning Center
W91. Information Systems Operations
W92. 304 Vassar Street
134. Mail Services (off map)
East Campus
MAP 26
Draper Laboratories
Portland St
Albany St
Vassar St
Main St
Broadway
Ames St
Dock St
Charlotte's Wy
Carleton St
Hayword St
Wadsworth St
Amherst St
Kendall/MIT
32 Stata Center
54 Green Building
Killian Court
50 Walker Memorial
Media Lab Extension
N10 Annex Lot
Memorial Dr
Memorial Dr
Charles River

Northeastern University

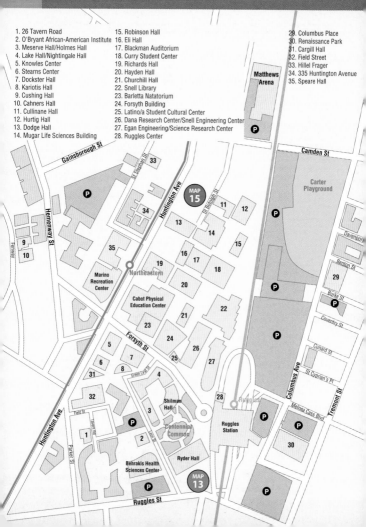

1. 26 Tavern Road
2. O'Bryant African-American Institute
3. Meserve Hall/Holmes Hall
4. Lake Hall/Nightingale Hall
5. Knowles Center
6. Stearns Center
7. Dockster Hall
8. Kariotis Hall
9. Cushing Hall
10. Cahners Hall
11. Cullinane Hall
12. Hurtig Hall
13. Dodge Hall
14. Mugar Life Sciences Building

15. Robinson Hall
16. Eli Hall
17. Blackman Auditorium
18. Curry Student Center
19. Richards Hall
20. Hayden Hall
21. Churchill Hall
22. Snell Library
23. Barletta Natatorium
24. Forsyth Building
25. Latino/a Student Cultural Center
26. Dana Research Center/Snell Engineering Center
27. Egan Engineering/Science Research Center
28. Ruggles Center

29. Columbus Place
30. Renaissance Park
31. Cargill Hall
32. Field Street
33. Hillel Frager
34. 335 Huntington Avenue
35. Speare Hall

Northeastern University

General Information

NFT Maps: 13 & 15
Address: 360 Huntington Ave, Boston, MA 02115
Phone: 617-373-2000
Website: www.northeastern.edu

Overview

Northeastern University has come a long way from being a commuter school with a fairly unimpressive urban campus. In recent years, the university has emerged as an important national research institution with sparkly new academic, athletic, and residential facilities. NU originally began as a five-year school with an academic model called "Practice-Oriented Education," a program that combines education and internships (co-op). The school added more four- and five-year options, along with online study for a number of degrees. Northeastern University is ranked 115th among the nation's top 500 universities by *U.S. News & World Report*.

Founded in 1898 as a part-time night school, Northeastern is located on more than 66 acres along Huntington Avenue and served by three Green Line E train stops. The current enrollment at NU is approximately 15,000 full-time undergraduate students and 2,200 graduate students with a male-to-female ratio that is pretty evenly matched. However, cultural diversity isn't something for which the university is known. The most popular degree programs on offer are in Business, Health, and Engineering/Technology.

Tuition

Undergraduate tuition costs run at about $26,990 per year with room and board adding up to an additional $10,800. Books, lab fees, and personal expenses, as always, are extra. Graduate student tuition and fees vary by college, as do individual online courses.

Sports

The Northeastern Huskies compete in Division I with varsity teams in nine men's and ten women's sports. The school's various teams had their finest collective performance ever in the 2002-03 season. The Huskies sent four teams to the NCAA playoffs and won a total of seven conference titles—Northeastern's most ever in both categories.

Culture on Campus

While Northeastern University doesn't offer much in the way of the arts, it is located in a prime spot for cultural enrichment. Huntington Avenue, also known as "Avenue of the Arts," runs through the urban campus, making it easy to visit the neighborhood museums. Among the most notable are the Isabella Stewart Gardner Museum, a ten-minute walk from the center of campus, and the Museum of Fine Arts (page 292), a four-minute walk from the main quad. Massachusetts College of Art is also located just a few T stops away and Symphony Hall is next door.

Departments

Admissions... 617-373-2200
(TTY) 617-373-3100
Library... 617-373-2354
Registrar.. 617-373-2300
Athletics Department 617-373-2672
Athletics Ticket Office 617-373-4700

Undergraduate:

Admissions... 617-373-2200
School of Arts & Sciences 617-373-3980
Bouve College of Health Sciences........ 617-373-3321
School of Business Administration 617-373-3270
School of Computer Science 617-373-2462
School of Criminal Justice 617-373-3327
School of Engineering 617-373-2152
School of Engineering Technology 617-373-2500
School of Nursing.. 617-373-3102
University College 617-373-2400

Graduate:

Bouvé College of Health Sciences........ 617-373-2708
School of Arts & Sciences 617-373-3982
School of Business Administration 617-373-5992
School of Computer Science 617-373-2464
School of Criminal Justice 617-373-3327
School of Engineering 617-373-2711
School of Engineering Technology 617-373-2500
Law School.. 617-373-2395
School of Professional Accounting 617-373-3244
School of Continuing Studies 617-373-2425

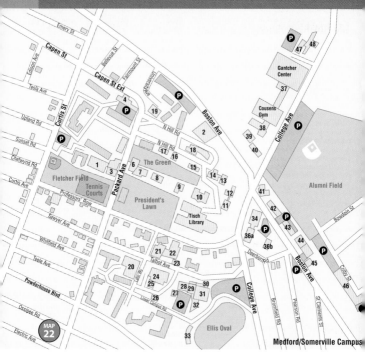

1. Mugar Hall
2. Dowling Hall
3. Goddard Hall
4. Granhoff Family Hillel Center
6. Dana Lab
7. Barnum Hall
8. Ballou Hall
9. Goddard Chapel
10. Eaton Hall
11. Paige Hall
12. Lincoln Filene Center
13. Braker Hall
14. East Hall
15. Packard Hall
16. Bendetson Hall
17. West Hall

18. Central Heating Plant
19. Lane Hall
20. Dewick-MacPhie Hall
21. Bookstore
22. Elizabeth Van Huyson Mayer
    Campus Center
23. 55 Talbot Ave
24. Pearson Chemical Laboratory
25. Michael Lab
26. Academic Computing Building
27. Costume Shop
28. Jackson Gym
29. Batch Arena Theatre
30. Remis Sculpture/ Leir Hall
31. Cohen Auditorium
32. Aidekman Arts Center

33. Baronian Field House
34. Anderson Hall
35. Robinson Hall
36a. Bromfield-Pearson
36b. Bromfield House
37. Hamilton Pool
38. Halligan Hall
39. 177 College Ave
40. Office Services
41. Curtis Hall
42. Psychology Building
43. Bray Laboratory
44. Central Services
45. Bacon Hall
46. Science and Technology Center
47. Eliot-Pearson Child
    Development Center

General Information

NFT Map:	22
Tufts Admin Building:	169 Holland St, Somerville, MA 02144
Medford/Somerville Campus:	Medford, MA 02155
Boston Campus:	136 Harrison Ave, Boston, MA 02111
North Grafton Campus:	200 Westboro Rd, North Grafton, MA 01536
Tufts General Phone:	617-628-5000
Website:	www.tufts.edu

Overview

There's a perception that Tufts is a school for kids who didn't get into Harvard, just two Red Line stops away. This is (mostly) not true. Tufts possesses academic prowess in its own right, especially in its engineering, veterinary, international relations, and science departments. The Fletcher School is the country's oldest graduate school of international affairs, and its prestige and strong curriculum draw students from across the globe.

The university has three campuses. The main Medford/Somerville campus is where approximately 5,500 students, mostly liberal arts undergrads, live and learn. The Medford/Somerville campus also houses the School of Engineering, the Graduate School of Arts and Sciences, and the School of Special Studies. Tufts prides itself on diversity: a whole center is devoted to lesbian, gay, bisexual, and transgender students, and on any given day the "viewpoints" section of The Tufts Daily—the school's impressive and professional-looking student newspaper—will have several pieces about the LGBT community.

The centrally located Boston campus houses the School of Medicine, School of Dental Medicine, Sackler School of Graduate Biomedical Sciences, Jean Mayer USDA Human Nutrition Research Center on Aging, and The Gerald J. and Dorothy R. Friedman School of Nutrition Science and Policy.

Tuition

In the 2005-2006 academic year, undergraduate tuition fees totaled $31,828. Room and board cost an additional $10,982. Books, service fees, activity fees, and personal expenses are extra. Graduate student tuition, fees, and expenses vary by college.

Sports

If you ever find yourself at Tufts University and, more specifically, in the office of the Athletic Director, you might notice a peanut butter jar with ashes in it. Don't be frightened; it's only Jumbo. Jumbo is the elephant mascot of Tufts University. P.T. Barnum, of the Barnum and Bailey Circus, was one of the University's original trustees. His prize act was an elephant named Jumbo, who was hit by a train and killed in 1885. His stuffed body was donated to Tufts, where it was stored in a museum on campus that eventually became a student lounge. Sadly, however, the museum burned in 1975 and Jumbo went up with it. The ashes in the jar are said to be those of Jumbo, though university officials say they have no evidence that that is the case. Luckily, they have his tail in a cardboard folder in their archives.

If that isn't enough to attract you to the sports, then maybe the recent successes of the golf and women's sailing teams will pique your interest.

There's also an old campus joke: "What's Brown and Blue and loses every weekend?" Answer: "The Tufts football team." It's not really funny, but often accurate.

Culture on Campus

If sports aren't your thing, cultural activities are plentiful at Tufts. In the Aidekman Arts Center on the Medford/Somerville campus, you'll find the Tufts University Art Gallery. Again, the mantra seems to be diversity, diversity, and more diversity. The Gallery's mission is to explore art through all of its cultural complexities.

Over 70 students make up the Tufts Symphony Orchestra, which performs regularly throughout the school year. The Department of Drama and Dance is where all of the performing artists can be found — its students perform regularly at the Balch Arena Theater.

Departments

Undergraduate Admissions	617-627-3170
Graduate and Professional Studies	617-627-3395
The Fletcher School	617-627-3040
School of Medicine	617-636-7000
School of Dental Medicine	617-636-6828
Sackler School of Graduate Biomedical Sciences	617-636-6767
School of Nutrition and Science Policy	617-636-3737
School of Veterinary Medicine	508-839-5302
Athletics Department and Ticket Office	617-627-3232
Balch Arena Theater	617-627-3493
Tufts Symphony Orchestra	617-627-4042
Tisch Library	617-627-3460

Continuing Education in Boston

Harvard, MIT, Boston College… the city of Boston has long been associated with academic achievement. But even if you're not ready to matriculate at one of the city's famed institutions of higher learning, Boston can still be a great place to learn everything from basic Arabic to authentic Italian cooking.

For those looking to change careers—or simply get ahead in a current position—many of the area's renowned schools offer continuing education or professional development classes. Tuition at Harvard Extension School is very reasonable and comes with unbeatable name recognition.

Those who are feeling less cerebral can try gymnastics at Cambridge's Jam'nastics or take a golf lesson at CityGolf. Got an urge to indulge your creative side? Explore painting or sculpture with a studio art class at the MFA or learn the craft of glass-blowing at Diablo Glass and Metal.

Adrenaline junkies can hop the commuter rail and head out to Trapeze School, hidden in the Jordan's Furniture complex in suburban Reading.

Continuing Education and Professional Development

Boston College Woods College of Advancing Studies, www.bc.edu, 617-552-3900, 140 Commonwealth Ave, Chestnut Hill

Boston Language Institute, www.bostonlanguage.com, 617-262-3500, 648 Beacon St, Boston

Boston University Metropolitan College, www.bu.edu/met, 617-353-6000, 755 Commonwealth Ave, Boston

Harvard Extension, www.dce.harvard.edu/extension, 617-495-4024, 51 Brattle St, Cambridge

Northeastern University, www.ace.neu.edu, 617-373-2400, 360 Huntington Ave, Boston

Little Bit of Everything

Boston Center for Adult Education, www.bcae.org, 617-267-4430, 5 Commonwealth Ave, Boston

Cambridge Center for Adult Education, www.ccae.org, 617-547-6789, 42 Brattle St, Cambridge

Arts and Lifestyle

Beadworks, www.beadworksboston.com, 617-247-7227, 167 Newbury St, Boston and 617-868-9777, 23 Church St, Cambridge

Boston Wine Tasting Classes, www.invinoveritas.com, 617-784-7150, 336 Washington Ave, Brookline

Cambridge School of Culinary Arts, www.cambridgeculinary.com, 617-354-2020, 2020 Massachusetts Ave, Cambridge

Diablo Glass and Metal, www.diabloglassandmetal.com, 617-442-7444, 123 Terrace St, Boston

Grub Street Writing Center, www.grubstreet.com, 617-695-0075, 160 Boylston St, Boston

Massachusetts College of Art, www.massart.edu, 617-879-7000, 621 Huntington Ave, Boston

Museum of Fine Arts, www.mfa.org, 617-267-9300, 465 Huntington Ave, Boston

Spark Craft Studios, www.sparkcrafts.com, 617-718-9132, 50 Grove St, Somerville

Athletics and Dance

Boston Sailing Center, www.bostonsailingcenter.com, Lewis Wharf, Boston

CityGolf Boston, www.citygolfboston, 617-357-4653, 38 Bromfield St, Boston

Fred Astaire Dance Studios, www.fadsboston.com, 617-247-2435, 179 South St, Boston

GottaDance Cambridge, www.gottadance.org, 617-864-8675, 11 Garden St, Cambridge and 7 Temple St, Cambridge

Jam'nastics, www.jamnastics.org, 617-354-5780, 199 Columbia St, Cambridge

Trapeze School, boston.trapezeschool.com, 781-942-7800, 50 Walkers Brook Dr, Reading

Overview

Bostonians don't just live by the water—they venture out onto it, too. A testament to the popularity of H_2O-based activities is the slew of yacht clubs and boating centers that hug the shores of the Charles River, fill up Boston Harbor, and even creep up-river as far as Watertown. Boston Harbor's reputation for being one of the country's dirtiest waterways has changed since the government spent $3.7 billion on a huge cleanup effort. The efforts have resulted in a harbor that's now supposedly clean enough to swim in without donning a chemical suit. Still, you won't find many athletes doing their morning breaststroke in the harbor, and some boaters still abuse its waters by disposing of cans, bottles, and bags of trash by chucking them overboard. If you witness such atrocities, record the boat's number and report it to the Boston Police Harbor Patrol (617-343-4721). With any luck, the sizeable fines will force them to sell their boats and start collecting cans for recycling.

Boston Harbor's 34 beautiful islands have been designated a National Recreation Area. On George's Island you will find the historic Fort Warren, a former Civil War prison. The trails across 48-acre Lovell's Island pass through dunes, forests, and the ruins of Fort Standish. Amenities include a supervised swimming beach, picnic areas, and 11 campsites. Deer Island is home to the Waste Water Treatment Plant. Wildlife, plant life, and beautiful beaches abound on most of the islands. If you want to venture a bit farther out, consider Buzzards Bay to the south, touching more than 280 miles of the Massachusetts coastline. The bay stretches from Rhode Island Sound to the Cape Cod Canal. Calmer waters inside the bay make for good sailing conditions.

Back on the Charles (don't even *think* about pronouncing the "r"), crew is a popular sport, particularly among the local colleges and universities. Many of the clubs and organizations offer instruction to the general public. The Head of the Charles Regatta, held every fall, is the world's largest two-day rowing event. The race schedule includes single and team events and draws competitors from around the world. Check out www.hocr.org for more information.

The nonprofit Community Boating Inc. (located between the Charles/MGH Red Line stop and the Hatch Shell) offers summer kayaking, windsurfing, and sailing lessons for kids aged 10-17 for just $1. (Participants must be able to swim 75 yards.) Visit www.community-boating.org for more information.

Boston is also home to the CRASH—B World Indoor Rowing Championships, held annually in February at the Reggie Lewis Track & Athletic Center at Roxbury Community College. More information is available at www.crash-b.org.

Sailing/Boating Centers

Piers Park Sailing	95 Marginal St, East Boston	617-561-6677	www.piersparksailing.org; hire/lessons/racing/sale
Boston Harbor Sailing Club	100 High St, Boston	617-720-0049	www.bostonharborsailing.com
Boston Harbor Shipyard & Marina	256 Marginal St, East Boston	617-561-1400	www.bhsmarina.com; moorings/lessons
Community Boating	21 David Mugar Way, Boston	617-523-1038	www.community-boating.org; sailing lessons
Lincoln Sailing Center	PO Box 492, Hingham	781-741-5225	www.lincolnsailing.org; non-profit/lessons/sailing/rowing
Courageous Sailing Center	One 1st Ave, Charlestown	617-242-3821	www.courageoussailing.org; lessons/racing
Boston Sailing Center	The Riverboat at Lewis Wharf	617-227-4198	www.bostonsailingcenter.com; hire/courses/lessons/racing
MIT Sailing	134 Memorial Drive, Cambridge	617-253-4884	www.mit.edu/activities/mit-sailing; lessons/racing
Boston Harbor Sailing Club	58 Batterymarch St, Boston	617-720-0049	www.bostonharborsailing.com; moorings/hire/lessons/racing/clothing

Yacht Clubs

Bass Haven Yacht Club	10 McPherson Dr, Beverly	978-922-9712	www.basshavenyachtclub.com
Boston Yacht Club	1 Front St, Marblehead	781-631-3100	www.bostonyc.com
Braintree Yacht Club	9 Gordon Rd, Braintree	781-843-9730	
Corinthian Yacht Club	1 Nahant St, Marblehead	781-631-0005	www.corinthianyc.org
Danversport Yacht Club	161 Elliott St, Danvers	978-774-8622	www.danversport.com
Eastern Yacht Club	47 Foster St, Marblehead	781-631-1400	www.easternyc.org
Hull Yacht Club	Fitzpatrick Way, Hull	781-925-9739	www.hullyc.org
Jeffries Yacht Club	565 Sumner St, East Boston	617-567-9656	www.jeffriesyachtclub.com
Jubilee Yacht Club	126 Water St, Beverly	978-922-9611	www.jubileeyc.net
Metropolitan Yacht Club	39 Vinedale Rd, Braintree	781-843-9882	www.metyc.com
New Bedford Yacht Club	208 Elm St, South Dartmouth	508-997-0762	www.nbyc.com
Old Colony Yacht Club	235 Victory Rd, Dorchester	617-436-0513	
Peninsula Yacht Club	671 Sumner St, Boston	617-464-7901	www.pycboston.org
Plymouth Yacht Club	34 Union St, Plymouth	508-746-7207	www.plymouthyachtclub.org
Sandy Bay Yacht Club	5 T Wharf, Rockport	978-546-9433	www.sandybay.org
South Boston Yacht Club	1849 Columbia Rd, South Boston	617-268-6132	www.southbostonyc.com
Squantum Yacht Club	646 Quincy Shore Dr, Quincy	617-770-4811	www.squantumyc.org
Wianno Yacht Club	101 Bridge St, Osterville	508-428-2232	www.vsb.cape.com/~wianno/
Winthrop Yacht Club	649 Shirley St, Winthrop	617-846-9774	www.win-yc.org

Rowing Clubs

Community Rowing (Apr–Oct)	Nonantum Rd, Newton	617-964-2455	www.communityrowing.org
Whaling City Rowing Club	5 Dover St, New Bedford	508-517-1251	www.whalingcityrowing.com

General Information

City of Boston Bicycling: www.ci.boston.ma.us/transporta-tion/bike.asp
City of Cambridge Bicycling: www.ci.cambridge.ma.us/CDD/et/bike/index.html
MassBike : www.massbike.org
Charles River Wheelmen: www.crw.org
Rubel BikeMaps: www.bikemaps.com
Hub on Wheels: www.hubonwheels.org

Overview

City Hall shows its grasp on reality is as tenuous as Washington's with the "Don't Be a Road Warrior!" safe cycling campaign. On the city's narrow, congested, and craggy streets, filled with malicious drivers, if you're not a Road Warrior, you're likely a pedestrian. Make no mistake, Boston is tough for cyclists.

That said, Boston and the surrounding cities are making efforts to increase the accessibility and safety of bike transportation. Relatively flat and compact, it's often quicker on a bike to get across the city, and you'll find, even in the middle of winter, hardy cyclists trekking through the city, delivering packages, and heading to class. Bike-only or mixed-use bike/pedestrian paths run through most of the area's parks, paralleling major roads such as the Riverway, Storrow Drive, and Memorial Drive. While getting "doored" is a serious threat in Central Square, a much-needed repaving of Mass Ave has smoothed the bike lane connecting Boston to Harvard.

Cycling is not all fun and games. Danger lurks around every non-perpendicular corner. Be especially wary of:

- **Drivers**—Some would hit you just to spice up their commute. They're notoriously self-centered, erratic, prone to underestimate your speed, and quick to double-park to dash in for liquor or donuts.
- **Potholes**—They can sneak up on you, especially at night. Some are big enough to swallow you whole.
- **Trolley Tracks**—Green Line tracks will flip you over and buckle your wheel, especially in parts of Mission Hill, Jamaica Plain, and in Cleveland Circle. If you're going to cross the tracks, take them at a 90-degree angle.
- **Bridges**—All the bridges across the Charles are narrow and heavily trafficked.
- **Pedestrians**—If they aren't darting across the street, they're on the paths listening to their iPods and ignoring everybody and everything.

If you plan on biking in Boston and you have a brain that you'd like to keep, invest in a helmet and a battery-powered red light to place below your seat or on your back. Front lights and rear reflectors are the law after dark.

The city offers many options for recreational biking, including the popular 11-mile Minuteman Bikeway through Lexington and the 17-mile Charles River Bikeway growing past Watertown. Shorter but handy for commuting, the Southwest Corridor sends you from Northeastern along the Orange Line to Forest Hills. Recent funding should improve one of the serious flaws of the Boston bike system: a lack of cross-trail connections, crossing lights, or route markings. This makes them less than ideal for outing with small children. Of particular danger to families are the many bridge intersections along the south Charles River Bikeway.

For something a little longer and farther away, the Bay Circuit Trail winds its way 150 miles from Newburyport on the North Shore to Duxbury on the South Shore, creating a "C" shape around Boston. Cycling enthusiasts refer to it as "Boston's outer Emerald Necklace." You'll find the bay racers skipping the summer crowds on the Minuteman for spins along around Concord and many of the cycle shops sponsor club teams. The Charles River Wheelmen is one of the nation's oldest bicycle clubs with a year round calendar of rides and site full of cue sheets. For the ultra-distant riders, the BMB (Boston-Montreal-Boston) ride draws randonneurs from across the country for the grueling 90 hour, 1,200K ride.

Rubel BikeMaps produces maps of riding paths and trails throughout the Greater Boston area and is well worth five bucks. You'll likely want both the Boston map and the Eastern Mass map. They can be purchased at most bike shops, bookstores, or on the Rubel website. Take it to the State House with MassBike, the primary lobbying and bicycle advocacy group in the state. They maintain an extensive website of all things pedal-powered in Massachusetts. Hub on Wheels is a new addition to the city and organizes free tours to offbeat Boston during the summer, DIY guides to biking Jewish boston, the Underground Railroad, and other routes are on their web site, and they organize a city bike rally and ride in early October.

Bikes and Mass Transit

Bikes are allowed on the Red, Orange, and Blue Lines, on the MBTA Commuter Rail with some limitations, on the Crosstown (CT) buses, and on the MBTA ferries at all times. Bikes are not permitted on the Green Line, the Mattapan Trolley, or other buses. On the subway and commuter rail, bikes are permitted during non-rush hours (roughly 10 am–2 pm and after 7pm). Bikes are allowed at all subway stations except Park Street, Downtown Crossing (except to transfer), and Government Center. Crosstown buses are equipped with bike racks and can be used at any time. Other bus services do not provide racks and bikes are not permitted on board.

If you're traveling on commuter rail, wait for the conductor's instructions before entering or exiting the train. On subways, head for the rear of the train. You're only allowed to enter the last carriage and, even then, there's a two-bikes-per carriage limit. There is no additional fee for bikes on any public transportation. See the MBTA website for schedules (www.mbta.com) for schedules.

Bike Shops and Makers

Boston's got a great variety of shops. While most will have a low-end city cruiser or two, it's worth getting to know your local shops for their specialties, whether the high-end racing bikes at ATA or fixies at Beacon Street Oddly enough, Boston's most famous shop and mechanic, Sheldon Brown, are way out in West Newton at Harris Cyclery. However, if you don't mind getting your hands dirty, we applaud the rent-by-the-hour stands and geniuses at Broadway Bicycle School.

- **Ace Wheelworks** • 145 Elm St, Somerville • 617-776-2100
- **ATA Cycle** • 1773 Massachusetts Ave, Cambridge • 617-354-0907
- **Back Bay Bicycles** • 366 Commonwealth Ave, Boston • 617-247-2336
- **Beacon Street Bicycle** • 842 Beacon St, Boston • 617-262-2332
- **Bicycle Bill's** • 253 North Harvard St, Allston • 617-783-5636
- **Bicycle Exchange** • 2067 Massachusetts Ave, Cambridge • 617-864-1300
- **Bikes Not Bombs** • 59 Amory St, Roxbury • 617-442-0004
- **Broadway Bicycle School** • 351 Broadway, Cambridge • 617-868-3392
- **Cambridge Bicycle** • 259 Massachusetts Ave, Cambridge • 617-876-6555
- **Community Bicycle Supply** • 496 Tremont St, Boston • 617-542-8623
- **Federico's Bike Shop** • 126 Emerson St, Boston • 617-269-1309
- **Ferris Wheels Bicycle Shop** • 64 South St, Jamaica Plain • 617-522-7082
- **Harris Cyclery** • 1353 Washington St, West Newton • 617-244-1040
- **International Bicycle Center** • 89 Brighton Ave, Brighton • 617-783-5804
- **Jamaica Cycle** • 667 Centre St, Jamaica Plain • 617-524-9610
- **Paramount Bicycle Repair** • 860 Broadway, Somerville • 617-666-6072
- **Park Sales & Service** • 510 Somerville Ave, Somerville • 617-666-3647
- **Revolution Bicycle Repair** • 753 Atlantic Ave, Boston • 617-542-4327
- **Ski Market** • 860 Commonwealth Ave, Boston • 617-731-6100

When out on the road, what's better than showing off some Yankee ingenuity? Boston's been a center of bike fabrication since Columbia popularized the really-high-wheel in 1877. Here are some sweet handcrafted builders welding new traditions:

- **A.N.T.** • 24 Water St, Holliston • 508-429-3350
- **Independent Fabrication** • 86 Joy St, Somerville • 617-666-3609
- **Seven Cycles** • 125 Walnut St, Watertown • 617-923-7774

Overview

If you like the idea of lowering your center of gravity and darting around at high speeds on tiny wheels or thin blades, then Boston is the place for you. The city is jam-packed with parks and rinks that accommodate inline skaters in the summer and ice skaters in the winter.

Inline Skating

Boston drivers are no more sympathetic to skaters than they are to bikers. If you're skating for recreation, it is probably best to stick to the numerous places designated for outdoor activities. A favorite haunt of Boston skaters is Harvard's Arnold Arboretum (125 Arborway, Jamaica Plain, 617-524-1717), which offers one of the most scenic (and hilly) skates in the area. The best thing about this place is that skaters are welcome everywhere. There are two or three miles of paved paths and you don't have to worry about cars (although you might find yourself dodging quite a few fellow skaters, particularly on sunny weekends).

Boston Common (see page [190]) is another popular skating destination, but the pedestrian traffic on the Common makes skating quite challenging. The Common is usually crowded with tourists and business folk who don't take too kindly to being mowed down by skaters. The upside, though, is that you can take in some impressive cityscapes as you zip around. The best way to get there is to take the T to Park Street. Note: Wearing skates on the T is prohibited.

For a great view of the bridges that stretch over the Charles River, try the Charles River Bike Path. The trail runs along both sides of the river between the Galen Street Bridge in Watertown and River Street Bridge in Boston, and from the Science Museum to Watertown Square. The path is about 8.5 miles each way.

Beacon Hill Skate Shop (135 Charles St S, 617-482-7400) rents top-of-the-line inline skates, roller skates, and ice skates. Rentals cost $10/hour, $15/day, and $20 overnight. Beacon Hill Skate Shop accepts cash only and requires you to leave a credit card as a deposit. All rentals come with safety equipment.

Ice Skating

On crisp winter days, when the cold makes it almost unbearable to be outside, the thought of skating on Boston Common's famous Frog Pond motivates many Bostonians to leave the comfort of their homes—either that or the thought of standing around Frog Pond heckling skaters. Skating is free for children 13 and under and for everyone else. Skate rental is $5 for children and $8 for everyone else. Lockers are available for a dollar. Regulars might consider buying individual season passes for $100 or a family pass for $150. Lunchtime passes are valid Mon-Fri, 11 am to 3 pm (holidays excluded), and cost $60. Frog Pond is open Sun-Thurs 10 am-9 pm (except Mon when the rink closes at 5 pm) and Fri-Sat 10 am-10 pm. For more information, call 617-635-2120.

The Larz Anderson Park in Brookline is a good back-up for when Frog Pond gets too crowded (and it will). Larz Ander-son Park is located on a former 64-acre estate and is the largest park in Brookline. In addition to the outdoor skate rink, the park has picnic areas, ball fields, and an incredible view of Boston. The only downside is that the skating rink is only open a few months every year, from December to February. Skating fees cost $4 for adults and $3 for kids ($7 and $4, respectively, for non-residents). The rink is open Tues and Thurs 10 am-12 pm, Fri 7:30 pm-9:30 pm, Sat-Sun 12 pm-5 pm. After a construction-shortened 2006 season, the park will probably sell season passes again for 2007. For more information, call 617-739-7518.

Ice Skating Rinks

If you have your own skates, you might opt for one of the following rinks run by the Department of Conservation and Recreation, where skating in the winter is free. Call rinks for hours of operation.
Bajko Memorial Rink, 75 Turtle Pond Pkwy, Hyde Park, 617-364-9188
Jim Roche Community Ice Arena, 1275 VFW Pkwy, West Roxbury, 617-323-9512
Daly Memorial Rink, 1 Nonantum Rd, Brighton, 617-527-1741
Devine Memorial Rink, 995 Morrissey Blvd, Dorchester, 617-436-4356
Emmons Horrigan O'Neill Memorial Rink, 46 Union St, Charlestown, 617-242-9728
Flynn Skating Rink, 2 Woodland Rd, Medford, 781-395-8492
Kelly Outdoor Skating Rink, 1 Murphy Terr, Jamaica Plain, 617-727-7000
LoConte Memorial Rink, 97 Locust St, Medford, 781-395-9594
Murphy Memorial Rink, 1800 William J Day Blvd, South Boston, 617-269-7060
Porazzo Memorial Rink, 1 Constitution Beach, East Boston, 617-567-9571
Reilly Skating Rink, 355 Chestnut Hill Ave, Brighton, 617-277-7822
Skating Club of Boston, 1240 Soldiers Field Rd, Brighton, 617-782-5900
Simoni Memorial Rink, 168 Gore St, Cambridge, 617-982-8166
Steriti Memorial Rink, 561 Commercial St, Boston, 617-523-9327
Veterans Memorial Rink, 570 Somerville Ave, Somerville, 617-623-3523

Skateboarding

The Charles River Skatepark, 40,000 square feet of pipes, ramps, and rails, is being constructed at North Point Park along the Charles River where Cambridge meets Charlestown. Scheduled to open sometime in 2007, it will be one of the largest skateparks in the country, perfect for catching air like Tony Hawk or busting backside lipslides like Ryan Sheckler. For info, go to www.charlesriverconservancy.org/projects/skatepark.

Gear

Beacon Hill Skate Shop, 135 Charles St S, Boston, 617-482-7400
Coliseum Skateboard, 150 Huntington Ave, Boston, 617-399-9900
True East Skate Shop, 32 Province St, Boston, 617-451-8999

General Information

Boston Parks and Recreation Office
Phone: 617-635-4505
Hotline: 617-635-PARK
Website: www.cityofboston.gov/parks

Brookline Recreation Department
Phone: 617-730-2083
Website: www.townofbrooklinemass.com/
recreation/Tennis.html

Cambridge Recreation Department
Phone: 617-349-6200
Website: www.cambridgema.gov

Department of Conservation and Recreation
(Division of Urban Parks)
Phone: 617-626-1250
Website: www.mass.gov/dcr/recreate/tennis.htm

Outdoor Courts—Open to the Public

These public courts operate on a first-come, first-served basis. Most courts are not equipped with lights, so get there early to get your game in. Although many courts are in good condition, some have pretty major divots, à la the Boston Garden's parquet floor, making the ball spin in unexpected directions. Courts are managed by the city or the town recreation department, or by the Commonwealth's Department of Conservation and Recreation's Division of Urban Parks (DCR). Until recently, the DCR was the Metropolitan District Commission (MDC), so the courts might still be labeled with the wrong acronym. Don't let it affect your game! Many locals also use the well-maintained school courts in the university-rich area. Each school has a different policy regarding outsiders depending on season, location, and the mood of the athletic director on a particular day. Contact the schools or just take your chances.

Tennis Courts

	Address	Type	Map
Charlesbank Park (DCR)	Charles St	Public, 4-courts	1
North End Park (DCR)	Commercial St	Public, 2-courts	2
Boston Common	Boylston St & Charles St	Public, 2-courts	3
Pagoda Park	Kneeland St	Public, 1-court	4
Cook Street Play Area	Hill St & Cook St	Public, 1-court	8
Porzio Park	Maverick Sq	Public, 2-courts	9
Boston Athletic Club	653 Summer St	Private	10
Marine Park (DCR)	Day Blvd	Public, 1-court	11
Clifford Playground	Norfolk Ave & Proctor St	Public, 1-court	12
Carter Playground	Columbus Ave & Camden St	Public, 5-Courts	13
Jeep Jones Park	King St	Public, 1-court	13
Malcolm X Park	Dale St & Bainbridge St	Public, 2-Courts	13
Trotter School Playground	Humboldt Ave & Waumbeck St	Public, 1-court	13
Mission Hill Deck (DCR)	Southwest Corridor Park	Public, 2-courts	14
South Street Mall	South St & Carolina Ave	Public, 2-courts	14
Stony Brook Deck (DCR)	Southwest Corridor Park	Public, 2-courts	14
Amory Clay Tennis Courts	Amory St	Public	16
Longwood Playground Park	Newall Rd off Kent St	Public, 3-courts	16
Waldstein Playground	37 Dean Rd	Public, 8-courts	17
Cassidy Playground	Beacon St & Acacia Ave	Public, 2-courts	18
Rogers Park	Lake St & Foster St	Public, 2-courts	18
Coolidge Playground	Kenwood St b/w Harvard St & Columbia St	Public, 1-court	19
Devotion Playground	Steadman St off Harvard St	Public, 3-courts	19
Driscoll School	Washington St	Public, 2-courts	19
Ringer Playground	Allston St & Griggs Pl	Public, 2-courts	19
Anderson Courts	Pemberton St & Haskell St	Public	22
George Dilboy Field (DCR)	Alewife Brook Pkwy	Public, 2-courts	22
Saxton J Foss Park (DCR)	McGrath Hwy & Broadway	Public, 2-courts	24
Hoyt Field	Western Ave & Howard St	Public	27
Riverside Press Park	River St & Memorial Dr	Public	27
Harvard Street Park	Harvard St & Clark St	Public	28
Joan Lorentz Park at Cambridge Public Library	Broadway & Ellery St	Public	28

Public Courses

	Address	Phone	Par	Fees (WD/WE)	Map
Fresh Pond Golf Course	691 Huron Ave, Cambridge	617-349-6282	35/70	$31 weekday /$37 weekend	21
Franklin Park Golf Course	1 Circuit Dr, Dorchester	617-265-4084	70	$23-26 weekday / $29-34 weekend	n/a
Presidents Golf Course	357 W Squantum St, Quincy	617-328-3444	70	$30 weekday /$39 weekend	n/a
Putterham Meadows Golf Club	1281 W Roxbury Pkwy, Chestnut Hill	617-730-2078	71	$27 weekday /$32 weekend	n/a

Driving Ranges

	Address	Phone	Fees (WD/WE)	Map
Boston Golf Academy	Radisson Hotel, 200 Stuart St, Boston	617-457-2699	$10/bucket (get free parking for 2 hours)	3
City Golf Boston	38 Bromfield St, Boston	617-357-4653	$9/bucket	3

Bowling

Bowling: the lost art. The pined-over puppy love of today's 20- and 30-somethings. Stolen away by glove-wearing, trophy-wielding, middle-aged suburban leagues. However, the shoes aren't just making a comeback as streetwear among the hipsters. Believe it or not, bowling's back, baby—all over Boston, in fact. And the '70s babies can't stay away.

Most central and T-accessible (and most resembling a bar, because…well, it IS one) is **Kings (Map 16)**. Ditto for **Lucky Strike (Map 16)** except that it's 18-plus. While bowling is not the main event at these venues, it sure as shootin' is at **Boston Bowl**! Join hordes of families and assorted teeny boppers in the 44-lane alley (offering both candlepin and tenpin lanes equipped with optional bumpers and touch-screen score monitors), and warm up or cool down with an arcade game or 70. Far less futuristic—in fact, downright retro—is the **Milky Way Lounge (Map 14)**, which also offers live music. For a casual, no-frills bowl-a-rama, throw on your league shirt and head to **Lanes & Games** or **Lucky Strike** (the Dorchester one).

Bowling Lanes

	Address	Phone	Fees	Map
Boston Bowl	820 Morrissey Blvd	617-889-1552	$2.70–$4.25 per person/per game; $3.55 for shoes, $2.55 for kids under	32, 12
Central Park Lanes	10 Saratoga St	617-567-7073	$1.50–$2 per person/per game; $.75 for shoes	9
Kings	10 Scotia St	617-266-2695	$6.50 per person/per game; $4 for shoes	16
Lanes & Games	195 Concord Turnpike	617-876-1533	$3 per person/per game; $1.50–$2 for shoes	n/a
Lucky Strike Lanes	289 Adams St	617-436-2660	$3 per person/per game; $1.50–$2 for shoes	32
Lucky Strike Lanes/Jillian's	145 Ipswich St	617-437-0300	$9.45 per person/per game (includes shoes); $5.95 per person for each additional game	16
Milky Way Lounge & Lanes	403-405 Centre St	617-524-3740	$25 per lane (shoes included)	22
Sacco's Bowl Haven	45 Day St	617-776-0552	$2.50 per person/per game; $1 shoes	10
South Boston Candlepin	543 E Broadway	617-464-4858	$3.50 per person/per game; $1.50 shoes	14

Sports • **Hiking**

Hiking in Boston

While it may not be the greatest city for driving, Boston is a great walking city. Whether you're in the mood for a casual stroll or a major trek, the city offers a surprisingly wide array of hikes and walks from which to choose. The trails closest to the city tend to be more scenic walks than hikes—appropriate for strolling students or families who want to get out and about in the city. If you're hungering for some real hiking, you'll need to be prepared for a drive. Boston's outskirts offer plenty of rigorous hiking trails with breathtaking views of the city and a taste of Massachusetts nature. If none of that is hardcore enough for you, the White Mountains of New Hampshire are just a Zipcar (see page 258) away.

A great source for information about various Boston trails is *Exploring in and Around Boston on Bike and Foot* by Lee Sinai (Appalachian Mountain Club Books).

Boston Harbor Islands

Seven miles from downtown Boston, this cluster of pretty much undiscovered islands is a great day trip to walk among historical forts and bucolic landscapes, birdwatch, or do some beachcombing. The inexpensive ferry from Long Wharf drops you off at Georges Island, where you can explore Fort Warren, a former Civil War prison that supposedly has its own ghost, "The Lady in Black." From there you can take free shuttles to the other islands. Peddock's Island has the longest coastline of all the islands and the most diverse set of trails. Grape Island takes you through forests, orchards, and rocky shoreline. Lovells has sand dunes and swimming beaches. Spectacle Island, perennially set to open, has a renewable energy visitor center and five miles of trails. There is camping on Peddocks, Grape, Lovells, and Bumpkin, but you must pack in and pack out everything yourself. Georges Island is open 9 am until sunset in the summer. Return ferry tickets cost $10, $8 seniors, and anywhere from free to $8 for children, depending on their age. For more information, go to www.bostonislands.com or call 617-223-8666 for schedules.

HarborWalk

With the cleaning up of Boston Harbor (though we still wouldn't swim in it) and the removal of the Central Artery, the waterfront has become more beautiful and accessible to pedestrian traffic. Finally realizing that people are attracted to a picturesque waterfront, Boston decided to capitalize on its coastal setting and incorporate it into the life of the city. The HarborWalk is a multi-use attraction consisting of walkways, parks, benches, artwork, and swimming pools extending from Chelsea to Neponset. Currently 44 miles long, it is 75% complete and meanders through diverse waterfront neighborhoods with views of the Harbor Islands and Boston skyline. It is really quite pleasant on warm summer nights to wander among the boats and the lights of the city and revisit neighborhoods from a whole new perspective. Plans are to eventually link it to the city's inland parks and the future Rose Kennedy Greenway.

Arnold Arboretum

Harvard's Arnold Arboretum, located in Jamaica Plain, occupies 265 acres and boasts a dizzying array of woody plants, more than 700 of which are over 100 years old. You can take a free guided tour of the grounds (call 617-524-1718 for tour schedules) or amble along the three-mile trail at your own pace. The arboretum welcomes dogs as long as they're kept on their leashes. The botanical haven is just two blocks away from the Forest Hills T stop (Orange Line) and parking is available outside the main gate. Restrooms are located next to the entrance gate in the Hunnewell Visitor Center. The grounds are open every day of the year during daylight hours. For more information, visit www.arboretum.harvard.edu.

Fresh Pond Reservation

This is a favorite of local residents and Harvard students. Located just one mile from the university and six miles from downtown Boston, the Fresh Pond Reservation offers a rather easy 2.5-mile paved trail around comely Fresh Pond, the 155-acre reservoir. The trail has become a hot spot for joggers, cyclists, and skaters. If you take your dog, be sure to check out the pooper-scooper dispensers! But it's not just the athletic types that reap the benefits of the reservation—the reservoir provides drinking water to many residents and businesses in Cambridge. To reach the reservation by train, take the Red Line to Alewife (last stop). By car, follow Route 2 east or west to Fresh Pond Parkway. The reservation lies on the corner of Huron Avenue and Fresh Pond Parkway. You'll find the best entrance to the reservation directly across from Wheeler Street. Parking in the reservation is reserved for cars with a Cambridge permit. There is parking after hours at the Tobin School, or take bus #72, #74, #75, or #78. For more information, visit www.friendsoffreshpond.org or call 617-349-6319.

Mount Auburn Cemetery

Hailed as America's first landscaped cemetery and a National Historic Landmark, Mount Auburn provides two miles of leisurely walking, alternating between paved walkways and unpaved footpaths, and is considered one of the best birding spots in the state. Aside from the 86,000 graves, the cemetery is home to over 5,000 native and foreign trees. Located just 1.5 miles west of Harvard Square, the cemetery can be reached via Route 2 or 3 to Route 16 at the Mount Auburn/Brattle Street intersection on Fresh Pond Parkway. If you follow Mount Auburn Street (Rte 16) west for two blocks, you will reach the entrance. Contact the Friends of Mount Auburn Cemetery (617-547-7105) for information about guided tours and lectures or visit their website at www.mountauburn.org. No dogs allowed.

Forest Hills Cemetery

Jamaica Plain's Forest Hills Cemetery is overshadowed in popularity (perhaps unfairly) by Mount Auburn Cemetery. Established in 1848, it's one of the country's oldest burial grounds, featuring 275 acres of beautifully sculpted landscape. The cemetery offers guided tours ($5-$8) or brochures and maps to help visitors create their own (free) tours of the grounds and its famous residents, including Eugene O'Neill and e.e. cummings. One of its most impressive features is Lake Hibiscus, which hosts the Buddhist-inspired lantern lighting festival held annually in the summer season. Another highlight is the Sculpture Path, a revolving exhibit of work by contemporary local and national artists. The cemetery is located conveniently next to the Forest Hills T stop. If you're driving, take the Arborway east over the Casey Overpass and follow signs for the cemetery exit, located on the right, on Shea Circle. The grounds are open year-round during daylight hours. For more information, visit www.foresthillscemetery.com or call 617-524-0128.

Hammond Pond Reservation

Hammond Pond is located behind a suburban mall in Chestnut Hill—an unlikely place to find a reservation. You can see the department stores as you hike through the 200 acres of woodlands. It's also one of the few outdoor places in Boston where you can rock climb. The best place to start is at the entrance to the reservation, located on the left of Hammond Pond at the north side of the parking lot. Walk through the metal gate and remain on the wide main path through the woods. If you're interested in rock climbing, you'll see rocks to your left a little way along the path. If climbing rocks is not your thing, continue on for two miles of easy walking or try fishing in the pond. Hammond Pond Reservation can be reached by foot from the Chestnut Hill T stop. Hammond Pond Reservation is open year-round during daylight hours. For more information, call 617-698-1802.

Breakheart Reservation

Hidden amidst strip malls and fast-food joints along Route 1, this 640-acre hardwood forest is a treasure for hikers lucky enough to stumble across it. The reservation offers many miles of scenic views and plenty of strenuous trails to get your heart pumping. Fishing, bird watching, cross-country skiing, swimming, and biking are other attractions that lure nature lovers out to Breakheart. As there's really no way to get to there by mass transit, you'll have to drive. Take Route 1 to the Lynn Fells Parkway exit towards Melrose and Stoneham. Turn right onto Forest Street, and follow the signs to Breakheart Reservation. A good place to begin your hike is on the paved Pine Tops Road, is located next to the parking lot adjacent to the headquarters building. For more information, call 781-233-0834.

Skyline Trail

This seven-mile trail is located in Blue Hills Reservation (near Milton), the largest open space within 35 miles of Boston. The Skyline Trail winds through rocky hills and provides scenic views of the city. With an elevation gain of 2,500 feet, this hike is not for the faint of heart. This is a strenuous hike that will take at least half a day. But don't fret! If you're not up for a real workout, there are plenty of less challenging trails in the park and the color-coded trail map available at the headquarters building will help you find your way around. To get there, take Route 138 to Exit 3 towards Houghton's Pond. After exiting, turn right at the stop sign onto Hillside Street and travel about a mile until you reach Houghton's Pond. The trail is open year-round from sunrise until sunset. Also in the Reservation is the Ponkapoag Pond trail, a four-mile loop around the pond, the highlight of which is a boardwalk trail (two miles roundtrip) through a rare Atlantic white cedar swamp. It's fun and different, but be warned: Wear waterproof shoes. Seriously. The boardwalk is made up of half submerged logs.

Middlesex Fells Reservation Eastern Section

Located seven miles north of Boston, Middlesex Fells is a 2,000-acre reservation where you'll find some of the area's most challenging hikes, many of which are considered some of the Boston area's best kept secrets. (If anyone asks, you didn't hear about it from us.) Middlesex Fells is off I-93 past the Stone Zoo. Parking is available on Pond Street. The beginning of the trail is located on the south side of Pond Street and begins behind a Virginia Wood sign near Gate 42. The trail is approximately 5.5 miles long, but can be extended to 16 miles if you connect trails. All of the hikes in this area are fairly strenuous and involve climbing and descending rocky slopes.

Moose Hill Wildlife Sanctuary

This is the oldest and second-largest Massachusetts Audubon Society (MAS) sanctuary. Moose Hill covers 2,000 acres that teem with wildlife and offers more than 25 miles of well-marked trails. One trail in particular, the Warner Trail, provides an exceptional view of the surrounding area from 491 feet. (You have to earn the view by climbing up Bluff Head.) Admission is $4 for adults, $3 for seniors and children aged 3-12. Members enter for free. Trails are open daily from dawn to dusk. The best way to get to Moose Hill is off Route 128/I-95 S. Take Exit 10. At the end of the ramp, make a left towards Sharon Street; then travel a quarter-mile and turn right onto Route 27 towards Walpole. After half a mile, turn left onto Moose Hill Street. Follow the MAS signs to the parking lot on the left. Find your way to the Visitor Center. All of the trails stem from there. For more information call 781-784-5691.

Walden Woods

Henry David Thoreau's account of his two-year stay in Walden is credited with sparking the conservation movement. Indeed, though nestled between railroad tracks and busy Route 2, Walden Pond is still a peaceful and pleasant setting for an afternoon walk no matter what season. The 102-foot deep Walden Pond is just one part of the 2680-acre Walden Woods. There is an easy loop trail around the pond, with a side path that takes you to the site of Thoreau's house (a replica sits in the parking lot). If you get too hot, you can always stop for a quick dip. Easy interconnecting trails link up with the neighboring Walden Woods and Lincoln Conservation Trust. The main parking area is on Route 126 off of Route 2. Parking ($5) is limited to 350 spaces and fills up quickly on hot summer days. If there is no ranger at the gate, you will need exact change for the annoying automated ticket machine, inevitably causing longer delays than dealing with a live person. On crowded days, there are designated times of the day when they let people in. Call ahead at 781-259-4700, and visit www.walden.org for more information.

General Information

City of Boston Swimming:	www.cityofboston.gov/bcyf/search.asp
Department of Conservation Resources:	www.mass.gov/dcr/recreate/swimming.htm
MIT Zesiger Center:	web.mit.edu/zcenter/aquatics/index.html
YMCA of Greater Boston:	www.ymcaboston.org
New England Masters Swimming:	www.swimnem.org

Overview

With your swimming options including universities, the oldest Y in the country, and few local gyms, it's easier to skip the many poorly maintained pools of the city with their odd hours. While the city's pools are the cheapest option, you'll find the city's website little help in locating pools and the only way to get schedules is to call each pool directly. The largest indoor pool in Boston is at MIT's Zesiger Center, running short course all winter and changing lanes to a 50m for summer. Day passes are available. New England Masters maintains a comprehensive listing on swimming clubs, workout locations, and stroke clinics.

In the summer, the DCR operates many outdoor pools and public beaches along the Bay and at local ponds. Unsurprisingly, preference is given to family time and the general chaos of children. Two summertime favorites include taking a dip in Walden Pond (get there early, as it often closes due to overcrowding) and strolling the busy beach at Revere with its easy access via the Blue Line and many ice cream counters.

Where to Swim

	Address	Phone	Fees	Map
Boston Harbor Island National Park Beach	Ferry leaves from Long Wharf outside Marriott Hotel, 296 State St	617-223-8666	Free (but unavoidable $10-12 ferry ticket)	2
Constitution Beach	Orient Heights, E Boston	617-626-4973	Free	n/a
Crane Beach	Argilla Rd, Ipswich	978-356-4354	$2 per car for members / $7 per car for non-members	n/a
Nantasket Beach	Nantasket Ave	617-727-8856	Free	n/a
Revere Beach	Revere Beach Blvd	617-727-8856	Free	n/a
Mirabella Pool	585 Commercial St	617-635-5235	$10 adults, kids under 5 free	2
Boston Chinatown Neighborhood Center Pool	885 Washington St	617-635-5129	$32 per year adults, $12 children	3
Brighton/Allston Pool	380 N Beacon St	617-254-2965	Free	5
Central Branch YMCA Pool	316 Huntington Ave	617-536-6950	Membership $55.60 per month, plus $100 joining fee	5
Blackstone Community Center	50 W Brookline St	617-635-5162	$25 per year, children $5	7
Charlestown Community Center	255 Medford St	617-635-5169	$25 per year adults, $5 children	8
Harborside Community Center	312 Border St	617-635-5114	$25 per year adults, $5 children	9
Paris Street Pool	113 Paris St	617-635-5122	$20 per year adults, $5 children	9
Condon Community Center	200 D St	617-635-5100	$5 adults, $3 youth	10
Curley Community Center	1663 Columbia Rd	617-635-5104	$50 per year	11
Madison Park Community Center	55 New Dudley St	617-635-5206	$10 per year adults, $4 children	13
Curtis Hall Community Center	20 South St	617-635-5193	$25 per year adults, $5 children	14
Hennigan Community Center	200 Heath St	617-635-5198	$25 per year adults, $5 children	15
Clougherty Pool	Bunker Hill St	617-635-5173	Free	16
Dealtry Memorial Pool	114 Pleasant St	617-923-0073	Free	16
Brookline Swimming Pool	60 Tappan St	617-713-5435	Residents pay $5 (adult) and $3 (under 18) per visit, non-residents pay $7 (adult) and $4 (under 18)	16 17
Oak Square YMCA	615 Washington St	617-782-3535	Membership $55.60 per month plus $100 joining fee	18
McCrehan Memorial	356 Rindge Ave	617-354-9154	Free	22
Cambridge Family YMCA	820 Massachusetts Ave	617-661-9622	Members only, membership starts at $77 per month	27
Veterans Memorial Pool	719 Memorial Dr	617-354-9381	Free	27
Mason Pool	159 Norfolk Ave	617-635-5241	$10 per year (adult), $5 (under 18)	28

General Information

NFT Map: 16
Address: 4 Yawkey Wy
             Boston, MA 02215
Phone: 617-267-9440
Website: www.redsox.com

Overview

Crouched beneath the giant Citgo sign just outside Kenmore Square, Fenway Park is the crooked little heart of Boston—a place where locals from all walks of life sit arm-to-arm, enjoying a deep love of the Sox and an even deeper hatred of the Yankees.

Fenway is old. The first game at Fenway Park, played on April 20, 1912, got bumped off the front page of the newspapers by the breaking news of the Titanic sinking a few days earlier. In spite of Fenway's age, the owners of the Sox aren't about to cede control of its excellent location, so the "lyric little bandbox" looks to be around for a few more years. To boost revenue in this smallest of big-league parks (only 33,871 seats), management has put seats on top of the Green Monster, brought in the Rolling Stones, built an enormous public-access sports bar (Game On), and converted Yawkey Way from a street into a street fair where you can get an early start on paying too much for beer or, on warmer days, watch Dennis Eckersley and his magnificent hair engage in pre-game banter with the hairenvious Tom Caron.

Fenway Park is hands down the best venue for watching a major-league baseball game. Because the park is so small, there are few bad seats—even the bleacher seats offer decent views. Just try not to get stuck in the right field grandstand, where the seats don't face home plate for some ridiculous reason and you have to crane your neck left to see anything other than the Monster or Manny Ramirez daydreaming in left field.

Truly patriotic citizens of Red Sox Nation should take the Fenway Park tour. A tour leaves from Yawkey Way every hour Mon-Sat 9 am-4 pm and Sun 12 pm- 4 pm. To get more information (recommended), call the Tours Hotline on 617-226-6666 or email tours@redsox.com.

How to Get There—Driving

Driving isn't the best idea—parking is tight and traffic gets bad on game days. If you must drive, take I-93 to Exit 26 (Storrow Drive). Take the Fenway exit off Storrow Drive and turn right onto Boylston Street for parking.

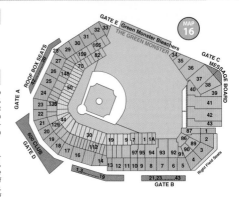

Parking

Fenway does not provide parking. Area garages and lots charge between $5 and $25, but they tend to fill up quickly, as does the limited street parking.

How to Get There—Mass Transit

Take the Green Line to Kenmore and follow the crowd to the ballpark. If you're on the D train of the Green Line, use the Fenway stop. The MBTA Commuter Rail's Worcester/Framingham line also goes to Yawkey, a short walk from Fenway Park. There's also a free game-day-only shuttle that connects Gate B at Fenway Park with the Ruggles stop, served by the T's Orange Line and the MBTA Commuter Rail's Attleboro/Stoughton, Needham, and Franklin lines. Subway fare is $1.25; commuter rail fares range from $1.25 to $6.

How to Get Tickets

For individual game and season ticket information, call the Red Sox box office at 877-REDSOX9 or visit the team's website. Ticket prices in "traditional" seats range from $12 to $95. Prices for seats above the Monster and in the Right Field Roof Tables Area range from $25 to $130. If there are no team tickets left, check StubHub.com, eBay, or boston.craigslist.org, but read the fine print and beware of scams. And one can always rely on the many scalpers trawling Kenmore Square on game day. Prices for scalped tickets will be higher during the playoffs and for any game against the Yankees.

General Information

Address: One Patriot Pl
           Foxborough, MA 02035
Phone: 508-543-8200
Websites: www.gillettestadium.com
           www.patriots.com
           www.revolutionsoccer.net

Overview

As far as NFL franchises go, the New England Patriots were a joke until Bill Parcells took over as head coach in 1993 and Robert Kraft bought the team in 1994. The team continued to play in a mediocre stadium until 2002. Old Schaefer/Sullivan/Foxboro Stadium was an unsightly, obsolete, charmless concrete slab, but the Pats sent it packing in style. The last game at Foxboro Stadium was the hotly debated "Snow Bowl" vs. the Oakland Raiders. Depending on your loyalties, QB Tom Brady either fumbled or "tucked" the ball during a key late-game possession. (It was a tuck.) The Pats won, propelling them to victory in the 2002 Super Bowl—the first in a series of three championships in four years.

Upper Level, Corner/End Zone · Lower Level, Corner/End Zone
Upper Level, Sideline · Lower Level, Sideline
Mezzanine Level, Corner/End Zone · * N/A=Non-Alcoholic Section

The 2002 season was ushered in by the opening of Gillette Stadium, which was supposed to be called CMGI Field until CMGI, a floundering Internet company, found itself without the dough for the lucrative naming rights deal. The stadium has been accessorized with a 12-story lighthouse and a replica of the Longfellow Bridge at one end of the field.

With a seating capacity of 68,000, Gillette Stadium does triple duty, also acting as the home of Major League Soccer's New England Revolution and a major concert venue. It can be a good place to catch big names like the Rolling Stones or U2, but, given the size of the stadium, make sure to bring a pair of binoculars if you have anything but the best seats.

How to Get There—Driving

From Boston, take I-93 S to I-95 S; take I-95 S to Exit 9 (Wrentham) onto Route 1 S. Follow Route 1 S approximately three miles to Gillette Stadium (on the left).

Parking

The lots open four hours before Pats games and three hours before concerts and other events, leaving plenty of time for tailgating—an opportunity fans use to the fullest. General Seating ticket holders should enter lot P2, P5, or P10 from Route 1. Follow signs for "General Stadium Parking." Disabled parkers and limos should head for P2, buses for P5, and RVs for P10. For Patriots games, car parking costs $35, RV and limo parking costs $125, and bus parking costs $200. Prices vary for other Gillette events.

How to Get There—Mass Transit

MBTA commuter rail trains leave South Station for Foxboro Station on game days. A round-trip ticket costs $10. The train departs from the stadium 30 minutes after the game.

How to Get Tickets

With the Pats' status as a dynasty now official (including an NFL-record 21-game winning streak), tickets get snapped up. To get on the season ticket waiting list, visit the Patriots' website and have $75 a seat on hand for a deposit. For regular tickets (or concert tickets), call Ticketmaster at 617-931-2222. Game tickets range from $49 to $99. The ubiquitous scalpers can be found roaming the parking lots and approaches to the stadium. StubHub.com, eBay, and boston.craigslist.org also accommodate folks who are selling and buying tickets, but be careful—season ticket holders have been known to lose their seats after being caught selling extra tickets online.

General Information

NFT Map: 1
Address: 150 Causeway St
Boston, MA 02114
Phone: 617-624-1805
Celtics: 617-854-8000
Bruins: 617-624-1900
Websites: www.tdbanknorthgarden.com
www.bostonceltics.com
www.bostonbruins.com

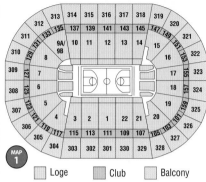

☐ Loge   ☐ Club   ☐ Balcony

Overview

Greater Boston's long regional sports nightmare is over. Once again Celtics and Bruins fans can accurately say that their teams compete in "the Garden." The original Boston Garden, which opened in 1928, was, by the time of its demise, fully equipped with obstructed views, rats, a dank odor, a lack of ale, and a crusty old guy playing the organ. As with most truly awful buildings, it was beloved by Bostonians. In footage of the Celts' 1984 NBA finals victory over the Lakers, fans crowd the sidelines and rush the court with time left on the clock. Bruins games could be even less civil and, correspondingly, even more fun.

But then in 1995, both the Celtics and the Bruins said goodbye to the Boston Garden and moved next door to a new arena, then known as the FleetCenter (though it took years for the new name to catch on among the area's stubborn traditionalists). When Fleet was acquired by Bank of America, the newcomers realized that no one in Boston would ever actually say "Bank of America Center." Eventually, TD Banknorth agreed to pay $6 million a year for the naming rights. The 19,600-seat TD Banknorth Garden has all that you would expect from a modern arena—rocket-launched t-shirts, luxury box TVs, and airline and casino promotions during timeouts—but still holds on to touches of tradition, including the Celts' legendary parquet floor. Nonetheless, even with the relative success of the Celts and Bs in recent years, the new venue just doesn't seem to inspire the same sort of love from fans as did its dilapidated predecessor.

In addition to sporting events, the TD Banknorth Garden hosts the circus and concerts from Metallica to Avril Lavigne.

How to Get There—Driving

If at all possible, don't. If you have to, try these routes. From the north, take I-93 S to Exit 26A (Leverett Circle/Cambridge). Follow the signs (if construction hasn't relocated them) towards North Station/TD Banknorth Garden. Take a right at the end of the ramp; the arena will be on your left. From the south, take I-93 N to Exit 26 (Storrow Drive). After the exit, keep left and follow the signs (see above warning) for TD Banknorth Garden. Watch out, it's a left-hand exit. The Garden will be on your left.

Parking

Reason number two not to drive. The TD Banknorth Garden doesn't have its own parking facilities, but there are several nearby garages ready and willing to gouge you, including a parking facility underneath the arena.

How to Get There—Mass Transit

The TD Banknorth Garden sits atop the North Station commuter rail station, which services the northern suburbs. Directly underneath is a new "superstation" that finally puts North Station's Green Line and Orange Line T stops in the same location. The Charles/MGH Red Line stop and the Bowdoin Blue Line stop are less than a ten-minute walk away. Commuter rail fares range from $1.25 to $6.

How to Get Tickets

To get Celtics season tickets, call 866-4CELTIX or visit the Celtics' website. They offer full-season, half-season, and multi-game packages. Individual ticket prices range from $10 nosebleed seats to $750 courtside seats. The midrange $55 end-court seats offer an excellent value.

To get Bruins season tickets call 617-624-BEAR or visit the Bruins' website. The Bs offer full-season, half-season, and ten-game packages, with individual ticket prices ranging from $10 to $99, topping out with the mysteriously un-priced Premium Club. (If you have to ask, you can't afford them.)

If you don't have tickets but have cash to burn, scalpers can be found on Causeway Street on game days.

History

The story begins just after World War II. When the good people at the Massachusetts Department of Public Works noticed the increasing popularity of automobiles and the stream of people leaving the city for the suburbs, they decided to make plans to build some major highways. The first highway to be completed was I-93, the Central Artery, hailed at the time as "a futuristic highway in the sky."

It soon became apparent that I-93 totally sucked. It was ugly, disruptive to neighborhoods, and boasted a high accident rate due to the excessive number of entry and exit ramps along the 1.5-mile stretch through the city. Recognizing that the Central Artery was a disaster, community groups fought successfully to stop other major highway projects. Two plans that never came to fruition were the Inner Belt (unbuilt I-695), which would have taken traffic around I-93 via a new, ten-lane BU bridge, and the Southwest Corridor Highway (unbuilt I-95), which would have run from the 93/128 split up through Hyde Park and JP to central Boston.

While averting construction of two new highways was a small victory for city dwellers, I-93 was still operating at triple its capacity, resulting in traffic jams at most hours of the day. The solution to the congestion was to dig a highway under the city—a solution that rather resembled performing open-heart surgery on a fully awake patient. Planning the project took the entirety of the 1980s and construction finally began in September 1991. After fifteen years and almost fifteen billion dollars, the project is almost finished.

What is the Big Dig?

As most Bostonians know, the substantially completed "Central Artery/Tunnel Project" was, as the Massachusetts Turnpike Authority puts it, "the largest, most complex and technologically challenging highway project ever." The most important element of the Big Dig is the routing of I-93 from the Central Artery to a new (and leaky) tunnel. Other major aspects of the Dig include the extension of the Mass Pike to Logan Airport through the Ted Williams Tunnel, the construction of the Zakim Bridge, the erection of the Leverett Circle Connector Bridge, and a complete overhaul of the roads and traffic patterns around Logan Airport. The 2006 opening of the Albany Street off-ramp from I-93 S marked the point when all of the Dig's tunnels and bridges and their connection and ramps to surface roads were open to general traffic.

But when, exactly, does a civil engineering project of this magnitude "end"? Is it when the last orange pylon is removed from the road, or when the litigation finally wraps up? The new I-93 tunnel (O'Neill Tunnel) sprouted a leak in 2004 shortly after opening to traffic. In its design for the tunnel, contractor Bechtel/Parsons Brinckerhoff recommended an approach that had never been used for another highway tunnel in the US, rejecting the more conventional design of lining the huge slurry walls with a concrete "tunnel box" in favor of making the slurry walls the tunnel's *only* walls. When the tunnel construction later necessitated waterproofing, the lack of interior walls caused some major problems. The *Boston Globe* reports that lawmakers, lawyers, and federal and state transportation agencies are investigating two kinds of leaks—small leaks where the rough slurry walls meet the tunnel roof and much larger breaches in the slurry walls themselves, the result of structural weaknesses caused by debris left in the walls by contractors. Bechtel insists that construction subcontractors are responsible for both types of leaks. Critics in the legislature say that for $2 billion, Bechtel should have been able to design a tunnel that wasn't doomed to leak. So, as fingers are pointed over the next several years, drivers using the tunnel should be mindful of standing water and workers patching the walls.

Development Plans

With the demolition of the old, elevated I-93 viaduct, construction is proceeding on the new Rose Kennedy Greenway, a 27-acre green space extending from Chinatown to the North End and the TD Banknorth Garden. Development in this area will (supposedly) include a new tree-lined boulevard, several miles of new and refurbished sidewalks, 600 street lights, nearly 900 trees with irrigation, numerous plazas, and 14 new parks with public art, water features, and other amenities. About a quarter of the space has been set aside for construction of low-rise retail, commercial, and residential space. Post-Dig developers also hope to incorporate the construction of parks and other pedestrian-friendly spots along the Fort Point Channel, along the Charles River between the Museum of Science and the North End, and in East Boston.

For updates on all the exciting plans, check out www.masspike.com/bigdig/index.html.

General Information

Mass Highway Department:
www.mhd.state.ma.us
Massport: www.massport.com
Big Dig: www.masspike.com/bigdig

Overview

The first bridge built in the American colonies (a pile bridge, incidentally) was erected in 1660 to connect Cambridge and Brighton. Unsurprisingly, said bridge no longer stands. Fast-forward 350 years and you'll find no fewer than ten bridges spanning the Charles River between Brighton and the Inner Harbor, including the Boston University Bridge, the Harvard Bridge (aka the Mass Ave Bridge), and the Longfellow Bridge (and its salt-and-pepper-shaker towers), all of which offer great views of the skyline. (The view from the BU Bridge is our favorite.) Other bridges further upstream cross the river at River Street, Western Avenue, JFK Street/North Harvard Street (the Larz Anderson Bridge), and Gerry's Landing Road/Soldiers Field Road (the Eliot Bridge).

Without question, the Big Kahuna of Boston's bridges is the Leonard P. Zakim Bunker Hill Bridge. The bridge, which connects downtown with Charlestown, has become the city's favorite new landmark—no postcard of the Boston skyline seems complete without it. The Zakim's towers were designed to reflect the shape of the nearby Bunker Hill Monument. Unlike the other bridges crossing the Charles, the Zakim is not open to pedestrians. The Charlestown Bridge, now somewhat overshadowed by the Zakim, connects the North End and Charlestown and was once the scene of many Irish/Italian gang fights.

The old green lady crossing the Mystic River and connecting Charlestown with Chelsea is the Tobin Bridge. The three lanes on the lower level of the Tobin run northbound; the three lanes on the upper level run southbound. Drivers heading south on the Tobin must pay a toll (30 cents with a resident commuter permit and $3 for everyone else).

The Evelyn Moakley Bridge, built in the mid-1990s over the Fort Point Channel to divert traffic from the historic-but-decaying Northern Avenue Bridge, is itself decaying at an alarmingly fast pace. Be careful walking across the bridge at high tide.

And remember: The Callahan Tunnel takes you *to* the airport (no toll) and the Sumner Tunnel takes you *from* the airport (yes, toll).

Bridge	Engineer (E); Architect (A)	Length	Opened
Boston University Bridge	Desmond and Lord (A)		1928
	John Rablin (E)		
Charlestown (N Washington St) Bridge			1901
Congress Street Bridge			1930
Eliot Bridge	Maurice Witner (A)		1950
	Burns & Kennerson (E)		
Evelyn Moakley Bridge	Ammann & Whitney (A)	800'	1996
	Modern Continental (E)		
Harvard Bridge	William Jackson (E)	364.4 smoots, one ear	1891
Larz Anderson Bridge	Wheelright, Haven, and Hoyt (A)		1915
	John Rablin (E)		
Leverett Circle Connector Bridge	HNTB Corporation (E)	830'	1999
Longfellow Bridge	Edmund M. Wheelwright (A)	1,768'	1906
	William Jackson (E)		
Malden (Alford St) Bridge		2420'	
Northern Avenue Bridge		636'	1908
River Street Bridge	Robert Bellows (A)	330'	1926
	John Rablin (E)		
Summer Street Bridge	John Cheney (A)		1899
	William Jackson (E)		
Tobin Memorial Bridge	JE Grenier Co (A)	1,525'	1950
Weeks Footbridge	McKim, Mead, and White (A)		1924
	John Rablin (E)		
Western Avenue Bridge	John Rablin (E)	328'	1924
Zakim Bunker Hill Bridge	Christian Menn (designer)	1,457'	2002
	Miguel Rosales (A)		
	HNTB Corporation (E)		

Tunnel	Engineer	Length	Opened
Callahan Tunnel			1961
O'Neill Tunnel	Bechtel/Parsons Brinckerhoff (E)		2003
Sumner Tunnel			1934
Ted Williams Tunnel	Jacobs Engineering Group (designer)	8,500'	1995
	Bechtel/Parsons Brinckerhoff (E)		

Airline	Terminal	Phone Number
Aer Lingus	E	800-474-7424
AeroMexico	E	800-237-6639
Air Canada	C	888-247-2262
Air Canada Jazz	E	888-247-2262
Air France	E	800-237-2747
Air Jamaica	E	800-523-3515
AirTran	C	800-247-8726
Alaska Airlines	B	800-252-7522
Alitalia	E	800-223-5730
America West	B	800-235-9292
American (except int'l arrivals)	B	800-433-7300
American (int'l arrivals only)	E	800-433-7300
American Eagle	B	800-433-7300
ATA	B	800-225-2995
British Airways	E	800-347-9297
Cape Air	C	800-352-0714
Continental	C	800-525-0280
Delta Air Lines	A	800-221-1212

Airline	Terminal	Phone Number
Delta Connection	A	800-221-1212
Delta Shuttle	A	800-221-1212
Icelandair	E	800-223-5500
JetBlue	C	800-538-2583
KLM	E	800-374-7747
Lufthansa	E	800-645-3880
Midwest	C	800-452-2022
Northwest	E	800-225-2525
SATA	E	800-762-9995
Song	A	800-221-1212
Swiss	E	877-359-7947
TACA	E	800-535-8780
United	C	800-241-6522
United Express	C	800-241-6522
US Airways	B	800-428-4322
US Airways Express	B	800-428-4322
US Airways Shuttle	B	800-428-4322
Virgin Atlantic	E	800-862-8621

General Information

Website: www.massport.com/logan
Phone:
Customer Service: 617-561-1800
Ground Transportation Info: 800-23-LOGAN
Logan Lost and Found: 617-561-1714
Parking Office: 617-561-1673

Overview

The 18th-busiest airport in the United States, Logan International Airport features all the serpentine security lines and two-mile gate runs of most major airports and is located in an area of the country where weather can ground planes at any time of the year. But why dwell on negatives? Thanks to the completion of the Big Dig and the extension of the Silver Line, getting to Logan is easier now than ever.

Jutting into the harbor from East Boston, Logan opened in 1923 as the "temporary occupant" on landfill originally intended to be a port. By 1939, flying contraptions had proven their worth and the site was made permanent. The airport is named after Lt. General Edward Lawrence Logan, a local and a Harvard grad who served in the Spanish-American War, the Massachusetts House of Representatives, and the Senate. Logan also chaired the Metropolitan District Commission, a now-defunct organization that managed everything from swimming pools to the upkeep of major roadways such as Storrow Drive and the Riverway.

The decade-long Logan Modernization Project, now moving into its later stages, has been taking the airport through a bewildering maze of construction and renovation. Within the past few years, the airport opened a completely overhauled Terminal A, a new T station, an extended Silver Line, a new arrivals hall in international-serving Terminal E, and improved access to the Central Parking Garage. The final piece of the project, a two-year, $14 million initiative to standardize and improve the airport's signage, is under way.

In 2006, Massport "merged" Terminal D into Terminal C. The international terminal, presently known as Terminal E, will be re-designated as "Terminal D" sometime in 2007. You know, to simplify things.

How to Get There—Driving

To get to Logan from the west, take the Mass Pike (I-90) E through the Ted Williams Tunnel until the highway ends. From the south, use I-93 N and take Exit 20 to I-90 E. From the north, take I-93 S and follow the signs to the Callahan Tunnel. Check www.massport.com for traffic and construction updates.

Parking

Hourly and daily parking are available at Central Parking Garage, Terminal B Garage, and Terminal E Parking Lots 1 and 2. Rates range from $2 to $24 during the day and $22 to $24 for overnight parking. The Economy Parking lot charges a daily rate of $16 and a weekly rate of $96.

How to Get There—Mass Transit

Seriously, take the T. It's a quick ride on the Blue Line from downtown to the Airport stop. A free shuttle bus that runs 4am–1am, will take you from the T stop to your terminal. Or take the Red Line to South Station and transfer to the Silver Line bus, which stops at each airport terminal. If you're coming in from the 'burbs, check out the Logan Express buses that service Braintree, Framingham, Peabody, and Woburn. A Park-and-Ride system is in place, and although the prices for parking and buses vary, they will always be cheaper than taking a cab. If you're downtown near the water, the MBTA's Harbor Express water taxi can get you from Long Wharf to the airport in less than ten minutes.

How to Get There—Taxi

It's hard to get to Logan from anywhere except Eastie for less than $20. Boston Cab: 617-262-2227; Checker Taxi: 617-494-1500; City Cab: 617-536-5100; Green Cab (Somerville): 617-623-6000; Cambridge Cab: 617-776-5000.

Rental Cars

Alamo   800-327-9633
Avis   800-831-2847
Budget   800-527-0700
Dollar   800-800-4000
Hertz   800-654-3131
National   800-227-7368
Enterprise   800-325-8007 (off-airport)
Thrifty   800-367-2277 (off-airport)

Hotels

Courtyard Boston Tremont • 275 Tremont St • 617-426-1400
Embassy Suites • 207 Porter St • 617-567-5000
Hampton Inn • 230 Lee Burbank Hwy • 781-286-5665
Hilton • 85 Terminal Rd • 617-568-6700
Holiday Inn • 225 McClellan Hwy • 617-569-5250
Hyatt • 101 Harborside Dr • 617-568-1234 • 800-633-7313
Marriott Long Wharf • 296 State St • 617-227-0800
Omni Parker House • 60 School St • 617-227-8600
Ramada Inn • 75 Service Rd • 617-287-9100
Wyndham Downtown • 89 Broad St • 617-556-0006

MBTA Buses

Website: www.mbta.com
Phone: 617-222-5000

Every day, intrepid T bus drivers pilot their behemoth vehicles down too-narrow streets filled with angry drivers, errant pedestrians, unfortunate bikers, and, in the winter, ice and snow. (A simple "thank you" to the driver as you get off the bus isn't too much to ask.) MBTA buses run everywhere the subway doesn't, and some places it does. Usually at least one of any bus route's end points is a subway station. The T also runs several popular express buses from outlying neighborhoods to downtown along the Mass Pike and other highways.

The T is in the process of replacing the bulk of its aging diesel fleet with new Compressed Natural Gas (CNG) buses. Identifiable by their blue strip and the low roar of their engines, the new buses reduce emissions by up to 90 percent and, so far, are cleaner on the inside as well (just give them a few years). Some buses on busy routes feature low floors and articulated midsections, such as those used along the Silver Line and JP's 39 bus.

The MBTA has discontinued its popular but unprofitable Night Owl service (is a public service supposed to be profitable, anyway?). The Night Owl used to run buses along the subway routes until 2:30 am on Friday and Saturday nights, helping late-night partiers with a lift home. No word from the MBTA on whether this service will ever re-appear.

Most buses cost 90 cents, some longer rides cost $1.55, and fares on the express buses range from $2.20 to $3.45. Monthly bus passes are $31 and subway/bus combos cost $71. Students, seniors, and disabled persons can purchase monthly passes at reduced rates. Bus passes can be bought at several T stations or online at www.mbta.com.

Silver Line

Website: www.allaboutsilverline.com
Phone: 617-222-5000

Although the Silver Line appears on the MBTA's subway map, it is actually a high-speed bus line (a "state-of-the-art Bus Rapid Transit system", no less) that, according to the MBTA, "combines the quality of rail transit with the flexibility of buses." The MBTA's public relations materials may be as gassy as the CNG used by some of the new buses, but in fact the new

system provides much-needed additional public transport options for Roxbury residents and is proving handy to airport travelers, Moakley Courthouse staff, and people working at construction sites along the waterfront.

The Silver Line is being constructed in three phases. Completed Phase I runs between Downtown Crossing and Dudley Square in Roxbury. Phase II, also completed, runs from South Station to Logan Airport, Boston Marine Industrial Park, and City Point. (The MBTA is waffling on its original plan to extend the Silver Line to the Andrew T stop in South Boston/Dorchester).

Phase III will make it possible to use the Silver Line to travel all the way from Dudley Square to Logan Airport. Phase III will link Phase I and Phase II with a mile-long underground tunnel, which will run beneath Essex Street and Boylston Street and make new connections to the Orange Line (at the Chinatown T stop) and the Green line (at the Boylston T stop). Phase III is scheduled to be completed in 2010, but because there hasn't yet been a decision taken on how the buses will actually *get into* the tunnel, it's anyone's guess when Phase III will go on-line.

The Silver Line Waterfront is $1.25 per ride (subway passes are valid) and the Silver Line Washington Street is 90 cents per ride (bus passes are valid).

Cambridge EZRide

Website: www.masscommute.com/tmas/crtma/ezgen.htm
Phone: 617-839-4636

Cantabrigians who traverse the Charles each morning on their daily commute should check out the EZRide bus service, whose cheery sky-blue coaches run through Cambridge to North Station. The EZRide route begins in Cambridgeport and passes through University Park, Kendall Square, and East Cambridge, making a dozen or so stops along the way.

EZRide operates Monday through Friday only, and does not run on holidays. Service in the morning runs from approximately 6:15 am to 10 am; afternoon service runs from 3:30 pm to 7:30 pm.

A trip on EZRide costs $1. Students, seniors, disabled persons, and children aged 5-11 traveling with an adult pay 50 cents. Flashing an MIT ID lets you ride for free.

Greyhound

NFT Map: 4
Website: www.greyhound.com
Phone: 800-231-2222

Greyhound buses leave from the South Station bus terminal and they'll take you *anywhere*. It ain't the Concorde, but it'll eventually get you to one of its 3,700 stations across North America. Round-trip tickets to New York cost $55-$65, round-trip to Washington DC is $132, and Boston to Philadelphia is $110 round-trip.

South Station is on Atlantic Avenue, one block down from Summer Street. The bus terminal is the taller building behind the rail building.

To get to South Station from the Mass Pike (I-90), take Exit 24A. This exit drops you onto Atlantic Avenue—the bus terminal is on the right side. From I-93 N, take Exit 20 and follow signs for Downtown and South Station. At the lights, continue straight onto Atlantic Avenue.

From I-93 S, take Exit 23 onto Purchase Street, make a left on Kneeland Street, continue to the end of the street, and then take a left onto Atlantic Avenue. On-street parking is scarce. If you're pinched, try the bus terminal's parking garage. The entrance is on Kneeland Street.

The Red Line T line has a stop at South Station, also the end point for the southern routes of the commuter rail.

Chinatown Buses

If you want to get to New York City for *really* cheap, take a Chinatown bus. A round-trip ticket will only cost you $30 on Boston Deluxe, Fung Wah, Lucky Star, or Sunshine. Chinatown buses range from small coaches (especially on the Fung Wah) to full-blown buses with bathrooms and TVs (but we recommend using the bathrooms only in emergency situations).

If you take a late Chinatown bus from NYC, you will get into Boston after the T closes, meaning you'll have to pay for a cab that will cost more than the 200-plus-mile journey from New York.

Boston Deluxe

www.ivymedia.com/bostondeluxe; 617-354-2101
Christian Science Plaza, 175 Huntington Ave (Map 5)
Pick up the Boston Deluxe near the Prudential Center for trips to New York City and Hartford. New York-bound buses depart at 8:30 am, 1 pm, 4 pm, and 6 pm and drop off at Broadway and 32nd Street as well as E 86th Street and Second Avenue. Buses to Hartford depart at 8:30 am, 1 pm, and 6 pm and drop off at 365 Capitol Ave (Charter Oak Supermarket). Both routes cost $30 round-trip.

Fung Wah Bus

www.fungwahbus.com; 617-345-8000
South Station, 700 Atlantic Ave (Map 4)
Buses to New York depart every hour on the hour, from 7 am until 10 pm, with an additional trip at 11:30 pm. Round-trip tickets cost $30. Buses leave from Gate 25 at South Station (left side) and drop off at 139 Canal Street in New York's Chinatown.

Lucky Star Bus

www.luckystarbus.com; 617- 426-8802
South Station, 700 Atlantic Ave (Map 4)
Buses to New York depart every hour on the hour, from 7 am until 8 pm. There are also departures at 11:30 pm and 2 am. Round-trip tickets cost $30 (add $10 for the 2 am trip). Buses leave from Gate 13 at South Station and drop off at Christie and Hester Streets in New York's Chinatown.

Sunshine Travel

www.sunshineboston.com; 617-328-0862
31 Harrison Ave, Boston (Map 4);
McDonald's Plaza, Fields Corner, Dorchester (Map 32)
Along with buses departing hourly for NYC ($15 each way), Sunshine Travel offers two-, three-, and four-day tours to places like Tennessee (four days, $168), Chicago (four days, $268), Washington DC (three days, $109), Niagara Falls (two days, $89), and destinations in eastern Canada ($109-$288). Buses to the Mohegan Sun in Connecticut depart five times daily, picking up in Dorchester then Boston. Round-trip tickets cost $20, and you'll receive a $20 gambling voucher and a $15 dining voucher if you're 21 years of age or older.

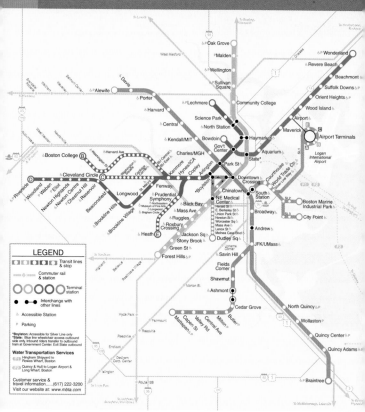

General Information

Website: www.mbta.com
Phone: 617-222-5000

Overview

Maps of the T show its four subway lines (Red, Orange, Blue, and Green) and the Silver Line (the T's mash-up of a subway line and a bus). All of the T

lines except the Green Line's B train move you across the city at a decent clip. But if you need to get from Davis Square (Somerville) to Cleveland Circle (Brighton), well... it's not easy. Despite the proximity of the two places, you have to go downtown on one line (Red) and back out on another (Green)—an 11-mile trip connecting destinations that are 6.5 miles apart. Another T peeve is that the last trains depart from stations between midnight and 1 am, even though last call at Boston bars is between 1 and 2 am. (Some Redcoat traditions live on.) Late-night revelers are left to shell out for cabs.

The Red Line: The T's flagship line, the Red Line runs from Alewife in Cambridge through Davis Square, Harvard Square, MIT, the Esplanade, the Common, Southie, and Dorchester. At the JFK/UMass stop, the line splits in two: The Ashmont train goes to Dorchester (with a connecting trolley to Mattapan), and the Braintree train runs through Quincy. A fun game to play on the Red Line: Bet with your friends about which student riders and professorial-looking types will get off at which university stops.

The Green Line: This is the oldest operational subway in the country, and it shows. Not a grown-up subway like the Red, Orange, and Blue Lines, the Green Line features light-rail "trolleys"—130-foot-long green Twinkies—that shoot you beneath the city of Boston before emerging onto streets and getting stuck in traffic.

The Green Line runs from Lechmere in Cambridge as far as Kenmore in Boston. Stops along the way include the Museum of Science, TD Banknorth Garden, Faneuil Hall, the Common, Back Bay, and Fenway Park. At Kenmore, the B (Boston College), C (Cleveland Circle), and D (Riverside) trains diverge and emerge from the ground as trolleys. The E train parts ways two stops back at Copley. The B is the slowest train because god forbid the Boston University kids walk anywhere. Lots of stops + lots of red lights = long rides. The B takes you through BU, Allston, Brighton, and as far as Boston College. The C runs along Beacon Street through Coolidge Corner (in Brookline) to Cleveland Circle (in Brighton). When getting off the train at Cleveland Circle, note the trolley making a wide circular turn through four-way traffic, which, inexplicably, leads to a lot of accidents. The D runs through Fenway and Brookline Village to Chestnut Hill before hitting several Newton neighborhoods. The E (Heath Street) train splits before Kenmore at Copley and services Symphony Hall, Mission Hill, Northeastern University, the Museum of Fine Arts, and Longwood Medical Area. Don't believe the maps that tell you E trains terminate at Forest Hills. This service was "temporarily" suspended in 1986—meanwhile, the 39 bus will take you from Heath Street to Forest Hills.

Somerville residents have been patiently waiting for the arrival of a long-promised extension of the Green Line. This extension, which would value the Green Line from Lechmere through exhaust-clogged Union Square to West Medford, is now expected to open no sooner than 2011, and even that delayed date could be pushed back.

The Orange Line: The Orange Line worked as an elevated trolley running above Washington Street until the 1980s. Today, it's a legitimate train that runs below the Southwest Corridor Park. The park and the Orange Line follow a path originally designed for the extension of I-95 through Boston. Community groups defeated the proposal in 1979, convincing officials to put a subway and park on the land instead. The Orange Line runs from Oak Grove in Malden to Forest Hills in Jamaica Plain. Stops along the way include Sullivan Square, Bunker Hill Community College, TD Banknorth Garden, Faneuil Hall, Downtown Crossing, Chinatown, New England Medical Center, Back Bay/South End, as well as a few stops in Roxbury and Jamaica Plain.

The Blue Line: Who rides the Blue Line? MBTA rider ship figures show a little over 55,000 daily boardings on the Blue Line, compared to 154,000 on the Orange, 210,500 on the Red, and about 205,000 on the Green. Running from Bowdoin Street downtown to Wonderland in Revere, this is the line you want to ride if you're going fishing, flying, or betting on horses and dogs. On your way east, you'll pass the Aquarium, Logan Airport, Suffolk Downs, and Revere Beach before winding up at Wonderland and its dog track. The stations at Aquarium and Logan have been renovated and made more accessible; other stations on the Blue Line are due to get the same treatment over the next couple of years.

The Silver Line: This is actually a high-speed bus line. See page 246 for all the salacious details.

Parking

Your chances of finding parking increase as you move further away from downtown, but generally only end cap stations and suburban stations provide day parking. Garages and lots fill up quickly on weekdays. Prices vary. Parking in resident-only spots will result in a ticket and, in some areas, a keying.

Fares and Passes

A ride on the subway costs $1.25, but if you board the outbound Green Line west of Kenmore (or Symphony on the E train), you'll ride for free. Monthly subway passes cost $44 and combo subway/bus passes cost $71. Passes are sold at certain T stops and in some stores. To find out where to buy a pass or to purchase one online, visit www.mbta.com. The MBTA has started to replace subway tokens with the magnetic-stripe CharlieCard and the paper CharlieTicket. (The "Charlie" moniker was taken from the Kingston Trio's 1959 hit, "Charlie on the MTA.")

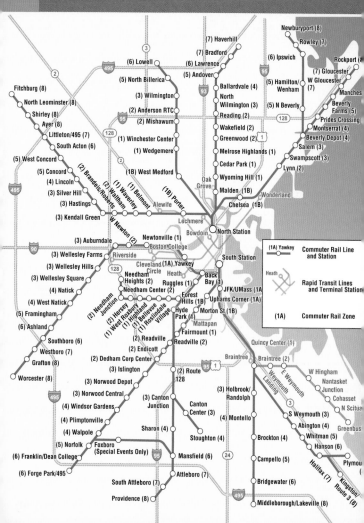

Fitchburg (8)

North Leominster (8)

Shirley (8)

Ayer (8)

Littleton/495 (7)

South Acton (6)

(5) West Concord

(5) Concord

(4) Lincoln

(3) Silver Hill

(3) Hastings

(3) Kendall Green

(2) Brandeis/Roberts

(2) Waltham

(1) Belmont

(1B) West Medford

(1) Waverley

(3) Auburndale

(1) Wedgemere

(1) Winchester Center

(2) Mishawum

(2) Anderson RTC

(3) Wilmington

(5) North Billerica

(6) Lowell

(7) Haverhill

(7) Bradford

(6) Lawrence

(5) Andover

Ballardvale (4)

North Wilmington (3)

Reading (2)

Wakefield (2)

Greenwood (2)

Melrose Highlands (1)

Cedar Park (1)

Wyoming Hill (1)

Malden (1B)

Chelsea (1B)

Newburyport (8)

Rowley (7)

(6) Ipswich

Rockport (8

(7) Gloucester

W Gloucester (7)

Manches

Beverly Farms (5)

Prides Crossing

Montserrat (4)

Beverly Depot (4)

Salem (3)

Swampscott (3)

Lynn (2)

(5) Hamilton/Wenham

(5) N Beverly

W Newton (2)

(3) Wellesley Farms

(3) Wellesley Hills

(3) Wellesley Square

(4) Natick

(4) West Natick

(5) Framingham

(6) Ashland

Southboro (6)

Westboro (7)

Grafton (8)

Worcester (8)

Newtonville (1)

Boston College

Riverside

Needham Heights (2)

Needham Center (2)

(2) Needham Junction

(2) Hersey

(2) West Roxbury

(1) Highland

(1) Bellevue

(1) Roslindale Village

(2) Readville

(2) Endicott

(2) Dedham Corp Center

(3) Islington

(3) Norwood Depot

(3) Norwood Central

(4) Windsor Gardens

(4) Plimptonville

(4) Walpole

(5) Norfolk

(6) Franklin/Dean College

(6) Forge Park/495

Foxboro (Special Events Only)

South Attleboro (7)

Providence (8)

Cleveland Circle (1A) Yawkey

Heath

Ruggles (1)

Forest Hills (1B)

Hyde Park (1)

Fairmount (1)

Readville (2)

(2) Route 128

(3) Canton Junction

Canton Center (3)

Sharon (4)

Stoughton (4)

Mansfield (6)

Attleboro (7)

North Station

South Station

Back Bay (1)

JFK/UMass (1A

Uphams Corner (1A)

Morton St (1B)

Mattapan

Braintree

Braintree (2)

Quincy Center (1)

(3) Holbrook/Randolph

(4) Montello

Brockton (4)

Campello (5)

Bridgewater (6)

Middleborough/Lakeville (6)

E Weymouth

Weymouth Landing

S Weymouth (3)

Abington (4)

Whitman (5)

Hanson (6)

Halifax (7)

Kingston Route 3 (8

W Hingham

Nantasket Junction

Cohasset

N Scitu

Greenbus

Plymou

Lechmere

Bowdoin

Alewife

Porter

Oak Grove

Wonderland

Legend

(1A) Yawkey — Commuter Rail Line and Station

Heath — Rapid Transit Lines and Terminal Station

(1A) — Commuter Rail Zone

General Information

Website: www.mbta.com
Phone: 617-222-3200 or 800-392-6100

Overview

The commuter rail is a series of train lines that service the outer limits of Greater Boston, the suburbs, and points as far out as Worcester and Providence, Rhode Island. Northbound routes leave from North Station, and southbound routes depart from, believe it or not, South Station. Compared to the commuter rail systems of other East Coast cities, Boston's trains make for a relatively pleasant experience. Massachusetts is working to renovate all of the stations, outfitting them with new platforms, electronic signaling, and new ramps and elevators to make them handicapped accessible. As with any major transit network, there are occasional (read: daily) delays on the commuter rail. Still, a ride on the rails is 1,000 percent less stressful than driving in and out of the city every day.

The commuter rail is also a great option for day-trippers going in either direction. Taking the train allows inbound visitors to enjoy, rather than just get lost in, the city. City-dwellers who want to escape the familiar urban landscape can head up to Gloucester for a day at the beach, venture to Plymouth for a history lesson, or just explore a new city down in Providence.

The MBTA has decided to restore long-suspended commuter rail service to the South Shore on what is known as the Greenbush Line. Cost for the project was projected to be $479 million, but the Big Dig has taught Bostonians to be distrustful of such estimates. Work on the line, which will offer a commuting alternative for folks in Braintree, Weymouth, Hingham, Cohasset, and Scituate, began in 2003. Service was originally scheduled to begin in spring 2006; current estimates predict some time in mid-2007. To learn more about the Greenbush Line, visit the project's website at www.cbbgreenbush.com.

If you're looking at the commuter rail map for the first time, you might think that the lack of a connection between North Station and South Station is a mistake. Well, it's a mistake, but not on the part of the mapmakers. To get from one station to another, you'll have to use the T (and transfer to a second T), take a cab, or walk. No, we're not kidding. For additional information about North Station and South Station, see the next page.

Parking

Parking is available at every commuter rail station except Ayer, Belmont, Endicott, Foxboro, Greenwood, Hastings, Mishawum, Morton Street, Natick, Newtonville, Plimptonville, Prides Crossing, Porter, Silver Hill, Uphams Corner, Waverley, West Newton, Windsor Gardens, and Yawkey. Rates vary, with some as low as $2 per day.

Fares and Passes

Commuter rail tickets range in price from $1.25 to $6. Tickets can be purchased on the train, but depending on how busy the train is and the ticket-taker's mood, a surcharge may be added to the price. Kids 5-11, high school students, seniors, and disabled persons ride for half-price. Children under five and blind people ride free. The cost of monthly passes ranges from $106 to $198, depending on the zone. Some monthly passes offer varying perks like free subway, bus, and ferry use. Passes are sold at certain T stops and other locations (usually a local shop close to the station), as well as online at www.mbta.com.

MAP
1

TO
Bunker Hill
Monument
North Station

PAGE
241

Commercial St

Charlestown Bridge

Causeway St

North
Station

Canal St

N Washington St

Battery St

Merrimack St

Market St

New Chardon St

Cross St

New Sudbury St

Haymarket

Bowdoin

Cross St

Christopher
Columbus
Park

Cambridge St

Clinton St

Government
Center

City
Hall

Quincy Market

Aquarium

Somerset St

Bowdoin St

State

PAGE
196

State St

Ashburton Pl

Congress St

Kilby St

East
India Row

Beacon St

School St

Broad St

Park Street

Washington St

Franklin St

Milk St

Oliver St

Pearl St

High St

Boston
Common

Temple Pl

Downtown
Crossing

Summer St

Purchase St

Atlantic Ave

Northern Av

Seaport Blvd

Tremont St

Essex St

Fort Point
Channel

MAP
4

Boylston

Chinatown

Lincoln St

Atlantic Ave

South
Station

Congress St Bridge

Dorchester Ave

General Information

NFT Maps: 1 & 4
Websites: www.amtrak.com/stations/bon.html (North)
www.amtrak.com/stations/bos.html (South)
www.amtrak.com (Amtrak)
www.mbta.com (MBTA)
Amtrak: 800-872-7245 (800-USA-RAIL)
MBTA: 617-222-5215

Overview

North Station and South Station are the main Amtrak and MBTA Commuter Rail depots in Boston. North Station, near the North End and underneath TD Banknorth Garden, sits above the T's new "superstation" that (finally) connects the Green Line and Orange Line. South Station, on Atlantic Avenue and Summer Street at the gateway to South Boston, is served by MBTA and Amtrak and also has a bus terminal, a food court in the domed arrival hall, a bar, a newsstand, and a bookstore.

Traveling between Stations

There is a one-mile gap between the two Amtrak stations. The North Station stop is on the Orange and Green Lines of the MBTA subway, and the South Station stop is on the Red Line. Yes, it *is* crazy that the stations aren't on the same line and don't directly connect to each other. No, they're *not* going to do anything to correct the problem in the near future. Yes, they *could* have rolled it into the Big Dig project, since they were digging under the city anyway. No, we *don't* know why they didn't. And yes, it *does* seem odd that they spent billions to improve automobile transportation while ignoring public transportation. As it stands, travelers going from New York to Maine have to get off the train at South Station and either take a cab, take two subway trains, or walk to get to North Station to continue their journey.

How to Get There—Driving

Both stations are located off I-93 in downtown Boston. For North Station, take Exit 26 (Storrow Drive), and for South Station, take Exit 23 (Purchase Street/South Station). To get to South Station from the Mass Pike (I-90), take Exit 24B to Atlantic Avenue.

Parking

The MBTA says there's no parking at either station, but "street or private parking may exist." Helpful, huh? In fact, both North Station and South Station are served by nearby, expensive parking garages, and neither station offers much in the way of street parking. Lovely.

How to Get There—Mass Transit

North Station is on the T's Green and Orange Lines. South Station is on the Red Line.

Amtrak

Amtrak trains leave out of North Station and South Station going north to Portland, Maine and south to NYC and beyond. When you go north, they call it the Downeaster (that's Mainer for "near Canada"). When you go south, they call it a bunch of things, including "the Federal," "the Acela," and the mundanely titled "Regional." The Acela is Amtrak's flagship route, offering "high-speed" service from South Station to NYC, Philly, and DC, with stops along the way. On a good day, the Acela chugs from Boston to New York in 3.5 hours, which is still only slightly faster than a bus and, at $81 a ticket, costs much more than taking one of the Chinatown buses (see page [247]).

Baggage Check

Three items of baggage weighing up to 50 lbs each may be checked up to 30 minutes prior to train departure. For an additional fee of $10 per bag, three additional pieces can be checked. Each passenger is allowed two carry-on items on board. No dangerous, fragile, valuable items, animals, or household goods can be checked. Bikes, skis, and other odd-shaped equipment usually count as one checked bag and should not be carried aboard the train. With the exception of service animals, all pets are prohibited on Amtrak trains.

How to Get Tickets

To purchase train tickets, call Amtrak or visit their website. The website sometimes offers discounts for purchasing on-line, so it's worth checking the website before heading to the station.

Going to New York

One-way fares start at $54 and the journey takes about 4.5 hours from South Station. You could cut an hour off your commute by riding express on the Acela, but the comfort and convenience will cost ya ($81 to be exact).

Going to Philadelphia

One-way fares start at $69, and the ride takes about six hours. Fares on the speedier Acela Express start at $157 and cut about an hour off of the journey.

Going to Washington DC

A trip to Washington on the regular Amtrak train will cost you at least $76 and will take you between eight and nine hours. Acela Express tickets start at $170 and the trip takes between six and seven hours.

General Information (Ferries)

MBTA: www.mbta.com; 617-222-5215
Harbor Express: www.harborexpress.com;
617-222-6999

Overview

The MBTA Commuter and Excursion Boat Service connects Boston to Logan Airport and is one of the best routes in and out of Charlestown and other shore side communities. One thing that makes the T boat better than any other form of Boston transportation is the fun factor. On a nice day, paying a buck and a half for a quick jaunt across the harbor feels like a steal. And on any day, not having to deal with Boston traffic is priceless. The views of the city from the water are gorgeous, and since the routes are in the Inner Harbor, the ride remains relatively smooth even in bad weather. There is also that delicious old-time feeling that comes with ferrying across the harbor. You'll want to keep in mind that boat schedules are more limited than bus schedules (particularly on weekends) and are more susceptible to disruptions due to inclement weather.

Most ferries operated by the MBTA leave from Long Wharf and travel to the Charlestown Navy Yard (F4), the Fore River Shipyard in Quincy (F2), and Pemberton Point in Hull (F2H). The F1 boat travels between Rowes Wharf and Hingham Shipyard.

The F2 and the F2H boats, catamarans operated by Harbor Express, stop at Logan Airport, but not at all times of the day—check the MBTA website for timetables. During rush hour (and decent weather) the Harbor Express is a sensible choice for getting to the airport. It takes a mere seven minutes to get to the airport dock from Long Wharf and about 25 minutes from Quincy and Hull. From the airport dock, take the free Water Shuttle bus 66 to the terminals. The 66 bus takes about 15 minutes to visit all terminals and return to the dock.

All ferry stops are accessible to wheelchair users. Bicycles can also be taken on board for free.

Parking

Parking for commuter ferry stops in the Inner Harbor is available only on the street or in a garage. Parking in Quincy costs $1 for a day and $6 overnight. In Hingham, parking costs $1 for a day and $1.75 overnight. Free parking is available at Hull High School.

Fares

A trip on a boat between destinations in the Inner Harbor costs $1.50 (pay a crewmember when boarding the boat). Trips from Hull, Quincy, and Hingham to the Inner Harbor (Rowes Wharf or Long Wharf) cost $6 ($3 for kids, seniors, and disabled persons). Trips from Quincy and Hull to Logan Airport on the Harbor Express are $12 ($10 for seniors, $3 for kids 5-11). Pay a crewmember when boarding the boat.

General Information (Water Taxis)

City Water Taxi: www.citywatertaxi.com;
617-422-0392
Rowes Wharf
Water Taxi: www.oms.net/rwwatertaxi/contact.htm
617-406-8584
Massport: www.massport.com/logan/
getti_typeo_water.html;
800-23-LOGAN

Overview

On the charmed waters of the Inner Harbor, two water taxi companies ply their trade. During the warmer months, water taxis provide an enjoyable way to cross the Inner Harbor. Both water taxi companies stop at the Logan Airport dock.

City Water Taxi

City Water Taxi provides on-call service between April 1 and November 30 (Mon–Thurs 7 am–10 pm; Sun 7 am–8 pm). In addition to the airport dock, City Water Taxi serves 15 other points, including Bank of America Pavilion, Fan Pier, Charlestown Navy Yard, Black Falcon Terminal, and all the major wharves in the Inner Harbor. (To get to the Boston Convention and Exhibition Center, aim for the World Trade Center.) To catch a City Water Taxi from the airport, take Massport's 66 bus to the airport dock. Use the call box at the dock to call for a boat if there isn't one already there. From other destinations, call City Water Taxi to arrange a pick-up.

Tickets are sold on board the boat. Fares to downtown points and Logan Airport cost $10 one-way and $17 round-trip. To Charlestown, North Station, or Black Falcon Terminal, the fare is $15. If you're alone and riding to North Station or Black Falcon Terminal, the fare is $20.

Rowes Wharf Water Taxi

Operating year-round, Rowes Wharf Water Taxi provides on-call service to points in the Inner Harbor (from Oct 1–May 31, service only Mon–Fri 7 am–7 pm; from June 1–Sept 30, daily 7 am–7 pm). After-hours service is available upon request. Rowes Wharf Water Taxi serves Rowes Wharf, Logan Airport, Fan Pier, and the World Trade Center. To hail a boat from the airport dock, use the company's call box; from other destinations, give them a call from your own phone.

Tickets are sold on board. The fare costs $10 one-way and $17 round-trip.

General Information

Websites:
Boston: www.cityofboston.gov/transportation/
             driveandpark.asp
Brookline: www.town.brookline.ma.us/
             transportation
Cambridge: www.cambridgema.gov/traffic
Somerville: www.ci.somerville.ma.us
Mass. RMV: www.state.ma.us/rmv

Phones:
Boston: 617-635-4680
Brookline: 617-730-2177
Cambridge: 617-349-4700
Somerville: 617-625-6600, ext. 7900

Overview

In Boston, driving is art. The roads are a blank canvas and cars the paintbrush. Perhaps this is why there are so few road signs in the city; Picasso, after all, didn't do paint-by-numbers. The lack of signs means that finding your way in the city depends on a heady mix of practice and intuition.

The road system in Boston grew organically as the city expanded and merged with small farming villages such as Brighton, Dorchester, and Roxbury. Little, if any, urban planning took place. The result is the chaos of today, an exasperating, exhilarating tangle of streets that are a source of pride to those who master them.

Depending on who you ask, Boston drivers are either the best in the country or the most frightening. As a rule, however, they are both aggressive and competent. Years of experience have taught them precisely how far they can push the envelope on sudden lane changes and risky passing maneuvers.

For the novice, it may be intimidating, but the initial challenge makes the eventual mastery all that much more satisfying.

Survival Tips

- **Learn the Vocabulary:** In driving, as in other areas, Bostonians have their own distinct vocabulary. Therefore, it is wicked important to know the following terms:
  · Rotary- Known in other parts of the country as a roundabout or traffic circle. Poor rotary skills are near the top of most Bostonians driving pet peeve lists, so it is important to remember that vehicles already in the rotary have right-of-way.
  · Square- A location at which several feeder streets connect in odd formations and strange angles (e.g. Harvard or Davis). Squares are rarely, if ever, square.
  · Masshole- From the mouths of out-of-staters, a derogatory term. For a true Boston driver, a label worn with pride.
  · The Expressway- Refers to the Southeast Expressway, the southern half of the length of I-93 that runs through the city. Common usage: "The Expressway is a parking lot."
  · *@%$ you- A helpful driving tip frequently offered by fellow motorists.

- **Be aggressive:** Drive the streets of Boston, don't let the streets drive you. Other drivers express their displeasure with such assertiveness, but, secretly, they respect it.

- **Be color blind:** A yellow light (and the first ten seconds of a red light) are generally considered the functional equivalent of a green light.

- **Plan Very Carefully:** Once you deviate from your planned route, one-way streets and unexpected turns may make it hard to get back on track. And once your route is in place…

- **Triple-check your directions:** Because of the paucity of road signs in Boston, driving directions are likely to be heavily landmark-based. Be wary of landmarks like "that bridge with the construction on it" or "that Dunkin' Donuts on the corner," since that could be any block in the city. If someone tells you to take a right or a left, ask *how much* of a right or a left.

- **Get lost anyway:** There's really no good way of preparing for what's in store. Just do it. Leave yourself some extra time and learn to enjoy being lost. We promise, one day it will start making sense.

General Information

Websites:
Boston: www.cityofboston.gov/transportation/parking.asp
Brookline: www.town.brookline.ma.us/transportation/parking/parking.html
Cambridge: www.cambridgema.gov/Traffic/index.cfm
Somerville: www.ci.somerville.ma.us

Phones:
Boston: 617-635-4680
Brookline: 617-730-2230
Cambridge: 617-349-4700
Somerville: 617-625-6600

Overview

When parking within the city, patience is a cardinal virtue; with a few exceptions (near Fenway during Sox games come to mind), careful circling of a target area will eventually yield results. If patience fails, a willingness to pay the often outrageous fees at a parking garage is also helpful. There are, however, bargains to be found; the rates at the Post Office Square garage are amazing considering its location and the Cambridgeside Galleria charges only $1 per hour.

Depending on where you live, you might want to reconsider ever owning a car. The North End and Allston are crowded neighborhoods with narrow streets jam-packed with parked cars. As it becomes colder and snowier in Boston, the residents become fiercely protective of their parking spots, using traffic cones, lawn chairs, and other assorted paraphernalia to claim their freshly shoveled out spaces. Somerville, Cambridge, and Brookline, however, aren't quite as bad for parking, in part due to vast "resident-only parking" zones (generally resented by non-residents).

Ultimately, if you live in Boston and own a car, you will receive at least one ticket a month. Maybe there was street cleaning the night before. Maybe there was a parking ban because of snow. Or maybe you got towed because there's a construction project and you missed the half-hidden "Tow Zone" sign that workers positioned conveniently on the sidewalk under a discarded pizza box. It doesn't matter what you do and how careful you are—*they will get you*—so just add it to the monthly budget.

How to Get Permits

In Somerville, take a lease or a current bill with your address and your registration to 133 Holland Street. In Boston, take your registration and a current bill with your address to City Hall, Room 224, at Government Center. All Brookline wants is $15 and apparently they don't care where you live. Brookline Town Hall is at 333 Washington Street. In the People's Republic of Cambridge, you need your registration saying that either you or your car (it's not clear which) weighs less than 2.5 tons and proof of residency. You can visit the website and download the form and send copies of the above with a check for $8 (bargain!) to Cambridge Traffic, Parking & Transportation, Resident Parking, 238 Broadway, Cambridge, MA 02139.

Towing

Cars get towed for snow emergencies, street cleaning, and other emergency situations, so keep an eye out for Nor'easters, third Thursdays, and massive construction. If your car gets towed, it'll cost you at least $100 to get it back.

The Boston BTD Tow Lot is located at 200 Frontage Road, near the Andrew T stop in Dorchester/Southie. The City of Boston website says that "walking is not encouraged" due, obviously, to the Big Dig. Cabs can be hailed at the Andrew T stop.

Brookline, Somerville, and Cambridge use private, commercial lots to store your newly towed car. Call one of the numbers above, and they'll (hopefully) be able to tell you where your car is.

The Somerville tow lot is, for reasons unknown, Pat's Auto Body on McGrath Highway near Union Square.

Cambridge either has a top-secret tow lot, or it rotates. If your car gets towed, they ask you to call the police (617-349-3300), who will presumably then tell you where your car is.

Brookline has a similarly clandestine car imprisonment system. A call to their transportation/parking office should unearth your car.

Tickets

Because it allows them to take your money immediately, all four places offer online ticket payment. Tickets are dispensed for offenses such as double-parking, expired meters, non-resident parking on a resident-only street, street cleaning violations, and the city/town needing money. Regardless of the city, you're looking at about 50 bucks per infringement.

Car Rental

If you need a car for more than 24 hours at a time, try one of the many old-fashioned car rental places in Boston.

Map 1 • Beacon Hill / West End

Avis	3 Center Plz	617-534-1400
Dollar	209 Cambridge St	617-723-8312

Map 2 • North End / Faneuil Hall

Enterprise	1 Congress St	617-723-8077

Map 3 • Downtown Crossing / Park Square / Bay Village

Budget	24 Park Plz	617-497-3669
Hertz	30 Park Plz	617-338-1500

Map 4 • Financial District / Chinatown

Alamo	270 Atlantic Ave	617-557-7179
Dollar	30 Rowes Wharf	617-367-2654
Hertz	Summer St & Atlantic Ave	617-338-1503
National	70 E India Row	617-557-7179
Select Car Rental	1 Lincoln St	617-737-0371

Map 5 • Back Bay (West) / Fenway (East)

Avis	41 Westland Ave	617-534-1400
Enterprise	800 Boylston St	617-262-8222
Select Car Rental	39 Dalton St	617-236-6088

Map 6 • Back Bay (East) / South End (Upper)

Dollar	110 Huntington Ave	617-578-0025
Hertz	10 Huntington Ave	617-338-1506
Hertz	145 Dartmouth St	617-338-1500

Map 9 • East Boston

Affordable Auto	84 Condor St	617-561-7000

Map 12 • Newmarket / Andrew Square

Enterprise	230 Dorchester Ave	617-268-1411
Hertz Local Edition	371 Dorchester Ave	617-268-4660

Map 16 • Kenmore Square / Brookline (East)

Select Car Rental	500 Commonwealth Ave	617-532-5060

Map 18 • Brighton

Rent A Wreck	2022 Commonwealth Ave	617-254-9540

Map 19 • Allston (South) / Brookline (North)

Budget	95 Brighton Ave	617-497-3608
Enterprise	292 Western Ave	617-783-2240
Enterprise	996 Commonwealth Ave	617-738-6003
Hertz	414 Cambridge St	617-787-2894
Hertz Local Edition	226 Harvard Ave	617-566-9801
U-Save Auto & Truck	25 Harvard Ave	617-254-1000

Map 20 • Harvard Square / Allston (North)

Alamo	1663 Massachusetts Ave	617-661-8747
Avis	1 Bennett St	617-534-1400
Hertz	24 Eliot St	617-338-1520
National	1663 Massachusetts Ave	617-661-8747
Thrifty	110 Mt Auburn St	617-876-2758

Map 21 • West Cambridge

Enterprise	48 New St	617-354-2302

Map 23 • Central Somerville / Porter Square

Enterprise	377 Summer St	617-628-2266
Hertz	646 Somerville Ave	617-625-7958

Map 24 • Winter Hill / Union Square

American Auto	90 Highland Ave	617-776-4640

Map 25 • East Somerville / Sullivan Square

Enterprise	37 Mystic Ave	617-625-1766

Map 26 • East Cambridge / Kendall Square / MIT

Enterprise	1 Broadway	617-577-0404

Map 27 • Central Square / Cambridgeport

Budget	66 Anglim St	617-497-3614
Enterprise	25 River St	617-547-7400

Map 28 • Inman Square

U-Save Auto & Truck	70 Prospect St	781-321-3300

Zipcar General Information

Website: www.zipcar.com
Phone: 617-491-9900

Background

Zipcar rents out cars by the hour. The company, which now runs similar services in DC, New Jersey, New York, and elsewhere, was founded at MIT: "People would achieve transportation nirvana by having a transit pass and a Zipcar in their pockets. The result would be reduced congestion, fewer auto emissions, more green space, and a revolution in urban planning." That's Cambridgian for "Give us $8.75/hr, we'll give you a Jetta." This seems like the smartest idea on wheels if you live in congested areas like the North End, Allston, or Harvard Square and you need to get somewhere the T can't take you. For infrequent drivers, even the $100 (refundable) deposit, $25 application fee, and minimum annual fee of $50 still make Zipcar service cheaper than owning a car.

How It Works

If you're 21 or older, in possession of a valid driver's license, and you've completed the online application, all you need to do is call or go online to reserve one of the hundreds of cars available at zipcar.com. (You get to choose from a fleet of BMWs, Minis, pick-ups, and others.) Your Zipcard unlocks the car that has been reserved for you, which you pick up at the most convenient of their many locations. Cars must be returned to the same spot where they were picked up. The car unlocks when a valid Zipcard is held to the windshield; your card will only open the car during the time you have reserved it.

Costs

The cost of Zipcar varies depending on the pick-up location, but rates start at $8.75 an hour. A reservation for 24 hours, the maximum amount of time that a car can be reserved, starts at about $63. The first 125 miles are free; each additional mile costs 30 cents. Membership costs are additional. Make sure to return your car on time, as Zipcar charges exorbitant hourly late fees on unreturned cars.

General Information

All Emergencies: 911
Crime Stoppers: 800-494-TIPS
Boston Area Rape Crisis Center (BARCC): 617-492-RAPE
State Police: 617-727-7775
Boston: www.ci.boston.ma.us/police
Brookline: www.brooklinepolice.com
Cambridge: www.ci.cambridge.ma.us/~CPD/
Somerville: www.ci.somerville.ma.us

Statistics

	2005	2004	2003	2002	2001
Murder	73	61	39	60	39
Rape & Attempted	268	269	263	369	361
Robbery & Attempted	2,649	2,428	2,759	2,533	2,524
Aggravated Assault	4,113	4,159	4,113	3,994	4,412
Burglary & Attempted	4,531	4,545	4,344	3,830	4,222
Larceny & Attempted	15,957	17,526	17,069	17,824	17,608
Vehicle Theft	4,717	5,545	6,463	7,096	8,194

Police Stations

	Address	Phone	Map
District A-1	40 New Sudbury St	617-343-4240	1
District D-4	650 Harrison Ave	617-343-4250	7
District A-7	69 Paris St	617-343-4220	9
District C-6	101 W Broadway	617-343-4730	10
District B-2	135 Dudley St	617-343-4270	13
District E-13	3345 Washington St	617-343-5630	14
Brookline Police Department	350 Washington St	617-730-2222	17
District D-14	301 Washington St	617-343-4260	18
Somerville Police Department	220 Washington St	617-625-1600	24
Cambridge Police Department	5 Western Ave	617-349-3300	27

Louis Prang St

Short St

Plymouth St

Pilgrim Rd

Brookline Ave

Beth Israel
Deaconess
Medical Center
(BID)

BID

BID

BID

Judge Baker
Children's
Center

Harvard
Institute of
Medicine

Tetlow St

Palace Rd

Ave Louis Pasteur

Channing Lab/BWH

CH

CH

CH

Blackfan St

CH

MAP
15

Longwood Ave

MAP
16

Autumn St

Joslin
Diabetes
Center

Longwood
Galleria

Binney St

CH

Harvard Medical
School (HMS)

Harvard
Dental
School

HMS

Longwood
Medical
Area

Deaconess Rd

BIDMC

Dana-Farber
Cancer Institute
(DFCI)

Jimmy Fund Wy

Children's
Hospital (CH)

Beth Isreal
Deaconess
West-Campus
(BID)

CH

DFCI

CH

Peabody St

Shattuck St

CH

Harvard School
of Public Health

HMS

Huntington Ave

Riverway

BID

Brigham and
Women's
Hospital (BWH)

Francis St

Countway
Library

Brigham
Circle

Worthington St

Wigglesworth St

Fenwood Rd

Vining St

Fenwood Road

Tremont St

Torpie St

S Whitney St

Saint Alphonsus St

Brookline Ave

Jamaica Wy

New Whitney St

Mission Park Dr

Kempton St

St Albans Rd

Alleghany St

Mission Park

Shepherd Ave

Franklin St

Mission St

Pequot St

Wait St

Delling St

Calumet St

Riverway

Pearl St

Worthington St

Copenger St

Eldora St

Sunset St

Sachem St

Hillside St

Parker Hill Tor

Parker Hill

Iroquois St

Fisher Ave

Fisher St

Jamaicaway

Coburn St

Back of
the Hill

Hospitals

Boston's medical facilities rank among the best in the world. Many medical firsts happened in Boston, including the:

· First public demonstration of anesthesia during surgery, at Massachusetts General Hospital (1846).
· First identification and analysis of appendicitis, at Massachusetts General Hospital (1886).
· First surgical procedure to correct a congenital cardiovascular defect, performed by Dr. Robert Gross (1938).
· First successful fertilization of a human ovum in a test tube, by researchers at Peter Bent Brigham Hospital (1944).
· First successful pediatric remission of acute leukemia, achieved by Dr. Sidney Farber (1947).
· First isolation of the polio virus, at Children's Hospital (1948).
· First successful kidney transplant, at Peter Bent Brigham Hospital (1954).
· First demonstration of the effectiveness of an oral contraceptive, by Dr. John C. Rock (1959).

The Longwood Medical Area (see map on the facing page) compresses a dozen medical institutions into a handful of blocks below Mission Hill. These institutions, including **Brigham and Women's Hospital (Map 15)**, **Beth Israel Deaconess Medical Center (Map 16)**, **Children's Hospital (Map 15)**, **Dana-Farber Cancer Institute (Map 15)**, **Joslin Diabetes Center (Map 16)**, the **CBR Institute for Biomedical Research (Map 16)**, and **Harvard's** medical, dental, and public health schools, comprise what is probably the world's leading center for health care and medicine.

Massachusetts General Hospital (Map 1), which opened in 1811, is the oldest and largest hospital in New England. Each year MGH admits over 45,000 in-patients, processes over 76,000 emergency visits, and, at its West End main campus and four satellite facilities, handles more than 1.5 million outpatient visits.

Emergency Rooms	Address	Phone	Map
Massachusetts Eye and Ear Infirmary	243 Charles St	617-523-7900	1
Massachusetts General	55 Fruit St	617-726-2000	1
Tufts-New England Medical Center	750 Washington St	617-636-5000	3
Boston Medical Center	1 Boston Medical Ctr Pl	617-638-8000	7
Brigham and Women's Hospital	75 Francis St	617-732-5500	15
Children's Hospital	300 Longwood Ave	617-355-6000	15
Beth Israel Deaconess Medical Center	110 Francis St	617-667-7000	16
Mount Auburn	330 Mt Auburn St	617-492-3500	21
Somerville	230 Highland Ave	617-591-4500	23
Cambridge	1493 Cambridge St	617-665-1000	28

Other Hospitals	Address	Phone	Map
Boston Shriners Hospital	51 Blossom St	617-722-3000	1
Spaulding Rehabilitation Hospital	125 Nashua St	617-573-7000	1
Jewish Memorial Hospital & Rehabilitation Center	59 Townsend St	617-989-8315	13
Arbour Hospital	49 Robinwood Ave	617-522-4400	14
VA Boston-Jamaica Plain Campus	150 S Huntington Ave	617-232-9500	14
Dana-Farber Cancer Institute	44 Binney St	866-408-3324	15
New England Baptist Hospital	125 Parker Hill Ave	617-754-5800	15
CBR Institute for Biomedical Research	220 Longwood Ave	617-734-9500	16
Joslin Diabetes Center	1 Joslin Pl	617-732-2400	16
Franciscan Hospital for Children	30 Warren St	617-254-3800	18
St Elizabeth's Medical Center	736 Cambridge St	617-789-3000	18
The Boston Center	14 Fordham Rd	617-783-9676	19
Youville Hospital & Rehabilitation Center	1575 Cambridge St	617-876-4344	28

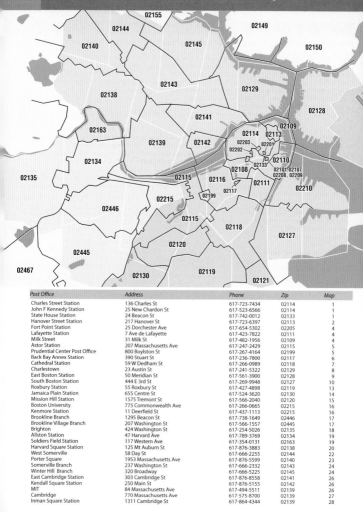

Post Offices & Zip Codes

Map labels: 02155, 02149, 02144, 02145, 02150, 02140, 02143, 02129, 02138, 02128, 02141, 02163, 02142, 02109, 02114, 02113, 02139, 02134, 02203, 02201, 02202, 02110, 02135, 02108, 02133, 02101, 02107, 02208, 02209, 02115, 02116, 02111, 02210, 02199, 02117, 02446, 02215, 02115, 02118, 02127, 02120, 02445, 02119, 02467, 02130, 02121

Post Office	Address	Phone	Zip	Map
Charles Street Station	136 Charles St	617-723-7434	02114	1
John F Kennedy Station	25 New Chardon St	617-523-6566	02114	1
State House Station	24 Beacon St	617-742-0012	02133	1
Hanover Street Station	217 Hanover St	617-723-6397	02113	2
Fort Point Station	25 Dorchester Ave	617-654-5302	02205	4
Lafayette Station	7 Ave de Lafayette	617-423-7822	02111	4
Milk Street	31 Milk St	617-482-1956	02109	4
Astor Station	207 Massachusetts Ave	617-247-2429	02115	5
Prudential Center Post Office	800 Boylston St	617-267-4164	02199	5
Back Bay Annex Station	390 Stuart St	617-236-7800	02117	6
Cathedral Station	59 W Dedham St	617-266-0989	02118	7
Charlestown	23 Austin St	617-241-5322	02129	8
East Boston Station	50 Meridian St	617-561-3900	02128	9
South Boston Station	444 E 3rd St	617-269-9948	02127	10
Roxbury Station	55 Roxbury St	617-427-4898	02119	13
Jamaica Plain Station	655 Centre St	617-524-3620	02130	14
Mission Hill Station	1575 Tremont Ave	617-566-2040	02120	15
Boston University	775 Commonwealth Ave	617-266-0665	02215	16
Kenmore Station	11 Deerfield St	617-437-1113	02215	16
Brookline Branch	1295 Beacon St	617-738-1649	02446	17
Brookline Village Branch	207 Washington St	617-566-1557	02445	17
Brighton	424 Washington St	617-254-5026	02135	18
Allston Station	47 Harvard Ave	617-254-5511	02134	19
Soldiers Field Station	117 Western Ave	617-354-0131	02163	19
Harvard Square Station	125 Mt Auburn St	617-876-3883	02138	20
West Somerville	58 Day St	617-666-2255	02144	22
Porter Square	1953 Massachusetts Ave	617-876-5599	02140	23
Somerville Branch	237 Washington St	617-666-2332	02143	24
Winter Hill Branch	320 Broadway	617-666-5225	02145	24
East Cambridge Station	303 Cambridge St	617-876-8558	02141	26
Kendall Square Station	250 Main St	617-876-5155	02142	26
MIT	84 Massachusetts Ave	617-494-5511	02139	26
Cambridge	770 Massachusetts Ave	617-575-8700	02139	27
Inman Square Station	1311 Cambridge St	617-864-4344	02139	28

General Information

Websites:
Boston: www.bpl.org
Brookline: www.town.brookline.ma.us/library
Cambridge   www.ci.cambridge.ma.us/~cpl
Somerville: www.somervillepubliclibrary.org

Phones:
Boston: 617-536-5400
Brookline: 617-730-2370
Cambridge: 617-349-4040
Somerville: 617-623-5000

Overview

The Boston Public Library, founded in 1848, was the first publicly supported municipal library in the United States, and is the only public library in the United States that is also a Presidential library, that of John Adams. It is also the first library to open and operate neighborhood branches. The BPL now operates 27 branch libraries, each of which offers free wireless Internet access. Check out the details on the BPL's website. For more information on the BPL's main branch and just how much cultural heat it's packing, see page 185.

Brookline, Cambridge, and Somerville have their own public libraries, which are part of the Minuteman System. The Brookline Public Library houses government documents, Russian and Chinese materials, Brookline high school yearbooks and newspapers, DVDs, videos, new books, and local newspapers. The Cambridge Public Library's Main Library has

occupied the same building since 1889, and is currently undergoing renovations and expansion slated for completion in 2008. It is temporarily located in the old Longfellow School at 359 Broadway. The Cambridge History and Local History Collections will be made available to the general public within the next two years, when the Main Library renovations are complete. The 93-year-old Somerville Public Library is also considering new construction in the future. Both Cambridge and Somerville libraries offer residents free passes to visit the Children's Museum, Harvard University Museum of Natural History, the JFK Library and Museum, the Museum of Fine Arts, the New England Aquarium, the Roger Williams Park Zoo, and others. To reserve FREE tickets, call 617-623-5000 (Somerville) or 617-349-4040 (Cambridge). For more information about hours, collections, and special events, check the library websites.

Library	Address	Phone	Map
Boston Public Library	700 Boylston St	617-536-5400	6
Boudreau	245 Concord Ave	617-349-4017	21
Brighton	40 Academy Hill Rd	617-782-6032	18
Brookline Main Library	361 Washington St	617-730-2370	17
Cambridge Main Library	359 Broadway	617-349-4030	28
Central Square	45 Pearl St	617-349-4010	27
Charlestown	179 Main St	617-242-1248	8
Connolly	433 Centre St	617-522-1960	14
Coolidge Corner	31 Pleasant St	617-730-2380	19
Dudley	65 Warren St	617-442-6186	13
East Boston	276 Meridian St	617-569-0271	9
Faneuil	419 Faneuil St	617-782-6705	18
Honan-Allston	300 N Harvard St	617-787-6313	19
Jamaica Plain	12 Sedgwick St	617-524-2053	14
Kirstein Business	20 City Hall Ave	617-523-0860	3
The Mary Baker Eddy Library	200 Massachusetts Ave	617-450-7000	5
North End	25 Parmenter St	617-227-8135	2
O'Connell	48 Sixth St	617-349-4019	26
O'Neill	70 Rindge Ave	617-349-4023	22
Parker Hill	1497 Tremont St	617-427-3820	15
Somerville East	115 Broadway	617-623-5000	24
Somerville Main Library	79 Highland Ave	617-623-5000	24
Somerville West	40 College Ave	617-623-5000	22
South Boston	646 E Broadway	617-268-0180	11
South End	685 Tremont St	617-536-8241	7
Valente	826 Cambridge St	617-349-4015	28
Washington Village	1226 Columbia Rd	617-269-7239	10
West End	151 Cambridge St	617-523-3957	1

General Information • FedEx

* Last pick-up

Map 1 • Beacon Hill / West End   *

Drop Box	1 Bowdoin Sq	8 pm
Drop Box	101 Merrimac St	8 pm
Drop Box	165 Cambridge St	8 pm
Drop Box	1 Beacon St	7 pm
Drop Box	131 Beverly St	7 pm
Drop Box	170 Canal St	7 pm
Drop Box	50 Staniford St	7 pm
Drop Box	7 Bulfinch Pl	7 pm
Drop Box	15 New Sudbury St	6:30 pm
FedEx Kinko's	2 Center Plaza	7 pm
Self-Service	60 Garden St	6 pm
Self-Service	55 Fruit St	6 pm
Self-Service	185 Cambridge St	5:30 pm
Self-Service	25 New Chardon St	4 pm

Map 2 • North End / Faneuil Hall   *

FedEx Kinko's	60 State St	8:30 pm
Drop Box	66 Long Wharf	8 pm
Drop Box	1 Boston Pl	7:15 pm
Drop Box	343 Commercial St	7:15 pm
Drop Box	1 Congress St	7 pm
Drop Box	240 Commercial St	7 pm
Drop Box	260 Tremont St	7 pm
Drop Box	77 N Washington St	7 pm
Drop Box	200 State St	6:45 pm
Drop Box	10 Saint James Ave	6:30 pm
Drop Box	28 State St	6:30 pm
Drop Box	98 N Washington St	6:30 pm
Prince Postale	71 Prince St	5 pm
Drop Box	141 Tremont St	4 pm

Map 3 • Downtown Crossing / Park Square / Bay Village   *

FedExStaffed	333 Washington St,	9 pm
FedEx Kinko's	211 Congress St	8 pm
Drop Box	270 Congress St	8 pm
Drop Box	99 Summer St	8 pm
Drop Box	45 School St	7:30 pm
Drop Box	50 Milk St	7:30 pm
Drop Box	260 Franklin St	7:15 pm
Drop Box	10 Park Plaza	7 pm
Drop Box	265 Franklin St	7 pm
Drop Box	35 Kneeland St	7 pm
Drop Box	75 Arlington St	7 pm
Drop Box	821 Washington St	7 pm
Drop Box	136 Harrison Ave	6:30 pm
Drop Box	73 Tremont St	6:30 pm
Drop Box	750 Washington St	6:30 pm
FedEx Kinko's	125 Tremont St	6 pm
Drop Box	31 Milk St	6 pm
Drop Box	470 Atlantic Ave	6 pm
Drop Box	80 Boylston St	6 pm
Drop Box	99 High St	6 pm
Self-Service	7 Ave de Lafayette	5 pm
Mail Boxes Etc	276 Washington St	5 pm

Map 4 • Financial District / Chinatown   *

Self-Service	1 Lincoln St	8 pm
Drop Box	4 Blackfan Circle	8 pm
Drop Box	88 Broad St	7:45 pm
Drop Box	1 Financial Center	7:30 pm
Drop Box	1 International Pl	7:30 pm
Drop Box	150 Federal St	7:30 pm
Drop Box	100 Federal St	7:15 pm
Self-Service	25 Dorchester Ave	7 pm
Penfield's	250 Franklin St	7 pm
FedEx Kinko's	10 Post Office Sq	7 pm
Drop Box	100 Summer St	7 pm
Drop Box	125 Summer St	7 pm
Drop Box	225 Franklin St	7 pm
Drop Box	155 Federal St	6:45 pm
Drop Box	21 Custom House St	6:45 pm
FedEx Kinko's	225 Washington St	6:30 pm
Drop Box	1 Federal St	6:30 pm
Drop Box	101 Arch St	6:30 pm
Drop Box	745 Atlantic Ave	6 pm
Drop Box	75 Federal St	6 pm
Drop Box	85 Franklin St	6 pm
Drop Box	45 Batterymarch St	5:30 pm
Self-Service	600 Atlantic Ave	4:30 pm
Drop Box	175 Federal St	4:30 pm

Map 5 • Back Bay (West) / Fenway (East)   *

Drop Box	200 Clarendon St	8 pm
Drop Box	815 Boylston St	8 pm
Drop Box	95 Berkeley St	7:30 pm
Drop Box	116 Huntington Ave	7 pm
Self-Service	900 Boylston St	6:30 pm
Self-Service	207 Massachusetts Ave	6:30 pm
Penfields	10 Huntington Ave	6 pm
Penfields	39 Dalton St	6 pm
Drop Box	800 Boylston St	4 pm

Map 6 • Back Bay (East) / South End (Upper)   *

Drop Box	699 Boylston St	7:45 pm
Drop Box	31 Saint James Ave	7:30 pm
Drop Box	101 Huntington Ave	7 pm
Drop Box	162 Columbus Ave	7 pm
Drop Box	197 Clarendon St	7 pm
Drop Box	399 Boylston St	7 pm
Drop Box	80 E Concord St	7 pm
Drop Box	818 Harrison Ave	7 pm
FedEx Kinko's	575 Boylston St	6 pm
FedEx Kinko's	187 Dartmouth St	6 pm
Drop Box	142 Berkeley St	6 pm
Drop Box	88 E Newton St	6 pm
Drop Box	700 Albany St	5:30 pm
Drop Box	500 Boylston St	5 pm
Drop Box	745 Boylston St	4 pm

Map 7 • South End (Lower)   *

Self-Service	85 E Concord St	8 pm
Self-Service	715 Albany St	7 pm

Map 8 • Charlestown   *

Self-Service	23 Austin St	7:30 pm
Drop Box	101 Main St	7:30 pm
Self-Service	20 City Sq	7 pm
Drop Box	149 13th St	7 pm
Drop Box	1 Thompson Sq	6:45 pm
Drop Box	1 Main St	6 pm
Drop Box	465 Medford St	6 pm
Drop Box	1 Constitution Plz	5:45 pm

Map 9 • East Boston   *

FedEx	142 Harborside Dr	8:45 pm
Drop Box	2 Central Sq	7:30 pm
Drop Box	430 W Broadway	7:30 pm
Self-Service	50 Meridian St	7 pm
Drop Box	256 Marginal St	6:30 pm
Drop Box	280 Summer St	6:30 pm
Drop Box	1 Harborside Dr	6 pm
Drop Box	580 Chelsea St	6 pm

Map 10 • South Boston (West) / Fort Point   *

Drop Box	313 Congress St	8 pm
FedEx Kinko's	415 Summer St	7:30 pm
Drop Box	68 Fargo St	7:30 pm
Drop Box	25 Thomson Pl	7 pm
Drop Box	88 Black Falcon Ave	6:30 pm
Drop Box	1 Gillette Way	6 pm
Drop Box	2 Seaport Lane	6 pm

Map 11 • South Boston (East)   *

FedEx	775 Summer St	9:30 pm
Drop Box	100 Newmarket Sq	7:15 pm
Drop Box	212 Northern Ave	6:30 pm
Drop Box	1 Design Center Pl	6 pm

Map 12 • Newmarket / Andrew Square   *

Self-Service	55 Roxbury St	7 pm
Drop Box	1 Widett Circle	6 pm

Map 13 • Roxbury   *

Drop Box	1135 Tremont St	7 pm
Drop Box	550 Huntington Ave	7 pm
Self-Service	1620 Tremont St	6:45 pm
Self-Service	716 Columbus Ave	6:30 pm
Drop Box	221 Longwood Ave	6:30 pm
Self-Service	346 Huntington Ave	6 pm
Self-Service	370 Huntington Ave	6 pm
Self-Service	43 Leon St	6 pm
Drop Box	20 Shattuck St	6 pm
Drop Box	677 Huntington Ave	6 pm

Map 14 • Jamaica Plain *

Drop Box	670 Centre St	7 pm

Map 15 • Fenway (West) / Mission Hill *

Self-Service	401 Park Dr	8 pm
Self-Service	1 Blackfan Circle	7:30 pm
Drop Box	75 Francis St	7:30 pm
Self-Service	10 Brookline Pl W	7 pm
FedEx Staffed	44 Binney St	7 pm
--Mobile Unit		
Drop Box	180 Longwood Ave	7 pm
Drop Box	188 Longwood Ave	7 pm
Self-Service	11 Leon St	6 pm
Drop Box	300 The Fenway	6 pm
Drop Box	44 Binney St	6 pm
Drop Box	300 Longwood Ave	5:30 pm
Drop Box	200 Longwood Ave	5 pm
Self-Service	125 Parker Hill Ave	4 pm
Self-Service	15 Deerfield St	4 pm
Drop Box	150 S Huntington Ave	4 pm

Map 16 • Kenmore Square / Brookline (East) *

Drop Box	1 Joslin Pl	6:30 pm
Drop Box	771 Commonwealth Ave	7:15 pm
Self-Service	364 Brookline Ave	7 pm
Drop Box	110 Francis St	7 pm
Drop Box	1 Brookline Pl	6:30 pm
Drop Box	375 Longwood Ave	6:30 pm
Drop Box	44 Cummington St	6:30 pm
Drop Box	675 Commonwealth Ave	6:30 pm
Drop Box	1 Autumn St	6:30 pm
Self-Service	1 Overland St	6:15 pm
Self-Service	1 Deaconess Rd	6 pm
FedEx Kinko's	115 Cummington St	6 pm
Drop Box	590 Commonwealth Ave	5 pm
Drop Box	330 Brookline Ave	5 pm
Drop Box	890 Commonwealth Ave	4 pm

Map 17 • Coolidge Corner / Brookline Hills *

Self-Service	138 Harvard St	7:30 pm
FedEx Kinko's	1370 Beacon St	6:30 pm
Self-Service	1295 Beacon St	6 pm
Mail Boxes Etc	258 Harvard St	6 pm
Self-Service	235 Cypress St	5 pm
Self-Service	207 Washington St	5 pm

Map 18 • Brighton *

Self-Service	1660 Soldiers Field Rd	9 pm
Self-Service	736 Cambridge St	7 pm
Self-Service	20 Guest St	6:30 pm
Self-Service	424 Washington St	6:30 pm
Drop Box	119 Braintree St	6:30 pm
Drop Box	12 Oxford St	4 pm

Map 19 • Allston (South) / Brookline (North) *

Drop Box	881 Commonwealth Ave	7:30 pm
Drop Box	1065 Commonwealth Ave	7 pm
Drop Box	1505 Commonwealth Ave	6:30 pm
Drop Box	214 Lincoln St	6:30 pm
Signal Graphics	450 Cambridge St	3 pm

Map 20 • Harvard Square / Allston (North) *

Drop Box	1 Brattle Sq	7:30 pm
Drop Box	20 University Rd	7:30 pm
Drop Box	35 Oxford St	7:30 pm
Self-Service	1 Mifflin Pl	7 pm
Self-Service	48 Quincy St	7 pm
Self-Service	79 JFK St	7 pm
Drop Box	147 Sherman St	7 pm
Drop Box	1563 Massachusetts Ave	7 pm
Drop Box	33 Kirkland St	7 pm
Drop Box	50 Church St	7 pm
Self-Service	1350 Massachusetts Ave	6:30 pm
Self-Service	230 Western Ave	6 pm
Drop Box	124 Mt Auburn St	5 pm

Map 22 • North Cambridge / West Somerville *

Drop Box	48 Grove St	7 pm
Self-Service	167 Holland St	6:30 pm
Self-Service	90 Sherman St	6:30 pm
Self-Service	5 Cameron Ave	6:30 pm
Self-Service	186 Alewife Brook Pkwy	6:30 pm
Drop Box	150 Cambridge Park Dr	6:30 pm
Drop Box	2067 Massachusetts Ave	6:30 pm
Self-Service	175 Packard Ave	6:15 pm
Self-Service	62 Whittemore Ave	6 pm
Drop Box	199 Alewife Brook Pkwy	6 pm

Map 23 • Central Somerville / Porter Square *

Self-Service	815 Somerville Ave	7 pm
Drop Box	1972 Massachusetts Ave	7 pm
Drop Box	500 Rutherford Ave	7 pm
Self-Service	52 Roland St	6:30 pm
Self-Service	237 Washington St	6:30 pm
Self-Service	1815 Massachusetts Ave	6 pm
Self-Service	36 Bay State Rd	5:30 pm

Map 24 • Winter Hill / Union Square *

Self-Service	5 Middlesex Ave	6:45 pm
Drop Box	100 Fellsway W	6:30 pm
Drop Box	66 Union Sq	6 pm

Map 25 • East Somerville / Sullivan Square *

Drop Box	529 Main St	6:30 pm

Map 26 • East Cambridge / Kendall Square / MIT *

Drop Box	25 1st St	8 pm
Self-Service	55 Cambridge Pkwy	7:30 pm
Drop Box	1 Memorial Dr	7:15 pm
Drop Box	4 Cambridge Center	7 pm
Self-Service	31 Ames St	6 pm
Self-Service	5 Cambridge Center	6 pm
FedEx Kinko's	600 Technology Sq	6 pm
Drop Box	1 Broadway	6 pm
Drop Box	245 1st St	5:30 pm
Self-Service	400 Technology Dr	5 pm
Self-Service	300 3rd St	4:30 pm
Drop Box	222 3rd St	4:30 pm
Drop Box	43 Thorndike St	4 pm
Self-Service	One Kendall Sq	4 pm

Map 27 • Central Square / Cambridgeport *

Drop Box	38 Sidney St	7:45 pm
Self-Service	26 Landsdowne St	7:30 pm
Self-Service	141 Portland St	7 pm
Drop Box	1033 Massachusetts Ave	7 pm
Drop Box	201 Broadway	7 pm
Drop Box	950 Cambridge St	7 pm
Drop Box	955 Massachusetts Ave	7 pm
Drop Box	1010 Massachusetts Ave	6 pm
Drop Box	432 Columbia St	6:30 pm
Drop Box	790 Memorial Dr	6:30 pm
Drop Box	359 Green St	6 pm
Drop Box	64 Sidney St	6 pm
Drop Box	675 Massachusetts Ave	6 pm
Drop Box	840 Memorial Dr	6 pm
Drop Box	875 Massachusetts Ave	6 pm
Drop Box	21 Erie St	5 pm
Drop Box	350 Massachusetts Ave	5 pm

Map 28 • Inman Square *

Drop Box	120 Beacon St	7 pm

Though Boston is chiefly known for its college-town feel, there is plenty for the younger set to enjoy. You're bound to find something to hold the attention of your little ones among the many, MANY museums and parks.

The Best of the Best

- **Best Kid-Friendly Restaurant:** Full Moon (344 Huron Ave, Cambridge, 617-354-6699). Full Moon is the brainchild of two restaurateurs who also happen to be moms. The result is a restaurant that features a sophisticated menu with an extensive wine list for adults and a tasty assortment of kids' tried-and-true favorites. With sippy cups, toy buckets at every table, and a play area stocked with pretty much every toy imaginable, Full Moon gives you "grown-up dining with a kid-friendly twist."
- **Quaintest Activity:** Swan Boats in the Public Garden (Public Garden, Boston, 617-522-1966). Owned and operated by the same family for over 120 years, the swan boats have directly inspired two children's classics: Robert McCloskey's *Make Way for Ducklings* and E.B. White's *The Trumpet of the Swan*. The people-paddled boats can hold up to 20 passengers during the 15-minute cruise around the lagoon and under the world's smallest suspension bridge. An inexpensive and adorable treat for all. Open Apr-Sept.
- **Funnest Park:** Rafferty Park (799 Concord Ave, Cambridge). One of the area's best-hidden playgrounds, this wooded park provides tons of fun stuff for older children, including a new metal climbing structure with a twisty slide, wobbly bridge, boat-shaped sand box, and a mini schoolhouse with a chalkboard roof. Basketball courts, tennis courts, and a baseball field reside next door.
- **Coolest Bookstore:** Curious George Goes to Wordsworth (1 JFK St, Harvard Square, Cambridge, 617-498-0062). With floor-to-ceiling shelves packed with books for children of all ages, there's something for everyone in this charming jungle-themed bookstore. And if you're tired of reading, they've got TOYS.
- **Best Rainy Day Activity:** Children's Museum (300 Congress St, Boston, 617-426-8855). This world-renowned museum has designed early learning experiences for kids of all ages with its inventive hands-on exhibits. Permanent exhibits include the Japanese House, where children experience the culture of Kyoto, Japan through a replica of a silk merchant's house, as well as a Hall of Toys, in which children can look at toys of the past, but not touch.
- **Cutest Event:** The Annual Ducklings Day Parade (Boston Common). Held every year on Mother's Day, the parade commemorates Robert McCloskey's children's book *Make Way for Ducklings* set on Boston Common. Children come dressed as their favorite duckling character and ready to parade.
- **Neatest Store:** Irving's Toy and Card Shop (371 Harvard St, Brookline, 617-566-9327). Since 1939, Irving's has been a favorite neighborhood source for ice cream, candy, and little nostalgic toys galore. This small store is packed with everything you never knew you needed from kazoos, to jacks, to tiny plastic farm animals.

Shopping Essentials

- **Nine Months Maternity and Infant Wear** (mom & baby clothes) 286 Newbury St, Boston, 617-236-5523
- **Barefoot Books Store** (kids' books) 1771 Massachusetts Ave, Cambridge, 617-349-1610
- **Barnes & Noble:**
  395 Washington St, Downtown, 617-426-5184
  325 Harvard St, Brookline, 617-232-0594
  660 Beacon St, Boston University, 617-638-5496
  800 Boylston St, Prudential Center, 617-247-6959
- **Black Ink** (stamps):
  101 Charles St, Boston, 617-723-3883
  5 Brattle St, Cambridge, 617-497-1221
- **Boing!** (toys) 729 Centre St, Jamaica Plain, 617-522-7800
- **Borders Books & Music:**
  10-24 School St, Boston, 617-557-7188
  100 Cambridgeside Pl, Cambridgeside Galleria, Cambridge, 617-679-0887
- **Calliope** (toys & kids' clothes) 33 Brattle St, Cambridge, 617-876-4149
- **The Children's Book Shop** (kids' books) 237 Washington St, Brookline, 617-734-7323
- **Co-op for Kids at the Harvard Co-op** (kids' books) 1400 Massachusetts Ave, Harvard Square, Cambridge, 617-499-2000
- **Curious George Goes to Wordsworth** (kids' books & toys) 1 JFK St, Harvard Square, Cambridge, 617-498-0062
- **Discovery Channel Store** (educational gifts) 40 South Market Building, Faneuil Hall, 617-227-5005
- **Fish Kids** (kids' clothes) 1378A Beacon St, Coolidge Corner, Brookline, 617-738-1006
- **Henry Bear's Park** (kids' books & toys) 361 Huron Ave, Cambridge, 617-547-8424
- **KB Toys** (toys) 100 Cambridgeside Pl, Cambridgeside Galleria, Cambridge, 617-494-8519
- **Oilily** (up-scale kids' clothes) 32 Newbury St, Boston, 617-247-9299
- **The Red Wagon** (kids' toys & clothes), 69 Charles St, Boston, 617-523-9402
- **Sloane's Children's Shoes** (kids' shoes) 1349 Beacon St, Coolidge Corner, Brookline, 617-739-0582
- **Stellabella Toys** (toys) 1360 Cambridge St, Inman Square, Cambridge, 617-491-6290

Parks for Playing

Kids need fresh air. And singing into the rotating fan doesn't count. Take them out for a swing. In addition to the roomy Boston Common and Cambridge Common, Boston boasts many smaller neighborhood parks:

- **Charlesbank/Esplanade Playground** (Charles St at Longfellow Bridge). This large play area features several climbing structures, slides, and swings for all ages with a nearby snack bar, open during the summer months.
- **Christopher Columbus Park** (Atlantic Ave & Commercial Wharf, Boston). One large climbing structure dominates this playground that is mostly geared towards the six-and-under set.
- **Clarendon Street Playground** (Clarendon St & Commonwealth Ave, Boston). This fenced and gated area provides ample scope for the imagination of children of all ages. The park features several climbing structures, slides, swings, and a sand area, along with a larger, open area for games of tag and soccer.
- **Constitution Beach** (Orient Heights, East Boston). Lifeguarded swimming areas, a bathhouse with a snack bar, tennis courts, and a playground with lots of climbing and sliding prospects make this a great destination to take the kids.
- **Emerson Park** (Davis Ave & Emerson St, Brookline). The Park boasts one of the town's oldest spray pools, with lots of trees for shade and a casual open space for tag.

- **Green Street Playground** (Green St, Jamaica Plain). On summer days, the city turns on the water, and kids in bathing suits splash around in the fountains. Families set up picnics around the periphery, and there is a sandy jungle gym and swingset area nearby.
- **Huron Avenue Playground** (Huron Ave, Cambridge). This newly renovated play area has two climbing structures for children of all ages, as well as a play train and spray fountain for the summer months. The lack of tree shade may bother some parents.
- **Langone Park** (Commercial St, Boston). This park features a brand-new playground with multi-age, multi-level climbing structures, and a swing set hovering on the edge of the harbor, great for that flying-across-water feeling. There are also three bocce courts and a baseball field.
- **Larz Anderson Park** (Newton, Avon, & Goddard Sts, Brookline). The largest park in Brookline holds an enclosed playground, picnic areas, ball fields, and an outdoor skating rink open December though February.
- **Millennium Park** (VFW Pkwy & Gardner St, West Roxbury). This park is larger than the Boston Common and TD Banknorth Garden combined and located on the site of the former Gardner Street landfill. The park provides picnic areas, play structures, and hiking and walking trails, as well as access to the river for boating and fishing.
- **Myrtle Street Playground** (Myrtle St & Irving St, Boston). Situated at the top of Beacon Hill, this playground features several climbing structures, a glider, a fire pole, swings, and a crazy daisy.
- **Public Garden** (Between Arlington St & Charles St, Boston). The first public botanical garden in the US, the Public Garden has 24 acres of flowers and green in the middle of the busy city. Among the park's winding pathways and tranquil lagoon are the prized bronze statues of a mama duck and her brood commemorating Robert McClosky's famous children's book, *Make Way for Ducklings*.
- **Rafferty Park** (799 Concord Ave, Cambridge). One of the area's highest-elevation playgrounds, this wooded park provides tons of fun activities for older children, including a new metal climbing structure with a twisty slide, wobbly bridge, boat-shaped sand box, and a mini-schoolhouse with a chalkboard roof. Basketball hoops, tennis courts, and a baseball field reside next door.
- **Raymond Street Park** (Walden St & Raymond St, Cambridge). Located on the shady side of the field, this playground is split up into two sections: one sandy, sunken area for the younger toddlers and one area for older children, equipped with a large climbing structure. Play gear ranges from a bridge to swing sets, including one handicapped swing seat.
- **Stoneman Playground** (Fairfield Ave & Massachusetts Ave, Cambridge). This playground is divided into a toddler area and an older children's space, with entertaining activities for both groups. Supervised model sailboat racing and fishing takes place on Sundays in the summer months.

Rainy Day Activities

It rains in Boston. A lot. It's also one of the windiest cities in the country. Foul weather can drench even the highest aspirations for outdoor fun. Here are some dry alternatives:

Museums with Kid Appeal

- **Museum of Afro-American History** (46 Joy St, Boston, 617-725-0022). The first publicly funded grammar school built for African-Americans now has interactive exhibits for kids. www.afroammuseum.org.

- **Children's Museum** (300 Congress St, Boston, 617-426-8855). This world-renowned museum has designed early learning experiences for children of all ages with its inventive hands-on exhibits. Permanent exhibits include the Japanese House, where children get to experience the culture of Kyoto, Japan through a replica of a silk merchant's house, as well as a Hall of Toys where children can look at toys of the past, but not touch. www.bostonkids.org
- **New England Aquarium** (Central Wharf, 617-973-5200). Among the many exhibits you'll find here are the sea lion show and a supervised hands-on demonstration that allows children to touch sea stars, snails, and mussels. Whale-watching trips and summer classes are also offered through the aquarium. www.neaq.org
- **Larz Anderson Auto Museum** (Larz Anderson Park, 15 Newton St, Brookline, 617-522-6547). Located in the grand Carriage House, the museum features an extensive exhibit on the history of the automobile, as well as America's oldest car collection. www.mot.org
- **Museum of Science** (Science Park, 617-723-2500). This award-winning interactive science museum features permanent and changing exhibits, including a Virtual Fish Tank, where children see life through the eyes of a fish. The museum also houses the Charles Hayden Planetarium, featuring sky and laser shows, and the five-story IMAX Mugar Omni Theater. Various science classes are also available. www.mos.org

Other Indoor Distractions

- **The Clayroom** (1408 Beacon St, Brookline, 617-566-7575). Paint your own pottery place. Great for parties. www.clayroom.com
- **Lanes and Games** (195 Concord Turnpike, Rte 2, Cambridge, 617-876-5533). Candlepin bowling and ten-pin lanes for the whole family. www.lanesgames.com
- **Puppet Showplace Theater** (32 Station St, Brookline, 617-731-6400). This 100-seat theater has staging shows for Boston's young brood for over 30 years. The company stages classic puppet shows, as well as many original productions. Shows are recommended for children five and older. Great for parties. www.puppetshowplace.org

Outdoor *and* Educational

For when you've come to realize your children are a little too pale from sitting inside and playing video games all day.

- **Boston Duck Tours** (departure points: Prudential Center and Museum of Science, information: 617-267-DUCK). The Boston Duck is an original WWII amphibious landing vehicle that takes guests on an 80-minute tour (rain or shine) around the city by land and by sea. Kids are encouraged to quack at passersby. Tickets are sold inside the Prudential Center and Museum of Science beginning at 8:30 am. An additional ticketing location is at Faneuil Hall. Operating season: March 27th – Nov 26th. www.bostonducktours.com
- **Zoo New England** (1 Franklin Park Rd, Boston, 617-541-LION). The zoo holds all the standard zoo fare, plus the Butterfly Landing exhibit, a tented outdoor area where you can walk among more than 1,000 butterflies in free flight. Adults: $9.50, seniors: $8, children (2-12): $5.50, under 2 free, and half-price tickets the first Sat of each month 10 am-12 pm. www.zoonewengland.com

Classes

Boston kids can participate in any number of structured activities that could help to mold and shape them like the blobs of clay that they are.

- **Boston Ballet School** (19 Clarendon St, Boston, 617-695-6950). Ballet classes for kids ages three and up. www.bostonballet.org
- **Boston Casting** (129 Braintree St, Suite 107, Allston, 617-254-1001). Acting classes for kids ages five and up. www.bostoncasting.com
- **Boston Children's Theatre** (321 Columbus Ave (Studio/Office), Boston, 617-424-6634). "Theatre for children by children," this theatre group has children involved in all phases of production. The theatre also offers acting classes and a summer creative arts program, in which kids learn stage combat, clowning, and juggling. www.bostonchildrenstheatre.org
- **Brookline Arts Center** (86 Monmouth St, Brookline, 617-566-5715). A non-degree school for the visual arts, the Brookline Arts Center offers classes for children ages two to teen in subjects ranging from jewelry-making to sculpture. www.brooklineartscenter.com
- **Cambridge Multicultural Arts Center** (41 Second St, Cambridge, 617-577-1400). A program designed for Cambridge residents to promote cross-cultural interchange using dance, music, writing, theater, and the visual arts. www.cmacusa.org
- **Community Music Center of Boston** (34 Warren St, Boston, 617-482-7494). A music program designed to promote musical development through experimental learning for kids of all ages. The center also offers visual arts classes, summer programs, and individual instruction. www.cmcb.org
- **French Library and Cultural Center** (53 Marlborough St, Boston, 617-912-0400). French classes for children ages three to ten. www.frenchlib.org
- **Full Moon** (344 Huron Ave, Cambridge, 617-354-6699). This kid-friendly restaurant offers cooking classes for parents and children ages three and up. www.fullmoonrestaurant.com
- **Grace Arts Project** (Grace United Methodist Church, 56 Magazine St, Cambridge, 617-864-1123). The program offers non-sectarian classes in music.
- **Grub Street Writers, Inc.** (565 Windsor St, Somerville, 617-695-0075). Boston's only private writing school offers workshops and summer courses for young adults. www.grubstreet.org
- **Happily Ever After** (799 Concord Ave, Cambridge, 617-492-0090). The classes use fitness with creative stories and games for children aged three to six. Great for birthday parties. www.evergreendayschool.org
- **Hill House** (127 Mt. Vernon St, Boston, 617-227-5838). A non-profit community center that offers activities such as inline skating, karate, and youth soccer teams to downtown residents. www.hillhouseboston.org
- **Jeanette Neill Children's Dance Studio** (261 Friend St, Boston, 617-523-1355). Since 1979, the program has offered children ages three to 12 an "intelligent dance alternative" with its focus on education, not preparation. www.jndance.com
- **Jose Mateo's Ballet Theatre** (Old Cambridge Baptist Church, 400 Harvard St, Cambridge, 617-354-7467). A professional performance company that provides ballet instruction for children ages three through 18. www.ballettheatre.org

- **Longy School of Music** (1 Follen St, Cambridge, 617-876-0956). Music instruction for children ages 1 to 18. www.longy.edu
- **Made By Me in Harvard Square** (1685 Massachusetts Ave, Cambridge, 617-354-8111). A paint-your-own-pottery studio. Great for birthday parties. www.made-by-me.com
- **Make Art Studio** (44 N Bennett St, Boston, 617-227-0775). Children ages four to 13 are encouraged to "choose their own medium" with guidance and instruction in small, age-appropriate classes.
- **Mudflat Studio** (149 Broadway, Somerville, 617-628-0589). For the past 30 years, the studio has offered hand-building, pot throwing, and individual workshops for children ages four and up. www.mudflat.org
- **Museum of Fine Arts** (465 Huntington Ave, Boston, 617-267-9300). The museum offers weekday and Saturday instruction that combines gallery study and creative expression for children ages five to 18. www.mfa.org/education/courses.htm
- **New School of Music** (25 Lowell St, Cambridge, 617-492-8105). Newborns and up are provided with musical instruction for all levels of interest and skill, as well as musical theater classes for the older kids. www.cambridgemusic.org
- **North Cambridge Family Opera** (2 North St, Cambridge, 617-492-4095). Adults and children ages seven to 14 can participate in theatrical and operatic production. www.familyopera.com
- **North End Music and Performing Arts Center** (Paul Revere Mall, between Hanover St and Unity St, Boston, 617-227-2270). The center offers classes in music, language, and the performing arts to North End residents. www.nempac.com
- **New England Conservatory** (290 Huntington Ave, Boston, 617-585-1130). Music lessons for kids ages four and up at the oldest independent school of music in the US. www.newenglandconservatory.edu
- **Oak Square YMCA** (615 Washington St, Brighton, 617-782-3535). The center offers instruction in swimming, gymnastics, basketball, and art as well as after school programs for kids of all ages. www.ymcaboston.org
- **The Skating Club of Boston** (1240 Soldiers Field Rd, Brighton, 617-782-5900). Classes for skaters and hockey players of all levels. www.scboston.org
- **Topf Center for Dance Education** (551 Tremont St, Boston, 617-482-0351). The center provides underserved youth access to classes in jazz, tap, ballet, hip hop, and African dancing. www.topfcenter.org
- **Upon a Star** (441 Stuart St, Studio 4, Boston, 617-797-5562). Music and movement classes for children ages 14 months to three. www.uponastar.com
- **Wang YMCA of Chinatown** (8 Oak St W, Boston, 617-426-2237). Activities ranging from swimming instruction to music and art classes for children of all ages. www.ymcaboston.org
- **Wheelock Family Theatre** (180 The Riverway, Boston, 617-879-2147). The Theatre offers classes for kids ages four to 17. www.wheelock.edu/wft

For more information, visit www.gocitykids.com

Websites

Boston Gay Men's Chorus · www.bgmc.org
Now in its 24th year, the BGMC, through its collaboration with The Boston Pops, was the first gay chorus in the world to be recorded with a major orchestra on a major label.

craigslist · boston.craigslist.org
General community site (for straights, gays, and everyone else) that offers heavily trafficked "men seeking men" and "women seeking women" sections, as well as other community-related listings and information.

EDGE Boston · www.edgeboston.com
Gay Boston news and entertainment.

Gay & Lesbian Advocates & Defenders (GLAD) · www.glad.org
New England's leading legal rights organization dedicated to ending discrimination based on sexual orientation.

Greater Boston Business Council · www.gbbc.org
Promotes the vitality of Boston's LGBT business and professional community.

Out In Boston · www.outinboston.com
Local news and events, personal ads, business ads, chat, and community message boards.

PinkWeb · www.pinkweb.com
The LGBT yellow pages for New England and beyond.

Provincetown Business Guild · www.ptown.org
A gay and lesbian guide to P'town.

Publications

Bay Windows—New England's largest gay and lesbian newspaper is a weekly publication that prints local, national, and international news as well as community events and guides. www.baywindows.com.

In Newsweekly—News and entertainment weekly, including a calendar of events and a club guide. www.innewsweekly.com.

Bookstores

Calamus Bookstore · 92B South St, Boston · 617-338-1931 · www.calamusbooks.com

Sports

Beantown Softball League · www.beantownsoftball.com
LGBT softball since 1978.

Boston Bay Blades · www.bayblades.org/boston
For rowers and scullers.

Boston Boasts Squash League · www.bostonboasts.com
The country's oldest and largest gay and lesbian squash league.

Boston Gay Basketball League · www.bgbl.com
The country's largest LGBT basketball league.

Boston Strikers · www.bostonstrikers.com
Indoor and outdoor soccer league for gay and straight players of all levels.

Cambridge-Boston Volleyball Association · www.gayvolleyball.net
Indoor league with three levels of play.

Chiltern Mountain Club · www.chiltern.org
New England's largest LGBT outdoor recreation club.

East Coast Wrestling Club · www.eastcoastwrestlingclub.org
Gay men's wrestling group for athletes of all abilities.

FLAG Flag Football · flagflagfootball.tripod.com/flagflagfootballonline
Plays a full fall season and an abbreviated spring season.

FrontRunners Boston · www.mindspring.com/~frontrunners/index.htm
Welcomes joggers, walkers, and runners of all experience levels.

PrideSports Boston · 617-937-5858 · www.geocities.com/pridesportsboston
Gay & lesbian athletic alliance with more than 20 sports clubs.

Health Centers & Support Organizations

Boston Alliance of Gay Lesbian Bisexual and Transgender Youth · 617-227-4313 · www.bagly.org
For young people 22 and under.

Dignity Boston · 617-421-1915 · www.dignityboston.org
An inclusive community of LGBT Catholics.

Fenway Community Health · 7 Haviland St, Boston · 617-267-0900 · www.fenwayhealth.org
Provides high-quality medical and mental health care to Boston's gay and lesbian community; also a leader in HIV care.

Gay Men's Domestic Violence Project · 800-832-1901 · www.gmdvp.org
Offers shelter, guidance and resources to allow gay, bisexual, and transgender men in crisis to remove themselves from violent situations and relationships; also operates a 24-hour free-of-charge crisis center.

The Network · 617-423-SAFE · www.thenetworklared.org
Provides information and resources for battered lesbian, bisexual, and transgendered women.

Annual Events

Boston Pride Week · 617-262-9405 · www.bostonpride.org
Begins on a Friday in June with a flag raising at City Hall; the parade and festival usually take place on the Saturday of the following weekend.

Boston Gay/Lesbian Film/Video Festival · 617-267-9300 · www.mfa.org
Usually held in May at the MFA.

Mass Red Ribbon Ride · 617-450-1100 · www.massredribbonride.org
This bike ride across the state raises money for AIDS organizations. Takes place annually in August.

Venues – Lesbian

- **Dyke Night Productions** · www.dykenight.com
- **Toast** (Fridays) · 70 Union Sq, Somerville · 617-623-9211 · www.toastlounge.com
- **Tribe** (at **Felt**) · 533 Washington St, Boston · 617-350-5555 · www.tribenightclub.com

Venues – Gay

- **The Alley** · 14 Pi Alley, Boston · 617-263-1449 · www.thealleybar.com
- **Aria** · 246 Tremont St, Boston · 617-338-7080 · www.ariaboston.com
- **Avalon** (Sundays) · 15 Lansdowne St, Boston · 617-262-2424 · www.avalonboston.com
- **Buzz** (Saturdays @ Club Europa) · 51 Stuart St, Boston · 617-267-8969 · www.buzzboston.com
- **Chaps** (Wednesdays & Sundays) · 101 Warrenton St, Boston · 617-587-0000 · www.chapsboston.com
- **Club Cafe** · 209 Columbus Ave, Boston · 617-536-0966 · www.clubcafe.com
- **Dedo** (Upstairs) · 69 Church St, Boston · 617-338-9999
- **Eagle** · 520 Tremont St, Boston · 617-542-4494
- **Embassy** (Thursdays) · 36 Lansdowne St, Boston · 617-536-2100
- **Fritz** · 26 Chandler St, Boston · 617-482-4428 · www.fritzboston.com
- **Jacque's** · 79 Broadway St, Boston · 617-426-8902 · www.jacquescabaret.com
- **Machine** (Thurs-Sat) · 1256 Boylston St, Boston · 617-226-2986 · www.ramrodmachine.com
- **Paradise** · 180 Massachusetts Ave, Cambridge · 617-868-3000 · www.paradisecambridge.com
- **Ramrod** · 1254 Boylston St, Boston · 617-226-2986 · www.ramrodmachine.com
- **Rise** (members only, after-hours) · 306 Stuart St, Boston · 617-423-7473 · www.riseclub.us

After years of suffering from a shortage of hotel accommodations, Boston's hotel market has finally warmed up. Developers, encouraged by an improving economic climate and continued high demand for rooms, have moved forward with several large projects, most of which are located on or near the waterfront, where developers hope to leverage locations close to the Boston Convention & Exhibition Center. But it's not all just about harbor views and cafeteria-sized restaurants—boutique hotels are also popping up in various locations around town. Newcomers in the boutique market include **Hotel 140 (Map 6)** (a historic building in the shadow of the Hancock Tower), sleek **Nine Zero (Map 3)** (on Tremont Street), the **Bulfinch Hotel (Map 1)** (near North Station) and the **Beacon Hill Hotel (Map 1)** (on Charles Street, near the Common). **Jurys' (Map 6)** first Boston location has opened in the fully renovated former headquarters of the Boston Police Department. Another recently-opened property, the **Hampton Inn & Suites (Map 12)** (near Newmarket Square) may not be as luxurious as Jurys, but its suites are a decent option for long-term stays, and its proximity to I-93 and the Mass Pike make it easy to get to other locations.

But Boston residents shouldn't let tourists have all the fun. Even if you're not staying the night, it's worth popping into one of Boston's classic hotels to soak up the atmosphere. The lobby of the **Fairmont Copley Plaza (Map 6)** exudes luxuriousness, as does its acclaimed restaurant, the Oak Room. Genteel rivals the **Four Seasons (Map 3)** and the **Ritz Carlton (Map 3)** (the oldest Ritz in the country) both

overlook the Public Garden. The Ritz serves the city's best-known high tea, and the Four Seasons has the recently renovated Aujourd'hui, one of Boston's finest restaurants. Across the Common, towards the financial district, the **Omni Parker House (Map 3)** stands as a Boston institution and a literary landmark. If you're killing time in Back Bay, check out the charming and cozy lobby of the **Lenox (Map 6)**. Playing up its proximity to techie heaven is the **University Park Hotel @ MIT (Map 26)**, decorated with tributes to the art of engineering. In Harvard Square, the **Charles Hotel (Map 20)** offers nightly jazz at the Regatta-bar as well as organic fine dining at Henrietta's Table. And if you're suffering from wanderlust of the spirit, ask about the weekend retreats at the **Monastery of the Society of St. John the Evangelist (Map 20)**.

Marriott's Custom House (Map 2) is located in one of Boston's most prominent historic landmarks, the Custom House Tower. The original Custom House building, completed in 1847, was described by Walt Whitman as the "noblest work of architecture in the world." The tower was added in 1915. The open-air observation deck on the 26th floor is open to the public and offers prime views of the harbor and the open spaces created by the demolition of the Central Artery.

See the average room rates listed below? Pretty expensive, huh? Whether you're booking for yourself or the in-laws, call the hotels to ask about specials and check websites such as hotels.com, Orbitz, Travelocity, and All-Hotels for discounts. Maybe you'll get lucky.

Map 1 • Beacon Hill / West End

		Phone	Rate	Rating
Beacon Hill Hotel	25 Charles St	617-723-7575	245-365	★★★
Bulfinch Hotel	107 Merrimac St	617-624-0202	179	★★★
Charles Street Inn (B&B)	94 Charles St	617-314-8900	265-350	
Holiday Inn	5 Blossom St	617-742-7630	229	
John Jeffries House (B&B)	14 David G Mugar Wy	617-367-1866	95-175	
Onyx Hotel	155 Portland St	617-557-9955	199	★★★★
Shawmut Inn	280 Friend St	617-720-5544	99	★★★
XV Beacon Hotel	15 Beacon St	617-670-1500	295-450	

Map 2 • North End / Faneuil Hall

Boston Marriott Long Wharf	296 State St	617-227-0800	339-449	★★★★★
Golden Slipper (floating B&B)	Lewis Wharf	781-545-2845	175	
Harborside Inn	185 State St	617-723-7500	129-149	
Marriott's Custom House	3 McKinley Sq	617-310-6300	230-300	
Millennium Bostonian Hotel	26 North St	617-523-3600	149-399	★★★★

Map 3 • Downtown Crossing / Park Square / Bay Village

Boston Park Plaza Hotel	64 Arlington St	617-426-2000	159-209	★★★
Courtyard Boston Tremont	275 Tremont St	617-426-1400		
Doubletree Boston	821 Washington St	617-956-7900	152-309	★★★
Four Seasons Hotel	200 Boylston St	617-338-4400	425	★★★★★
Hyatt Regency Boston	1 Ave de Lafayette	617-912-1234	235-270	★★★★★
Milner Hotel	78 Charles St S	617-426-6220	109	★★
Nine Zero Hotel	90 Tremont St	617-772-5800	269-450	★★★★★
Omni Parker House	60 School St	617-227-8600	209-229	
Radisson Hotel Boston	200 Stuart St	617-482-1800	105-195	★★★
Ritz-Carlton Boston	15 Arlington St	617-536-5700	375-475	★★★★★
Ritz-Carlton Boston Common	10 Avery St	617-574-7100	375-475	★★★★★

Map 4 • Financial District / Chinatown

Boston Harbor Hotel	70 Rowes Wharf	617-439-7000	288	★★★★
The Langham Hotel	250 Franklin St	617-451-1900	275-555	★★★★
Westin Boston Waterfront	245 Summer St	617-532-4600	n/a	
Wyndham Boston	89 Broad St	617-556-0006	179-199	★★★★

General Information • **Hotels**

Map 5 • Back Bay (West) / Fenway (East)

436 Beacon Street	436 Beacon St	617-536-1302	69-149	
Commonwealth Court Guest House	284 Commonwealth Ave	617-424-1230	79-140	
Eliot Hotel	370 Commonwealth Ave	617-267-1607	215-280	★★★★
Hilton Boston Back Bay	40 Dalton St	617-236-1100	209-252	★★★★
Hosteling International	12 Hemenway St	617-536-9455	32 (dorm), 80 (private room)	
Midtown Hotel	220 Huntington Ave	617-262-1000	89-239	★★
Newbury Guest House (B&B)	261 Newbury St	617-437-7666	120-160	★★★
Oasis Guest House	22 Edgerly Rd	617-267-2262	69-149	
Sheraton Boston Hotel	39 Dalton St	617-236-2000	149	
YMCA	316 Huntington Ave	617-536-7800	46 (men only)	

Map 6 • Back Bay (East) / South End (Upper)

Boston Marriott Copley Place	110 Huntington Ave	617-236-5800	299-324	★★★★★
Charlesmark Hotel	655 Boylston St	617-247-1212	139-179	★★★
The College Club	44 Commonwealth Ave	617-536-9510	75-160	
Colonnade Hotel	120 Huntington Ave	617-424-7000	199-285	★★★★
Copley House	239 W Newton St	617-236-8300	80-135 per night, 425-825 per week	
Copley Inn	19 Garrison St	617-236-0300	85-150	
Copley Square Hotel	47 Huntington Ave	617-536-9000	159	★★★
Courtyard by Marriott Copley Place	88 Exeter St	617-437-9300	199-239	★★★
Fairmont Copley Plaza Hotel	138 St James Ave	617-267-5300	399-529	★★★★
Hotel 140	140 Clarendon St	617-585-5600	169	
International Guest House	237 Beacon St	617-437-1975	95 (shared room), 135 (private room)	
Jewel of Newbury	254 Newbury St	617-536-5523	225	★★★★★
John Hancock Hotel & Conference	40 Trinity Pl	617-933-7700	89-139	
Jurys Boston Hotel	350 Stuart St	617-266-7200	215-275	★★★★
Lenox Hotel	61 Exeter St	617-536-5300	179-209	★★★★
Westin Copley Place	10 Huntington Ave	617-262-9600	259	★★★★

Map 7 • South End (Lower)

Chandler Inn	26 Chandler St	617-482-3450	79-143	★★
Clarendon Square Inn (B&B)	198 W Brookline St	617-536-2229	119-289	
Encore Bed & Breakfast	116 W Newton St	617-247-3425	130-190	
Rutland Square House	56 Rutland Sq	617-247-0018		
YWCA/Berkeley Residence	40 Berkeley St	617-375-2524	56 (men & women)	

Map 8 • Charlestown

Bunker Hill Bed & Breakfast	80 Elm St	617-241-8067	135-145	
Constitution Inn	150 2nd Ave	617-241-8400	107-139	
Residence Inn Tudor Wharf	34 Charles River Ave	617-242-9000	199-249	

Map 9 • East Boston

Embassy Suites Boston at Logan	207 Porter St	617-567-5000	199	★★★
Hilton Boston Logan	1 Hotel Dr	617-568-6700	209-259	★★★★
Hyatt Harborside at Logan	101 Harborside Dr	617-568-1234	189-385	★★★

Map 10 • South Boston (West) / Fort Point

Nolan House (B&B)	10 G St	617-269-1550	95 (shared bath), 125 (private bath)

Map 11 • South Boston (East)

Seaport Hotel	1 Seaport Ln	617-385-4000	229

Map 12 • Newmarket / Andrew Square

Best Western Inn Roundhouse Suites	891 Massachusetts Ave	617-989-1000	149-159	
Hampton Inn & Suites Boston Crosstown Center	811 Massachusetts Ave	617-445-6400	125-145	★★★
Holiday Inn Express	69 Boston St	617-288-3030	88-200	★★★★

Map 15 • Fenway (West) / Mission Hill

Best Western Longwood Medical	342 Longwood Ave	617-731-4700	179-349	★★
Howard Johnson	1271 Boylston St	617-267-8300	155	

Map 16 • Kenmore Square / Brookline (East)

Anthony's Town House	1085 Beacon St	617-566-3972	88	
Beacon Inn	1087 Beacon St	617-566-0088	79-129	
Buckminster Hotel	645 Beacon St	617-236-7050	109	★★
Gryphon House (B&B)	9 Bay State Rd	617-375-9003	149-208	
Holiday Inn Boston at Brookline	1200 Beacon St	617-277-1200	140-170	

Hotel Commonwealth	500 Commonwealth Ave	617-933-5000	239-259	★★★★
Longwood Inn (B&B)	123 Longwood Ave	617-566-8615	86 (private bath), 71 (shared bath)	

Map 17 • Coolidge Corner / Brookline Hills

Beacon-Plaza	1459 Beacon St	617-232-6550	55 (shared bath), 85 (private bath)	
Bertram Inn (B&B)	92 Sewall Ave	617-566-2234	119-229	
Coolidge Corner Guest House	17 Littell Rd	617-734-4041	79-149	
Courtyard by Marriott Brookline	40 Webster St	617-734-1393	179-219	
Samuel Sewall Inn (B&B)	143 St Paul St	617-713-0123	119-179	

Map 18 • Brighton

Best Western Terrace Inn	1650 Commonwealth Ave	617-566-6260	119	
Days Inn	1800 Soldiers Field Rd	617-254-0200	79-109	

Map 19 • Allston (South) / Brookline (North)

Abercrombie's Farrington Inn	23 Farrington Ave	617-787-1860	65-95	
Days Hotel	1234 Soldiers Field Rd	617-254-1234	98-138	★★★★
Doubletree Guest Suites	400 Soldiers Field Rd	617-783-0090	109-129	★★★

Map 20 • Harvard Square / Allston (North)

Charles Hotel	1 Bennett St	617-864-1200	149-599	★★★★
Harvard Square Hotel	110 Mt Auburn St	617-864-5200	139	★★★
The Inn at Harvard	1201 Massachusetts Ave	617-491-2222	119-475	★★★★
Mary Prentiss Inn (B&B)	6 Prentiss St	617-661-2929	159-199	
Monastery of the Society of St John the Evangelist	980 Memorial Dr	617-876-3037	60	
Sheraton Commander Hotel	16 Garden St	617-547-4800	145	

Map 21 • West Cambridge

Best Western Hotel Tria	220 Alewife Brook Pkwy	617-491-8000	129-169	★★★

Map 22 • North Cambridge / West Somerville

A Cambridge House, B&B Hotel Inn	2218 Massachusetts Ave	617-491-6300	129-149	★★★
Meacham Manor	52 Meacham Rd	617-623-3985	85	
Morrison House (B&B)	221 Morrison Ave	617-627-9670	65-120	

Map 24 • Winter Hill / Union Square

Holiday Inn Boston/Somerville	30 Washington St	617-628-1000	124	★★★★
La Quinta Inn & Suites	23 Cummings St	617-625-5300	109-139	★★★

Map 25 • East Somerville / Sullivan Square

Hampton Inn Boston/Cambridge	191 Monsignor O'Brien Hwy	617-494-5300	149	★★★
Marriott Cambridge	2 Cambridge Ctr	617-494-6600	139-309	★★★
Residence Inn by Marriott - Cambridge	6 Cambridge Ctr	617-349-0700	269-300	★★★★
Royal Sonesta Hotel Boston	5 Cambridge Pkwy	617-806-4200	149-189	★★★★

Map 26 • East Cambridge / Kendall Square / MIT

Holiday Inn Express Hotel & Suites	250 Monsignor O'Brien Hwy	617-577-7600	112-139	★★★
Hotel Marlowe	25 Land Blvd	617-868-8000	249-279	
Hyatt Regency Cambridge	575 Memorial Dr	617-492-1234	255-295	★★★★
Kendall Hotel	350 Main St	617-577-1300	209-249	
Radisson Hotel Cambridge	777 Memorial Dr	617-492-7777	129-199	★★★
University Park Hotel at MIT	20 Sidney St	617-577-0200	179-229	
Windsor Inn	85 Windsor St	617-868-8812	79-199	

Map 27 • Central Square / Cambridgeport

Cambridge Bed & Muffin	267 Putnam Ave	617-576-3166	88	

Map 28 • Inman Square

Amory Guest House (B&B)	62 Amory St	617-308-4237	68	
A Bed & Breakfast in Cambridge	1657 Cambridge St	617-868-7082	125-160	
A Friendly Inn at Harvard (B&B)	1673 Cambridge St	617-547-7851	107	
Harding House (B&B)	288 Harvard St	617-876-2888	105 (shared bath), $135 (private bath)	
Irving House at Harvard (B&B)	24 Irving St	617-547-4600	100 (shared bath), $150 (private bath)	
Prospect Place (B&B)	112 Prospect St	617-864-7500	115 (shared bath) $135 (private bath)	

If you've just moved to Boston and need a crash course on the "sights," you must check out the **Freedom Trail** (see page 191). Yes, it's touristy, but it's the best self-guided tour of Revolution-era Boston and gives you the skinny on aspects of Boston colonial history that every resident should know. To gain a better appreciation of just where it is you live, hit the top of the **Prudential Tower** (Map 5) for a bird's eye view, which will show you that Boston has a lot more hills and water than you might have suspected. For a more human perspective, get familiar with the Charles River with a stroll along the **Esplanade** (Map 6), or for a walk with an impressive view of Beacon Hill and Back Bay, cross the **Harvard Bridge** (Map 26) and take a stroll along Memorial Drive in Cambridge. For a nice rest, grab a snack in Harvard Square, and a find a tree in **Harvard Yard** (Map 20) under which to chill.

If winter keeps you from strolls outside—there's plenty to see indoors. The **Museum of Fine Arts** (Map 15) (see page 292) is world-class. Across the street, the **Isabella Stewart Gardner Museum** (Map 15) has a first-rate collection, and the setting (inspired by a 15th-century Venetian palace) is stunning. The ornate interior of **Trinity Church** (Map 6) and the Sargent Murals at the **Boston Public Library** (Map 6) (see page 185) are also impressive. Boston's best concert halls are in the neighborhood, so why not catch

a show at internationally acclaimed **Boston Symphony Hall** (Map 5) or one of the many free shows at the New England Conservatory's **Jordan Hall** (Map 5). You'll also not want to overlook the many museums of Harvard, notably the **Fogg Art Museum** (Map 20) (focusing on Western art) and the **Natural History Museum** (Map 20) (with its brilliant glass flowers).

If you've already checked out Boston's big hits, there are plenty of quirky spots to fill your time. See the skull of Phineas Gage, the 19th century medical oddity who survived a thirteen-pound rod of steel shot through his brain at the **Warren Anatomical Museum** (Map 15). **The Boston Athenaeum** (Map 1) has a true crime account bound with the criminal's skin. If that's not to your sense of everlasting life, you could sip coffee in the North End and wander over to see if Peter Baldassari is home and his folksy **All Saints Way** (Map 2) is open. Roxbury has the only scale Nubian tomb at the Museum of the **National Center for Afro-American Artists** (Map 13). The **Mapparium** (Map 5) at the Christian Science Center highlights the ambitions of Mary Baker Eddy and her clean-living movement. Those with a more criminal bent can find mobster haunts like "Whitey" Bulger's old Southie **liquor store** (Map 10) or the garage of the **Brink's Job** (Map 2) in the North End.

Map 1 · Beacon Hill / West End

Abiel Smith School	46 Joy St	Center of 19th century African-American Boston.
Acorn Street	b/w West Cedar St & Willow St, running parallel to Chestnut St,	The most photographed street in America.
Boston Athenaeum	10 1/2 Beacon St · 617-227-0270	Old books, including one true crime account bound in the author's skin.
Leonard P Zakim Bunker Hill Bridge	I-93 & Charles River	World's widest cable-stayed bridge. Boston's newest landmark.
Longfellow Bridge	Cambridge St & Charles St	The "salt and pepper shaker bridge."
Louisburg Square	b/w Mt Vernon St & Pinckney St	Charming square with elegant homes, including John Kerry's.
Make Way for Ducklings	Charles St & Beacon St	Inspired by the Robert McCloskey children's book.
Massachusetts General Hospital	55 Fruit St · 617-726-2000	The Ether dome, site of first use of ether, contains an antique surgical museum.
TD Banknorth Garden	150 Causeway St · 617-624-1050	Looking for the FleetCenter? This is it.

Map 2 · North End / Faneuil Hall

All Saints Way	Battery St & Hanover St	Peter Baldassari's folksy, handcrafted devotional alley.
Boston Tea Kettle	63 Court St	Long before Starbucks, this gigantic 1873 copper kettle was steaming.
The Brink's Job	165 Prince St	Where Brink's Gang robbery occurred in 1950; now used for TD Banknorth Center parking.
Christopher Columbus Park	Atlantic Ave	Destruction of the Artery gives this park new breath.
City Hall	1 City Hall Plz · 617-635-4000	The box Faneuil Hall came in.
Faneuil Hall	Congress St at North St · 617-523-1779	Faneuil Hall (that is, the building) dates from 1742.
Holocaust Memorial	Congress St at Union St · 617-457-8755	Six glass towers, with victims' numbers representing six camps.
New England Aquarium	Central Wharf · 617-973-5200	Check out penguin snack-time.
North End Playground	Commercial St & Foster St	Site of the famous Great Molasses Flood.
Old North Church	193 Salem St · 617-523-6676	One if by land, two if by sea.
Paul Revere House	19 North Sq · 617-523-2338	Where Paul was born and raised.
Union Oyster House	41 Union St · 617-227-2750	Oldest restaurant in America, skip food but saddle up to oyster bar.

Map 3 · Downtown Crossing / Park Square / Bay Village

Arlington Street Church	351 Boylston St · 617-536-7050	Congregation dates from 1729, building from 1861.
Boston Irish Famine Memorial	School St & Washington St	Statue commemorating the Great Hunger of the 1840s.
Colonial Theater	106 Boylston St · 617-426-9366	Boston's oldest continuously operating theater, since 1900.
Four Seasons Hotel	200 Boylston St · 617-338-4400	The preferred local home of the Rolling Stones.
Granary Burying Ground	Tremont St & Park St · 617-635-4505	Featuring John Hancock, Mother Goose, many others.
Old South Meeting House	310 Washington St · 617-482-6439	Where Sam Adams gave the order for the Boston Tea Party.
Old State House	206 Washington St · 617-720-1713	Oldest surviving public building in Boston.
Omni Parker House	60 School St · 617-227-8600	One-time employees include Ho Chi Minh and Malcolm X.
Opera House	539 Washington St · 617-259-3400	Beaux-Arts landmark open again after many years.
State House	Beacon St at Park St · 617-727-3679	Finished in 1797. Gold dome added later.
Swan Boats	Arlington St & Boylston St · 617-522-1966	Since 1877. Ideal for wee ones.
Wang Center	270 Tremont St · 617-482-9393	Eye-popping, opulent interior. A must see.

Map 4 · Financial District / Chinatown

Boston Harbor Hotel	70 Rowes Wharf · 617-439-7000	The "building with a hole in the middle."
Chinatown Gate	Beach St & Hudson St	Everything under the sky is for the people.
Custom House Tower	3 McKinley Sq	Boston's first "skyscraper," completed in 1915.
Federal Reserve	600 Atlantic Ave · 617-973-3463	Easy-to-spot concrete monolith, built in 1983.
South Station	Atlantic Ave & Summer St	Busier train station, with the new Silver Line and bus terminal.

Map 5 · Back Bay (West) / Fenway (East)

Burrage House	314 Commonwealth Ave	Nineteenth-century French-Renaissance mansion. Private.
Christian Science Center	175 Huntington Ave · 617-450-3790	Mother Church, Mapparium, reflecting pool. Quite nice.
Church Park	221 Massachusetts Ave · 617-437-7328	Stylish concrete residential/retail complex.
Hynes Convention Center	900 Boylston St · 617-954-2000	Still a convention center, for now.
Jordan Hall	30 Gainsborough St	Hundred-year-old theater seats over 1,000 and has remarkable acoustics.
Prudential Tower	800 Boylston St · 617-236-3100	The other tall building. Equally loved and reviled.
Symphony Hall	301 Massachusetts Ave · 617-266-1492	Home of the Boston Symphony Orchestra.

Map 6 · Back Bay (East) / South End (Upper)

Boston Public Library	700 Boylston St · 617-536-5400	The Sargent murals, Italianate courtyard, and café make up for the dismal addition.
Charles River Esplanade	n/a	Great place to run or read a book.
Commonwealth Ave	Arlington to Mass Ave	Boston's most distinguished promenade with oddest collection of statues.
Hatch Shell	Esplanade	Where the Pops play each July 4.
John Hancock Tower	200 Clarendon St	New England's tallest building, designed by I.M. Pei.
Old South Church	645 Boylston St · 617-536-1970	Northern Italian Gothic, finished in 1875.
Trinity Church	206 Clarendon St · 617-536-0944	Romanesque, with massive open interior.

Map 7 · South End (Lower)

Cathedral of the Holy Cross	1400 Washington St · 617-542-5682	Mother church of the Archdiocese of Boston.
SoWa Building	450 Harrison Ave	A converted warehouse, now home to several galleries.

Map 8 · Charlestown

Bunker Hill Monument	Monument Ave · 617-242-5641	Battle actually took place on nearby Breed's Hill.
Charlestown Navy Yard	Constitution Rd & Warren St · 617-242-5601	Home of the *USS Constitution* ("Old Ironsides").
Tobin Memorial Bridge	US-1	Lovingly photographed in Mystic River.
Warren Tavern	2 Pleasant St · 617-241-8142	One of Paul Revere's favorite watering holes.

Map 9 · East Boston

LoPresti Park	Sumner St & Jeffries St	Best view of the Boston skyline and harbor for landlubbers.

Map 10 · South Boston (West) / Fort Point

Boston Convention & Exhibition Center	415 Summer St · 617-954-2100	The Southie Starship.
Children's Museum	300 Congress St · 617-426-8855	Featuring the giant Hood milk bottle.
Institute of Contemporary Art	100 Northen Ave · 617-266-5152	New Location
South Boston Liquor Mart	295 Old Colony Ave · 617-269-3600	Bostonians know who Whitey is.

General Information · **Landmarks**

Map 11 · South Boston (East)

Bank of America Pavilion	290 Northern Ave · 617-728-1690	Music venue.
Black Falcon Terminal	1 Black Falcon Ave · 617-330-1500	Heavily trafficked cruise boat terminal.
Boston Design Center	1 Design Center Pl · 617-338-6610	For interior design junkies; several dozen showrooms.
L Street Tavern	658 E 8th St · 617-268-4335	Infinitely better than "Cheers", Damon's pub in that movie.
World Trade Center Boston	200 Seaport Blvd · 617-385-5090	Event space that's part of "The Seaport Experience."

Map 12 · Newmarket / Andrew Square

Suffolk County House of Correction	20 Bradston St · 617-635-1000	Just so you know.

Map 13 · Roxbury

Highland Park	Fort Ave & Beech Glen	Little visited Fort Hill monument with great views.
Islamic Cultural Center	1 Malcolm X Blvd	Largest mosque in the Northeast.
Museum of the National Center for Afro-American Artists	300 Walnut Ave · 617-442-8614	Puddingstone mansion holds Nubian tomb model, afternoon hours.
Roxbury Center for Arts	182 Dudley St · 617-541-3900	A historic building, but a less than historic center for cultural activity.
Shirley-Eustis House	33 Shirley St · 617-442-2275	Eighteenth-century royal governor's country estate.

Map 14 · Jamaica Plain

Arnold Arboretum	125 Arborway · 617-524-1718	The most famous collection of trees in America, an oasis.
Doyle's Café	3484 Washington St · 617-524-2345	A century's worth of pols have slapped backs here.
First Church, Unitarian Universalist	6 Eliot St · 617-524-1634	The first church in Jamaica Plain, ca. 1853. Impressive stone façade, creepy graveyard.
The Loring-Greenough House	12 South St · 617-524-3158	Built as a country estate in 1760. Open for tours.
Samuel Adams Brewery	30 Germania St · 617-368-5080	Love the product, but not much of an experience.
Spontaneous Celebrations	75 Danforth St · 617-524-6373	JP community arts organization.

Map 15 · Fenway (West) / Mission Hill

Diablo Glass & Metal	123 Terrace St · 617-442-7444	Public access art studio; also offers classes.
Isabella Stewart Gardner Museum	280 The Fenway · 617-278-5180	Eccentric collection highlighting the Renaissance and the pleasures of having money. A gem.
Mission Church Basilica	1545 Tremont St · 617-445-2600	Mission Hill landmark. Recently renovated.
Museum of Fine Arts	465 Huntington Ave · 617-267-9300	Arguably, one the top museums in the country. Go for the Copleys.
Warren Anatomical Museum	10 Shattuck St · 617-432-6196	Phineas Gage's skull and other medical oddities.

Map 16 · Kenmore Square / Brookline (East)

BU Bridge	Essex St & Mountfort St	Arguably Boston's best river/skyline view.
Citgo Sign	Commonwealth Ave & Beacon St	Beloved Kenmore Square landmark.
Fenway Park	4 Yawkey Wy · 617-267-9440	Home to the Red Sox since 1912.

Map 17 · Coolidge Corner / Brookline Hills

Frederick L. Olmstead Home	99 Warren St	Genius of American landscapes, the ultimate home office.

Map 19 · Allston (South) / Brookline (North)

John F Kennedy Birthplace	83 Beals St · 617-566-7937	Understated residential home, open only in summer.
The Publick Theater	1400 Soldiers Field Rd · 617-332-0546	Outdoor theater along the Charles.

Map 20 · Harvard Square / Allston (North)

Fogg Art Museum	32 Quincy St · 617-495-9400	Fine collection, more humane scale than the MFA.
Harvard Stadium	Soldiers Field Rd	The nation's oldest stadium.
Harvard Yard	b/w Broadway, Quincy St, Peabody St, & Massachusetts Ave	The core of the campus--full of historical landmarks.
John Harvard Statue	Harvard Yard	The "statue of the three lies."
Out of Town News	0 Harvard Sq · 617-354-7777	The sensible Harvard Square rendezvous spot.
The Pit	0 Harvard Sq	Favorite hang-out for the counter-culture kids.

Map 22 · North Cambridge / West Somerville

Somerville Theater	55 Davis Sq · 617-625-4088	Late-run movies and live music.
Spark	50 Grove St · 617-718-9132	DIY arts and craft workshop.

Map 23 · Central Somerville / Porter Square

Powderhouse	College Ave & Broadway	Revolutionary War-era gunpowder store, park centerpiece.
The Round House	36 Atherton St	Round since 1856. Not open to the public.
Somerville Museum	1 Westwood Rd · 617-666-9810	Great exhibits of Somerville history.

Map 24 · Winter Hill / Union Square

Prospect Hill Monument	Munroe St b/w Prospect Hill Ave & Walnut St	Excellent view of Boston from Somerville.
Somerville City Hall	93 Highland Ave · 617-625-6600	A classic New England municipal building.

Map 25 · East Somerville / Sullivan Square

Schrafft's Building	529 Main St	Once the country's largest candy factory.

Map 26 · East Cambridge / Kendall Square / MIT

Harvard Bridge	Massachusetts Ave	364 smoots and an ear, the Harvard Bridge leads to MIT.
Kendall /MIT T Station	Main St	Every T Stop should have musical instruments by MIT students.
Stata Center	32 Vassar St	Frank Gehry's curvy and colorful MIT building.

Map 27 · Central Square / Cambridgeport

Cambridge City Hall	795 Massachusetts Ave · 617-349-4000	Recently got a needed facelift.
Edgerton Center & Strobe Alley	77 Massachussetts Ave, MIT · 617-253-4629	4th floor of Bldg 4 displays of slow-mo destructive photography and tech.
Necco Building/Novartis	250 Massachusetts Ave	Yet another candy company leaves Cambridge.
Simmons Hall	229 Vassar St · 617-253-5107	Agressively modernist MIT dorm by Stephen Holl.
University Park	Massachusetts Ave & Sidney St	Complex of cool structural and landscape architecture.

Map 28 · Inman Square

Julia Child's Home	103 Irving St	The kitchen was dismantled and moved to the Smithsonian.

Map 29 · West Roxbury

Millennium Park	VFW Pkwy & Gardner St	Clear your head by flying a kite.

Map 30 · Roslindale

Forest Hills Cemetery	95 Forest Hills Ave · 617-524-0128	This 250 acre beautiful cemetery is not only home to such literary greats as e.e. cummings but is also great spot to picnic and bike ride.
Roslindale Square	Washington St & Belgrade Ave	Or, Roslindale Village.

Map 31 · Mattapan / Dorchester (West)

Franklin Park Zoo [Bear Cages]	1 Franklin Park Rd · n/a	The abandoned bear cages outside the zoo's fences that make for a creepy outing.
United House of Prayer	206 Seaver St [Elm Hill Av] · 617-447-0105	Impressive Mishkan Tefila synagogue, now church and soul food kitchen

Map 32 · Dorchester (East)

All Saints Church	209 Ashmont St	A landmark of the American Gothic style.
Commonwealth Museum	220 Morrissey Blvd · 617-727-9268	Operated by the Massachusetts Historical Society.
The James Blake House	735 Columbia Rd	Built in 1648, Boston's oldest house.
John F Kennedy Museum	Morrissey Blvd & Columbia Pt · 617-514-1600	Houses 21 permanent exhibits examining JFK's life and work.

Map 33 · Hyde Park

Stony Brook Reservation	Washington St & Turtle Pond Pkwy	Great option for biking and hiking.

Overview

There's always something going on in Boston—the list below is just a smattering of the hundreds of annual parades, festivals, and wing-dings. Note that the dates indicated below for September through December reflect schedules for 2007, and the dates indicated for January through August reflect schedules for 2008. As always, it's a good idea to check an event's website when making plans. Now get out and enjoy!

- **First Night** · Dec. 31/Jan 1 · www.firstnight.org · Family-oriented First Night got its start in Boston. Celebrate the new year with live performances, interactive events, and in most years, bitter cold. The purchase of a First Night Button gains you admission to participating performance centers.
- **Boston Wine Expo** · Late Jan · www.wine-expos.com/boston · Largest consumer wine event in the country, with a long bill of celebrity chefs to boot.
- **Chinese New Year** · Late Jan-Early Feb · Fireworks, parades, and special banquets in Chinatown.
- **Black History Month Music Celebration** · Feb · www.berkleebpc.com · A series of concerts at the Berklee Performance Center.
- **Winter Restaurant Week** · early March · www.restaurantweekboston.com · Local eateries offer specially priced lunches and dinners. A chance to sample meals you could never otherwise afford!
- **New England Spring Flower Show** · Early March · www.masshort.org · Flower and craft exhibition at the Bayside Expo Center.
- **St. Patrick's Day Parade** · Mar 19 · www.saintpatricksdayparade.com/boston · Marching through Southie since 1737.
- **Red Sox Opening Day** · Early Apr · www.redsox.com · Unofficial holiday.
- **Boston Marathon/Patriots Day** · Apr 17 · www.baa.org · Pseudo local holiday with the 111th running of the marathon and an early Red Sox game.
- **Wake Up the Earth Festival** · Early May · www.spontaneouscelebrations.org · Hippies and children alike enjoy stilt walking, puppets, live bands, and community bonding in Jamaica Plain.
- **Walk for Hunger** · May 7 · www.projectbread.org · 20-mile walk whose proceeds fund over 400 emergency food programs each year.
- **Anime Boston** · May 26-28 · www.animeboston.com · Japanese animation convention at the Hynes Convention Center.
- **Feast of the Madonna di Anzano** · Jun 3-4 · www.anzanoboston.com · Procession and gala feast in the North End Italian community.
- **Scooper Bowl** · Jun 6-8 · www.jimmyfund.org · World's biggest all-you-can-eat ice cream festival. Proceeds go to the Jimmy Fund.
- **Boston Gay Pride Parade** · Jun 10 · www.bostonpride.org · New England's largest, capping a week of pride events.
- **Bloomsday** · Jun 16 · www.artsandsociety.org · Celebration of James Joyce's *Ulysses* at BU.

- **Bunker Hill Parade** · Jun 18 · www.charlestownonline.net · Celebration of Bunker Hill Day in Charlestown.
- **Boston Globe Blues and Jazz Festival** · Late Jun · Jazz and blues on the waterfront.
- **Boston Harborfest** · Jun 28-July 4 · www.bostonharborfest.com · Over 200 events celebrating Boston's colonial and maritime history through reenactments, concerts, and historical tours.
- **Boston's Fourth of July** · Guess · www.july4th.org · Ridiculously crowded Boston Pops concert and fireworks on the Esplanade.
- **Khoury's State Spa Big Man Run** · Late Jul · www.clydesdale.com · A 4.8-mile race through Somerville during which runners stop three times to consume a hot dog and a beer.
- **Feast of St. Agrippina** · Aug 4-6 · Featuring a procession, block party, and a giant tug-of-war.
- **Feast of the Madonna del Soccorso** · Aug 17-20 · www.fishermansfeast.com · Boston's longest-running Italian festival.
- **Restaurant Week** · Late Aug · www.bostonchefs.com/news · Discounted *prix-fixe* meals at scores of area restaurants—a terrific bargain.
- **Boston Carnival** · Late Aug · www.bostoncarnival.com · Celebration of Caribbean culture in Dorchester.
- **Boston Film Festival** · Sep 9-13 · www.bostonfilmfestival.org · Plenty to please the most finicky cinephile.
- **Boston Tattoo Convention** · Sep 8-10 · www.bostontattooconvention.com · Celebrating the newly legal (in Mass) art form.
- **Boston Freedom Rally** · Sep 18 · www.masscann.org · That ain't freedom they're smoking.
- **Boston Folk Festival** · Sep 16-17 · www.wumb.org/folkfest · Pickin' and grinnin'.
- **Opening Night at the Symphony** · Early Oct · www.bso.org · Kicks off Maestro Levine's second season at the BSO.
- **Harvard Square Oktoberfest** · Oct 2 · www.harvard-square.com · Don't expect liters of free beer.
- **Head of the Charles** · Oct 21-22 · www.hocr.org · The world's largest two-day rowing event.
- **Belgian Beer Fest** · Oct 29 · www.beeradvocate.com/fests · Sluit je aan bij de Bierrevolutie!
- **Boston Jewish Film Festival** · www.bjff.org · Now in its 17th season.
- **Boston International Antiquarian Book Fair** · Mid-Nov · www.bostonbookfair.com · The country's longest running antiquarian book fair features autographs, photographs, maps, and more.
- **Prudential Center Christmas Tree Lighting** · Dec 3 · www.prudentialcenter.com · Each year Nova Scotia thanks Boston for helping Halifax recover from a 1917 disaster by sending down a huge tree.
- **Boston Tea Party Re-enactment** · Mid-Dec · www.oldsouthmeetinghouse.org · A fine excuse to don your tri-cornered hat.
- **Boston Common Menorah Lighting** · Late Dec · www.cityofboston.gov/arts · Celebrating the first night of Hanukkah.

Television

2	WGBH	(PBS)	www.wgbh.org
4	WBZ	(CBS)	www.wbz4.com
5	WCVB	(ABC)	www.thebostonchannel.com
7	WHDH	(NBC)	www1.whdh.com
25	WFXT	(FOX)	www.fox25.com
27	WUNI	(Univision)	www.wunitv.com
38	WSBK	(UPN)	www.upn38.com
44	WGBH	(PBS)	www.wgbh.org
56	WLVI	(WB)	wb56.trb.com
66	WUTF	(Telefutura)	www.univision.com
68	WBPX	(PAX)	www.paxboston.tv

AM Radio

590	WEZE	Christian radio	www.wezeradio.com
680	WRKO	Talk	www.wrko.com
740	WJIB	Instrumental Pop/Light Oldies	
850	WEEI	Sports	www.weei.com
950	WROL	Religious	
1030	WBZ	News/Talk/Sports	www.wbz.com
1060	WBIX	Business Talk	
1090	WILD	Urban	
1150	WJTK	Religious	
1260	WMKI	Radio Disney	
		radio.disney.go.com/mystation/Boston/	
1510	WWZN	Sports	www.1510thezone.com
1600	WUNR	Leased	

FM Radio

88.1	WMBR	MIT	www.wmbr.mit.edu
88.9	WERS	Emerson College	www.wers.org
89.7	WGBH	NPR News/Classical	
			www.wghb.com
90.3	WZBC	Boston College	
90.9	WBUR	NPR/BU	www.wbur.org
91.5	WMFO	Tufts University	www.wmfo.org
91.9	WUMB	Folk/Jazz	www.wumb.org
92.9	WBOS	Modern AC	www.wbos.com
94.5	WJMN	Hip-Hop/R&B	www.jamn.com
95.3	WHRB	Harvard University	
			www.whrb.org
96.9	WTKK	Talk	www.wtkk.com
98.5	WBMX	Modern AC	www.mix985.com
100.7	WZLX	Classic Rock	www.wzlx.com
101.7	WFNX	Modern Rock	www.wfnx.com
102.5	WCRB	Classical	www.wcrb.com
103.3	WODS	Oldies	www.oldies1033.com
104.1	WBCN	Modern Rock	www.wbcn.com
104.9	WBOQ	Soft Rock	
			www.northshore1049.com
105.7	WROR	Classic Rock	www.wror.com
106.7	WMJX	Soft Rock	www.magic1067.com
107.3	WAAF	Active Rock	www.waaf.com
107.9	WXKS	Pop	www.kissfm.com

Print Media

Bay Windows	www.baywindows.com	617-266-6670	LGBT newsweekly.
Beacon Hill Times	www.beaconhilltimes.com	617-523-9490	Newsweekly serving Beacon Hill.
Boston Business Journal	www.bizjournals.com/boston	617-330-1000	Business weekly.
Boston Globe	www.boston.com	617-929-2000	Daily broadsheet.
Boston Haitian Reporter	www.bostonhaitian.com	617-436-1222	Free monthly for Haitian-American community.
Boston Herald	www.bostonherald.com	617-426-3000	Daily tabloid.
Boston Irish Reporter	www.bostonirish.com	617-436-1222	News from and about the Irish in Boston.
Boston Metro	www.metropoint.com	617-338-7985	Weekday tabloid aimed at commuters.
Boston Magazine	www.bostonmagazine.com	617-262-9700	Glossy monthly.
Boston Phoenix	www.bostonphoenix.com	617-536-5390	Progressive news and entertainment listings.
Boston Review	www.bostonreview.net	617-258-0805	Leftish politics and culture magazine.
Boston Russian Bulletin	www.russianmass.com	617-277-5398	Russian community news, in Russian.
Brookline TAB	www.townonline.com/brookline	617-566-3585	Brookline newsweekly.
Cambridge Chronicle	www.townonline.com/cambridge	617-577-7149	Cambridge newsweekly.
Cambridge TAB	www.townonline.com/cambridge	617-497-1241	Cambridge newsweekly.
Dig	www.weeklydig.com	617-426-8942	Humor, news and nightlife.
Dorchester Reporter	www.dotnews.com	617-436-1222	Dorchester news.
Improper Bostonian	www.improper.com	617-859-1400	Free entertainment and lifestyle magazine.
In Newsweekly	www.innewsweekly.com	617-426-8246	LGBT news and entertainment.
Jamaica Plain Gazette	www.jamaicaplaingazette.com	617-524-2626	JP news.
The Jewish Advocate	www.thejewishadvocate.com	617-367-9100	News about Boston's Jewish community.
Mass High Tech	www.masshightech.com	617-242-1224	Technology news.
Mattapan Reporter	www.bostonneighborhoodnews.com	617-436-1222	Mattapan neighborhood news.
Pilot	www.rcab.org/Pilot/storyIndex.html	617-746-5889	Catholic monthly.
Sampan	www.sampan.org	617-426-9492	Chinese/English bimonthly.
Somerville Journal	www.townonline.com/somerville	617-625-6300	Weekly Somerville news.
Stuff@Night	www.stuffatnight.com	617-859-3333	Entertainment listings and "what's hot."

And this is good old Boston.
The home of the bean and the cod.
Where the Lowells talk to the Cabots,
And the Cabots talk only to God.

—John Collins Bossidy (a toast given
at a Harvard alumni dinner in 1910)

Useful Phone Numbers

General Info	411
Emergencies	911
Boston City Hall	617-635-4000
Brookline Town Hall	617-730-2000
Cambridge City Hall	617-349-4000
Somerville City Hall	617-625-6600
Boston Board of Elections	617-635-4635
Brookline Town Clerk	617-730-2010
Cambridge Board of Elections	617-349-4361
Somerville Board of Elections	617-625-6600, ext. 4200
Boston Police Headquarters	617-343-4200
Keyspan Energy Delivery	617-469-2300
NStar	617-424-2000
Comcast	888-633-4266
Verizon	800-256-4646

Websites

www.notfortourists.com/boston-home.aspx—
The Boston site written by the people, for the people.
www.cityofboston.gov—Boston government resources.
www.cambridgema.gov—
Cambridge government resources.
www.ci.somerville.ma.us—
Somerville government resources.
www.town.brookline.ma.us—
Brookline government resources.
www.boston.com—Website of the Boston Globe.
boston.craigslist.org—
Classifieds in almost every area, with personals, apartments
for rent, musicians, job listings, and more.
boston.citysearch.com—
Portal channeling the Yellow Pages.
www.boston-online.com—
Forums and fun facts; guide to Boston English.

We're the First!!!

- America's first public park (Boston Common, 1634)
- America's first college (Harvard, founded in 1636)
- America's first public school (Boston Latin, 1645)
- America's first public library (Boston Public Library, 1653)
- America's first post office (Richard Fairbanks' Tavern, 1639)
- America's first regularly issued newspaper (Boston News-Letter, 1704)
- America's first lighthouse (Boston Harbor, 1716)
- First flag of the American colonies raised on Prospect Hill (January 1, 1776)
- America's first published novel (The Power of Sympathy by William Hill Brown, 1789)
- First demonstration of surgical anesthesia (1845)
- First telephone call (Alexander Graham Bell, 1876)
- America's first subway (1897)
- First person-to-person network email (BBN Technologies, 1971)
- First "First Night" New Year's celebration (1976)

Boston Timeline

A timeline of significant Boston events (by no means complete)

1620	Mayflower arrives in Plymouth.
1630	Dorchester founded by Gov. John Winthrop.
1630	City of Boston chartered.
1634	Boston Common, first public park in America, opens.
1636	Harvard College opens.
1639	America's first canal cut near Dedham.
1645	Boston Latin School, first public school in America, opens.
1692	Witchcraft trials begin in Salem.
1693	Society of Negroes founded.
1704	First regularly issued American newspaper, the Boston News-Letter.
1706	Benjamin Franklin born.
1716	First American lighthouse built (Boston Harbor).
1770	Boston Massacre.
1773	Boston Tea Party.
1775	Revolutionary War begins at Lexington and Concord.
1775	Battle of Bunker Hill.
1776	First flag of the American colonies raised on Prospect Hill in Somerville.
1776	British evacuate Boston.
1780	John Hancock becomes first elected Governor of Massachusetts.
1788	Massachusetts ratifies Constitution.
1795	The "new" State House built.
1796	John Adams, of Quincy, elected second president.
1806	African Meeting House, first church built by free African-Americans, opens.
1820	Maine separates from Massachusetts.
1824	John Quincy Adams elected sixth president.
1826	Union Oyster House opens.
1831	William Lloyd Garrison publishes first abolitionist newspaper, the Liberator.
1837	Samuel Morse invents electric telegraph machine.
1845	Sewing machine invented by Elias Howe.
1846	Boston dentist William T.G. Morton publicly demonstrates the use of anesthesia in surgery.
1846	From 1846 to 1849, 37,000 Irish people flee the Potato Famine for Boston.
1860	From 1860 to 1870, the Back Bay is filled in, greatly increasing the landmass of Boston.
1863	University of Massachusetts at Amherst chartered.
1868	From 1868 to 1874, Boston annexes Charlestown, Brighton, Roxbury, West Roxbury, and Dorchester.
1872	Boston Globe prints its first newspaper.
1872	Great Fire.
1876	First telephone call by Alexander Graham Bell.
1877	Helen Magill becomes first woman Ph.D. in US (at BU).
1882	John L. Sullivan becomes bare-knuckle boxing champ.
1886	Irish Echo newspaper founded.
1888	Construction begins on new building for Boston Public Library.
1892	JFK grandfather John F. "Honey Fitz" Fitzgerald elected to state senate.
1894	Honey Fitz elected to US Congress.
1896	First US public beach opens in Revere.
1897	First American subway opens.
1900	Symphony Hall opens.
1901	Boston Red Sox play first game against New York Yankees.
1903	Red Sox (then the Americans) win first World Series.
1906	Honey Fitz becomes first Boston-born Irish-American mayor.
1912	Fenway Park opens.
1914	James Michael Curley elected mayor for the first time.
1915	Custom House Tower completed, tallest building in Boston at time.

1919 Great Molasses Flood kills 21 in the North End.
1920 Red Sox owner Harry Frazee sells Babe Ruth to Yankees for $100,000.
1920 Irish-Italian gang fights begin.
1924 Boston Bruins play first game.
1924 World's first mutual fund established.
1927 Sacco and Vanzetti wrongly executed for robbery shootings.
1928 Boston Garden opens.
1928 First computer invented at MIT.
1929 Bruins win their first Stanley Cup trophy.
1934 JFK's father, "Old Joe" Kennedy, named SEC chairman.
1941 Ted Williams hits .406, last player to hit over .400.
1942 Fire at Cocoanut Grove nightclub kills 491 people.
1946 JFK elected to Congress.
1946 Boston Celtics play first game.
1946 Red Sox lose World Series after tragic player error.
1947 Microwave oven invented at Raytheon.
1947 Polaroid camera invented.
1947 Dr. Sidney Farber introduces chemotherapy.
1950 Red Auerbach becomes Celtics coach.
1952 Boston Braves play final game in Boston, move to Milwaukee.
1956 Celtics draft Bill Russell.
1957 Massachusetts Turnpike opens.
1958 Celtics win first of 16 championships.
1958 Demolition of the West End neighborhood begins.
1959 Central Artery opens.
1960 Boston Patriots play first game.
1960 John F. Kennedy elected 35th president.
1960 Ted Williams homers in last at-bat for Red Sox.
1962 From 1962 to 1964, Boston Strangler kills 13 women. Albert DeSalvo is convicted and killed in prison.
1963 JFK assassinated in Dallas.
1964 Prudential Tower built.
1965 Havlicek steals the ball! Celtics win championship.
1966 Bobby Orr plays first game as a Bruin.
1966 Edward W. Brooke becomes first African-American elected to US Senate since Reconstruction.
1967 Red Sox's Impossible Dream season ends in defeat.
1971 First e-mail sent by BBN Technologies.
1973 John Hancock building, tallest in Boston, nears completion—giant windows start falling out.
1974 Federal court declares "de facto segregation" of Boston public schools; orders desegregation by busing. Demonstrations and violence ensue.
1975 Carlton Fisk hits 12th inning Game 6 homer, does baseline foul pole dance. Sox go on to lose Game 7.
1975 Gangster Whitey Bulger begins relationship with FBI agents, reign as Boston's biggest crime lord.
1976 First "First Night" New Year's celebration.
1978 Blizzard of '78 paralyzes Southern New England.
1978 Bucky Dent! Sox lose to Yanks.
1986 Celtics draft pick Len Bias dies of a drug overdose.
1986 Red Sox lose World Series Game 6 to Mets after excruciating 10th inning error, go on to lose Game 7.
1987 Big Dig construction begins in Charlestown.
1987 Cleanup of Boston Harbor begins.
1988 Governor Michael Dukakis runs for president, rides tank, loses to Bush the First.
1993 Celtics captain Reggie Lewis dies.
1993 Former Mayor Ray Flynn named ambassador to Vatican.
1993 Thomas M. "Mumbles" Menino elected Boston's first Italian-American mayor.
1995 Boston Garden closes; FleetCenter opens.
1995 Whitey Bulger goes on the lam after his FBI handlers are indicted.

1998 *Boston Globe* columnists Patricia Smith and Mike Barnicle fired over fabrications and plagiarism, respectively.
2001 Jane Swift becomes first female governor of Massachusetts.
2001 Planes that destroy NYC World Trade Center leave Logan Airport.
2002 After a 0-2 start, New England Patriots win their first Super Bowl.
2002 Ted Williams dies, cryogenically frozen in two pieces.
2002 Catholic clergy sexual abuse scandal explodes; Cardinal Bernard Law resigns amid controversy.
2003 Billy Bulger forced to resign as UMass president due to controversy about his gangster brother, Whitey.
2004 Supreme Judicial Court rules that gay couples have the right to marry.
2004 Demolition of Central Artery.
2004 Sox win World Series for first time since 1918.
2004 Beacon Hill resident John Kerry fails to unseat President Bush.
2005 New England Patriots win their third Super Bowl in four years.

15 Essential Boston Movies

The Boston Strangler (1968)
The Thomas Crown Affair (1968)
Love Story (1970)
The Paper Chase (1973)
Between the Lines (1977)
The Verdict (1982)
The Bostonians (1984)
Glory (1989)

Far and Away (1992)
Good Will Hunting (1997)
A Civil Action (1998)
Monument Ave (1998)
Next Stop, Wonderland (1998)
Mystic River (2003)
The Departed (2006)

15 Essential Boston Songs

"Boston" — The Byrds
"Charlie on the MTA" — The Kingston Trio
"Dirty Water" — The Standells
"Down at the Cantab" — Little Joe Cook & the Thrillers
"Government Center" — Jonathan Richman
"Highlands" — Bob Dylan
"I Want My City Back" — The Mighty Mighty Bosstones
"Massachusetts" — The Bee Gees
"Roadrunner" — Jonathan Richman
"Rock and Roll Band" — Boston
"Sweet Baby James" — James Taylor
"Tessie" — Dropkick Murphys
"The Ballad of Sacco & Vanzetti" — Joan Baez
"Twilight in Boston" — Jonathan Richman
"UMass" — The Pixies

15 Essential Boston Books

All Souls, Michael Patrick McDonald
The Autobiography of Benjamin Franklin
Black Mass, David Lehrer and Gerard O'Neill
The Bostonians, Henry James
Dark Tide: The Great Boston Molasses Flood of 1919, Stephen Puleo
Faithful, Stewart O'Nan and Stephen King
The Handmaid's Tale, Margaret Atwood
The House of the Seven Gables, Nathaniel Hawthorne
Infinite Jest, David Foster Wallace
John Adams, David McCullough
Johnny Tremain, Esther Forbes
Little Women, Louisa May Alcott
Make Way for Ducklings, Robert McCloskey
The Trumpet of the Swan, E.B. White
Walden, Henry David Thoreau

281

Self Storage / Van & Truck Rental

Self Storage

	Address	Phone	Map
Planet Self Storage	33 Traveler St	617-426-7229	7
Storage USA	150 William F McClellan Hwy	617-568-0009	9
Planet Self Storage	135 Old Colony Ave	617-268-8282	10
Castle Self Storage	39 Old Colony Ave	617-268-5056	12
Planet Self Storage	100 Southampton St	617-445-6776	12
Public Storage	290 Southampton St	617-445-6287	12
Storage USA	235 North Beacon St	617-782-1177	18
Storage USA	130 Lincoln St	617-787-4325	19
Yellow Brick Self Storage	138 Harvard Ave	617-254-5007	19
Cambridge Self Storage	445 Concord Ave	617-876-5060	21
Storage USA	460 Somerville Ave	617-625-1000	23
Storage USA	14 McGrath Hwy	617-623-7690	25
C-Free Self Storage	86 Joy St	617-625-6410	28
Planet Self Storage	39 Medford St	617-497-4800	28
U-Haul Center Of Somerville	151 Linwood St	617-625-2789	28

Van & Truck Rental

	Address	Phone	Map
Budget	33 Traveler St	617-426-7886	7
Ryder	280 W 1st St	617-269-8000	10
U-Haul	985 Massachusetts Ave	617-442-5600	12
U-Haul	1579 Columbus Ave	617-445-0405	14
U-Haul	240 N Beacon St	617-782-0355	18
Budget	95 Brighton Ave	617-497-3608	19
Budget	420 Rutherford Ave	617-242-8044	25
U-Haul	844 Main St	617-354-0500	27
U-Haul	151 Linwood St	617-625-2789	28

WiFi

WiFi	Address	Phone	Map		Address	Phone	Map
Starbucks	1 Charles St	617-742-2664	1	Starbucks	1655 Beacon St	617-232-5940	17
Starbucks	222 Cambridge St	617-227-2959	1	French Press Coffee	2201 Commonwealth Ave	617-254-2266	18
Starbucks	97 Charles St	617-227-3812	1	Starbucks	1660 Soldiers Field Rd	617-782-1325	18
Boston Bean Stock Coffee	97 Salem St	617-725-0040	2				
Starbucks	2 Atlantic Ave	617-723-7819	2	Infusions Tea Spa	110 Brighton Ave	617-254-1122	19
Starbucks	63 Court St	617-227-2284	2	Starbucks	277 Harvard St	617-739-3453	19
Starbucks	84 State St	617-523-3053	2	Starbucks	473 Harvard St	617-738-8005	19
Rachel's Kitchen	12 Church St	617-423-3447	3	Upper Crust	286 Harvard St	617-739-8518	19
Starbucks	12 Winter St	617-542-1313	3	Peet's Coffee & Tea	100 Mt Auburn St	617-492-1844	20
Starbucks	143 Stuart St	617-227-7332	3				
Starbucks	240 Washington St	617-720-2220	3	Shay's Lounge	58 JFK St	617-864-9161	20
Starbucks	27 School St	617-227-7731	3	Simon's Coffee House	1736 Massachusetts Ave	617-497-7766	20
Starbucks	62 Boylston St	617-338-0067	3				
Les Zygomates	129 South St	617-542-5108	4	Starbucks	1662 Massachusetts House	617-491-0442	20
Starbucks	1 Financial Ctr	617-428-0080	4				
Starbucks	1 International Pl	617-737-4688	4	Starbucks	31 Church St	617-492-7870	20
Starbucks	101 Federal St	617-946-0535	4	Starbucks	36 JFK St	617-492-4881	20
Starbucks	211 Congress St	617-542-4439	4	Tealuxe	0 Brattle St	617-441-0077	20
Espresso Royale	286 Newbury St	617-859-9515	5	Starbucks	220 Alewife Brook Pkwy	617-876-1070	21
Espresso Royale	44 Gainsborough St	617-859-7080	5				
Starbucks	151 Massachusetts Ave	617-236-4335	5	Starbucks	260 Elm St	617-623-4497	22
				Carberry's Bakery & Coffee House	187 Elm St	617-666-2233	23
Starbucks	273 Huntington Ave	617-536-6501	5				
Starbucks	350 Newbury St	617-859-5751	5	Starbucks	711 Somerville Ave	617-776-6783	23
Starbucks	10 Huntington Ave	617-867-0491	5	Beantowne Coffee House	One Kendall Sq	617-621-7900	26
Starbucks	165 Newbury St	617-536-5282	6				
Starbucks	441 Stuart St	617-859-0703	6	Starbucks	100 Cambridgeside Pl	617-621-9507	26
Starbucks	443 Boylston St	617-536-7177	6				
Starbucks	755 Boylston St	617-450-0310	6	Starbucks	6 Cambridge Ctr	617-577-7511	26
Tealuxe	108 Newbury St	617-927-0400	6	1369 Coffee House	757 Massachusetts Ave	617-576-4600	27
Francesca's	564 Tremont St	617-482-9026	7				
Starbucks	627 Tremont St	617-236-7879	7	Starbucks	655 Massachusetts Ave	617-354-5471	27
Sorelle	100 City Sq	617-242-5980	8				
Emack & Bolio's	736 Centre St	617-524-5107	14	1369 Coffee House	1369 Cambridge St	617-576-1369	28
June Bug Café	403A Centre St	617-522-2393	14				
Sweet Finnish	761 Centre St	617-522-5200	14	Diesel Café	257 Elm St	617-629-8717	28
Starbucks	283 Longwood Ave	617-277-5202	15	Starbucks	468 Broadway	617-491-9911	28
Espresso Royale	736 Commonwealth Ave	617-277-8737	16				
Starbucks	874 Commonwealth Ave	617-734-3691	16				
Starbucks	15 Harvard St	617-232-5063	17				

Internet

Internet	Address	Phone	Map		Address	Phone	Map
FedEx Kinko's	2 Center Plz	617-973-9000	1	FedEx Kinko's	575 Boylston St	617-536-2536	6
FedEx Kinko's	60 State St	617-523-8174	2	FedEx Kinko's	715 Albany St	617-414-2679	7
FedEx Kinko's	125 Tremont St	617-423-0234	3	FedEx Kinko's	415 Summer St	617-954-2203	10
FedEx Kinko's	10 Post Office Sq	617-482-4400	4	FedEx Kinko's	115 Cummington St	617-358-2679	16
FedEx Kinko's	211 Congress St	617-482-0701	4	FedEx Kinko's	1370 Beacon St	617-731-3100	17
FedEx Kinko's	900 Boylston St	617-954-2725	5	FedEx Kinko's	252 Washington St	617-723-7263	18
NewburyOpen.net	252 Newbury St	617-267-9716	5	FedEx Kinko's	1 Miffin Pl	617-497-0125	20
FedEx Kinko's	187 Dartmouth St	617-262-6188	6	FedEx Kinko's	600 Technology Sq	617-494-5905	26

Gas Stations

Exxon	239 Cambridge St	1
Shell	584 Columbus Ave	5
Mobil	273 E Berkeley St	7
Shell	1 Rutherford Ave	8
Mobil	470 Meridian St	9
Shell	52 Meridian St	9
Hess	151 Old Colony Ave	10
Gulf	888 Dorchester Ave	12
Mobil	85 Southampton St	12
Sunoco	785 Tremont St	13
Exxon	1420 Boylston St	15
Mobil	1301 Boylston St	15
Shell	1241 Boylston St	15
Shell	525 Huntington Ave	15
Texaco	914 Huntington Ave	15
Gulf	25 Washington St	16
Mobil	345 Boylston St	17
Econogas	1550 Commonwealth Ave	18
Exxon	198 Western Ave	19
Hess	219 Cambridge St	19
Mobil	343 Fresh Pond Pkwy	21
Sunoco	515 Concord Ave	21
Hess	709 McGrath Hwy	24
Hess	123 Cambridge St	25
Mobil	816 Memorial Dr	27
Shell	207 Magazine St	27
Shell	820 Memorial Dr	27
Hess	287 Prospect St	28

Copy Shops

FedEx Kinko's	2 Center Plz	617-973-9000	1
Copy Cop	601 Boylston St	617-267-9267	6
FedEx Kinko's	187 Dartmouth St	617-262-6188	6
FedEx Kinko's	1 Miffin Pl	617-497-0125	20

Bowling (yes, bowling)

Boston Bowl (open 24 hours)	820 Morrissey Blvd, Dorchester	617-825-3800	32

Restaurants

Bova's Bakery	134 Salem St	617-523-5601	2
South Street Diner	178 Kneeland St	617-350-0028	4
IHOP	1850 Soldiers Field Rd	617-787-0533	18

Plumbers

Beacon Hill Plumbing	617-723-3296
Drain Doctor	617-547-6969
Drain King	617-439-3929
John's (Brookline)	617-277-1447
Metro Sewer & Drain	617-426-8939
Plumbing Express	617-288-0777
Roto-Rooter	617-267-1489
Sudden Service	617-367-8300

Veterinary

MSPCA Angell Memorial Animal Hospital	350 S Huntington Ave	617-522-7282	14
Brookline Animal Hospital	678 Brookline Ave	617-277-2030	16

Convenience Stores

White Hen Pantry	250 Cambridge St	617-367-8238	1
Store 24	177 State St	617-367-0034	2
White Hen Pantry	342 Hanover St	617-723-5569	2
Store 24	141 Massachusetts Ave	617-353-1897	5
Store 24	281 Huntington Ave	617-267-5668	5
Store 24	717 Boylston St	617-424-6888	6
Store 24	140 Main St	617-241-7865	8
White Hen Pantry	205 Maverick St	617-569-7069	9
Store 24	684 Centre St	617-524-9893	14
Store 24	542 Commonwealth Ave	617-424-8856	16
Store 24	1912 Beacon St	617-738-4874	18
Store 24	241 Market St	617-783-9193	18
White Hen Pantry	462 Washington St	617-787-3719	18
Store 24	509 Cambridge St	617-782-3900	19
Store 24	957 Commonwealth Ave	617-783-5466	19
White Hen Pantry	1868 Massachusetts Ave	617-547-7255	23
Store 24	321 Broadway	617-497-6275	28

Pharmacies

CVS	2 Center Plz	617-523-3653	24-Hours	1
Walgreens	841 Boylston St	617-236-8130	Prescription counter closes at 10PM	5
CVS	587 Boylston St	617-437-8414	24-Hour pharmacy	6
CVS	210 Border St	617-567-5147	24-Hour pharmacy	9
Walgreens	1 Central Sq	617-569-5278	24-hour prescription counter	9
CVS	211 Alewife Brook Pkwy	617-661-6422	24-Hour pharmacy	21
CVS	36 White St	617-876-5519	24-Hour pharmacy	23
Brooks	14 McGrath Hwy	617-776-3003	24-Hour pharmacy	25

Boston lost yet another movie theater recently with the closing of Loews Copley Plaza. It was cramped and uncomfortable, and the screens were only slightly larger than Post-Its, but at least it provided filmgoers with a backup venue to catch second-run and small-audience movies. (The theater space has morphed into the new outpost of clothier Barneys New York.) This leaves the City of Boston with (just) two theaters showing the new Will Smith vehicle or Pixar whimsy: **Loews Boston Common (Map 3)** and **AMC Theatres Fenway 13 (Map 16)**. Both offer stadium seating and the latest and greatest in concessions marketing. Loews also operates Somerville's **Loews Assembly Square (Map 24)** and Cambridge's **Loews Fresh Pond (Map 22)**.

To see a movie not primarily marketed to teenagers, check what's on at **Landmark Kendall Square Cinema (Map 26)**, **Brattle Theatre (Map 20)**, the **Harvard Film Archive (Map 20)**, the **Museum of Fine Arts (Map 15)**, or the art-deco landmark **Coolidge Corner Theatre (Map 17)**.

If you've never been to "Motion Picture Mondays" at the **Wang Center (Map 3)**, make a plan to go. The series features classic films, and there's that sumptuous interior. Better still, admission is free.

Huge-screen freaks should hit the **Mugar Omni Theater (Map 1)** at the Museum of Science and the **Simons IMAX Theatre (Map 2)** at the New England Aquarium. If you just *have* to shop for furniture before seeing a movie, you owe yourself a trip to **Jordan's Furniture** out in Natick where, for reasons we're still struggling to determine, there's an on-site 3-D IMAX theater. (Coming soon: Bernie & Phyl retaliate by building a drive-in behind their Saugus showroom…)

Movie Theater	Address	Phone	Map
AMC Theatres Fenway 13	201 Brookline Ave	617-424-6266	16
Brattle Theatre	40 Brattle St	617-876-6837	20
Coolidge Corner Theatre	290 Harvard St	617-734-2500	17
Harvard Film Archive	24 Quincy St	617-495-4700	20
Institute for Contemporary Art	100 Northern Ave	617-266-5152	10
Landmark Kendall Square Cinema	One Kendall Sq	617-499-1996	26
Loews Boston Common	175 Tremont St	617-423-3499	3
Loews Cineplex Assembly Square	35 Middlesex Ave	617-628-7000	24
Loews Cineplex Fresh Pond	168 Alewife Brook Pkwy	617-661-2900	22
Loews Cineplex Harvard Square	10 Church St	617-864-4580	20
MIT Film Series	77 Massachusetts Ave	617-253-3791	26
Mugar Omni Theatre	Science Park	617-723-2500	1
Museum of Fine Arts	465 Huntington Ave	617-369-3770	15
National Amusements Circle Cinemas	399 Chestnut Hill Ave	617-566-2170	18
Simons IMAX Theatre	Central Wharf	866-815-4629	2
Somerville Theatre	55 Davis Sq	617-625-5700	22
Wang Center	270 Tremont St	617-482-9393	3

Newbury Street has Boston's largest and densest concentration of art galleries. You've probably passed by the several dozen galleries on Newbury Street many times without taking a look at what's inside, but popping into just a few of them will give you some idea of the broad scope of what's on offer (even if your budget means you're more likely to be striking deals at the MFA's gift shop). Commercial art fans should check out **International Poster Gallery's (Map 6)** expansive collection of Italian, travel, and Soviet-era posters. The gallery of the **Copley Society of Boston (Map 6)**, also on Newbury Street, hosts several competitions over the course of the year, including showcases of student work.

While Newbury Street galleries may have the city's most established spots, the interesting developments are happening in the South End, where a number of galleries have opened or relocated. The center of the action is the converted warehouse at 450 Harrison Avenue between Thayer Street and Randolph Street. (Take the Silver Line to East Berkeley Street, walk one block to Harrison Avenue, and hang a right.) Big names at the "SoWa Building" include **Bernard Toale Gallery (Map 7)**, **Kingston Gallery (Map 7)**, and **Genovese/Sullivan (Map 7)**. If you're interested in what's emerging in Boston's contemporary art scene, head to SoWa on the first Friday of the month to see the new exhibits. (At the very least, it's an excuse to get dressed up and consume some free wine.)

Elsewhere in Boston, consider seeing what's on display at Inman Square's **Zeitgeist Gallery (Map 28)** (which also hosts fantastic performances and events), the **Fort Point Arts Community Gallery (Map 10)**, Roxbury's **Hamill Gallery of African Art (Map 13)**, and Kenmore Square's **Panopticon Gallery of Photography (Map 15)**. Cheaper rents are attracting artists to East Boston, where **Maverick Gallery (Map 9)** has recently opened its doors.

All areas codes are 617.

Map 2 • North End / Faneuil Hall

Mayor's Art Gallery	1 City Hall Plz, 3rd floor	635-3245
Scollay Square Gallery	1 City Hall Plz, 3rd floor	635-3245

Map 3 • Downtown Crossing / Park Square / Bay Village

Barbara Krakow Gallery	10 Newbury St	262-4490
Beth Urdang Gallery	14 Newbury St	424-8468
Howard Yezerski Gallery	14 Newbury St	262-0550
Miller Block Gallery	14 Newbury St	536-4650

Map 5 • Back Bay (West) / Fenway (East)

Gargoyles, Grotesques & Chimeras	262 Newbury St	536-2362
St George Gallery	245 Newbury St	450-0321
Kaji Aso Gallery	40 St Stephen St	247-1719

Map 6 • Back Bay (East) / South End (Upper)

Acme Fine Art	38 Newbury St	585-9951
Alianza Gallery	154 Newbury St	262-2385
Alpha Gallery	38 Newbury St	536-4465
Arden Gallery	129 Newbury St	247-0610
Artful Hand Gallery	100 Huntington Ave	262-9601
Chase Gallery	129 Newbury St	859-7222
Childs Gallery	169 Newbury St	266-1108
Copley Society	158 Newbury St	536-5049
DTR Modern Galleries	167 Newbury St	424-9700
Eclipse Gallery	164 Newbury St	247-6730
French Library and Cultural Center	53 Marlborough St	912-0400
Galerie d'Orsay	33 Newbury St	266-8001
Gallery NAGA	67 Newbury St	267-9060
International Poster Gallery	205 Newbury St	375-0076
Judi Rotenberg Gallery	130 Newbury St	437-1518
Judy Ann Goldman Fine Art	14 Newbury St	424-8468
Kidder Smith Gallery	131 Newbury St	424-6900
L'Attitude Gallery and Sculpture Garden	218 Newbury St	927-4400
Lanoue Fine Art	160 Newbury St	262-4400
Martin Lawrence Galleries	77 Newbury St	369-4800
Mercury Gallery	8 Newbury St	859-0054
Newbury Fine Arts	29 Newbury St	536-0210
Nielsen Gallery	179 Newbury St	266-4835
Pepper Gallery	38 Newbury St	236-4497
Pucker Gallery	171 Newbury St	267-9473
Richardson-Clarke Gallery	38 Newbury St	266-3321
Robert Klein Gallery	38 Newbury St	267-7997
Rolly-Michaux Gallery	290 Dartmouth St	536-9898
The Society of Arts and Crafts	175 Newbury St	266-1810
Victoria Munroe Fine Art	179 Newbury St	523-0661
Vose Galleries	238 Newbury St	536-6176

Map 7 • South End (Lower)

Allston Skirt Gallery	65 Thayer St	482-3652
Ars Libri	500 Harrison Ave	357-5212
BCA Mills Gallery	539 Tremont St	426-8835
Berenberg Gallery	4 Clarendon St	536-0800
Bernard Toale Gallery	450 Harrison Ave	482-2477
bf Annex	450 Harrison Ave	451-3344
Boston Sculptors Gallery	486 Harrison Ave	482-7781
Bromfield Art Gallery	450 Harrison Ave	451-3605
Gallery AA/B	535 Albany St	574-0022
Gallery Katz	450 Harrison Ave	423-6328
Gallery Kayafas	450 Harrison Ave	482-0411
Genovese/Sullivan Gallery	450 Harrison Ave	426-9738
Jules Place	1200 Washington St	542-0644
Kingston Gallery	450 Harrison Ave	423-4113
Mario Diacono Gallery	500 Harrison Ave	560-1608
MPG Contemporary	450 Harrison Ave	357-8881
OHT Gallery	450 Harrison Ave	423-1677
OSP Gallery	450 Harrison Ave	778-5265
Qingping Gallery Teahouse	231 Shawmut Ave	482-9988
Samson Projects	450 Harrison Ave	357-7177
Soprafina	73 Thayer St	728-0770
Space Other	63 Wareham St	451-3500

Map 9 • East Boston

Maverick Gallery	37 Maverick Sq	569-1233

Map 10 • South Boston (West) / Fort Point

Crump McCole Gallery	200 Seaport Blvd	330-1133
Fort Point Arts Community Gallery	300 Summer St	423-4299
Studio Soto	63 Melcher St	426-7686

Map 11 • South Boston (East)

Artists Foundation	516 E 2nd St	464-3559
Diana Levine Art Gallery	1 Design Center Pl	338-9060

Map 12 • Newmarket / Andrew Square

HallSpace	31 Norfolk Ave	989-9985

Map 13 • Roxbury

Hamill Gallery of African Art	2164 Washington St	442-8204

Map 14 • Jamaica Plain

JP Art Market	36 South St	522-1729

Map 15 • Fenway (West) / Mission Hill

Grossman Gallery at School of the Museum of Fine Arts	230 Fenway	369-3718
Panopticon Gallery of Photography	502C Commonwealth Ave	267-8929

Map 16 • Kenmore Square / Brookline (East)

Boston University Art Gallery	855 Commonwealth Ave	353-3329
Boston University Sherman Gallery	775 Commonwealth Ave	358-0295
Brookline Arts Center	86 Monmouth St	566-5715

Map 17 • Coolidge Corner / Brookline Hills

Artana	1378 Beacon St	879-3111
Gateway Gallery	62 Harvard St	734-1577

Map 19 • Allston (South) / Brookline (North)

Brookline Community Center for the Arts	14 Green St	738-2800

Map 20 • Harvard Square / Allston (North)

Baak Gallery	35 Brattle St	354-0407
Cambridge Artists Cooperative	59A Church St	868-4434
University Place Gallery	124 Mt Auburn St	876-0246

Map 21 • West Cambridge

Kathryn Schultz Gallery	25 Lowell St	876-0246
Mobilia Gallery	358 Huron Ave	876-2109

Map 22 • North Cambridge / West Somerville

Nave Gallery	155 Powderhouse Blvd	625-4823

Map 24 • Winter Hill / Union Square

Brickbottom Gallery	1 Fitchburg St	776-3410
Scat Gallery	90 Union Sq	628-8826

Map 26 • East Cambridge / Kendall Square / MIT

Art Interactive	130 Bishop Richard Allen Dr	498-0100
Cambridge Mulitcultural Art Center	41 Second St	577-1400
MIT List Visual Arts Center	20 Ames St, Building E15	253-4680

Map 28 • Inman Square

Art Attack	108 Beacon St	441-3833
Cambridge Arts Council Gallery	344 Broadway	349-4380
Out of the Blue Gallery	106 Prospect St	354-5287
Zeitgeist Gallery	1353 Cambridge St	876-6060

Even bad books are books and, therefore, sacred.
—Gunther Grass (*The Tin Drum*)

Big

As in so many other US cities, **Barnes & Noble (Map 3, Map 5, Map 16, Map 19)** and **Borders (Map 3, Map 26)** are the big dogs on the Boston bookstore scene. If you're shopping for a book, but not also for a low-fat latte or a high-fat chocolate croissant, get familiar with the large independents **Brookline Booksmith (Map 19)** and **Harvard Book Store (Map 20)** (unaffiliated with the university). Both focus on new titles but have cellars that handle used books.

Used

Davis Square's **McIntyre & Moore Books (Map 22)** sells an array of used books, with a bent toward scholarly works. A good place to find used guidebooks and fiction is **Rodney's Bookstore (Map 17, Map 27)**, with locations in both Central Square and Brookline. Downtown Crossing's **Brattle Book Shop (Map 3)** is a well-known used book specialist—check out the outdoor bookracks on dry days. Also in Central Boston, and worth checking out for antiquarian books, are **Lame Duck Books (Map 20)** and **Commonwealth Books (Map 3, Map 16)**.

Specialty

Quantum Books (Map 26) is the best computer bookstore in the city. For little kids, take a look at Brookline's **Children's Book Shop (Map 17)**. Slightly

older kids who dig gaming will enjoy **Pandemonium (Map 27)**. **Ars Libri (Map 7)** has an exemplary collection of rare and out-of-print fine art books. The only remaining LGBT bookstore in Boston is **Calamus (Map 4)** near South Station. A big tip of the chapeau is due to **Schoenhof's Foreign Books (Map 20)** for its broad selection. **Lucy Parsons Center (Map 6)**, in the South End, stocks many progressive titles. **Trident Booksellers & Café (Map 5)** stocks books and a good variety of mainstream and alternative magazine titles, in addition to serving a mean breakfast.

Cambridge

Several years ago there were more than 25 bookstores in Harvard Square, the greatest concentration of bookstores in the city (and perhaps the country). No longer. Blame high rents, online retail, large chains dominating the market, or a general waning interest in the printed arts, but the sad fact is that many fine shops have packed it in. The closing of NFT's favorite travel bookshop, **Globe Corner Travel (Map 20)**, is particularly discouraging. **The Harvard Coop (Map 20)** isn't your father's school bookstore—today it's managed by Barnes & Noble. Cheaper space outside Harvard Square had to have attracted the owners of independent **Porter Square Books (Map 23)** and Inman Square's **Lorem Ipsum (Map 28)**. **Grolier Poetry Book Shop (Map 20)**, a national poetry landmark, has somehow managed to remain open in its tiny space on Plympton Street.

Map 1 • Beacon Hill / West End

DiscountMedbooks.com	79 Beacon St	617-523-3221	Medical Books
Suffolk University Bookstore	148 Cambridge St	617-227-4085	Schoolbooks and campus merchandise.

Map 3 • Downtown Crossing / Park Square / Bay Village

Barnes & Noble	395 Washington St	617-426-5184	General.
Black Library Booksellers	Washington St & Summer St	617-442-2400	African-American Literature
Borders	10 School St	617-557-7188	General.
Brattle Book Shop	9 West St	617-542-0210	Used; outdoor racks when warm.
Commonwealth Books	134 Bolyston St	617-338-6328	Scholarly, used, antiquarian.
Emerson College Bookstore	120 Bolyston St	617-824-8696	Schoolbooks and campus merchandise.
Peter L Stern & Co	55 Temple Pl	617-542-2376	Antiquarian, especially first editions.
Suffolk Law School Book Store	110 Tremont St	617-227-8874	Schoolbooks and campus merchandise.

Map 4 · Financial District / Chinatown

Barbara's Best Sellers	720 Atlantic Ave	617-443-0060	In South Station.
Calamus Bookstore	92 South St	617-338-1931	Gay & lesbian.
Central China Book Co	44 Kneeland St	617-426-0888	Chinese.
Cheetah Trading	214 Lincoln St	617-451-1309	Chinese.
F A Bernett	144 Lincoln St	617-350-7778	Rare and scholarly art and architecture.
Rand McNally	84 State St	617-720-1125	Travel.
Tufts Medical Bookstore	116 Harrison Ave	617-636-6628	Schoolbooks and campus merchandise.

Map 5 · Back Bay (West) / Fenway (East)

Barnes & Noble	111 Huntington Ave	617-247-6959	General.
Berklee College of Music Bookstore	1080 Boylston St	617-267-0023	Schoolbooks and campus merchandise.
Trident Booksellers	338 Newbury St	617-267-8688	Independent; eclectic.

Map 6 · Back Bay (East) / South End (Upper)

Brentano's at Copley Place	100 Huntington Ave	617-859-9511	General.
Bromer Booksellers	607 Boylston St	617-247-2818	Fine, rare, and unusual.
Buddenbrooks Fine & Rare Books	31 Newbury St	617-536-4433	Fine, rare.
Lucy Parsons Center	549 Columbus Ave	617-267-6272	Progressive.
Thomas G Boss Fine Books	234 Clarendon St	781-431-2037	High-end, fine art books

Map 7 · South End (Lower)

Ars Libri	500 Harrison Ave	617-357-5212	Rare and out-of-print books on art.
Boston University Medical Center Bookstore	700 Albany St	617-638-5496	Schoolbooks and campus merchandise.

Map 9 · East Boston

Pathfinder Books	12 Bennington St	617-569-9169	Political books.
Studium Spanish Bookstore	268 Bennington St	617-569-1253	Spanish.

Map 13 · Roxbury

Roxbury Community College Bookstore	1234 Columbus Ave	617-442-8150	Schoolbooks and campus merchandise.

Map 14 · Jamaica Plain

Albatross Books	10 Parley Ave	617-739-2665	Antiquarian.
Boston Book Co	705 Centre St	617-522-2100	Antiquarian.
Jamaicaway Books & Gifts	676 Centre St	617-983-3204	Multicultural.
Rhythm & Muse	470 Centre St	617-524-6622	Independent.

Map 15 · Fenway (West) / Mission Hill

Brown & Connolly Medical Book Store	1315 Boylston St	617-262-5162	Medical Texts.
Emmanuel College Bookstore	400 The Fenway	617-264-7697	Schoolbooks and campus merchandise.

Arts & Entertainment · **Bookstores**

Map 15 · Fenway (West) / Mission Hill—*continued*

Mass College of Pharmacy & Art Bookstore	625 Huntington Ave	617-739-4772	Textbooks.
Medical Center Coop	333 Longwood Ave	617-499-3300	Schoolbooks and campus merchandise.
Northeastern University Bookstore	360 Huntington Ave	617-373-2286	Schoolbooks and campus merchandise.
Simmons College Book Store	300 The Fenway	617-521-2054	Schoolbooks and campus merchandise.
Wentworth Book Store	550 Huntington Ave	617-445-8814	Textbooks.

Map 16 · Kenmore Square / Brookline (East)

Barnes & Noble	660 Beacon St	617-267-8484	General/schoolbooks and campus merchandise.
Boston Book Annex	908 Beacon St	617-266-1090	Used.
Comicopia	464 Commonwealth Ave	617-266-4266	Comics.
Commonwealth Books	526 Commonwealth Ave	617-236-0182	Used.

Map 17 · Coolidge Corner / Brookline Hills

Book World	77 Harvard St	617-739-5768	Russian.
Brandeis Book Stall	12 Sewall Ave	617-731-0208	General.
Children's Book Shop	237 Washington St	617-734-7323	Children's.
Horai-san	242 Washington St	617-277-4321	New age/spiritual.
Mundi International	1362 Beacon St	617-277-1199	Foreign languages.
New England Comics	316 Harvard St	617-566-0115	Comics.
Petropol	1428 Beacon St	617-232-8820	Russian.
Rodney's Bookstore	1362 Beacon St	617-232-0185	General.

Map 18 · Brighton

Russian Bookseller Outlet	403 Washington St	617-787-5384	Russian.

Map 19 · Allston (South) / Brookline (North)

Barnes & Noble	325 Harvard St	617-232-0594	General.
Brookline Booksmith	279 Harvard St	617-566-6660	Independent; used book cellar.
Harvard Business School Co-op	117 Western Ave	617-499-3245	Business.
Israel Book Shop	410 Harvard St	617-566-7113	Judaica.
Kolbo Fine Judaica	437 Harvard St	617-731-8743	Judaica.
Korean Book & Video	156 Harvard Ave	617-782-8874	Korean.
New England Comics	131 Harvard Ave	617-783-1848	Comics.
Russian Bookstore	1217A Commonwealth Ave	617-783-1590	Russian.

Map 20 · Harvard Square / Allston (North)

Atherton Antiquarian	5 JFK St, 4th Floor	617-547-2664	Old, rare books.
Canterbury's Book Shop	1675 Massachusetts Ave, Ste 1	617-864-9396	Antiquarian and scholarly Books.
Curious George Goes to Wordsworth	1 JFK St	617-498-0062	Children's.

Grolier Poetry Book Shop	6 Plympton St	617-547-4648	Poetry books.
Harvard Book Store	1256 Massachusetts Ave	617-661-1515	Independent, with an academic bent.
Harvard Coop	1400 Massachusetts Ave	617-499-2000	General/schoolbooks and campus merchandise.
Harvard Law School Coop	14 Everett St	617-499-3255	Law.
Lame Duck Books	12 Arrow St	617-868-2022	Rare Books, manuscripts, art
Million Year Picnic	99 Mt Auburn St	617-492-6763	Comics.
New England Comics	14A Eliot St	617-354-5352	Comics.
Raven Used Books	52-B John F Kennedy St	617-441-6999	Scholarly used.
Revolution Books	1156 Massachusetts Ave	617-492-5443	Revolution.
Robin Bledsoe Books	1640 Massachusetts Ave	617-576-3634	Out-of-print books on horses and art.
Schoenhof's Foreign Books	76A Mt Auburn St	617-547-8855	Foreign languages.

Map 21 • West Cambridge

| Bryn Mawr Book Store | 373 Huron Ave | 617-661-1770 | Used and rare, stocked by donations. |

Map 22 • North Cambridge / West Somerville

| Kate's Mystery Books | 2211 Massachusetts Ave | 617-491-2660 | New and used mysteries. |
| McIntyre & Moore Books | 255 Elm St | 617-629-4840 | Scholarly used. |

Map 23 • Central Somerville / Porter Square

Barefoot Books	1771 Massachusetts Ave	617-349-1610	Picture books for the wee.
Comicazi	380 Highland Ave	617-666-2664	Comics.
Porter Square Books	25 White St	617-491-2220	Fiercely independent!
Unicorn Books	1971 Massachusetts Ave	617-876-4448	Spiritual and self-help books, candles, and crystals

Map 26 • East Cambridge / Kendall Square / MIT

Borders	100 Cambridgeside Pl	617-679-0887	General.
MIT Co-op	3 Cambridge Ctr	617-499-3200	Schoolbooks and campus merchandise.
MIT Press Bookstore	292 Main St	617-253-5249	MIT Press authors and quality trade.
Quantum Books	4 Cambridge Ctr	617-494-5042	Computer, technical.

Map 27 • Central Square / Cambridgeport

Bookmarx	550 Massachusetts Ave	617-354-2876	At the center for Marxist Education.
Pandemonium	4 Pleasant St	617-547-3721	Sci-fi, fantasy, and gaming.
Rodney's Bookstore	698 Massachusetts Ave	617-876-6467	Used, out-of-print, remainders.
Seven Stars	731 Massachusetts Ave	617-547-1317	New Age.
Stratton Center Co-op	84 Massachusetts Ave	617-499-3240	Schoolbooks and campus merchandise.

Map 28 • Inman Square

| Lorem Ipsum | 157 Hampshire St | 617-497-7669 | Used. |

MAP
15

Fine Arts
Restaurant

Courtyard

Upper
Rotunda

Escalator

Library

SECOND FLOOR

Closed to the Public

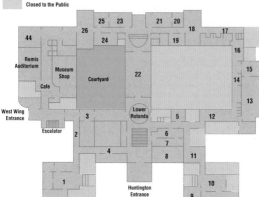

Remis
Auditorium

Museum
Shop

Courtyard

Cafe

West Wing
Entrance

Lower
Rotunda

Escalator

Huntington
Entrance

FIRST FLOOR

1. Japanese Art
2. Islamic Art
3. Brown Gallery
4. Indian Art
5. Egyptian Mummies
6. Graphics
7. Musical Instruments
8. Nubian Art
9. Etruscan Art
10. Greek Art
11. Near-Eastern Art
12. 18th Century American Furniture
13. 18th Century French Art
14. 18th Century Boston
15. English-Silver
16. 19th Century American
17. American Federal
18. Copley & Contemporary
19. American Neoclassical & Romantic
20. American Folk Painting
21. 19th Century Landscape
22. American Modern
23. American Masters
24. Early 20th Century American & European
25. Chinese Art
26. Egyptian Art
27. Roman Art
28. Medieval Art
29. Euro Decorative Arts
30. Impresses
31. 19th Century French & English
32. Post-Impressionism
33. Coolidge Collection
34. 18th Century Italian
35. Dutch & Flemish Art
36. Renaissance
37. Spanish Chapel
38. Baroque Art
39. Himalayan Art
40. Tapestries
41. Special Exhibitions

General Information

NFT Map: 15
Address: 465 Huntington Ave
            Boston, MA 02115
Phone: 617-267-9300
Website: www.mfa.org

Overview

The Museum of Fine Arts is Boston's largest and most famous art institution. The extensive permanent collection of paintings and sculpture, as well as the various lectures, films, concerts, and special traveling exhibitions, offer something for one-time sightseers and regular visitors alike. While you're there soaking up a little sophistication, enjoy a meal at one of the museum's three restaurants, and buy an artifact from the gift shop or some of their little postcards with the pretty paintings on them. Why? Because the museum needs the money. Though it's one of the largest art museums in the country, it receives little public funding. This, in part, accounts for the high admission fee. But don't worry: You get what you pay for.

The MFA is in the middle of a mammoth project that will increase the size of the museum by 28%. To replace the old east wing of the museum, the MFA is building a new wing which will feature its Art of the Americas collection. Check the MFA's website for details about the project and the exciting-sounding Glass Courtyard.

Hours

The museum is open Mon, Tues, Sat, and Sun 10 am–4:45 pm, and Wed-Fri 10 am–9:45 pm. Special exhibitions close 15 minutes before the museum closes. The gift shop is open until 5:30 pm on Saturdays and Sundays.

Admission Fees

Admission to the MFA costs $15 for adults, $13 for seniors and college students, and $6.50 for kids 7-17 on school days until 3 pm (free at all other times). School groups are charged $5 per student, but may enter for free after 3 pm.

Paid admission entitles visitors to one free visit within ten days of ticket purchase. On Wednesday evenings 4 pm–9:45 pm, admission is by voluntary contribution.

Tickets for entry can be purchased at the museum. Tickets for concerts, films, lectures, or special exhibitions can be purchased at the museum or online at www.mfa.org.

How to Get There—Driving

From the north, take I-93 S to Exit 26 (Storrow Drive). From Storrow Drive, take the Fenway/Kenmore exit. From the exit, take a left at the first traffic light, heading toward Boylston Street inbound. At the second traffic light, bear right onto The Fenway and proceed to the next set of lights. After passing through two stone gates, take the first right onto Hemenway Street and proceed to the end of the street. Take a left onto Forsythe Way and then a right onto Huntington Avenue. The museum is located a few lights down and on your right. Go past the museum and turn right onto Museum Road to reach the museum's parking lots.

From the south, take I-93 N to Exit 18 and follow the signs for Massachusetts Avenue. Turn right on Massachusetts Avenue, go past Columbus Avenue, and then turn left onto St. Botolph Street. Drive one block and turn right onto Gainsborough Street. Drive one block and turn left onto Huntington Avenue. The museum will be a couple of blocks down on your right. Go past the museum and turn right onto Museum Road to reach the museum's parking lots.

From the west, take the Mass Pike (I-90) E. Upon approaching the Boston city limits, look for Exit 22 (Prudential Center/Copley Square), the first exit after the Cambridge/Brighton toll plaza. You will enter a tunnel and Exit 22 will be on your right. Once on the exit ramp, get into the left lane (Prudential Center) and follow the exit to Huntington Avenue. Follow Huntington Avenue past the Christian Science Center (go through the underpass) and Northeastern University. The museum is located a few lights down on the right. Drive past the museum and turn right onto Museum Road to reach the museum's parking lots.

Parking

There is limited parking available at the museum, including two parking lots on Museum Road. Museum members pay $2.50 for each half-hour, $12 maximum. Non-members pay $3.50 for each half-hour with a $22 maximum for the day. A far cheaper option is public transportation.

How to Get There—Mass Transit

The museum is close to the Green Line's Museum stop (E train only) or the Orange Line's Ruggles stop. You can also take the 39 bus to the Museum stop or the 8 bus, 47 bus, or CT2 bus to the Ruggles stop.

Arts & Entertainment • **Museums**

If you're familiar with every painting at the **Gardner (Map 15)**, every print in the **MFA (Map 15)**, every fish in the **Aquarium (Map 2)**, and every cobblestone on the **Freedom Trail**, then it's time to take it to the next level by ferreting out some of the city's hidden treasures and discovering something new about some old favorites.

The new facility of the Institute of California of Contemporary Art, whose design evokes a laptop, opened in the fall of 2006. If you're looking for a reason to make your way over to Fan Pier, here it is.

Release your inner child on a Friday night at the **Boston Children's Museum (Map 4)**—from 5 pm to 9 pm, admission is just $1. Or, engage your inner adult at the **Museum of Science (Map 1)** with a cocktail (yes, a real cocktail), a movie in the Mugar Omni Theater, or free star-gazing at the Gilliland Observatory.

If you want to take in some art during a drive out of town, check out the **DeCordova Museum and Sculpture Park** in Lincoln (not far from Route 2 and Route 128). The DeCordova's 35 acres of woodlands is the largest sculpture garden in New England. The contemporary American outdoor sculpture park changes its exhibitions on a regular basis. Admission to the sculpture park is $9 for adults, $6 for students, seniors, and children ages 6-12. Children five and under, as well as active duty military personnel, are admitted free. For more information, visit www.decordova.org.

And if none of that is enough, step into a whole new world, literally, at the **Mapparium (Map 5)**—an enormous glass globe with a walkway through the center.

Museum	Address	Phone	Map
Ancient and Honorable Artillery Company	Faneuil Hall, 4th Fl	617-227-1638	2
Arthur M Sackler Museum	485 Broadway	617-495-9400	20
Boston Athenaeum	10 1/2 Beacon St	617-227-0270	1
Boston Children's Museum	300 Congress St	617-426-8855	10
Boston Tea Party Ship & Museum	Congress St Bridge	617-269-7150	10
(closed for renovations, scheduled to re-open sometime in 2007)			
Busch-Reisinger Museum	32 Quincy St	617-495-9400	20
Carpenter Center for Visual Arts	24 Quincy St	617-495-3251	20
Commonwealth Museum	220 Morrissey Blvd	617-727-9268	32
Fogg Art Museum	32 Quincy St	617-495-9400	20
Gibson House Museum	137 Beacon St	617-267-6338	6
Harrison Gray Otis House	141 Cambridge St	617-227-3956	1
Harvard Mineralogical & Geological Museum	24 Oxford St	617-495-3045	20
Harvard Museum of Comparative Zoology	26 Oxford St	617-495-3045	20
Harvard Museum of Natural History	26 Oxford St	617-495-3045	20
Institute of Contemporary Art	100 Northern Ave	617-266-5152	10
Isabella Stewart Gardner Museum	280 The Fenway	617-566-1401	15
JFK National Historic Site	83 Beals St	617-566-7937	19
John F Kennedy Museum	Morrissey Blvd & Columbia Pt	617-514-1600	32
Larz Anderson Auto Museum	15 Newton St	617-522-6547	n/a
Loring-Greenough House	12 South St	617-524-3158	14
Mapparium/Christian Science Museum	200 Massachusetts Ave	617-450-7000	5
MIT List Visual Arts Center	20 Ames St	617-253-4680	26
MIT Museum	265 Massachusetts Ave	617-253-4444	26
Museum of Afro-American History	46 Joy St	617-725-0022	1
Museum of Bad Art (MOBA)	580 High St	781-444-6757	n/a
Museum of Fine Arts	465 Huntington Ave	617-267-9300	15
Museum of Science	Science Park	617-723-2500	1
National Center for Afro-American Artists	300 Walnut Ave	617-442-8614	13
New England Aquarium	Central Wharf	617-973-5200	2
Nichols House Museum	55 Mt Vernon St	617-227-6993	1
Old South Meeting House	310 Washington St	617-482-6439	3
Old State House	206 Washington St	617-720-1713	3
Paul Revere House	19 North Sq	617-523-2338	2
Peabody Museum of Archaeology and Ethnology	11 Divinity Ave	617-496-1027	20
The Semitic Museum at Harvard University	6 Divinity Ave	617-495-4631	20
Somerville Museum	1 Westwood Rd	617-666-9810	23
The Sports Museum	150 Causeway St	617-624-1234	1
USS Constitution Museum	Charlestown Navy Yard	617-426-1812	8
Warren Anatomical Museum	10 Shattack St	617-432-9196	15

It's not quite the city that never sleeps, but Boston's nightlife is vast and varied, catering not only to teeming masses of college students but to young professionals and aging hipsters as well. There is something to suit every urge. Unable to completely cast off the heavy cloak of Puritanism, however, Boston tries its hardest to make sure you don't have too much fun by forcing the bars to close by 1 or 2 am. But what's dumber: this blue-law hangover or putting the T to bed for the night even earlier? After-hours joints exist, but are for members-only. As bartenders are fond of saying, "You don't have to go home, but you can't stay here." Despite these best efforts, though, the variety of bars, dance clubs, and live music venues keep growing, so you'll be able to find just the right spot to be seen, be picked up, dance, throw some spears, or sit and share a pint with a friend while you catch a live band. Remember that clubs are always in flux, so it makes sense to call ahead and confirm what's up before rounding up your crew and hitting the town.

Beer

Like with Dunkin' Donuts, you can't throw a shillelagh in this town without hitting an Irish pub. Some of the best Guinness this side of the Atlantic can be found (usually poured by authentic Irish hands) at many of these fine establishments. If stout is not your thing, there are several good microbreweries around town including **Boston Beer Works (Map 1)**, **Cambridge Brewing Company (Map 26)**, and **John Harvard's Brew House (Map 20)**. Large (we mean large) beer selections can be found at **Sunset Grill & Tap (Map 19)**, **Bukowski's (Map 5, Map 28)**, **Roggie's (Map 18)**, and to a smaller degree, **Christopher's (Map 23) and Doyle's (Map 14)**. **Redbones (Map 22)** barbecue joint has a beer wheel you can spin if you're have trouble making up your mind. If you insist on going straight to the source, take a tour and quaff some samples at the **Harpoon (Map 11)** and **Sam Adams (Map 14)** breweries.

Sports

Almost every bar in Boston becomes a sports bar when the Sox or Pats are playing. It's a good thing, too, since tickets to actual games are prohibitively expensive and the Sox decided to broadcast their games only on cable. If you're desperate to see your (non-Boston) team or follow every March Madness game, try **Sports Depot (Map 19)**, **The Four's (Map 1)**, **Stadium (Map 10)**, **Champions (Map 6)**, **Tequila Rain (Map 16)**, or **Lir (Map 5)**.

Elegant

Sometimes you just need to dress up and treat yourself to see how the other half lives. For a change of pace from drunken sports fans and bottles of Bud, or for a good way to impress a date, sip a cocktail in the refined elegance of **Parker's Bar (Map 3)**, **City Bar (Map 6)**, or **Rowes Wharf Bar (Map 4)**. Have a nice romantic evening taking in the view of the Boston skyline at **Top of the Hub (Map 5)** in the Prudential Center. Or don your coolest duds for some cocktails and people-watching at **Whiskey Park (Map 3)** or **Sonsie (Map 5)**.

Dive

The smoking ban threatened the livelihoods of many a beloved Boston dive, and while some have revamped their image to draw in different crowds, the few hardy stalwarts are still alive and still a dive. Go get lost at **Sullivan's Tap (Map 1)**, **Pete's Pub (Map 2)**, **Silhouette Lounge (Map 19)**, **Punter's Pub (Map 15)**, or **T.C. Lounge (Map 5)**, or more upscale dives that feature live bands like the **Midway Café (Map 14)** and **Abbey Lounge (Map 28)**. While not quite dives good local color can be absorbed at the **Sligo Pub (Map 22)** and the **Beacon Hill Pub (Map 1)**.

Live Music

For such a small city, Boston has a thriving live music scene, its local community of musicians nurturing each other and able to get lots of exposure in a wide array of venues. The Cars, Bonnie Raitt, The Mighty Mighty Bosstones, Sropkick Murphys, and Aerosmith are just a few names to come out of this town. Whether you're in the mood for rock, blues, roots, punk, folk, rockabilly, jazz, or yes, even bluegrass, somebody in Boston is playing it. Pretty much everything but country.

While huge national acts play at the Garden and Tweeter Center, many also opt for smaller venues like the 2,800-seat **Orpheum Theater (Map 3)** for its great acoustics, or the newly renovated **Opera House (Map 3)**. For more intimate shows that attract the major players, check out the **Somerville Theatre** (www.somervilletheatreonline.com/somerville, 617-625-5700, and the **Regent Theatre** (www.regenttheatre.com, 781-646-4849, 7 Medford St, Arlington). Berklee College has graduated the likes of Branford Marsalis, Melissa Etheridge, and Donald Fagen, and at its **Berklee Performance Center (Map 5)** (www.berkleebpc.com, 617-747-2261) you can catch performances by big names and famous alumni or cheap concerts by teachers and students. Who knows? You may be watching the next John Mayer. Other places to catch national acts in a club atmosphere are the spacious **Roxy (Map 3)**, **Axis (Map 16)**, and **Avalon (Map 16)**. Avalon shows usually start early at 7 pm, so they can clear the room in time for the 10 pm clubbers. Rumor has it they once forced Bob Dylan off the stage to make way for a DJ.

For jazz, you can grab dinner and a show at the classy **Regattabar (Map 20)** or **Scullers (Map 19)**. Both in Cambridge, they host world-class performers. If you're on a budget, check out smaller venues like **Ryles (Map 28)** in Inman Square, **Good Life (Map 4)** in Downtown Crossing, and **Wally's (Map 5)** in the South End, a tiny neighborhood bar where you'll sometimes find Berklee students sitting in with the evening's combo.

Rock 'n rollers head to **Paradise Rock Club (Map 19)**. If the downstairs is packed, go upstairs for a bird's-eye view of the band. If you get tired of moshing, the adjoining **Paradise Lounge (Map 19)** features smaller bands in a more relaxed setting. In Central Square, lines form out the door for **T.T. the Bear's Place (Map 27)**. At next door's **Middle East (Map 27)**, one of the coolest clubs around, you can grab some grape leaves before heading to one of its three rooms of music. **Harper's Ferry (Map 19)** gets a good mix of rock, blues, and New Orleans funk. And if you're pining for some old school blues and rock, head to the **Cantab (Map 27)** on the weekend for the still standing Little Joe Cook and the Thrillers. Smaller bars to catch a good groove include **Sky Bar (Map 23)**, **O'Briens (Map 19)**, **Midway Café (Map 14)**, **PA's Lounge (Map 24)**, **Great Scott (Map 19)**, and **Abbey Lounge (Map 28)**.

Folkies and singer-songwriters worship at the altar that is **Club Passim (Map 20)**, a 40-plus-year-old landmark dedicated to promoting independent musicians. Joan Baez, Bob Dylan, and Muddy Waters have all graced its stage. Be warned that they do not sell drinks, just coffee, tea, and vegetarian meals. And if you're ready to pull off that old banjo of yours, return to the **Cantab (Map 27)** on Tuesday nights for its bluegrass pickin' party.

You can find reggae, hip-hop, and afrobeat at **Western Front (Map 27)**. Latin music and salsa dancing heat up **Green Street Grill (Map 27)**, **Mojito's Lounge (Map 3)**, and **Milky Way Lounge (Map 14)**.

Can't decide what mood you're in? For every kind of musical act, both local faves and national legends, **Johnny D's (Map 22)** in Somerville reigns supreme. The **Lizard Lounge (Map 20)**, a laid-back neighborhood

hang in Cambridge, hosts an eclectic mix of music and performances seven nights a week, ranging from punk to acoustic, rock and roll, experimental, and poetry slams.

Many pubs and bars feature local bands or musicians, often for free or a minimal cover charge. It's a great way to get to know the scene. Check weekly listings for schedules. Probably the best of these is **Toad (Map 23)**. The room is small, and you usually have to sneak past the bass player to get to the bathroom, but the wide variety and high quality of bands make this a popular gathering place.

Clubs

If you're new to Boston clubbing, start with the strip of clubs situated along Lansdowne Street. These clubs draw a huge student and Euro crowd and, as they're all located near Fenway Park, get particularly busy when the Sox are in town. Among the many good clubs on Lansdowne is **Avalon (Map 16)** which for years, has hosted a huge, very popular gay night on Sundays. If you feel like mixing your clubbing with a game of billiards or ping pong, head to **Jillian's (Map 16)** around the corner. Central Boston has smaller clusters of clubs in the Theater District (such as the **Roxy (Map 3)**, **Aria (Map 3)**, the **Big Easy (Map 3)**, or **Venu (Map 3)**), around Faneuil Hall (such as **Boston Rocks (Map 2)**, **Vertigo (Map 2)**, and **The Rack (Map 2)**), and in Downtown Crossing (**Felt (Map 3)** or the salsa heaven **Mojito's (Map 3)**). If you're in Cambridge, check out **Phoenix Landing (Map 27)**, which morphs from an Irish pub into a dance club on most nights. **Jacque's (Map 3)** is Boston's oldest drag club, with shows on most nights. Many clubs have 18+ nights and gay nights, so check their schedules.

Map 1 • Beacon Hill / West End

21st Amendment	150 Bowdoin St	617-227-7100	Favorite of the State House crowd.
6B	6 Beacon St #B	617-742-0306	Martinis and snacks for the after-work crowd.
Beacon Hill Pub	149 Charles St	617-625-7100	Dive popular with young Hill residents.
Boston Beer Works	112 Canal St	617-896-2337	Cavernous suds shop near the Garden.
Cheers	84 Beacon St	617-227-9605	If you must.
The Four's	166 Canal St	617-720-4455	Sports tavern across from the Garden.
Greatest Bar	262 Friend St	617-367-0544	Big deal.
The Harp	85 Causeway St	617-742-1010	Pack in after an evening at the Garden.
Hill Tavern	228 Cambridge St	617-742-6192	Middling Beacon Hill hangout.
Seven's	77 Charles St	617-523-9074	Sturdy Beacon Hill local.
Sullivan's Tap	168 Canal St	n/a	Dive. Proper before Celtics and Bruins games.

Map 2 • North End / Faneuil Hall

Bell in Hand Tavern	45 Union St	617-227-2098	Welcoming thirsty travelers since the 18th century.
Black Rhino	21 Broad St	617-263-0101	Nothing too special, but has a roof deck.
Black Rose	160 State St	617-742-2286	Tourist-crowded, unremarkable. Try somewhere else first.
Boston Rocks	245 Quincy Market	617-726-1110	Generic nightclub.
Boston Sail Loft	80 Atlantic St	617-227-7280	Big outside deck on the water, good crowds.
Club Q	25 Union St	857-829-3766	DJ four nights a week.
Green Dragon Tavern	11 Marshall St	617-367-0055	Pretend you're Sam Adams while having the same.
McFadden's	148 State St	617-227-5100	Eek!
Ned Devine's	Quincy Market	617-248-8800	Sizeable "Irish" bar. Best avoided.
Paddy O's	33 Union St	617-263-7771	The name tells you it's Oirish, you know.
Parris	Quincy Market	617-248-8800	Tucked inside the less impressive Ned Devine's.
Pete's Pub	108 Blackstone St	617-523-9424	Dive.
Purple Shamrock	1 Union St	617-227-2060	Giggly and bland.
The Rack	24 Clinton St	617-725-1051	Billiards bar. Boob city (double entendre intended).
Sanctuary	189 State St	617-573-9333	For the young and fashion-aware.
Tia's on the Waterfront	200 Atlantic Ave	617-277-0828	Warm-weather party house.
Vertigo	126 State St	617-723-7277	Downtown hot spot.

Map 3 • Downtown Crossing / Park Square / Bay Village

Aria	246 Tremont St	617-338-7080	DJs Tuesday through Saturday.
Big Easy	1 Boylston Pl	617-351-7000	Helping you hook up. No baseball caps.
Chaps	101 Warrenton St	617-587-0000	Gay: Latin/house W'day, T dance Sunday.
Felt	533 Washington St	617-350-5555	Club/upscale pool hall. DJ most nights.
Intermission Tavern	228 Tremont St	617-451-5997	Food and drink in the theater district.
Jacque's	79 Broadway	617-426-8902	Drag, but all welcome. Nightly cabaret.
Matrix	275 Tremont St	617-542-4077	Large dance club.
MJ O'Connor's	27 Columbus Ave	617-482-2255	Large Irish pub. Outdoor seating when warm.
Mojitos Lounge	48 Winter St	617-817-2533	For those who like their salsa hot.
Parker's Bar	60 School St	617-227-8600	Elegant. Try the Boston Creme martini.
Roxy	279 Tremont St	617-338-7699	Large, popular dance club. Matrix is downstairs.
Rumor	100 Warrenton St	617-442-0045	Tuesday's the big night here.
Teatro	177 Tremont St	617-778-6841	Drinks in a dark and pretentious setting.
Venu	100 Warrenton St	617-338-8061	Always changing; check before you go.
West Street Grille	15 West St	617-423-0300	Not for the impatient.
Whiskey Park	64 Arlington St	617-542-1483	Swank, popular. Dress up.

Map 4 • Financial District / Chinatown

An Tain	31 India St	617-426-1870	For after work; DJs on Thursday, Friday.
Aqua	120 Water St	617-720-4900	Nice glass walls, anyway.
Elephant & Castle	161 Devonshire St	617-350-9977	Large pub handy for groups. Skip the food.
Good Life	28 Kingston St	617-451-2622	Martinis and jazz.
JJ Foley's	21 Kingston St	617-338-7713	Attracts a big after-work crowd.
Jose McIntyre's	160 Milk St	617-451-9460	Casual DJ and dance spot. Popular and simple.
Les Zygomates	129 South St	617-542-5108	Comprehensive wine list, pleasant bar.
Mr Dooley's Boston Tavern	77 Broad St	617-338-5656	Irish. Popular after-work drinking spot.
News	150 Kneeland St	617-426-6397	Leather District late-night spot.
Rowes Wharf Bar	70 Rowes Wharf	617-439-7000	Relax with scotch and an armchair.
Times Restaurant and Bar	112 Broad St	617-357-8463	Irish. Live music and DJs.
Umbria	295 Franklin St	617-338-1000	Italian restaurant goes club at night.

Map 5 • Back Bay (West) / Fenway (East)

Bukowski's	50 Dalton St	617-437-9999	100+ beers served with loud, eclectic music.
Crossroads	495 Beacon St	617-262-7371	Dive popular for its late last call.
Dillon's	955 Boylston St	617-421-1818	Revisiting the Roaring '20s.
Kings	10 Scotia St	617-266-2695	Bowling, pool, TV sports. Goofy but fun.
The Last Drop	421 Marlborough St	617-262-5555	Supposed latest last call in Boston.
Lir	903 Boylston St	617-778-0089	Upscale Irish. Large, handy for sports watchers.
Match	94 Massachusetts Ave	617-247-9922	More for cocktails than food. Stylish, DJ.
Our House East	52 Gainsborough St	617-236-1890	Branch of Allston college-kid hangout.
Pour House	907 Boylston St	617-236-1767	Wide beer selection, cool bartenders.
Sonsie	327 Newbury St	617-351-2500	People-watching mainstay. Nice French-doors street exposure.
TC's Lounge	1 Haviland St	617-247-8109	Dive for Berklee people and locals.
Top of the Hub	800 Boylston St	617-536-1775	Great view from the top of the Pru.
Wally's Café	427 Massachusetts Ave	617-828-1754	Cramped jazz landmark. For everyone at least once.

Map 6 • Back Bay (East) / South End (Upper)

Anchovies	433 Columbus Ave	617-266-5088	Easy-going neighborhood joint.
Champions	110 Huntington Ave	617-937-5658	Sports. Foods wins no trophies.
City Bar	61 Exeter St	617-933-4800	At the Lenox Hotel.
Clery's	113 Dartmouth St	617-262-9874	Bar with food. Location is its best attribute.
Club Café	209 Columbus Ave	617-536-0966	Gay: restaurant in front, scoping in back.
Rattlesnake	384 Boylston St	617-859-8555	Hit the roof deck in the summer.
Rise	306 Stuart St	617-423-7473	For clubbing after 2 am. Arrive as a member.
Saint	90 Exeter St	617-236-1134	Nitery for aspiring Paris Hiltons.
Vox Populi	755 Boylston St	617-424-8300	Strangely soulless.

Map 7 • South End (Lower)

Delux Café	100 Chandler St	617-338-5258	Small, hip spot with good eats, music.
Eagle	520 Tremont St	617-542-4494	Casual gay local, mostly denim and leather.
Franklin Café	278 Shawmut Ave	617-350-0010	Mainly a restaurant, but a good bar choice too.
Pho Republique	1415 Washington St	617-262-0005	Fave of South End drinking set.

Map 8 • Charlestown

Sullivan's Pub	85 Main St	617-242-9515	Relaxed pub off of Thompson Square.
Tavern on the Water	1 Pier 6 at E 8th St	617-242-8040	Good on a warm afternoon. Skyline view.
Warren Tavern	2 Pleasant St	617-241-8142	One of Paul Revere's favorite watering holes.

Map 9 • East Boston

Kelly Square Pub	84 Bennington St	617-567-4627	Neighborhood local, try the ribs.
Pony Lounge	411 Chelsea St	617-567-9775	Karaoke on weekend nights.
Trainor's Café	127 Maverick St	617-567-6995	Neighborhood local.

Map 10 • South Boston (West) / Fort Point

Blackthorn Pub	471 W Broadway	617-269-1159	Real Irish. Pours a mean Guinness.
The Cornerstone	16 W Broadway	617-269-9553	Broadway Square, erm, cornerstone. Parking in rear.
The Junction	110 Dorchester St	617-268-6429	Low-key neighborhood spot.
Lucky's	355 Congress St	617-357-5825	Well-liked retro cocktail lounge. Music most nights.
The Quiet Man	11 W Broadway	617-269-9878	Pub. Try the steak tips.
Shenanigans	332 W Broadway	617-269-9509	Popular watering hole.
Stadium	232 Old Colony Ave	617-269-5100	Two parts sports bar, one part dance club.

Map 11 • South Boston (East)

Boston Beer Garden	734 E Broadway	617-269-0990	Had a makeover recently. Long wine list too.
Corner Tavern	645 E 2nd St	617-269-9891	Locals only.
Harpoon Brewery	306 Northern Ave	617-574-9551	Brewery tours, seasonal special events.
L Street Tavern	658 E 8th St	617-268-4335	No nonsense local. Appeared in *Good Will Hunting*.
Murphy's Law	837 Summer St	617-269-6667	Occasional live acoustic acts.
Playwright	658 E Broadway	617-269-2537	For socializing and television watching.

Map 12 • Newmarket / Andrew Square

Aces High	551 Dorchester Ave	617-269-7637	Check out their "new drinks and decor."
Dot Tavern	840 Dorchester Ave	617-288-6288	Neighborhood local.
Sports Connection Bar	560 Dorchester Ave	617-268-4119	Featuring a "big screen TV".

Map 13 • Roxbury

C&S Tavern	380 Warren St	617-442-7023	Neighborhood local.
El Mondonguito	221 Dudley St	617-522-3672	A decent dive bar.
Slade's	958 Tremont St	617-442-4600	Dancing, mostly R&B and hip-hop.

Map 14 • Jamaica Plain

Brendan Behan Pub	378 Centre St	617-522-5386	Well-liked Irish local. Relaxed atmosphere.
Costello's Tavern	723 Centre St	617-522-9263	Now with live music on some nights.
Doyle's Café	3484 Washington St	617-524-2345	Trusty Irish landmark. Serves decent pubgrub, great Bloody Marys.
Jeanie Johnston Pub	144 South St	617-983-9432	Darts, karaoke, live music, local flavor.
Midway Café	3496 Washington St	617-524-9038	Local watering hole featuring a variety of live bands.
Milky Way Lounge & Lanes	403 Centre St	617-524-3740	Hipster lounge with colorful décor, live music, candlepin bowling.
Samuel Adams Brewery	30 Germania St	617-368-5080	Tours and samples.

Map 15 • Fenway (West) / Mission Hill

Curtin's Roadside Tavern	1592 Tremont St	617-739-9826	Neighborhood local.
Flann O'Brien's	1619 Tremont St	617-566-7744	Spirited Brigham Circle local.
Linwood Grill & BBQ	69 Kilmarnock St	617-267-8644	Live music in room adjoining barbecue spot.
Machine	1256 Boylston St	617-536-1950	Large gay club.
Punter's Pub	450 Huntington Ave	n/a	Student dive.
Ramrod	1254 Bolyston St	617-266-2986	Gay denim-and-leather crowd; various theme nights.

Map 16 • Kenmore Square / Brookline (East)

An Tua Nua	835 Beacon St	617-262-2121	Pub and dance club popular with twentysomethings.
Audubon Circle	838 Beacon St	617-421-1910	Chill out with tasty bar food.
Avalon	15 Lansdowne St	617-262-2424	Popular "superclub." Huge gay night on Sunday.
Axis	13 Lansdowne St	617-262-2437	DJs, occasional live acts.
Bill's Bar and Lounge	5 1/2 Lansdowne St	617-421-9678	Predominantly student crowd. Mostly rock.
Boston Billiard Club	126 Brookline Ave	617-536-7665	Capacious, down the street from Fenway Park.
Cask 'n' Flagon	62 Brookline Ave	617-536-4840	Just behind the Green Monster. Nothing special.
The Dugout	722 Commonwealth Ave	n/a	Babe Ruth's dive bar of choice.
Embassy	36 Lansdowne St	617-536-2100	Dress to impress. Mostly hip-hop.
Foundation Lounge	500 Commonwealth Ave	617-859-9900	For sake connoisseurs.
Game On!	82 Lansdowne St	617-351-7001	Yet another sports bar near Fenway.
Jillian's	145 Ipswich St	617-437-0300	Uber gaming and lounge establishment.
The Modern	36 Lansdowne St	617-536-2100	Dress to impress.

PJ Kilroy's	822 Beacon St	617-266-3986	Liked by Sox fans and students.
T's Pub	973 Commonwealth Ave	617-254-0807	An institution; free champagne on your birthday.
Tequila Rain	3 Lansdowne St	617-437-0030	Woooo! Woooo!
Tiki Room	1 Lansdowne St	617-351-2580	Trader Vic's for students.
Who's on First?	19 Yawkey Wy	617-247-3353	Fun Fenway dive.

Map 17 • Coolidge Corner / Brookline Hills

The Last Drop	596 Washington St	617-787-1111	Sibling of Marlborough Street bar.
Matt Murphy's Pub	14 Harvard St	617-232-0188	Popular Irish pub. Good food and music.
The Public House	1648 Beacon St	617-277-2880	Focus here is on the beers.
Washington Square Tavern	714 Washington St	617-232-8989	Pub/restaurant with slightly overpriced food.

Map 18 • Brighton

CitySide	1960 Beacon St	617-566-1002	Hit the patio if it's nice outside.
Green Briar	304 Washington St	617-789-4100	Pub with frequent live rock.
Irish Village	224 Market St	617-787-5427	Popular, relaxed local.
Joey's	416 Market St	617-254-9381	Don't ask for Joey.
Mary Ann's	1937 Beacon St	n/a	BC student dump.
Roggie's	356 Chestnut Hill Ave	617-566-1880	52 beers, televised soccer.
Soho	386 Market St	617-562-6000	Sleek, large dining spot-cum-nightclub.

Map 19 • Allston (South) / Brookline (North)

Avenue Bar & Grille	1249 Commonwealth Ave	617-782-9508	Cheap drafts and college kids.
Big City	138 Brighton Ave	617-782-2020	For beer and pool, not food and service.
Bus Stop Pub	252 Western Ave	617-254-4086	Townie bar with sports.
Common Ground	85 Harvard Ave	617-783-2071	Defending Allston.
Great Scott	1222 Commonwealth Ave	617-566-9014	Loud live music in a small dark place.
Harper's Ferry	156 Brighton Ave	617-254-9743	Good place for live, unthreatening rock and blues.
Harry's Bar & Grill	1430 Commonwealth Ave	617-738-9990	Casual and roomy, with a mostly neighborhood crowd.
The Kells	161 Brighton Ave	617-782-9082	Now with revamped Asia-by-way-of-Ikea theme.
Kinvara Pub	34 Harvard Ave	617-7839400	Old Irish men and drunk sophomore girls.
Model Café	7 N Beacon St	617-254-9365	Allston staple, with all the usual suspects.
O'Brien's	3 Harvard Ave	617-782-6245	Live rock, mostly local acts.
Our House	1277 Commonwealth Ave	617-782-3228	So mellow that patrons fall asleep on the couches.
Paradise Rock Club & Lounge	967 Commonwealth Ave	617-562-8800	Major rock acts. Tasty food and smaller bands in Lounge.
Reel Bar	477 Cambridge St	617-783-3222	Mixing up punk and DJs in small space.
Scullers Jazz Club	400 Soldiers Field Rd	617-562-4111	Live jazz most nights. In the Doubletree.
Silhouette Lounge	200 Brighton Ave	617-254-9306	A room full of darts and drunks.
Sports Depot	353 Cambridge St	617-783-2300	Good choice for March Madness drinking.
Sunset Grill & Tap	130 Brighton Ave	617-254-1331	Hundreds of beers to choose from, food until 1 am.
Tonic	1316 Commonwealth Ave	617-566-6699	Red lights, leather seats...yawn.
White Horse Tavern	116 Brighton Ave	617-254-6633	Always hopping, great for sports.
Wonder Bar	186 Harvard Ave	617-351-2665	Wannabe Soho, patronized by wannabe yups.

Map 20 • Harvard Square / Allston (North)

Cambridge Common	1667 Massachusetts Ave	617-547-1228	Local restaurant hang above the Lizard.
Charlie's Kitchen	11 Eliot St	617-492-9646	Old School by the old school. Great jukebox.
Club Passim	47 Palmer St	617-492-7679	Folk singer-songwriter landmark and vegetarian restaurant.
Grendel's Den	89 Winthrop St	617-491-1160	Harvard Square mainstay.
Hoffa's Swiss Alps	114 Mt Auburn St	617-354-5300	Weiner schnitzel and salsa dancing.
John Harvard's Brew House	33 Dunster St	617-868-3585	Large and loud, good for crowds.
Lizard Lounge	1667 Massachusetts Ave	617-547-0759	Great spot to kick back to live music.
Noir	1 Bennett St	617-861-8010	More pretentious than sophisticated.
Redline	59 JFK St	617-491-9851	A decent spot, but too often cramped.
Regattabar	1 Bennett St	617-661-5000	Serious jazz club.
Shay's Lounge	58 JFK St	617-864-9161	Lo-fi wine bar and pub with outdoor seating.
Temple Bar	1688 Massachusetts Ave	617-547-5055	Popular and impressed with itself.
West Side Lounge	1680 Massachusetts Ave	617-441-5566	For those who find Temple Bar too pretentious.

Map 22 • North Cambridge / West Somerville

The Burren	247 Elm St	617-776-6896	Well-known Irish; live music.
Jimmy Tingles, Off Broadway Theater	255 Elm St	617-591-1616	Comedy club.
Johnny D's Uptown	17 Holland St	617-776-2004	Music nightly, wide variety.
PJ Ryan's	239 Holland St	617-625-8200	Brick and beer bar.
Redbones	55 Chester St	617-628-2200	Don't dig on swine? Then come spin the beer wheel.
Sligo Pub	237A Elm St	617-625-4477	A landmark of sorts.
Somerville Theatre	55 Davis Sq	617-625-5700	Occasional live music.

Map 23 · Central Somerville / Porter Square

Christopher's	1920 Massachusetts Ave	617-876-9180	Large selection of drafts, friendly staff, warm food.
On the Hill Tavern	499 Broadway	617-629-5302	DJs Thursday through Saturdays.
Samba Bar & Grill	608 Somerville Ave	617-718-9177	Brazilian vibe.
Sky Bar	518 Somerville Ave	617-623-5223	Live rock.
Toad	1912 Massachusetts Ave	617-497-4950	Cramped but fun. Live music nightly.

Map 24 · Winter Hill / Union Square

The Independent	75 Union Sq	617-440-6022	Irish pub on one side, upscale bar on the other.
Khoury's State Spa	118 Broadway	617-776-0571	Large, easy-going joint. Pool, darts.
PA's Lounge	345 Somerville Ave	617-776-1557	Cool spot for live modern rock.
Sally O'Brien's	335 Somerville Ave	617-666-3589	Local bands, local sports, decent pub food.
Tir Na Nog	366A Somerville Ave	617-628-4300	Irish through and through. Music every night.
Toast	70 Union Sq	617-623-9211	Basement lounge. DJs most nights.

Map 25 · East Somerville / Sullivan Square

Good Time Emporium	30 Assembly Square Dr	617-628-5559	Enormous. TVs, arcade games, batting cage, etc.

Map 26 · East Cambridge / Kendall Square / MIT

Cambridge Brewing Company	One Kendall Sq, Bldg 100	617-494-1994	Decent microbrews. Some outdoor seating.
Flattop Johnny's	One Kendall Sq, Bldg 200	617-494-9565	Cambridge's best large pool hall.
Pugliese's	635 Cambridge St	617-491-9616	Cambridge's oldest family-owned bar.

Map 27 · Central Square / Cambridgeport

All Asia	334 Massachusetts Ave	617-497-1544	Restaurant squeezes in live bands most nights.
Asgard	350 Massachusetts Ave	617-577-9100	Enormous "Celtic" gastropub.
Cantab Lounge	738 Massachusetts Ave	617-354-2685	Legendary quasi-dive. Little Joe Cook still plays.
The Cellar	991 Massachusetts Ave	617-876-2580	Stuck between Central and Harvard? Here you go.
Enormous Room	567 Massachusetts Ave	617-491-5550	Trendy couch lounge with tasty bar food.
The Field	20 Prospect Ave	617-354-7345	Dark and gritty Irish pub.
The Middle East	472 Massachusetts Ave	617-864-3278	Venerable venue that gets high-profile music bookings.
Middlesex	315 Massachusetts Ave	617-868-6739	Rotating DJ line-up, fun modular seating.
Miracle of Science	321 Massachusetts Ave	617-868-2866	Energetic mainstay, always playing cool music.
People's Republik	880 Massachusetts Ave	617-492-8632	Toast 'til 2:00.
Phoenix Landing	512 Massachusetts Ave	617-576-6260	Irish pub with club music every night.
Plough & Stars	912 Massachusetts Ave	617-441-3455	Well-loved local. Frequent live music.
River Gods	125 River St	617-576-1881	Hipster house. DJs spin frequently.
TT the Bear's Place	10 Brookline St	617-492-2327	Live rock nightly. Showcases local bands.
Western Front	343 Western Ave	617-492-7772	Mostly reggae and world, occasional hip-hop.

Map 28 · Inman Square

Abbey Lounge	3 Beacon St	617-441-9631	Boston's "best dive bar"? You decide. Music nightly.
B-Side Lounge	92 Hampshire St	617-354-0766	Well-loved local. Live music and good local color.
Bukowski's	1281 Cambridge St	617-497-7077	100+ beers. More chill than its Boston brother.
The Druid	1357 Cambridge St	617-497-0965	Well-liked Irish pub.
Kirkland Café	425 Washington St	617-491-9640	Relaxed neighborhood bar, live bands.
Ryles Jazz Club	212 Hampshire St	617-876-9330	Two-level club with jazz, world, Latin.
Thirsty Scholar Pub	70 Beacon St	617-497-2294	Laid-back neighborhood local. Good food, too.

Map 32 · Dorchester (East)

Banshee	934 Dorchester Ave	617-436-9747	Irish pub.
dBar	1236 Dorchester Ave	617-265-4490	Hip, gay bar. Food till 10pm, then the dancing starts.
Harp & Bard	1099 Dorchester Ave	617-265-2893	Patio makes this a summertime Irish standout.
Lucky Strike Lanes	289 Adams St	617-436-2660	No relation to trendy Fenway palace, candlepin for the serious.

Hungry?

Seafood

Legal Sea Foods (Map 3, Map 6, Map 26) has the highest profile among local fishmongers and deserves its good reputation. **McCormick and Schmick's (Map 2, Map 3)** sells quality fish in a chophouse atmosphere. Worth the trip to Inman Square is **East Coast Grill & Raw Bar (Map 28)**, which also excels at barbecue. For something cheaper in Cambridge, try **Dolphin Seafood (Map 27)**; in Somerville, **Out of the Blue (Map 22)**. In the summer, get out of the city and eat your seafood by the seashore.

Italian

Boston is blessed with numerous outstanding Italian restaurants. In the North End, **Mamma Maria (Map 2)** and **Bricco (Map 2)** are two among many standouts. For a fine Italian meal elsewhere in Central Boston, reserve a table at **Domani Map 6)**, **Teatro (Map 3)**, or **Grotto (Map 1)**. Brookliners should look into **La Morra (Map 17)**. On the other side of the river, **La Groceria (Map 27)** is very reliable and **Vinny's at Night (Map 25)** dishes out Southern Italian to a loyal following. Roslindale's **Delfino (Map 30)** has legions of local fans.

Pizza

Few foods inspire as much passion (and contentiousness) as pizza; as such, identifying Boston's best pizza is a thankless task. Our favorites? In no particular order: **Penguin Pizza (Map 15)**, **Pizzeria Regina (Map 2)**, **Santarpio's (Map 9)**, **Emma's (Map 28)**, **Joe V's (Map 7)**, **Cambridge, 1 (Map 20)**, and **Armando's (Map 21)**.

East Asian

As with the North End and its Italian food, Chinatown has scads of high-quality restaurants. If you're looking for full-on dim-sum craziness, try **Chau Chow City (Map 4)** or **Emperor's Garden (Map 3)** for weekend brunch. If you want more sedate surroundings in Chinatown, try **New Shanghai (Map 4)**. Want Thai? Try **House of Siam (Map 6)** (in the South End) or **Dok Bua (Map 17)** (in Brookline). Korean? Try **Koreana (Map 28)** (near Inman Square). Sushi? Try **Osushi (Map 4, Map 6)** (in the Financial District and Back Bay) or **Montien (Map 3)** (in the Theater District). Cambodian? Try **Elephant Walk (Map 16, Map 22)** (two locations, one near Porter Square, the other near Kenmore Square). Vietnamese? Try **Sunrise (Map 32)** or **Ba-Le (Map 32)** (both in Dorchester).

South Asian

Central Square (home to reliable standby **India Pavilion (Map 27)**) is no longer the only place to get good Indian food. Consider trying Brookline's **Rani Indian Bistro (Map 17)**, Harvard Square's **Tamarind Bay (Map 20)**, Jamaica Plain's **Bukhara (Map 14)**, Dorchester's **Shanti: Taste of Indian (Map 32)**, or Kenmore Square's **India Quality (Map 16)**. For something different (and pleasant), try the Afghan cuisine at East Cambridge's **Helmand (Map 26)**. Still waiting for Boston's first Iraqi restaurant…

Bars

Better known as drinking and meeting spots, but also serving damn good grub, are **The Asgard (Map 27)**, **Audubon Circle (Map 16)**, **B-Side Lounge (Map 28)**, **Blarney Stone (Map 32)**, **Grendel's Den (Map 20)**, **James's Gate (Map 14)**, **Matt Murphy's Pub (Map 17)**, **Miracle of Science (Map 27)**, **The Paradise (Map 19)**, and **Silvertone Bar & Grill (Map 3)**.

Grease

Diner enthusiasts should try **Mike's City Diner (Map 7)**, **Breakfast Club Diner (Map 19)**, or **Rosebud Diner (Map 22)**. For a big breakfast, consider **Sound Bites (Map 23)**, **Broken Yolk (Map 23)**, **Brookline Lunch (Map 27)**, or the slightly more civilized **Trident Bookstore & Café (Map 5)**. Speaking of that Iraqi restaurant, we'd settle for The Tasty magically re-appearing…

Top-End

Want to celebrate a special occasion? Have your concierge reserve a table downtown at **Aujourd'hui (Map 3)**, **Excelsior (Map 3)**, **The Federalist (Map 1)**, **Mantra (Map 3)**, **No. 9 Park (Map 3)**, or **Radius (Map 4)**, in the South End at **Hamersley's Bistro (Map 7)** or **Masa (Map 7)**, around Back Bay at **Mistral (Map 6)**, **L'Espalier (Map 5)**, **Grill 23 (Map 6)**, **Great Bay (Map 16)**, or **Clio (Map 5)**, or over the river at **Harvest (Map 20)**, **Rialto (Map 20)**, **EVOO (Map 28)**, **Oleana (Map 28)**, or **Rendezvous (Map 27)**.

Key: $: Under $10 / $$: $10–$20 / $$$: $20–$30 / $$$$: $30–$40 / $$$$$: $40+
* : Does not accept credit cards. / † : Accepts only American Express. / †† : Accepts only Visa and Mastercard
Time listed refers to kitchen closing time on weekend nights.

Map 1 · Beacon Hill / West End

75 Chestnut	75 Chestnut St	617-227-2175	$$$$	11 pm	Featuring a Sunday jazz brunch.
Angus Beef Steakhouse	107 Merrimac St	617-742-6487	$$$	2 am	Another steak place.
Anthem	138 Portland St	617-523-8383	$$$	11 pm	Home of the Fried Twinkie.
Artu	89 Charles St	617-227-9023	$$$	11 pm	Affordable Italian. Fresh ingredients. Take-out panini.
Beacon Hill Bistro	25 Charles St	617-723-1133	$$$$	11 pm	Elegant cooking in a cozy space.
Café Podima	156 Cambridge St	617-227-4959	$	11 pm	Sandwiches and such, frozen yogurt.
The Federalist	15 Beacon St	617-670-2515	$$$$$	10:30 pm	A thoroughly top-end experience.
Figs	42 Charles St	617-742-3447	$$$	10 pm	Beacon Hill branch of upscale pizza chain.
Grotto	37 Bowdoin St	617-227-3434	$$$	10 pm	Good-value Italian in a Beacon Hill basement.
Harvard Gardens	316 Cambridge St	617-523-2727	$$	11 pm	More for meeting and drinking than eating.
Hungry I	71 1/2 Charles St	617-227-3524	$$$$	10 pm	French. Cozy spot for intimate meals.
King & I	145 Charles St	617-227-3320	$$	10 pm	No-brainer for decent, inexpensive Thai.
Lala Rokh	97 Mt Vernon St	617-720-5511	$$$	10 pm	Alluring Persian in a pleasant Beacon Hill townhouse.
Ma Soba	156 Cambridge St	617-973-6680	$$$	11 pm	Sleek Asian fusion.
Panificio	144 Charles St	617-227-4340	$	9 pm	Paninis, pastries. Try the formaggio.
The Paramount	44 Charles St	617-720-1152	$$	11 pm	Popular local spot for all three meals. Fantastic brunch.
Phoenicia	240 Cambridge St	617-523-4606	$$	10 pm	Excellent grape leaves.
Pierrot	272 Cambridge St	617-725-8855	$$$$	10 pm	Authentic French bistro.
Ristorante Toscano	41 Charles St	617-723-4090	$$$	10 pm	Try the North End first.
Torch	26 Charles St	617-723-5939	$$$$	10:30 pm	French and Italian influenced. A safe bet.
Upper Crust	20 Charles St	617-723-9600	$$	11 pm	Quality, crisp-crust pizza.
Viva Burrito	66 Staniford St	617-523-6390	$††	9:30 pm	Putting volume ahead of flavor.

Map 2 · North End / Faneuil Hall

Antico Forno	93 Salem St	617-723-6733	$$$	10:30 pm	A home-style North End stand-out. Great pizza.
Billy Tse	240 Commercial St	617-227-9990	$$$	11 pm	Pan-Asian near the waterfront.
Bonne Chance	77 Canal St	617-742-3115	$*	3 pm	Bakery, sandwiches.
Boston Sail Loft	80 Atlantic Ave	617-227-7280	$$	11 pm	Serviceable seafood with a good view.
Bova's Bakery	134 Salem St	617-523-5601	$*	24-hrs	Open 24 hours.
Bricco	241 Hanover St	617-248-6800	$$$$	12 am	Boutique Italian cuisine. Rather popular.
Caffe Paradiso	255 Hanover St	617-742-1768	$	2 pm	Coffee and cannoli. Local landmark.
The Daily Catch	323 Hanover St	617-523-8567	$$$*	11 pm	For those who can stand the heat in the kitchen.
Galleria Umberto	289 Hanover St	617-227-5709	$*	2:30 pm	Ideal for a tasty, cheap lunch.
Green Dragon Tavern	11 Marshall St	617-367-0055	$$	2 am	Pretend you're Sam Adams while having the same.
Haymarket Pizza	106 Blackstone St	617-723-8585	$*	7:30 pm	Enjoy a great slice in the company of pigeons.
Houston's	60 State St	617-573-5977	$$$	11 pm	Great apps, burgers and cocktails.
L'Osteria	104 Salem St	617-723-7847	$$$	11 pm	Family-style red sauce joint.
La Famiglia Giorgio's	112 Salem St	617-367-6711	$$	10:30 pm	Home-cooked Italian, student dinner discounts.
La Summa	30 Fleet St	617-523-9503	$$$	10:30 pm	More low-key than most North End places.
Lucca	226 Hanover St	617-742-9200	$$$$	12:15 am	Stylish Northern Italian.
Mamma Maria	3 North Sq	617-523-0077	$$$$	11 pm	High-end Italian in a charming townhouse.
McCormick & Schmick's	Faneuil Hall Marketplace	617-720-5522	$$$$	12 am	Enormous fresh seafood selection in steakhouse atmosphere.
Pizzeria Regina	11 1/2 Thacher St	617-227-0765	$$*	12 am	Original location of local landmark.
Prezza	24 Fleet St	617-227-1577	$$$$	10:30 pm	High-end Italian.
Ristorante Fiore	250 Hanover St	617-371-1176	$$$	11 pm	Only rooftop deck in the North End.
Sage	69 Prince St	617-248-8814	$$$$	10:30 pm	Italian/American. Might trouble claustro-phobics.
Sel de la Terre	255 State St	617-720-1300	$$$$	10 pm	A taste of Provence.
Taranta	210 Hanover St	617-720-0052	$$$	11 pm	Larger than most upscale North End spots.
Theo's Cozy Corner	162 Salem St	617-241-0202	$*	n/a	Cozy diner. Killer hash browns.
Union Oyster House	41 Union St	617-227-2750	$$$	10 pm	Authentic New England experience since 1826.
Via Valverde	233 Hanover St	617-742-8240	$$$$	11 pm	Great place to splurge. Huge wine list.

Map 3 · Downtown Crossing / Park Square / Bay Village

Aujourd'hui	200 Boylston St	617-351-2071	$$$$$	10:30 pm	Sublime French, delightful room.
Buddha's Delight	5 Beach St	617-451-2395	$$	10:30 am	All-vegetarian Asian.
Chacarero	426 Washington St	617-542-0392	$*	6 pm	Unique Chilean sandwich. Lunch, take-away only.

Dedo	69 Church St	617-338-9999	$$$$	1 am	Rib-eye for the queer guy.
Emperor's Garden	690 Washington St	617-482-8898	$$$	10:30 pm	Dim sum for the masses.
Excelsior	272 Boylston St	617-426-7878	$$$$	11 pm	Opulent food, crowd. Cool wine elevator.
Herrera's Mexican Grille	11 Temple St	617-426-2350	$*	4 pm	Good and cheap Cali-Mex.
Intermission Tavern	228 Tremont St	617-451-5997	$$	1:30 am	Drinks and burgers until 1:30 am.
Jacob Wirth	31 Stuart St	617-338-8586	$$	11 pm	German-y. Local institution since 1868.
Know Fat!	530 Washington St	617-451-0043	$	9 pm	Healthy burgers and sandwiches.
Legal Sea Foods	26 Park Plz	617-426-4444	$$$	12 am	Fresh fish, famous chowder. Legal's sleekest space.
Locke-Ober	3 Winter Pl	617-542-1340	$$$$	11 pm	Re-opened. Still has the Brahmin vibe.
Mantra	52 Temple Pl	617-542-8111	$$$$	10 pm	French/Indian in a stylish former space.
McCormick & Schmick's	34 Columbus Ave	617-482-3999	$$$	11 pm	$2 "social hour" bar menu is a great deal.
New Saigon Sandwich	696 Washington St	617-542-6296	$*	6:30 pm	Cheap sandwiches, boxed lunches. Day only.
No 9 Park	9 Park St	617-742-9991	$$$$	11 pm	Consistently rated among Boston's best.
Penang	685 Washington St	617-451-6373	$$	11:30 pm	Well-established Malaysian out of NYC.
Pigalle	75 Charles St S	617-423-4944	$$$$	10:30 pm	Modern French cuisine in an intimate setting.
Rachel's Kitchen	12 Church St	617-423-3447	$*	2 pm	Friendly breakfast/lunch corner shop.
Rock Bottom Brewery	115 Stuart St	617-742-2739	$$	12:30 am	Better food than most brewpubs.
Sam LaGrassa's	44 Province St	617-357-6861	$$	n/a	Monster sandwiches. Try the pastrami.
Silvertone Bar & Grill	69 Bromfield St	617-338-7887	$$*	12 am	Great after-work lounge with tasty home cooking.
Smith & Wollensky	101 Arlington St	617-423-1112	$$$$$	12:30 am	The castle has been taken.
Teatro	177 Tremont St	617-778-6841	$$$	12 am	Sleek Italian next to Loews Cinema.
Tequila Mexican Grill	55 Bromfield St	617-482-8822	$*	4 pm	Muy sabroso hole-in-the-wall.
Via Matta	79 Park Plz	617-422-0008	$$$	11 pm	Stylish Italian, stylish crowd.

Map 4 · Financial District / Chinatown

Andale	125 Summer St	617-737-2820	$*	n/a	Tamales, burritos for takeaway.
Chau Chow City	83 Essex St	617-338-8158	$$	4 am	Dim sum above. Open late.
J Pace & Son	1 Federal St	617-227-4949	$	5 pm	Hot and cold Italian for take-away.
Julien	250 Franklin St	617-451-1900	$$$	10 pm	Elegant French in the Langham Hotel.
Les Zygomates	129 South St	617-542-5108	$$$	11:30 pm	French bistro. Comprehensive wine list, pleasant bar.
Meritage	70 Rowes Wharf	617-439-3995	$$$$$	11 pm	Serious about pairing food with wine.
Milk Street Café	50 Milk St	617-542-3663	$	3 pm	Dependable lunch option. Also in Post Office Square.
New Shanghai	21 Hudson St	617-338-6688	$$	11 pm	Critically acclaimed Shanghainese.
News	150 Kneeland St	617-426-6397	$$$	5 am	Terrific Leather District late-night spot.
Noodle Alcove	10 Tyler St	617-542-5857	$$	11 pm	Fresh, hot noodles, knife-cut and hand-pulled.
Ocean Wealth	8 Tyler St	617-423-1338	$$	3 am	Cantonese seafood specialists.
Osushi	101 Arch St	617-330-1777	$$$	11 pm	Copley fave now open in the Financial District.
Peach Farm	4 Tyler St	617-482-1116	$$	3 am	Family-style Cantonese. Cool seafood tanks.
Peking Tom's	25 Kingston St	617-482-6282	$$$	2 am	High-energy "Chinese."
Pho Hoa	17 Beach St	617-423-3934	$	11 pm	Phat pho.
Pizza Oggi	131 Broad St	617-345-0022	$$	9:30 pm	Outdoor tables.
Pressed Sandwiches	2 Oliver St	617-482-9700	$	n/a	Potential ironic indie band name.
Radius	8 High St	617-426-1234	$$$$$	11 pm	A Financial District jewel. Expensive, worth it.
Sakurabana	57 Broad St	617-542-4311	$$$	9:30 pm	Good bet for low-key sushi.
Shabu-Zen	16 Tyler St	617-292-8828	$$	12 am	Japanese in Chinatown. Go with a group.
South Street Diner	178 Kneeland St	617-350-0028	$	24-hrs	Open all night.
Sultan's Kitchen	116 State St	617-570-9009	$*	4 pm	Terrific Turkish. A great lunch choice.
Taiwan Café	34 Oxford St	617-426-8181	$$*	1 am	For opponents of the PRC's "one China" policy.
Umbria	295 Franklin St	617-338-1000	$$$	11 pm	Replaced Il Panino; still doubles as a club.

Map 5 · Back Bay (West) / Fenway (East)

Bangkok City	167 Massachusetts Ave	617-266-8884	$$$	10:30 pm	Solid Thai served in a large, blue room.
Bangkok Cuisine	177A Massachusetts Ave	617-262-5377	$$$	10:30 pm	Less fancy than Bangkok City, but just as tasty.
Betty's Wok & Noodle Diner	250 Huntington Ave	617-424-1950	$$	11 pm	Reliable, if uninspiring, stir-fry joint.
Cactus Club	939 Boylston St	617-236-0200	$$	12 am	Loud, popular. There's better Tex-Mex nearby.
Café Jaffa	48 Gloucester St	617-536-0230	$	11 pm	Affordable, delicious Middle Eastern.
Capital Grille	359 Newbury St	617-262-8900	$$$$$	11 pm	Arise, Sir Loin!
Casa Romero	30 Gloucester St	617-536-4341	$$$	11 pm	Mexican. Decent but not inspiring.
Clio	370A Commonwealth Ave	617-536-7200	$$$$	11 pm	Sublime spot in the Eliot Hotel.
Croma	269 Newbury St	617-247-3200	$$	10 pm	Pizza. You can do better.
Island Hopper	91 Massachusetts Ave	617-266-1618	$$	12 am	Malaysian, Chinese, Thai.
L'Espalier	30 Gloucester St	617-262-3023	$$$$$		One of Boston's best.

Arts & Entertainment • **Restaurants**

Key: $: Under $10 / $$: $10–$20 / $$$: $20–$30 / $$$$: $30–$40 / $$$$$: $40+
* : Does not accept credit cards. / † : Accepts only American Express. / †† : Accepts only Visa and Mastercard
Time listed refers to kitchen closing time on weekend nights.

Map 5 • Back Bay (West) / Fenway (East)–continued

Lir	903 Boylston St	617-778-0089	$$$	1 am	Upscale Irish. Large, handy for sports watchers.
Other Side Cosmic Café	407 Newbury St	617-536-9477	$	12:30 am	Good for a bite and beer on nice days.
Pour House	909 Boylston St	617-236-1767	$	10 pm	Wonderful, cheap bar food. Opens at 8 am.
Shanti: Taste of India	277B Huntington Ave	617-867-9700	$$$	11 pm	Refined curry house behind Symphony Hall.
Sonsie	327 Newbury St	617-351-2500	$$$$	11 pm	People-watching mainstay. Nice French-doors street exposure.
Spike's Junkyard Dogs	1076 Boylston St	617-266-0909	$*	2 am	Perfect summer eats.
Tapeo	266 Newbury St	617-267-4799	$$$	11 pm	Tapas. Sip sangria outside on warm days.
Top of the Hub	800 Boylston St	617-536-1775	$$$$	11 pm	Hoity-toity dining atop the Prudential tower.
Trident Booksellers & Café	338 Newbury St	617-267-8688	$	11:30 pm	All-day breakfast in a cool bookstore.
Vinny T's	867 Boylston St	617-262-6699	$$$	11 pm	Red sauce theme park. Count on leftovers.
Wine Cellar	30 Massachusetts Ave	617-236-0080	$$$$	11:30 pm	Fondue fight! Seriously, best avoided.

Map 6 • Back Bay (East) / South End (Upper)

33	33 Stanhope St	617-572-3311	$$$$	11 pm	Enticing menu, snazzy digs. Patio too.
Abe & Louie's	793 Boylston St	617-536-6300	$$$$	12 am	Popular local steakhouse.
b.good	131 Dartmouth St	617-424-5252	$*	10 pm	Healthy, quick lunches.
Bangkok Blue	651 Boylston St	617-266-1010	$$	11 pm	Standard Thai. Some outdoor seating.
Blackfin Chophouse & Raw Bar	116 Huntington Ave	617-247-2400	$$$$	11 pm	Another steak place. Is it Atkins? What?
Bomboa	35 Stanhope St	617-236-6363	$$$	12 am	Brazilian hot-spot. Have a mojito or caipirinha.
Brasserie Jo	120 Huntington Ave	617-425-3240	$$$	11 pm	French brasserie near Symphony Hall. Usually very busy.
Charlie's Sandwich Shoppe	429 Columbus Ave	617-536-7669	$*	1 pm	Been here forever. A good lunch choice.
Claremont Café	535 Columbus Ave	617-247-9001	$$$	12 am	(Too) popular for weekend brunch. Good scones, though.
Davio's	75 Arlington St	617-661-4810	$$$	11 pm	Good food, but it's about the river view.
Domani	51 Huntington Ave	617-424-8500	$$$	11 pm	Eat like there's no er, "tomorrow".
Grill 23 & Bar	161 Berkeley St	617-542-2255	$$$$$	11 pm	Classic steakhouse. Ideal for business dinners.
House of Siam	542 Columbus Ave	617-267-1755	$$	11 pm	Solid Thai cuisine in pleasant surroundings.
Jae's	520 Columbus Ave	617-421-9405	$$$	11 pm	Try the crispy Pad Thai. Sushi also.
Jae's	711 Boylston St	617-236-1777	$$$	2 am	Newer location of pan-Asian mini-chain.
L	234 Berkeley St	617-266-4680	$$$	10 pm	Just not all that.
Laurel	142 Berkeley St	617-424-6664	$$$	10 pm	Five-star meals at two-star prices.
Legal Sea Foods	800 Boylston St	617-266-6800	$$$	11 pm	At the Pru, sporting a new look.
Mistral	223 Columbus Ave	617-867-9300	$$$$	11:30 pm	Superb. Great bar, too. Look sharp.
Montien	63 Stuart St	617-338-5600	$$$	11 pm	Really, the best and biggest sushi. No kidding.
Osushi	10 Huntington Ave	617-266-2788	$$$	11 pm	Sushi in the Westin Copley.
Parish Café	361 Boylston St	617-247-7777	$$	1 am	Inventive sandwiches. Full bar too.
Rouge	480 Columbus Ave	617-867-0600	$$$	10:30 pm	Well-done barbecue and other American fare.

Map 7 • South End (Lower)

Addis Red Sea	544 Tremont St	617-426-8727	$$	11 pm	Ethiopian. Get jiggy with some injera.
Aquitaine	569 Tremont St	617-424-8577	$$$$	11 pm	A solid French bistro.
B&G Oysters	550 Tremont St	617-423-0550	$$$	11 pm	Stylish oyster shop. Good wine list.
Caffe Umbra	1395 Washington St	617-867-0707	$$$	11 pm	Increasingly popular; justly so.
Delux Café	100 Chandler St	617-338-5258	$$*	10:30 pm	Small, hip spot with good eats, music.
Dish	253 Shawmut Ave	617-426-7866	$$$	11 pm	Popular bistro. Outdoor seating.
El Triunfo	147 E Berkeley St	617-542-8499	$*	8 pm	Cheap tacos.
Emilio's	536 Tremont St	617-423-4083	$	11 pm	Solid choice for pizza and subs. Delivery.
Equator	1721 Washington St	617-536-6386	$$	11 pm	Mostly Thai. A welcome addition to this area.
flour bakery + café	1595 Washington St	617-267-4300	$	6 pm	Also serves dinners for take-away.
Franklin Café	278 Shawmut Ave	617-350-0010	$$$	1:30 am	Delicious late-night option.
Garden of Eden	571 Tremont St	617-247-8377	$$	11 pm	Popular bruncheonette. Associated with Lionette's next door.
Hamersley's Bistro	553 Tremont St	617-423-2700	$$$$	10:30 pm	Outstanding. Deserves its reputation.
Joe V's	315 Shawmut Ave	617-426-0862	$$$	11 pm	Relatively unknown. Great food, pleasant room.
The Little Window	42 Plympton Ave	617-426-7200	$*	3 pm	Take-away only.
Masa	439 Tremont St	617-338-8884	$$$$	11 pm	Southwestern. A stylish South End secret.
Metropolis Café	584 Tremont St	617-247-2931	$$$	11 pm	Try the cranberry pancakes for brunch.
Mike's City Diner	1714 Washington St	617-267-9393	$*	3 pm	A trusty not-too-greasy spoon.
Morse Fish	1401 Washington St	617-262-9375	$$	9 pm	The neighborhood's only fish shack.
Nicole's	639 Tremont St	617-266-0223	$	11 pm	Pizza, sandwiches and their ilk.
Nightingale	578 Tremont St	617-236-5658	$$$	10:30 pm	Chirpy, cheery, and delicious.
Pho Republique	1415 Washington St	617-262-0005	$$$	12:30 am	Vietnamese gets the South End treatment.
Picco	513 Tremont St	617-927-0066	$$	11 pm	Pizza and ice cream handy to BCA.
Red Fez	1222 Washington St	617-338-6060	$$$	12 am	Open late. Red fez not required for entry.
Sibling Rivalry	523 Tremont St	617-338-5338	$$$$	11 pm	Attractive space, good food, outdoor dining when warm.

Arts & Entertainment · **Restaurants**

Stella	1525 Washington St	617-247-7747	$$$	11 pm	Stylish, whitish spot, mostly Italian menu.
Thai Village	592 Tremont St	617-536-6548	$$	10:30 pm	Not as good as House of Siam.
Tremont 647	647 Tremont St	617-266-4600	$$$	10:30 pm	One of the South End's best.
Union Bar and Grille	1357 Washington St	617-423-0555	$$$$	12 am	Still the best food on Washington Street.

Map 8 · Charlestown

Figs	67 Main St	617-242-2229	$$$	10:30 pm	Charlestown branch of upscale pizza chain.
Ironside Grill	25 Park St	617-242-1384	$$	11 pm	Formerly managed by Raymond Burr.
Jenny's Place	320 Medford St	617-242-9474	$*	9 pm	Subs too. Nice view of the, erm, Autoport.
Meze Estiatorio	100 City Sq	617-242-6393	$$$	11 pm	Delicious Greek in a well-windowed room.
Navy Yard Bistro & Wine Bar	1 1st Ave	617-242-0036	$$	10 pm	Mid-priced bistro fare near the ships.
Ninety Nine	29 Austin St	617-242-8999	$$	11 pm	Take your stepkids.
Olives	10 City Sq	617-242-1999	$$$$	10:30 pm	Mediterranean mecca.
Paolo's Trattoria	251 Main St	617-242-7229	$$$	10:30 pm	Italian, including wood-oven-cooked pizzas.
Sorelle	1 Monument Ave	617-242-2125	$*	3 pm	Tasty sandwiches, baked goods, alcohol too.
Sorelle	100 City Sq	617-242-5980	$	9 pm	Tasty sandwiches, baked goods, alcohol too.
Tangierino	83 Main St	617-242-6009	$$$	11:30 pm	Rockin' Moroccan.
Warren Tavern	2 Pleasant St	617-241-8142	$$	10:30 pm	One of Paul Revere's favorite watering holes.

Map 9 · East Boston

Café Belo	254 Bennington St	617-561-0833	$	10 pm	Brazilian cafeteria.
Café Italia	150 Meridian St	617-561-6480	$$	12 am	For enjoying jazz with coffee and dessert.
Café Meridian	271 Meridian St	617-561-6622	$$	11 pm	Relaxing Colombian restaurant
El Buen Gusto	295 Bennington St	617-561-6333	$$	11 pm	Upscale Salvadoran taqueria.
Jeveli's	387 Chelsea St	617-567-9539	$$	10 pm	Italian. Has a bar.
La Frontera	290 Bennington St	617-569-8600	$*	11 pm	Mexican/Salvadoran hole in the wall.
La Terraza	19 Bennington St	617-561-5200	$$	11:30 pm	Straight-forward Colombian cooking. Try the flan.
Rincon Limeno	409 Chelsea St	617-569-4942	$	10 pm	Specializing in Peruvian rotisserie chicken.
Santarpio's Pizza	111 Cheslea St	617-567-9871	$*	12 am	Thin and crispy. No need to dress up.
TacoMex	65 Maverick Sq	617-569-2838	$	11 pm	Tongue taco, a sign of real Mexican.
Taqueria Cancun	192 Sumner St	617-567-4449	$$	11 pm	Don't count on tequila slammers.

Map 10 · South Boston (West) / Fort Point

6 House	28 W Broadway	617-268-6697	$$	10 pm	Open air, long bar.
Amrheins	80 W Broadway	617-268-6189	$$	11 pm	Has been here since Southie was mostly German.
Barking Crab	88 Sleeper St	617-426-2722	$$	10:30 pm	Make a mess while viewing the harbor skyline.
Blue Wave Bar & Grill	343 Congress St	617-790-0720	$$	11 pm	Skip this one.
The Daily Catch	2 Northern Ave	617-772-4400	$$$*	11 pm	Italian seafood specialists' Moakley Court-house spot.
Fresh Tortillas	475 W Broadway	617-269-0061	$	11 pm	Mexican take-out.
Lucky's	355 Congress St	617-357-5825	$$	12 am	Well-liked retro cocktail lounge. Music most nights.
R&L Delicatessen	313 Old Colony Ave	617-269-3354	$	11 pm	For large sandwiches.
Salsa's Mexican Grill	118 Dorchester St	617-269-7878	$$	10 pm	Legit Mexican. Newly expanded.
Stadium	232 Old Colony Ave	617-269-5100	$$	1 am	Not into sports? Don't eat here.
Teriyaki House	32 W Broadway	617-269-2000	$	1 am	Japanese, some other Asian. Good value.

Map 11 · South Boston (East)

Aura	1 Seaport Ln	617-385-4300	$$$$	n/a	Seafood for doing deals over.
Boston Beer Garden	732 E Broadway	617-269-0990	$$	11 pm	Casual. Long wine list too.
Café Porto Bello	672 E Broadway	617-269-7680	$$*	11 pm	Straight-forward, honest Italian.
Kelly's Landing	81 L St	617-268-8900	$$	11 pm	The "original" is back, specializing in seafood.
L Street Diner	108 L St	617-268-1155	$	10 pm	Southie standby.
Playwright	658 E Broadway	617-269-2537	$$	11 pm	For socializing and television watching.
Summer Street Grille	653 Summer St	617-269-2200	$$	11 pm	Undemanding American at the BAC.

Map 12 · Newmarket / Andrew Square

224 Boston Street	224 Boston St	617-265-1217	$$$	11 pm	A cut above its neighbors. New American.
Alex's Pizza	580 Dorchester Ave	617-464-3663	$$	12 am	Steak subs and pizza, late nights near the T.
Avenue Grille	856 Dorchester Ave	617-288-8000	$$	9 pm	Always something tasty here. A good choice.
Baltic Deli & Café	632 Dorchester Ave	617-268-2435	$	8 pm	Foods from the old country.
Café Polonia	611 Dorchester Ave	617-269-0110	$$	10 pm	Polish. Small, inviting, authentic. Have a Zywiec.
Restaurante Laura	688 Columbia Rd	617-825-9004	$$	10 pm	Scary outside, lovely Cabo Verde inside. Live music.
Singh's Roti Shop	692 Columbia Rd	617-282-7977	$	9 pm	Huge roti. Also try the channa doubles.
Taqueria Casa Real	860A Dorchester Ave	617-282-3135	$	8 pm	Mexican; good hot sauce options.

(305)

Arts & Entertainment • **Restaurants**

Key: $: Under $10 / $$: $10–$20 / $$$: $20–$30 / $$$$: $30–$40 / $$$$$: $40+
* : Does not accept credit cards. / † : Accepts only American Express. / †† : Accepts only Visa and Mastercard
Time listed refers to kitchen closing time on weekend nights.

Map 12 • Newmarket / Andrew Square—continued

Venetian Garden	1269 Massachusetts Ave	617-288-9262	$$	11 pm	A '60s time warp for Rat Pack Mexican food.
Victoria	1024 Massachusetts Ave	617-442-5965	$$	12 am	Diner. Good choice before hitting the highway.
World Seafood Restaurant	400 Dorchester Ave	617-269-1456	$$*	8 pm	Fishmonger with fish, chips and decent crab cakes.

Map 13 • Roxbury

Bob the Chef's	604 Columbus Ave	617-536-6204	$$	12 am	For those needing a soul food fix.
Breezeway Bar and Grill	153 Blue Hill Ave	617-541-5400	$$	2 am	Decent American. Occasional live music.
Merengue	156 Blue Hill Ave	617-445-5403	$$	10 pm	Dominican. Tropical vibe. Gets props from the Sox.
Roxbury Rotisserie	475 Dudley St	617-989-0627	$	6 pm	Great chicken at this clean, tidy hole in the wall.
Pepper Pot	208 Dudley St	617-445-4409	$	12 am	Caribbean.
Stash's Grille	150 Dudley St	617-989-0200	$	12 am	Pizza, etc. next to Dudley transpo center.

Map 14 • Jamaica Plain

Ban Chiang House	707 Centre St	617-522-2299	$$	11 pm	Passable Thai.
Bella Luna	405 Centre St	617-524-6060	$$	11 pm	Popular pizza and pasta next to the Milky Way.
Bon Savor	605 Centre St	617-971-0000	$$	10 pm	French creperie.
Bukhara	701 Centre St	617-522-2195	$$	11 pm	Well-liked Indian bistro.
Café D	711 Centre St	617-522-9500	$$$††	11 pm	Dressed-up comfort food. Cool newspapered walls.
Centre Street Café	699 Centre St	617-524-9217	$$	10 pm	Groovy, particularly for brunch.
Cha Fahn	763 Centre St	617-983-3575	$$	11 pm	Serves a light dinner/lunch menu.
Dogwood Café	3712 Washington St	617-522-7997	$$	12 am	Casual; excellent wood-fired pizzas.
Doyle's Café	3484 Washington St	617-524-2345	$$*	11 pm	Extensive decor, decent pub grub.
Great Wall	779 Centre St	617-522-0277	$	11 pm	Cheap and tasty take-out.
James's Gate	5 McBride St	617-983-2000	$$	11 pm	Laid-back Irish gastropub.
JP Seafood Café	730 Centre St	617-983-5177	$$	10:30 pm	Japanese-Korean.
La Pupusa Guanaca	378 Centre St	617-524-4900	$	9 pm	Little-known Salvadoran snack counter.
Purple Cactus Burrito & Wrap	674 Centre St	617-522-7422	$	10 pm	Satisfactory storefront.
Sorella's	388 Centre St	617-524-2016	$*	2 pm	Worth waiting for famous, diner-style breakfasts.
Tacos El Charro	349 Centre St	617-983-9275	$$	11 pm	Actual Mexican food.
Ten Tables	597 Centre St	617-524-8810	$$$	10:30 pm	Short, precise, inspired menu.
Wonder Spice Café	697 Centre St	617-522-0200	$$	10:30 pm	Tasty Cambodian/Thai. Well named.
Zesto's	460 Centre St	617-524-2004	$$$*	11 pm	Great fresh subs, OK pizza.
Zon's	2 Perkins St	617-524-9667	$$	11 pm	Home-cooking for hipsters.

Map 15 • Fenway (West) / Mission Hill

Bravo	465 Huntington Ave	617-369-3474	$$$$	3 pm	At the MFA. Stick with the art.
Brigham Circle Diner	737 Huntington Ave	617-277-2730	$*	2:30 pm	Good hash browns.
Brown Sugar Café	129 Jersey St	617-266-2928	$$	11 pm	Overrated Thai.
Chacho's	1502 Tremont St	617-445-6738	$	9 pm	Pizza and subs.
El Pelon Taqueria	92 Peterborough St	617-262-9090	$	11 pm	Great value in a Fenway storefront.
Huntington Pizza & Café	764 Huntington Ave	617-566-1177	$	11:30 pm	Pretty clear, huh?
Il Mondo Pizza	682 Huntington Ave	617-277-7161	$	11:30 pm	Unremarkable pizza.
Linwood Grill & BBQ	81 Kilmarnock St	617-247-8099	$$	11 pm	Satisfactory barbecue. Live music in adjoining room.
Longwood Grille & Bar	342 Longwood Ave	617-232-9770	$$	10 pm	Hotel restaurant serving medical community.
Mississippi's	103 Terrace St	617-541-4411	$	5 pm	Good for a hot lunch.
Penguin Pizza	735 Huntington Ave	617-277-9200	$	1 am	Recommended, and not just for the name.
Rod Dee II	94 Peterborough St	617-859-0969	$*	11 pm	Ideal for Thai take-out.
Solstice Café	1625 Tremont St	617-566-5958	$$	12 am	Casual; good lunch and dinner choices.
Sorento's	86 Peterborough St	617-424-7070	$$	12 am	Darn good pasta and pizza.
Squealing Pig	134 Smith St	617-566-6651	$	1 am	Toasties and cheap beer.

Map 16 • Kenmore Square / Brookline (East)

Ankara Café	472 Commonwealth Ave	617-437-0404	$	12 am	Turkish place popular with student snackers.
Audubon Circle	838 Beacon St	617-421-1910	$$	11 pm	Chill out with tasty bar food.
Bertucci's	4 Brookline Pl	617-731-2300	$$	11 pm	Brick oven pizza chain. Good, but not exceptional.
Boston Beer Works	61 Brookline Ave	617-536-2337	$$	12 am	Cavernous suds shop across from Fenway Park.

Café Belo	636 Beacon St	617-236-8666	$		Brazilian cafeteria.
Chef Chang's House	1004 Beacon St	617-277-4226	$$	10:30 pm	Not exemplary, but not a bankbuster.
Cornwall's	654 Beacon St	617-262-3749	$$	12 am	Eat only to soak up pints.
Eastern Standard	528 Commonwealth Ave	617-532-9100	$$	12 am	New, casual spot at the Hotel Common wealth.
Elephant Walk	900 Beacon St	617-247-1500	$$$	11 pm	French-Cambodian local legend.
Ginza	1002 Beacon St	617-566-9688	$$$	1:30 am	Sushi/Japanese. Pompous, overpriced.
Great Bay	500 Commonwealth Ave	617-532-5300	$$$$	11 pm	Elegant seafood, exquisite desserts.
India Quality	484 Commonwealth Ave	617-267-4499	$$	11 pm	Quality Indian.
New England Soup Factory	2 Brookline Pl	617-739-1899	$	9 pm	Creative, home-style soups. Recommended.
Noodle Street	627 Commonwealth Ave	617-536-3100	$	11 pm	Unexpected bistro fare transcend everyday Asian fare.
Petit Robert Bistro	468 Commonwealth Ave	617-375-0699	$$$	11 pm	Traditional bistro fare. Try the skate wing.
Sol Azteca	914A Beacon St	617-262-0909	$$$	11 pm	Satisfying Mexican fusion. Try the mole.
Taberno de Haro	999 Beacon St	617-277-8272	$$	11 pm	Solid tapas spot.

Map 17 • Coolidge Corner / Brookline Hills

Baja Betty's Burritos	3 Harvard Sq	617-277-8900	$*	9 pm	Tops taqueria.
Boca Grande	1294 Beacon St	617-739-3900	$	11 pm	Lots of good taqueria fare. Consider ordering carnitas.
Bottega Fiorentina	41 Harvard St	617-738-5333	$	8 pm	Tuscan sandwiches to go.
Brookline Family Restaurant	305 Harvard St	617-277-4466	$$	11 pm	Turkish. Save room for dessert.
Café Mirror	362 Washington St	617-779-9662	$	5:30 pm	Sandwiches and small bites.
Café St Petersburg	236 Washington St	617-277-7100	$$	11 pm	Boston's finest Russian restaurant. Na zdrov'e!
Chef Chow's House	230 Harvard St	617-739-2469	$$	10 pm	Yummy Chinese food, nice ambience.
Dok Bua	411 Harvard St	617-277-7087	$	11 pm	Authentic Thai; doubles as a grocery.
Fireplace	1634 Beacon St	617-975-1900	$$$	11 pm	Warning: food also capable of inducing nap.
Fugakyu	1280 Beacon St	617-738-1268	$$$	1:30 am	Sushi, very popular. Be prepared to wait.
Golden Temple	1651 Beacon St	617-277-9722	$$	2 am	Inauthentic Chinese.
Khao Sarn	250 Harvard St	617-566-7200	$$	11 pm	Relax and enjoy excellent Thai.
La Morra	48 Boylston St	617-739-0007	$$$$	10:30 pm	Popular Northern Italian.
Matt Murphy's Pub	14 Harvard St	617-232-0188	$$	11 pm	Well-liked Irish pub. Good food.
Pho Lemongrass	239 Harvard St	617-731-8600	$$	12 am	Pho, Brookline-style.
Rani Indian Bistro	1353 Beacon St	617-734-0400	$$	11 pm	Hyderabadi cuisine, apparently.
Rod Dee	1430 Beacon St	617-738-4977	$*	11:30 pm	Cheap, satisfying Thai.
Seoul Kitchen	349 Washington St	617-787-2822	$$	11 pm	Japanese/Korean, with some sushi and Thai.
Tsunami	10 Pleasant St	617-277-8008	$$$	11 pm	Satisfactory sushi spot.
Village Fish	22 Harvard St	617-566-3474	$$	11 pm	Neighborhood standby.
Village Smokehouse	1 Harvard St	617-566-3782	$$	11 pm	Best barbecue in Brookline.
Washington Square Tavern	714 Washington St	617-232-8989	$$$	11 pm	Decent American food, slightly overpriced.

Map 18 • Brighton

Bamboo	1616 Commonwealth Ave	617-734-8192	$$	11 pm	Very good Thai at Washington Street.
Bangkok Bistro	1952 Beacon St	617-739-7270	$$	11 pm	Thai for the BC crowd.
Bluestone Bistro	1799 Commonwealth Ave	617-254-8309	$$	12 am	Pizza and pasta, small and hopping.
Cityside Bar & Grill	1960 Beacon St	617-566-1002	$$	10:30 pm	More for watching television than dining.
Devlin's	332 Washington St	617-779-8822	$$$	11 pm	A little better than other places around here.
Green Briar	304 Washington St	617-789-4100	$$	11 pm	Generic pub food. Stick with beer.
IHOP	1850 Soldiers Field Rd	617-787-0513	$	24-hrs	Pancakes anytime.
Jasmine Bistro	412 Market St	617-789-4676	$$	10 pm	Hungarian-French-Lebanese. Somehow this works.
Soho	386 Market St	617-562-6000	$$$	12 am	Sleek, large dining spot-cum-nightclub.
Tasca	1612 Commonwealth Ave	617-730-8002	$$	11 pm	Tapas, Spanish wine.

Map 19 • Allston (South) / Brookline (North)

Anadolu Café	1022 Commonwealth Ave	617-264-9800	$$	12 am	Turkish delight.
Bagel Rising	1243 Commonwealth Ave	617-789-4000	$*	6 pm	Funky bagel joint.
Big City	138 Brighton Ave	617-782-2020	$	1 am	For the beer and pool, not food and service.
Bottega Fiorentina	313B Harvard St	617-232-2661	$	8 pm	Tuscan sandwiches to go.
Breakfast Club Diner	270 Western Ave	617-783-1212	$$*	2 pm	The shiniest diner found outside New Jersey.
Brown Sugar Café	1033 Commonwealth Ave	617-787-4242	$$	11 pm	Crowded, overrated Thai.

Arts & Entertainment · **Restaurants**

Key: $: Under $10 / $$: $10–$20 / $$$: $20–$30 / $$$$: $30–$40 / $$$$$: $40+
*: Does not accept credit cards. / † : Accepts only American Express. / †† : Accepts only Visa and Mastercard
Time listed refers to kitchen closing time on weekend nights.

Map 19 · Allston (South) / Brookline (North)–*continued*

Buddha's Delight	404 Harvard St	617-739-8830	$$	11 pm	All-vegetarian Asian.
Buk Kyung II	151 Brighton Ave	617-254-2775	$	11 pm	Popular Chinese-influenced Korean.
Café Brazil	421 Cambridge St	617-789-5980	$$	11 pm	Authentic, home-style Brazilian.
Camino Real	48 Harvard Ave	617-254-5088	$$	10 pm	Good-value Colombian.
Charlie's Pizza & Café	177 Allston St	617-277-3737	$	1 am	Middle Eastern counter food, student-style, and wireless.
El Cafetal	479 Cambridge St	617-789-4009	$$	10 pm	Co-yum-bian.
Grasshopper	1 N Beacon St	617-254-8883	$$	11 pm	Hip Asian vegan.
Grecian Yearning	174 Harvard Ave	617-254-8587	$*	n/a	Classic diner.
Harry's Bar & Grill	1430 Commonwealth Ave	617-738-9990	$$	1 am	Casual and roomy, with a mostly neighborhood crowd.
Indian Dhaba Roadside Diner	180 Brighton Ave	617-787-5155	$	11:30 pm	Curried goodness. Not actually a diner.
La Mamma Pizza	190 Brighton Ave	617-783-1661	$	1 am	Stick with the empanadas and Chilean specialties.
Madina Market's Kitchen	72 Brighton Ave	617-878-4400	$	10 pm	No-charm Pakistani hole in the wall. Superb tandoori, naan.
Paris Creperie	278 Harvard St	617-232-1770	$$	11 pm	A variety of sweet and savory crepes.
Rangoli	129 Brighton Ave	617-562-0200	$$		Emphasizes South Indian.
Redneck's Roast Beef	140 Brighton Ave	617-782-9444	$††	3 am	Open til 3 am; great drunk food.
Reef Café	170 Brighton Ave	617-202-6366	$	12 am	One of the best Lebanese joints in Boston.
Rubin's	500 Harvard St	617-731-8787	$$		Old-style Kosher and all the fixin's.
Saigon	431 Cambridge St	617-254-3373	$$*	10 pm	Pleasant Vietnamese, good value.
Spike's Junkyard Dogs	108 Brighton Ave	617-254-7700	$*	1 am	Quick sausage fix.
Sunset Grill & Tap	130 Brighton Ave	617-254-1331	$$	n/a	Huge Mexican platters and tons of great beer.
Super 88 Food Court	1095 Commonwealth Ave	617-787-2288	$*	8 pm	Boston's largest Asian food court.
Upper Crust	286 Harvard St	617-739-8518	$	11 pm	Hit or miss pizza, now wireless hot spot.
V Majestic	164 Brighton Ave	617-782-6088	$*	10:30 pm	Perhaps Allston's best cheap Vietnamese.
Zaftigs Delicatessen	335 Harvard St	617-975-0075	$$	10 pm	Comfort food for breeders who brunch.

Map 20 · Harvard Square / Allston (North)

9 Tastes	50 JFK St	617-547-6666	$$	10:30 pm	Good Thai in a cheery basement.
Algiers	40 Brattle St	617-492-1557	$	11:30 pm	An excellent, and oddly tourist-free, lunch and coffee spot.
b. good	24 Dunster St	617-354-6500	$$	11 pm	Healthier fast food.
Border Café	32 Church St	617-864-6100	$$	12 am	Feeding students quality Tex-Mex for many years.
Caffe Paradiso	1 Eliot Sq	617-868-3240	$	11:30 pm	For students getting their just desserts.
Cambridge, 1	27 Church St	617-576-1111	$$	12 am	Tasty pizzas, salads. Relaxed, stripped-down space.
Casablanca	40 Brattle St	617-876-0999	$$$	11 pm	Still popular with the Harvard crowd.
Charlie's Kitchen	10 Eliot St	617-492-9646	$	1:30 am	Old School at the old school.
Chez Henri	1 Shepard St	617-354-8980	$$$	10:30 pm	French/Cuban bistro.
Crazy Doughs	36 JFK St	617-492-4848	$	11 pm	Pizza in The Garage.
Greenhouse Coffee Shop	3 Brattle St	617-354-3184	$*	12 am	Affordable, old-style coffee shop.
Grendel's Den	89 Winthrop St	617-491-1050	$	1 am	For the laid-back academic. Reasonable prices.
Harvest	44 Brattle St	617-868-2255	$$$$	11 pm	Excellent. Nice garden terrace.
Hi-Rise Bread Company	56 Brattle St	617-492-3003	$*	5 pm	Tasty, but bring some extra cash.
Hoffa's Swiss Alps	114 Mt Auburn St	617-354-5300	$$	10 pm	Weinerschnitzel and salsa dancing.
Iruna	56 JFK St	617-868-5633	$$	10 pm	Spanish restaurant tucked away off JFK.
John Harvard's Brew House	33 Dunster St	617-868-3585	$$	12:30 am	Large and loud, good for crowds.
Mr & Mrs Bartley's Burger Cottage	1246 Massachusetts Ave	617-354-6559	$*	9 pm	Campusy burger joint across from the Yard.
Pho Pasteur	35 Dunster St	617-864-4100	$$	11 pm	Reliable Vietnamese.
The Red House	98 Winthrop St	617-576-0605	$$$	11 pm	Seasonal menus served in an old red house.
Rialto	1 Bennett St	617-661-5050	$$$$$	11 pm	Probably Cambridge's finest restaurant.
Sabra Grill	20 Eliot Sq	617-868-5777	$*	10 pm	Tasty, cheap Greek food.
Sandrine's	8 Holyoke St	617-497-5300	$$$$	10:30 pm	Have a flammekueche - hard to say, easy to eat.
Shilla	57 JFK St	617-547-7971	$$$	12:30 pm	Quiet, subterranean Japanese/Korean.
Tamarind Bay	75 Winthrop St	617-491-4552	$$	10:30 pm	Try the bhuna paneer.
UpStairs on the Square	91 Winthrop St	617-864-1933	$$$$	11 pm	Neoclassical food in an expressionist room.
Veggie Planet	47 Palmer St	617-661-1513	$$*	10:30 pm	At Club Passim. Mostly for pizzas, some vegan.

Map 21 • West Cambridge

Armando's	163 Huron Ave	617-354-8275	$*	11:30 pm	Cheap and delicious pizza.
Aspasia	377 Walden St	617-864-4745	$$$$	10 pm	Mediterranean prepared with care.
Full Moon	344 Huron Ave	617-354-6699	$$	9 pm	For a night out with the children.
Hi-Rise Bread Company	208 Concord Ave	617-876-8766	$*	5 pm	Tasty, but bring some extra cash.
Il Buongustaio	369 Huron Ave	617-491-3133	$*	10 pm	Very good pizzas, calzones, paninis.
Trattoria Pulcinella	147 Huron Ave	617-491-6336	$$$$	11 pm	For those not going to the North End.

Map 22 • North Cambridge / West Somerville

Amelia's Kitchen	1137 Broadway	617-776-2800	$$	10:30 pm	Basic Italian fare.
Anna's Taqueria	236 Elm St	617-666-3900	$*	11 pm	Fastest burritos in town.
Antonia's Italian Bistro	37 Davis Sq	617-623-6700	$$††	11 pm	Solid choice for the carb-starved.
Bhoja	235 Elm St	617-440-6011	$*	9 pm	Exotic sandwich combos.
Café Barada	2269 Massachusetts Ave	617-354-2112	$	9 pm	Relaxed Middle Eastern.
Dave's Fresh Pasta	81 Holland St	617-623-0867	$††	7:30 pm	Homemade pasta and sauces
Diesel Café	257 Elm St	617-591-0308	$	1 am	Coffee and sandwich shop with an attitude.
Diva Indian Bistro	246 Elm St	617-629-4963	$$	1 am	Flashy and tasty, but pricey.
Elephant Walk	2067 Massachusetts Ave	617-492-6900	$$$	11 pm	French-Cambodian local legend.
Frank's Steak House	2310 Massachusetts Ave	617-661-0666	$$	10:30 pm	Average, uninviting.
Gargoyles on the Square	219 Elm St	617-776-5300	$$$$	10:30 pm	Deservedly popular Davis Square haunt.
House of Tibet	235 Holland St	617-629-7567	$$	9:30 pm	Delicious. But where's the yak butter?
Jasper White's Summer Shack	149 Alewife Brook Pkwy	617-520-9500	$$$	11 pm	Seafood. More a hangar than a shack.
Jose's	131 Sherman St	617-354-0335	$$	12 am	So-so Mexican cantina.
Joshua Tree	256 Elm St	617-623-9910	$$	10 am	Achtung, baby.
Martsa on Elm	233A Elm St	617-666-0660	$$	11 pm	Tibetan.
Namaskar	236 Elm St	617-623-9911	$$$	10:45 pm	Above-average Indian with good variety.
Nick's Roast Beef	20 College Ave	617-625-1497	$	11 pm	Sandwiches and such.
Out of the Blue	215 Elm St	617-776-5020	$$$††	10 pm	Good value for seafood, Italian. Colorful room.
Qingdao Garden	2382 Massachusetts Ave	617-492-7540	$	11 pm	Casual, delicious. Sells dumplings-to-go in bulk.
Redbones	55 Chester St	617-628-2200	$$*	12:30 am	Don't dig on swine? Then come for the beers.
Rosebud Diner	381 Summer St	617-666-6015	$$	12 am	Wise choice for a comfort food fix.
Sauce	400 Highland Ave	617-625-0200	$$	11 pm	Nothing special.
Soleil Café	1153 Broadway	617-625-0082	$	4 pm	Breakfast, lunch. Closed Sundays.

Map 23 • Central Somerville / Porter Square

Anna's Taqueria	822 Somerville Ave	617-661-8500	$*	11 pm	Fastest burritos in town.
Blue Fin	1815 Massachusetts Ave	617-497-8022	$$	10:30 pm	Not the best sushi, but maybe the cheapest.
Broken Yolk	136 College Ave	617-628-6621	$	3:30 pm	Mmm, pancakes.
Christopher's	1920 Massachusetts Ave	617-876-9180	$$	12 am	Good for relaxing on a wet day.
Kaya	1924 Massachusetts Ave	617-497-5656	$$$	12 am	Japanese/Korean. Decent food, uninspiring vibe.
Lil Vinny's	525 Medford St	617-628-8466	$$	11 pm	Spin-off of East Somerville's Vinny's at Night.
Lyndell's Bakery	720 Broadway	617-625-1793	$	6 pm	Old-fashioned bakery.
Naturals Café	187 Elm St	617-666-2233	$	8 pm	All natural fast-food.
Passage to India	1900 Massachusetts Ave	617-497-6113	$$	11 pm	Good Indian, served late.
RF O'Sullivan's	282 Beacon St	617-492-7773	$††	1 am	Quite possibly the best burgers in Boston.
Rustic Kitchen	1815 Massachusetts Ave	617-354-7766	$$$	11 pm	Hand-made pasta.
Sound Bites	708 Broadway	617-623-8338	$*	3 pm	For filling breakfasts.
Sugar & Spice	1933 Massachusetts Ave	617-868-4200	$$	11 pm	Thai.
Tu y Yo	858 Broadway	617-623-5411	$$	10 pm	Authentic Mexican - no burritos here.

Map 24 • Winter Hill / Union Square

Café Belo	120 Washington St	617-623-3696	$	10 pm	Brazilian cafeteria.
Great Thai Chef	255 Washington St	617-625-9296	$$††	10:30 pm	It's Thai, it's great, there's a chef.
Machu Picchu	25 Union Sq	617-623-7972	$	10 pm	Peruvian. Definitely worth trying.
Neighborhood Restaurant & Bakery	25 Bow St	617-623-9710	$*	4 pm	Big, good breakfasts + patio = summer morning bliss.
Sherman	257 Washington St	617-776-4944	$*	7 pm	Good lunch spot; comes recommended by Mr. Peabody.
Taqueria la Mexicana	247 Washington St	617-776-5232	$	10 pm	The real deal. Terrific flautas.

Map 25 • East Somerville / Sullivan Square

Beijing Taste	99A Cambridge St	617-241-5077	$	12 am	For emergencies only.
Mount Vernon	14 Broadway	617-666-3830	$$	11 pm	Sleepy spot with occasional lobster specials.
Vinny's at Night	76 Broadway	617-628-1921	$$$	10:30 pm	Quality home-style Italian tucked behind a deli.

309

Arts & Entertainment • **Restaurants**

Map 26 • East Cambridge / Kendall Square / MIT

Aceituna	605 W Kendall St	617-252-0707	$$	8 pm	Mediterranean for lunch at the Genzyme building.
Bambara	25 Land Blvd	617-868-4444	$$$	11 pm	Hit-or-miss at Hotel Marlowe.
Black Sheep Café	350 Main St	617-577-1300	$$	10:30 pm	In the Kendall Hotel. Go for breakfast.
The Blue Room	One Kendall Sq	617-494-9034	$$$$	11 pm	Terrific food, popular. Somehow elegant and casual.
The Cheesecake Factory	100 Cambridgeside Pl	617-252-3810	$$$	12:30 am	Done shopping? Unsatisfied? Continue your consumption here.
Court House Seafood	498 Cambridge St	617-491-1213	$$	6 pm	One step removed from bobbing for fish.
Desfina	202 Third St	617-868-9098	$$	1 am	Greek for geeks.
Helmand	143 First St	617-492-4646	$$$	11 pm	Delightful, authentic. Family ties with Afghanistan's president.
Legal Sea Foods	5 Cambridge Ctr	617-864-3400	$$$	11 pm	Above the Kendall T stop.
Second Street Café	89 Second St	617-661-1311	$$*	n/a	Plenty of fresh, inexpensive choices.

Map 27 • Central Square / Cambridgeport

Asgard	350 Massachusetts Ave	617-577-9100	$$	2 am	Enormous "Celtic" gastropub.
Asmara	739 Massachusetts Ave	617-864-7447	$$	11:30 pm	The only Ethiopian restaurant in Cambridge.
Atasca	50 Hampshire St	617-621-6991	$$	11 pm	Prodigious Portuguese. Smaller sibling is around the corner.
Brookline Lunch	9 Brookline St	617-354-2983	$*	5 pm	Popular diner. For food, not service.
Café Baraka	80 1/2 Pearl St	617-868-3951	$$*	10:30 pm	North African.
Carberry's	74 Prospect St	617-576-3530	$	8 pm	Bakery items and good sandwiches.
Cuchi Cuchi	795 Main St	617-864-2929	$$$	11:30 pm	You either love this place or hate it.
Dolphin Seafood	1105 Massachusetts Ave	617-661-2937	$$	10 pm	Unpretentious fish house.
Green Street Grill	280 Green St	617-876-1655	$$$	10:30 pm	Great Caribbean food with a slow burn. Mellow bar.
Hi-Fi Pizza & Subs	496 Massachusetts Ave	617-492-4600	$	3 am	Soak up the beer you drank at T.T.s.
India Pavilion	17 Central Sq	617-547-7463	$$	11 pm	Reliable Indian. A decent value.
La Groceria	853 Main St	617-497-4214	$$$	10 pm	Still there. Still good.
Mary Chung	464 Massachusetts Ave	617-864-1991	$$*	11 pm	Going strong.
Middle East	472 Massachusetts Ave	617-492-9181	$$	12 am	Cheap and tasty. Not just for partying!
Miracle of Science	321 Massachusetts Ave	617-868-2866	$$	1 am	Energetic neighborhood mainstay. Great burgers, quesadillas.
Moody's Falafel Palace	25 Central Sq	617-864-0827	$*	n/a	Located in what was once a White Castle.
Picante Mexican Grill	735 Massachusetts Ave	617-576-6394	$	11:30 pm	Cali-Mex. Pretty good salsas.
Pu Pu Hot Pot	907 Main St	617-491-6616	$	10:30 pm	Chinese. Much better than it sounds.
Rendezvous	502 Massachusetts Ave	617-576-1900	$$$$	11 pm	Great addition to Central Square.
Salts	798 Main St	617-876-8444	$$$$	11 pm	New ownership, higher prices.
Sonora Mexican Grill	319 Western Ave	617-576-6672	$	10 pm	Tiny taqueria.
Tavern in the Square	720 Massachusetts Ave	617-868-8800	$$	1 am	Ah, good! Central needed a meat market…
ZuZu!	474 Massachusetts Ave	617-492-9181	$$	11 pm	Funky, colorful. Make a meal of maza.

Map 28 • Inman Square

Amelia's Trattoria	111 Harvard St	617-868-7600	$$$	10:30 pm	The best Italian in this area.
Argana	1287 Cambridge St	617-868-1247	$$$	11 pm	Engaging North African.
B-Side Lounge	92 Hampshire St	617-354-0766	$$$	1 am	Hip spot that deserves its reputation.
Café Kiraz	119 Hampshire St	617-868-2233	$	9 pm	Subs and shwarma.
City Girl Café	204 Hampshire St	617-864-2809	$$	9 pm	Comfy and cool. Try the lasagna.
Dali	415 Washington St	617-661-3254	$$$	11 pm	Fun tapatia. Worth the wait.
East Coast Grill & Raw Bar	1271 Cambridge St	617-491-6568	$$$$	10:30 pm	Awesome seafood, barbecue. Try the Hell Sausage.
Emma's Pizzeria	40 Hampshire St	617-864-8534	$$	10 pm	Design your own gourmet pie. Worth waiting.
EVOO	118 Beacon St	617-661-3866	$$$$	11 pm	Creative cuisine. Possibly Somerville's best restaurant.
Koreana	154 Prospect St	617-576-8661	$$	12 am	One of the area's better Korean restaurants.
Magnolia's	1193 Cambridge St	617-576-1971	$$	10 pm	Southern. Try the fried chicken.
Midwest Grill	1124 Cambridge St	617-354-7536	$$	11 pm	Brazilian sword-play.
Ole Mexican Grill	11 Springfield St	617-492-4495	$$	11 pm	Food, drinks & a good atmosphere. Better Mexican in Cambridge.
Oleana	134 Hampshire St	617-661-0505	$$$$	11 pm	Top-notch Mediterranean. Patio seating in warm weather.
Pho Lemon	228 Broadway	617-441-8813	$	10:30 pm	Vietnamese. Not fancy, but good value.
S&S Restaurant	1334 Cambridge St	617-354-0777	$$	12 am	Serving deli, comfort food for eighty years.
Sweet Chili	1172 Cambridge St	617-864-4500	$$	11 pm	Thai.
Toscanini and Sons	406 Washington St	617-666-2770	$*	9 pm	Scrumptious café food and, of course, great ice cream.

Map 29 · West Roxbury

Corrib Pub	2030 Centre St	617-469-4177	$$	10:30 pm	American, hugely popular with neighborhood residents.
Real Deal	1882 Centre St	617-325-0754	$	9 pm	Sandwiches and other lunchables.
Samia Bakery	1894 Centre St	617-323-5181	$	8 pm	Syrian.
Spring Street Café	320 Spring St	617-327-6066	$$	3 pm	Mostly Italian, also open for breakfast.
Tony's Place	188 Baker St	617-323-3550	$	11 pm	Italian basics.
Vintage	1430 VFW Pkwy	617-469-2600	$$$$	11 pm	Steakhouse for locals unwilling to drive downtown.
West on Centre	1732 Centre St	617-323-4199	$$$	11 pm	Casual American; plenty of brick and mahogany.
West Roxbury Pub & Restaurant	1885 Centre St	617-469-2624	$$	9 pm	Irish pub serving American staples.

Map 30 · Roslindale

Birch Street Bistro	14 Birch St	617-323-2184	$$	10:30 pm	Inviting place to kick back for dinner.
Café Apollonia	146 Belgrade Ave	617-327-6910	$$	10:30 am	Authentic Albanian. Of course, who would know?
Delfino	754 South St	617-327-8359	$$$	10 pm	Tiny, popular spot serving good-quality Italian.
Diane's Bakery	9 Poplar St	617-323-1877	$*	1 pm	Croissant sandwiches, snack cakes.
Pleasant Café	4515 Washington St	617-323-2111	$$	11:30 pm	Pizza and other basics.
Primavera	289 Walk Hill St	617-522-1186	$$&&	9:30 pm	Mostly Italian.
Village Sushi & Grill	14 Corinth St	617-363-7874	$$	10 pm	Sushi and other Japanese, Korean dishes.
Yucatan Tacos	1417 Centre St	617-323-7555	$*	8 pm	"Authentic Mexican food," apparently.
Ali's Roti	1188 Blue Hill Ave	617-298-9850	$	10 pm	Caribbean curry wraps.
Bon Appetit	1138 Blue Hill Ave	617-825-5544	$$	11 pm	Haitian food supposedly makes you a better lover.
Brothers	1638 Blue Hill Ave	617-298-5224	$	7 pm	Southern. Huge side portions.
Flames	461 Blue Hill Ave	617-989-0000	$$	11 pm	Unusually stylish for this neighborhood.
Flames	663 Morton St	617-296-4972	$$	11 pm	Jamaican. Serves ackee!
Hummingbird Grill	736 Blue Hill Ave	617-822-0242	$$	11 pm	Drunken crab is the Caribbean specialty here.
Jamaica Jerk & Grill	1210A Blue Hill Ave	617-296-1436	$*	10 pm	Patties and curried peas at this tiny two-table place.
Lenny's Tropical Bakery	1195 Blue Hill Ave	617-296-2587	$*	9 pm	Double parking for the patties.
Picasso Creole Cuisine	1296 Blue Hill Ave	617-296-1300	$	10 pm	Haitian home-style cooking.
Pit Stop Bar-B-Q	888A Morton St	617-436-0485	$	12 am	A rib shack, literally. Stick to the ribs.
Simco's on the Bridge	1509 Blue Hill Ave	617-296-3800	$*	5 pm	Boston's best hotdogs since the 1930s.
United House of Prayer Kitchen	206 Seaver St	617-445-3246	$*	6 pm	Friendly soul food in basement of Boston's old stadt shul.

Map 32 · Dorchester (East)

Ashmont Grill	555 Talbot Ave	617-825-4300	$$$	11 pm	Bringing flair to Peabody Square.
Ba-Le Restaurant	1052 Dorchester Ave	617-265-7171	$*	10 pm	Crisp Vietnamese sandwiches.
Blarney Stone	1505 Dorchester Ave	617-436-8223	$$	11 pm	Hodgepodge of good pub-type food.
CF Donovan's	112 Savin Hill Ave	617-436-6690	$$	1 am	Friendly neighborhood restaurant/bar.
Charlie's Place	1740 Dorchester Ave	617-265-3111	$	10:30 pm	Pizza and steak sandwiches.
Chef Lee's II	554 Columbia Rd	617-436-6634	$$	8 pm	Second location of Boston soul food institution.
Chris's Texas BBQ	1370 Dorchester Ave	617-436-4700	$$	11 pm	Neighborhood institution.
dbar	1236 Dorchester Ave	617-265-4490	$$$	10 pm	So chic, you could be in Downtown Crossing.
Moonlight Terrace	756 Dudley St	617-436-4586	$*		Pizzeria.
Phillips Old Colony House	780 Morrissey Blvd	617-282-7700	$$$$	10 pm	Brunch to impress your grandmother visiting from Iowa.
Pho 2000	198 Adams St	617-436-1908	$$	10 pm	Pho and other Vietnamese dishes.
Pho Hoa	1356 Dorchester Ave	617-287-9746	$	11 pm	Phat pho.
Restaurante Cesaria	266 Bowdoin St	617-282-1998	$$	11 pm	Cape Verdean.
Shanti: Taste of India	1111 Dorchester Ave	617-929-3900	$$	11 pm	Popular spot, good quality.
Sunrise	1157 Dorchester Ave	617-288-7314	$	10 pm	Pho and other ethereal delights.

Map 33 · Hyde Park

Angie's	984 Hyde Park Ave	617-361-9811	$$*	10 pm	Haitian and other Caribbean dishes.

It's difficult to typecast of Boston shoppers. This is due in part to the varied levels of crazy inhabiting its people – ranging from the Burberry-sporting, Beacon-Hill-dwelling elite to the thrift-shop-shopping Cambridge funksters in Doc Martens. The city's extremes of climate (the adage being, "if you don't like the weather, wait five minutes") compel most Bostonians to spend their weekends popping into nice warm (or cool, depending on the season) shops that range from uncomfortably exclusive to quietly quaint to downright weird. And, in addition to the extreme consumerist lifestyle of many of its dwellers, the city also has its share of psychotic, insane though rugged outdoor athletes, for whom purveyors of gear spread evenly throughout the city. The fleet of moving trucks clogging this college town on the first of every month from March through October keeps the furniture-and-housewares-hawkers in business. Despite the few malls that have weaseled their way onto the scene, the dependable disparity and constant movement of the city results in a throbbing, colorful, and sometimes shocking mass of consumers.

Clothing

For the labradoodle-walking yuppies in our midst, the Boston shopping scene certainly delivers. Start in the Back Bay on Newbury Street at **Louis Boston (Map 6)** then head across the street to **Brooks Brothers (Map 6)** and similar venues. More reasonably priced but still plenty preppy is **Eddie Bauer (Map 3)** downtown. On the other side of the coin, Boston has a ton to offer those seeking funkier duds – you just need to know where to look. The **Garment District (Map 28)** in Cambridge is a gargantuan thrift/vintage store with everything from '60s sweaters to contemporary second-hand treasures—contrary to New York, it's a store, not a neighborhood. Poke around the North End's tiny shops and you'll eventually stumble onto the treasures to be found in **Karma (Map 2)**. **Cibeline (Map 22)** in Davis Square is amazing for designer vintage. Even upscale Newbury Street has its share of vintage chic – the **Army Barracks (Map 5)** is an old fave. And Boston is really a walking city (you know, when it's not hailing), so outfit your feet with shoes from **Berks (Map 20)**, **The Tannery (Map 6, Map 20)** in Back Bay and Harvard Square, or **DSW (Map 2)** in Downtown Crossing.

For the Home/Apartment/Dorm

Though driving through Brookline and Beacon Hill on September 2—after most apartments have been vacated and their perfectly usable furniture left on the curb—is a fabulous way to outfit your own digs, you may wish to take a gander at the furniture 'n' stuff offered throughout a city that's constantly turning over. Despite the terrific selection and prices offered by the obvious **Crate and Barrel (Map 6, Map 20)**, beware the slalom of newly-engaged couples registering for gifts. **Bowl and Board (Map 17)** is similar, but more diverse as far as neat little whosits for every room in the home. Crowded, annoying, one-stop house shopping can be achieved at the wicked huge **Bed Bath & Beyond (Map 16)** in Kenmore. **Economy Hardware (Map 5, Map 16, Map 19, Map 27)** is always a safe – albeit pricey – bet for furniture, gadgets, even paint (oh, and hardware). Check out counter-intuitive spots like **Urban Outfitters (Map 20, Map 5)**, **Absolutely Fabulous (Map 28)**, or even **TJ Maxx (Map 3, Map 19)** and **Marshall's (Map 3, Map 6, Map 12)** for finishing touches like pretty pillows,

cool lamps, and funky artwork. Antique hunters will be kept happy at **Cambridge Antique Market's (Map 26)** five floors of yesteryear.

Sports

Ready, set … Cross-country ski? Whatever the season, you can find what you're looking for at **City Sports (Map 3, Map 6, Map 19, Map 23)**. Boston's also a biker city (but more the Schwinns than the Harleys). Riders can get tune-ups, gear, and honest advice at **International Bicycle Center (Map 19)**. **REI (Map 6)** is also good for bikes along with anything you might need for a cliff-hangin' good time. **Marathon Sports (Map 17)** in Brookline lets you test drive the sneakers on the sidewalk and makes sure you leave with exactly the right pair.

Electronics

Thanks to its many universities, hospitals, and research facilities, Boston is awash with computer-loving dweebs. **Micro Center (Map 27)** is swarmed on the weekends. Two centrally located **Best Buys (Map 16, Map 26)** feature their usual merchandise and crowds. The PC-user-repellant **Apple Store (Map 26)** in the Cambridgeside Galleria is one stylin' geek boutique.

Music

The rise of the iPod has given Bostonians yet another excuse to keep eyes forward and not interact with fellow human beings that dare cross their path. But there are still plenty of options for those in search of disks and vinyl. **Newbury Comics (Map 2, Map 5, Map 20, Map 21)** delivers on their offer of "a wicked good time" with not only music, but movies, novelties, and general craziness. The **Virgin Megastore (Map 5)** is a great place to listen before you buy. For those in search of vinyl, vintage, and generally hard-to-find tunes, stroll along Mass Ave in Cambridge to find **Cheapo Records (Map 27)**, **Massive Records (Map 27)**, **Skippy White's (Map 27)**, **Stereo Jack's (Map 20)**, and a number of others. Comm Ave near BU and Harvard Square are also places to troll for rare stuff with stores like **In Your Ear (Map 19)**, **Nuggets (Map 16)**, and **Planet Records (Map 20)**.

Food

You literally cannot go wrong once you set foot in the North End. **Mike's Pastry (Map 2)** and **Modern Pastry (Map 2)** are just two of about a thousand places to try. Equally tempting treats can be found at **Athan's Bakery (Map 17)** in Brookline and **Cremaldi's (Map 27)** in Cambridge. If ever you lived abroad and are feeling nostalgic, **Cardullo's (Map 20)** in Harvard Square is a sure place to grab imported anything from Branston Pickle to real Italian gelato. For ice cream, **Christina's Homemade (Map 27)** in Inman Square is a favorite. Popular spots also include **JP Licks (Map 5, Map 14, Map 19)** and **Emack & Bolio's (Map 5, Map 17, Map 31)**, both with lines out the door in summer months. **Zathmary's (Map 17)** in Coolidge Corner has a great salad bar and fabulous prepared stuff priced in accordance with the neighborhood.

Malls and 'hoods

If you're going to make an afternoon of it, you might as well hit up a neighborhood with a lot to offer – including a bite in between stops and plenty of people – watching for when the cash runs out. **Downtown Crossing (Map 3)** is a high – energy center of rabid consumerism, very convenient to the T and boasting the gigantic department store **Macy's (Map 3)** (which has recently gobbled up the beloved Filene's), discount stores (**Marshall's (Map 3)**, **TJ Maxx (Map 3)**), and other joints like **H&M (Map 3)** where you can get lost for hours. Clothes aren't the only thing for which to shop here – there are jewelers, shoe stores, and street vendors and performers. It's also within walking distance of **Faneuil Hall (Map 2)**. One could easily spend a solid afternoon wandering around **Harvard Square (Map 20)**. **Newbury Comics (Map 20)** and **Little Tibet (Map 20)** are great for gift shopping (for yourself or anyone else). Stop for a snack at **Cardullo's (Map 20)**, or recharge at **Tealuxe (Map 20)**, and while you're sipping or munching, flip through a book at the **Coop (Map 20)** or **Harvard Book Store (Map 20)**. Walk the length of

Newbury Street (Map 5), and you'll find everything from bookstores (**Trident Booksellers and Café (Map 5)** is a must) to house stuff (**Kitchen Arts (Map 6)**) to ice cream (**Emack & Bolio's (Map 5)**) to art (**International Poster Gallery (Map 6)**), plus clothes and clothes and clothes. Though most of what's found on Newbury is decidedly pricey, things do get more reasonable as you get closer to Mass Ave. **Boylston Street (Map 6)** runs parallel to Newbury with offerings like **Anthropologie (Map 6)**, **City Sports (Map 6)**, **Tweeter Etc. (Map 6)**, and **Shreve, Crump & Lowe (Map 6)**. And yes, as much as we hate to admit it, Boston does have a few "malls" – though they are well camouflaged and the word "mall" does not actually appear in their titles. **The Shops at Prudential Center (Map 5)** include **Sephora (Map 5)**, **Lord & Taylor (Map 6)**, and several others and also cuts through to the even higher-end **Copley Place (Map 6)**. The **Cambridgeside Galleria (Map 26)** is a multi-leveled mecca containing **Best Buy (Map 26)** and the **Apple Store (Map 26)**, with restaurants and vendors throughout.

Map 1 • Beacon Hill / West End

Black Ink	101 Charles St	617-723-3883	A blend of quirky and handy gifts.
DeLuca's Market	11 Charles St	617-523-4343	Good deli, pricey fruit, wine, and beer downstairs.
Eugene Galleries	76 Charles St	617-227-3062	A treasure chest of old maps, prints, books.
The Flat of the Hill	60 Charles St	617-619-9977	Quirky gifts. Lots of pink.
Hilton's Tent City	272 Friend St	617-227-9242	Four floors of outdoors needs since 1947.
Moxie	51 Charles St	617-557-9991	Shoes, bags, accessories.
The Red Wagon	69 Charles St	617-523-9402	Pricey kids' clothes and toys.
Savenor's Market	160 Charles St	617-723-6328	For a variety of gourmet goodies.
Wish	49 Charles St	617-227-4441	Trendy, upscale women's clothing and accessories.

Map 2 • North End / Faneuil Hall

Bova's Bakery	134 Salem St	617-523-5601	Pastries, also deli and pizza. Open 24 hours.
Brooks Brothers	75 State St	617-261-9990	Branch of venerable Back Bay clothier.
Dairy Fresh Candies	57 Salem St	617-742-2639	Big selection of candy imported from Italy.
Fresh Cheese	81 Endicott St	617-570-0007	Also sells dozens of oils and vinegars.
Green Cross Pharmacy	393 Hanover St	617-227-3728	Old-world pharmacy. Also sells Italian sundries.
Holbrows Flowers	100 City Hall Plz	617-227-8057	Convenient to Government Center T stop.
Karma	26 Prince St	617-723-8338	Upscale consignment shop.
Maria's Pastry Shop	46 Cross St	617-523-1196	Sweet tooth heaven.
Mike's Pastry	300 Hanover St	617-742-3050	The most famous of the North End Italian bakeries.
Modern Pastry	257 Hanover St	617-523-3783	Boston's best cannoli? You decide.
Monica's Salumeria	130 Salem St	617-742-4101	Homemade takeout and Italian groceries.
Newbury Comics	1 Washington Mall	617-248-9992	Downtown location of successful music/novelties chain.
Roche-Bobois	585 Commercial St	617-742-9611	Interior design and furnishings.
Salumeria Italiana	151 Richmond St	617-523-8743	Well-regarded Italian specialties store.
Salumeria Toscana	272 Hanover St	617-720-4243	Imported Italian specialties, heat-and-serve meals.
Stanza dei Sigari	292 Hanover St	617-227-0295	17-year-olds take note: hookahs available.

Map 3 • Downtown Crossing / Park Square / Bay Village

Beacon Hill Skate Shop	135 Charles St S	617-482-7400	Rentals available. Also has hockey gear.
Borders	10 School St	617-557-7188	All you've come to expect, plus sidewalk sales.
Bromfield Camera & Video	10 Bromfield St	617-426-5230	Decent selection of new and used cameras.
City Antiques	362 Tremont St	617-423-7600	Used furniture and furnishings.
City Sports	11 Bromfield St	617-423-2015	Covers all the basics in apparel and equipment.
DSW	385 Washington St	617-556-0052	Oodles and oodles of sho[odl]es.
Eddie Bauer Outlet	500 Washington St	617-423-4722	Good deals on quality clothing.
H&M	350 Washington St	617-482-7001	Inexpensive sportswear from Swedish megamerchant.
Jack's Joke Shop	226 Tremont St	617-426-9640	More than just fake vomit.
LJ Peretti	2 1/2 Park Sq	617-482-0218	Oldest family-run tobacconist in the country.
Macy's	450 Washington St	617-357-3000	Once Jordan Marsh.
Marshall's	350 Washington St	617-338-6205	Discount clothing and other stuff.
Old Town Camera	226 Washington St	617-227-0202	Photo equipment, film developing.
Staples	25 Court St	617-367-1747	Printer ink and other more reasonably priced supplies.
Staples	25 Winter St	617-426-2290	Smaller than the Court Street branch.
TJ Maxx	350 Washington St	617-695-2424	Off-price apparel and housewares.
Windsor Buttons	35 Temple Pl	617-482-4969	Buttons, darning needs.

Map 4 • Financial District / Chinatown

Anna's Dessert House	66 Harrison Ave	617-542-7903	One of Chinatown's better bakery/dessert shops.
Boston Costume Company	69 Kneeland St	617-482-1632	Rentals and sales.
Silky Way Boston	38 Kneeland St	617-423-2264	For your martial arts and herbal medicine needs.

Map 5 • Back Bay (West) / Fenway (East)

Army Barracks	328 Newbury St	617-547-1657	Surplus store. Lots of coats, T-shirts.
Back Bay Bicycle	366 Commonwealth Ave	617-247-2336	Accurately monikered.
CD Spins	324 Newbury St	617-267-5955	A good choice for selling back CDs.
Daddy's Junky Music	159 Massachusetts Ave	617-247-0909	Comprehensive store serving the Berklee community.
DeLuca's Market	239 Newbury St	617-262-5900	Good deli, expensive fruit, wine, and beer downstairs.
Economy Hardware	219 Massachusetts Ave	617-536-4280	Hardware, household needs, cheap furniture. Very popular.
Emack & Bolio's	290 Newbury St	617-536-7127	Innovative ice cream flavors.
John Fluevog	302 Newbury St	617-266-1079	Buy your guy some nicer shoes.
Johnson Artist Materials	355 Newbury St	617-536-4065	Tony. Also a selection of stationery.
JP Licks	352 Newbury St	617-236-1666	Well-liked ice cream shop.
Luna Boston	286 Newbury St	866-910-3900	Handbags.
Matsu	259 Newbury St	617-266-9707	Gifts, accessories, good women's clothes.
Newbury Comics	332 Newbury St	617-236-4930	Now featuring a large DVD section.
Orpheus	362 Commonwealth Ave	617-247-7200	Focusing on classical music.
Sephora	800 Boylston St	617-262-4200	A makeup wonderland - play before you buy.
Sweet-N-Nasty	90 Massachusetts Ave	617-266-7171	Cakes for all [adult] occasions.
Trident Booksellers & Café	338 Newbury St	617-267-8688	Cool independent bookstore with tons of magazines.
Urban Outfitters	361 Newbury St	617-236-0088	Funky clothes, apartment stuff and novelties.
Utrecht Art Supply Center	333 Massachusetts Ave	617-262-4948	Serious art store near Symphony Hall.
Virgin Megastore	360 Newbury St	617-896-0950	Soon to have condos on upper floors.

Map 6 • Back Bay (East) / South End (Upper)

All Things Chocolate	31 St James Ave	617-423-9400	For that funny valentine of yours.
Amazing Express	57 Stuart St	617-338-1252	Sex; a vestige of the erstwhile Combat Zone.
Anthropologie	799 Boylston St	617-262-0545	Good for gifts and conversation pieces. Some clothes.
Brooks Brothers	46 Newbury St	617-267-2600	Flagship store of company operating since 1818.
City Sports	480 Boylston St	617-267-3900	Covers all the basics in apparel and equipment.
Crate & Barrel	777 Boylston St	617-262-8700	Back Bay location of Chicago behemoth.
First Act Guitar Studio	745 Boylston St	617-226-7899	Guitars made, guitars played, in-store concerts.
Hempest	207 Newbury St	617-421-9944	Don't ask if they sell sweaters.
International Poster Gallery	205 Newbury St	617-375-0076	Prints and posters from around the world.
Kitchen Arts	161 Newbury St	617-266-8701	Broad range of kitchen needs and esoterica.
Lindt Master Chocolatier	704 Boylston St	617-236-0571	Nifty gifts for your Swiss miss.
Lord & Taylor	760 Boylston St	617-262-6000	Featuring new facade.
Louis Boston	234 Berkeley St	617-262-6100	High-end men's and women's designer clothing.
Lush	166 Newbury St	617-375-5874	British cosmetics merchant.
Marc Jacobs	81 Newbury St	617-425-0707	Will he make it in fashion-challenged Boston?
Marshall's	500 Boylston St	617-262-6066	Discount clothing and other stuff.
Neiman Marcus	5 Copley Pl	617-536-3660	Needless Markup?
Paper Source	338 Boylston St	617-536-3444	DIY paper crafts and quirky gifts.
Saks Fifth Avenue	1 Ring Rd	617-262-8500	Boston branch of New York playa.
Shreve, Crump & Low	440 Boylston St	617-267-9100	Boston jewelers since 1796.
Stil	170 Newbury St	617-859-7845	Au courant clothes and accessories.
Tannery	400 Boylston St	617-267-0899	Boots, leather, coats, sneakers. Hit-or-miss service.
Teuscher Chocolates	230 Newbury St	617-536-1922	For the chocoholic.
Tweeter Etc	350 Boylston St	617-262-2299	Audio and video equipment.
Winston Flowers	131 Newbury St	617-266-1058	Well-established high-end flower shop.

Map 7 • South End (Lower)

Aunt Sadie's	18 Union Park St	617-357-7117	Fabulous candles, other gifts.
Bobby from Boston	19 Thayer St	617-423-9299	Vintage clothing.
Brix Wine Shop	1284 Washington St	617-542-2749	Upscale wine shop.
The Butcher Shop	552 Tremont St	617-423-4800	Sweet meats. Also a wine bar serving specialties.
Community Bicycle Supply	496 Tremont St	617-542-8623	South End bike shop.
Fresh Eggs	58 Clarendon St	617-247-8150	Cheery home accessories store.
Ilex	73 Berkeley St	617-422-0300	Florist.
Kosmos Market	683 Tremont St	617-236-4480	Good deli options.
Lekker	1317 Washington St	617-542-6464	Unique home furnishings.
Lionette's	577 Tremont St	617-778-0360	Food shop associated with Garden of Eden.
Picco	513 Tremont St	617-927-0066	Ice cream handy to the BCA.
Posh	557 Tremont St	617-437-1970	Gifts, home furnishings and accessories.
South End Formaggio	268 Shawmut Ave	617-350-6996	Cheese, cured meats, dry goods and wine.
Uniform	511 Tremont St	617-247-2360	Top clothes for lads.

Map 8 · Charlestown

A Wild Flower	73 Main St	617-242-4214	Florist.
Bunker Hill Florist	1 Thompson Sq	617-242-2124	Florist.
Doherty's Flowers	223 Main St	617-242-1300	Main Street florist.
The Joy of Old	85A Warren St	617-242-6066	Coming soon: "The Joy of Gay Old."

Map 9 · East Boston

Brazilian Soccer House	110 Meridian St	617-569-1164	The place to get your soccer kit.
Globos y Fiesta	52A Bennington St	617-569-4908	Order your piñatas here.
Lilly's Flower Shop	512 Saratoga St	617-567-5177	Day Square florist.
Liverty Stadium Bookstore	268 Bennington St	617-569-1253	Los libros en español.
Lolly's Bakery	158 Bennington St	617-567-9461	Quality pañaderia.
Salvy the Florist	8 Chelsea St	617-567-3331	Florist.

Map 10 · South Boston (West) / Fort Point

Machine Age	354 Congress St	617-482-0048	Modern furniture in a huge space.

Map 11 · South Boston (East)

EP Levine	23 Drydock Ave	617-951-1499	High-end photo shop.
Miller's Market	336 K St	617-268-2526	Apparently, the coldest beer in town.
Stapleton Floral	635 E Broadway	617-269-7271	Florist.

Map 12 · Newmarket / Andrew Square

Home Depot	5 Allstate Rd	617-442-6110	Got wood?
Marshall's	8D Allstate Rd	617-442-5050	Discount clothing and other stuff.

Map 14 · Jamaica Plain

Boing! JP's Toy Shop	729 Centre St	877-264-6400	Friendly toy shop.
Boomerangs	716 Centre St	617-524-5120	Used clothing.
Bread & Butter Baking Co.	3346 Washington St	617-983-8688	Lovingly made breads and sweets.
CD Spins	668 Centre St	617-325-7400	A good choice for selling back CDs.
City Feed and Supply	66 Boylston St	617-524-1657	Popular neighborhood grocery, meeting spot.
Eye Q Optical	7 Pond St	617-983-3937	Designer eyeglasses.
Fat Ram's Pumpkin Tattoo	380 Centre St	617-522-6444	Skilled ink artists with degrees in fine art.
Ferris Wheels Bicycle Shop	66 South St	617-522-7082	JP bike shop.
Fire Opal	683 Centre St	617-524-0262	Upscale craft gallery.
Gadgets	671 Centre St	617-524-6800	Kitchen stuff, mostly.
JP Licks	659 Centre St	617-524-2020	Popular ice cream shop.
Petal & Leaf	461 Centre St	617-524-2227	Friendly staff, fun gifts and fresh flowers.
Pluto	603 Centre St	617-522-0054	Clothes, housewares, gifts.

Map 16 · Kenmore Square / Brookline (East)

Artemisia	506 Commonwealth Ave	617-266-3030	Florist. Also gifts, indoor touches.
Bed Bath & Beyond	401 Park Dr	617-536-1090	For when holes are growing in your towels.
Best Buy	401 Park Dr	617-424-7900	Awful, annoying electronics retailer.
Blick Art Materials	401 Park Dr	617-247-3322	Art-supply megashop.
Boston Bicycle	842 Beacon St	617-236-0752	Selection geared toward messengers, plenty of fixies.
Economy Hardware	1012 Beacon St	617-277-8811	Hardware, household needs, cheap furniture. Very popular.
Guitar Center	750 Commonwealth Ave	617-738-5958	Also has drums, keys, etc.
Hunt's Photo and Video	520 Commonwealth Ave	617-778-2222	Good selection of used cameras.
Nantucket Natural Oils	508 Commonwealth Ave	617-437-9800	Aromatherapy and perfumes.
Nuggets	486 Commonwealth Ave	617-536-0679	Sells only used recordings. Quite fun to browse.
REI	401 Park Dr	617-236-0746	Seattle co-op for the gearhead.
Ski Market	860 Commonwealth Ave	617-731-6100	Skis or bicycles depending on the season.
Staples	401 Park Dr	617-638-3292	Printer ink and more reasonably priced supplies.
Tomb/SWITS	186 Brookline Ave	617-375-9487	Pretend you're Indiana Jones.
Tweeter Etc	880 Commonwealth Ave	617-738-4411	Audio and video equipment.
University Computers	533 Commonwealth Ave	617-353-1800	BU store; ask about student discounts.

Map 17 · Coolidge Corner / Brookline Hills

Athan;s Bakery	1621 Beacon St	617-734-7028	Exquisite baked goods, chocolates, gelato and espresso.
Beacon Kosher	1706 Beacon St	617-734-5300	Gets very crowded on Fridays.
Bowl & Board	1354 Beacon St	617-566-4726	Home furnishings and housewares.
Catering by Andrew	402 Harvard St [Fabyan St]	617-731-6585	Shabbat bakery, Thursdays and Fridays only.
EC Florist & Gifts	224 Washington St	617-232-3693	Florist.

Map 17 • Coolidge Corner / Brookline Hills–*continued*

Emack & Bolio's	1663 Beacon St	617-731-6256	Innovative ice cream flavors.
Eureka Puzzles	1354 Beacon St	617-738-7352	Old-timey gamers' heaven.
Marathon Sports	1638 Beacon St	617-735-9373	Run! Run! Run!
Paper Source	1361 Beacon St	617-264-2800	DIY paper crafts and quirky gifts.
Party Favors	1356 Beacon St	617-566-3330	Satisfies your sweet tooth and your inner party animal.
Petropol	1428 Beacon St	617-232-8820	Russian books and CDs.
Pier 1 Imports	1351 Beacon St	617-232-9627	Brought to you by Fat Actress Kirstie Alley.
Russian Village	1659 Beacon St	617-731-2023	Foodstuffs, deli, CDs/videos.
Serenade Chocolates	5 Harvard Sq	617-739-0795	Tastes of Vienna.
Ten Thousand Villages	226 Harvard St	617-277-7700	Free-trade, handmade crafts from around the world.
Wild Goose Chase	1431 Beacon St	617-738-8020	Crafts, gifts. A flea market, Brookline-style.
Zathmary's	299 Harvard St	617-731-8900	Specialty foods emporium.

Map 18 • Brighton

Amanda's Flowers	347 Washington St	617-782-0686	Florist.
Boomerangs	298 Washington St	617-787-0500	Used clothes.
CompUSA	205 Market St	617-783-1900	Has the basics, but service could be sharper.
Staples	1660 Soldiers Field Rd	617-254-4822	Printer ink and other more reasonably priced supplies.

Map 19 • Allston (South) / Brookline (North)

Berezka International Food	1215 Commonwealth Ave	617-787-2837	Russian goods for the slavophile.
Bicycle Bill's	253 N Harvard St	617-783-5636	Quality, no-attitude, neighborhood bike shop.
Bob Smith's Wilderness House	1048 Commonwealth Ave	617-277-5858	Everything for your outdoor adventures.
Brookline News and Gifts	313 Harvard St	617-566-9634	Since 1963, chances are they have what you're looking for.
City Housewares	434 Harvard St	617-278-6333	Inexpensive yet stylish kitchen goods.
City Sports	1035 Commonwealth Ave	617-782-5121	Covers all the basics in apparel and equipment.
Clear Flour	178 Thorndike St	617-739-0600	Lines out the door for Boston's honest bread.
Coco Cosmetics	192 Harvard Ave	617-782-1547	Trendy bright shop seems out of place. The future of Allston?
Eastern Mountain Sports	1041 Commonwealth Ave	617-254-4250	Gear for the New England outdoor enthusiast.
Economy Hardware	144 Harvard Ave	617-789-5552	Hardware, household needs, cheap furniture. Very popular.
Herrell's Ice Cream	155 Brighton Ave	617-782-9599	Attracts a loyal following.
In Your Ear	957 Commonwealth Ave	617-787-9755	Good selection of independent, experimental music.
International Bicycle Center	89 Brighton Ave	617-783-5804	Two floors of bikes, one of Boston's largest.
Jasmine Sola Warehouse Store	965 Commonwealth Ave	617-562-0004	Newbury Street style at warehouse prices.
JP Licks	311 Harvard St	617-738-8252	Popular Boston ice cream institution.
Kolbo Fine Judaica	437 Harvard St	617-731-8743	Good place for Jewish gifts.
Kupel's Bake & Bagel	421 Harvard St	617-566-9528	Old school bagel joint.
New England Comics	175 Harvard Ave	617-783-1848	Study break reading material, some independent comics.
Pixi Accessories	175 Harvard Ave	617-782-1150	Not quite Bjork, but fun.
Re:Generation Records & Tattoo	155 Harvard Ave	617-782-1313	Good addition to the Allston punk scene.
Richman's Zipper Hospital	318 Harvard St	617-277-0039	The place to go for fixing zippers and tailoring.
Staples	214 Harvard Ave	617-566-8605	Printer ink and other more reasonably priced supplies.
Stingray Body Art	1 Harvard Ave	617-254-0666	Huge tattoo parlor with sassy boutique.
TJ Maxx	525 Harvard St	617-232-5420	Off-price apparel and housewares.
Urban Renewals	122 Brighton Ave	617-783-8387	Thrift shop with clothes, gifts and kitsch.
Vespa Boston	22 Brighton Ave	617-254-4000	Imagine you are in Italy with its better drivers.
Wulf's Fish Market	409 Harvard St	617-277-2506	Respected fishmonger.

Map 20 • Harvard Square / Allston (North)

Abodeon	1731 Massachusetts Ave	617-497-0137	Retro housewares.
Alpha Omega	1380 Massachusetts Ave	617-864-1227	Jewelry, large selection of watches.
Berk's Shoes	50 JFK St	888-462-3757	Arm yourself with the right kicks for the neighborhood.
Black Ink	5 Brattle St	617-497-1221	A blend of quirky and handy gifts.
Bob Slate	1288 Massachusetts Ave	617-547-1230	Popular stationery store. Art supplies too.
Cambridge Naturals	1670 Massachusetts Ave	617-492-4452	Quality selection of all things yogi.
Cardullo's Gourmet Shoppe	6 Brattle St	617-491-8888	Going for more than sixty years. Expensive, recommended.
City Sports	44 Brattle St	617-492-6000	Moved from Dunster Street.
Crate & Barrel	48 Brattle St	617-876-6300	Harvard Square location of Chicago behemoth.
Harvard Coop	1400 Massachusetts Ave	617-499-2000	Good for books, maps, and school stuff.
Herrell's Ice Cream	15 Dunster St	617-497-2179	Try the hot fudge.
Hidden Sweets	25 Brattle St	617-497-2600	Bulk candy and other crap.
LA Burdick Homemade Chocolates	52D Brattle St	617-491-4340	Sublime confections and some killer hot chocolate.
Leavitt & Pierce	1316 Massachusetts Ave	617-547-0576	Best tobacconist in Cambridge. Chess sets too.
Little Tibet	1174 Massachusetts Ave	617-868-1030	Far-eastern clothing, jewelry, incense and more.
Museum of Useful Things	49 Brattle St	617-576-3322	Museum/shop celebrates the Beauty of Function.
Newbury Comics	36 JFK St	617-491-0337	A zoo on weekends.

Nini's Corner	1394 Massachusetts Ave	617-547-3558	What are sundries? This place sells sundries.
Nomad	1741 Massachusetts Ave	617-497-6677	Cool stuff from all over.
On Church Street	54 Church St	617-497-7070	Replaced CD Spins here.
Oona's	1210 Massachusetts Ave	617-491-2654	Nifty little vintage shop.
Out of Town News	0 Harvard Sq	617-354-7777	The sensible Harvard Square rendezvous spot.
Planet Records	54B JFK St	617-492-0693	CDs, some vinyl. Grab a $1 "mystery bag."
Proletariat	36 JFK St	617-661-3865	Cool clothes and other fun nonsense.
Staples	57 JFK St	617-491-1166	Printer ink and other more reasonably priced supplies.
Stereo Jack's	1686 Massachusetts Ave	617-497-9447	Specializing in jazz, blues, and the like.
Tannery	11A Brattle St	617-491-0810	Boots, leather, coat, sneakers. Hit-or-miss service.
Tealuxe	0 Brattle St	617-441-0077	Good spot to hide from Harvard Square crowds.
Tess and Carlos	20 Brattle St	617-864-8377	Chi-chi clothes.
Twisted Village	12B Eliot St	617-354-6898	Focusing on experimental, modern psychedelic music.
Urban Outfitters	11 JFK St	617-864-0070	Funky clothes and apartment stuff. Great bargain basement.

Map 21 · West Cambridge

Formaggio Kitchen	244 Huron Ave	617-354-4750	Cheese and other gourmet imports.
Henry Bear's Park	361 Huron Ave	617-547-8424	Chi-chi toy store.
Newbury Comics	211 Alewife Brook Pkwy	617-491-7711	Fresh Pond location of successful music/novelties chain.
Staples	186 Alewife Brook Pkwy	617-547-3948	Printer ink and other more reasonably priced supplies.

Map 22 · North Cambridge / West Somerville

Asierica	2259 Massachusetts Ave	617-492-5040	Funky, arty objects for your home.
Bicycle Exchange	2067 Massachusetts Ave	617-864-1300	Porter Square bike shop.
Black & Blues	89 Holland St	617-628-0046	Unusual clothing.
CD Spins	235 Elm St	617-666-8080	A good choice for selling back CDs.
China Fair	2100 Massachusetts Ave	617-864-3050	Inexpensive kitchen gear and housewares.
Chinook Outdoor Adventure	93 Holland St	617-776-8616	For when your fleece coat has finally had it.
Cibeline	85 Holland St	617-625-2229	Party clothes, whatever your mood.
McKinnon's Choice Meat Market	239A Elm St	617-666-0888	Smart choice before a barbecue.
Modern Brewer	2304 Massachusetts Ave	617-498-0400	Everything for your home-brewing needs.
Nellie's Wildflowers	72 Holland St	617-625-9453	Florist.
Poor Little Rich Girl	416 Highland Ave	617-684-0157	Good spot to shop for fun clothes.

Map 23 · Central Somerville / Porter Square

Ace Wheelworks	145 Elm St	617-776-2100	Davis Square bike shop.
Big Fish, Little Fish	55 Elm St	617-666-2444	Pet store with more than just fish.
Bob Slate	1975 Massachusetts Ave	617-547-8624	Popular stationery store. Art supplies too.
Cambridge Music Center	1906 Massachusetts Ave	617-547-8263	Sells instruments and hard-to-find sheet music.
City Sports	1815 Massachusetts Ave	617-661-1666	Covers all the basics in apparel and equipment.
Joie de Vivre	1792 Massachusetts Ave	617-864-8188	Silly gifts, nostalgic toys, good stocking stuffers.
Lyndell's Bakery	720 Broadway	617-625-1793	Tasty pastries.
Paper Source	1810 Massachusetts Ave	617-497-1077	DIY paper crafts and quirky gifts.
Roach's Sporting Goods	1957 Massachusetts Ave	617-876-5816	100 years of sporting goods, camp supplies, and guns.

Map 24 · Winter Hill / Union Square

Bombay Market	359 Somerville Ave	617-623-6614	Good Indian grocery, Bollywood movies.
Bostonian Florist	92 Highland Ave	617-629-9300	Florist.
Christmas Tree Shops	177 Middlesex Ave	617-623-3428	Everything including the kitchen sink.
Mudflat Studio	149 Broadway	617-628-0589	Pottery classes and studios.
Reliable Market	45 Union Sq	617-623-9620	Overflowing East Asian grocer.
Ricky's Flower Market	9 Union Sq	617-628-7569	Great outdoor market. Mind the traffic, though.
Saini Sweet Shop	65 Summer St	617-623-2603	Indian desserts.

Map 25 · East Somerville / Sullivan Square

Home Depot	75 Mystic Ave	617-623-0001	Got wood?
Vinny's Superette	76 Broadway	617-628-1921	Damn good Italian cold-cuts.

Map 26 · East Cambridge / Kendall Square / MIT

Apple Store	100 Cambridgeside Pl	617-225-0442	Mac heaven in the Galleria.
Best Buy	100 Cambridgeside Pl	617-577-8866	Awful, amazing electronics retailer.
Calumet Photographic	65 Bent St	617-576-2600	High-end photo shop.
Cambridge Antique Market	201 Monsignor O'Brien Hwy	617-868-9655	Five floors to keep you busy.
Mayflower Poultry	621 Cambridge St	617-547-9191	Live poultry, fresh killed.

Map 27 · Central Square / Cambridgeport

Buckaroo's Mercantile	5 Brookline St	617-492-4792	Kitsch niche.
Cambridge Bicycle	259 Massachusetts Ave	617-876-6555	Bike shop near MIT.
Cheapo Records	645 Massachusetts Ave	617-354-4455	A treasure trove of older tunes.
Cremaldi's	31 Putnam Ave	617-354-7969	Gourmet shop.
Economy Hardware	438 Massachusetts Ave	617-864-3300	Hardware, household needs, cheap furniture. Very popular.
Hubba Hubba	534 Massachusetts Ave	617-492-9082	Focusing on the naughty bits.
Looney Tunes	1001 Massachusetts Ave	617-876-5624	Records covered with the finest dust.
Massive Records	1105 Massachusetts Ave	617-576-1887	Massive selection of vinyl, other DJ treats.
Micro Center	730 Memorial Dr	617-234-6400	Computer have-it-all. Avoid going on Saturdays.
Pearl Art & Craft Supplies	579 Massachusetts Ave	617-547-6600	Arts and crafts, Central Square style.
Sadye & Company	182 Massachusetts Ave	617-547-4424	Good antiques store.
Shalimar	571 Massachusetts Ave	617-868-8311	Huge selection of spices.
Skippy White's	538 Massachusetts Ave	617-491-3345	Mostly R&B, soul, Motown, other oldies.
Ten Thousand Villages	694 Massachusetts Ave	617-876-2414	Free-trade, handmade crafts from around the world.
Toscanini's	899 Main St	617-491-5877	In our opinion, Boston's best ice cream.
University Stationery	311 Massachusetts Ave	617-547-6650	A friendly little shop near MIT.

Map 28 · Inman Square

Absolutely Fabulous	1309 Cambridge St	617-864-0656	Inman Square maxi-boutique.
Christina's Homemade Ice Cream	1255 Cambridge St	617-492-7021	Clever flavors; good spice shop next door.
The Garment District	200 Broadway	617-876-5230	Vintage threads, costumes, clothing by-the-pound.
Inman Square Market	1343 Cambridge St	617-354-8697	Independent quickie mart.
Royal Pastry	738 Cambridge St	617-547-2053	Caters to a devoted clientele.
Target	180 Somerville Ave	617-776-4036	Oh, you know.
Wine Cask	407 Washington St	617-623-8656	Wine, cheese, specialties.

Map 29 · West Roxbury

Irish Cottage	1898 Centre St	617-323-4644	Food, kitsch. Gag us with a shamrock.
Jack Davis Florist	2097 Centre St	617-323-6006	Florist.

Map 30 · Roslindale

18 Birch Street	18 Birch St	617-323-3269	Hodgepodgerie.
Blooms & Greens	4014 Washington St	617-524-5556	Florist.
Emack & Bolio's	2 Belgrade Ave	617-323-3323	Innovative ice cream flavors.
Exotic Flowers	609 American Legion Hwy	617-247-2000	Florist.
Formax Bread Baking Company	27 Corinth St	617-325-8852	Sandwiches, too.
Solera	10 Corinth St	617-469-4005	Wine.
Village Books	751 South St	617-325-1994	Beloved community bookstore.
Zia	22 Birch St	617-327-1300	Boutique.

Map 31 · Mattapan / Dorchester (West)

Brigham's Ice Cream	1621 Blue Hill Ave	617-298-6398	Step back in time at this ice cream parlor.
Dark Horse	2297 Dorchester Ave	617-298-1031	Antiques.
Hip Zepi USA	612 Blue Hill Ave	617-778-2455	All the pants are baggy at this hip hop store.
Le Foyers Bakery	132 Babson St	617-298-2233	Long lines for patties at this Haitian bakery.
Rainbow Apparel	474 Blue Hill Ave	617-427-1932	Discount clothes for the ladies.
Taurus Records	1282 Blue Hill Ave	617-298-2655	Small shop is best source for reggae, tons of singles.

Map 32 · Dorchester (East)

Asian Bookstore	1392 Dorchester Ave	617-822-9996	Tidy bookstore specializing in Vietnamese books.
Coleen's Flowershop	912 Dorchester Ave	617-282-0468	Cute florist on Dot Ave.
Greenhills Irish Bakery	780 Adams St	617-825-8187	Soda bread, scones and sandwiches with blood pudding.
P.J. Bait Shop	1397 Dorchester Ave	617-288-7917	Rods, reels and fishing licenses.

Map 33 · Hyde Park

Capone Foods [Garfield Av]	14 Bow St	617-629-2296	All your specialty food shop needs.
Marascio's Market	1758 River St	617-361-6847	Italian specialties.
Ron's Gourmet Ice Cream	1231 Hyde Park Ave	617-364-5274	Candlepins too!
Tutto Italiano	1889 River St	617-361-4700	Deli. A mayoral favorite.

Boston may not have the Great White Way, but the theater scene—including musical venues—is alive and vibrant; you just might have to look a little harder for it. Where to start looking? Well, the most enthused patron of theatre in the region is Larry Stark of theatermirror.com. If there's a production taking place anywhere within 100 miles, Larry and his cast of writers are all over it. The *Boston Phoenix* and *Dig* will also point you to good productions.

Broadway in Boston runs popular mainstream shows (e.g. *Wicked*, *Swan Lake*, *Les Miserables*) at Boston's flagship theatres such as the **Wang Center for the Performing Arts (Map 3)**, neighboring **Shubert Theater (Map 3)**, and the newly-restored **Opera House (Map 3)**. These theatres also produce readings, dance, and a wide variety of performances. Also of note in the Theater District: **Tribe Theatre (Map 6)** and the **Charles Playhouse (Map 3)**, which runs long-running favorites *Blue Man Group* and *Shear Madness*.

Away from the clamor of the Theater District down Tremont Street, you'll find the **Boston Center for the Arts (Map 7)**, containing four performance spaces that accomodate fare ranging from Forbidden Broadway to one-man shows.

The Lyric Stage Company (Map 6) nearby on Clarendon Street showcases wide-ranging seasons. The **Huntington Theatre (Map 5)** is the other major theatre in the area.

For something a little different, check out the **Puppet Showplace Theater (Map 17)** in Brookline. For laughs, try Inman Square's **ImprovBoston (Map 28)** or the North End's **ImprovAsylum (Map 2)** (both, despite the names, do more than just improv).

If you're more of a choir and orchestra person, keep your eye on what's playing at the **Sanders Theatre (Map 20)**. Located in Harvard's Memorial Hall, Sanders Theatre offers terrific acoustics in a classic interior. Built to offer a 180-degree perspective for the audience, the theater was inspired by a Christopher Wren design. And of course, the Boston Symphony Orchestra at Symphony Hall **(Map 5)** has a thing or two to offer as far as classical music goes.

You can pick up half-price, same-day tickets at the BosTix booth in Copley Square or at Faneuil Hall Marketplace (both accept cash only). You can find out performances for which tickets are available at www.bostix.org.

Theater	Address	Phone	Map
BCA Plaza Black Box	539 Tremont St	617-426-5000	7
Berklee Performance Center	136 Massachusetts Ave	617-747-2261	5
Blackman Auditorium/Studio Theatre	360 Huntington Ave	617-373-2247	15
Boston Center for the Arts	527 Tremont St	617-426-5000	7
Boston Children's Theater	321 Columbus Ave	617-424-6634	5
Boston Playwrights' Theatre	949 Commonwealth Ave	617-353-5443	5
Charles Playhouse	74 Warrenton St	617-426-6912	3
Colonial Theatre	106 Boylston St	617-426-9366	3
Cutler Majestic Theatre at Emerson College	219 Tremont St	617-824-8000	3
Devanaughn Theatre at The Piano Factory	791 Tremont St	617-247-9777	13
Footlight Club	7A Eliot St	617-524-3200	14
Huntington Theatre Company	264 Huntington Ave	617-266-0800	5
ImprovAsylum	216 Hanover St	617-263-6887	2
ImprovBoston	1253 Cambridge St	617-576-1253	28
Jimmy Tingle's Off Broadway	255 Elm St	617-591-1616	23
Jorge Hernández Cultural Center	85 W Newton St	866-811-4111	7
Kresge Little Theatre	48 Massachusetts Ave	617-253-6294	27
Loeb Drama Center	64 Brattle St	617-547-8300	20
Lyric Stage Company	140 Clarendon St	617-437-7172	6
Nancy and Edward Roberts Studio Theater	539 Tremont St	617-426-5000	7
Opera House	539 Washington St	617-259-3400	3
Orpheum Theatre	1 Hamilton Pl	617-679-0810	3
The Publick Theatre	1400 Soldiers Field Rd	617-782-5425	19
Puppet Showplace Theatre	32 Station St	617-731-6400	17
Remis Auditorium	465 Huntington Ave	617-369-3770	15
Sanders Theatre	45 Quincy St	617-496-2222	20
Semel Theatre at Emerson College	10 Boylston Pl	617-824-8364	3
Shubert Theatre	265 Tremont St	617-482-9393	3
Stuart Street Playhouse	200 Stuart St	617-426-4499	3
Symphony Hall	301 Massachusetts Ave	617-266-1492	5
Theater at Zero Arrow Street	0 Arrow St	617-547-8300	20
Theatre Cooperative	277 Broadway	n/a	24
Tower Auditorium	621 Huntington Ave	617-879-7000	15
Tribe Theater	67 Stuart St	617-510-4447	6
Virginia Wimberley Theatre	539 Tremont St	617-266-0800	7
Wang Center for Performing Arts	265 Tremont St	617-482-9393	3
Wang Theatre	270 Tremont St	617-482-9393	3
Wheelock Family Theatre	180 The Riverway	617-879-2000	16
Wilbur Theatre	106 Boylston St	617-423-4008	3

Arts & Entertainment • Symphony Hall

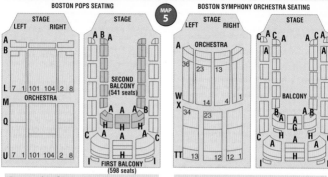

General Information

NFT Map: 5
Address: 301 Massachusetts Ave, Boston, MA 02115
Website: www.bostonsymphonyhall.org
Phone: 617-266-1492
Tickets: 617-266-1200; www.bso.org

Overview

Boston Symphony Hall, home of the Boston Symphony Orchestra and Boston Pops, is regarded as one of the finest concert halls in the world. Modeled after the German Leipzig Gewandhaus and the old Boston Music Hall, Symphony Hall was the first American hall designed to maximize acoustics, thanks to Harvard physics professor Wallace Clement Sabine (and to think you slept through your physics class!). Classical music connoisseurs recognize the hall as a space that produces a near-perfect sound experience. The Hall, designed by New York architects McKim, Mead, & White, opened in 1900, replacing the Boston Music Hall, which was in the way of the burgeoning subway system. The hall seats 2,625 people in the Boston Symphony Orchestra (BSO) season and 2,371 in the Boston Pops Orchestra season. Don't leave without checking out the Aeolian-Skinner organ with 67 stops and 5,130 pipes. Free tours offer an insight into the history and features of Symphony Hall.

Symphony Hall contains dozens of museum-like items documenting notable events in its history. You can learn just what was so revolutionary about the acoustics and famous composers. Excitement and pride leaps from a reprinted Boston Globe article documenting the first performance.

In the past the Hall has hosted auto shows, mayoral inaugurations, meetings of the Communist Party, and a performance by Harry Houdini. You can also celebrate New Year's style here as the orchestra performs in the background. (Bring your tux.) The tradition of hosting non-traditional events looks set to continue. In recent years, the US Open Squash Tournament has been held at Symphony Hall, using portable glass courts placed just below the stage.

If you're looking to throw your own Diddy-like party, function rooms and hall spaces can be rented for private functions. Renting out Symphony Hall for a night costs between $4,700 and $6,200. Five different function spaces are available for rent and cost between $700 and $2,700 per night.

How to Get Tickets

You can purchase tickets to any of the Symphony Hall performances online at www.bso.org, in person at the Symphony Hall box office, or by phone on 617-266-1200 or 617-638-9283 (TDD/TTY).

How to Get There—Driving

From the north, take I-93 to the Storrow Drive (Exit 26). Once you're on Storrow Drive, bear left towards Copley Square/Back Bay. Turn right onto Beacon Street. Turn left onto Clarendon Street. Turn right onto St. James Avenue. Bear left onto Huntington Avenue. Symphony Hall is on the corner of Huntington Avenue and Massachusetts Avenue.

From the south, take I-93 to Exit 18 and follow signs toward Massachusetts Avenue. Turn right onto Massachusetts Avenue.

From the west, take the Mass Pike (I-90) to the Prudential Center/Copley Square (Exit 27) and merge onto Huntington Avenue. Symphony Hall is on the corner of Huntington Avenue and Massachusetts Avenue.

Parking

There are two pay parking garages on Westland Avenue, another parking garage on Gainsborough Street next to Jordan Hall at the New England Conservatory, and very limited street parking. The Prudential Center Garage offers discount parking with the presentation of a performance ticket stub from the same day if you enter the garage after 5 pm.

How to Get There—Mass Transit

The Green Line's E train stops at Symphony Hall. Other Green Line trains that stop at the Hynes Convention Center will get you close. Another option is to take the Orange Line to the Massachusetts Avenue stop.

The 1 bus, which runs down Massachusetts Avenue from Harvard Square to Dudley Square, stops mere feet from Symphony Hall.

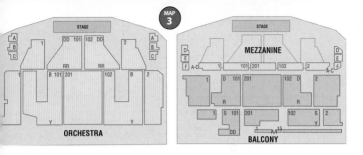

General Information

NFT Map:	3
Address:	One Hamilton Pl, Boston, MA 02108
Website:	www.ticketmaster.com/venue/8318
Phone:	617-679-0810
Ticketmaster:	www.ticketmaster.com

Overview

When you look down a street or alleyway in a major city, what do you expect to find? A theater is probably not among those answers, but that's just what you'll see at One Hamilton Place. The Orpheum has been around since 1852, and despite renovations, it can still feel like its age, which many consider part of the charm. (Apparently, they have not heard of this thing called The Internet either...) The Orpheum originally had an eye on high-brow stuff: Tchaikovsky along with the Boston Symphony Orchestra made debuts there. Now, it packs in close to 3,000 people to witness an eclectic lineup of acts ranging from Larry the Cable Guy to an Evening with Hall and Oates to the latest popular music acts. Tickets often go quickly and every seat is a good one, though leg room is notably sparse.

How to Get Tickets

Tickets can be purchased from the Orpheum Theater Box Office Mon–Sat, 10 am–5 pm. Tickets can also be purchased online at www.ticketmaster.com or by calling 617-679-0810.

How to Get There—Driving

From the north, take I-93 S to Exit 24A (Government Center). At the bottom of the ramp, bear right onto New Chardon Street. At the second set of lights, take a left onto Cambridge Street. Stay on the right-hand side of Cambridge Street, which will become Tremont Street as soon as you pass City Hall Plaza (on your left). Drive two blocks farther on Tremont Street. The Orpheum will be on your left on Hamilton Place.

From the south, take I-93 N to Exit 23 (Government Center). At the end of the ramp, follow signs for Government Center/Faneuil Hall. At the set of lights, make a left onto North Street. Drive a quarter-mile to the end of North Street, then make your first right onto State Street, which turns into Court Street after a few feet. Follow Court Street to the end, then make a left at the fork onto Tremont Street. Drive two blocks farther on Tremont Street. The Orpheum will be on your left on Hamilton Place.

From the west, take the Mass Pike (I-90) E to Exit 24B, which will dump you onto I-93 N. From there follow the directions above for driving from the south.

Parking

Street parking will be scarce, especially during event hours. The closest parking lot is on Tremont Street.

How to Get There—Mass Transit

Take the Red or Green Line to the Park Street stop or the Orange Line to Downtown Crossing. The theater is just a short walk from both stops. It's directly across from the Park Street Church.

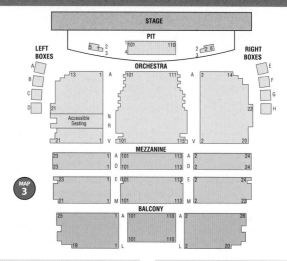

General Information

NFT Map: 3
Address: 265 Tremont St, Boston, MA 02116
Website: www.wangcenter.org
Phone: 617-482-9393
Tele-charge: www.telecharge.com, 800-447-7400

Overview

Part of the not-for-profit Wang Center for the Performing Arts, the Shubert Theatre is the "Little Princess" to the Wang Theatre's "Grand Dame." The 1,600-seat venue opened in 1910 and has since undergone two major renovations. The theater's elaborate entranceway was destroyed during the widening of Tremont Street in 1925, and in 1996, $6 million was spent restoring and improving the theater's original ornate French Renaissance architecture. The intimacy within the Shubert remained intact, and the theater is now the home of many Boston arts organizations as well as several touring companies. Broadway shows, including such classics as *The King and I* and *South Pacific*, debuted at the Shubert before making their way to Broadway.

How to Get Tickets

You can purchase tickets for the Shubert Theatre online at www.telecharge.com or by calling Tele-charge at 800-447-7400.

How to Get There—Driving

From the north, take I-93 S to Exit 23 (South Station), which dumps you onto Purchase Street. Immediately after the Chinatown Gate (on your right), take a right onto Kneeland Street. Go straight for several blocks and then turn left onto Tremont Street. The Shubert Theatre is on your right.

From the south, take I-93 N to Exit 20 (South Station) and immediately get into the left-hand lane. The sign overhead will read "Detour South Station via Frontage Road." Take this left exit off the ramp and follow Frontage Road north to South Station. Turn left onto Kneeland Street. Go straight for several blocks, and then turn left onto Tremont Street. The Shubert Theatre is on your right.

From the west, take the Mass Pike (I-90) E to Exit 24A. Turn left onto Kneeland Street. Go straight for several blocks and then turn left onto Tremont Street. The Shubert Theatre is on your right.

Parking

Your best bets are the parking lot on the corner of Tremont and Stuart Streets, the lot at the Radisson Hotel on Stuart Street, the Kinney Motor Mart on Stuart Street, or the Fitz-Inn lot on Kneeland Street.

How to Get There—Mass Transit

The Orange Line's New England Medical Center stop and the Green Line's Boylston Street stop are both one block away from the theater. The Red Line's Park Street stop on Tremont Street is three or so blocks from the theater.

General Information

NFT Map: 3
Address: 270 Tremont St, Boston, MA 02116
Website: www.wangcenter.org
Phone: 617-482-9393
Tele-charge: www.telecharge.com,
               800-447-7400

Overview

Surviving several name changes and heavy renovation over the years, the Wang Theatre has remained a prominent feature of the Boston theater scene. With 3,600 seats, it is the larger of the two performance spaces operated by the Wang Center for the Performing Arts (the other is the famous Shubert Theatre across (see page 322) the street).

Opened in the "Roaring Twenties" (1925) as the Metropolitan Theatre, the venue was considered to be a "magnificent movie cathedral" with its ornate interior resembling something from Louis XIV's palace. Renamed the Music Hall in 1962, the theater became home to the then-fledgling Boston Ballet. As the years passed, the shiny gem began to lose some of its luster, and control of the property was transferred to a non-profit organization known as The Metropolitan Center in 1980. Some minor renovations were made, but it wasn't until 1983, when Dr. An Wang stepped in to resuscitate the theater, that things took a turn for the better. Since the restoration, the theater has played host to such classics as *Les Miserables* and *The Phantom of the Opera* and still houses one of New England's largest movie screens, used for the weekly Motion Picture Mondays film series. The *Nutcracker at the Wang* (snicker...) holiday tradition is no more—Macaulay Culkin's favorite ballet has been replaced by "The Radio City Christmas Spectacular" featuring high-kicking Rockettes wearing reindeer antlers.

How to Get Tickets

You can purchase tickets for the Wang Theatre online at www.telecharge.com or by calling Tele-charge at 800-447-7400. The Wang Theatre Box Office, open Monday through Saturday from 10 am until 6 pm, sells tickets without the nasty service charges levied by external vendors.

How to Get There—Driving

From the north, take I-93 S to Exit 23 (South Station), which dumps you onto Purchase Street. Immediately after the Chinatown Gate (on your right) take a right onto Kneeland Street. Go straight for several blocks and then turn left onto Tremont Street. The Wang Theatre is on your left.

From the south, take I-93 N to Exit 20 (South Station) and immediately get into the left-hand lane. The sign overhead will read "Detour South Station via Frontage Road." Take

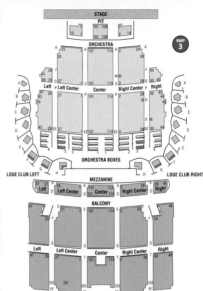

this left exit off the ramp and follow Frontage Road north to South Station. Turn left onto Kneeland Street. Go straight for several blocks, turn right onto Tremont Street. The Wang Theatre is on your left.

From the west, take the Mass Pike (I-90) to Exit 24A. Turn left onto Kneeland Street. Go straight for several blocks and then turn left onto Tremont Street. The Wang Theatre is on your left.

Parking

Your best bets are the parking lot on the corner of Tremont and Stuart Streets, the lot at the Radisson Hotel on Stuart Street, the Kinney Motor Mart on Stuart Street, or the Fitz-Inn lot on Kneeland Street.

How to Get There—Mass Transit

The Orange Line's New England Medical Center stop and the Green Line's Boylston Street stop are both one block away from the theater. The Red Line's Park Street stop on Tremont Street is three or so blocks from the theater.

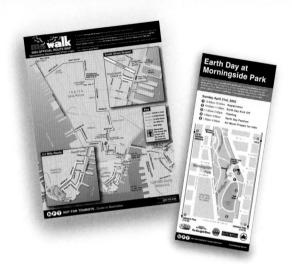

Map 6 • Washington Sq./NYU/SoHo

Blown up and hung.

Your favorite **NFT** map as a poster. Any **Not For Tourists** map can be made into a 24"x 36" poster. These large wall maps are taken directly from the pages of the **Not For Tourists** Guidebooks.

Order at www.notfortourists.com

Not For Tourists™
New York City · Brooklyn · Los Angeles · Chicago · San Francisco · Boston · Washington DC · Atlanta · Philadelphia

www.notfortourists.com

zipcars

live in your neighborhood

For work or play

...unexpected necessities...

Black Ink
Harvard Square
5 Brattle Street
Cambridge

Black Ink
Beacon Hill
101 Charles Street
Boston

www.BlackInkBoston.com

pure. simple. mintwater.™

Made with pure water and real mint, Metromint relieves your thirst,
relaxes your mind, freshens your breath, and revives your soul.
No sweeteners. No preservatives. No calories. Nothing but all-natural
ingredients and surprisingly vibrant taste. Available at Whole Foods,
D'Agostino, Gourmet Garage, and other specialty retailers.

METROMINT.

FASHION MUSIC ART LIFESTYLE

YRB MAGAZINE

www.yrb.us

Boston

Street	Page	Grid
Beechland St	30	B1
Beechmont St	33	A1/A2
Beechmont Ter	33	A2
Beechwood St	31	A2
Beethoven St	14	A2
Belden Sq	32	A1
Belden St	32	A1
Belfort St	32	A1
Belgrade Ave		
(1-257)	30	B1
(258-499)	29	A2
Belgrade Ter	29	A2
Belgravia Pl	2	A2
Bell Ct	10	B1
Bellaire Rd	29	A2
Belle Ave	29	B1
Bellevue St [DO]	32	A1
Bellevue St [WR]		
(1-307)	29	A2/B2
(308-399)	33	A1
Bellevue Ter	23	A1
Bellevue Hill Rd		
(1-54)	29	A2
(55-199)	33	A1
Bellflower St	12	B2
W Bellflower St	12	B2
Bellingham Pl	1	B1
Bellvista Rd	19	B1
Belmore Ter	14	A2
Belnap Rd	33	B1
Belnel St	31	B1
Belton St	32	B2
Belvidere St	5	B2
Bennet Pl	9	A1
N Bennet Pl	2	A1
Bennet St	4	B1
N Bennet St	2	A1
N Bennett Ct	2	A1
Bennett St	18	A1/A2
Bennington St	9	A1/A2
Benson St	18	A2
Bent Ct	10	B2
Bentham Rd	32	B1
Bentley St	18	A2
Benton St	13	A1
Beram St	33	A1
Berkeley St		
(1-83)	7	A1/A2
(84-399)	6	A2/B2
E Berkeley St	7	A2
Berkshire St	32	B1
Bernard Pl	11	B1
Bernard St	31	A2
Bernice St	32	B2
Berry St	32	B2
Bertram St	19	A1
Bertson Ave	29	A1
Berwick St	29	A1
Beryl St	30	B1
Bethune Way	13	B1
Beverly St		
(1-125)	2	A1
(126-299)	1	A2
Bexley Rd	30	B1/B2
Bickford Ave	15	B1
Bickford St	14	A2
Bicknell St	31	A2
Bigelow Cir	18	A1
Bigelow St	18	A1
Billings Ln	30	A1
Billings St	29	B1
Bills Ct	15	A2
Bilodeau Rd	31	A2
Biltmore St	14	B2
Binford St	10	A1
Binney St	15	A1
Birch Rd	29	B2
Birch St	30	B1
Birchcroft Rd	33	A2
Birchland Ave	29	B2
Birchland Ter	29	B2
Birchwood St	29	B2
Bird St		
(1-153)	32	A1
(154-199)	13	B2
Bishop St	14	B2
Bismarck St [JP]	14	A2
Bismarck St [MT]	31	B1
Bispham St	32	B1
Black Falcon Ave	11	A1
Blackfan St	15	A1
Blackstone St	2	B1
Blackwell St	32	B2
Blackwood St	5	B2
Blagden St	5	A1
Blaine St	19	A1
Blake St		
(1-63)	33	A2
(64-199)	31	B2
Blakemore St	30	B2
Blakeville St	32	A1
Blanchard St	13	A1
Blanche St	32	B2
Blandford St	16	A2
Blanvon Rd	30	B2
Blenford Rd	18	B2
Bloomfield St	32	B1
Bloomington St	32	B2
Blossom Ct	1	A1
Blossom St	1	A1
Blue Hill Ave		
(1-358)	13	B2
(359-1699)	31	A1/A2/B1
Blue Ledge Dr	33	A1
Blue Ledge Ter	33	A1
Bluefield Ter	31	B1
Blueview Cir	29	B2
Blueview Rd	29	B2
Board Aly	2	B1
Boates Ct	4	A2
Bobolink St	33	A1
Bodwell St	32	A1
Bogandale Rd	29	B2
Bolster St	14	A2
Bolton St	10	A1/B2
Bonad Rd	29	A2
Bonair St	29	A1/A2
Bond St	7	A2
Bonnel Ter	13	A1
Bonner Ter	13	A1
Boradial St	2	A1
Border St	9	A1/B1
Boriken St	7	A1
Boston Pl	2	B1
Boston St	12	B2
Boston Fish Pier	11	A1
Boston Medical Center Pl	7	B1
Bostonia Ave	18	B1
Bosworth St	3	A2
Bothwell Rd	18	A1
Boulevard Ter	29	B2
W Boundary Rd	29	B2
Bourne St	30	B2
Bournedale Rd	30	B2
Bourneside St	32	B1
Boutwell St	32	B2
Bow St		
(1-26)	33	B2
(27-199)	23	A2
Bowditch Rd	30	A1
Bowdoin Ave	31	A2
Bowdoin St	1	B2
Bowdoin St [DO]		
(1-92)	31	A2
(93-499)	32	A1/B1
Bowdoin Park	32	A1
Bowen St	10	B1
Bower St	13	B1
Bower Ter	14	B1
Bowker St	1	A2
Bowman St	32	B2
Boxford Ter	29	A2
Boyd St	32	B1
Boyden St	31	B2
Boylston Pl	3	B1
Boylston Pl [JP]	14	A2
Boylston Sq	3	B2
Boylston St		
(1-440)	3	B1/B2
(442-699)	6	A1/A2
(700-1155)	5	A2/B1/B2
(1156-1499)	15	A1/A2
Boylston St [JP]	14	A2/B2
Boynton St	14	B1/B2
Brackett St	18	A1
Bradbury St	19	A1
Braddock Park	6	B1
Bradeen St	30	B2
Bradfield Ave	30	B1
Bradford Cir	30	B1
Bradford Rd	31	B2
Bradford St	7	A2
Bradlee Ct	33	A2
Bradlee Ln	33	A2
Bradlee St [DO]	31	A2
Bradlee St [HP]	33	A2
Bradlee Park	33	A2
Bradshaw St	31	A2
Bradston St	12	A1
Bradstreet Ave	30	B2
Bradwood St	29	A2
Braeburn Rd	33	A1
Braemore Rd	18	B2
Braewood St	33	A1/A2
Bragdon St		
(1-40)	13	B1
(41-109)	14	B1
Brahms St	30	B1
Brainard St	33	B1
Brainerd Rd	19	B1
Braintree St	19	A1
Branch St	1	B1
Branchfield St	31	B2
Branton St	32	B2
Branwin Harris Way	13	A2
Brattle Way	1	A2/B2
Bray St	13	B1
Bremen Pl	9	B1
Bremen St	9	A1/A2/B1
S Bremen St	9	B1
Bremen Ter	30	A2
Brenen St	9	A2
Brent St	32	B1
Brenton St	31	A2
Brentwood St	19	A1
Brewer St	14	B1
Brewster St	11	B1
Bridge Ct	1	B1
Bridge St		
(1-99)	31	B1
(340-399)	29	B1
Brier Rd	29	B2
Briercliff Ter	31	B1
Briggs Pl	7	A2

Street Index

Street	No.	Grid
Brigham St	9	B1
Brighton Ave	19	A1/A2
Brimmer St	1	B1
Brinsley St	31	A2
Brinton St	13	B1
Bro Joseph A Herran Way	29	B1
Broad St		
(1-49)	2	B1
(50-199)	4	B1
Broadlawn Park	29	A1
Broadway	3	B1
E Broadway		
(481-567)	10	B2
(568-999)	11	B1/B2
W Broadway	10	A1/B1/B2
Brock St	18	A1/B1
Brockton St	31	B1
Bromfield St	2	B1
Bromley St	15	B2
Bronsdon St	18	A2
Bronx Rd	29	B2
Brook Ave	13	B2
Brook Farm Rd	29	A1/A2
Brook Marshall Rd	13	A2
Brookdale St	30	B2
Brookfield St	30	B1
Brookford St	13	B2
Brookledge St	31	A1
Brookley Rd		
(1-17)	14	B2
(18-56)	30	A2
(57-118)	31	A1
Brookline Ave	16	A2/B1
E Brookline St	7	B1/B2
W Brookline St	7	B1
Brooks St	9	A1
Brooks St [BR]	18	A1
Brooksdale Rd	18	A1
Brookside Ave	14	B2
Brookvale St	31	B2
Brookview St	31	B1
Brookway Rd	30	A2/B2
Brookway Ter	30	B2
Brookwood Ter	16	B1
Brown Ave	30	B1/B2
Brown Ter	14	B1
Browning Ave	31	A2
Brownson Ter	30	A1
Bruce St	32	B1
Brucewood St	29	A2
Brunswick St	31	A2
Brush Hill Ter	33	B2
Brushwood Cir	33	B2
Bryant Rd	29	B2
Bryon Rd	29	A1
Buchanan Rd	30	A1/B1
Buckingham St	33	B1
Buckley Ave	14	A2
Bucknam St	15	B1
Buick St	19	A2
Bulfinch Pl	1	A2/B2
Bullard St	31	A2
Bullock St	10	A1/A2
Bumstead Ct	3	B2
Bungalow Rd	29	B2
Bunker St	33	B1
Burard St	29	A1
Burbank St	5	B1
Burgess St	32	A1
Burgoyne St	32	B1
Burke St [RX]	13	A1
Burke St [SB]	10	B1
Burley St	33	B2
Burlington Ave	16	A2
Burmah St	31	B1
Burnett St	14	B2
Burney St	15	B2
Burnham Pl	11	B1
Burnside Ave	29	A1
Burr St	14	A2
Burrage St	14	A1
Burrell St	12	B1
Burrill Pl	11	B1
Burroughs Pl	14	B1
Burroughs St	14	B1
Burrwood Rd	29	A2
Burt St	32	B1
Burton Ave	13	B2
Burwell Rd	29	A2
Bush St	7	B2
Bushnell St	32	B1
Business St	33	B1/B2
Business Ter	33	B1
Bussey St	30	A1
Buswell St	16	A1
Butland Ct	11	B2
Butler Pl	2	A1
Butler Row	2	B1
Butler Sq	2	B1
Butler St	10	A2
Butler St [DO]	31	B2
Buttonwood Ct	12	B2
Buttonwood St		
(1-21)	32	A1
(22-199)	12	B2
Bynner St	14	A1/A2
Byrd Ave	30	B2
Byron St	1	B1
C St		
(1-24)	11	A1
(59-550)	10	A1/A2/B1
Cabot St	13	A1
Caddy Rd	31	B2
Cahners Pl	6	B2
Calder St	31	A1
Caledonian Ave	29	B1
Call St	14	B2
Callahan Pl	20	B1
Callahan Tunl	2	B1
Callender St	31	B1/B2
Calumet St	15	B1
Calvin Pl	10	A2
Calvin Rd	30	A1
Cambria St	5	B2
Cambridge St	1	B1/B2
Cambridge St [AL]		
(1-567)	19	A1/A2
(568-799)	18	A2/B2
Cambridge Ter	19	A1
Cambridge Street Ave	1	B1
Camden St	13	A1/A2
Camelia Rd	33	A2
Camelot Ct	18	B2
Cameron St	32	A1
Camp Rd	29	B2
E Campbell Pl	13	A2
Canaan St	31	B1
Canal St		
(1-103)	2	A1/B1
(104-199)	1	A2
Candor Pl	14	B2
Canterbury St	30	B2
Canton Pl	7	A1
E Canton St	7	B2
W Canton St		
(1-173)	7	A1
(174-299)	6	B1
Capen Pl	31	B2
Capen St	31	B2
Capital St	29	A1
Capstan Way	11	A2
Cardington St	13	B1
Carleton St	6	B1
Carlford Rd	30	B1
Carlisle St	13	B2
Carlos St	31	B1
Carlotta St	32	B1
Carlson Cir	29	A2
Carlson Rd	33	B2
Carmel St	15	B2
Carmela Ln	32	B1
Carmen St	31	A2
Carmody Ct	10	B2
Carol Ave	19	B1
Carol Cir	29	B2
Carolina Ave	14	B1/B2
Carolina Pl	14	B2
Carpenter St	10	B1
Carroll St	29	A1
Carrolton Rd	29	B2
Carruth St	32	B1
Carson St	32	A1
Cary St	31	A1
Caryll St	31	B2
Caspar St	29	A1
Caspian Way	32	A2
Cass St	29	B2
Cassnet St	32	B1
Castle Ct [EB]	9	B1
Castle Ct [RX]	7	A2
Castlegate Rd	31	A2
Castlerock St	32	A2
Castleton St	14	A1
Cataumet St	14	B1
Catawba St	13	B1
Catenaccia Way	30	A2
Catherine St	30	B2
Caton St	31	B1
Causeway St		
(1-159)	1	A2
(160-299)	2	A1
Cawfield St	32	A1
Cazenove St	6	B2
S Cedar Pl	32	A1
Cedar Rd	29	B2
Cedar Sq	13	B1
Cedar St [MT]	31	A2/B2
Cedar St [RX]	13	A1/B1
W Cedar St	1	B1
Cedar Grove St	32	B2
Cedar Lane Way	1	B1
Cedar Park	13	A1
Cedarcrest Cir	29	B1
Cedarcrest Ln	29	B2
Cedarcrest Rd	29	B2
Cedarcrest Ter	29	B2
Cedarwood Rd	30	A1
Cedric St	12	B1
Cedrus Ave	30	B1
Cefalo Rd	29	A2
Celia Rd	29	B2
Cemetery Rd	31	A1
Cenacle Rd	18	B1
Centervale Park	32	B1
Centola St	18	A2
Central Ave [HP]	33	A2/B2
Central Ave [MT]	31	B2
Central Sq	9	A1
Central St	2	B1/B2
Central Wharf	2	B2
Centre Ave	32	B1
Centre Ct	32	B1
Centre Ln	29	B2
Centre Pl [DO]	32	B1

Street Index

Street	Page	Grid
E Concord St	7	B1
W Concord St	7	A1/B1
Condor St	9	A1/A2
Congress St		
(2-40)	2	B1
(42-301)	4	A1/A2
(302-399)	10	A1/A2
Congreve St	30	B1
Coniston Rd	30	B1
Connolly St	13	A2
Conrad St	32	A1
Conry Cres	30	A1
Constance Rd	29	B1
Constitution Rd	31	B1
Constitution Wharf	2	A2
Converse St	18	A1
Conway St	30	B1
S Conway St	30	B1
Cookson Ter	31	B1
Coolidge Rd [AL]	19	A1
Coolidge Rd [DO]	32	B1
Cooper St	2	A1
Copeland Pl	13	B2
Copeland St	13	B2
Copeland Park	13	B2
Copenger St	15	B1
Copley St	14	A2
Coppersmith Way	9	B1
Copps Hill Ter	2	A1
Corbet St	31	B2
Corcoran Cir	33	B2
Corcoran Dr	33	B2
Corey Ave	4	B1
Corey Rd	19	B1
Corey St	29	A2
Corey Ter	29	A2
Corinne Rd	18	A1
Corinth St	30	B1
Corman Rd	31	B1
Cornauba St	30	B1/B2
Cornelia Ct	15	B2
Cornell St		
(1-17)	33	A1
(18-385)	30	B1
(386-399)	29	A2
Cornhill St	2	B1
Cornwall St	14	B2
Corona St		
(1-42)	31	A2
(43-99)	32	B1
Coronado Rd	31	B1
Cortes St	3	B1
Corwin St	32	B1
Cottage Ct	13	B2
Cottage Pl [EB]	9	B1
Cottage Pl [HP]	33	B1
Cottage Rd	29	B2
Cottage St [EB]	9	B1
Cottage St [SB]	10	B1
E Cottage St		
(1-233)	12	B1/B2
(234-282)	32	A1
W Cottage St	13	B2
Cotton St	30	B1
Cottrell St	12	B2
Cotuit St	29	A1
Countryside Dr	31	B2
Court Sq	2	B1
Court St	2	B1
Courtland Rd	31	B1
Courtney Rd	29	A2
Coventry St	13	A1
Covington St	10	B2
Cowing St		
(1-42)	33	A1
(43-199)	29	B2
Cowper St	9	A2
Craft Pl	30	A2
Craftsman St	19	A1
Craftson Way	15	B1
Cragmere Ter	31	B1
Crandall St	30	B1
Crane St	33	A2
Cranmore Rd	33	B2
Cranston St	14	A2
Crawford St		
(1-106)	31	A1
(107-199)	13	B1
Creek Sq	2	B1
Crehore Rd	29	A2
Creighton St	14	A2
Crescent Ave	32	A1
N Crescent Circuit	18	B1
S Crescent Circuit	18	B1
Crest St	29	A2
Cresthill Rd	18	A1
Creston St		
(1-63)	31	A2
(64-99)	13	B2
Creston Park	13	B2
Crestwood Park	13	B1
Cricket Ln	29	A2
Crispus Attucks Pl	13	B1
Crockers Ln	29	B2
Crockett Ave	32	B2
Croftland Ave	32	B1
Cromwell Rd	33	A2
Crosby Sq	13	A2
Cross Rd	29	B2
Cross St	2	B1/B2
Cross St [HP]	33	B1
Crossland Pl	18	B2
Crossman St	31	B1
Crosstown Ave	29	B1
Crowell St	31	B2
Crowley Rogers Way	10	A1/B1
Crown Path	31	A2
Crown St	33	A2
Crown Point Dr	29	B2
Croydon St		
(1-77)	31	B1
(78-99)	33	A2
Culbert St	31	B1
Cumberland St	5	B2
Cummings Rd	18	B2
Cummings St	12	A1
Cummington St	16	A1/A2
Cummins Hwy		
(1-411)	30	B1/B2
(412-614)	33	A2
(615-964)	31	B1
Cumston Pl	7	B1
Cumston St	7	B1
Cunard St	13	A1
Cunningham St	13	B2
Curlew St	29	B2
Curley St	30	B2
Currier St	31	B1
Curtis St	9	A2
Curve St	4	B1
Cushing Ave	32	A1
Cushman Rd	18	A2
Custer St	14	B1
Custom House St	4	A2
Cuthbert Rd	29	B2
Cutler St	11	B1
Cutter Rd	29	A1
Cygnet St	19	A1
Cypher St	10	A1/A2
Cypress Rd	13	A2
Cypress St	29	B1
Cypress Ter	29	B1
D St	10	A1/A2/B1
Dabney St	13	B1
Dacia St	13	B2
Dacy St	33	B1
Dade St	13	A2
Dakota St		
(1-34)	31	A2
(35-199)	32	B1
Dale St [RS]	33	A1/A2
Dale St [RX]	13	B1/B2
Dalessio Ct	10	A1/B1
Dalin Pl	13	B2
Dalkeith St	13	B2
Dalrymple St	14	A2
Dalton St	5	A2/B2
Daly St	32	B1
Damon Pl	33	B1
Damon St	33	B1
Damrell St	10	B1
Dana Ave	33	B2
Dana Rd	29	B2
Danbury Rd	33	A2
Dane St	14	B1
Danforth Pl	13	A1
Danforth St	14	A2
Dania St	31	B1
Dania Ter	31	B1
Daniel Ct	33	B1
Danny Rd	33	B1
Danube St	13	B2
Danville St	29	A2
Darius Ct	10	B1
Darling St	15	B1
Darlington St	31	B2
Dartmouth Pl	7	A1
Dartmouth St		
(1-83)	7	A1
(84-399)	6	A1/B1/B2
Davenport St	13	A1
Davern Ave	32	A1
David Rd	30	A1
Davidson Ave	32	A1
Davis Ct	9	A1
Davison St	33	A2/B2
Davitt St	32	A2
Dawes St		
(1-111)	12	B2
(12-99)	32	A1
Dawes Ter	32	A1
Dawson St	32	B1
Day St	14	A2
Dayton St	32	B1
Deacon St	7	B1
Deaconess Rd		
(1-44)	16	B1
(45-99)	15	A1
Deady Ln	11	B1
Dean St	13	B2
Dean Way	11	B2
Dearborn St	13	A1
Deblois St	7	B1
Decatur Ave	15	B2
Decatur St	9	B1
Deckard St	13	B1
Dedham Blvd	33	B1
Dedham Pky	33	A1/B1
Dedham St [HP]	33	B1
Dedham St [WR]	29	A1/B1
E Dedham St	7	B2
W Dedham St	7	A1
Deer St	32	A1

Street	Map	Grid
Deerfield St	16	A2
Deering Rd	31	B1
Deforest St	33	A1
Degautier Way	13	A2
Delaney St	18	B2
Delano Ct	30	B1
Delano St	32	B1
Delano Park	30	B1
Delaware Pl	18	A2
Delford St	30	B1
Delhi St	31	B1
Dell Ave	33	A2
Dell Ter	33	A2
Delle Ave	15	B2
Dellmore Rd	30	B2
Delmont St	32	B1
Delnore Pl	31	B1
Delore Cir	30	B1
Denby Rd	19	A1
Dennis St	13	B2
Dennison St	13	B1
Denny St	32	A2
Dent St	29	A1/A2
Denton Ter	30	B1
Denvir St	32	B1
Derne St	1	B2
Deroma Rd	29	B2
Derry Rd	33	A2
Design Center Pl	11	B1
Desmond Rd	31	B2
Desoto Rd	29	B2
Destefano Rd	30	B2
Dever St	32	B1
Devine Way	10	B1
Devon St	31	A2
Devonshire St		
(1-95)	2	B1
(96-299)	4	A1
Dewar St	32	A1
Dewey St	13	B2
Dewey Ter	13	B2
Dewitt Dr	13	A1/A2
Dewolf St	32	A1
Dexter St	12	B2
Dickens St	32	B1
Dickinson Rd	18	B1
Dietz Ct	33	B1
Dietz Rd	33	B1
Dix St	10	B2
Dixfield St	13	B1
Dixwell St	13	B1
Dodge Rd	33	B1
Dolans Ct	14	B2
Dolphin Way	11	A2
Don St	31	B1
Donald Rd	31	A1
Doncaster St	33	A2
Donna Ter	33	B1
Donnybrook Rd	18	A2
Donwood Ter	31	B1
Doolin Pl	10	B1
Doone Ave	31	B2
Dorchester Ave		
(1-48)	4	A2/B2
(49-910)	12	A2/B2
(911-2080)	32	A1/B1
(2081-2299)	31	B2
W Dorchester Ave	12	A2
Dorchester St		
(1-383)	10	B1/B2
(384-669)	12	B2
Dore St	3	B1
Doris St	32	A1
Dorr St	13	A1
Dorset St	12	B2
Douglas Ct	2	A1
Douglas St	10	B2
Douglas Park	13	A2
Dove Ct	13	B2
Dove St	13	B2
Dow Rd	29	A1
Downer Ave	32	A1
Downer Ct	32	A1
Downey Ct	13	B2
Dracut St	32	B1
Drake Pl	9	B1
Draper St	32	A1/B1
Draper's Ln	7	A1
Drapper Rd	33	B2
Drayton Ave	32	A1
Dresden St	14	A2
Dresser St	10	B2
Driftwood Rd	30	B1
Driscoll Dr	31	B2
Dromey St	13	B2
Druce Ct	32	A1
Druid St	31	B2
Drummond St	31	A2
Drury Rd	33	B1
Dry Dock Ave	11	A1
Dudley St		
(1-616)	13	A1/A2/B2
(617-899)	32	A1
Dudley Ter	32	A1
Duke St	31	B1
Dumas St	31	B1
Dunbar Ave	31	B2
Dunbarton Rd	29	B2
Dunboy St	18	A1
Duncan Pl	32	B1
Duncan St	32	B1
Duncan Ter	32	B1
Duncklee St	18	A1
Dunford St	13	B1
Dungarven Rd	31	A1
Dunkeld St	13	B2
Dunlap St	31	B2
Dunmore St	13	B2
Dunn St	32	A1
Dunning Way	30	A2
Dunns Ter	32	B2
Dunreath St	13	B2
Dunreath Ter	13	B2
Dunster Rd	14	B1
Dunwell St	29	B1
Durant St	29	A1
Durham St	6	A1
Durland St	18	A1
Durnell Ave	30	B1
Dustin St	18	A2
Duval St		
(1-20)	19	A1
(21-99)	18	A2
Duxbury Rd	31	B2
Dwight St	7	A2
Dwinell St	29	A1/A2
Dyer Ave	10	B2
Dyer Ct	31	B2
Dyer St	31	B2
E St		
(1-27)	29	B1
(145-599)	10	A2/B1/B2
(600-675)	11	A1
Eagle Ct	9	A2
Eagle St	29	B2
E Eagle St	9	A1/A2
W Eagle St	9	A1
Earhardt Rd	30	B1
Earl St	10	B1
Earnshaw St	29	B1
East Pl	4	B2
East St		
(1-99)	4	B1/B2
(354-361)	10	B2
East St [DO]	32	A1
Eastbourne St		
(1-16)	29	A2
(17-99)	30	B1
Eastburn Pl	18	B1
Eastburn St	18	B1
Eastern Ave	2	A2
Eastland Rd	30	B2
Eastman St	32	A1
Eastmont Rd	33	B1
Easton Ave	33	B2
Easton St	19	A1
Eastwood Ct	29	B1
Eastwood Circuit	29	B1
Eatonia St	19	A1/A2
Edgar Allan Poe Way	3	B1
Edge Hill St	14	A2
Edgebrook Rd	29	B1
Edgemere Rd	29	B2
Edgemont St	30	B1
Edgerly Pl	3	B1
Edgerly Rd	5	B1/B2
Edgewater Dr	31	B1
Edgewood St	13	B2
Edgewood Park	13	B2
Edinboro St	4	A1
Edison Green	32	A1
Edith St	33	B2
Edna Rd	32	B1
Edson St [DO]	31	B2
Edson St [HP]	33	B1
Edson Ter	33	B1
Edwardson St	33	A2
Edwin St	32	B1
Egan Way	18	A2
Egleston St	14	A2/B2
Egremont Rd	18	B2
Eileen Cir	15	B1
Elba St	32	A1
Elbert St	13	B1
Elbow St	9	B1
Elder St	32	A1
Eldon St [DO]	31	A2
Eldon St [RS]	30	B1
Eldora St	15	B1
Eldridge Rd	30	B2
Eleanor St	18	A2
Electric Ave	18	A1
Elene St	31	B1
Elgin St	29	A2
Elinor Rd	29	B2
Eliot Pl	3	B2
Eliot Pl [JP]	14	B1
Eliot St	3	B1
Eliot St [JP]	14	B1
Eliot Ter	13	B1
Elizabeth St	31	A1
Elkins St	11	B1

Street Index

Street Index

Street Index

Street Index

Street Index

Cambridge

Street Index

Street Index

Street Index

Charlestown

Somerville

Street Index